THE AGRARIAN
HISTORY OF ENGLAND
AND WALES

THE AGRARIAN
HISTORY OF ENGLAND
AND WALES

GENERAL EDITOR

JOAN THIRSK
Reader in Economic History in the
University of Oxford

I·1

PREHISTORY

THE AGRARIAN HISTORY OF
ENGLAND AND WALES

★ Already published

PREFACE
BY THE GENERAL EDITOR

The first volume of the *Agrarian History* was planned, as an integral part of the series after the setting up of the original 1956 Committee, by the late Professor H. P. R. Finberg, who took an active part in its earlier stages. As he stated in his preface to Volume I, Part II, the historians responsible for the period AD 42–1042 "left the archaeologists behind (but we hope not far behind)", and their contributions were, therefore, published first. The present volume, after various vicissitudes, now appears under the authorship of Professor Stuart Piggott and Dr P. J. Fowler, and covers the period from the beginnings of British agriculture in the fourth millennium BC to the eve of the Roman Conquest, together with a survey of the history of livestock from prehistory to AD 1042 by Dr M. L. Ryder.

JOAN THIRSK

ADVISORY COMMITTEE

FOR THE AGRARIAN HISTORY OF
ENGLAND AND WALES
1980

THE AGRARIAN
HISTORY OF ENGLAND
AND WALES

VOLUME I

I. PREHISTORY

EDITED BY

STUART PIGGOTT

Professor Emeritus of Archaeology
University of Edinburgh

CAMBRIDGE UNIVERSITY PRESS

CAMBRIDGE

LONDON   NEW YORK   NEW ROCHELLE

MELBOURNE   SYDNEY

1981

Published by the Press Syndicate of the University of Cambridge
The Pitt Building, Trumpington Street, Cambridge CB2 IRP
32 East 57th Street, New York, NY 10022, USA
296 Beaconsfield Parade, Middle Park, Melbourne 3206, Australia

First published 1981

Printed in Great Britain
at the University Press, Cambridge

Library of Congress Cataloguing in Publication Data
Main entry under title:
The Agrarian history of England and Wales.
General editor, v.: Joan Thirsk.
Includes bibliographies.
CONTENTS: v. 1, pt I. Prehistory, edited by
S. Piggott. – v. 1, pt II. AD 43–1042, edited by
H. P. R. Finberg. – [etc.] – v. 8. 1914–39, by
E. H. Whetham.
1. Land use, Rural – England – History – Collected works.
2. Agriculture – England – History – Collected works.
3. Land use, Rural – Wales – History – Collected works.
4. Agriculture – Wales – History – Collected works.
I. Finberg, H. P. R., ed. II. Thirsk, Joan, ed.
HD593.A62   333.7′6′0941   66–19763
ISBN 0 521 08741 4

CONTENTS

Early Prehistory
By STUART PIGGOTT
Professor Emeritus of Archaeology
University of Edinburgh

Later Prehistory
By P. J. FOWLER
Secretary, Royal Commission on Historical Monuments (England)
Formerly Reader in Archaeology, University of Bristol

Livestock

By M. L. RYDER

Principal Scientific Officer, Agricultural Research Council
Animal Breeding Research Organisation, Edinburgh, and Honorary Lecturer, University of Edinburgh

TABLES

ILLUSTRATIONS

PREFACE

The first half of the 1970s have not been the easiest years in which to write about the agrarian history of Britain in the last four millennia BC. Even accepting that no time is absolutely right for such a task, these years have been particularly marked by changes in British archaeology. Dr Fowler's conceptual framework on which an early draft (subsequently discarded) was written in 1972 disintegrated and is not yet reconstructed. New uncertainties about chronology, with all their implications for cultural history, are far and away the most disconcerting, exacerbated by Local Government boundary changes in 1974 and the adoption of the metric system. With the three basic parameters of time, place, and size in a state of flux, it is a little difficult to pin the subject down for coherent exposition. Furthermore, the subject itself possesses three characteristics, two of them 'new', which do not help.

First, as a product of the past, the agrarian evidence on which to base description and interpretation is of poor quality. Much that has to be taken into account was acquired by crude methodology; hardly any of it has been produced by research directed towards the resolution of agrarian problems. The value of the evidence for present purposes is then usually accidental and often incidental to the circumstances or objectives by which it was acquired. Secondly, while these chapters were being written, a great deal of what was left of the data in the field was being damaged or finally destroyed. We share a realistic despondency with others that, however plausible our models, it is no longer possible in fact to reconstruct any more than certain aspects of agrarian life in later prehistoric Britain. A high proportion of the evidence is already, irretrievably, lost. Thirdly, and largely as a result of the intensive land-exploitation behind the last point, the amount of data now known to exist has exploded quantitatively; yet, because they have not yet in the main been studied and published, they cannot be synthesized here. The known bias in the published evidence, leaning heavily on Wessex, well-preserved remains, and the activities of a few individuals, is actually much worse than is immediately apparent. The next decade of research will demonstrate this fact.

In view of the dynamic state of later prehistoric studies and the unavoidably interim nature of the following, it is only proper to state that Dr Ryder's text was written in 1970, and that Dr Fowler's text was mainly written in the latter half of 1975, and an earlier draft by Professor Piggott re-written at the same time. Amendments and additions to the last two contributions were made during 1976 but a clear horizon was provided by the Council for British Archaeology's Conference on 'The Effect of Man on the Landscape: the Lowland Zone' in December 1975. That has been taken into account, but two subsequent conferences (Newcastle University, January 1976; Bristol University May 1976 – see Appendix 3) have not. They were significant occasions for the study of later prehistoric agriculture, marking the beginnings of a new phase of development. Dr Fowler's chapters in particular summarize the base from which that development, with its new ideas and objectives, can proceed.

It is our personal regret that our original editor did not live to receive these pages, and we thank the present editor for her sorely tried patience and for all her encouragement and help. Professor Piggott's indebtedness to previous workers in the field of agrarian archaeology goes back to O. G. S. Crawford and Eliot and E. C. Curwen, and continued in Christopher Hawkes, who was inspired to see Dr Fowler as a 'fields' man. Collin Bowen taught him in the field and both he and Charles Thomas have given considerable general and specific assistance in writing these chapters. We are most grateful to them all. The help of others is acknowledged in the footnotes. Material assistance, also gratefully acknowledged, has come from the Research Funds of the University of Bristol and its Department of Extra-Mural Studies. Unwittingly, the BBC was also of enormous help in getting Dr Fowler around the British Isles to see current work while the material for these chapters was being collected.

S. PIGGOTT, *University of Edinburgh*

December 1976   P. J. FOWLER, *University of Bristol*

ACKNOWLEDGMENTS

Apart from the helpful suggestions given by the appropriate co-authors, Dr Ryder wishes to thank the following: Mr R. A. Harcourt and Miss B. A. Noddle for freely supplying unpublished bone data, and much helpful discussion on the interpretation of findings, and Mr C. L. Cram and Mr G. W. I. Hodgson for supplying data. He is grateful to the following for reading and commenting on the sections indicated in brackets: Mr Harcourt (Autumn killing); Dr Marca Burns (goats); Mr I. L. Mason (goats, cattle, horses and parts of the husbandry sections); Mr G. R. Bishop, OBE (pigs); Dr G. Clayton and Dr D. G. M. Wood-Gush (poultry); Mr B. A. Cooper (bees).

EARLY PREHISTORY

By STUART PIGGOTT

Professor Emeritus of Archaeology
University of Edinburgh

"The progress of British agriculture in these prehistoric times is largely a matter of conjecture,..."

Warmsley's Rural Estate Management
(5th edn, London, 1969, p. 7)

CHAPTER I

PLANTS, ANIMALS, AND MAN IN BRITAIN

INTRODUCTION: THE NATURE OF THE EVIDENCE

So far as the beginnings of agrarian history in Britain are concerned, they may properly be thought of as the concern of archaeologists seeking to recover the economic patterns of pre-literate human societies in their relationship to the animal and plant populations with which they shared this island. This evidence, being non-literate, is to that extent non-historical, and, indeed, much of it falls within the disciplines of zoology and botany, but it is susceptible to interpretation in historical terms. The status of archaeology as a discipline has recently been the matter of active discussion, and a 'new archaeology', or rather a 'new prehistory', as it seems to exclude the archaeology of historically documented cultures, has been framed in terms which would regard its methodology as that of an "experimental social science" and "concerned with the formulation of general rules of cultural behaviour". However, such a conceptual model is not necessarily endowed with unique validity, and here we prefer to see our aims as essentially historical, and appropriate therefore as a preface to the main theme of agrarian history, based on the documentary evidence of literate societies.[1]

Prehistory by its nature is, however, non-historical in so far that it deals with non-literate peoples, and can therefore have no documented chronology in calendar years. Since 1950, progressive refinements in techniques and theory have now made available a natural time-scale to about 50,000 years before the present, based on the radioactive decay of an isotope of carbon with an atomic weight of 14. This radiocarbon or C-14 method of dating has revolutionized prehistoric chronology within the limits to which it extends, and is used throughout this volume, but must be taken with two provisos. The first is that dates, by reason of the method, can only be expressed as statistical probabilities, normally to one standard deviation – there is one chance in three that the 'true' date may be outside these limits, one in twenty outside twice the limits. For our purpose the dates will be given in the form '*c.* 2860' and the margin of error left unexpressed. The second point is that recent

[1] The situation is well summarized by B. G. Trigger, *Beyond History, the Methods of Prehistory*, New York, 1968; 'Aims in prehistoric archaeology', *Ant.* XLIV, 1970, pp. 26–37.

work has shown that radiocarbon 'years' have not a one-to-one equivalence with historical calendar years, but diverge from them consistently but irregularly back to about 6,000 radiocarbon years before the present. Again for our use we will cite uncorrected dates, since complete agreement on the detailed conversions needed has not been reached, except where reference is needed to new time-spans implied by an extended scale.[2] Radiocarbon dates are expressed as 'bc'; historical or calibrated dates as 'BC'.

The initial situation in Britain as elsewhere in the Old World is the presence of man as a rare component of the large mammalian fauna, exploiting, with increasing degrees of self-consciousness, his fellow-animals and the plant cover in which both found themselves with the establishment of modern climatic conditions after the final withdrawal of the ice-sheets from *c.* 10,000 bc. In such situations lies the ultimate genesis of the animal and plant husbandry which forms the basis for the subsistence-economies of agrarian societies as we know them from historically documented contexts and infer them from archaeological evidence. But the relationship between man and other animals, especially the larger mammals, can cover a very wide range of symbiotic associations, all related to man's need as an omnivore for a protein intake derived from meat, and his consequent role as a predator among his fellow mammals. Such gradations of association between a human group and an animal group, such as a herd of deer, for instance, can spread from random killing when opportunity presents, to organized hunting, rounding-up of herds for slaughter, ranging (in the sense of nineteenth-century cattle ranging in America), more purposive herding, and ultimately captive domestication and selective breeding. At no one point in the spectrum of relationships can one select a 'beginning of animal husbandry' or of agriculture, even were there zoological agreement on the diagnostic features of an animal's skeleton which initially distinguish domestic stock from the wild congeners, though if man interferes with the natural plant cover to improve grazing and therefore hunting conditions by, for instance, deliberate forest fires, this may be perceptible in the palaeobotanical record. Similarly, relationships between man and plants may range from selection, weeding, or encouraging the growth of wild edible species, uninterruptedly to full plough agriculture, and at most stages the transition is imperceptible to the archaeologist.

These circumstances are of crucial importance in assessing the

[2] British dates are fully published in Council for British Archaeology, *Archaeological Site Index to Radiocarbon Dates for Great Britain & Ireland*, 1971, and Supplements. Corrections are discussed in T. Watkins (ed.), *Radiocarbon: Calibration and Prehistory*, Edinburgh, 1975.

situations in which fully agrarian societies were formed either in the Old or New World: the 'Neolithic Revolution' is perhaps now a rather tired old concept, and shifts of relationships or intensity of exploitation can be thought of as potentially possible in more than one geographical area independently. For Britain, as we shall see, the problem of an indigenous emergence of agrarian economies does not arise, as introduction from the European continent can be demonstrated, but we must take cognisance of the original population, conventionally Mesolithic hunter-gatherers, contrasted with intrusive Neolithic farmers, and consider the possible modes of animal and plant exploitation that they could have shared with the newcomers, and have contributed to the subsequent development of prehistoric agrarian societies from the later fourth millennium BC. There may have been, in some respects, less incompatibility between economies than has sometimes been thought.[3]

The evidence for the inference or assumption of agrarian communities in prehistory falls into three classes: zoological, botanical, and archaeological, in the sense of being defined by human artifacts (though in a sense a domestic sheep or cultivated strain of barley is as much an artifact as is a cart or a ploughed field). This archaeological evidence can be either primary (a surviving plough) or secondary (a quern which could grind cultivated corn or wild acorns). Direct inferences can be made from the former, indirect or collateral inferences from the latter. The presence of settlements that can be inferred to be stable and continuously occupied need not be correlated with an agrarian economy; these can exist on a basis of any assured food supply, as the fishing community at Lepenski Vir on the Danube shows in the sixth millennium bc, or Lautereck, in Württemburg rather later, or the permanent villages of the British Columbian Indians with an economy based on river fish and sea-mammals in recent times. Permanent, as distinct from recurrent, occupation of a settlement is in fact often very difficult to demonstrate archaeologically.

The zoological evidence for an agrarian community would theoretically take the form of the presence in the food refuse of a settlement of a significant percentage of animal bones which can unequivocally be assigned to domestic stock and not to the indigenous wild animal population. Difficulties can arise here when, as we saw above, the status of 'domesticated' is uncertain and the osteological criteria for determining it not established. But such circumstances hardly occur in

[3] For the background of the ideas expressed here, cf. P. J. Ucko & G. W. Dimbleby (eds.), *The Domestication and Exploitation of Plants and Animals*, London, 1969; E. S. Higgs and M. R. Jarman, 'The origins of agriculture: a reconsideration', *Ant.*, XLIII, 1969, pp. 31–41; P. W. Wilkinson, 'Neolithic postscript', *ibid.*, XLV, 1971, pp. 193–6; E. S. Higgs (ed.), *Papers in Economic Prehistory*, Cambridge, 1972.

Britain, where a complete intrusive agricultural economy seems to have been introduced from the European continent, except in the instance of the dog, already domesticated in Britain at an earlier period. British Neolithic farm stock was all descended from an imported nucleus of already domesticated animals, even if subsequent interbreeding with, for instance, wild cattle and swine took place.

The contribution of the study of early plant communities – palaeobotany – is more extensive but not always unambiguous, and comprises three classes of evidence. The first is concerned with the natural plant cover of an area when this is able, unimpeded, to reach the botanical climax whereby all suitable ecological niches are occupied by appropriate species. As the occurrence and distribution of plant species are ultimately dependent on climatic factors, changes in the composition of the flora can be themselves indices of climatic change; owing to the highly resistant qualities and markedly characteristic forms of the pollen of all species, this can become embedded and survive in ancient soils and peat deposits, and be used to assess the proportionate incidence of the various species at a given point of archaeologically or geologically determined time. The natural sequence of change in the north European botanical climax during the 10,000 years or so of post-glacial time is now known with considerable precision, and disturbances, such as a marked decline in the proportion of tree pollen in the total count, and the concurrent appearance of species proper to open country, or weeds of cultivation or even cereals, may indicate human interference and forest clearance for cultivation or pasture. Such phenomena are not always as simple to interpret as may appear at first sight, and we shall find examples of these in Britain. In general, though, the palaeobotanical evidence derived from pollen analysis, supplemented by macroscopic remains where these survive, has proved an extremely sensitive indicator of man's activities in the wooded landscape of Britain encountered by the first stone-using agricultural immigrants from *c.* 3500 bc, or in calendar years from about 4400 BC.

The second botanical technique is the most direct but in its nature dependent on fortunate circumstances of survival: the identification of extant edible plant remains, either seeds such as cereal grain or nutritious cultivated species, such as the oily seeds of flax, or, in the form of straw, husks, glumes, and other identifiable debris characteristic of the crops grown by agriculturalists. Similarly, wild vegetable remains such as seeds, pips, stones, or other indigestible fragments can add to our knowledge of the dietary range of prehistoric peoples. Charring or incomplete burning offer good chances of survival in most conditions, and by an extension of this the third botanical technique has been devised – the identification of seed impressions in baked clay (pottery, hearths, burnt daub, etc.) where the original seed has been destroyed by burning but has left an accurate cast in the substance in which it was accidentally embedded in the circumstances of household manufacture in primitive conditions of cleanliness and tidiness. This elegant technique has contributed enormously to our knowledge of cereal cultivation in prehistoric Britain.

Purely archaeological evidence, while of prime importance, is limited. The survival of wooden agricultural implements such as digging-sticks, hoes, ards, or ploughs is naturally restricted to exceptional natural circumstances such as water-logging in peat or marshlands; so too is the survival of even fragments of vehicles such as carts or wagons demanding traction by domestic animals. Settlements are not always unambiguously agrarian in character, and the identification of pits as certainly for storage of farm produce, or of post-settings as necessarily supporting granaries, is fraught with uncertainties. More decisive are surviving traces of enclosures bounding plots or fields of cultivated soil, or even, in buried land-surfaces, traces of plough-furrows or spade digging. And the fencing of tilled fields or the demarcation of pre-sumptive cattle enclosures or ranch areas can sometimes at least be inferred, if difficult to demonstrate conclusively. As we noted, querns and grinding stones, though necessary in cereal preparation, need not be devoted to grain alone, or even to cultivated seeds; sickles and reaping knives, again an adjunct to cereal farming, can equally well be used for reeds, and grain can be collected by such alternative means as plucking. On the whole, however, we can recognize in the material equipment of our earliest agriculturalists the set of instruments of husbandry common to their continental ancestors, which continue, some in metal rather than in stone, throughout pre-industrialized farming virtually to the present day.

THE DEVELOPMENT
OF THE POST-GLACIAL CLIMATE

The sequence of changes in the natural plant cover, and in particular of the composition of the forest which formed the main constituent of the botanical climax, as average temperatures rose with the final withdrawal of the ice-sheet, has been worked out by means of pollen analysis for northern Europe over the past half-century. With the advent of radiocarbon dating the vegetational phases or zones, for long firmly established as a relative chronological scheme, could be assigned dates with increasing precision, and the correlation of vegetational zones with archaeological evidence for human occupation gave an added dimension to the natural and man-made environment for a period of some 10,000 years before the present.[4] In the earlier studies of the climatic phases, reflected in the changing plant cover, names such as 'Boreal' or 'Atlantic' were used to describe the assumed type of climate of a given period, but these have largely been replaced by the more neutral numbering of zones, in Britain from I (Early Post-glacial, or, from a characteristic plant, the older Dryas phase) to VII (Sub-Atlantic or Modern). For our purposes we shall be almost wholly concerned with Zones VI (Boreal), VIIa (Atlantic), and VIIb (Sub-Boreal), and for the first demonstrably agricultural settlements, VIIb.

The zone boundaries have now been fairly firmly fixed in terms of radiocarbon years, and in round figures these are: V/VI, c. 7500 bc; VI/VIIa, c. 5500 bc; VIIa/VIIb, c. 3500 bc. This last transition date is roughly equivalent to the average of those from the earliest archaeological sites attributable to agriculturalists, in the British Isles, and the botanical characteristics distinguishing VII from VIIa include a marked decline in the proportions of tree pollen, particularly that of the elm, and the appearance of species associated with cleared or open country. This has posed the problem as to whether, unlike the natural climatically induced changes which mark the boundaries of the other zones, the VIIa/VIIb transition is wholly or predominantly the result of the appearance of man as an active agent in the landscape, reducing the forest for agricultural clearance, or lopping trees to provide cattle-fodder. This is a complex question affecting north-western continental Europe as well as Britain, and clearly with far-reaching consequences for our concepts of the beginnings of agrarian colonization of the area, and must be discussed in detail in a later section.

An additional natural factor affecting the British Isles is the formation of the English Channel, whereby Britain became an island detached from the continental land-mass, so that all subsequent human contacts had of necessity to be made across the sea in boats. The date of the final insulation of Britain has not been precisely determined, but there is general agreement that it took place about the beginning of, or early in, Zone VIIa, around 5500 bc. Not only would the Channel have limited human contacts in both directions but it would have inhibited any further colonization of plant or animal species spreading northwards as the climate ameliorated, unless these two were deliberately introduced

⁴ J. G. Evans, 'Notes on the environment of early farming communities in Britain', in D. D. A. Simpson (ed.), *Economy and Settlement in Neolithic and Early Bronze Age Britain and Europe*, Leicester, 1971, pp. 11–26; J. G. Evans, *The Environment of Early Man in the British Isles*, 1975; W. Pennington, *The History of British Vegetation*, London, 1969; J. D. Ovington, *Woodlands*, London, 1965; cf. H. H. Lamb, *The Changing Climate*, London, 1966. Full documentation of date in H. Godwin, *The History of the British Flora*, Cambridge, 1st ed. 1956; plants and animals in R. G. Pearson, *Animals and Plants of the Cenozoic Era*, London, 1964.

by man. A species of thistle (*Cirsium*), flourishing on the French side of the Straits of Dover but unknown across the Channel in England, has been instanced as a good case in point.[5]

THE PLANT, ANIMAL, AND HUMAN POPULATION BEFORE *c.* 4000 BC

"Let us imagine then what kind of countrie this was in the time of the Ancient Britons", wrote John Aubrey in the 1660s. "The whole island was anciently one great forest", he went on, "and the inhabitants almost as savage as the beasts whose skins were their only rayment." He remembered that there was more woodland in Wiltshire even in his youth and realized how the countryside could be swiftly changed from forest to grassland. At the Royal Society on one occasion the poet Edmund Waller had posed the question "whether Salisbury plaines were always plaines", in the sense of open grassland or prairies: this usage goes back in America to the eighteenth century. It was in fact to the New World that Aubrey's intuitive intelligence turned when he gave his view that one might think of the Indians of Jamaica or Virginia who "did burn down great woods to cultivate the soil" and "plaines were there made by firing the woods to sowe corne. They do call these plaines Savannas. Who knowes but Salisbury plaines, &c, might be made long time ago, after this manner, and for the same reason?" When we come to talk of the botanical climax of temperate forests in Britain, with forest clearances apparently initially made by primitive communities without evidence of the knowledge of textiles, and furthermore, when we use recent ethnographical parallels to suggest that the 'slash-and-burn' technique was most likely employed by early agriculturalists, we are no more than using our scientific knowledge to come to conclusions startlingly similar to those brilliantly apprehended by Aubrey over three centuries ago.[6]

The palaeobotanical evidence for the plant cover of Britain at the beginning of Zone VIIa, the Atlantic climatic phase, is consistent over most of the country, and is marked by the almost universal replacement of the birch and pine woodlands of VI, the Boreal period, by deciduous forest of the mixed oak type, dominated by oak and elm, as a result of a rise in average annual temperatures, which even allowed warmth-loving trees like lime to colonize southern England. The process, starting in Zone VI, reached its maximum in the subsequent phase, and

---

[5] Pennington, *op. cit.*, I, p. 54.

[6] J. Aubrey, *Wiltshire Topographical Collections*, ed. J. E. Jackson, 1862, 4; *idem., The Natural History of Wilts.*, ed. J. Britton, London, 1847 (repr., Newton Abbot, 1969), p. 10.

with the formation of the Channel our insular post-glacial flora took on its characteristic insular pattern. The deciduous forests were reaching mountain altitudes of up to 760 m, even in Scotland as far north as Ben Lawers (lat. 56° 30′). This is moving towards the northern geographical boundary of the range of oak, though it has been recognized in VIIa contexts even further north. Pine, widespread in Boreal times, became a northern tree, especially characteristic of the north-east Scottish Highlands; in the lower coastal areas to the east, birch had reached a dominant position in Zone VI and continued as an important forest component; alder reached its maximum in VIIb. Mixed oak forest was also present, never in great quantity, but at its optimum development around the Boreal–Atlantic transition. In north-east Caithness, approaching lat. 59°, the pine–birch forests were at their maximum in Zone VI, and early in Zone VIIa they appear to have been replaced by a landscape dominated by heather (*Calluna*), grass, and sedge.[7] Even in the island of Harris, there is evidence of woodland conditions and neolithic clearance. Archaeological evidence suggests, as we shall see, that the Orkneys, northwards across the Pentland Firth, and the still more remote Shetlands (lat. 60°) were virtually treeless in the early second millennium.

In general, therefore, we have to think of the whole of Britain, except at high altitudes and in salt-marsh areas, carrying forest cover at the period of the Post-glacial botanical climax from *c.* 5500 bc. Archaeologically, as we shall see, the human population was that of hunters and gatherers, stone-using, and in sparsely scattered communities, conventionally labelled 'Mesolithic'. Over most of Britain, the forests were predominantly deciduous, dominated by stands of oak, elm, and to a less extent ash, though birch was abundant in what are now the Somerset fens; in northern Scotland pine was the main constituent of the mountain forests, birch and alder on the lower coastal areas east of the Highland massif. The reduction of this almost universal forest cover has been the work of man over the millennia, and the earliest phases of this predatory action in prehistory will be traced in ensuing sections of this volume. There are two types of British landscape, however, which merit discussion, since they have in recent centuries been open areas with little or no forest cover, and the high antiquity of this botanical situation has only recently been called into question in a scientific manner. These are first the heathlands of, for instance, the

---

[7] S. E. Durno, 'Certain aspects of vegetational history in N.E. Scotland', *Scott. Geog. Mag.*, 73, 1957, pp. 176–84; 'Pollen analysis of peat deposits in E. Sutherland and Caithness', *ibid.*, 74, 1958, pp. 127–35; 'Pollen analysis peat deposits in the E. Grampians', *ibid.*, 75, 1959, pp. 102–11; J. G. Evans, 'Habitat change on the calcareous soils of Britain: the impact of neolithic man', in Simpson, *op. cit.*, pp. 27–74.

Pennines, North Yorkshire, and the Norfolk Breckland; Hardy's Egdon Heath; Betjeman's Sandy Surrey; or Heywood Sumner's pre-Raphaelite New Forest. The second is the chalk downs of Sussex, where Kipling glimpsed prehistory, or of Wessex and Salisbury Plain, where Edmund Waller asked his searching question. Heathland and downland have caught the imagination of the generations by their stark, treeless contrast with the mild pastoral slopes of the rest of southern England, and in the instance of the chalk hills and plateaux have for long been cited by archaeologists and human geographers as open areas inviting early colonization and cultivation. All recent research, however, points to their man-made character, as Aubrey thought might have been the case in Wiltshire, and the heathlands present a similar situation.

The status of the British heathlands has been the subject of study since Godwin's analysis of the Hockham Mere pollen sequence in relation to the Breckland landscape of today, and continued by Dimbleby at over thirty sites, ranging from the North Yorkshire moors to Dorset, Hampshire, Surrey, and Sussex.[8] In many instances the beginning of the decline of previous forest cover goes back to the fifth millennium bc or to approximately equivalent chronological horizons in Zone VIIa, and the process clearly accelerates in subsequent periods. On a number of occasions it is possible to associate the earliest forest clearance with the presence of stone-using hunter-gatherers of Mesolithic cultural traditions, and with the advent of agriculturalists the areas which were to deteriorate from woodland to heathland owing to poor soil conditions would have rapidly increased. Intensified grazing by wild animals, such as deer, after initial clearances by man could lead to leaching and the impoverishment of acid soils, with the development of the typical heathland flora. These instances of early human interference with the tree cover in Britain are discussed in more detail later in the book.

The chalk downs, basic in contrast to the acidic soil of the heaths, have in the past presented a problem in interpretation owing to the fact that pollen grains have a poor chance of survival in alkaline soils, and peat sequences rarely occur in near relationship to the well-drained Chalk. It has recently been shown, however, that adequate pollen samples are not impossible to collect on occasion, even from unpromising soils,[9] and indicate the local plant population in the usual way.

[8] H. Godwin, 'Age and origin of the 'Breckland' heaths of East Anglia', Nature, 154, 1944, p. 6; G. W. Dimbleby, The Development of British Heathlands and their Soils, Oxford, 1962. A man-made origin for the comparable 'landes' of Brittany has also been suggested: W. van Zeist, 'A palaeobotanical study of some bogs in Western Brittany...', Palaeohistoria, 10, 1964, pp. 157–80, esp. p. 170.

[9] G. W. Dimbleby, 'Pollen analysis of terrestrial soils', New Phytol., 56, 1957, pp. 12–28; idem., 'Soil pollen analysis', J. Soil Science, 12, 1961, pp. 1–11; idem. in I. F. Smith (ed.), Windmill Hill and Avebury, Oxford, 1965, pp. 34–8.

Reassessment of the condition of the Wiltshire Chalk in glacial times has shown the inevitability of its having been covered, in Post-glacial times, by a soil cover with fertile and non-acidic humus, mixed with the upper layer of mineral soil, which would normally support deciduous forest: the change to open grassland could only have come about as the result of human cultivation and subsequent erosion. Added to this, the incidence of land molluscs from buried soils can be interpreted in terms of open or shady habitats, implying woodland, scrub, or open country.[10] All the evidence is consistent in indicating that the Chalk was originally covered with deciduous forest, growing on a brown-earth soil, and that human inroads on this began at the VIIa/VIIb transition by the action of agriculturalists clearing forests for fodder, pasture, or cultivation.

The post-glacial animal population of Britain is not susceptible to study by means comparable to those used in botany, which, as we have seen, to a large degree depend on the enormous natural wastage of pollen in the process of fertilization in plants, and the accident of a high survival-value of the pollen-rain as it becomes incorporated in natural deposits of soil or peat. Our knowledge of the fauna which formed a biological counterpart of the flora just described within Zones VI and VIIa depends on the survival of skeletal or other remains either as fossils in recent natural deposits, or in contexts determined by man who, as an omnivorous predator, exploited animals for food or for other products such as antlers or furs, and left the inedible residue of such operations – animal bones or molluscs shells – in his middens. In such contexts of course we do not have a random sample of species, but only those with nutritive value, and these chosen for what may seem quite irrational reasons, or for their palatability by themselves or in conjunction: "we are still not very knowledgeable as to why people eat some foods and reject other foods".[11] The absence or presence of animal bones or mollusc shells among the debris of a prehistoric site will therefore depend on selection partly made on grounds of utility (for food bait, or as raw material for artifacts) and partly in response to the tradition of the group as to what may and what may not be eaten,

[10] J. G. Evans, 'Periglacial deposits on the chalk of Wiltshire', *Wilts. Arch. Nat. Hist. Mag.*, 63, 1968, pp. 12–26; 'Land mollusca from the neolithic enclosure on Windmill Hill', *ibid.*, 61, 1966, pp. 91–2; 'Interpretation of land snail faunas', *Lond. Univ. Inst. Arch. Bull.*, VIII/IX, 1968–9, pp. 109–16; 'Habitat change on the calcareous soils of Britain: the impact of neolithic man', in D. D. A. Simpson (ed.), *Economy and Settlement in Neolithic and Early Bronze Age Britain and Europe*, Leicester, 1971, pp. 27–74; *Land Snails in Archaeology*, 1972.

[11] J. Yudkin, 'Archaeology and the nutritionist', in P. J. Ucko and G. W. Dimbleby (eds.), *The Domestication and Exploitation of Plants and Animals*, London, 1969, pp. 547–52.

in terms of totem, tabu, or custom. In a recent study of a Bushman group of hunter-gatherers it was recorded that although they recognized and named 223 local animal species, 54 were regarded as edible and of these only 17 species were regularly hunted.[12]

With these provisos we have to consider an animal population adapted to the temperate forests of mixed oakwood, or pine and birch in the north, near to that surviving to the present day, but with several large mammalian species now extinct and of course without recent introductions (such as the fallow deer).[13] To this we must add the sea mammals, fresh water and ocean fish, crustaceans and molluscs, for all of which we have evidence of human consumption. Nor must we altogether forget the possibility of edible insects. One animal appears to have been domesticated among British and European hunter-gatherers, the dog. It has been identified at Star Carr and Thatcham in the eighth millennium bc, and is also known in Scandinavia, and in later Mesolithic contexts. It is generally assumed that it was used in hunting, but its initial captivity as a food animal has been suggested.[14]

From the view of human exploitation the large mammals form the most significant animal population as providers of meat. In general, as in Post-glacial times the tundra landscape was replaced by woodland, the reindeer, bison, and wild horse of this environment were replaced by the aurochs (or wild cattle) and elk in the birch, pine, and hazel forests of Zones IV and V; by Zone VI, with the beginning of the spread of mixed oak woodlands, we have the red and roe deer, the wild boar and brown bear as additional large mammals, while the elk became extinct or retreated to more northerly latitudes. The basic fauna of later prehistoric Britain was, indeed, established at this time, and, with minor modifications made by man as predator, continued into the early Middle Ages. Thenceforward, increasing forest clearance reduced it to its present minimal status. Naturally, after the formation of the English Channel around 6000 bc and the Zone VI/VIIa transition, no new species could colonize Britain from the continent, and any additions to the wild or domestic fauna could only be sea-borne and by human agency. Apart from stray finds of bones in geological deposits of

[12] R. B. Lee, 'What hunters do for a living...', in R. B. Lee and I. De Vore, *Man the Hunter*, Chicago, 1968, pp. 30–48.

[13] The identification of fallow deer antler in the Neolithic context (*c.* 2400 bc) at the Giants' Hills long barrow in Lincolnshire must be an error. J. W. Jackson in C. W. Phillips, 'Excavation of the Giants' Hill long barrow...', *Archaeologia*, 85, 1936, p. 95. *Cervus dama* appears to be a Norman introduction. J. Ritchie, *The Influence of Man on Animal Life in Scotland*, Cambridge, 1920, p. 284; C. Matheson, *Changes in the Fauna of Wales within Historic Times*, 1932, p. 72.

[14] J. Murray, *The First European Agriculture*, Edinburgh, 1970, p. 18; E. S. Higgs and M. R. Jarman, 'The origins of agriculture: a reconsideration', *Ant.*, XLIII, 1969, p. 36.

Post-glacial date, our best conspectus of the fauna from an early hunter-gatherer site is that from Star Carr in Yorkshire, of *c.* 7500 bc; another contemporary site is at Thatcham in Berkshire. Of later dates are the specialized inventories of Mesolithic communities, mainly based on fishing in west Scotland, which may be as late as the fourth millennium bc, and a list of wild animals has been compiled associated with Neolithic agriculturalists from *c.* 3000–1500 bc.[15] Here one must remember we are dealing with agricultural peoples in whose economy hunting had an unimportant place, so that absolute numbers of bones of wild species are drastically reduced.

The most important large mammal of the temperate woodlands of Britain between *c.* 6000–3000 BC and onwards into later prehistory, was the red deer, *Cervus elaphus.* Faunal remains from archaeological sites show its preponderance as a source of food and, in respect of its antlers, of raw material for tools: the hide, imperceptible in the archaeological record, could have been equally valued. The antlers were collected either from the heads of stags killed between October and March, or after shedding in April but before they had been gnawed and eaten by the deer themselves. The Star Carr evidence, combined with that for the elk indicated below, implies a hunting season spread over the winter months, from October to April. The size of the red deer in its natural environment would have made it a notable contribution to the meat diet from its sheer size and weight; this is discussed again in a later section. But we have to think of beasts at least a third greater in meat weight than the impoverished specimens feeding on the poor diet of Scottish deer 'forests' today. The roe deer (*Capreolus capreolus*) has not on the whole made the adaptation to reduced circumstances in recent times that the Scottish red deer population achieved, and has remained a woodland species slightly reduced in size from prehistoric standards. In the period under consideration it was widely hunted, but to a lesser degree than red deer.

The elk (*Alces alces*) presents a somewhat different picture as an animal now extinct in Britain, though surviving for instance in Sweden, where the modern animal is unaltered in size from its prehistoric forebears. It was present in some quantity in the eighth millennium bc site of Star Carr, and in less quantity at Thatcham, but no Neolithic records for the period *c.* 3000–1500 bc exist: Post-glacial finds, not in archaeological contexts, total eight from England and twenty from Scotland.[16] It must be remembered that Neolithic fauna lists are almost wholly southern

[15] F. C. Fraser and J. E. King, 'Faunal remains', in J. G. D. Clark, *Excavations at Star Carr*, Cambridge, 1954, pp. 70–95; J. E. King, 'Report on Animal Bones', in J. Wymer, 'Excavations at...Thatcham, Berks.', *Proc. Prehist. Soc.*, 28, 1962, pp. 355–61; S. Piggott, *Neolithic Cultures of the British Isles*, Cambridge, 1954, pp. 10–13.

[16] Fraser and King., *op. cit.*, p. 92.

English, and the elk may have been a casualty not only as a result of
forest clearance but of the change from predominantly pine and birch
forest to mixed oak woodlands.[17] In such a context a northward retreat
of the species might be envisaged, with a longer survival in Scotland
in forest conditions still of this type in later prehistory. At Keiss in
Caithness there is a record in a context which could be early medieval,
and in the Lowlands it was extant in the first–second centuries AD as
the finds from the Newstead Roman fort demonstrate.[18]

Wild cattle (urus or aurochs: *Bos primigenius*) were another component
of the Pleistocene mammalian fauna surviving into Post-glacial times,
and at Star Carr they were the second most important food animals after
red deer. They continue to occur, in small numbers, in Neolithic and
even slightly later contexts, and reached formidable dimensions:
although variable and showing marked differences in size between bulls
and cows, they "did not decrease in size in Northern Europe between
the Mesolithic and the Bronze Age". Although usually assumed to be
a forest dweller, it has been pointed out that its huge horn-span would
preclude or hamper movement among dense stands of timber, and the
possibility of 'woodland' and 'plains' form (like the American bison)
should not be overlooked.[19] And like the other ungulates just discussed,
Bos primigenius must by its grazing have tended to extend open areas
in the woodlands, so that the indigenous wild deer and cattle population
might themselves be unconscious agents in forest reduction, side-by-side
with the deliberate efforts of man. The relation of a wild cattle
population in Britain, at the time of the introduction of domesticated
stock, to the incoming herds will be discussed at a later stage.

Before leaving the ungulates, we may notice in passing the evidence
for the survival of the reindeer (*Rangifer tarandus*) in Scotland into
Post-glacial, prehistoric, and perhaps even into historic times.[20] The

---

[17] Cf. J. E. King in Wymer, *op. cit.* But the modern elk population in Sweden has
in fact increased after agricultural clearance of woodland. J. D. Ovington, *Woodlands*,
London, 1965, p. 56.

[18] J. A. Smith, 'Notice of the discovery of remains of the Elk...', *Proc. Soc. Ant.
Scot.*, 9, 1870–71, p. 297; J. Ritchie, *op. cit.*, p. 348; J. C. Ewart, 'Animal remains', in
J. Curle, *A Roman Frontier Post and its People...*, 1911, pp. 362–77. Birch and hazel
were predominantly present in the tree remains. H. F. Tagg, 'Vegetable remains', *ibid.*,
pp. 353–61. Ewart's statement that *Alces* was present 'at several Romano-British villages
in England' (*ibid.*, p. 376n) is inexplicable.

[19] C. Grigson, 'Absolute size differences of aurochs and cattle', in Ucko and
Dimbleby, *op. cit.*, pp. 277–94. Cf. P. A. Jewell, 'Cattle from British archaeological
sites', in A. E. Mourant and F. E. Zeuner (eds.), *Man and Cattle*, Roy. Anthrop. Inst.
Symp., London, 1963, pp. 80–101; F. W. Shawcross and E. S. Higgs, 'The excavation
of a *Bos primigenius* at Lowe's Farm, Littleport', *Proc. Camb. Ant. Soc.*, 54, 1961, pp.
3–16 (Bronze Age survival).

[20] Ritchie, *op. cit.*, pp. 338–46; J. A. Smith, 'Notice of the remains of Rein-Deer...',
Proc. Soc. Ant. Scot., 8, 1869–70, p. 186.

question of the wild horse (*Equus* sp.) also deserves comment. Survival from the Pleistocene of an animal, ultimately to be ancestral to Ewart's 'Forest' and 'Celtic' types, must be assumed in Britain as elsewhere in north-western Europe: a wild forest species survived in Poland until the eighteenth century.[21] It was present at Thatcham, though not at Star Carr, but there are at least fourteen occurrences in Neolithic (third millennium bc) contexts in Sussex, Wessex, and the Cotswolds, and six from Caithness and Orkney in Scotland. Its presence in Ireland in a Beaker context of *c.* 2000 bc has been interpreted as the introduction of a domesticate.[22] It seems to have been a food animal but rarely consumed; the wild boar (*Sus scrofa*) on the other hand is common, though not in large proportions, throughout our period, and like the cattle, raises questions of possible relationships between wild and domestic breeds, once the latter had been introduced. The brown bear (*Ursus arctos*) can of course provide some bulk of meat, and is attested in Neolithic contexts: it survived until historical times, but its significance in prehistoric times, together with other animals such as the beaver (*Castor fiber*), and others such as the Neolithic wild cat (*Felis sylvestris*) at Windmill Hill,[23] is more likely to be for its fur than its nutritive value.

The sea mammals, notably the whales and seals, have been studied in their economic relationship to prehistoric man in Britain and Europe in a series of magisterial studies by Grahame Clark.[24] The whales (within which order dolphins and porpoises as well as baleen, rorqual, and the toothed whales are included) were obvious sources of meat either when hunted, or as a massive protein windfall when stranded, and the importance of the latter was soon recognized in medieval legislation: at Chichester in the twelfth century a whale stranded on cathedral property belonged to the bishop (except for the tongue, a royal prerogative), but he only got a right flipper if it turned up elsewhere on the coast of his diocese. Strandings can be frequent (over 400 have been recorded for the British Isles in a dozen years), and bones of rorquals (including the huge blue-whale), were found with tools of

[21] Ewart, *op. cit.*; F. E. Zeuner, *A History of Domesticated Animals*, London, 1963, p. 310. Cf. J. Murray, *The First European Agriculture*, Edinburgh, 1970, p. 101; C. Grigson in P. Ashbee, 'The Fussell's Lodge long barrow...', *Archaeologia*, 100, 1966, pp. 69–70.

[22] To instances in S. Piggott, *op. cit.*, add *idem*, *The West Kennet Long Barrow*, 1962, p. 53; J. F. S. Stone *et al.*, 'Durrington Walls...', *Ant. J.*, 34, 1954, p. 176; M. Jope in I. F. Smith (ed.), p. 143. Cf. Ritchie, *op. cit.*, p. 71. Ireland, L. H. van Wijngaarden-Bakker, 'Animal remains...at Newgrange Co. Meath...', *Proc. Roy. Irish Acad.*, 74, C, 1974, p. 313.

[23] M. Jope in I. F. Smith (ed.), *Windmill Hill and Avebury*, Oxford, 1965, p. 143.

[24] J. G. D. Clark, 'Seal-hunting in the Stone Age of north-western Europe', *Proc. Prehist. Soc.*, 12, 1946, pp. 12–48; *idem.*, 'Whales as an economic factor in prehistoric Europe', *Ant.*, XXI, 1947, pp. 84–104; *idem.*, *Prehistoric Europe: the Economic Basis*, London, 1952.

hunter-gatherers in the Forth Estuary in a Zone VIIa context, and probably in a contemporary settlement in the island of Oronsay, together with grey and spotted seals, found also on Rigsa in Loch Sunart.

Little is known of the use of birds for food except from a few Mesolithic and Neolithic sites in the Hebrides and Orkneys, where fifteen species, including cormorant, gannet, pink-footed goose, and the extinct great auk, are represented.[25]

Finally, together with the sea mammals there were enormous potential protein resources in fish, in salt or fresh water, again exhaustively reviewed by Clark.[26] Coastal fishing by Mesolithic communities must have been both from the rocks and by line or nets from boats; black sea-beam from the shore, and conger, haddock, sea-bream, ballan wrasse, thornback ray, skate, and sharks from deeper water. Crabs were caught, perhaps in traps baited with ballan wrasse. Grey mullet could be netted or speared, as were fresh-water fish such as pike. To these must be added seafood such as cockles, winkles, scallops, mussels, and limpets (which could also have been used as bait in line-fishing) and, parenthetically, edible seaweeds such as laver and carrageen moss should not be forgotten.

The natural food resources of Britain *c.* 6000–3000 BC were practically limitless, though deficient mainly in the starches and carbohydrates provided by cereal crops. Here, however, we must remember the potential of wild seeds: the gruel eaten by Tollund man in the third/fifth centuries AD in Denmark included not only barley, oats, and linseed, but seeds of sixteen wild species, thus providing starch and fat.[27] Hazel nuts (*Corylus*) seem to have been everywhere collected and may have formed an important dietary item: deliberate encouragement of hazel growth for the purpose has been suggested. We will look more closely into the exploitation of these by man later. But as we shall see, at no time was the potential exploited to the full: human communities were always small and primitive; hunting and gathering is not always very efficient, nor is it carried out in terms of a conscious exploitation to the fullest degree of an environment's resources. To look at early man's relationship to his environment (including his fellow-men) in this way is making the cardinal error of importing into the past ideas motivating societies in the present, and to create a fictitious *Homo*

[25] S. Piggott, *Neolithic Cultures of the British Isles*, p. 12, for list; J. G. D. Clark, 'Fowling in prehistoric Europe', *Ant.*, XXII, 1948, pp. 116–30; D. Bramwell, 'Bird distribution in Britain during the late-glacial and post-glacial periods', *Merseyside Nat. Assoc. Bird Rep.*, 1959–60, pp. 51–8.

[26] J. G. D. Clark, 'The development of fishing in prehistoric Europe', *Ant. J.*, 28, 1948, pp. 45–85; idem., *Prehistoric Europe*. . ., 1952.

[27] H. Helbaek, 'Botanical study of the stomach contents of the Tollund man', *Aarbøger*, 1950, pp. 329–41.

economicus rather than a hunter who sees no reason to spend more than two or three hours a day on 'subsistence activities' so as to have plenty of time for sleeping and lazing about (as in Arnhem Land). Others would be loath to let hunting interfere with the pleasures of gambling (as is the practice among the Hadza) or visiting, entertaining, and dancing (as is customary in a Bushman tribe).[28] Even when we turn to agricultural communities, it is wrong to consider the prehistoric peasant as actuated by the same ethics of work, profit, and financial status as is man in the modern urbanized West.

It is time to bring man, our leading actor, on to the stage which we have spent some time in decorating with appropriate woodland sets and a walking-on cast of assorted animals. But it would have been misleading to introduce our principal character unsupported and spot-lighted on the bare boards of an uninhabited island. He can only be understood as a piece of natural history himself, and the first human settlement of Britain is simply a natural consequence of the northward expansion of plant and animal species to fill new biological niches as climate rendered this possible. Before the formation of the English Channel, in the interglacials and final glacial period, that part of Britain habitable south of the ice-sheets constituted a peripheral north-western corner of the ancient European continent, with its human population everywhere scanty, and, at the last glaciation, in the area to become southern England, likely to be reckoned in hundreds rather than thousands; 250 persons was an estimate made some time ago which may still not be far off the mark. With the formation of modern climatic conditions the process was not stopped, for "the presumption is that the main elements in the mesolithic population of Britain reached us from the Continent as part of the general northward march of flora and fauna that mark the transition to Post-glacial times."[29]

At the time of the occupation of the settlement sites at Star Carr in Yorkshire, or Thatcham in Berkshire, or (a little later) Broxbourne in Hertfordshire, the southern shore of the North Sea probably followed the 50 m submarine contour, and so would have run roughly from the North Yorkshire coast to the Skaggerak, and although the land between this and the present coast from Dover to Schleswig may have contained numerous areas of salt or fresh water, land communication was possible between what was then the British peninsula, and

[28] M. D. Sahlins, 'Notes on the original affluent society', in R. B. Lee and I. De Vore, *Man the Hunter*, Chicago, 1968, pp. 85–9; J. Woodburn, 'An introduction to Hadza ecology', in *ibid*. pp. 49–55; R. B. Lee, 'What hunters do for a living...', in *ibid.*, pp. 30–48.

[29] J. G. D. Clark, 'Notes on the Obanian with special reference to antler and bone-work', *Proc. Soc. Ant. Scot.*, 89, 1955–56, p. 102.

continental Europe from the coast of North France to Scandinavia and points east. In the subsequent land and sea changes we have lost heavily along our eastern coasts, and what would have been the shore-line of later Mesolithic and early Neolithic Britain around 4000–3000 BC has long vanished in the erosion and subsidence that continued from Winchelsea to Ravenser on the Humber into the Middle Ages. But the formation of the Channel, if it stopped further movement northward of plant or animal communities from the coast, failed to prevent man's colonization because he had invented the boat, whereby he "made himself amphibious without the necessity of even getting wet". The European contacts established overland were now continued by sea.

For over a century a 'Mesolithic' phase of human culture has been named as such, to indicate in the first place a stage technologically and chronologically intermediate between the 'Palaeolithic' and 'Neolithic' periods as originally defined by Lubbock in 1865, and in ecological terms coming to be defined as hunter-gatherers in a post-glacial context.[30] In Britain it is convenient to distinguish an Early phase, c. 8300–6500 bc, from a Late, c. 6500–3000, and in the first come our eighth millennium hunter-gatherer cultures represented by Star Carr or Thatcham, having affinities with what is now Scandinavia and the North European Plain. The sites in fact constitute the most westerly of a culture-province stretching eastwards to the Vistula and the Gulf of Riga, but already with distinctive insular characteristics, and they seem widespread in Britain as far west as Cornwall, and northwards to the southern Pennines. In north Britain and in Wales the situation is less clear at this time. In the later phase in Britain the flint industries show affiliations with the Late Mesolithic traditions of the Low Countries and north France, as might be expected before the final breach of the Straits of Dover; similarly, after this event insular qualities would naturally become apparent, however much cross-channel contacts may have been maintained. Although there is a theoretical point of chronological contact or overlap between the end of this phase and the first advent of agricultural colonists in Britain, no cultural contact can be perceived between the two.[31]

The later Mesolithic cultures of Britain are almost wholly known from their flint and stone equipment, owing to their prevalence on acid soils inimical to the preservation of bone. Many tools and weapons must have been composite, utilizing so-called microlithic flint blades and

---

[30] The modification of Lubbock's scheme was made immediately, in 1866, and was in international use by 1874. J. Wilkins, 'The Mesolithic', *Ant.*, 33, 1959, pp. 130–1; C. A. Moberg, 'The Mesolithic', *ibid.*, pp. 220–1.

[31] The most convenient up-to-date summary is P. A. Mellars, 'The palaeolithic and mesolithic', in C. Renfrew (ed.), *British Prehistory*, London, 1974, pp. 41–99.

points, but in southern and eastern England at least evidence for flint axe-blades of a distinctive type, is continuous through both Early and Late phases of the Mesolithic and can hardly be dissociated from tree-felling activities and forest clearance which, as we shall see, is indicated by other evidence. The paucity or absence of evidence in the north and west has suggested to some that sites in the latter region may represent specialized and seasonal hunting activities by the same communities as those identified in the south and east, an hypothesis which would have fundamental implications in any population estimates based on the number of recognized sites. Another feature which is becoming increasingly apparent is the transport and interchange (or 'trade') in certain stones over long distances. A characteristic chert from the Isle of Portland, where occupation of already coastal settlement-sites goes back to *c.* 5200 bc, was distributed as far as Land's End, the Cotswolds, and Sussex; flint itself must also have been sought as outcrops or beach pebbles far and wide; other pebbles of Cornish origin reached sites in Hampshire and Surrey. In the north, Arran pitchstone was traded as far east as Fife and the Tweed valley in Mesolithic hunter-gatherer contexts and on into the second millennium BC.[32] Here again, the immigrant neolithic agriculturalists would have found an already established network of communications not only along the coasts, but overland, and the possible volume of exchange in perishables imperceptible to the archaeologist can only be guessed at.

The Mesolithic flint axes already mentioned bring us to one of the most interesting aspect of man's activities in pre-agricultural Britain, the evidence for his active interference in the natural processes of plant growth by forest clearance. The first indication of such action is in fact as early as the Lower Palaeolithic, in a site of Great Interglacial date at Hoxne in Suffolk, where human occupation on a lake edge could be correlated with the surrounding plant cover. The inter-glacial climatic optimum supported a mixed oak forest, very comparable to that of Zone VIIa encountered by the first Neolithic colonists, but this was ended by an "abrupt fall both in the tree-pollen to non-tree pollen ratio and in the frequency of the tree pollen", followed by an increase in grasses and the appearance of *Plantago*. This is regarded by the botanists as being the result of "a catastrophe which caused the deforestation", probably a forest fire, but as likely to have been man-made and deliberate as accidentally by lightning. If man-made, it would mean

[32] S. Palmer, 'The Stone industries of the Isle of Portland...', *Proc. Prehist. Soc.*, 36, 1970, 82–115; W. F. Rankine, *The Mesolithic of Southern England*, Guildford, 1956; P. R. Ritchie, 'The stone-implement trade in third-millennium Scotland', in J. M. Coles and D. D. A. Simpson (eds.), *Studies in Ancient Europe*, Leicester, 1968, pp. 117–36.

deliberate clearance (presumably for hunting purposes) somewhere around 200,000 years ago.[33]

The Hoxne evidence is corroborated by similar circumstances recently observed at a contemporary site at Marks Tey in Essex, and in Post-glacial times the evidence for Mesolithic forest clearances is now accumulating. At Star Carr itself no interference could be traced, but at Flixton site 2, nearby and contemporary, a fall in birch and a rise in hazel pollen has been regarded as representing "an attack on the forest, using fire, destructive enough to cause a certain amount of soil erosion". In later Mesolithic contexts, near Malham Tarn, Yorks., at *c*. 4550 bc it appears that "woodland vegetation was being locally affected by human activity" and possibly too at Shippea Hill, Cambs., between *c*. 5650 and 4730 bc.[34] On the Cumberland coast there are traces of forest clearance at the beginning of Zone VIIa,[35] around 4000 bc, and though these are not directly associated with human artifacts, a Mesolithic site dated to *c*. 4050 bc lies less than 80 km by sea up the coast at Barsalloch in Wigtonshire. The date of the Mesolithic flints associated with charcoal, and evidence of slight forest reduction at White Gill in the Cleveland Hills, are uncertain, but here as in the south of England the beginning of the man-made heathland probably goes back to pre-Neolithic times.[36] At Oakhanger, Hants., and Iping, Sussex, there was definite evidence of forest clearance associated with Mesolithic occupation, dated at the first site to *c*. 4400 bc.[37] At Oakhanger too abundant pollen of an ivy-like species (cf. *Hedera*) seems inexplicable unless in some way associated with human activity; similar pollen occurs in a buried land-surface of the second millennium bc in Dorset. Comparable high percentages of *Hedera* pollen in Swiss Neolithic lake-side sites have been

[33] R. G. West and C. M. McBurney, 'The Quaternary deposits at Hoxne, Suffolk', *Proc. Prehist. Soc.*, 20, 1954, pp. 131–54. Pearson is overstating the case when he interprets the evidence as indicating 'a considerable amount of forest clearance and primitive agriculture, probably comparable to that carried out by the aborigines in the Indo-Malayan region today.' R. Pearson, *Animals and Plants of the Cenozoic Era*, London, 1964, p. 193.

[34] A. G. Smith, 'The influence of mesolithic and neolithic man on British vegetation', in D. Walker and R. G. West (eds.), *Studies in the Vegetational history of the British Isles*, Cambridge, 1970, pp. 81–96.

[35] D. Walker, 'The late Quaternary history of the Cumberland lowland', *Phil. Trans. Roy. Soc. B*, 251, 1966, pp. 1–120, esp. pp. 194–9.

[36] G. W. Dimbleby, *Development of British Heathlands...*, 1962

[37] F. W. Rankine et al., 'Further excavations at a mesolithic site at Oakhanger...', *Proc. Prehist. Soc.*, 26, 1960, pp. 246–62; P. A. M. Keef *et al.*, 'A mesolithic site on Iping Common...', *ibid.*, 31, 1965, pp. 85–92; Dimbleby, *op. cit.*, pp. 93, 97; J. Troels-Smith, 'Ivy, Mistletoe and Elm: Climate Indicators-Fodder Plants', *Dan. Geol. Undersøgelse*, IV, Series 4, no. 4, 1960.

interpreted as evidence of the use of flowering ivy as animal fodder. Further west, the possibility of Mesolithic forest clearance has been seen on Dartmoor and at Westward Ho! (c. 4635 bc).[38] Finally, in Scotland, on Beinn Eighe on Gairloch "three successive pine forests destroyed by fire in Boreal and Atlantic times" have been noted in the pollen sequence, and in Caithness and Sutherland "quite a spectacular reduction of tree pollen" and an increase in heather, grasses, and sedges have been noted at the Zone VI/VIIa transition, and no natural reason adduced. At Storrs Moss, inland from Morecambe Bay, Lancs., a site with evidence of tree-burning and timber-working, and with flint waste from an anomalous industry, was contained in Zone VIIa peat with a date of c. 3500 bc, and could as well be attributed to a Late Mesolithic as to an Early Neolithic context.[39] In sum, the evidence for Mesolithic hunter-gatherers as active agents in woodland clearance is impressive, and we may, as Simmons suggests, see situations similar to those among the North American Indians: "in the Hudson River and Lake Champlain regions the woods were burned in the autumn and again in the spring in order to make hunting easier, to improve the growth of grass and to surround game", and European settlers in new territory seem to have found areas of artificially created grazing land already available for annexation. So, too, the first Neolithic colonists in Britain may well have found a landscape which was hardly an untouched forest primeval, but already beginning to take on the character of an artifact. It is even possible, if unproven, that men and red deer populations were in the same sort of close relation as Lapps and reindeer today, so that the herding of large ruminants would not be a wholly novel concept. But the real basic distinction was in the growing of cereal crops, and the economic, nutritional, and social repercussions of mixed subsistence farming.[40]

As it first appears in Britain, the agrarian economy does not present itself as an inevitable development from, or a technological increment to, the hunting and gathering traditions of the Post-glacial millennia.

[38] I. G. Simmons, 'Evidence for vegetation changes associated with mesolithic man in Britain', in P. J. Ucko and G. W. Dimbleby (eds.), *The Domestication and Exploitation of Plants and Animals*, London, 1969, pp. 110–19; D. M. Churchill and T. Wymer, 'The kitchen midden site at Westward Ho!', *Proc. Prehist. Soc.*, 31, 1965, pp. 74–84.

[39] S. E. Durno and D. N. McVean, 'Forest history of the Beinn Eighe Nature Reserve', *New Phytol.*, 78, 1959, p. 235; S. E. Durno, 'Pollen analysis of peat deposits in eastern Sutherland and Caithness', *Scott. Geog. Mag.*, 74, 1958, pp. 27–135. Storrs Moss, T. G. E. Powell *et al.*, 'Excavations in Zone VII peat at Storrs Moss, Lancashire...', *Proc. Prehist. Soc.*, 37, 1971, pp. 112–37.

[40] I. G. Simmons, *op. cit.*, p. 113; 'The Ecological setting of Mesolithic man in the Highland Zone' in J. G. Evans, S. Limbrey and H. Cleere (eds.), *The effect of man on the landscape: the Highland Zone*, London, 1975, 57; P. Mellars, 'Ungulate populations...and the Mesolithic landscape' in *ibid.*, p. 49.

It is introduced, with other technologies such as pottery-making, as a wholly alien and incompatible social order, that would not give added satisfaction to the life of a Mesolithic hunter, nor offer him a tempting alternative life-style. The Botswana Bushmen had no envy of the agriculturalists and pastoralists in their territory – a large proportion of their diet consists of highly nutritious nuts, and why, they asked, should they cultivate, when there was so many nuts in the world? The crofters of the Scottish Highlands in the eighteenth century had no desire to change their very inefficient agrarian and social order, and make themselves prosperous sheep-farmers on the Lowland model. We should not think of a change from hunting and gathering to mixed farming as being in any way an inevitable event involving concepts of 'progress'. "Can we", asked Collingwood, "speak of progress in happiness or comfort or satisfaction? Obviously not... the problem of being comfortable in a medieval cottage is so different from the problem of being comfortable in a modern slum that there is no comparing them; the happiness of a peasant is not contained in the happiness of a millionaire."[41] The first establishment of an agrarian economy in Britain can only have been the result of the imposition of a new social order, as different from that which it came to supersede as was the importing of European patterns of life into the New World after Columbus to the traditional hunter-gatherer communities of the Americas. Opinion is at the moment divided on the question of a possible figure for the Mesolithic population of Britain, ranging from a small number (estimated on analogy with Caribou Eskimo densities) of perhaps 10,000 persons, to unspecified preferences for a much higher figure. If very small, the submergence or virtual extinction of this population becomes a possibility. At all events the archaeological evidence and the chronological determinations together seem to exclude any cultural exchange or indeed perceptible contact between Mesolithic and Neolithic communities in Britain.

[41] R. G. Collingwood, *The Idea of History*, ed. T. M. Knox, Oxford, 1946, p. 330. Collingwood was anticipated by Samuel Johnson: "A peasant and a philosopher may be equally *satisfied* but not equally *happy*...A peasant has not capacity for having equal happiness with a philosopher". Johnson to Boswell, February 1766.

CHAPTER II

THE FIRST AGRARIAN SOCIETIES
IN BRITAIN FROM 4000 BC

THE PROBLEM OF THE 'ELM DECLINE' OF *c.* 3000 bc

As we saw in the previous chapter, the boundaries agreed upon by botanists in defining the successive zones in the Post-glacial are dependent upon changes in the proportion of plant species, themselves reflecting climatic changes, and especially in the dominant types of forest trees. In Zone VI, the Boreal phase, pine is dominant; the change to VIIa, the Atlantic climatic stage is marked around 5500 bc by an increasing proportion of birch, which in southern Britain soon itself made way for the overwhelming preponderance of mixed oak forest. This VI/VIIa boundary is fixed then as a result of wholly natural changes in climate and in the botanical climax. But the boundary between Zones VIIa and VIIb, the Atlantic and Sub-Boreal, is drawn at the point in the sequence where a sudden change in forest growth and in the occurrence of certain other species of plant is of so curious a nature that it is still a matter of discussion whether it should be attributed to natural or to manmade causes, or to both. And this is not merely a question of palaeobotanical interest, because, if of human origin, the phenomenon argues not only forest clearance, but a specific type of animal husbandry among the first Neolithic agriculturalists in north-western Europe. The problem must therefore be examined before we turn to any archaeological evidence.[1]

In Britain, unlike Scandinavia and other continental areas, there is no clearly recognizable climatic change reflected in the plant history of Zones VIIa and VIIb, the Atlantic and Sub-Boreal phases, although attention has recently been drawn to cold spells such as the Piora oscillation as being significant. But what is seen in the British, in common with the other north-west European, pollen-diagrams is a marked recession in the proportion of *Ulmus* pollen taking place suddenly at a chronological point fixed in many instances around 3000 bc. This 'Elm Decline' is the factor which has led botanists to take it as denoting a boundary between Zones VIIa and VIIb; with it appear

---

[1] Summary of the situation in W. Pennington, *The History of British Vegetation*, London, 1969, pp. 62–70; J. G. Evans, 'Notes on the environment of early farming communities in Britain', in D. D. A. Simpson (ed.), *Economy and Settlement in Neolithic and Early Bronze Age Britain and Europe*, Leicester, 1971, pp. 11–26.

on occasion the pollen of grasses and of a well-known weed commonly associated with human activity, the plantain. The species may, on occasion, appear a little later in the stratigraphic sequence than the 'Elm Decline' associated with a general drop in all tree pollen percentages. The fact that the radiocarbon dating technique, which provided an absolute chronology for the vegetation zones, also demonstrates that in Britain the earliest Neolithic sites so far identified also cluster around a date rather before 3000 bc has naturally supported the view that the Elm Decline was a manmade phenomenon associated with the earliest immigrant agrarian societies in these islands (for the Irish evidence is concordant).

The case for a natural origin has been made more than once, since the manmade origin of the Elm Decline was first put forward, first in 1944, and again in the later 1950s, by various scholars. Frenzel has suggested a cold phase, associated with the Piora oscillation perceptible in the Alps, and points out, for instance, that an elm decline dated to *c.* 3100 bc took place on Mt Acker in the Harz Mountains at a height of over 825 m, where there was no evidence of Neolithic settlement and forest clearance was inherently unlikely at such an altitude.[2] The problem was recently reviewed by a Dutch botanist[3] who drew attention to the nature of plant communities in unstable boundary zones – between wet and dry, rich and poor in nutrients, fresh-water or salt – which would encourage the growth of *Plantago* and species of allied habitat. Conditions favourable to colonization and growth of such plant populations could equally well be produced by a grazing, trampling, and dunging by wild animals such as deer and aurochs, as by the similar activity of man with domestic herds. In Chapter I (p. 20) we noted the Lower Palaeolithic evidence for forest clearance at Hoxne, which was followed by colonization by *Plantago*, and it occurred again with likely evidence of clearance in a late Mesolithic context at Westward Ho! Van Waateringe sums up by pointing out two possible situations: plantain and other weeds of cultivation can certainly indicate early cultivation by man, or, as in the northern temperate zone, short-term alternations of wet and dry periods could produce the botanically unstable context favourable to such growth. To be reasonably certain, one should only accept the Elm Decline and *Plantago* incidence if this is accompanied by unambiguous cereal pollen and archaeological material. Elm infections, such as the fungal 'Dutch elm disease', carried by elm-bark beetles, or the viral phloem necrosis (specifically New World) have been

---

[2] B. Frenzel, 'Climatic change in the Atlantic/Sub-Boreal transition...', in J. S. Sawyer (ed.), *World Climate from 8000 to 0 BC.*, London, 1966, pp. 99–123.

[3] W. Groenman-van Waateringe, 'The elm decline and the first appearance of *Plantago maior*', *Vegetatio*, 15, 1968, pp. 292–6.

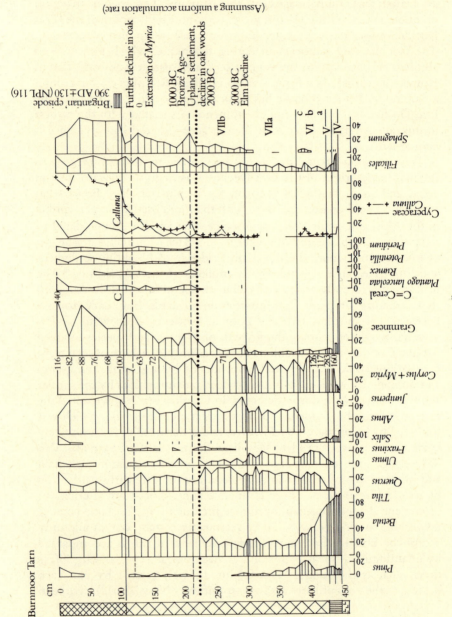

Burnmoor Tarn

Percentage total tree pollen

(Assuming a uniform accumulation rate)

390 AD ± 130 (NPL 116)
Brigantian episode
Further decline in oak
Extension of *Myrica*
1000 BC
Bronze Age–
Upland settlement,
decline in oak woods
2000 BC
3000 BC
Elm Decline

ruled out as plausible explanations for the phenomenon by botanists. The sudden incidence of the fungal disease among the British elm population in 1971 might, however, be thought to present a phenomenon of selective killing which could be represented in pollen diagrams in the same terms in antiquity.

The views against the human origin of the Elm Decline have been given in fairness, but on the whole its manmade nature seems to be generally held by palaeobotanists and archaeologists alike, and must now be examined in detail. The primary assumption made by Troels-Smith, who first presented the case in detail, was that the Elm Decline, as it first appears in the pollen diagrams, was not merely the product of human forest clearance for pasture or arable, but the result of a distinctive form of husbandry whereby cattle were over-wintered or wholly fed, not by grazing, but by humanly provided fodder in the form of leaves lopped from elm trees. In some pollen sequences there appears at a slightly later date evidence of all tree pollens declining in frequency, while grasses and open-country weeds increase: this was interpreted as normal forest clearance for agriculture, and given the name of *landnam*, from the Viking phrase for 'land-taking' in new territory.[4] The combined evidence would therefore imply a primary agrarian colonization of an area, with an economy based on elm-lopping for cattle-fodder, followed by some woodland regeneration, and a second occupation involving indiscriminate forest clearance for mixed farming.

The case for elm-lopping is supported by an impressive body of evidence for the practice of using elm and other leaves for fodder over large areas of the Old World in the historical past, and in a few regions (e.g. the lower Himalayas) at the present time. The material is set out by Troels-Smith and by Heybroek, and there is no doubt of the antiquity and prevalence of the practice at least back to classical times, and its long survival, especially for overwintering, in regions of poor

[4] Pennington, *op. cit.*; J. Iversen, *Land Occupation in Denmark's Stone Age*, Danske Geol. Undersøg., II, 1941, p. 66; J. Troels-Smith, 'Ivy, Mistletoe and Elm: Climate Indicators–Fodder Plants', *ibid.*, IV, 1960, p. 4; H. M. Heybroek, 'Diseases and lopping for fodder as possible causes of a prehistoric decline of *Ulmus*', *Acta Bot. Neerlandica*, 12, 1963, pp. 1–11.

Fig. 1. Example of a pollen diagram, here illustrating Post-glacial vegetation history in the south-west of the Lake District as represented at Burnmoor Tarn. The wavy line indicates the revertence of *Betula*, previously thought to indicate the opening of the Sub-Atlantic period. This horizon is now seen to be non-synchronous, by comparison of pollen diagrams, and is interpreted as an anthropogenic effect, resulting from destruction of upland oak woods by the clearance episode which precedes the horizon of sustained expansion of *Betula* (from W. Pennington in D. Walker & R. G. West (eds.), *Studies in the Vegetational History of the British Isles*, Cambridge 1970, Fig. 15a).

pasture or an impoverished peasantry. In Britain, Mascall in 1627 recommended elm leaves for fattening cattle, while John Evelyn in 1664 wrote that elm leaves "suffered to dry upon the branches...will prove a great relief to cattle, in winter and scorching summers, when hay and fodder is dear: they will eat them before oats, and thrive exceedingly well with them". Their food value is confirmed by modern figures on the nutritive index scale, where elm leaves equal or exceed the values of best meadow hay.[5] The leaves of other trees may also be lopped for fodder, and Evelyn says of ash "the very dead leaves afford, like those of the Elm, relief to our cattle in winter". In eighteenth-century Lancashire

the woodlanders of High Furness were charged with the care of flocks and herds [and] in winter, to browse them with the tender sprouts and sprigs of the hollies and ash...the holly-trees are carefully preserved for that purpose, where all other wood is cleared off; and large tracts of common pasture are so covered with these trees, as to have the appearance of a forest of hollies. At the shepherd's call the flock surround the holly-bush, and receive the croppings at his hand, which they greedily nibble up, and bleat for more...The mutton so fed has a remarkable fine flavour.[6]

But, if nutritious, leaf-fodder is bulky, and considerable lopping is needed to make adequate provision for even a small number of beasts. In Yugoslavia in recent times leaf-fodder for over-wintering alone (90–150 days) was estimated to require the loppings of 1 ha for 10 sheep, and cattle need 5 or 6 times as much as sheep; in Sweden, Sjöbeck's figures, again for overwintering, were 1,000 kg of leaf sheaves per cow.[7] For fodder throughout the year these figures would have to be proportionately multiplied, with a cow consuming something like 3,000 kg of elm-leaves, the product of about 10 ha of forest stands of elm. At such rates it would not be surprising to find the proportions of arboreal pollen-rain perceptibly altered by the advent of pastoralists with such an economy in a given area.

Unfortunately, archaeological evidence or corroboration for such a Neolithic economy existing in Europe is limited to two instances in Switzerland, and a piece of not wholly conclusive evidence from Denmark. At the Michelsberg culture settlement at Thayngen-Weier, surviving in waterlogged conditions, the floor of one structure was strewn with leafy branches of elm, birch, oak, lime, maple and ash, presumably fodder, and the dung of stalled sheep was also found on

[5] Heybroek, op. cit.

[6] J. Thirsk, review of Heybroek in Agric. Hist. Rev., 12, 1964, pp. 58–9, quoting T. West, Antiquities of Furness, London, 1774, p. xlv.

[7] Heybroek, op. cit., p. 7, quoting Petroviç; J. G. D. Clark, Prehistoric Europe: the Economic Basis, London, 1952, pp. 124–5, quoting Sjöbeck.

the site. At the Egolzwil site, "stacks of leaves, twigs of mistletoe and, indeed, all forms of wasteland hay" were found.[8] In Denmark (as also at Thayngen-Weier) a find of a small wooden bowl, carved from 'Bird's Eye' or pollarded elm wood, is contemporary with the local elm decline, but pollarding need not necessarily be done for fodder. So the thesis that the decline in elm pollen around 3000 bc can be equated with the local appearance of cattle-herders lopping selectively for fodder, though very attractive and inherently plausible, cannot be conclusively demonstrated anywhere by a strict correlation of the pollen phenomenon with archaeological evidcence, though the Swiss site shows the practice to have been known there at the requisite time. In Britain, it remains an unconfirmed hypothesis, though at Shippea Hill, Cambs., Neolithic occupation and charcoal occurred in the peat coincidentally with the Elm Decline and radiocarbon dates of c. 3500 bc.[9]

THE CONTINENTAL ARCHAEOLOGICAL BACKGROUND

As we saw in Chapter I, contacts between Britain and the Continent can be shown to have existed in earlier Mesolithic, pre-agricultural contexts from the Channel to the Baltic, and it is not surprising that the archaeological evidence for the affiliations of our first Neolithic colonists should equally suggest contributions from the same stretch of what by c. 3000 bc was a coastal littoral. Boats were certainly in use by the Mesolithic population, as the island settlements of Teviec and Hoëdic, off Brittany, show in the west at c. 4500 bc, and are represented by actual finds as well as occupied islands in the north-east: a dug-out canoe, fire-hollowed and nearly three metres long from Pesse in Drenthe province of the Netherlands, dates from c. 6000 bc, around the time of the formation of the English Channel. At Mouligna, near Biarritz, the pollen evidence has been held to imply some forest clearance at c. 3100 bc associated with a Mesolithic (Asturian) stone industry,[10] and in Brittany forest clearances with *Plantago* and a characteristic elm decline, have been detected in the pollen sequences at Brignogan and Yeun-Elez, at the latter place with dates of c. 3450 bc.[11] At the Tourbière de Poigny in the Paris basin a primary elm

[8] W. U. Guyan, 'Das jungsteinzeitliche Moordorf von Thayngen-Weier', in W. U. Guyan et al., *Das Pfahlbauproblem*, 1955, pp. 223–72, 261, 270. Radiocarbon dates of c. 3100–3000 bc; C. F. W. Higham, 'Stock rearing as a cultural factor in prehistoric Europe', *Proc. Prehist. Soc.*, 33, 1967, pp. 84–106, 93.

[9] J. G. D. Clark and H. Godwin, 'The neolithic in the Cambridgeshire Fens', *Ant.*, XXXVI, 1962, pp. 10–23.

[10] F. Oldfield, 'The coastal mud-bed at Mouligna...', *Pollen et Spores*, 2, 1960, pp. 57–70.

[11] W. van Ziest, 'A palaeobotanical study of some bogs in Western Brittany...',

decline appeared in the middle of Zone VIIa, and a second at its end, dated to c. 3730 bc.[12] In the Netherlands, the same phenomenon was noted at c. 3000 bc in pollen sequences around Emmen, but van Waateringe has made the point that no Neolithic culture of equivalent date has so far been identified in the area.[13] In Denmark, as we have seen, the elm decline marking the Atlantic–Sub-Boreal climatic transition has been associated with tree-lopping pastoralists, but no direct correlation has been made, though at Muldbjerg the elm decline is earlier than a settlement of Early Neolithic character, c. 2820 bc. We have then a general situation of forest clearance, or elm decline, or both, along the north-west European sea-board, but in no instance attributable to an archaeologically defined Neolithic culture. The Irish evidence, while showing characteristics distinguishing it from both Britain and the Continent, is in substantial agreement with the general situation just outlined.[14] It remains to review the purely archaeological evidence for British Neolithic origins.

The writer, and others, have discussed the question of the origins of the Neolithic cultures of the British Isles at some length over recent years, and so only a brief outline of the likely situation is necessary here.[15] It has to be taken in the wider context of a long-term spread of farming culture across Europe from south-east to north-west which can be documented by radiocarbon dates as beginning in the seventh millennium BC and reaching the Channel coasts of the continent by the middle or second half of the fourth. Many archaeological 'cultures' are involved, differentiated by variants in material culture, but all are stone-using and all share the essential features of cereal cultivation

Palaeohistory, 10, 1964, pp. 157–80; 'Recherches palynologiques en Bretagne occidentale', *Norois*, 37, 1963, pp. 5–19; I. Roux and Arlette Leroi-Gourhan, 'Les défrichements de la période atlantique', *Bull. Soc. Prehist. France*, 61, 1964, pp. 309–15.

[12] Jalut, G. 'Analyse pollinique de la Tourbière de Poigny', *Pollen et Spores*, 8, 123–33.

[13] W. van Zeist, 'Some radiocarbon dates from the raised bog near Emmen...', *Palaeohistory*, 4, 1955, pp. 113–18; W. Groenman-van Waateringe, 'The elm decline and the first appearance of *Plantago maior*', *Vegetatio*, 15, 1968, pp. 292–6.

[14] A. G. Smith, 'Influence of mesolithic and neolithic man on British Vegetation', in D. Walker and R. G. West (eds.), *Studies in the Vegetational History of the British Isles*, Cambridge, 1970, pp. 81–96.

[15] Views current to 1950 summarized in S. Piggott, *Neolithic Cultures of the British Isles*, Cambridge, 1954; modifications in *ibid.*, 'Windmill Hill – east or west?', *Proc. Prehist. Soc.*, 21, 1955, pp. 96–101; 'The British neolithic cultures in their continental setting', in J. Bohm and S. de Laet (eds.), *L'Europe à la fin de l'age de la pierre*, Praha, 1961, pp. 557–74; 'The beginning of the Neolithic in the British Isles', in H. Schwabedissen (ed.), *Fundamenta: Monographien zur Urgeschichte*, Bd 3, T. 6, Köln, 1965, pp. 172–84; J. G. D. Clark, 'Radiocarbon dating and the expansion of farming culture...', *Proc. Prehist. Soc.*, 31, 1965, pp. 58–73; 'The invasion hypothesis in British archaeology', *Ant.*, XL, 1966, pp. 172–89.

(wheat or barley) and animal husbandry based on cattle, sheep and/or goats, pigs and dogs in variable proportions. Whatever may be their ultimate origins, by the time farming communities were colonizing north-west Europe they were bringing with them their own flocks and herds, and their corn, both with a long and respectable domesticated ancestry behind them.[16]

Broadly speaking the archaeological cultures likely to be contributing to the initial settlement of agriculturalists in Britain can be placed in two blocks, those of the French later Neolithic cultures on the west, and those of the Late Neolithic cultures of the North European Plain and south Scandinavia on the east. Our knowledge of the agrarian economy of these groups varies in accordance with the standards of excavation and subsequent analysis of material, but in general it is thin. The bone assemblies from the French sites show very small percentages of wild animals: hunting was almost wholly rejected as a meat source, and was mainly of red deer, with very rare aurochs. In the domestic herds cattle predominated, particularly in the centre and north of France, and two sizes have been noted, but not certainly assigned to breeds rather than attributed to size variation due to sex: the smaller type is slightly more frequent. Sheep and goats have been distinguished, occurring in proportions approximating to those of pig. Domesticated dogs are of types comparable with the Swiss 'Turbary' breed, and there is a possible representative of the domestic horse at one site. Among the cereal crops wheat is most evident, and einkorn, emmer, bread wheat, and spelt have been recorded, as well as six-row barley.[17]

When we look eastward we have more detailed studies, and a somewhat different picture. Wild animals here play a more important part in the meat consumption, at times constituting one-third of the total bones on a site, including red deer, aurochs and horse. In the overall view, cattle predominate, though Danish sites mentioned below show a concentration on pigs: the cattle are large, of the *primigenius*-derived type, and local domestication has been suggested in the Netherlands. Pigs are second only to cattle in Poland and elsewhere, and sheep or goats form a small proportion of the stock. Horse occurs and may have been domesticated, and the dogs are again of *Canis f. palustris* or related types. Wheat again predominates, most commonly emmer, and barley is rare.[18]

Detailed studies of the bones from three Danish sites of mid third

[16] Clark, 'Radiocarbon dating...', *op. cit.*; H. T. Waterbolk, 'Food production in prehistoric Europe', *Science*, 162, 1968, pp. 1093–102; J. Murray, *The First European Agriculture*, Edinburgh, 1970; 'Some aspects of ovicaprid and pig-breeding in Neolithic Europe', in J. M. Coles and D. D. A. Simpson, *Studies in Ancient Europe*, Leicester, 1968, pp. 71–81.

[17] Murray, *op. cit.*, pp. 57–9.   [18] *Ibid.*, pp. 60–4.

millennium date show what information can be obtained from good series by proper analytical means. Here is mostly pig in the ratio of one-half to one-third, with cattle representing about a quarter, and sheep and goats a quarter to one-eighth. Wild animals were almost totally absent. The pigs had been bred up to the age of about two years before killing, and the cattle were maintained to maturity by overwintering. Sheep were concentrated on the coastal sites, it is suggested to avoid the foot-rot and liver-fluke likely near stagnant fresh water, and died or were killed below shearling age, presumably for food rather than wool. A few adults goats may have been kept for milking.[19]

A recent overall survey of Mesolithic and earliest Neolithic stone industries in south-east and central Europe has made it clear that two quite distinct cultural traditions were involved, and that not only had the hunter-gatherers and the first agriculturalists mutually exclusive areas of settlement, but agrarian economies appeared as entities introduced from outside, and neither as a result of the acculturation of a Mesolithic population nor of any independent autochthonous development. In north-west Europe the situation appears somewhat different. The Lautereck rock-shelter in Württemburg, for instance, shows a riverside settlement of Mesolithic carp-fishers acquiring pottery from Neolithic sources from before 4000 bc and for some time afterwards, and the early Neolithic flint industries in the south Netherlands show a mixture of intrinsic and indigenous traditions suggesting a mixing of population and culture. In the Baltic area the final Mesolithic cultures adopted many intrusive technologies, including pottery-making and cattle-raising, and evidence of domestic animals (cattle and ovicaprids) appears in late Mesolithic contexts in France.[20] The hunter-gatherer economies of north-western Europe seem to have had a vigour and individuality recalling for instance the exceptional qualities of the Indians of the north-west coast of America.[21] In Britain, however, as we shall see, archaeological evidence of contacts between Mesolithic and Neolithic communities hardly exists.

[19] C. F. W. Higham, 'The economic basis of the Danish Funnel-necked Beaker (TRB) culture', *Acta Arch.*, 40, 1969, pp. 200–9; cf. *idem*, 'Stock rearing as a cultural factor in prehistoric Europe', *Proc. Prehistor. Soc.*, 33, 1967, pp. 94–103.

[20] R. Tringham, 'A preliminary study of the early neolithic and latest mesolithic blade industries in south-east and central Europe', in J. M. Coles and D. D. A. Simpson (eds.), *Studies in Ancient Europe*, Leicester, 1968, pp. 45–70; W. Taute, 'Das Felsdach Lautereck...', *Palaeohistoria*, 12, 1967, pp. 483–504; J. Troels-Smith, 'The Ertebølle culture and its background', *ibid.*, pp. 505–28; R. R. Newell, 'The flint industry of the Dutch Linearbandkeramik', in P. J. Modderman *et al.*, *Linearbandkeramik aus Elsloo und Stein*, Niederlandse Oudheden, III, 1970, pp. 144–83; Murray, *op. cit.*, pp. 22–9; Waterbolk, *op. cit.*

[21] Cf. W. Suttles, 'Coping with abundance: subsistence on the north-west coast', in R. B. Lee and I. De Vore, *Man the Hunter*, Chicago, 1968, pp. 56–68.

COLONIZATION AND FOOD POTENTIAL

The practical considerations involved in the introduction of the first agrarian economies into the British Isles have been reviewed by Case, and his main points are as follows.[22] The earliest Neolithic economy we can detect in Britain is already "mature and non-experimental", and bears every sign of having been introduced complete from outside; in other words, we must envisage the physical transference across the sea of "not only men, women, children and infants, but breeding and milking stock, winter fodder, sown crops, seed corn, fodder grain and much else besides". Such a complete farming system would be particularly vulnerable at many points. In the first place, the initial transfer and subsequent conservation of seed corn must have presented a hazard – "any wet will spoil seed; salt water will ruin it", and hardly less hazardous would be the establishment of the first patches of crop and preserving it from damage or destruction by wild animals and birds. The animal husbandry of the economy depended on importing actual cattle, pigs, goats and sheep in boats on sea voyages not all by the shortest cross-Channel ferry route; Cherbourg to Christchurch, for instance, is 120 km, St Malo to Weymouth 200 km. In-calf animals were presumably taken in the initial colonizing movements, and then came the difficulty of maintaining the livestock once established against such hazards as that of cows being serviced by wild bulls. In order to obtain pasture on arrival, or trees suitably leafy for lopping, the most likely months for such expeditions would have been after the main agricultural activities of the year, from March to July, and before winter set in around late October. Like others who have considered the problem, Case opts for skin-boats of the *umiak* or curragh type as the most likely type of craft, envisaging boats paddled rather than rowed, up to the size of a 32-ft (9.75 m) whaling *umiak*, with a possible load of three tons (*c*. 3,000 kg) of crew, stores, a couple of dogs, two adult cows, and two calves, or about six pigs or ten sheep. If dug-out canoes were used in this or similar contexts, it is worthwhile remembering that one having an internal capacity of 3 × 2 × 20 ft (*c*. 1 × 0.6 × 6 m) would carry a load of 2½ tons (*c*. 2,500 kg) leaving 6 ins. (15 cm) of freeboard; such giant craft as the canoe from Brigg, Lincs., of *c*. 850 bc, and 45 ft (13.7 m) long, would carry 10 tons (*c*. 10,000 kg) with a freeboard of 1 ft (30 cm). The weight of crew can be roughly estimated as 14 12-stone (76 kg) men to 1 ton (1,000 kg). A recent full-sized experiment with a 20 ft (6 m) replica skin-boat showed that it could easily carry a ton load with over a foot of freeboard amidships.

[22] H. Case, 'Neolithic explanations', *Ant.*, XLIII, 1969, pp. 176–86; C. Green *et al.*, 'Neolithic comments', *ibid.*, XLIV, 1970, pp. 105–14.

Case further envisages the possibility of several stages in any colonizing venture, beginning with coastal exploration, and here the long-standing Mesolithic sea-links between Britain and the Continent that we have seen must have existed, should be given weight. The Neolithic cultures of Europe north of the Alps in the late fourth millennium BC were essentially land-based by long tradition and geographical circumstance, even if with abundant inland navigation on rivers and lakes. The colonization of the British Isles must have involved the acquisition of practical seafaring skills no less than the reframing of a land-locked mentality to accommodate concepts of the sea as a potential link rather than a barrier between land masses. Even if we cannot demonstrate it archaeologically, it is difficult to think that no contact existed between those who were turning their thoughts to the establishment of agricultural colonies overseas in the British Isles and the older Mesolithic communities who had maintained connections by boat up the Atlantic, Channel, or North Sea coasts for millennia. If indeed no such contacts existed, we have to see a remarkable coincidence in the pattern of Early Neolithic settlement with its cultural elements implying contributions from a stretch of European coastline, repeating the Mesolithic range.

While one naturally assumes the earliest Neolithic colonization of Britain to have been strictly coastal, one must also realize that since the early third millennium bc changing sea-levels and erosion have together removed this Neolithic coastline throughout southern and eastern Britain, though by compensation contemporary shorelines in the north now lie above the modern tide-mark. It would therefore be theoretically possible to assume the loss of virtually all settlements of the entrance phase of colonization. It would be reasonable to assume, however, that the land sought out for primary occupation would be that with minimal tree cover, potentially good arable soil, favourably placed for sunlight and shelter, and with minimum bog or salt marsh. Such areas would in fact develop at the seaward edge of woodlands as a result of the operation of natural factors constituting 'unstable boundary zones' in terms of their plant cover, and would offer natural pastures to wild grazing animals.[23] We have already touched on the likelihood of considerable forest clearance being effected by the indigenous large ungulate population, notably red deer, elk, and aurochs. Deer are recognized by modern foresters as a menace: "deer damage trees by browsing and by debarking when they remove the velvet from their antlers", and open conditions once established would lead to further browsing, preventing forest recovery or encroachment. In conjunction

[23] W. Groenman-van Waateringe, 'The elm decline and the first appearance of *Plantago maior*', *Vegetatio*, 15, 1968, p. 293.

with the aurochs such clearance might be considerable – "cattle will eat the coarse grasses almost non-selectively, and leave a sward cropped so that the deer can enjoy the finer grasses" when browsing on marginal open land.[24] Up to a point, the creation and maintenance of open spaces might even increase the large mammal population (as with the elk in modern Sweden), or, as we saw, Mesolithic man may well have been acting deliberately in this matter. Coastal situations would also attract the large ungulates as a source of salt: modern cattle need 100 g per head per day, and in the Scottish Highlands today the red deer population may make long overnight journeys to the coast for salt if necessary, for up to 32 km across agricultural land. This salt problem must incidentally have faced Neolithic herdsmen, for once cattle are kept in one place, they must be provided with salt in some form.[25] Coastal pasture, as we saw in Neolithic Denmark, might well have had the added advantage of freedom from liver-fluke for a sheep population[26] and from malaria for men.

The identification and interdisciplinary study of coastal sites in north Britain, where the old shoreline may still exist, might well throw light on at least secondary colonization in that region. Childe many years ago suggested correlations between potentially lighter wooded soils, such as alluvial gravels, and Neolithic settlement in west Scotland, and at Northton in the Isle of Harris we have evidence of Neolithic forest clearance and occupation, followed by woodland regeneration and subsequent clearance once more in Beaker times, and on both occasions probably for pasture rather than arable.[27] As we shall see, the poverty of our knowledge of the real relationship between prehistoric man and his environment in Britain is lamentable at all periods, and the Neolithic entrance phase is no exception. What we can perceive, however, is that the establishment of a new form of economy was in no sense a conscious exploitation of resources by means more effective than those of the hunters and gatherers, but the introduction of a novel form of subsistence-pattern that may have been no more efficient in providing an adequate and balanced diet than that which it eventually supplanted.

[24] J. D. Ovington, *Woodlands*, 1965, pp. 54–7; C. Lucas, 'Herd management suggestions on the basis of park stocks', in M. M. Bannerman and K. L. Blaxter, *The Husbanding of Red Deer*, Inverness, 1970, p. 33.
[25] A. E. Nenquin, *Salt: a Study of Economic Prehistory*, Diss. Arch. Gandenses, VI, Brugge, 1961, p. 140.
[26] Higham, *op. cit.*; C. Matheson, 'Note on the liver-fluke as a suggested factor in early human distribution', in C. Fox, *Personality of Britain*, 4th ed., Cardiff, 1947, p. 94.
[27] J. G. Evans, 'Habitat change...', in D. D. A. Simpson (ed.), *Economy and Settlement in Neolithic and Early Bronze Age Britain and Europe*, Leicester, 1971, pp. 27–74; V. G. Childe, 'Neolithic settlement in the west of Scotland', *Scott. Geog. Mag.*, 50, 1934, pp. 18–25.

CLEARANCE, SETTLEMENT, AND ORGANIZATION

Whatever marginal forest clearance may have been effected by indigenous large mammals or non-agricultural human communities in Britain, the advent of the first agricultural peoples must have been intimately bound up with reduction of the woodland cover on a scale and with a conscious deliberation far beyond what had gone before. However we interpret the phenomenon of 'Elm Decline', the *landnam* episodes in the pollen sequences seem unambiguous, and with cereal cultivation as a part of the basic subsistence-economy, open areas exposed to air and sunlight were a necessity of existence to Neolithic communities. On the Continent the problem had brought about the invention of the requisite tool millennia before; the stone-bladed, wooden-hafted axe, and stone axe-blades chipped and ground into shape have, since the recognition of a 'Stone Age' early in the nineteenth century, been seen as the distinctive 'type-fossil' of a 'Neolithic' phase, even if we now realize that they were on occasion used by hunting and gathering communities in northern Europe. The first agricultural colonists of Britain were by long tradition expert lumberjacks.

It follows then that the essential equipment first carried by the settlers from the fourth millennium bc would be tree-felling axes, hafted, with a supply of spare axe-blades to replace those broken during work, and presumably suitable stones for grinding and sharpening blunted tools, for their natural occurrence in new territory could not be counted upon. Not all stones provide the qualities of inherent toughness, suitability for flaking, grinding, and polishing, and relative abundance in concentrated areas of accessible raw material, needed for such purposes: in Britain the two types are a range of igneous rocks in the west and north, and flint from the Cretaceous Chalk, and possibly other deposits where it occurs in nodules of sufficient size for an axe-blade. The situation in north and west Europe was similar, showing a complementary distribution of stone resources in the more westerly region, and flint to the east, that echoed the British geological pattern. While some communities had local sources of stone to exploit, others were relatively or absolutely remote from supplies, so that complex systems of exchange or 'trade' developed, with the transmission of stones over long distances. To take a single instance among many, a Neolithic settlement of *c.* 4000 bc in the Rhineland obtained its flint from nearly 80 km away, and while most of the stone for axe-blades came from relatively local sources, raw material and finished products were also obtained from a locality in Silesia, some 700 km away.[28] Britain, by the third millennium bc, can

[28] K. Schietzl, *Müddersheim*, Köln, 1965.

show examples of almost equally extended relationships established for the same purpose.

To meet the need, centres of exploitation of stone and flint were developed, in systems of organization that can only be guessed at on anthropological analogy;[29] axe-blades were produced in bulk to supply the needs of the farmers engaged primarily in forest clearance and secondarily in the timber-working demanded by the construction of houses, burial and ceremonial structures, fen causeways, dug-out boats, and other wooden equipment. The clearance of woodland for agriculture in Britain, as elsewhere in Europe, is intimately bound up with the provision of axe-blades of adequate quality and in sufficient quantity, and the means taken to achieve this form as essential a part of our agrarian history as does the development of iron-working in later times in relation to the production of agricultural tools and eventually machines.

The application of radiocarbon dating in combination with petrological and other analysis of the rocks concerned is beginning to give a picture of the opening up of outcrop workings, open-cast quarrying, and even deep mining for the raw material for axe-blades in Europe and Britain from the later fourth millennium bc. In Brittany, the production of a certain desirable stone was certainly spread over the centuries between c. 3000–2000 bc at Plussulien near St Brieuc: a few axe-blades of this stone from southern England could even have been brought by first-generation colonists.[30] Similar working-sites or 'axe factories' were soon developed in west Britain, evidently as a result of an urgent need coupled with an adroit exploitation of practical field geology on the part of the early colonists. Four types of Cornish rocks were in use by 3000 bc; the working sites at Graig Lwyd in North Wales were active by c. 2800–2600 bc and those further north in Great Langdale in the Lake District by c. 2700 bc. The products of these major working centres were widely dispersed, from Scotland to the English Channel coast, as were those of the Tievebulliagh centres in Antrim, Northern Ireland, where working may have started at the Zone VIIa/VIIb transition, concurrently with the local decline in tree pollen and the presumed first advent of agriculturalists in the region. A Scottish working-site at Craig na Caillich near Killin was in operation c. 2500–2200 bc. What is impressive is the early identification of suitable sources of stone, and the rapid widespread distribution of their products.

[29] For some of the problems involved, cf. J. G. D. Clark, 'Traffic in Stone Axe and Adze Blades', *Econ. Hist. Rev.*, 18, 1965, p. 1; C. Renfrew, 'Trade and Culture Process in European Prehistory', *Curr. Anthrop.*, 10, 1969, p. 151; B. Stjernquist, 'Models of commercial diffusion in prehistoric times', *Scripta Minora Lund.*, 1965–66, 1967.

[30] E. D. Evens *et al.*, 'Fourth report...on the petrological identification of stone axes', *Proc. Prehist. Soc.*, 28, 1962, pp. 209–66; C. T. le Roux, 'A stone axe factory in Brittany', *Ant.*, XLV, 1971, pp. 283–8.

Eastwards on the North European Plain, open-cast workings for flint in the Kimmeridge Clay at Orónsko in Poland were operated by hunter-gatherer communities as early as the Zone VI/VIIa transition, *c.* 5500 bc. The main exploitation of flint for axe-blades, however, was that of the first agriculturalists of the Funnel-Beaker culture, and the huge mines at Krzemionki were in operation *c.* 2850–2650 and very probably as early as *c.* 3000 bc.[31] In southern Sweden, the Kvarnby mines were in operation *c.* 2900 bc. In Belgium the mines and axe-blade factories in Mesvin were working by *c.* 3400 bc, and a date of *c.* 2280 bc from Spiennes can hardly be early in its history of extensive axe-production.[32] The sequence of mining flint for axe-blades in Britain is most interesting. In Sussex, operations were in progress as early as at Mesvin, *c.* 3400 bc at Church Hill Findon, and almost equally early at Blackpatch and Harrow Hill (*c.* 3000), and from *c.* 2800 bc at Cissbury. Wiltshire was producing axe-blades at Easton Down by *c.* 2500, while in Norfolk the famous Grimes Graves mines operated on present showing not before *c.* 2300, and mainly around 2000 bc.[33] One is tempted to see reflected in this activity the progress of initial forest clearance for agriculture, carried out by colonists fully acquainted with flint-mining techniques, who moved from Sussex into Wessex and later north-east to attack the woodlands on what were to become the Breckland heaths. Armed with axes with blades of south-eastern flint or westerly stones, the first agricultural colonists and their immediate descendants must, in the first few centuries of the third millennium, have been making noticeable inroads on the forest cover of Britain.

On ethnological analogy, the method of clearance employed by prehistoric farmers in Europe and Britain has generally been considered to be the technique of combined tree-felling and controlled burning known variously as slash-and-burn, swidden, or *Brandwirtschaft*. It must be remembered, however, that this type of clearance has only been demonstrated in an archaeological context firmly related to Neolithic occupation: the Dalladies evidence from north-east Scotland referred to below is one of the few instances. This has a worldwide distribution among primitive peoples in a forest environment, and we saw how contemporaneous New World practices suggested themselves to John Aubrey when thinking of the prehistoric deforestation of Salisbury Plain. In Europe it survived longest on the edges of the northern forests

[31] K. Jazdzewski, *Poland*, 1965, pp. 56–7, 86–7; J. A. Bakker *et al.*, 'TRB and other C14 dates from Poland', *Helinium*, 9, 1969, p. 216.

[32] M. G. Lefranc and P. H. Moisin, 'Le néolithique ancien en Belgie', *Hannonia Prehist.*, 1, 1965, p. 405; H. Bakker *et al.*, 'British Museum natural radiocarbon measurements, VII', *Radiocarbon*, 13, 1970, p. 158.

[33] Bakker *et al.*, *op. cit.*; 'British Museum natural radiocarbon measurements, VI', *Radiocarbon*, 11, 1969, pp, 285–6.

of birch and conifers, and indeed may still be practised in Carelia, north of lat. 64°, on the boundaries of Finland and the USSR. Clark has summarized the recent evidence of a century or more ago. In the spring, small trees were grubbed up and larger trees ringed, to be felled later; the actual burning took place in summer, with the anticipation of subsequent rain to wash the fertilizing ash into the soil, and tree stumps were left standing, as they would present no obstacle to light ploughs of ard type or to primitive bush-harrows, and still less to hoe cultivation. The first crop, sown in the ash-laden soil, could be phenomenal yields of rye from 50- and 80-fold as against the normal 15- to 20-fold – but the subsequent decline was so disastrous that in north Carelia only one year's crop was taken off the cleared land and in the south of the province no more than two were occasionally achieved. A study of the same agricultural technique as it survived in northern Russia until modern times provides us with additional important details. Sites for new forest clearance were selected where possible on river banks, and especially on peninsulas formed by river bends; bog was naturally avoided and the chance of good hunting in the adjacent uncleared forest was a factor borne in mind. Natural woodland in the areas under consideration were mainly of birch, alder, spruce, and pine, and of these trees stands of alder were preferred, as they yielded more ash on burning than the other species: alder–birch woods were next in preference, and pine was avoided. The quality of the soil was judged from the scrub cover and undergrowth, and a good showing of wild raspberries, bilberries, and whortleberries was looked for, while heather and the other ericoids were shunned.

Upon selection, the first tasks were tree killing and felling. Even with iron axes in use these might be inadequate for large trees; these were ringed by stripping the bark and sometimes the sapwood, on occasion up to a man's height. These trees might take from five to fifteen years to die, and crops were often sown under standing dead or dying trees in otherwise cleared land. Felling was usually carried out in June, at a time free of agricultural work when the dry summer season lay ahead, and, when felled, trunks were left to dry for from one to three years.

Burning was usually carried out in the spring, less often in the autumn, against the prevailing wind, and it was aimed to burn well into the top humic layer. A secondary burning followed – 'the black work' – which gathered together the charred and still unburnt vegetation together in piles for re-burning to ash. The sowing was then done immediately in the warm ashes and soil, without ploughing or harrowing, the seed being broadcast and then covered by dragging branches over it as a primitive bush-harrow. The crop yield for the first year was very good but quickly dwindled to an uneconomic yield in three years, when the area was abandoned. When the land was reused, a long fallow of anything between fifteen and sixty years could be allowed, but the usual interval was between twenty and forty years.

If these recent situations can be accepted as valid in antiquity (and there is no inherent reason against this), one factor stands out, namely, the length of time the *Brandwirtschaft* operation can take before a crop is reaped. If full clearance were aimed at, intervals of from six to eighteen years could elapse before sowing, and even cultivation among dead trees (which would throw less shade than when alive and in leaf) might wait for three years or more, especially in wet spells. It is in these terms that we must think of our Neolithic *landnam*, and not as a process which could clear and crop a forested area within a matter of months. Even after this effort, a maximum of three years' use of a cornfield was all that was won, and, if the Russian figures for long fallow are taken, it would seem that the minimal period of time would have been the space of a human generation before it was cultivated again.[34] It was therefore an extremely wasteful process, in that continued new clearance was necessary until the old clearances were sufficiently regenerated by a natural long fallow to be suitable for new burning and cultivating with subsequent cropping. And as there would come a point when the cleared land was inconveniently far from the settlement, this in turn would be shifted to a new position nearer to virgin forest unless some agrarian system of fallowing, rotation, or manuring had been devised. Upon such factors the whole question of maintaining stable populations in permanent settlements depends, and it is extremely difficult from archaeological evidence to know when this was achieved, wholly or in part, by the earliest agricultural peoples of Britain.

In addition to forest clearance for directly agricultural purposes, the constant need of wood for fuel among human populations must be reckoned as a factor, for cooking, heating, and ritual purposes. The demands are naturally linked to climatic conditions, and New World figures ranging from about 1–2 lb (0.45–0.9 kg) per family per day are probably underestimates for prehistoric Britain. A warning against taking the charcoals from prehistoric hearths as necessarily a random sample of available combustible vegetable matter is contained in the observations of anthropologists on 'preferred' or 'accustomed' fuels, as when Bear Lake Indians on the move dragged sledges of forest firewood into areas where abundant heather would have provided the necessary domestic fuel.[35]

[34] J. G. D. Clark, *Prehistoric Europe: the Economic Basis*, London, 1952, pp. 92–4. Cf. also T. Shaw, 'Tree-felling by fire', *Ant.*, XLIII, 1969, p. 52; for Russia, W. Linnard, 'Terms and techniques in shifting cultivation in Russia', *Tools and Tillage*, I, part 3, 1970, pp. 192–7.

[35] R. F. Heizer, 'Domestic fuel in primitive society', *J. Roy. Anthrop. Inst.*, 93, 1963, pp. 186–94.

A practical experiment in forest clearance by Neolithic techniques carried out in Denmark in 1952–53 enables us to amplify our knowledge extrapolated from ethnography.[36] An area of the Draved Forest in south Jutland was attacked by an archaeologist and two professional tree-fellers, using ancient flint axe-blades, hafted in modern replicas of Neolithic wooden hafts. It was found, once the technique of using short sharp strokes rather than the long swinging blow of the modern woodsman had been recognized and adopted, that an oak-tree about one foot in diameter could be felled in 30 minutes, and that 3 men could clear about ⅛ acre (0.05 ha) in 4 h work, a rate equivalent to 1 man clearing 1 acre (0.4 ha) in 96 working hours. The trees were felled so as to fall north–south for good drying, and once thrown, they and the undergrowth were set on fire and kept burning continuously day and night. Part only of the felled area was burnt, the remainder being kept as a control. Immediately after burning, both areas were sown with primitive strains of wheat (einkorn and emmer), and naked barley.

The results were illuminating. The cereal growth on the unburnt acid forest soil was negligible, but on the burnt area an excellent grain crop was produced in the first year; the second year's crops showed a rapid decline and it was estimated that at most three years' crops could have been taken from the corn-plot. The natural regeneration also showed interesting contrasts over the years. On the unburnt area ferns and other plant species already present in the forest increased owing to the removal of shade by tree-felling, but on the burnt area, in addition to a comparable increase in ferns, a new flora colonized the ground, including plantain, Compositae such as dandelions, thistle, and daisies, and certain mosses from windblown spores, three of them recognized in North America as constant concomitants of the regeneration of burnt-down forests. Later, tree seedlings began to appear, beginning with the light-loving birch, and willow, hazel, aspen, and lime. The experimental circumstances on the burnt ground were in fact repeating those inferred from pollen diagrams following the *landnam* phenomenon.

At Ordrup in Denmark, Iversen found a charcoal layer in the peat section at the *landnam* horizon, followed by a primary tree regeneration represented by birch, which has also been noticed as a primary colonist after forest burning in modern Finland. Athough no direct archaeological demonstration in the form of charcoal layers have been found in Neolithic *landnam* horizons in Britain, the presumptive evidence of

---

[36] There seems to be no full publication of the Draved experiment. See, however, J. Iversen, 'Forest clearance in the Stone Age', *Scient. Amer.*, 194, 1956, and 'Le défrichement de la forêt pendant l'âge de la pierre', *Naturalistes Belges*, 41, 1960, pp. 53–64; W. Pennington, *The History of British Vegetation*, London, 1969, p. 67; J. D. Ovington, *Woodlands*, London, 1965, pls. 2–5.

Brandwirtschaft as a means of forest clearance in advance of cereal agriculture is strong. A Neolithic long barrow at Dalladies in Kincardineshire, north-east Scotland, was found to have been constructed from sods of turf cut from land recently cleared by burning, with dates ranging between *c.* 3240 and 2580 bc.[37] As a footnote to the Draved figures, for speed of clearance we may take Atkinson's estimate that a family of five or six persons, eating grain in some form at a figure approximating to the bread ration of classical times (ten bushels per head per year), would need the consumption-crop off about ten acres (*c.* 4 ha). This could then be cleared by three able-bodied members of the household in around two months – a perfectly reasonable figure. Assuming then further annual clearance to compensate for exhausted land, a third of a square mile (0.86 km²) could have been cleared in a century by three or four generations of the hypothetical single family, if natural forest growth were kept in check.[38]

That early forest clearance in third millennium Britain need not have been wholly occasioned by the needs of agriculture and domestic fuel, the evidence for timber constructions on a fair scale shows. The tree-felling at Storrs Moss *c.* 3500 bc already referred to suggested to the excavators not only "the most initial stages of a certain kind of human interference with the environment where small-scale encroachment of marginal woodland is preliminary to inroads on close forest" but also "the working and abandonment of timber on the site, in the form of plank-splitting and trimming for tenon jointing".[39] In the Somerset Levels timber causeways of corduroy or brushwood construction were being made over swampy ground from before 3000 bc, linking up areas of dry sandy soil and likely to have been used for driving cattle as well as for human passage. Here the consumption of felled and cut wood was considerable: the so-called 'Abbot's Way' track has been identified for over 2.5 km, and it was estimated that its corduroy construction of split alder logs would have required over 21,000 linear yards (*c.* 19,200 m) of timber, plus 50,000 birchwood pegs and an unknown quantity of stringers along the edges of the same wood. Other tracks were constructed with smaller stems and branches laid endways longitudinally or on bundles of birch brushwood, while one of the Chilton Tracks was made of poles of hazel, 6–7 ft (1.8–2.1 m) long, implying the products of coppice areas of some size. A recent

[37] S. Piggott, 'Excavation of the Dalladies long barrow...', *Proc. Soc. Ant. Scot.*, 104, 1971–2, p. 23.

[38] R. J. C. Atkinson, 'Old mortality...', in J. M. Coles and D. D. A. Simpson (eds.), *Studies in Ancient Europe*, Leicester, 1968, pp. 83–93; cf. S. Piggott, *Ancient Europe*, Edinburgh, 1965, p. 68, n. 52, for corn consumption figures.

[39] T. G. E. Powell *et al.*, 'Excavations in Zone VII peat at Storrs Moss...', *Proc. Prehist. Soc.*, 37, 1971, pp. 112–87.

discovery on the Walton Track showed it to be constructed of well-made hurdles of coppiced hazel, nearly 3 m long and just over 1 m wide, and traces of comparable hurdle-work have been found in contemporary long barrows.[40] In sum, the local forest clearance necessary simply to initiate and keep in repair a footpath system between settlements, or between settlements and grazing areas, must have been significant.

Similarly, timber consumption for building purposes must not be forgotten. As we shall shortly see, our very scanty evidence for Neolithic settlements in Britain hardly informs us beyond the fact that timber buildings were used, but funerary monuments even from the late fourth millennium, and ceremonial structures from the middle of the third, show us a lavish use of massive tree-stems. The timber revetment of the Fussell's Lodge long barrow in Wiltshire, comprised of whole or split oak treetrunks from 0.3 m in diameter to 0.6–0.9 m and up to at least 3.6 m in height, would have consumed in all a linear run of 660 m of timber of appropriate scantling. In normal conditions of natural woodland oaks of such sizes would be expected to occur at a frequency of about 12 to 0.4 ha, so that the 100 or so stems needed would represent a selective choice from oak stands in about 4 ha of forest. This long barrow dates from c. 3240 bc and is one of our earliest Neolithic monuments: its counterparts, incorporating timber mortuary houses or revetments, are widespread from Wessex north-eastwards to Yorkshire and Scotland, and in the main lie within the first half of the third millennium bc.[41]

From the middle of the millennium ceremonial centres were coming into being in Wessex and elsewhere, which comprised not only circular embanked enclosures of the 'henge monument' class, but large concentric settings of rings of timber uprights, either free-standing or roofed. However interpreted, these sanctuary sites again demanded timber on a considerable scale, the more so if they were in fact roofed structures. At the best-known of these sites, Woodhenge, Wilts., one ring comprised 16 uprights of 1 m diameter timbers, and the whole monument (which may be of more than one building period) a total of 156 uprights of varying scantlings. It has been calculated that in the closely adjacent circular structure within the henge monument of Durrington Walls a total of over 900 m of timber would have been needed for the uprights alone and more than 135 m for roofing – a total

---

[40] J. M. Coles et al., 'Prehistoric roads...the Sweet Track, Proc. Prehist. Soc., 30, 1973, p. 256; 'A neolithic hurdle...', Ant., L, 1976, p. 57.
[41] P. Ashbee, 'The Fussell's Lodge long barrow...', Archaeologia, 100, 1966, pp. 1–80, esp. pp. 35–6; for tree frequencies, K. Jessen in P. Nørlund, Trelleborg, Nord. Fortidsminder IV, i, Copenhagen, 1948, pp. 173–9; long barrows in general, P. Ashbee, The Earthen Long Barrow in Britain, London, 1970.

weight of timber of about 26,500 kg, the product of 3.6 ha of oak forest.[42] The Durrington structure dates from the Late Neolithic period, *c*. 2000 bc, and Woodhenge is roughly contemporary. The implications of such structures, if interpreted as roofed buildings, on the presumptive nature of as yet unidentified Neolithic domestic houses in Britain, is obvious.

In any attempt to place such forest clearance for agricultural or other purposes in its social context as the earliest phase of British agrarian history, we should now naturally turn to the types of settlement and their distribution pattern, and see what social inferences might reasonably be drawn from them. Two difficulties immediately present themselves, the first being the long duration of stone-using agricultural economies in Britain, and the large element of social evolution and change that this must imply. We have to turn to the recent correlations of radiocarbon dates with calendar dates, obtained by dendrochronology, already touched on for an estimate of this period of time. In radiocarbon 'years' the time-span involved would be from *c*. 3500 bc, the entrance phase of initial colonization, to *c*. 1500 bc, when the final Late Neolithic cultures in the north, surviving for nearly half a millennium after the beginnings of non-ferrous metallurgy in Britain, came to an end. This period of 2,000 radiocarbon years, however, when adjusted to the real time-scale, becomes *c*. 4400–1900 BC, in calendar years, thus adding another half-millennium to our estimated duration of the British Neolithic cultures. Over such a period of time it would clearly be very unwise to assume that there were no changes in the patterns of society; they may well have been very different, in the first few centuries of this 2,500 year span, from those of the final phase. To this may be added the supposition that the geographical diversity of Britain would favour the development of local variants on any basic cultural pattern that may be thought to have characterized the initial settlements. Such conditions contrast with the archaeological evidence for the first agricultural communities in Neolithic Europe being on the central loess or the northern plain, where natural circumstances favoured uniformity rather than diversity. We must therefore beware of generalizing too far in time or space from a few pieces of evidence widely scattered in both dimensions. We can perhaps at least visualize Early, Middle, and Late Neolithic phases, with dates, reverting to the conventional radiocarbon notation, from *c*. 3500–2750 bc (Early); *c*. 2750–2000 bc (Middle) and *c*. 2000–1500 bc (Late).

Any attempt at drawing conclusions about the social pattern or patterns within Britain over this period is rendered peculiarly difficult by the paucity of information on settlements or dwelling sites. Instances

[42] G. Wainwright, 'Woodhenges', *Scient. Amer.*, 223, 1970, pp. 30–8.

of human occupation attested by finds of pottery, flint, and stone, foods, hearths, rubbish or storage pits, and occasional post-structures, sometimes to be interpreted as houses, are widely scattered throughout Britain, while two exceptional stone-built settlements in Orkney, and several stone houses in Shetland, all Late Neolithic, are so peripheral as not to be representative. What can be said, however, is that in no instance have the exiguous remains recovered elsewhere in Britain been capable of interpretation as population centres larger than a farm or homestead; they are certainly not fragments of otherwise unexcavated sites of village status as would normally be the case on the European continent. The Shetland sites, which have associated field boundaries, emphasize the croft-like nature of the settlements there in the earlier second millennium bc; Skara Brae, partly eroded by the sea, has now only five certain dwelling-houses and two or three ancillary chambers; Rinyo is of unknown extent but may be approximately the same size, covering about 1100 m². A Late Neolithic site at Grandtully, Perths. (c. 2000 bc), when completely excavated, showed an occupied area of only about 150 m², with a single large pit, holes of uncertain purpose, and no evidence of a house.[43] In the south of England, Hazard Hill in Devon was estimated to cover over 15,000 m², but excavation (of a small area admittedly) produced no evidence beyond hearths, pits, and four post-holes forming no pattern. At the contemporary site of Haldon the scatter was spread over 600 m², and a single rectangular post-framed house was found.[44] At Hurst Fen, Mildenhall, occupation scatter was traced over an estimated 16,000 m², but excavation of nearly 2,000 m², revealed no house plans, a few stake-holes, and some 200 shallow pits.[45] These, with others of similar type widely distributed in Neolithic contexts in south-east England, have normally been identified as 'storage pits', with the assumption that the material stored was grain (on Iron Age analogies), but this has not yet been demonstrated directly.[46] Where houses have been identified, they are normally rectangular, ranging from 7 × 3.5 m at Haldon and Clegyr Boia to 6 × 4 m at Ronaldsway in the Isle of Man, and at Fengate 8.5 × 7 m, and are of light post or bedding-trench construction: at Skara Brae the roughly square or rounded stone houses measure about 6 × 6 m internally, and

[43] D. D. A. Simpson and F. M. B. Cooke, 'Photogrammetric planning at Grandtully, Perthshire', *Ant.*, XLI, 1967, p. 220.

[44] C. H. Houlder, 'A neolithic settlement on Hazard Hill, Totnes', *Trans. Devon Arch. Exp. Soc.*, 21, 1963, p. 2; Haldon, S. Piggott, *Neolithic Cultures of the British Isles*, Cambridge, 1954, p. 33. The former site dates from c. 2800 bc.

[45] J. G. D. Clark, 'Excavations at the Neolithic site at Hurst Fen, Mildenhall, Suffolk', *Proc. Prehist. Soc.*, 26, 1960, p. 202.

[46] N. H. Field et al., 'New neolithic sites in Dorset and Bedfordshire...', *Proc. Prehist. Soc.*, 30, 1964, p. 352.

the Shetland houses, again of stone, and oval in plan, had in typical examples inner areas ranging from 11 × 6 m to 8 × 4.5 m.[47] Allowing for differences in shape, the floor areas of the known houses are remarkably consistent, and differ little from the dimensions of earlier Neolithic houses in Eastern Europe. There they are normally interpreted as representing, in social terms, units of the 'natural' or 'nuclear' family type, conventionally set at about five persons. Scanty though our British Neolithic evidence is, its implication is consistent, and we are certainly not dealing with social situations involving 'extended' or 'undivided' families in the manner perhaps implied by the long-house tradition of many central European Neolithic cultures.[48] The evidence for massive circular ritual timber structures, almost certainly roofed buildings of accomplished carpentry, within henge monuments like those at Durrington Walls, Woodhenge, Marden, or Mount Pleasant, prompts thought on the possibility of secular timber houses of comparable scale and sophistication still to be discovered in Late Neolithic Wessex at least.

With such scanty and uninformative primary evidence, inference as to social structure and organization can at best be very tentative. An interesting approach has recently been made by Colin Renfrew in respect of Neolithic Wessex,[49] on the basis of the manpower and concerted effort needed to construct the main types of ceremonial monuments in the area – long barrows, causewayed enclosures, and henge monuments. Good basic formulae, based on the experience of constructing experimental earthworks in recent years, are available for such a purpose. A long barrow with timber-work features could represent about 5,000 man-hours – stone-built barrows perhaps rather more. In Wiltshire and Dorset there are about 120 long barrows, each of which could have been built by a small population group of between 20 and 100 persons: they fall into territorial groups and the construction of any one could draw on a population of 10 km². Chronologically, the long barrows are the earliest of the three classes of monuments, from c. 3000 to c. 2700 bc, and so belong in our Early Neolithic phase. In the Middle Neolithic we see the construction of the roughly circular enclosures with multiple lines of ditches broken by frequent gaps, the 'causewayed camps' which, originally construed as ditched settlements, are now by general agreement regarded as in some sense communal ritual centres. Such an enclosure would demand around 100,000 man-hours (the estimate for Windmill Hill itself), and their relationship

[47] C. S. T. Calder, 'Stone Age house sites in Shetland', Proc. Soc. Ant. Scot., 89, 1955–6, p. 340. Radiocarbon dates of c. 1700–1600 bc have been obtained for these sites.

[48] S. Piggott, Ancient Europe, Edinburgh, 1965, pp. 40–52.

[49] C. Renfrew, 'Monuments, mobilization and social organization in Neolithic Wessex', in idem (ed.), The Explanation of Culture Change, London, 1973, pp. 539–58.

to the long barrows suggests that each served an area containing about 20 barrows, forming five major territorial units. The major henge monuments, such as Avebury or Durrington Walls, are engineering operations involving around a million man-hours, and since their distribution suggests a connection with five causewayed camp provinces it may be guessed that by the Late Neolithic stage, to which they belong, they drew on an increased population to construct them.

Taking these approximate figures, Renfrew suggests the use of a model of social organization in terms of 'chiefdoms', as defined by anthropologists. This structure would not be apparent in Early Neolithic times, but the causewayed enclosures would imply the emergence in Wessex of five chiefdoms, each with population groups centred on 20 long barrows and totalling between 400 and 2,000 persons. These emergent chiefdoms would become consolidated as the henge monuments took over and developed the idea of ceremonial centres from the causewayed enclosure prototypes, with population figures rising to some 5,000 persons in each province. Finally, the construction of such outstandingly grandiose monuments as Silbury Hill or the final phase at Stonehenge might have been made possible by a 'confederation' of chiefdoms or the temporary formation of a supra-chiefdom.

The model is attractive and the arguments persuasive for the Dorset–Wiltshire Chalk massif for which it was adopted. Outside this area, circumstances clearly differed widely. On the Sussex Downs, with only a dozen long barrows and four causewayed enclosures, one might claim two or four emergent chiefdoms with a much smaller population than in Wessex, but in Sussex there are no henge monuments to mark any further stage of social development. Beyond Sussex and Wessex the causewayed enclosures of Windmill Hill type are virtually absent, though henge monuments, usually small, are widely distributed as far north as Orkney, and certainly appear to form ceremonial centres, sometimes in association with ancillary monuments of cursus or avenue type. But their distribution is unrelated to that of long barrows and their date, where ascertained, is Late Neolithic, within the first half of the second millennium bc. Apart then from the recognition of communal ceremonial centres at this time over most of Britain with the presumption that these served local populations within some social system, likely enough of chiefdom type, we cannot form a very satisfactory model outside Wessex.

In seeking to assess the social context within which to place the evidence from stock-breeding and arable husbandry in Britain from c. 3000–1500 bc we can therefore do little more than repeat that the archaeological evidence, such as it is, favours a predominance of settlements of *Einzelhof* type over larger aggregations of village status.

If we then assume the long barrows to represent the ceremonial burial-places of a small proportion of the total population, and each barrow to represent the effort of a kinship group, we have a minimal picture for the early phase of colonization and consolidation. From this basis the Wessex evidence could be interpreted as demonstrating the emergence of social units of 'chiefdom' type. Elsewhere, with the partial exception of Sussex, we have only the presumptive small kinship groups associated with long barrows in the east, and stone chambered tombs in the west and north, until the appearance at the end of the Neolithic period of ceremonial centres incorporating henge monuments and associated not with the earlier long barrows or chambered tombs, but with contemporary and later single-grave burials, with or without a mound or cairn. The individuality of Wessex seems already apparent from an early stage, and this exceptional quality becomes characteristic of all its subsequent prehistory.

STOCK, PASTURE, AND ARABLE HUSBANDRY

We have already noted the problems presented by the alternative possibilities of feeding cattle on leaf-fodder rather than on pasture, and in the entrance phase of colonization, before cleared woodland had regenerated into some form of grassland, this would have seemed a likely situation. Natural grass or parkland would clearly be at a premium, though some might well have existed and been grazed by the wild aurochs. In modern conditions of hill pasture cattle and red deer can graze in satisfactory relationship, as we have seen, and such a situation could equally exist with wild cattle, especially at the margins of forest areas near fresh or salt water, where, as we saw, unstable vegetation zones associated with the growth of open-country plants could be produced by natural causes. If such grazing areas existed and were exploited by the first Neolithic colonists, the likelihood of contact between wild and domestic cattle would be enhanced, and interbreeding could be encouraged if desired; if not, vigilance would have been needed on the part of the herdsmen from the first. Coastal settlements, as we also noted earlier, would provide salt for cattle, be inimical to liver-fluke in sheep, and, unlike stagnant fresh water, not afford breeding-places for the anopheles mosquito.

The relatively large size of the British Neolithic domestic cattle, around that of a modern Jersey, provides an interesting factor in assessing their comparative value as a meat source. With a larder weight of about 158 kg, this far exceeds the red deer under modern Highland conditions (up to 90 kg maximum for an 8-year-old stag), but deer bred in English deciduous woodland and parkland are "3.6 times greater in relative biomass terms than that of Scottish populations" and attain maximum larder weights of up to 160 kg – extremely near to our estimated figure for the Neolithic domestic cattle population. [50] Even if not "beef to the heels, like a Mullingar heifer" they must have represented a protein supply completely equivalent to the deer population at least, on the hoof and under control, and it is not surprising that from the first the evidence for hunting wild animals is minimal, being 3.9 per cent of the food-bones from the primary phase at Windmill Hill, and 9.0 per cent at the Late Neolithic henge monument of Durrington Walls, where, incidentally, aurochs of up to 2 m high at the shoulder were being hunted. There was no need to hunt deer for their antlers, as these could be (and, as the evidence shows, normally were) collected when shed in the spring and before being eaten again by the stags.

Cattle preponderate on the British Neolithic sites where bones survived, and reports on the animals represented have been made; ovicaprids are consistently minimal in importance. An exceptional site is the Late Neolithic ceremonial monument of Durrington Walls, where we have a large bones series studied in some detail, giving figures of 63 per cent pig, 26 per cent cattle, 2 per cent sheep, and a single bone of goat in the total assembly of domestic and wild species.[51] Here it is stressed that the human selection behind food-bones on a ritual site, and those in normal domestic contexts, might be different, but we must also remember that Windmill Hill, providing the only large comparable series of bones, is itself almost certainly in some sense a ritual site, antecedent to the henge monuments of the type of Durrington Walls, so that less disparity may exist between the two populations than might be thought. In any case, the contrast is very striking, and attention has been drawn to European Neolithic cultures in which pig-breeding is dominant.[52] Oak forest is of course involved for feeding, and the well-known rural axiom that "pigs won't be druv" underlines the presence of stable agricultural communities in Neolithic Britain no less than the Domesday Book figures for pannage, in an historical context. Again swineherds to control interbreeding with wild stock are implied. Cattle-breeding primarily for meat supplies, but also for milk, is usually

[50] G. H. M. Bland, in M. M. Bannerman and K. L. Blaxter (eds.), *The Husbanding of Red Deer*, Inverness, 1970, pp. 22–5. Note that the lower weights for 'deer' in American publications on prehistoric food intake (e.g. C. Gabel, *Analysis of Prehistoric Economic Patterns*, 1967, pp. 26–7) are those of the smaller white-tailed deer.

[51] R. A. Harcourt, 'Animal bones...', in G. J. Wainwright and I. H. Longworth, *Durrington Walls: Excavations 1966–68*, London, 1971, p. 338.

[52] J. Murray, 'Some aspects of ovicaprid and pig breeding in neolithic Europe', in J. M. Coles and D. D. A. Simpson (eds.), *Studies in Ancient Europe*, Leicester, 1968, p. 71.

assumed, especially with a small ovicaprid population, but it should be remembered that not all cattle-breeders need be milk-drinkers, though milk consumption is usually taken to be an ancient custom in Europe.[53] The evidence from Windmill Hill, Durrington Walls, Skara Brae, and other less well-documented Neolithic sites is consistent in demonstrating overwintering of cattle and pigs over several years, and earlier guesses at autumn slaughter must be discounted.[54] Evidence for castration of cattle has been noted at two Late Neolithic sites, Skara Brae and Durrington Walls, but has not been detected in earlier series. The point is returned to again in connection with the use of oxen as draught animals.

Slaughtering, skinning, and the selection of joints for cooking is an aspect hardly studied in British prehistory largely owing to the lack of detailed analysis of material even when this has been preserved. With the myth of autumn slaughter at Windmill Hill went that of pole-axed cattle-skulls on that site, the perforations on the frontal regions of which have since been shown to be irrelevant or *post mortem*.[55] Attention has been paid to selection by Bradley (in an Iron Age context) and by Harcourt at Durrington Walls, while there is evidence that hides were removed still attached to the skull and the limb extremities: such hides have a long history of ritual usage over wide tracts of Europe and Asia, implied by archaeological evidence and demonstrated in recent times in pagan Siberian religious ceremonies. The wooden gable of the Fussell's Lodge Early Neolithic burial chamber and long barrow may have been graced with such a horned skin, and evidence of their incidental presence has been found at several other such tombs.[56] The discarded portions of the animal were of limited nutritious value and dishes such as ox-tail, cow's heel, or pig's trotters can only result from prolonged slow cooking with water in a closed vessel in a manner likely to be difficult or impossible with the Neolithic pottery resources available. This limitation would also inhibit the manufacture of a

[53] Milk consumption in immediately pre-Roman Britain is attested by Caesar and Strabo (though both may draw on Posidonius), as among the Germani and Suebi on the Continent.—S. Piggott, 'Native economies and the Roman occupation of North Britain', in I. A. Richmond (ed.), *Roman and Native in North Britain*, Edinburgh, 1958, p. 1. For the general problem cf. F. J. Simoons, 'The traditional limits of milking and milk use in southern Asia', *Anthropos*, 65, 1970, p. 547; 'The antiquity of dairying in Asia and Africa', *Geog. Rev.*, 61, 1971, p. 431.

[54] Harcourt, *op. cit.*, p. 349; E. S. Higgs and J. P. White, 'Autumn killing', *Ant.*, XXXVII, 1963, p. 282.

[55] I. F. Smith, *Windmill Hill and Avebury*, Oxford, 1965, p. 41.

[56] Harcourt, *op. cit.*; R. Bradley, 'Excavations on Portsdown Hill 1963–65', *Proc. Hants. Fd Club and Arch. Soc.*, 24, 1967, pp. 42, 53–4; P. Ashbee, *The Earthen Long Barrow in Britain*, London, 1970, pp. 74–7; S. Piggott, 'Heads and hoofs', *Ant.*, XXXVI, 1962, p. 110.

satisfactory animal glue, as Rousing has indicated in connection with the making of composite bows:[57] birch resin, used from Mesolithic times, and fish glues are, however, not excluded, though less satisfactory. Methods of skin preparation, tanning or curing can only be inferential beyond the obvious use of flint scrapers for removing subcutaneous tissue, and no better suggestion for the use of the characteristic Early or Middle Neolithic 'antler combs' has been made other than comparing them with the *kumotin* of the Point Barrow Eskimos, used for removing coarse hair from pelts.

In default of evidence of the spinning of wool or plant fibres or of textile manufacture in Neolithic Britain, skin is likely to have been used for the making of clothing of the tailored type, as represented among the Eskimo today; indeed, such usage seems to go back to Upper Palaeolithic times. It is also likely to have been used for ropes in the absence of suitable vegetable fibres. The only alternatives were straw or heather, which would not provide the strength needed for the transport and erection of large timbers or stones utilized in tombs and ceremonial monuments. Only rawhide ropes could have stood up to such strain. The great probability of skin-covered boats being used at this time, as well as dug-out canoes, would imply a demand for cow-hides, as traditionally used on Irish curraghs and Welsh coracles until the advent of modern tarred canvas.[58]

The dietary 'revolution' brought about by the introduction of agriculture to Britain, as elsewhere, was not so much an assured supply of protein in the form of domestic flocks and herds but the enlarged carbohydrate resources in the form of cereal crops. These additions to the hunter-gatherers' diet gave a much higher carbohydrate yield than did the seeds of wild plants. By the time Neolithic agricultural techniques were imported into Britain in the fourth millennium bc, the cultivated versions of the original large-grained cereal grasses of western Asia had become stable species whose habitat has been steadily pushed north and west, beyond the natural range of the wild prototypes, by Neolithic farmers. Cereal crops in antiquity were rarely grown completely pure, in the sense of consisting of 100 per cent of a single grain, but one species always predominated. The evidence for Neolithic cultivated cereals in Britain, largely in the form of impressions on pottery, with a few finds of actual carbonized grain, showed, when

[57] G. Rausing, *The Bow: Some Notes on its Origins and Development*, Lund, 1967, p. 146.

[58] For skin clothing, see S. Piggott, *Ancient Europe*, Edinburgh, 1965, pp. 104–6; for ropes, see R. J. C. Atkinson, 'Neolithic engineering', *Ant.*, xxxv, 1961, p. 292; for skin boats, P. Johnstone, 'The Bantry Boat', *ibid.*, xxxviii, 1964, p. 277; J. Hornell, *British Coracles and Irish Curraghs*, London, 1938.

assessed in 1952, the cultivation of both wheat and barley, in the proportions of 91.6 per cent wheat to 8.4 per cent barley, in the large Windmill Hill series (the remaining impressions being flax seeds and apple-pips). This proportion is confirmed by the far smaller series from elsewhere. The wheat crop was overwhelmingly of emmer (*Triticum diococcum*), with one or two identifiable grains of eincorn (*T. monococcum*) as a fortuitous component, and the barley was preponderantly the naked form of *Hordeum vulgare*, probably of the six-rowed variety.[59] Most of our evidence comes from southern England, but sporadic impressions of barley have been recorded on probable Middle Neolithic pottery from Moray and Orkney, and a find of burnt barley was made in the Late Neolithic site at the Ness of Gruting in Shetland, further discussed in a later chapter (p. 205). The appearance of seed impressions in pottery is dependent upon manufacturing techniques which allow of the accidental incorporation of such extraneous matter and cannot in itself be taken as a negation of cereal cultivation: impressions are very rare on all British Late Neolithic wares, and wholly absent in pottery of the Grooved Ware style.[60] Although querns provide evidence that the grain was ground to flour, it is wholly uncertain how it was cooked, and some form of bread is only one of several possibilities.

The flax-seed impressions from Windmill Hill seem to be those of *Linum usitatissimum*, and are among the earliest on record for north-west Europe. The plant is most likely to have been grown for the nutritious qualities of the oily linseed as a part of the diet rather than for its fibres in making linen thread and cloth: a comparable Swiss find of *c.* 3000 bc certainly suggests this, the seeds being found in what appear to be human faeces.

From Windmill Hill also are the impressions of the pips of wild crab-apples (*Pyrus malus*), showing that these were gathered and, perhaps, as in the Swiss Neolithic, split and dried for storage. It might be apposite here to turn in parenthesis from these wild apples to consider briefly some of the other potential wild plant resources which, while not directly attested archaeologically, are unlikely to have been wholly

---

[59] K. Jessen and H. Helbaek, *Cereals in Great Britain and Ireland in Prehistoric and Early Historic Times*, Køberhaun, 1944; H. Helbaek, 'Early crops in southern England', *Proc. Prehist. Soc.*, 18, 1952, p. 194; *idem*, 'Notes on the evolution and history of *Linum*', *Kuml*, 1959, p. 103; general background, *idem*. 'Commentary on the phylogenesis of *Triticum* and *Hordeum*', *Econ. Bot.*, 20, 1966, p. 350; H. H. Clark, 'The origin and early history of the cultivated barleys', *Agric. Hist. Rev.*, 15, 1967, p. 1; J. Murray, *The First European Agriculture*, Edinburgh, 1970.

[60] It is hardly justifiable to say of the communities making the latter ware that "the evidence suggests pastoralism and strandlooping, with no certain evidence for the cultivation of cereals, for not one grain impression has been identified with certainty on any sherd of Grooved Ware". Wainwright and Longworth, *op. cit.*, p. 266.

ignored by the Neolithic (and indeed the later) prehistoric communities of Britain.[61] Ethnographical parallels would suggest that inevitably even full farming communities would avail themselves of such resources – for North America north of Mexico it was reckoned that the Indians counted as food-plants 120 families, 444 genera, and 1,112 species, of which only 1 per cent was cultivated.[62] As well as crab-apples in Britain, other fruits could include sloe and wild cherry (*Prunus spinosus avium*), raspberry (*Rubus idaeus*), identified in Neolithic and Early Bronze Age contexts, blackberry (*R. fructicosus*), a constant British species from Atlantic times onwards, and almost certainly collected for eating in Roman times, and rose hips (*Rosa* sp.). A burial, probably of the early second millennium, at Walton-on-Naze contained in its stomach blackberry and rose seeds, as well as remains of orache (*Atriplex*). Hazel-nuts (*Corylus*) have been found as charred shells in both Mesolithic and Neolithic hearths and, as we saw, may have come from deliberately tended stances, and acorns (*Quercus*) could also have been eaten not only by pigs but by man, as they appear to have been in Neolithic East Europe. They need careful preparation to remove their bitter tannin content by pounding them to a meal that is then leached with water, leaving the main nutrient content of starch and fat. Although not strictly a 'nut', the pig-nut or earth-nut (*Conopodium majus*) appears to be a native and has an edible root. The field pea (*Pisum sativum*) seems a Roman introduction, and the broad bean (*Vicia faba*) though known as a cultivar in Neolithic western Europe, is not a British plant. Finally there are a number of plants with edible leaves and agreeable flavours, broadly salads and herbs, such as water-cress (*Nasturtium officinale*), chives (*Allium schoenoprasum*), wild thyme (*Thymus*) and mint (*Mentha*).

Nor should the large range of edible fungi be forgotten, and here one may touch on the possibility of the prehistoric use of the fly agaric (*Amanita muscaria*) as a hallucinogen. The topic is sadly clouded by irresponsible theorizing at worst, and at best by overenthusiastic elaboration and extrapolation, but the basic arguments for a widespread use of this fungus in attaining Shamanistic ecstatic states in antiquity, as in modern Siberia, seem too cogent to be ignored, and shamanism cannot be excluded as a possible component of Neolithic as of other primitive religions.[63] At a less exalted level we must remember that fermented drinks can be made from fruit or wild honey no less than

[61] Basic documentation in H. Godwin, *History of the British Flora*, Cambridge, 1956.
[62] H. E. Driver and W. C. Massey, 'Comparative studies of North American Indians', *Trans. Amer. Phil. Soc.*, N.S. 47, 1957, p. 2.
[63] R. G. Wasson, *Soma: the Divine Mushroom*, 1968; *idem*, 'The soma of the Rig Veda: what was it?', *J. Amer. Orient. Soc.*, 91, 1971, p. 169. On Shamanism, see S. Piggott, *The Druids*, London, 1968, p. 184.

from cereal crops, where in all ancient and modern contexts the provision of 'drink corn' is as important as the food grain, and is on occasion rated as the overriding alternative.[64]

Thanks largely to recent studies by Evans of the populations of land molluscs in relation to buried land surfaces, we can observe the sequence of agricultural operations on a dozen Neolithic sites, especially on southern English calcareous soils.[65] Some monuments (the Windmill Hill and Knap Hill Middle Neolithic enclosures in Wiltshire, for instance of *c.* 2950 and 2760 bc, respectively) had been built in a woodland environment, though presumably some clearance took place at the time of their construction. In more instances, however, while there was evidence of original forest cover, this had been cleared well before the construction of what is in almost all instances a long barrow. Two types of clearance are detectable, that associated with an undisturbed soil profile, as at the long barrows of Beckhampton Road (*c.* 3250 bc) and West Kennet in Wiltshire, Ascott-under-Wychwood in the Cotswolds (*c.* 2785 bc), Kilham on the Yorkshire Wolds (*c.* 2880 bc) and Dalladies in east Scotland (*c.* 3240–2580 bc), which could be interpreted to indicate pasture, or with disturbance or actual evidence of plough agriculture, as at Wayland's Smithy in Berkshire (*c.* 2820 bc), and Horslip (*c.* 3240 bc) and South Street (*c.* 2820 bc) in Wiltshire, at the latter site with the furrows of cross-ploughing discussed below. A disturbed clearance-surface was also found below Silbury Hill, *c.* 2725–2365 bc. At the Marden henge monument, in the Vale of Pewsey, of *c.* 1990 bc, similar evidence of cleared forest existed.

Three specific instances of sequences under Early Neolithic long barrows on the Chalk or oolite, and one under a Late Neolithic henge monument on Chalk, make interesting comparisons. At South Street, Avebury, the natural Post-glacial conditions would have been light woodland in the Boreal climatic phase (Zone VI) developing into high forest by Atlantic times (VIIa). There followed complete Neolithic clearance, followed by deep ploughing with an ard, with furrows crossed at right angles. There then followed some form of non-arable human occupation with the formation of grassland, and about 2800 bc the long barrow was built on this. Similar ard marks occurred under

[64] R. J. Braidwood *et al.*, 'Did man once live by beer alone?', *Amer. Anthrop.*, 55, 1953, p. 515.

[65] G. W. Dimbleby and J. G. Evans, 'Pollen and land-snail analysis of calcareous soils', *J. Arch. Science*, 1974, p. 117; J. G. Evans, 'Habitat on the calcareous soils of Britain: the impact of neolithic man', in D. D. A. Simpson (ed.), *Economy and Settlement in Neolithic and Early Bronze Age Britain and Europe*, Leicester, 1971, pp. 27–74; 'Durrington Walls: the pre-henge environment', in G. J. Wainwright and I. H. Longworth, *Durrington Walls: Excavations, 1966–68*, 1971, p. 329; J. G. Evans, *Land Snails in Archaeology*, London, 1972, esp. pp. 242–79.

the great bank of the Avebury henge monument. The subsequent agricultural prehistory of South Street, also elucidated, is discussed in a subsequent chapter. The Cotswold barrow at Ascott-under-Wychwood covered an original Post-glacial surface, lightly wooded and with a Mesolithic occupation. The site was abandoned and the tree canopy increased, to be cleared in Neolithic times and occupied in two phases, the second of which was c. 2800 and was followed by the construction of the barrow. At Durrington Walls the usual forest cover of the Chalk in the Atlantic period was followed c. 2500 by Neolithic clearance and a soil profile indicating cultivation. This was then abandoned, and grassland formed which was probably used as pasture and then abandoned for this purpose (this is suggested by the appearance of bracken pollen at this point) before the henge monument was built and used c. 2000–1500 bc. A simpler sequence from the Northton site in the Isle of Harris nevertheless shows a consistent picture: forest cover even in the north of the Hebrides was cleared in Neolithic times, followed by abandonment, woodland regeneration, and new clearance by makers of Beakers early in the second millennium bc. The Dalladies long barrow in east Scotland was built of turf and topsoil derived from an area cleared of woodland by the *Brandwirtschaft* method and for its construction nearly 0.7 ha of sods would have to have been cut, implying considerable areas of manmade pasture in a birch and alder environment.

We finally come to tillage, plough, and fields. Very little evidence survives and one can only hope for more coming to light when buried land surfaces are carefully excavated with attention to such problems. At Carn Brea in Cornwall, recent excavations have found probable traces of cultivation by hoe or spade rather than by plough, with small heaps of stones from field clearance, in an Early Neolithic context which could be late fourth millennium bc.[66] But the possible plough-furrows of this date under the Fussell's Lodge long barrow in Wiltshire were eventually rejected as such by the excavator.[67] The most remarkable find so far is the area of cross-ploughing under the South Street long barrow already referred to, ploughed and abandoned before c. 2810 bc. Here the furrows appeared to be cut in the solid Chalk subsoil to a depth of up to 15 cm, but this may well be the result of frost action and solution deepening lighter furrows; they ran in two series, more or less at right angles, in a familiar pattern of cross-ploughing widely known in Europe and in later British contexts. The longest observable furrow was 14 m long, suggesting traction with a light plough of ard type: the

[66] R. J. Mercer, 'The neolithic settlement on Carn Brea...', *Cornish Arch.*, 9, 1970, p. 53.

[67] P. Ashbee, 'The Fussell's Lodge long barrow...', *Archaeologia*, 100, 1966, p. 1.

South Street
Neolithic plough marks

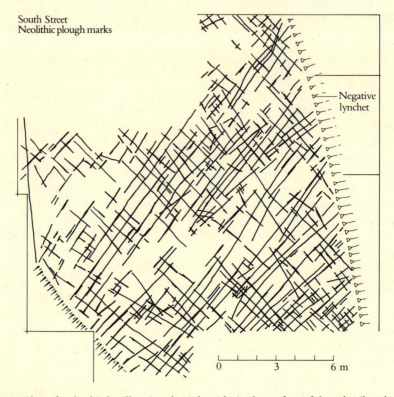

Negative
lynchet

0   3   6 m

Fig. 2. Plan of early third millennium bc ard-marks in the surface of the subsoil at the base of the soil profile sealed beneath the South Street long barrow, Avebury, Wilts. (after J. G. Evans).

implications of this are returned to later. The ard marks under the Avebury bank have not been extensively explored. Beneath a round barrow, the first phase of which dates from *c.* 2000 bc, at Earl's Farm Down, near Amesbury, Wilts., parallel grooves in the natural Chalk up to 15 cm deep ran down the hill slope 0.75 m to 1.4 m apart and in the absence of convincing natural explanations might be considered as possible plough traces.[68] Nothing is known of field sizes: at South Street the cross-ploughing could be traced for about 15 m in each direction and a fence of small posts running across this area bore no relation to it and was presumably of later date. The presence of

[68] P. J. Fowler and J. G. Evans, 'Plough-marks, lynchets and early fields', *Ant.*, XLI, 1967, p. 289; P. M. Christie, 'A barrow-cemetery of the second millennium B.C....', *Proc. Prehist. Soc.*, 33, 1967, p. 336.

abundant spores of bracken (*Pteridium aquilinum*) in the Neolithic soil below the South Street barrow has been interpreted not as natural invasion of land lying waste but of "bedding litter mucked out on arable land." Dry bracken only would have been used for litter, after the spores had ripened.

Our remaining evidence is from the Shetlands, northerly islands in the Arctic Ocean, where, however, agricultural stone-using communities were established by *c.* 1650 bc, growing barley and with their homesteads, field-boundaries, and clearance-heaps still visible on the ground.[69] As their pottery and other artifacts show, and the recent radiocarbon dates confirm, these sites are contemporary with the makers of Beaker pottery, who were also the first British workers in non-ferrous metal, so that the terms 'Neolithic' or 'Bronze Age' have little meaning, especially for settlements north of lat. 60°. They must, however, be mentioned both at the end of this section, and in the next chapter as well. We have already mentioned the oval stone houses with massive walls, which lie in irregular plots outlined by stone walls and containing clearance-heaps. More fieldwork is needed on these sites before we can be sure of the allocation of arable to each household: the Scord of Brouster site, usually regarded as a unit of five or six fields totalling about one hectare, looks from the published plan to be alternatively interpreted either as a single-house croft shifting its position, with a field of about half a hectare, three times over, or as the end-product of a croft enlarging itself to three times its original size. Actual burnt barley has been recovered from a similar site on the Ness of Gruting, but the crop, even during a climatic optimum, must have been small and chancy, so that even taken at its maximum field area Scord of Brouster can hardly have yielded a consumption-crop of more than about eighteen bushels (618 l) of barley on the usual reckoning for ancient yields.

The interest of the Shetland sites does not end here however, for from them, and less frequently in Orkney, come stone bars worked to a point which shows evidence of wear, broken-off points being the more common finds. These have been convincingly interpreted as stone plough-shares, "probably mounted in a mortice in the end of the plough-beam in the same manner as wooden shares are mounted in the composite variety known as the *bow-ard*".[70] The implication of the

---

[69] C. S. T. Calder, 'Stone Age house-sites in Shetland', *Proc. Soc. Ant. Scot.*, 89, 1955–6, p. 340; A. Fenton, 'Early and traditional cultivating implements in Scotland', *ibid.*, 96, 1962–3, p. 264. A radiocarbon date of *c.* 1560 bc was obtained by the British Museum laboratory (*Radiocarbon*, XIII, 1971, p. 177) and another of *c.* 1760 bc by Groningen (unpubl.) from the grain from the Ness of Gruting.

[70] Fenton, *op. cit.*, p. 267.

South Street furrows is of course the use of the traction ard before *c.* 2800 bc in southern England, and, by a millennium or so later, specialized ards with stone bar-shares were in use in the Shetlands and Orkneys. Further discussion must be left until later chapters but we may note in passing that an actual wooden ard from Denmark has a radiocarbon date of *c.* 1500 bc, and another in the Ukraine is dated to *c.* 1400 bc.[71]

In conclusion we must briefly set the foregoing evidence in its continental framework. While direct evidence is lacking, hoe agriculture has been assumed, on analogy, to have been the most likely method employed to break up the ground after slash-and-burn forest clearance had left the deforested area still encumbered with tree-stumps, though ploughing with a light ard is not impossible. And as we have seen, neither plough nor hoe was used in some recent Russian areas of *Brandwirtschaft*. The use of the traction-plough is bound up with the availability of suitable draught animals,[72] normally a pair of oxen, though strangely assorted animals can be used for this purpose and may not infrequently be seen in, for instance, the Near East today. The appreciation of castration as a means of obtaining docile and powerful oxen had been reached by Neolithic communities in central Europe by the fifth millennium BC,[73] and with the production of such draught animals the potentiality of plough agriculture is achieved. The use of paired draught for ploughing can apply equally to the traction of sledges or wheeled vehicles, but ploughing and the use of such transport are two separate technologies and one does not necessarily presuppose the other.

On present showing, the earliest evidence for plough agriculture in northern Europe is the group of ard-furrows preserved (as in Wiltshire) under a Neolithic long barrow, at Sarnowo No. 8, Włocławek, west of Warsaw, with a radiocarbon date not far from *c.* 3600 bc, and showing the remains of cereal pollen.[74] This then would suggest the use of a traction-plough of ard type, and of draught oxen in the early Funnel Beaker culture of Poland, for which there is corroborative evidence, including the presence of castrated animals. Ritual burials of

[71] G. Lerche, 'The radiocarbon-dated Danish ploughing implements', *Tools and Tillage*, I, 1968, p. 56; B. A. Schramko, 'Der Hakenplug der Bronzezeit in der Ukraine', *ibid.*, 1–4, 1971, pp. 223–4; with date of 1390±80 bc (Le: no lab. no.)

[72] A. G. Haudricourt and M. J-B. Delamarre, *L'homme et la charrue à travers le monde*, Paris, 1955; P. V. Glob, *Ard og plov i nordens oldtid*, Aarhus, 1951.

[73] J. Murray, *The First European Agriculture*, Edinburgh, 1970, p. 37.

[74] J. A. Bakker et al., 'TRB and other C14 dates from Poland', *Helinium*, IX, 1969, p. 224n.; L. Gabałowna, 'Radiocarbon dating of charcoal from the TRB cemetery...at Sarnowo (Barrow 8)...', *Prace i Materiały Muz. Arch. Łodz.*, Arch. Series, 17, 1970, p. 89.

cattle in pairs, suggesting a tradition of paired draught, go back in central and northern Europe to the earlier third millennium bc, if not to the late fourth, and some of these are contemporary and not unconnected with the earlier wheeled vehicles in this area; so also do models of yoked beasts. Traces of ard ploughing under barrows in the third and second millennium bc are not infrequent in, for instance, the Netherlands and Denmark, and perhaps it is no coincidence that the earliest surviving wooden disc wheels in northern Europe date from the end of the third millennium bc in both countries.[75] With the likelihood that an importance component of the British Neolithic agricultural economy is closely linked with the Late Neolithic cultures of northern Europe, we may perhaps look in that direction for the origins of our plough-agriculture, while the subsequent Dutch contacts, implicit in the Beaker connections of the early second millennium bc, may have strengthened these agricultural traditions. They are further discussed in the next section.

[75] J. D. van der Waals, *Prehistoric Disc Wheels in the Netherlands*, 1964; S. Piggott, 'The earliest wheeled vehicles and the Caucasian evidence', *Proc. Prehist. Soc.*, 34, 1968, p. 266.

LATER PREHISTORY

By P. J. FOWLER
Secretary of the Royal Commission on Historical Monuments (England)

CHAPTER I

LATER PREHISTORIC BRITAIN

THE SOURCES OF EVIDENCE

THE writing of history from non-documentary sources is a difficult, little understood task. It is perhaps as well, therefore, to mention briefly the main sources of evidence on which the following review is based. 'Review' is a word used advisedly here because the nature of the evidence for agrarian history in, roughly, the last two millennia BC, and the present (1975) state of study of that evidence, do not convincingly lend themselves to the writing of a historical narrative. This account must perforce confine itself to a survey and discussion of the evidence.

That evidence comes from several sources. Traditionally the most important for the period under review has been archaeology, and quantitatively most of our information comes indeed from archaeological investigations. Excavation has produced much of the evidence, not only in general terms of stratigraphical succession and artifactual association, but also as the various structures on which our picture of later prehistoric agricultural life is based. The farms and their buildings, the details of plan and settlement features like pits, these are the data excavation is good at recovering. Excavation also provides, more valuably than as casual finds, the artifacts of agriculture, the parts of ploughs and harness, the tools of the fields, the equipment for the processing of crops into palatable food. And sometimes it produces evidence of agrarian practice such as buried tracks or plough-marks. Furthermore, it is from excavation that the raw material comes for many of the palaeo-techniques of studying the past – the palaeobotanical evidence such as pollen, seeds and charcoal for microscopic examination; the animal bones which can allow inferences about species, diet, and economy; the fossil snail, insect, and parasite samples, eloquent of their man-influenced habitat; the buried soils containing their record of land-use; and, arguably most important, the contextual materials for date-estimation using the C-14 or other laboratory techniques. It is from excavation too that, in some ways, we come closest to prehistoric man by being able to examine the skeletons of individuals, sometimes with evidence of what they did and suffered in life and wore when buried. By implication at least, from such evidence we can also learn something of the communities they lived in, of societies' attitudes not only to death but to life.

63

Excavation, however, can never investigate more than a tiny fraction of the potentially available evidence which is still but a fraction, the surviving one, of the environmental and artifactual data which once existed. That fraction may be highly significant where, unlike most of the excavated evidence, it is obtained in controlled circumstances; but quantitatively it is always going to be small and, however important it may appear to be individually, without a context it is difficult to place it in an academic, let alone historical, perspective. Such assessment can only come from appreciation of the topographical and cultural background of the evidence that happens to be excavated. Without such minimum background data, it cannot be known whether any single excavated site, for example, is unique, unusual, or typical. Unless it is possible to place excavated evidence in one of these broad categories, the use of that evidence can easily be misleading. Little Woodbury (below, pp. 113–14) is a classic example. It is necessary to stress, therefore, that most of the potential evidence on and in the existing landscapes is going to continue to be discovered and studied by non-excavational methods – air photography, fieldwork, chance finds. Most of our information about the great variety and extent of the evidence not only comes, and will come, from such sources, but its investigation will be confined by the limitations of non-excavational field recording techniques.[1]

This point of view reflects the impact in recent decades of systematic air photography (Plate 1a), partly but not entirely for archaeological purposes, of systematic ground survey, and of opportunism in the face of the major land-disturbance which has characterized the middle decades of the twentieth century.[2] These three sources of evidence have overwhelmingly demonstrated over large areas of the British landscape

[1] For recent comment on this, see generally E. Fowler, *Field Survey in British Archaeology*, London, 1972, P. J. Fowler (ed.), *Archaeology and the Landscape*, London, 1972, and *Recent Work in Rural Archaeology*, Bradford-on-Avon, 1975. Cf. also, in a later context, C. C. Taylor, *Fieldwork in Medieval Archaeology*, London, 1974, and M. Aston and T. Rowley, *Landscape Archaeology*, Newton Abbot, 1974. The basic problem and the shift in emphasis about it are illustrated by comparing S. Piggott, *Approach to Archaeology*, London, 1959, and P. J. Fowler, *Approaches to Archaeology*, London, 1977.

[2] Air photography: RCHM, *A Matter of Time: an Archaeological Survey of the River Gravels of England*, London, 1960; systematic ground survey: see RCHM, RCAHM and RCAHM (S) volumes since c. 1960, H. C. Bowen, *Ancient Fields*, London, 1961, and the 'parish checklist' phenomenon discussed by C. Thomas in E. Fowler, *op. cit.*, and P. J. Fowler (ed.), *Archaeology and the Landscape*, and illustrated, *par excellence*, by V. Russell, *West Penwith Survey*, Truro, 1971; opportunism: P. Rahtz, *Rescue Archaeology*, Harmondsworth, 1974, and its quickly developing practice and rationale, e.g. P. Drewett, 'Rescue archaeology in Sussex, 1974', *Univ. London Inst. Arch. Bull.*, 12, 1975, pp. 13–70; P. A. G. Clack and P. F. Gosling, *Archaeology in the North*, Durham, 1976.

a range and spread of archaeological material, structural and artifactual, simply unknown to, indeed unconceptualized by, earlier generations of students. One is writing here not merely of many new sites but of whole landscapes and indeed of superimposed landscapes extending for many hectares in, for example, the river valleys of the Midlands, over much of the Lowland Zone, and on upland areas such as Dartmoor and the Yorkshire Wolds.[3] It appears that a high proportion of this evidence probably relates to agrarian history in the last two millennia BC and during the Roman period, but much of it has yet to be adequately recorded let alone investigated and studied. While, therefore, the existence of this landscape dimension amongst our sources of evidence is not in doubt, its assessment presents one of the most formidable challenges to British scholarship in the remaining decades of this century. In a very real sense this review is therefore premature, rather as would be a new medieval history following the discovery, but before the study, of a previously unsuspected Domesday Book of 1096.

Topographical evidence, nearly always an element of British arch-aeology, is then of prime importance. One effect of this, statistically at least, is to reduce quite staggeringly the significance of excavated evidence. If a crude guess be allowed, if only to give some perspective to an assessment of the sources of evidence, much less than 1 per cent of the quantity and extent of archaeological evidence now known to exist on and in the ground has been excavated; if we start to think of reliably excavated evidence, we are immediately thinking of a percen-tage to at least two places of decimals. The point must be emphasized because clearly a firm material foundation on which to build an authoritative agrarian model for the last two thousand years or so of British prehistory simply does not exist.

The documentary evidence is sparse and ambiguous and non-existent until the end of our period and is discussed in the context of Roman Britain later in the volume (Part II, 'Roman Britain', Chapter III). There is of course no pre-Roman indigenous literature, a fact of no mean importance, and the relevant post-Roman literary evidence can only be extrapolated backwards across a millennium with extreme caution. Its scope and its value and limitations are discussed in a Welsh, but largely

---

[3] D. Benson and D. Miles, *The Upper Thames Valley*, Oxford, 1972, T. Gates, *The Middle Thames Valley*, Oxford, 1975, and R. H. Leech, *The Upper Thames Valley in Gloucestershire and Wiltshire*, Gloucester, 1977, all subtitled *An Archaeological Survey of the River Gravels*; R. Hollowell, *Aerial Photography and Fieldwork in the Upper Nene Valley*, Leicester, 1971; RCHM, *op. cit.* and *Peterborough New Town...*, London, 1969, *An Inventory...Dorset*, ii–v, London, 1970–75, and the forthcoming Yorkshire and Northamptonshire volumes; E. Gawne & J. Somers Cocks, 'Parallel reaves on Dartmoor', *Trans. Devon. Assoc.*, 100, 1965, pp. 277–92.

British, i.e. Celtic, context below (Part II, pp. 281–88). The documentary evidence *sensu strictu*, then, comes entirely from the literate world of classical civilization, that is of foreigners looking across the English Channel into Britain, or, at best, writing on the Continent and including untested information brought back by other persons who, while they might be reporting from personal experiences, could equally well be relaying information at second hand. Caesar's evidence, supposedly direct, and that from Tacitus, overtly drawing on the accretion of British 'geography' as known to the informed Roman world of the later first century AD, must be looked at with these reservations in mind.[4]

The coinages current in Britain from the second half of the second century BC form a source of evidence halfway between the literary and the archaeological. Some are inscribed, all bear designs, and these attributes studied in relation to their chronologies and several distributions give one or two glimpses of later pre-Roman agriculture. The ear of barley on Cunobelinus's and Epaticcus's gold coins of the early first century AD is perhaps the most encouraging, but it should not blind us to Allen's statement that "We have no representations of houses or of farming...".[5] Nevertheless the coins are quite consistent and specific about other aspects of 'Belgic' life in south-eastern England and their lack of reference to agrarian aspects of what must surely have been one of the principal-producing regions of Britain is disappointing.

Nor is solace to be sought in the mainly non-representational 'Celtic' art of the period: its preoccupations with three-dimensional form and with the interplay of different materials, whatever their significance in the intellectual and aesthetic life of the time, did not allow the artists and craftsmen to stoop to the realities of daily work in a society structured on an agrarian base.[6] Britain also lacks the representational

[4] Classical literature as a source of late-prehistoric/early British history is discussed by A. L. F. Rivet, *Town and Country in Roman Britain*, London, 2nd ed. 1964, and S. S. Frere, *Britannia*, London, 1967 and A. Ross, *Everyday Life of the Pagan Celts*, London, 1970, pp. 28–32, all with source material and references. See also C. E. Stevens, 'Britain between the invasions (BC 54–AD 43): a study in ancient diplomacy', in W. F. Grimes, (ed.), *Aspects of Archaeology in Britain and Beyond*, London, 1951, pp. 332–44; on the sources of classical information about Britain, J. J. Tierney, 'The Celtic ethnology of Posidonius', *Proc. Roy. Irish Acad.* 60, part *c*, 1960, pp. 189–275; and, for a recent discussion in the light of current archaeological research, A. L. F. Rivet again in 'The rural economy of Roman Britain', in H. Temporini and W. Hause (eds.), *Aufstieg und Niedergang der römischen Welt*, Berlin, 1975, pp. 328–63, and H. C. Bowen in A. L. F. Rivet (ed.), *The Roman Villa in Britain*, London, 1969, esp. pp. 1–6.

[5] *Proc. Prehist. Soc.*, 24, 1958, p. 63.

[6] Cf. J. V. S. Megaw, *Art of the European Iron Age*, Bath, 1970, illustrating many insular works, and S. Piggott and G. E. Daniel, *A Picture Book of Ancient British Art*, Cambridge, 1951. For northern material, see now M. Macgregor, *Early Celtic Art in North Britain*, Leicester, 1976.

art of the second millennium displayed as petroglyphs across central Europe from northern Italy to Scandinavia, though the value of this evidence for British agriculture is, by implication, considerable (below, p. 215).[7] Why graphics of, for example, ard-scenes do not occur amongst the various rock-carvings of later prehistoric Britain is another curiosity of the insular evidence. Models of ards, in contrast, occur from the Roman period, as they do elsewhere in the Empire, but reservations must apply here as elsewhere in extrapolating backwards from the 'civilized' to the 'barbarian' world.[8] The same applies to all imperial art, whether or not made or found in Britain.

There remain two other, closely linked but distinct, sources of evidence: the ethnographical and the experimental. Both involve controversial approaches to technology, let alone life-styles, of any period in the past; but handled carefully, evidence from either or both sources can apparently be illuminating and may actually be so. Some of the discussion (below, pp. 232–42) on pastoral farming, for example, is influenced by current practice in part of north-west Spain,[9] while much of the discussion about farming in the last centuries before the Conquest is influenced by field experiments in England and Denmark over the last decade.[10] The establishment of a permanent 'Iron Age Farm' in 1973 on Little Butser Hill, Hants. (Plate I*b*) as a working 'hardware model' (sufficiently so to require planning permission from the Local Authority!) to test, and by testing to stimulate, theoretical models of later prehistoric farming represents a conceptual advance on, for example, yet more and bigger excavations producing more untested 'conclusions'. The experimental approach has theoretical limitations

[7] P. V. Glob, *Plov og Ard i nordens oldtid*, Aarhus, 1951; P. J. Fowler, 'Early prehistoric agriculture in Western Europe: some archaeological evidence', in D. D. A. Simpson (ed.), *Economy and Settlement in Neolithic and Early Bronze Age Britain and Europe*, Leicester, 1971, pp. 153–83.

[8] W. Manning, 'A group of Bronze Models...', *Ant. J.*, 46, 1966, pp. 50–9, and 'The Piercebridge plough group', *Brit. Mus. Quarterly*, 35, 1971, pp. 125–36.

[9] As observed by H. C. Bowen, P. J. Reynolds and P. J. Fowler, 1972–74, publication *forthcoming*.

[10] Generally, J. M. Coles, *Archaeology by Experiment*, London, 1973; Denmark, A. Steensberg, 'Some recent Danish experiments in Neolithic agriculture', *Agric. Hist. Rev.* 5, 1957, pp. 66–73, H. O. Hansen, *Reports from Experiments in Lejre 1968*, I, Lejre, Denmark, 1969; England, *Annual Reports*, 1973– , Butser Ancient Farm Project, following F. A. Aberg and H. C. Bowen, 'Ploughing experiments with a reconstructed Donnerupland ard', *Ant.*, xxxiv, 1960, pp. 144–7 and H. C. Bowen and P. D. Wood, 'Experimental storage of corn underground and its implications for Iron Age settlements', *Univ. London Inst. Arch. Bull.* 7, 1968, pp. 1–14, and contributing to, generally, P. J. Reynolds, *Farming in the Iron Age*, Cambridge, 1976, and, specifically, 'Experimental Iron Age storage pits: an interim report', *Proc. Prehist. Soc.*, 40, 1974, pp. 118–31. See now P. J. Reynolds, *Iron-Age Farm: the Butser Experiment*, London, 1979.

and must surmount grave practical problems (which is one reason for pursuing it); but among its merits is the contribution it can make towards an appreciation, not only of excavated data but also of the great bulk of landscape evidence which excavation will never touch and which modern land-use continuously erodes.

CHRONOLOGICAL OUTLINE (Fig. 3 and Appendix 1)

'Later prehistoric', a phrase already used here and inevitably to be repeated, is quite specifically used in this context to mean that period beginning with the 'horizon' in time provided by the appearance of the 'Beaker cultures' or 'Beaker folk' or, more exactly, by the appearance in the archaeological record of types of pottery which archaeologists call 'Beaker pottery' or simply 'Beakers'. The end of 'Later prehistoric' is, conventionally and here, AD 43 but for various reasons our review will stray a little later and thus consciously overlap to some degree with Part II. In sum, it would be convenient therefore – and such was the original intention – to be able to say that the 'Later prehistory' of this section covers the period of exactly 2000 years from 1900 BC to AD 100.

If we were to continue using the traditional 'Three Ages System' of British and indeed European archaeology, we would begin the story in the Late Neolithic and/or Early Bronze (or Copper) Age depending on whether Beakers were seen as primarily at the end of the stone-using tradition, specifically copper-using ('the first metallurgists') or beginning a new 'Age' of bronze-using communities. Whatever the preferred phraseology, Early, Middle, and Late Bronze Age then follow, sub-suming a Wessex culture, probably some Urn-folk, and certainly a Deverel–Rimbury culture. The Iron Age then succeeds, c. 550 BC, prompted, and at intervals revitalized, by continental invaders, and subdivided into Hallstatt, La Tène, and Belgic, or A, B, and C, or Early, Middle, and Late, according to fashion and the 'school' to which the writer belongs. The Iron Age 'ends', of course with the Roman invasion of Claudius in AD 43. It is proposed here to ignore all such 'Ages', and indeed the very concept on which they are based, to try to avoid the associated phraseology, and to use an absolute chronology deriving from C-14 estimates of dates bc.

Until recently, this would not have involved major changes in the span of 'later prehistory' since the 'Beaker horizon' remained at c. 2000 BC, and just enough C-14 estimates are now available to provide a framework for the last two millennia bc. Reassessment of the C-14 method of age estimation concurrently suggests, however, that, by and large, C-14 estimates are too young by varying amounts compared to calendar years or absolute time. The principle and mechanics of this 'second radiocarbon revolution' need not concern us but the results and implications do. Since, however, research into the controversy about C-14 calibration continues at the moment, we use here a chronological framework based on uncalibrated dates expressed in terms 'bc'. A select list of relevant estimates, correct to the end of 1974, with laboratory reference numbers and site names etc., is given below in APPENDIX 1.

To illustrate the current dilemma, however, so aggravating when wishing to attempt narrative history, let us briefly glance at some implications of a calibrated chronology before we perforce cast it aside. 'Later prehistory' would include some 2,500 years instead of 2,000 years. This is mainly the effect of pushing back to the middle centuries of the third millennium BC the origins of the Beaker period, although c. 2000 BC would still be central to it. In other words a period of time, represented distinctively by the use of particular types of pottery which seemed to be a few centuries long at most, could now stretch over a millennium. Agriculturally, this would be acceptable, although involving a major change of interpretation (cf. below, pp. 247–50). Apart from the increase in length of time involved, date-changes within the second millennium BC itself would be, from the agrarian point of view, either not of great moment or unnecessary. Two significant developments would nevertheless be conveniently relocated in time by calibrated C-14 dates, respectively for late in that millennium and early in the first. Farming settlements of a type once characteristic of what was regarded as a Late Bronze Age Deverel–Rimbury culture, i.e. after c. 1000 BC, and were then shown by C-14 to belong to the centuries immediately before 1000 bc would be, as a result of calibration, pushed back into the fourteenth and fifteenth centuries BC and potentially into the sixteenth. Indeed, they would overlap in date range with dates from Wessex culture contexts, including Stonehenge III, and of ceramic types characteristic of the Early Bronze Age. Such settlements would themselves overlap in time hill-top settlements which, chronologically speaking, are moving back into the 'vacuum' around and after 1000 BC left by the departure of the former Deverel–Rimbury farm into the second half of the second millennium. The appearance of hill-top settlements, perhaps but not yet certainly enclosed, in the centuries either side of 1000 BC is one of the more remarkable facets of current British archaeological research. Certainly the term 'hill-fort', hitherto synonymous with the concept of the 'the Iron Age', needs to be re-examined. Athough the introduction of iron technology, one of the most significant developments for later prehistoric agriculture in Britain, remains fixed in the seventh or sixth century BC, it is clear now that the origins of communal, enclosed settlements on hill-tops belong

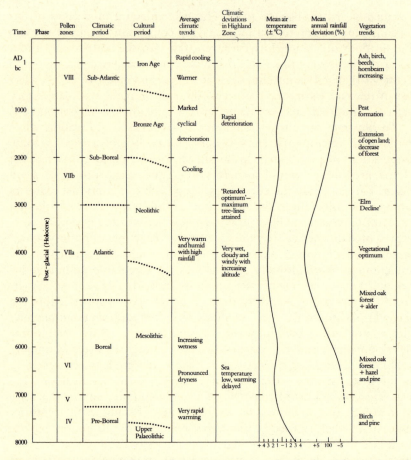

Fig. 3. An attempted correlation of various environmental and cultural factors through time in Post-glacial Britain (based on J. A. Taylor).

in the preceding half-millennium independently of either continental 'Celtic' immigrants or the new technology. The implications of this in agrarian and indeed social terms appear to be considerable (below, pp. 251–2), although it is not until the middle centuries of the millennium, so it will be argued, that the momentum of agrarian life perceptibly increases.[11]

[11] This brief summary of the chronological problem so crucial to agrarian history is expanded, for the Old World, in C. Renfrew, *Before Civilization*, Harmondsworth, 1973, and, for Britain, in C. Renfrew (ed.), *British Prehistory*, London, 1974, both fully referenced and the latter comprehensively for the 'Bronze Age' (though not the 'Iron Age'). Subsequent critical papers are R. J. C. Atkinson, 'British prehistory and the radiocarbon revolution', *Ant.*, XLIX, 1975, pp. 173–7 ("radiocarbon therapy...has left

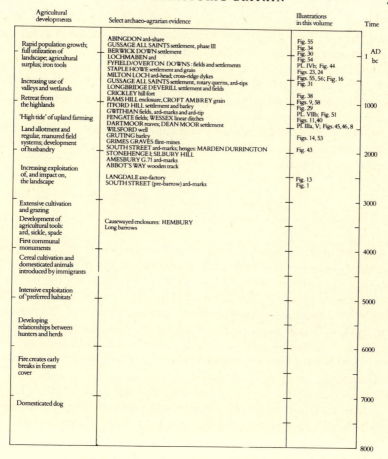

Agricultural developments	Select archaeo-agrarian evidence	Illustrations in this volume	Time
Rapid population growth; full utilization of landscape; agricultural surplus; iron tools	ABINGDON ard-share GUSSAGE ALL SAINTS settlement, phase III BERWICK DOWN settlement LOCHMABEN ard FYFIELD/OVERTON DOWNS : fields and settlements STAPLE HOWE settlement and grain	Fig. 55 Fig. 34 Fig. 30 Fig. 54 Pl. IVb; Fig. 44 Figs. 23, 24	AD 1 bc
Increasing use of valleys and wetlands	MILTON LOCH ard-head; cross-ridge dykes GUSSAGE ALL SAINTS settlement, rotary querns, ard-tips LONGBRIDGE DEVERILL settlement and fields CRICKLEY hill fort	Figs. 55, 56; Fig. 16 Fig. 31	
Retreat from the highlands	RAMS HILL enclosure, CROFT AMBREY grain ITFORD HILL settlement and barley GWITHIAN fields, ard-marks and ard-tip	Fig. 38 Figs. 9, 58 Fig. 29	1000
'High tide' of upland farming	FENGATE fields; WESSEX linear ditches DARTMOOR reaves; DEAN MOOR settlement	Pl. VIIb; Fig. 51 Figs. 11,40	
Land allotment and regular, manured field systems; development of husbandry	WILSFORD well GRUTING barley GRIMES GRAVES flint-mines SOUTH STREET ard-marks; henges: MARDEN DURRINGTON STONEHENGE I; SILBURY HILL AMESBURY G.71 ard-marks	Pl. IIIa, V; Figs. 45,46, 8 Figs. 14, 53 Fig. 43	2000
Increasing exploitation of, and impact on, the landscape	ABBOT'S WAY wooden track LANGDALE axe-factory SOUTH STREET (pre-barrow) ard-marks	Fig. 13 Fig. 1	
Extensive cultivation and grazing			3000
Development of agricultural tools: ard, sickle, spade	Causewayed enclosures: HEMBURY Long barrows		
First communal monuments			4000
Cereal cultivation and domesticated animals introduced by immigrants			
Intensive exploitation of 'preferred habitats'			5000
Developing relationships between hunters and herds			
Fire creates early breaks in forest cover			6000
Domesticated dog			7000
			8000

A final chronological phase, though unaffected by change C-14 dates, is equally controversial in its dating. Here, however, concern is with decades rather than centuries or millennia. In the second half of the second century BC, Britain, or at least its south-eastern segment, begins a period of Europeanization, a period of increasingly close contact with a continent no longer unaffected even on its north-western margins by the alien, classical culture of the Mediterranean world.[12] It is a period

the patient in a state of confusion and disturbance" eloquently expresses the basic difficulty for this study at the moment); R. M. Clark, 'A calibration curve for radiocarbon dates', *Ant.*, XLIX, 1975, pp. 251–66 and, with H. Suess, *Ant.*, L, 1976, pp. 61–3.

[12] Cf. D. W. Harding, *The Iron Age in Lowland Britain*, London, 1974, esp. pp. 201–26, with B. Cunliffe, *Iron Age Communities in Britain*, London, 1974, esp. pp. 59–106, both fully reviewed by T. G. E. Powell, 'Iron Age Britain retraced', *Ant.*, XLVIII, 1974, pp. 288–92.

with well-dated high-spots − 55/54 BC and AD 43/44 − both of which are significant from the agricultural point of view. Nor was 43 an end: from an agrarian point of view, it marked the culmination of a phase of development stretching back 2,000 years which was then further developed as, for the first time, much of Britain became part of a European political and economic community. It can be argued that, for better or for worse, the consequences of that were an intellectual legacy continually fostered by religious and military Europeans over nearly 2,000 subsequent years, but only realized for the secular and civilian British on 1 January 1973.

THE ENVIRONMENT[13] (Figs. 3−6)

Climate[14]

Later prehistoric agriculture took place within only two climatic phases on the conventional notation: the Sub-Boreal and the Sub-Atlantic, respectively covering Zones VIIb and VIII. Traditionally the former is characterized by a drier, less humid and more 'continental' climate than that of the preceding Atlantic phase (above, pp. 8−10). Presumably too, as far as Britain was concerned, a basically continental climate could give rise to more frequent and wider extremes of cold and heat than is produced by a basically Atlantic climate. The Sub-Atlantic phase is differentiated by a general deterioration caused by a shift back to prevailing westerly climatic conditions marked by increased precipitation and a fall in the mean annual temperature by 2−3 °C. No great imaginative effort is required to appreciate such a climate since we continue today − or at least have continued until very recently − to enjoy and suffer the attributes of a Sub-Atlantic climate. In such a context, the systematic weather records of the last century could well be indicative for the last millennium or so BC if only to suggest the significant regional and topographical differences prevailing in general and occurring simultaneously, with regard to both climate and weather

[13] Since this section was written, the topic has been synthesized, and is discussed in much greater detail than here, in J. G. Evans, *The Environment of Early Man in the British Isles*, London, 1975. Its excellent and up-to-date bibliography obviates to a large extent the need to repeat detailed references here. See also the second edition of the authoritative H. Godwin, *The History of the British Flora*, Cambridge, 1975, again published after this section was written.

[14] The subsection is very much influenced by the relevant papers read at the Council for British Archaeology (CBA) conference on *The Effect of Man on the Landscape: the Highland Zone* in March, 1974, subsequently published under that title as CBA Research Report, 11, 1975. The specific debt to Dr J. A. Taylor's paper, 'The role of climatic factors in environmental and cultural changes in prehistoric times' (pp. 6−19, including an excellent bibliography), is fully acknowledged.

respectively, within a broadly identifiable climatic phase such as the Sub-Atlantic.

The chronology of these two climatic phases now presents some difficulties. The change from Atlantic to Sub-Boreal traditionally occurred around the middle of the third millennium BC and indeed near the beginnings of the development of Neolithic or agricultural communities in Britain. Chronologically and archaeologically, any suspected association must now be discarded since crop and animal husbandry apparently began in Britain very much earlier (above, pp. 24ff.). A C-14 date of c. 2500 bc, when calibrated, gives an absolute date about the middle of the second half of the fourth millennium BC so presumably the Sub-Boreal climatic phase was well established by the time our later prehistoric period began. Beakers, henge monuments, Stonehenge and Silbury Hill, the great round barrow cemeteries, and the other outstanding material which highlight the archaeological record of the subsequent millennium were all apparently manufactured during a long period of predominantly warm, dry climate, slightly but significantly warmer and drier than the ensuing Sub-Atlantic phase.[15]

Pollen Zone VIII, which marks the onset of the Sub-Atlantic, has been regarded as about as clear an horizon in climatic history as, for example, the Beaker horizon in the archaeological record and, like Beakers, well-fixed in time. A climatic deterioration in the middle of the last millennium BC has been axiomatic to studies of late European prehistory, and, in the case of Britain, has been seen as at least influencing, if not actually causing, the beginnings of an immigrant, iron-using technology introduced from the Continent. As remarked above, adjustment to C-14 dates does not radically affect the later centuries BC and the change from Zones VII to VIII remains c. 700 BC.[16] But a few 'Late Bronze Age' dates which are significant in their association with evidence for climatic conditions indicate that deterioration probably started very much earlier, at least in western Britain, and was contemporary with both the 'Middle Bronze Age' small farmsteads of southern England and the hill-top settlements of the north and west (below, pp. 245–9). The Somerset Levels in particular, as so often, producing evidence to act as a touchstone for studies elsewhere, provide, for example, several C-14-dated trackways (e.g. Q52, Q908) which indicate that their construction across increasingly

[15] Both the remarkably well preserved vegetation of, and the land snails in, the central turf stack beneath Silbury Hill, Wilts., for example, indicated 'an environment of very dry, open grassland' at the time of construction – J. G. Evans, Land Snails in Archaeology, London, 1972, pp. 265–7 (with references and five previously unpublished mid-second millennium C-14 dates).

[16] As shown most recently in Taylor, op. cit., fig. 3.

wet bog was, if calibrated, probably in the eleventh century BC or earlier. The bog itself, of the raised peat variety, had been developing over former woodland since the early centuries of the third millennium bc and its growth over 1½–2 millennia was only terminated by freshwater flooding, presumably from increased rainfall.[17] A similar interpretation is offered for the rapid peat formation observed palynologically at the edge of Bloak Moss, Ayrs., between c. 1400– 1000 bc.[18]

It would be satisfactory to be able to summarize our two millennia by saying that the first half was warm and sunny and the second half cool and wet. While there may be an overall validity in such a generalization, it clearly must be qualified. In the first place, palaeoclimatology is a controversial subject anyway; secondly, a great deal of work is in progress and must be expected to produce results sounder than, and different from, those from the available data; thirdly, there is a great danger of a circularity developing in the discussions about past climate and weather in relation to man's activities, since much of the critical evidence used by climatologists comes from archaeological contexts excavated by those who look to the 'prehistoric weatherman' for the answers to the archaeologists' own questions about the climatic circumstances of their sites; and, fourthly, enough evidence has been accumulated to suggest, without certainty on any specific point in time and place, that variations in the elements of climate – temperature, rainfall, etc. – and in local topographical conditions that can affect climate – height above sea-level, sea-level itself – were sufficiently significant at specific sites at certain times to upset long-term trends and generally prevailing conditions.

The mean air temperature, for example, varies through time and indeed within climatic periods (Fig. 3). It was probably 3 °C higher at the beginning of the Sub-Boreal than at the end, dipping to about 1 °C in the second half of the third millennium and rising again slightly for much of the second millennium before dropping away relatively sharply in the eighth/seventh centuries to the onset of the Sub-Atlantic phase and to today's mean. Though generally wetter conditions, probably with relatively cool summers, then began to prevail, the air temperature rose to +1 °C again, peaking in the fourth/third centuries before dropping once more and, for the first time since the beginning of the Boreal, plunging Britain into an air temperature cooler than its mean today. While, therefore, the trend in air temperature over the whole of later prehistory is from +3 °C downwards towards today's mean, the oscillations producing two troughs and two peaks within that trend are significant for agrarian purposes. A variation of ±1 °C can

---

[17] *Somerset Levels Papers*, 1, 1975, p. 54. See Site Index for further references.
[18] J. Turner in Evans *et al.*, CBA Research Report, 11, p. 95.

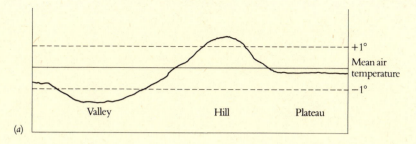

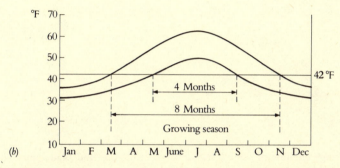

Fig. 4. Diagram to illustrate: (a) the critical effect on agricultural potential at different altitudes of minor variations in mean air temperature around the 'growth threshold'; (b) the effect of the annual temperature curve on agricultural potential (various sources).

be critical for the growth of certain crops and, as important, for the cropping potential of certain areas (Fig. 4). Such a variation can also smooth out growth differentials of contrasting regions. A rise of 2 °C in the mean air temperature could, for example, increase the agricultural potential of high areas more than for lowland areas since it could make the difference between whether they were cultivable or not. We see the reverse of this in late and post-medieval times with the retreat from the marginal intakes of the twelfth and thirteenth centuries AD broadly coinciding with a cooling of the air temperature and an increase in precipitation. The percentage differences are small: their effects, in lengthening the growing season or lowering the upper limits of cultivation, for example, can be critical for any given locality or indeed for a whole region (Figs. 4, 5).

The difficulties of establishing palaeo-climatic parameters, then relating them to cultural factors, and then exploring the relationship between man, climate, and the rest of the environment, has recently been expressed forcefully, clearly and succinctly:

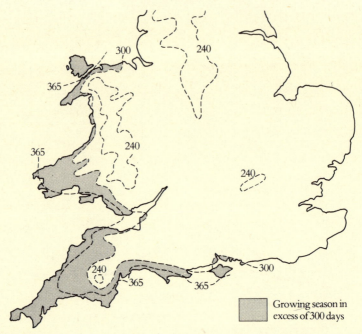

Fig. 5. Average duration of growth season (days) in England and Wales (after N. D. Johnson).

climate change and culture change may be conceived on two separate but complementary wavelengths. First, the macro-scale framework embracing the millennia presents the backcloth and general chronology, but, secondly, the actual changes at ground were governed by short-term periodicities in climate and weather and generated a metachronous mosaic of environmental or cultural responses. This is partly due to the inexorable march of palaeoecological research which is generating data and ideas at an increasingly accelerating rate. It is mainly due to the realisation, from a variety of interdisciplinary sources, that the only valid way to comprehend environmental and cultural changes is in *ecosystematic* terms, and that such changes were in reality local and regional rather than zonal or hemispheric.[19]

Soils[20]

In addition to climate and weather, another critical factor from the point of view of later prehistoric agrarian communities was obviously the soil itself. It would probably be more realistic to say 'soil' rather than 'the

[19] Taylor, *op. cit.*, p. 18.
[20] See now, S. Limbrey, *Soil Science and Archaeology*, London, 1975, esp. chaps. 5, 7, 8 and 15.

soil', since even on a relatively homogeneous geological base, like the Upper and Middle Chalks of Wessex or the Middle Terraces of the Upper Thames, variations in the soils not only occur but are of considerable local significance for those husbanding the land. Generalizations about the soils of later prehistoric Britain are then not only as difficult to make as those about the climate but they also suffer from similar limitations in helping towards an understanding of later prehistoric farming in practice. Soils too, like climate, change through time, arguably as a result of climatic change itself; but such changes through time, particularly local changes of the sort which almost by definition are those that have to be studied, can themselves be affected, perhaps even started, by human activities.

Soils, however, unlike climate, can be recovered physically and studied directly: their components, physical and chemical, organic and inorganic, exist in fact and not by inference, though of course their status 2,000 and more years ago is not necessarily provided by their condition as recovered in modern sampling. And their former use, as with former climates, has to be inferred. Nevertheless, fossil soils, preserved *in situ* beneath a man-made structure or in a natural deposit such as lake sediment or alluvial plain, provide often vivid insights into the changes occurring on and in the surface of the landscape from the third millennium onwards.[21]

In very general terms, soils were being degraded, in the sense of both physically losing constituents through erosion, and actually losing their capacity to support a 'natural' forest climax succession. The second loss implies a decreasing food production potential, probably reflected archaeologically by the evidence for manuring from the second millennium BC onwards (below, pp. 213–15). Some soils on limestone, for example, were apparently abandoned agriculturally during the process of food production before it had gone too far – presumably after an initial burst of high food production by communities not under land-pressure – but managed to revert to supporting woodland. Others also abandoned during the process, perhaps later, perhaps after more extensive exploitation, or perhaps in the face of a changing local environment, were sufficiently affected to be unable to support their former flora and, continuing to develop new characteristics, gave rise to a different vegetation and a new-looking landscape, e.g. moorland. By and large, examples of the former process will tend to be found today in the Lowland Zone and of the latter in the Highland Zone (Fig. 6). Major exceptions, however, would be much of the Wessex chalklands,

---

[21] See discussion of this point in R. J. C. Atkinson, 'Burial and population in the British Bronze Age' in F. Lynch and C. Burgess, eds., *Prehistoric Man in Wales and the West*, Bath, 1972, pp. 110–13.

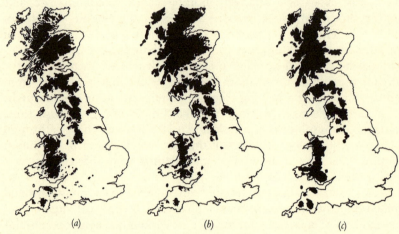

(a)   *(b)*   *(c)*

Fig. 6. Three environmental factors in Britain: (a) altitude, showing land over 800 ft (244 m); (b) rainfall, showing areas with 50+ ins. (127 cm) per annum; (c) moorland (various sources).

denuded of forest cover since the third millennium (Plate IIa), and many of the lowland heaths, developing from the early second millennium on overexploited, deteriorated Brown Earth soil podzolizing into Gley soils. On the other hand, the Moors of the south-west and parts of the Cumbrian Lakeland, for example, began to take on their present appearance from early in our period as a result of changes in the soils, and consequently in the vegetation, arising in large part from the activities of agrarian communities there in the third and second millennia BC (below, pp. 105–8).[22]

The Highland Zone has recently been defined by its characteristic soils:[23] Ranker, i.e. non calcarious, soils with O or A, and C or R, horizons; Gley, soils with mineral horizons due to long-term water-logging; Podzolic soils, characterized by a B horizon, i.e. "mineral material modified by physical, chemical or biological alteration so that it is differentiated by structure, colour or texture from horizons above and below"; and Organic soils with no master horizons at depths less than 50 cm. The other two main groups of soil, Calcareous and Brown Earth, also occur in the Highland Zone but are characteristic of lowland areas. The role of the various factors – the nature of the parent material, climate, relief, time, and biotic influences including man's activities –

[22] The general thesis in this paragraph is much influenced by the work of Professor G. W. Dimbleby: see Bibliography for references.

[23] D. F. Ball, 'Processes of soil degradation: a pedological point of view' in Evans *et al.*, CBA Research Report, 11, pp. 20–1.

individually and interacting is by no means clear, and present interpretations are variable. In some of the most recent work, for example,
the influence of the anthropogenic factor on soils in Wales is largely
discounted, while in Yorkshire and Scotland it is seen as significant. One
of the few certainties is that 'the farmers favoured the light soils' model
is a gross oversimplification, certainly by the second millennium;
another is that the present-day distribution of soil types does not
accurately reflect the distribution of basically the same range of types
in *c*. 2000 BC. Whether or not the cultural factor has been instrumental
or even influential in creating changing soils, there can be little doubt
that agrarian communities in *c*. 2000 BC had a much wider choice of
location of suitable soils for farming than did their counterparts at any
subsequent time before the introduction of mechanized land disturbance
and chemical fertilizers. On the other hand, though the choice was wide,
it was of potential fertility and, technologically speaking, was in part
theoretical; for although more of the landscape in the second millennium
contained potentially high-production soils than in, say, AD 500, much
of the potential was not attainable within the technological limits of
stone and bronze-using cultures. Undrained, swampy valleys and
heavily forested claylands, could not necessarily be exploited for
farming – perhaps there was no need to – so, in a sense, a sort of balance
was probably maintained between food potential and human need. It
was later on in the first millennium and in the Roman period that the
need arose for more extensive and more intense exploitation of the soil
and, then, improved technology made available a greater range of
exploitable landscape by releasing some of the hitherto unrealized
potential of 'less favourable' soils.

Flora[24]

Closely related to the soils were the preferred habitats of the contemporary, non-domesticated flora and fauna. Again in general terms, the
whole of later prehistoric times saw a continuous process of forest
clearance. The mixed oak forest of the climatic optimum of the Atlantic
phase had previously been in part cleared, some to regenerate, some to
disappear altogether, under the impact of earlier farming communities
and their grazing animals (above, p. 38). By about 2000 BC the

[24] For flora generally, see now Godwin, *The History of the British Flora*; W.
Pennington, *The History of British Vegetation*, London, 2nd edn, 1974, and the
bibliographies in them, and in Evans, *The Environment of Early Man*.... Some of the
principal references to original sources are given below in the Bibliography, pp. 289–98.
There are no comparable syntheses for the fauna, wild or domesticated, in the second
and first millennia BC but cf. generally F. E. Zeuner, *A History of Domesticated Animals*,
London, 1963.

impression gained from evidence collected from all over the British Isles is not so much of the impact of man on the 'natural' vegetation, considerable though that was, but of the regional diversity, the botanical variation, that that impact had created (Plate II*b*). The elm generally continued to decrease while ash became more prevalent; birch and heather spread, particularly on the podzolizing soils of upland plateaux and lowland drainage basins; the pine remained common in the north, while later in Zone VIII beech and hornbeam increased in the south.

In the south, however, particularly on the chalklands of the south-east and of Wessex, it is virtually certain that by 2000 BC at least parts of the downland had already become precisely that (Plate II*a*). Disafforestation had become extensive and permanent. There is "no evidence of widespread forest regeneration on the Chalk".[25] The harbingers of this state of affairs are the several studies of the environmental evidence and its implications from buried soils in fourth and third millennia contexts, particularly under Neolithic structures, where, with but four exceptions, "the environment immediately prior to burial of the soil profile was one of stable and dry short-turfed grassland".[26] That forest regeneration did not take place on much of the chalkland soils, not fortuitously preserved by being buried, is proved by the siting and development of the great Wessex barrow cemeteries in the first half of the second millennium. They simply could not have been placed with all the subtle relationships of spacing and intervisibility, barrow to barrow, cemetery to cemetery, in a closed environment.[27] Their existence demands an open landscape, and in Wessex its existence was maintained.

PEOPLES

The inhabitants of Britain in the last two millennia BC were basically of Indo-European stock. With really no evidence of any major immigrations since the early stages of the Neolithic well over a thousand years earlier, it seems not unreasonable to regard the inhabitants in *c.* 2000 BC as 'insular British'. Over the next 500 years, Beaker peoples were added to the insular stock, perhaps not in large numbers although culturally influential. The origins and racial status of the Beaker folk are currently matters of debate, as is the chronology and manner of their arrival in Britain,[28] and while it is likely that they spoke an Indo-

---

[25] Evans, *op. cit.*, p. 365.   [26] *Ibid.*, p. 364.

[27] As is perhaps best exemplified in south Dorset. See the detailed study and large accompanying map in RCHM, *Dorset*, II, 1970.

[28] D. L. Clarke, *Beaker Pottery of Great Britain and Ireland*, Cambridge, 1970; J. N. Lanting and J. D. van der Waals, 'British Beakers as seen from the Continent', *Helinium*, 12, 1972, pp. 20–46.

European language, it is perhaps unwise to press the suggestion that they were racially 'Celts' or at least the forerunners of the Celtic peoples who traditionally emerge and dominate the West European scene in the last millennium BC. In agrarian terms, nevertheless, the Beaker horizon seems to mark a break with the past after which we can begin to discern the elements of a farming way of life which alters little in its fundamentals until the social and technological innovations of the Roman period (below, pp. 259–62).

After *c.* 2000 BC it is at least arguable, and with justification, that the racial stock in Britain did not receive significant new blood until the mid/late second century BC. Certainly the next well-evidenced 'immigration', whatever its nature (below, pp. 82–3) is that referred to by Julius Caesar as having taken place before 55 BC but within living memory.[29] Between these two dates, *c.* 2000 BC and *c.* 100 BC, archaeological evidence indicates plentiful contact, varying from the apparently close to the slight, between Britain and the Continent (and Ireland) but there is no firm evidence for folk immigration of the sort which would affect the racial characteristics of insular agrarian society. Such a generalization certainly seems correct for the second millennium despite the clear indication of contact with, at different times, Brittany, Ireland, Holland, Scandinavia, the Rhine valley, and what subsequently became Northern Gaul. Doubtless people, in groups and individually, did cross the English Channel and the North and Irish Seas, and not only into Britain – as is indicated by evidence of 'Britons' in Holland from about the thirteenth/fourteenth centuries[30] – but it is unlikely that any such contacts and movements were of sufficient strength of themselves significantly to change the nature and number of Britain's population.

In the first millennium BC, more caution is needed for there are several occasions or periods on, and during, which the composition of Britain's population could have been affected. Around and immediately after *c.* 1000 BC, similarities in the completely new British 'hill-forts' (below, pp. 92–4) with those of the Upper Danube/South Germany area could be taken to suggest more than independent innovation or mere cultural contact and might indeed hint at the arrival of early, bronze-using 'Celts' or 'proto-Celts'.[31] In the eighth and seventh centuries, a time of considerable turmoil on the Continent, evidence in Britain could again be interpreted to suggest small but perhaps racially

[29] *De Bello Gallico,* v, p. 12.

[30] Cf. Cock Hill, *Sussex Arch. Coll.,* 99, 1961, pp. 78–101.

[31] Cf. 'The Late Bronze Age Problem...', in Harding, *The Iron Age in Lowland Britain,* pp. 129–33, and C. Burgess, 'The Bronze Age', in Renfrew (ed.), *British Prehistory,* pp. 165–231, esp. 219–20, and references.

significant incursions of Urnfield/Hallstatt peoples from the north-west European littoral and its hinterland.[32] Again in the sixth and fifth centuries, when the earliest iron objects appear in Britain, there is little doubt that their origin is in the same general area and the appearance of British counterparts, plus some of the exotic pottery traits, could suggest further arrivals of people who settled and bred.[33] Whatever the doubts, disputes, and ambiguities of this whole matter of invasions, immigrations, or insular isolation, from the anthropological point of view the issue to be resolved is that whereas about 1000 BC we can be fairly certain that Britain was populated by an insular stock largely unaffected by racial admixture for about a thousand years, by, say, 300 BC, the population can fairly be described in general as 'Celtic'.[34]

Whence cometh the Celts? While, as has become fashionable over the last decade, it is possible to reinterpret much of the British archaeological evidence of prehistoric change in terms of insular development, racial as distinct from cultural change requires external stimuli, and, if by the fourth century the population of Britain was in any meaningful sense 'Celtic', then new blood from the Continent must have been introduced in the preceding 700 years or so. This need not imply a quantitatively dominant flood of European immigrants, but it does require a racially significant addition to the insular stock, if only to act as a catalyst for the subsequent evolution of a characteristically insular version of Celtic society. A personal view is that the catalytic phase was in the eighth/seventh centuries, a period of folk movement on a European and indeed Mediterranean scale when rapid climatic deterioration was coinciding with technological innovation. The product was, at the two extremes of Europe, the literate, classical civilizations in the south-east and the agrarian, Celtic societies of the barbaric north-west.

In Britain, that Celtic society came to dominate the way of life in the latter half of the first millennium BC, but it was not completely inclusive. Non- or pre-Celtic peoples continued in parts of the north, developing the tradition of the ensuing millennium and more which saw their history, racial and otherwise, unfolding not quite independently of, but along different lines from, that in southern Britain. The

[32] Lanting and van der Waals, op. cit.; cf. Cunliffe, Iron Age Communities in Britain, chap. 2.

[33] Harding, op. cit., chap. 9; Cunliffe, op. cit.; cf. F. Hodson, Proc. Prehist. Soc., 28, 1962, pp. 140–55, and 30, 1964, pp. 99–110.

[34] In addition to the above, see, for example, J. G. D. Clark, 'The invasion hypothesis in British archaeology', Ant., XL, 1966, pp. 172–89, and the discussion arising in part from it by the editor in Renfrew (ed.), British Prehistory, chap. 1, esp. pp. 30–40. Percipient comments on the matter are in the reviews of Harding, op. cit. and Cunliffe, op. cit., by T. G. E. Powell in Ant., XLVIII, 1974, 288–92.

south and south-east and south-west coasts were open to the arrival of both people and ideas, thereby developing a pattern of regional differences in many ways hardened during the Roman period and reflected in early Scottish history.[35] Further west, in Ireland, the very nature of the population components in later prehistoric times is in dispute, though it is difficult to understand, along the lines of the argument in the previous paragraph, how the island later came to contain the classic and longest-surviving example of Celtic society without a racial admixture of its 'Bronze Age' population. Here too, the recent recognition of early 'hill-forts' in Ireland may not be irrelevant: certainly they offer an alternative to the confinement of the discussion of 'Celtic origins' within a La Tène artistic parameter.[36]

In the last two centuries before the Roman Conquest, southern Britain received further additions to its population. The 'Belgae' are currently in disarray, but for present purposes suffice it to say that two main incursions can be discerned, both crossing from north-western Gaul. The first, possibly after rather than before 100 BC, was politically and culturally significant, but perhaps not so racially or numerically. The second, a complex of movements between the Caesarian and Claudian invasions, certainly involved individuals and their retinues, but probably also saw the arrival of considerable numbers of settlers. They too were Celts, though somewhat modified by the intricacies of west European tribal history in previous centuries, not least in relation to the increasingly pervasive influence of Mediterranean peoples and cultures. That influence also affected south-eastern Britain in the decades before the Conquest and probably produced, then and subsequently, a small but perhaps significant addition to the racial composition of the British population.[37]

[35] Much of the new thought and current work on Scottish matters is reported and reflected in *Scott. Archaeol. Forum*, I– , 1969– .

[36] B. Raftery, 'Irish hill-forts' in C. Thomas (ed.), *The Iron Age in the Irish Sea Province*, London, 1972, pp. 37–58. Other alternatives are offered in the folk-life/cultural appraisals by E. E. Evans, e.g., *Irish Heritage*, Dundalk, 1942, and *Irish Folk Ways*, London, 1957; and, now, by F. Mitchell, *The Irish Landscape*, London, 1976, chaps. 4 and 5.

[37] On this vexed question see Frere, *Britannia*, pp. 20–6, summarizing earlier work; A. Birchall, 'The Aylesford–Swarling Culture: the problem of the Belgae reconsidered', *Proc. Prehist. Soc.*, 31, 1965, pp. 241–367; C.F. C. Hawkes, 'New thoughts on the Belgae', *Ant.*, XLII, 1968, pp. 6–16; Cunliffe, *op. cit.*, chap. 5; and, in contrast, Harding, *op. cit.*, chap. 12. Cf. now also W. Rodwell, 'Coinage, oppida and the rise of Belgic power in south-eastern Britain', in B. Cunliffe and T. Rowley (eds.), *Oppida, the Beginnings of Urbanisation in Barbarian Europe*, Oxford, 1976.

POPULATION (Fig. 7)

The first reasonably reliable data for estimating the population of England is in the Domesday Book. Estimates of course vary, but a figure of about 1½ million would represent a consensus view of the situation in 1086. The addition of Scotland, Wales, and those parts of England not included in the Domesday Survey does not radically affect the figure: we are still thinking of a number in the order of 1½ million, plus or minus two or three hundred thousand.[38] Estimates of earlier populations have been arrived at by various means: guesswork, counting backwards from the known and extrapolating, the establishment of minimum figures, the use of 'productivity models' based on ethnographic data. Every method has one characteristic in common: an assumption or result that the British population was always less before 1086 than it was in 1086. The assumption is at least questionable, though proof of any definite figure before the eleventh century is always going to be lacking.

Any estimate of the population figure for the later prehistoric period can at least begin by noting the two serious attempts to provide an indication of the order of numbers of which it is permissible to think for the Neolithic and Roman periods. For the fourth and third millennia to c. 2500 BC Atkinson suggests a figure of 140 for the 'long barrow population' of the Wessex chalkland.[39] The estimate was produced by using the known number of long barrows and their contained burials and by making certain assumptions. While "at first sight [these figures are] so small that one is inclined to reject them as a tenable estimate of the total 'long barrow population'",[40] extrapolation from them cannot avoid the implication that, given the longer time-span now involved, the population of Britain was very small. For example, Atkinson's long barrow count comes from only thirteen counties: if we multiply by five on the assumption that equivalent sites, not yet recognized, represent a similar population density evenly spread over the rest of Britain; multiply by two to counteract the assumption that, at the time, Wessex contained a denser population than elsewhere; and multiply by ten on the assumption that the Wessex 'long barrow population' and its

---

[38] Domesday Book actually records 283,242 persons. F. W. Maitland estimates 1,375,000 (*Domesday Book and Beyond*, Cambridge, 1897, Essay 3, part 2, Domesday Statistics) cf. J. C. Russell, *British Medieval Population*, Albuquerque, 1948, with *c*. 1,100,000. A. L. Poole, *From Domesday Book to Magna Carta 1087–1216*, 2nd ed., Oxford, 1955), p. 36, gives, 'at a rough guess', a twelfth-century population 'round the two million mark'.

[39] R. J. C. Atkinson, 'Old mortality: some aspects of burial and population in Neolithic England', in J. M. Coles and D. D. A. Simpson (eds.), *Studies in Ancient Europe*, Leicester, 1968, pp. 83–93. [40] Atkinson, *op. cit.*, p. 89.

equivalents elsewhere represent only 10 per cent of the total population, we arrive at an answer of 14,000. This is perhaps not far wrong for the number of inhabitants in Britain as the first metal technology was introduced to its scattered communities. Many would argue for a lower figure and it is difficult to conceive of a higher. It seems probable in any case that we should be thinking of an insular population in thousands, just possibly into the tens of thousands, in the second half of the third millennium BC.

Nearer to the end of later prehistory, Frere has estimated that the population of Roman Britain in c. 200 AD "may have amounted to about two million".[41] He envisaged London alone as having twice the total population suggested above for the whole of Britain 2,200 years earlier, and Colchester and Verulamium with about 15,000 inhabitants each. These urban figures compare realistically with the known populations of medieval towns, and are unlikely to have been much higher. On the other hand, Frere very considerably underestimates the density of settlements in the countryside of Roman Britain. If we take that factor into account and add the population of those British areas outside the frontiers of Roman Britain, there is an argument for pushing the total population of the whole of Britain well over three and possibly over four million in, say, the third century AD.

Though there are many problems in its demographic interpretation, the impact of aerial photography on settlement density and distribution in rural Britannia must not be underestimated, even if it cannot yet be accurately assessed. Nevertheless it makes a considerable difference that, on all reasonable grounds, we are now thinking of a British population in the early first millennium AD of between 2 and 4 million, perhaps more than twice the size of the population estimate of forty years ago[42] and, in any case, larger than the 1–1½ million estimate for the late eleventh century. If this is accepted, then even allowing generously for the thousands of troops and other 'Romans' introduced into Britain after the Conquest, and for a great increase in food productivity to support a larger population from mid first to mid third century (and both points are arguable), at the very least the population of pre-Roman Britain about the beginning of our era must have been well up to, and probably in excess of, the accepted Domesday figure. A late prehistoric population of 2 million is certainly conceivable and almost certainly nearer the mark than guesses of hundreds of thousands based, unconsciously or otherwise, on a premise that pre-1086 populations could not exceed that of Norman Britain. We are therefore apparently presented with a situation in later prehistoric Britain of having to explain how and why a basically

[41] Frere, *Britannia*, p. 261.
[42] R. E. M. Wheeler, in *Ant.*, IV, 1931, p. 95.

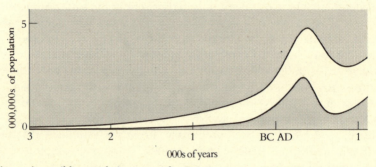

Fig. 7. A possible population curve for Britain, *c.* 3000 BC–AD 1100. The edges of the 'band of possibility' indicate maximum and minimum interpretations of present evidence (P. J. Fowler).

agrarian population grew, in round figures, from *c.* 10,000 to approaching 2,000,000 over some 2,500 years. Such figures require an average population growth rate of some 6 per cent per annum.

In looking at this perhaps surprising situation, we can start with two other recent studies which specifically face up to population parameters in the second and first millennia BC respectively. Atkinson followed up his essay on aspects of Neolithic population by applying similar methods to the burial mounds and their burials in the whole of southern Britain (defined, by the nature of the material, as south of a Tees–Mersey line).[43] His very tentative conclusion was that in the period 2500–1600 BC the average population of the area was about 2,000. Assuming a similar (but debatable) density of population in the northern part of Britain and even allowing for 100 per cent error factor in Atkinson's material or premises, the total population in Britain would still seem to have been of the order of 10,000 people. If we go further and, for example, argue that only half the total number of barrows and cairns has yet been found, or that their contained burials only represent one-quarter or even one-tenth of the population, we are still dealing with figures of the order of tens of thousands, not hundreds of thousands. Nevertheless, even within that order of numbers, there could be a critical significance between, at the one extreme, a more or less static population of *c.* 10,000 from the mid third millennium to the mid second millennium, and at the other extreme, a population rising from *c.* 10,000 to an absolute maximum of *c.* 100,000 in about 1,000 years. Whatever actually happened, these figures probably give the outside parameters, with a personal opinion favouring a rise in population to some tens of thousands by *c.* 1500 BC.

[43] R. J. C. Atkinson, 'Burial and population in the British Bronze Age', in F. Lynch and C. Burgess (eds.), *Prehistoric Man in Wales and the West*, Bath, 1972, pp. 107–16.

Contrast this speculation with those for only two counties, Hereford and Shropshire, a thousand years and more later.[44] Using somewhat controversial evidence and assumptions, the interesting point is that Stanford arrives at a figure *c.* 1400 BC very close to the estimate of population density from the Domesday Book, i.e. 22/24 per square mile (8/9 per km²); and by AD 50 a density of 29 per square mile (11 per km²) which compares with the 31 per square mile (12 per km²) of the 1377 Poll Tax returns. He argues that, for the hill-forts alone, the population rises from some 24,000 to 58,000 over 6 centuries. Despite the contentiousness of the basic evidence (below, pp. 112, 252) and the unacceptability of one of the basic premises, i.e. that the total population of the area lived in hill forts, the figures have an air of reality about them for an area containing in general one of the densest concentrations of hill forts in Britain. If we start applying figures of the same order to other areas – West Cornwall, Wessex, the Cotswolds, the Middle and Upper Thames, Sussex, the Wolds – where other concentrations of settlement evidence, not necessarily only in the form of hill forts, are known from about the middle of the first millennium onwards, we are soon thinking in terms of hundreds of thousands of people instead of the tens of thousands of a millennium earlier. Despite the recent assertion that Domesday figures may already have been approached by the end of the Bronze Age,[45] though accepting that this might be true for some favoured localities, e.g. Dorset, it would seem more reasonable to think in terms of a total population of Britain in the ½–1 million bracket by, say, *c.* 500 BC, thus requiring it merely to double in the next 500 years or so to provide the platform from which it could double again, in half the time, in the first half of the Roman period. Neither such postulates are far-fetched, as will be discussed below (pp. 259–62), and as is implied elsewhere in Part II of this volume dealing with Roman Britain (despite its total avoidance of the population question); the difficulty lies in raising a presumed population figure of merely a few tens of thousands to at least some hundreds of thousands in a thousand years or so. In thinking of the minimal ten-fold increase involved, it would at least appear to be an advance that, in our speculation, the critical period has been narrowed down to the half-millennium or so on either side of 1000 BC.

Anticipating arguments to be advanced below (pp. 249–59), two phases within that period can be suggested as appropriate for a rapid population growth above the average 5 per cent per annum increase over the whole millennium required by the general proposal. The first

[44] S. Stanford, 'The function and population of hill-forts in the central marches', in Lynch and Burgess, *op. cit.*, pp. 307–19.

[45] C. Burgess in Renfrew (ed.), *British Prehistory*, p. 166.

was in the fifteenth to thirteenth centuries, when we see archaeologically attested not only the *floruit* of Stonehenge and other evidence of technical accomplishment, e.g. the Wilsford shaft,[46] but also a development of organized landscapes, culminating in the appearance of the first 'fortified' hill-top enclosures. Surely all this signifies a growing communal cohesiveness under various social, political, and economic stimuli, among which population pressure could well be one of the most powerful. The fact itself that, after 1,000 years marked by the fashionable construction of great ceremonial monuments, such structures ceased to be built, suggests that the social investment, the 'spare' productive capacity, that they absorbed was henceforth not available or was being used in other activities. Though it is rather a 'chicken and egg' situation, one interpretation is that the needs of a growing population demanded intensified agrarian effort and left little spare capacity for communal frills.

The second phase was in the eighth to sixth centuries, when immigrants, climatic deterioration, and technological innovation all contributed to a dynamic situation of which population growth could well have been one of the products.

It is fully appreciated that much of the foregoing is speculative; yet in proposing a population model, attempting to be more precise than hitherto, it is facing up to one of the basic parameters of later British prehistory. Many writers have repeatedly stated that numbers of people, quantified populations, are fundamental to understanding of the period, not just so that we know how many people we are dealing with, but so that we can better understand the processes such as contact and exchange, conservatism, and innovation, which contribute towards cultural evolution.[47] In considering many aspects of the life of agrarian societies in particular, numbers are clearly crucial: put at its crudest, unless we have some idea of the consumer's needs, it is difficult to assess or even understand the input necessary for a satisfactory product. The figures tentatively suggested above are doubtless wrong, and certainly it is expected that they will be refined and improved; but it is hoped that they are of the right order and, in that sense, can provide a reasonable framework for much of the ensuing discussion.

[46] P. Ashbee, in *Ant.*, XXXVII, 1963, pp. 116–20; XL, 1966, pp. 227–8.
[47] E.g. R. J. C. Atkinson, 'Demographic implications', in E. Fowler (ed.), *Field Survey in British Archaeology*, pp. 60–6, a paper which partly stimulated a further discussion of population implications from which this section largely derives, see P. J. Fowler, 'Lowland landscapes...', in S. Limbrey and J. G. Evans (eds.), *The Effect of Man on the Landscape: The Lowland Zone*, CBA Research Report, 21, 1978, pp. 1–12.

SOCIETY

The archaeological evidence to which we are confined for much of later prehistory appears to afford clear indications of the ways in which the agrarian societies of the time organized themselves. Social organization, however, can be of immense complexity, compound of relationships which do not leave material traces, even – one might say particularly – in assumed primitive communities. Many examples exist of wrong interpretations having been placed on apparently straightforward evidence.[48] Nor is it in any way a justifiable assumption that in later prehistoric Britain we are dealing with societies which are in any realistic sense 'primitive'. Their primitive image exists because for the last 2,000 years they have been regarded and written about as such by their observers, *all of whom without exception have been outsiders*, either in space or in time. The near contemporary classical writers, notably Caesar, Tacitus, and Dio Cassius; Bede and all those he drew on; the medieval chroniclers up to and including Shakespeare; the Romantic discoverers of 'Ancient Britain', the British Imperial recognition of primitive savages, and the assumptions of our own urban-based viewpoint – all have contributed to continuous misunderstanding of the nature of later prehistoric society. Not a single voice from that society can speak in its defence, yet it has constantly been judged by its observers for what it was not.

Let us start by assuming that it was a complex and changing society. With our population parameters outlined above, we can also assert that it was a successful society; whether complex or not, it worked. It not only generated sustained population increase over 2,000 years, but did so, as far as we can see, without major disasters. There is no evidence at all for phases of social collapse or economic regression in our period, and archaeology certainly points to long-term technological development in a sense comparable to that of the last three hundred years. Even if we cannot adequately explain why it happened, we can recognize a very considerable achievement over some eighty generations in which a stone-using society became the advanced, iron-using society described by a slightly surprised Julius Caesar. Granted the political divisions of the first centuries BC and AD which made the conquest of southern Britain a relatively easy task in Roman military terms (cf.

[48] E.g., worryingly, R. Bonnichson, 'Millie's Camp: an experiment in archaeology', *World Arch.*, 4, 1973, pp. 277–91. For discussion of 'society' generally, cf. still C. Daryll Forde, *Habitat, Economy and Society*, London, 8th ed. 1963; G. Clark and S. Piggott, *Prehistoric Societies*, London, 1965; and, for the later part of our period here, Ross, *Everyday Life of the Pagan Celts* (despite the absence of farming from 'everyday life').

the British conquest of India in the eighteenth century), all the evidence nevertheless conveys an impression of social complexity, indeed cohesion, behind the field chaos created by an alien manner of warfare. The stratification and even sophistication in the 'Belgic' society of south-east Britain and in the non-Belgic societies beyond to the west and north, though they are easy enough to dismiss as 'barbaric', represented in reality· a stage in a dynamic process of social adaptation to rapid population growth and increasing agrarian productivity. Given the population parameters, flexibility must have been one of the characteristics of later prehistoric social organization, for there is all the difference between a structure suitable for ten or so thousands of people living at a very low population density, and that appropriate for a population in the region of a million living, in some areas, at a density approaching the norm of medieval rural England.

Archaeology, almost by definition, tends in social terms to emphasize the outstanding. Thus in the first five hundred years or so of later prehistory, compared to what went before, the record is dominated by the exotic Beaker material. It is difficult to avoid the implication of a dominant social element, metal technologists penetrating by this time conservative farming communities deficient, through the restricted social contact permitted by their small numbers, in internal stimuli.[49] While it has been argued that the Beaker people were prospectors searching for mineral deposits, the archaeological evidence nevertheless suggests that they were associating with the indigenous population. They do not appear to have ignored the scattered farming communities – which, as prospectors in an unknown landscape, they could have done – and therefore, precisely because they were scattered, arguably they sought them out and established some form of ascendancy over them. No precise information is available for the numbers involved but presumably we are thinking only of a few hundred, or at most a thousand or two, actual immigrants or direct descendants of immigrants added to the small existing population. While archaeological evidence too suggests the grafting of a strong Beaker influence on to the material culture of the later stone/early bronze-using societies, it is not known what this represents in terms of social structure. A hierarchical model with Beaker 'chieftains' is difficult to resist, though such need not necessarily imply the subjugation socially of the lower orders. A subjective but perhaps not too far-fetched analogy, involving the transference of a superior technology from one social environment to another, might be with a United Nations team of 'technical experts' operating in one of the developing countries of today's Third World.

Social distinctions of great clarity are implied by the evidence from

[49] As per R. J. C. Atkinson, in E. Fowler, op. cit., esp. figs. 20, 21.

around 2000 BC and during the first half of the second millennium (above, p. 47). Even if the 'Wessex Culture' is accepted as an insular phenomenon, yet not fully a culture as originally defined, its archaeological manifestations strongly indicate a distinctive class within the society of southern Britain and presumably one at the top of a hierarchy. The concept of 'Wessex chieftains', lording it over chiefdoms perhaps already old, as expressed in the tradition of focal community monuments, is certainly attractive.[50] From causewayed enclosures and long barrows through the great henge monuments of the third millennium to the major burial grounds of the earlier second millennium, a consistent element of social power drawing on communal effort seems to be represented. In other words, individuals or groups of people were able to focus part of the productive capacity of their fellows into the creation of places for dynastic or oligarchic display or for communal benefit, but not for the personal, practical use of the labourers themselves. The point is a favourite one and has recently been cogently re-argued in terms of a regional development within Wessex society and comparable contemporary communities elsewhere in southern Britain.[51] Whether chiefs so postulated were necessarily 'warrior chiefs' is a different matter – it seems unlikely to have been the case – but whatever the basis of their social supremacy, the model of such an aristocracy implies a greater number of people towards the base of the structure. That being so, it is difficult to accept that barrow burial was accorded to the mass of the population.[52] Of those people, therefore, at this period we still look in vain, both in death and in life. But they must have existed, for a hundred chiefs alone did not erect Stonehenge III.

In the second half of the second millennium BC, the evidence is different. Gone is the magnificence, the ostentation of the few, the building of major public monuments. It appears to be a quiet time, even a dull period, though agriculturally and socially it was of great

[50] Originally, S. Piggott, in *Proc. Prehist. Soc.*, 4, 1938, pp. 52–106, most recently discussed by C. Renfrew, *Before Civilization*, Harmondsworth, 1973, chap. 11; and in A. Fleming, 'Models for the development of the Wessex Culture' and C. Renfrew, 'Monuments, mobilisation and social organisation in Neolithic Wessex', in *idem* (ed.), *The Explanation of Cultural Change: Models in Prehistory*, London, 1973, pp. 539–58. C. Burgess, in Renfrew (ed.), *British Prehistory*, esp. pp. 303–6, provides bibliographical coverage.

[51] Renfrew, *The Explanation of Cultural Change*. Cf. also A. Fleming, 'Territorial patterns in Bronze Age Wessex', *Proc. Prehist. Soc.*, 37, 1971, pp. 138–66, and G. J. Wainwright, 'Religion and Settlement in Wessex, 3000–1700 bc', in P. J. Fowler (ed.), *Recent Work in Rural Archaeology*, pp. 57–71.

[52] *pace* R. J. C. Atkinson, 'Burial and population in the British Bronze Age', in F. Lynch and C. Burgess (eds.), *Prehistoric Man in Wales and the West*, Bath, 1972, pp. 107–16.

significance. From many parts of Britain comes similar evidence of small farming settlements and their fields, of concern with agrarian, practical, and technological matters. It appears to be a functional period, with emphasis on the basics of food production. In the south, large communal cemeteries replace the labour-intensive, single burial-mound rite and their cremations have none of the 'conspicuous' (or should it be 'hidden'?) 'waste' characteristic of the previous centuries. The chiefs have disappeared or, if present, they do not reveal themselves as chieftains are wont to do. The small community, perhaps just the family group, characterizes the landscape, and appears tied to the land in the daily grind of settled peasant farming which henceforth comes to represent the lot of so many in west European society. Of their allegiances, rights and duties, we are ignorant; whether they were 'free' farmers in their own right or in some sense tenants of communal or private landowners, we just do not know. The suggestion, to be discussed below (pp. 144–61) of large-scale landscape organization, if correct, implies the existence of some form of controlling influence, of some investment of power in groups or individuals; and it is conceivable that, behind the superficial dullness of the period, the energies of the counterparts, perhaps even the descendants, of the earlier chiefs were now being channelled into unostentatious land management instead of ceremonial circumstance – the post-Reformation landlord replacing the Renaissance prince?

This period ends with the appearance, for the first time, of non-ceremonial hill-top enclosures. 'Hill forts' probably have several origins but the end result is the same: a concentration of communal capital. An initial stockade, however, could have been built by a small independent group so it is not necessary to argue for tribal leaders and the like *ab initio*; but the appearance of truly defensive sites, coupled with the increasingly common appearance of fighting-equipment, betokens less settled conditions, the need to take a stand, the development of the property concept, all suggesting population pressures and the hardening of social relationships. Society, as its component communities took root in the landscape through the investment of their own capital in particular hill tops, in their own field system, in their own territory, was moving a long way indeed from the free-ranging way of farming life in earlier times when the problem would have been to meet other people. Now, in some areas anyway, the problem was becoming one of resisting other people. The perfectly understandable urge to move above potential visitors, to be able to see your land, was increasingly to become one of the characteristics of social behaviour over the next millennium. Since it had not manifested itself in earlier times – out of necessity anyway, for causewayed enclosures occur on low ground too, and long barrows are to be looked at, not seen from – this upward movement of social foci requires noting and some explanation. It is of course a long-term trend, not a sudden event, with its origins in the appearance of settlement foci as distinct from ceremonial centres back in the second millennium. This chronology firmly dissociates it from the introduction of an iron-based technology though we may link it with the beginnings of climatic deterioration.[53] The apparent contradiction in suggesting that hill-tops became more important as the climate began to be slightly less warm and slightly less dry and, as important to the farmer, the weather became less predictable, could be avoided if increasing population and therefore growing pressure on preferred localities were causal factors. Equally, less stable weather conditions could make higher land which had not already been overexploited more suitable for grazing than it had been in drier Sub-Boreal conditions?[54]

It is difficult to gauge the effects of such trends, particularly in their early stages, on social organization. As we move into the first half of the first millennium BC, however, aspects of the social structure begin to come into focus. For the first time, at hill-tops like Crickley Hill, Glos., we see the aggregation of settlement in a fortified enclosure; and the earlier unenclosed settlement on Itford Hill has been interpreted as a nucleated village. As far as we know, such relatively large communal units had not previously existed. This trend also continues to develop, with such settlements becoming larger and more common, until we see the massive, multi-vallate hill-forts, the *oppida* and the extensive 'open' settlements of the later centuries BC. But, as we glimpse now, mainly on air photographs, small farms and their characteristic surroundings not only continue but proliferate, henceforth increasingly enmeshed in a landscape network progressively more difficult for us to disentangle from the landscape of the Roman period (Plate I*a*).[55] Social structure is presumably reflected in these relict landscapes and, as the millennium progresses, the impression of an increasingly stratified society is con-

[53] P. J. Fowler, 'Lowland landscapes...', in Limbrey and Evans (eds.), CBA Research Report, 21, pp. 1–72, elaborating S. Piggott, 'A note on the climatic deterioration in the first millennium B.C. in Britain', *Scott. Arch. Forum*, 4, 1972, pp. 109–13.

[54] Cf. J. A. Taylor, in Evans *et al.*, CBA Research Report, 11, fig. 3.

[55] Most recently shown and discussed in D. R. Wilson (ed.), *Aerial Reconnaissance for Archaeology*, CBA Research Report, 12, London, 1975; RCHM, *Northamptonshire Inventory*, 1, London, 1975(1976), and *A Matter of Time*; Benson and Miles, *The Upper Thames Valley*; T. Gates, *The Middle Thames Valley:...*, Oxford, 1975; R. Leech, *The Upper Thames Valley in Gloucestershire and Wiltshire*, 1977; N. J. Higham and G. D. B. Jones, 'Frontier, forts and farmers: Cumbrian Aerial Survey 1974–5', *Archaeol. J.*, 132, 1975, pp. 16–53.

veyed. We see specialists at work in Late Bronze and Early Iron technology, their customers, presumably those who could afford to buy their products, perhaps even support their livelihood;[56] we see fighting men, perhaps retainers, in the weapons of the bronze-smith and the blacksmith of the eighth to sixth centuries; we see the leaders and the architects, the foremen and the labourers, in the hill forts and possibly even contract and design teams at work in their entrances; we see charioteers, artists, and, eventually, a religious caste, the druids;[57] we see carpenters, commercial potters, and farmers, herdsmen in the north and ploughmen in the south. We see those who dwelt communally in the large settlements, hill forts included, those who dwelt in the isolated grandeur of large country houses, those who dwelt in the smaller farms, and those who dwelt in caves.[58] And finally, we see those who dwelt in *oppida*, in a proto-urban state, and issued coins cast with their name and symbol.[59] On the eve of the Roman Conquest, the archaeological evidence for social complexity is supported by documentary evidence describing, at worst at second and third hand and with a bias which is obvious, those who tried to resist the benefits of Empire.[60] In social terms, the confrontation of Cortez and Aztecs or Puritan yeoman and Woodland Indian could hardly have been more vivid than that of Caesar and the Britons.

[56] The bulk of this field is now referenced in M. J. Rowlands, *The Organisation of Middle Bronze Age Metalworking*, British Archaeological Reports, 31, Oxford, 1976, pp. 432–46, and Burgess, *op. cit.*, pp. 291–329 for the Bronze Age; and in Cunliffe, *Iron Age Communities in Britain* and Harding, *The Iron Age in Lowland Britain*, for the Iron Age. For a bronze-smith at work in an Iron Age settlement, see *Ant.*, 47, 1963, pp. 109–30 and 50; 1976, pp. 32–9.

[57] S. Piggott, *The Druids*, London, 1968; Ross, *Everyday Life of the Pagan Celts*, chap. 6.

[58] In addition to Cunliffe, *op. cit.* and Harding *op. cit.*, hill-forts are now discussed in A. H. A. Hogg, *Hillforts of Britain*, London, 1975, and J. Forde-Johnston, *Hillforts of the Iron Age in England and Wales: a Survey of the Surface Evidence*, Liverpool, 1976, and D. W. Harding (ed.), *Hillforts: A Survey of Research in Britain and Ireland*, London, 1976, the last two published after this text was written, and all of them supplementary to, rather than replacing, M. Jesson and D. Hill (eds.), *The Iron Age and its Hill-Forts*, Southampton, 1971. For the north, A. L. F. Rivet (ed.), *The Iron Age in Northern Britain*, Edinburgh, 1966, and two books by R. W. Feachem, *A Guide to Prehistoric Scotland*, London, 1963; rev. ed. London, 1977, and *The North Britons*, London, 1965, cover much of the settlement range and the available literature, supplemented now by *Scott. Arch. Forum*, 1969– ; for the south, see especially H. C. Bowen, 'The Celtic background', in Rivet (ed.), *The Roman Villa in Britain*, pp. 1–48.

[59] See now B. Cunliffe and T. Rowley (eds.), *Oppida: the Beginnings of Urbanisation in Barbarian Europe*, Oxford, 1976, esp. pp. 325–39.

[60] For 'the bias', see J. J. Tierney, 'The Celtic ethnography of Posidonius', *Proc. Roy. Irish Acad.*, 60 C, 1960, pp. 189–275; see also Frere, *Britannia*, chaps. 3–5 and Rivet, *Town and Country in Roman Britain*, chap. 1, for a discussion of the resistance and the sources of evidence.

SETTLEMENT DISTRIBUTION

The archaeological evidence behind the previous discussions of people, population, and society lies in, or has been recovered from, the field. It consists of visible structures surviving and recorded on the ground (e.g. settlements and fields), and portable artifacts collected from the ground surface (e.g. worked flint); of a much larger and more extensive amount of information recorded on air photographs, an amount constantly being augmented and by no means yet assessed; of evidence from archaeological excavations; and of a considerable quantity of topographical/antiquarian literature and museum material, often recording information not otherwise available, e.g. about or from sites now destroyed or 'lost'. These data will be briefly described in terms of settlement distribution over Britain, first in the second millennium and then in the first.

Knowledge and understanding of the distribution and incidence of human settlement in Britain in later prehistoric times is conditioned by three factors above all: the accident of survival of detectable field monuments, the distribution of archaeologists themselves (or at least the pattern of those areas where they have chosen to work), and the environmental circumstances of preservation. To a large extent, to discuss regional differences may well, therefore, be reflecting secondary factors affecting the evidence rather than the realities of agrarian life 3,000 years ago.

In a broad band stretching from the Atlantic coast of western Britain to the ill-defined line – conventionally Exeter–Lincoln – east of which the older rocks literally fail to surface through the mantle of later deposits, prehistoric farming communities are represented by surviving structures, basically of stone. East of that line, with but rare exceptions, such evidence is not available, being replaced by less substantial earthworks, deliberately built, accidentally produced, or representing timber structures; and, more commonly now, by often ephemeral changes in soil and vegetation conditions, best recorded and appreciated from the air. In particular waterlogged environments, regardless of 'highland' or 'lowland' situation, the relevant evidence is preserved, superficially invisible, but more complete than elsewhere, as for example in the Somerset Levels (Plate IIb), the Fens, the Lake District, and along certain rivers, particularly by abandoned water-courses.

The known distribution of agrarian communities is therefore very uneven. They are of course implied fairly generally by the distribution of round barrows[61] but only in some areas can a firm relationship

[61] R. J. C. Atkinson in F. Lynch and C. Burgess (eds.), *Prehistoric Man in Wales and the West*, Bath, 1972, p. 111, fig. 1, and N. Thomas in P. J. Fowler (ed.), *Archaeology*

between cemetery and settlement be demonstrated or argued. Particular concentrations of burial and related sites need not necessarily imply a relatively large local population though, even allowing for the sanctity of particular areas like that around Stonehenge, it seems probable that most burials had not been brought very far, and therefore represent a population living within, say, 50 km of the focus of the cemetery. On the other hand, until it can be demonstrated that all the barrows in any given cemetery or area were built within a given time, the possibility that their construction was spread over several centuries must always invite caution in correlating barrow density with a high local population at any one time. Furthermore, although round barrow and cairn burial was generally practised throughout southern Britain in at least the first half of the second millennium, it is by no means certain that it applied throughout society or was equally followed in contemporary but neighbouring communities. The absence of barrows on the distribution map does not, therefore, necessarily mean an absence of settlement there.

Second millennium BC

The best known and apparently densest settlement areas in the second millennium, as represented by remains of actual settlements and fields, are in the south-west, Wessex and Sussex. In western Cornwall, several settlements – Trevisker, Gwithian, Bodrifty – have been excavated, and undoubtedly others are present amongst and under the proliferation of recently catalogued settlement evidence.[62] On Bodmin Moor, particularly on Dartmoor (Plate IIIa, Fig. 8), and to a lesser extent on Exmoor, surviving field monuments suggest a considerable extent of prehistoric farming, perhaps in some areas from Neolithic times but certainly during the second millennium and probably, again in some areas, into later centuries up to if not beyond the onset of the Sub-Atlantic climatic phase (below, pp. 169–70). But all these are now agriculturally marginal areas where later activity has not, until recently, posed much of a threat of destruction to the evidence, and the upstanding remains have exercised an obvious attraction for both field survey and excavation. In relation to the whole of the south-western peninsula, however, these areas are small, and results from them should not obscure our ignorance about the remainder – the river valleys of lowland plains and plateaux and of the coast itself especially – where

and the Landscape, p. 34, fig. 4. The fullest corpus of general distribution maps remains. Sir Cyril Fox, The Personality of Britain, Cardiff, 1932; 4th ed. Cardiff, 1947.

[62] V. Russell, West Penwith Survey, Truro, 1971.

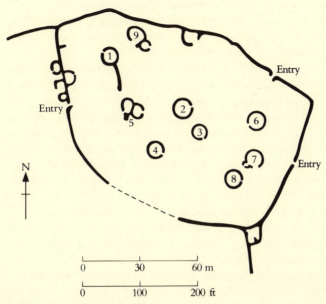

Fig. 8. Plan of enclosed settlement on Dean Moor, Dartmoor, Devon (after A. Fox).

basic questions about the existence (or not), rather than the nature, of habitation have yet to be tackled.[63]

The same sweeping generalization can, with little unfairness, also be applied to the whole of Wales. Despite the existence of well-attested communities and activities in the third millennium and a body of varied evidence, portable and monumental, from the second, agrarian knowledge until the last centuries BC is very limited. In the field, the record is dominated by round barrows and cairns, by cup-marks and standing stones, with settlements hardly known and fields almost non-existent. Yet clearly people were living in Wales, and it would seem likely that at least some of their domestic structures incorporated stone: perhaps some of the evidence remains to be recognized amongst the already recorded wealth of settlements and field systems in, for example, Caernarvonshire (Fig. 20) and Pembrokeshire, or among the moorland cairn fields which have so far been regarded mainly through funerary eyes. Speculation apart, however, second millennium Wales has little at the moment to contribute to British agrarian history though the potential is hinted at in a number of studies from the natural sciences.

[63] An up-to-date survey of the general south-west is Aileen Fox, *South West England 3500 BC–AD 600*, rev. ed. Newton Abbot, 1973.

Even if for many the economy was pastoral-based and left little artifactual evidence, second millennium farmers can surely be detected through the impact of their sheep, cattle, and horses on the environment.[64]

There is likewise little visible field evidence of settlement in the adjacent Severn estuary area, but recent and current work extending from a focus in the raised peat bog of the Brue valley out across the Somerset Levels shows how deceptive superficial appraisal can be (Plate IIb). The stratified archaeological evidence of timber trackways and the palaeobotanical evidence clearly indicate exploitation of the Levels, their 'islands', and their margins to north (Isle of Wedmore and perhaps the Mendip Hills) and south (the Polden Hills) in the fourth and third millennia. The C-14 evidence which is basic to the chronological framework of succession here is, however, sparse for the earlier second millennium, suggesting so far that timber trackways were not generally needed although other evidence indicates farming activities in the area. The reappearance of trackways in the later centuries of the millennium, however, strongly suggests attempts to continue such activities in the face of a rising water level. For present purposes, the key significance of the superficially invisible evidence from the Somerset Levels is its non-funerary nature for a period less than lavishly illuminated by settlement archaeology, its absolute and relative chronological succession, and its relationships to a detailed palaeobotanical record. It provides a classic example of an archaeologically blank area in terms of upstanding field remains producing scientific evidence of continued and probably continuous exploitation for food production through arable and pastoral farming and the older skills of hunting, shooting, and fishing.

Archaeologically, the Carboniferous Limestone range of the Mendip Hills immediately to the north presents a different and more conventional picture. The upland plateaux, rising to just over 1,000 ft (305 m) above OD, contain a density of round barrows comparable to that in south Dorset and around Avebury but, as in these examples, a lack of cohesive settlement evidence. Beaker activity is certainly attested, not least at Gorsey Bigbury, amongst occupation debris in a swallet nearby, and, stratified, at Mendip's western projection into the British Channel (Brean Down); but of the barrow-builders there are but glimpses in the caves and in stray finds.[65] A similar picture is presented for the

[64] E.g. J. A. Taylor, 'Chronometers and chronicles: a study of palaeo-environments in west central Wales', *Prog. Geog.*, 5, 1973, pp. 248–334. General background, H. N. Savory, 'The Bronze Age', in I. Ll. Foster and G. Daniel (eds.), *Prehistoric and Early Wales*, London, 1965, pp. 71–107.

[65] The most recent summary, fully referenced, is P. J. Fowler, 'Early Mendip', in R. Atthill, *Mendip: A New Study*, Newton Abbot, 1976, pp. 50–74 and 266–9; but for Beaker activities, see subsequently A. M. ApSimon *et al.*, 'Gorsey Bigbury, Cheddar,

second millennium on the Cotswolds stretching away to the north-east: again, there are hundreds of round barrows, somewhat less dense in their overall distribution, but little other evidence of settlement apart from almost ubiquitous (non-local) flints. Although no 'Bronze Age' settlements have been excavated, it is probable that some of the flint concentrations represent working and/or habitation sites and less frequent but similar evidence from the clay lowlands to the west might be interpreted likewise.[66]

The situation is very similar in Wessex except that, now, recultivation of formerly marginal land over the last two decades has removed much of the upstanding evidence (Plate IV*a*). Even so, though Wessex of the second millennium BC, with Stonehenge and its thousands of round barrows, is probably the best-established concept in British prehistory, relatively little evidence of actual settlements and fields has been recognized until recently (below, pp. 144–51). Nevertheless, while settlement earthwork remains may be infrequent, it has been clear from particular studies of, for example, the Bournemouth area, the Isle of Purbeck, and along the Wiltshire/Hampshire borders on Cranborne Chase and north-east of Salisbury (Fig. 40), that 'Bronze Age' occupation was more intense than mere surface appearances might suggest. Furthermore, many a barrow has been found to protect on, in, and under the buried land surface beneath it, evidence of earlier activity including actual habitation or cultivation (below, pp. 162–9). But here again, research and particularly excavation, recently, for example at Rams Hill, Berks. (Fig. 9) has concentrated on the high chalk downland, unconsciously to give an unbalanced regional picture of agrarian communities without much information about its, perhaps less intensive, counterpart along the valleys, on the heaths, and in or around the fringes of the considerable areas of 'natural' woodland.[67]   *206644*

A similar partial distribution of settlement can be seen in the

Somerset...', *Proc. Univ. Bristol Spelaeol. Soc.*, 14(2), 1976, pp. 155–83. The basic barrow data are in L. V. Grinsell, 'Somerset Barrows, Part II: North and East', *Proc. Somerset Archaeol. Natur. Hist.*, 115, 1971, pp. 43–137.

[66] The comparable modern summary for the Cotswolds is I. F. Smith, in C. and M. A. Hadfield, *The Cotswolds: A New Study*, Newton Abbot, 1973, pp. 76–84, 302–5. For barrows, see H. O'Neil and L. V. Grinsell, 'Gloucestershire barrows', *Trans. Bristol Glos. Arch. Soc.*, 79, part 1, 1960, pp. 1–148, with modern observations by J. H. Drinkwater, 'Barrows in Gloucestershire: patterns of destruction', in P. J. Fowler (ed.), 1972, *op. cit.*, pp. 129–56. On flints 'scatters, see L. V. Grinsell, 'The Royce Collection at Stow-on-the-Wold', *Trans. Bristol Glos. Soc.*, 83, 1964, pp. 1–33; E. K. Tratman, 'Flint implements from the Bath Downs', *Proc. Univ. Bristol Spelaeol. Soc.*, 13(2), 1973, pp. 153–69; and, in the Vale of Berkeley, P. J. Fowler, 'Archaeology and the M5 Motorway, Gloucestershire 1969–75: summary and assessment', *Trans. Bristol Glos. Arch. Soc.*, 95, 1977, 40–6.

[67] The best general survey is L. V. Grinsell, *The Archaeology of Wessex*, London, 1958, updated with C-14 in the slighter P. J. Fowler, *Regional Archaeologies: Wessex*,

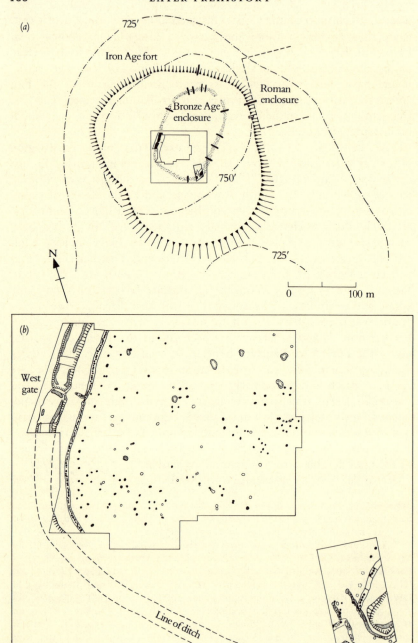

Fig. 9. Rams Hill, Berks.: (a) the successive enclosures on the hill top; (b) the excavated areas inside the southern part of the Bronze Age enclosure, showing entrances, ditch, palisade trenches, and internal post-holes and pits (after R. Bradley).

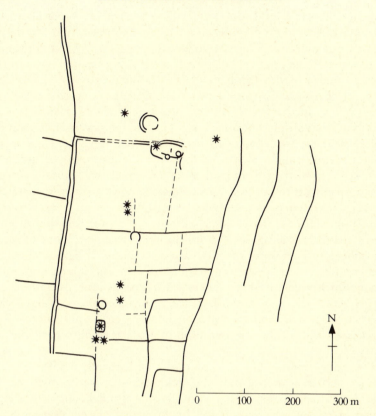

Fig. 10. New Barn Down, Clapham, Sussex: plan of settlement, fields and trackways of the later second millennium BC (after P. Drewett).

continuation of the chalk country to the east, though possibly significant differences can now be distinguished between the archaeology of the Wessex and Sussex Downs. The distribution of linear ditches, for example, seems confined to the former (below, pp. 233–6). Although, however, the best-known and best-studied sites lie on the downs (Fig. 10), the undifferentiated distribution of all 'Bronze Age' material brings out the importance of the coastal plain as an area of active land-use, and once again emphasizes the need for caution in using the evidence of extant surface structures alone.[68]

In Britain, south of the Thames, though speculation and some limited

London, 1967. The basic modern sources are the RCHM, *Dorset Inventories*, I–V (1952–75) and VCH, *Wilts*, I (1957, 1973); Hampshire, Berkshire, and the Isle of Wight have nothing comparable.

[68] The most useful general surveys are G. J. Copley, *An Archaeology of South-East England*, London, 1958, and R. Jessup, *South East England*, London, 1970.

evidence allows a consideration of farming areas in low-lying situations, the bulk of the attested evidence relates to the moors and the downs where upstanding remains have survived until recently; but in moving northwards to the Thames valley itself and the other major – and minor – river valleys of the Midland Plain, the picture to emerge is very different. It has clear implications for the similar but aerially unphotogenic valleys further south. A very great deal of settlement evidence is known from air photography to exist along the gravel terraces of the Middle and Upper Thames in particular (Plate I*a*), but what is not certain is how much of it is of the second millennium or indeed is prehistoric, as distinct from Roman or early medieval. Certainly many of the linear features, ring-ditches, and settlements are pre-Roman, and several excavated examples have been shown to be conventionally 'Neolithic' and/or 'Bronze Age'. Though it is probable that most of the ring-ditches indicate second millennium burial sites, some of them, and indeed of enclosures of other shapes, could well be non-funerary elements in a contemporary agrarian landscape. Though chronological data and many details of settlement form, density, and overall pattern are generally lacking in the area, it must be included as one of significant agrarian settlement and exploitation in the second millennium. The point is stressed by the concentration of artifacts of all types from the valley.[69]

The same is probably true of most, perhaps all, Midland valley gravels and can increasingly be demonstrated to be the case as investigation and chance discovery in advance of and during commercial gravel extraction proceeds apace. In the valley of the Warwickshire Avon, for example, cumulative aerial records have shown a tremendous, as yet barely assimilated, quantity of material amongst which are recognizable sites and features ascribable to prehistoric communities. Recent and continuing excavation which is both elucidating parts of the palimpsest and examining individual sites is supporting this interpretation for some elements in the complex and, though the significance of much is still to be assessed, agrarian activity along the valley in the second millennium cannot really be doubted.[70]

To the east, a similar picture, at least quantitatively, is emerging from

[69] The air photographic evidence is now conveniently assembled in the three Thames valley volumes referenced in n. 55, p. 93, above. Among artifact studies, see J. C. Barrett, 'Four Bronze Age cremation cemeteries from Middlesex', *Trans. Lond. Middlx Arch. Soc.*, 24, 1973, pp. 111–34.

[70] G. Webster and B. Hobley, 'Aerial reconnaissance over the Warwickshire Avon', *Archaeol. J.*, 121, 1964, pp. 1–22, followed by A. Oswald (ed.), 'Excavations of the Avon/Severn Research Committee at Barford, Warwickshire', *Trans. Proc. Birmingham Arch. Soc.*, 83, 1966–67, pp. 1–64; and 'Excavations at Beckford', *Trans. Worcs. Arch. Soc.*, 3, 1970–2, pp. 7–54.

the valleys draining into the North Sea. At the time of writing, however, while the English Royal Commission has provided both a general survey containing detailed local studies, particularly of the Welland Valley, and an extremely well-documented survey of the Peterborough areas embracing the Nene Valley, other work is currently in progress and/or unpublished. The Trent Valley, for example, still has a major contribution to make, and not just to the second millennium.[71] But again, the by now expected generalization can be made with some confidence: that the gravel terraces and, to an unknown extent, their hinterlands, were being exploited by agrarian communities in the second millennium BC. Their particular distribution and incidence along any of the individual valleys within the region is not known in detail, and it is indeed probable that the great majority of the elements visible in the landscape from the air will, on investigation, prove to be of late prehistoric or later date. The existence of evidence, usually less tangible, from earlier centuries nevertheless suggests settlement, perhaps locally intense, scattered fairly widely across the Midlands. The Fengate area (Fig. 11) immediately east of Peterborough, for example, has been and is the subject of detailed investigation in advance of destruction in a project similar in method and concept to that in the Somerset Levels. Its results, in terms of fields, settlements, land-use, and their changing relationships with each other and the 'natural' environment are crucial for the second millennium and will concern us more than once (below, pp. 104, 239).

In East Anglia, more is known about the Neolithic background, some elements of which, such as the mining of flint, certainly continued into the second millennium. Furthermore, external contacts during the earlier period are at least implied by the regional distribution of imported implements, with its two concentrations near the Rivers Lark and Ouse between the chalk downland and Breckland and in the Colchester area, respectively, well inland and markedly coastal. The subsequent distribution of Beaker material suggests an infilling of the landscape, again particularly in relation to river valleys, with the later distributions of round barrows and urnfields, respectively, almost entirely confined to Norfolk on the one hand and Suffolk and Essex on the other, which supports the former point. Such distribution also implies use of secondary agricultural areas like the Breckland and the Boulder Clay lands, perhaps to be compared with indications of the use of similar secondary, if not yet marginal, land in the Tertiary soils of

---

[71] RCHM, *A Matter of Time*; *Peterborough New Town*, 1969, *Northamptonshire I*; Trent Valley Archaeological Research Committee, *Annual Reports 1967–* , and see J. Hampton in Wilson (ed.), *Aerial Reconnaissance for Archaeology*, pp. 120–1, figs. 2 and 3.

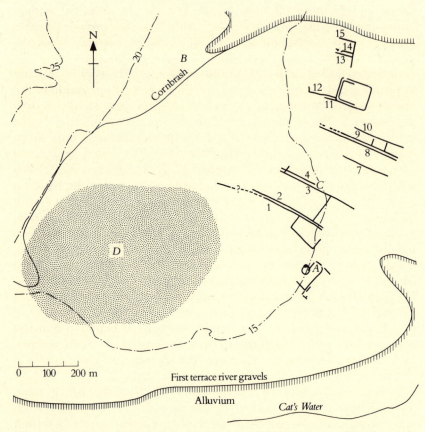

Fig. 11. Plan of excavated and crop-mark features at Fengate, just east of Peterborough. Nos. 1–4 and 7–15 are Bronze Age field ditches. *A*, Late Neolithic/Early Bronze Age settlement; *B*, Iron Age settlement; *C*, Beaker occupation features; *D*, approximate location of Neolithic and Iron Age settlement area (after F. Pryor).

Wessex and the North York Moors (above, p. 46 and below, pp. 173–6). Once again, however, it must be stressed in East Anglia that the settlement and, more particularly, the agrarian use of a region is being inferred from indirect evidence, mainly of funereal type and of portable material, in face of the great scarcity of actual settlement structures and direct agricultural evidence.[72]

North and east of the River Trent, the existence and distribution of relevant evidence has now been clarified by two important surveys on

[72] R. R. Clarke, *East Anglia*, London, 1960, is the most recent general survey; now overtaken by events – see the county journals and the new *East Anglian Archaeology*, 1974– .

which the following summary is very largely based.[73] The Carboniferous Limestone Peak District is geologically and topographically a great contrast with East Anglia but the state of knowledge about its agrarian history is similar. The stone monuments characterizing the area have in many cases at least been surveyed, and many of the barrows have been dug into, mostly last century, but the amount of reliable earlier agrarian information is very limited indeed. Although the wide distribution of surface-worked flints indicates upland land-use, few actual settlements and contemporary fields have been identified. Some of the caves were, however, inhabited, but their significance in the settlement distribution is not clear, mainly through lack of comparable evidence from 'open' sites. The point is emphasized by the current work in the Bar Brook area of Big Moor, where a settlement under excavation is one of the few of 'Bronze Age' date to be identified in the region (Plate IIIb).[74] Between Trent and Tyne, only nine 'extensive settlements' of the period have been claimed, though none is securely dated. Characterized by areas of scattered stone mounds (cairns or stone clearance heaps) irregular lengths of walling, and possible burial or occupation structures, these sites are difficult to recognize and interpret, but they represent a distinctive type of settlement evidence in northern Britain, which, by and large, can probably be referred to a time before the establishment of Sub-Atlantic climatic conditions and, therefore, to second or early first millennium date.

In the whole of northern England (Fig. 12) there is, purely in terms of the known distribution of surviving evidence, a marked dichotomy between upland and lowland areas, i.e. the crude distribution seems to echo the situation south of the Trent and the Wash. Surface evidence exists, or is known to have existed, on most of the high areas though not in the highest and most mountainous parts, e.g. the Lakeland mountain peaks. From the second millennium, certainly or presumptively, field evidence has been recorded or proposed from the Yorkshire Dales, the North York Moors, and some Cumbrian Fells in, for example, Furness. The type of 'extensive settlement' defined above is known in all three areas, with a scattering of 'isolated hut' sites along the Yorkshire coast and likewise on the lower hills west of the Pennines. But, while there are hints of communities living and farming in the valleys, not least from palynological studies, good archaeological evidence is to hand so far only in isolated examples (Fig. 13). While

[73] A. J. Challis and D. W. Harding, *Later Prehistory from the Trent to the Tyne*, British Archaeological Reports, 20 (i and ii), Oxford, 1975; P. A. G. Clack and P. F. Gosling, *Archaeology in the North*, Durham, 1976.

[74] A. Butterworth (ed.), *Archaeological Field Guide*, Sheffield, 1970, pp. 16–19 inc. two plans; *Trans. Hunter. Archaeol. Soc.*, 10, 1971, pp. 5–13.

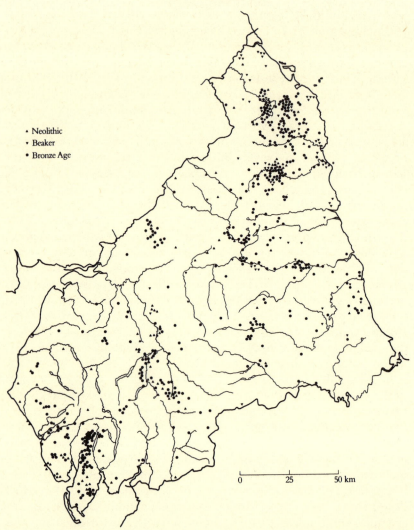

Fig. 12. Northern England, showing the general distribution of known sites, Neolithic–Iron Age (after P. A. G. Clack and P. F. Gosling).

therefore extensive use, probably locally intensive, of what is now moorland is evidenced in the mid and late second millennium in parts of Yorkshire and Cumbria, the incidence of other evidence is so far sparse or non-existent for much of the area between Trent and Tyne. Such a fact, however, should not totally obscure interpretive possibilities, not least in considering the implication of the upland bias in the distribution of the attested evidence.

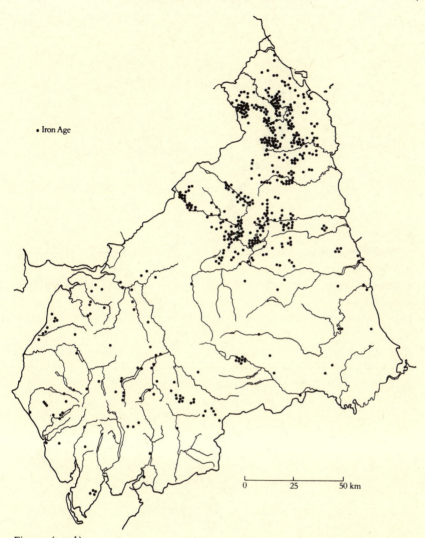

• Iron Age

0   25   50 km

Fig. 12 (*contd.*)

North of the Tees not just the second but also the first millennia are
so poorly represented in County Durham that the River Tyne has been
suggested as a 'cultural boundary' in later prehistory. There is, however,
very little field evidence from either County Durham, or Northumberland from the second millennium, though the latter has claimants in
its later centuries (Fig. 12). Earlier, the archaeological record is dominated
by the many Beaker burials, mostly in stone cists, tending to cluster

Neolithic

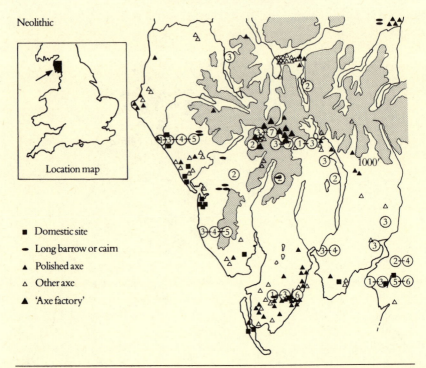

Location map

- ■ Domestic site
- ⬮ Long barrow or cairn
- ▲ Polished axe
- △ Other axe
- ▲ 'Axe factory'

Bronze Age

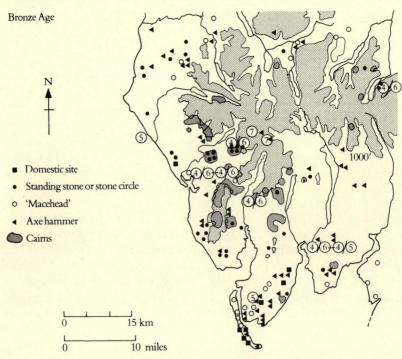

N

- ■ Domestic site
- ● Standing stone or stone circle
- ○ 'Macehead'
- ◀ Axe hammer
- ⬤ Cairns

0   15 km

0   10 miles

along the river valleys and the eastern coastal plain and particularly north of the River Coquet in the middle centuries of the millennium. As yet, this evidence lacks its settlement context. Round cairns, barrows, and cup-marked stones, in some quantity, can probably be referred to the centuries just before 1000 BC and it has also been opined that the origins of some of the settlements which appear in the first half of the first millennium may be sought during this time (below, p. 123). It is also possible that some of the cairn fields, of approximately 1000 BC in date, may be agrarian, by analogy with the Yorkshire examples, rather than funerary. Clearance of forest, well-evidenced in the second half of the second millennium in several studies in Cumbria and the Northumbrian moors, certainly pose the question of the date of their initial clearance.

The present border between Northumbria and Scotland has no significance in later prehistoric archaeology and the evidence immediately north of Cheviot is similar to that on its south, i.e. agriculturally sparse for the second millennium. Indeed the best published field evidence comes from Orkney and Shetland where, c. 1600 bc, cleared areas of presumptively arable land are still visibly associated with settlements (Fig. 14). Less conspicuous are examples of the recently recognized field systems associated with cairns or stone clearance heaps on the moorlands of southern and central Scotland and, from a Beaker horizon onwards, the vertical successions indicate occupation and changing land-usage at a few sand-dune sites along the Atlantic coast. Again the barrows, cairns, cup-marks, stone circles, and standing stones, together with a variety of conventional and portable archaeological material, attest what, by definition, must have been predominantly farming communities in second millennium Scotland, working in particular the eastern coastal plains perhaps; but direct agrarian evidence is sparse.[75]

Over second millennium Britain then, the picture from, on the whole, totally inadequate evidence is of widespread but generally patchy occupation and land-use. Certain areas, even whole regions,

[75] Of several books introducing Scotland's field archaeology, E. Mackie, *Scotland: An Archaeological Guide*, London, 1975, is the most recent.

Fig. 13. Environmental and archaeological evidence for land-use in the Lake District: (a) Neolithic; (b) Bronze Age. The numbers in circles indicate: (1) some interference with the forest cover before the Elm Decline, (2) Elm Decline without evidence for nearby clearance, (3) Elm Decline with evidence for nearby clearance, (4) a clearance phase after the Elm Decline, (5) arable farming inferred, (6) pastoral farming inferred, (7) peat bog formation. A horizontal line between figures indicates a sequence; an oblique stroke indicates synchronous changes. Land over 1000 ft (305 m) is hatched (after R. Bradley).

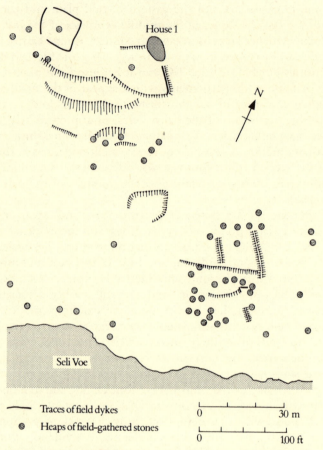

Fig. 14. House, arable plots and clearance cairns at Gruting, Shetland (after C. S. T. Calder).

stand out as supporting relatively intense and permanent settlement based on an agrarian economy: the major Midland river valleys, the chalk downlands and some of the uplands of the south-west. Elsewhere, we see hints of shifting agriculture and areas predominantly of pastoralists. Over the whole of the millennium, it seems probable that much of the primary agricultural land was used at least on occasions but it is impossible to know how much was in use simultaneously. At this stage we are mainly concerned to sketch in the nature of the evidence and its distribution, but we can already see that farming communities were active in all of the regions of Britain, that focal areas of more intensive land exploitation emerged or, in the case of Wessex, were consolidated during the second millennium BC, and that colonization of areas which had been marginal in Neolithic terms was proceeding.

First millennium BC

The landscape evidence of settlement in the last thousand years before the Roman conquest is much more plentiful than in the second millennium BC. Its most obvious manifestations are the 'hill-forts' of which well over a thousand have been identified.[76] Not all, however, originated after 1000 BC though it can be confidently asserted that the great majority was used at some time in the first millennium BC. In addition, hundreds of, on the whole smaller, unenclosed settlements are known, and thousands can reasonably be claimed to have existed in various regional forms.[77] Arable field systems have been plotted over many thousands of square kilometres (Plate IV), and it is now generally appreciated that even this extent is but a small fraction of the land that was under cultivation, periodically or otherwise, during these centuries. Furthermore, extensive areas of pasture, particularly in the north and west, must have existed, though their archaeological identification is difficult. Also difficult to find are the burial places of much of the population for most of the period, in marked contrast to the well-known types of burial site in the preceding millennium.

In the south-west, the settlement evidence on the ground exhibits a wide range of data, though the region notably lacks many of the objects which characterize the period elsewhere.[78] Settlements have survived in a variety of enclosed forms – cliff castles, hill-top 'forts', hill-slope forts, small rectangular and round enclosures – and in a variety of unenclosed forms, ranging from the nucleated "village' to the isolated hut.[79] The order of numbers of site complexes involved can at least be indicated as a result of the intensive, systematic survey of West Penwith in the further reaches of Cornwall, an order confirmed by subsequent field survey in other parts of the country.[80] While farmers may still have been cropping parts of Bodmin Moor and Dartmoor, the stone-walled fields and settlements were probably abandoned from early in the millennium, if not before. Large tracts of Dartmoor, for example, and indeed much of central Devon, contain virtually no known evidence of first millennium settlement at all.

Moving out of the south-western peninsula, regional variations in

[76] See n. 58, p. 94.

[77] OS, *Map of Southern Britain in the Iron Age*, Chessington, 1962.

[78] C. Thomas, 'The character and origins of Roman Dumnonia', in C. Thomas (ed.), *Rural Settlement in Roman Britain*, CBA Research Report, 7, London, 1966, pp. 74–98.

[79] Aileen Fox, *South West England*, provides a recent survey with references.

[80] V. Russell, *West Penwith Survey*, Truro, 1971; C. Thomas, 'The present significance of fieldwork in the light of the Cornish parochial check-list survey', in P. J. Fowler (ed.), *Archaeology and the Landscape*, pp. 75–95; *Corn. Arch.*, 1, 1962– , *passim*.

settlement forms immediately begin to appear. The hill-slope forts peter out, cliff castles disappear, the 'rounds' are simply not present. Up the Severn Basin, we move into hill-fort country: Somerset alone has fifty and more, and two of the densest concentrations in Britain are along the Cotswolds and in the Hereford/Shropshire area. The sites are characterized as much by the size and multivallation of the enclosures as by their frequency. Some indeed, enclosing over 100 acres (over 40 ha), are so large as to defy a defensive function in any military sense and have been suggested as large pastoral enclosures.[81] Smaller enclosures, perhaps comparable in function to the Welsh 'raths', also exist, particularly in the areas of broken country fringing the main chalk and limestone massifs. We see, too, some low-lying enclosures, particularly in the Vale of Berkeley. Large and small unenclosed settlements are not so well-recorded, and, probably as a result, appear to be less frequent. Some are known, particularly from late in the period, fringing the Somerset Levels,[82] which themselves contain the much publicized 'lake villages' near Meare and Glastonbury, remarkable really for their state of preservation as excavated rather than as an exotic type of settlement. Above them in the Mendips some of the caves in the soluble Carboniferous Limestone were used for habitation, metal-working, and burial,[83] while on the same formation the evidence from one particular locality, Brean Down, shows how use of one preferred settlement area cuts across regional and typological distinctions.[84] The unenclosed settlements which surely existed on the Cotswolds are reluctant to appear, though recent intensive survey by the Royal Commission on Historical Monuments has demonstrated both the reality of some and the presence of field systems more numerous and extensive than the few previously recorded examples.[85] The Cotswolds also bear a new type of major settlement, belonging to the last decades before the Conquest: the so-called *oppida*, visible in outline at Bagendon,

[81] G. J. Wainwright, 'The Excavation of an Iron Age Hillfort on Bathampton Down, Somerset', *Trans. Bristol Glos. Arch. Soc.*, 86, 1967, pp. 42–59, esp. p. 57.

[82] H. and T. J. Miles, 'Settlement sites of the late pre-Roman Iron Age in the Somerset Levels', *Somerset Arch. Nat. Hist.*, 113, 1969, pp. 17–55.

[83] J. Campbell et al., *The Mendip Hills in Prehistoric and Roman Times*, Bristol, 1970; R. Atthill (ed.), *Mendip: A New Study*, Newton Abbot, 1976; A. and R. Everton, 'Hay Wood Cave burials, Mendip Hills, Somerset', *Proc. Univ. Bristol Spelaeol. Soc.*, 13(1), 1972, pp. 5–29.

[84] *Proc. Univ. Bristol Spelaeol. Soc.*, 9(2), 1961, pp. 67–136; 10(3), 1965, pp. 195–258; 14(2), 1976, pp. 141–54; field systems, P. J. Fowler (ed.), *Recent Work in Rural Archaeology*, fig. 8.5.

[85] RCHM, *Iron Age and Roman Monuments in the Gloucestershire Cotswolds*, London, 1977.

north of Cirencester, and on Minchinhampton Common as tracts of countryside partly enclosed by banks and ditches.[86]

The whole of the triangle containing central southern Britain, defined by the Channel to the south, and the mainly chalk uplands from Lyme Bay in the south-west up to the escarpment into the Upper Thames valley and down to their attenuation at Beachy Head, came to be dominated, as in a sense it is today, by about 160 hill-forts – an average of 1 per 135 sq. km (but see below, pp. 251–5). These enclosures range from the very large (250 + ha) and usually univallate, through the large/medium ones of c. 125 ha, usually univallate, down to sites enclosing less than c. 10 ha. Some in this 'small' group fall into distinctive types like 'Little Woodbury' and 'banjo' enclosures; of these, some appear to be small enclosed farms, the Wessex equivalent to the Cornish 'round' (Fig. 15). There is a numerical shortage of settlements positively dated to the earlier centuries of this millennium, but after c. 600 BC the settlement evidence is almost quantitatively overwhelming and has not been synthesized regionally in detail. Often too the settlements exist in an archaeological context of ditches, field systems (Plate IV), and access networks, though seldom with their cemeteries (Fig. 16). The landscape appears to be thoroughly under control while being intensively exploited.[87] As in the Cotswolds, at the end of the period, *oppida* were added to the settlement diversity, with examples at Silchester, Winchester, and Selsey.

To the east is not so much visible evidence, though surface finds, excavation, and documentary evidence indicate that here too was a large rural population, albeit unevenly distributed. The Weald, for example, although exploited for iron, does not seem to have been densely occupied; and the low-lying area at the north foot of the South Downs is practically devoid of evidence. Fringing the North Downs, and along the Kentish coasts, however, is a spread of material continuing northwards into the London Basin.[88] Though little evidence remains on the ground because of London's centrifugal expansion, precisely because of that expansion, and the dredging of the Thames, a great deal of first-millennium material has come to light. Indeed, all the way up the Thames valley, right back to the Cotswolds, is more than enough

[86] RCHM, *op. cit.*, pp. 6–9, 81–4. Cf. E. M. Clifford, *Bagendon, a Belgic Oppidum*, Cambridge, 1961; H. C. Bowen, 'Air photography: some implications in the south of England', in E. Fowler (ed.), *Field Survey in British Archaeology*, pp. 38–49, Pls. I and II; and *idem*, 'Air photography and the development of the landscape...', in Wilson (ed.), *Aerial Reconnaissance...*, pp. 103–18, figs. 14–16. B. Cunliffe and T. Rowley (eds.), *Oppida: the Beginnings of Urbanisation in Barbarian Europe*, Oxford, 1976.

[87] Bowen, 'Air photography...', *op. cit.*; and see references given in n. 67, p. 99.

[88] See n. 68, p. 101.

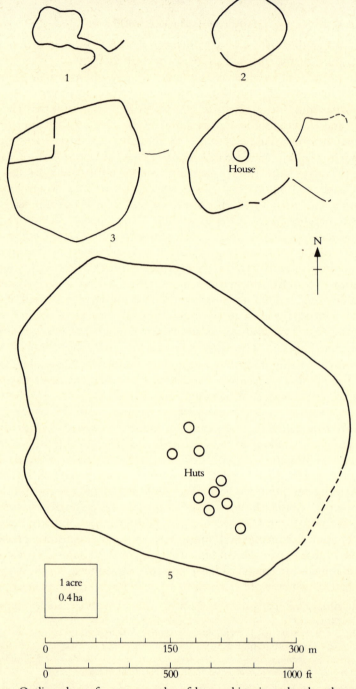

1

2

House

3

N

Huts

5

1 acre
0.4 ha

0   150   300 m

0   500   1000 ft

Fig. 15. Outline plans of some examples of late prehistoric enclosed settlements in Wessex: (1) Blagden Copse, Hurstbourne Tarrant, Hants., (2) Mancombe Down, Warminster, Wilts., (3) Farley Mount, Ashley, Hants., (4) Little Woodbury, Britford, Wilts., (5) Hog Cliff Hill, Maiden Newton, Dorset (after H. C. Bowen).

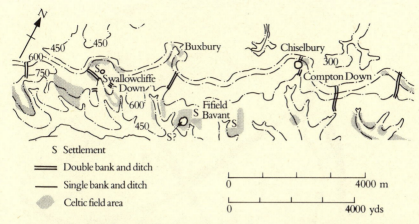

S   Settlement

===   Double bank and ditch

———   Single bank and ditch

▨   Celtic field area

Fig. 16. First-millennium land divisions defined by cross-ridge dykes on the Ebble–Nadder Ridge west of Salisbury, Wilts. S: Early Iron Age settlements (P. J. Fowler).

evidence to indicate that, from the middle of the millennium onwards at latest, it was intensively and probably continuously settled and farmed (Fig. 17).[89]

Broadly speaking, the distribution of settlement evidence thins out to the north. Along the continuation line of the Jurassic ridge north-eastwards into the Northamptonshire uplands only a dozen or so hill-forts are known, though detail of part of their context, particularly along the Nene valley, has recently been made available.[90] *Oppida* exist at Grim's Ditch in north Oxfordshire and at Braughing and Verulamium in Hertfordshire, with of course another further east at Colchester, Essex;[91] and right across the south-east Midlands, although sites surviving or known as earthworks are not as common as further south (Fig. 18), material and records are sufficiently frequent to indicate that, certainly late in the prehistoric period, the area was fairly intensely

[89] See n. 68, p. 101. The frequency of metal finds, including weapons, from the River Thames itself cannot surely all be explained as trans-riverine losses or 'ritual deposits': are not some settlement debris? Cf. C. B. Burgess, 'The Later Bronze Age in the British Isles and North Western France', *Arch. J.*, 125, 1968, pp. 1–45; E. M. Jope, 'Daggers of the Early Iron Age in Britain', *Proc. Prehist. Soc.*, 27, 1961, pp. 307–43, and 'The beginnings of La Tène Ornamental Style in the British Isles', and S. S. Frere (ed.), *Problems of the Iron Age in Southern Britain*, London, 1961, pp. 69–83; and D. W. Harding, *The Iron Age in the Upper Thames Basin*, Oxford, 1972. I acknowledge subsequent information and re-assurance on this point from R. Bradley.

[90] RCHM, *Northamptonshire*, I, 1975.

[91] Cunliffe and Rowley, *op. cit.*, esp. the paper by W. Rodwell which very considerably expands this curt sentence.

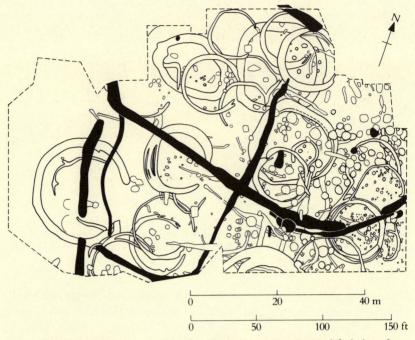

Fig. 17. Ashville Trading Estate, Abingdon, Berks. (now Oxon); simplified plan of part of unexcavated multi-period settlement complex on Second Terrace gravel in the Thames valley. This particular area was occupied by two ring-ditches in the second millennium and then successively occupied in two main phases through the second half of the first millennium. All features belonging to these three main phases, together with undated features, are shown in outline only. In the late first century BC/early first century AD, the area was divided up by linear ditches (solid black), apparently forming arable fields. Subsequent fields of the Roman period are not shown (after M. Parrington).

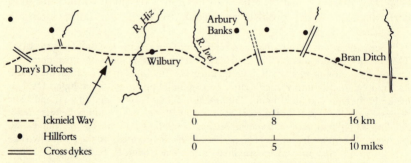

Fig. 18. Multiple lines of ditches crossing the course of the Icknield Way in the eastern Chilterns. Probably of late second or first millennium date, they have been interpreted as territorial boundaries (after J. F. Dyer).

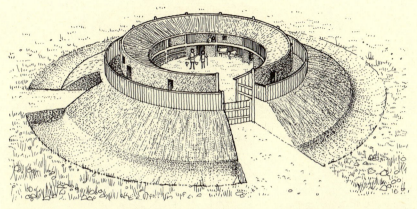

Fig. 19. A reconstruction of the West Harling Iron Age farmstead, assuming a penannular range of buildings around an open central courtyard instead of a conical roof over the whole. Approximate diameter between inner edges of ditch is 115 ft (35 m) (after J. R. C. Hamilton).

occupied. This is implied in particular by the evidence from burials in the century between the Invasions.[92]

To the north-east in East Anglia, the evidence becomes sporadic. Apart from some twenty or so hill-forts on the eastern extension of the Chilterns, little is visible on the surface, and fairly large areas of Suffolk and central Norfolk appear to be blank. A concentration of material around Cambridge is as likely to represent local antiquarian effort as a real centre, however; so presumably much in the region is yet to be discovered. By and large settlement evidence approximates to the line of the Icknield Way. A marked concentration along the Lark and Little Ouse valleys in the Mildenhall/Lakenheath/Thetford area includes the excavated West Harling settlement (Fig. 19) and several burial sites. Both here and further north, the late pre-Roman period is characterized by metal hoards of considerable wealth.[93]

A rather different situation exists over to the west in Wales.[94] In general, the country is one of hill-forts again, including many small embanked or stone-walled enclosures. They occur around much of the coastline, concentrating in the south-west, on the Gower and around the headwaters of the Severn. In the last area, they overlap with the otherwise almost distinct distribution of the larger hill-forts, spreading over and continuing northwards from the Herefordshire/Shropshire

[92] E.g. I. M. Stead, 'A La Tène III Burial at Welwyn Garden City', *Archaeologia*, 101, 1967, pp. 1–62.
[93] See n. 72, p. 104. Snettisham hoard, *Proc. Prehist. Soc.*, 20, 1954, pp. 27–86; 28, 1962, p. 20; 30, 1964, p. 280.   [94] For general reference, see p. 280 below.

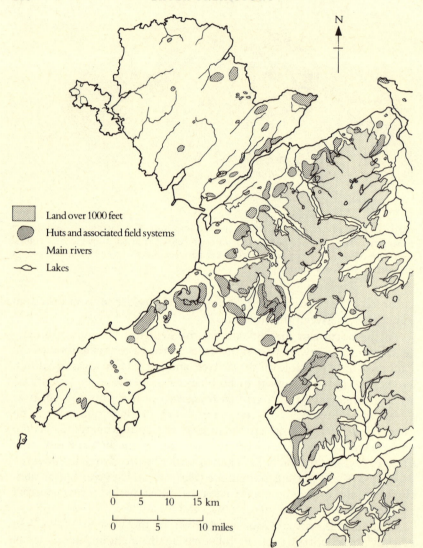

Fig. 20. Distribution of huts and associated field systems in relation to land above 1,000 ft (305 m) in north-west Wales (after N. D. Johnson).

group. Though the record is dominated by such sites, small enclosed sites of 'Iron Age' type have recently been photographed from the air in the valley of the Upper Severn[95] and some pre-Roman settlements of nucleated but mainly farmstead type exist in an apparently dispersed

[95] C. J. Spurgeon, 'Enclosures of Iron Age type in the Upper Severn Basin', in F. Lynch and C. Burgess (eds.), *Prehistoric Man in Wales and the West*, Bath, 1972, pp. 321–44.

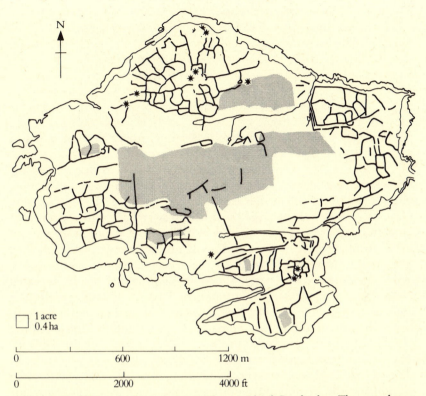

Fig. 21. Early fields and other remains on Skomer Island, Pembrokes. The central areas of stipple indicate ridge-and-furrow cultivation which has presumably flattened earlier field remains to give their present distribution its markedly peripheral character (after W. F. Grimes).

settlement pattern among the plentiful variety of field evidence collected from north Wales (Fig. 20).[96] In the extreme north-west, Anglesey has produced one of the best known and best dated of all iron hoards, from right at the end of 'Welsh prehistory', probably indicative of the fertility of the island from the farming point of view, then as now.[97] Field systems there, along much of the north Welsh littoral and sporadically elsewhere, as on Skomer Island (Fig. 21), are difficult to date, but certainly not all are of the Roman period.[98]

The west Midlands in the first millennium BC remain enigmatic.[99]

[96] RCAM, *Caernarvonshire*, I–III, 1956–64.
[97] C. Fox, *A Find of the Early Iron Age from Llyn Cerrig Bach, Anglesey*, Cardiff, 1946.
[98] Cf. pp. 176, 188 below; Skomer: *Arch. Camb.*, 101, 1951, pp. 1–20.
[99] No overall synthesis is available but see A. J. Challis and D. W. Harding, *Later Prehistory from the Trent to the Tyne*, Oxford, 1975, and Cunliffe, *Iron Age Communities in Britain*; and, for the end of the period, G. Webster, *The Cornovii*, London, 1975.

There are few earthwork sites but hints exist of early occupation on hill-tops, perhaps with enclosures. Much more plentiful is the air photographic evidence, particularly, but not entirely, from river valleys. The relatively little excavation of such evidence so far indicates second millennium activity, but suggests that widespread exploitation, perhaps after some forest regeneration, was later in the first millennium and in the Roman period. The generalization appears to be gaining some support from the current excavation at Beckford, Worcs., in the Carrant valley near Tewkesbury.[100] A straight length of ditch 124 m long has a mid second millennium C-14 date (Birm. 431), suggesting the possibility of a land allotment function similar to that argued for linear structures in very different situations on Dartmoor, the Wessex Chalk, and the Fengate fen-edge (below, p. 236). The occupation principally evidenced belongs, however, to an archaeologically complex settlement of the third to first centuries BC, followed by further activity in the Roman period, when the site was probably covered by a ditched field system. A pointer to what may have been happening in the region generally earlier in the first millennium is provided by the repeated observation of a stone-free, inorganic, buff-red clayey silt at the top of alluvial sections in the Lower Severn/Avon valleys. This, it is suggested, could be the result of widespread clearance followed by regular ploughing on the slopes of the valleys upstream from the flood-plains. The date for the deposition of the silt is *c.* 600 bc.[101]

In the east Midlands, the general picture is broadly similar with some clearance in the second millennium, partial regeneration, and the major forest removal from the mid first millennium onwards. Since most of the air photographic evidence, especially in the valleys of the Trent and Welland,[102] has not been tested, any generalization at the moment must be cautiously made. Apart from the countless settlements, which a guess would place mainly in the last centuries BC (Fig. 22) and the early centuries AD, currently undated field systems of regular appearance and wide extent have also been observed: whether they too fall into the planned landscapes of later prehistory (below, p. 151), or represent Roman mensuration, for example, is unknown. On balance, a later date seems more likely, but in any case there can be little doubt that much of the region was supporting extensive mixed-farming communities by the end of the prehistoric period. The complexities and local variety behind such a generalization are well illustrated by the current excavation of, and interim results from, the settlement at Dragonby, Lincolns., in

[100] *Curr. Arch.*, 45, 1974, pp. 293–7.
[101] F. W. Shotton, 'Archaeological inferences from the study of alluvium in the Lower Severn–Avon valleys', in Limbrey and Evans (eds.), CBA Research Report, 21, pp. 27–32.   [102] RCHM, *A Matter of Time*; see n. 71, p. 103.

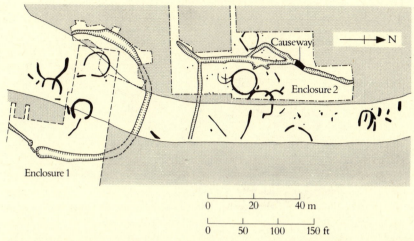

Fig. 22. Settlement complex on clay discovered, extensively exposed and partly excavated during industrial development at Moulton Park, Northampton. Enclosure 1 contained at least two successive late prehistoric houses; Enclosure 2, also with 'Belgic'-type pottery, contained at least three houses and a possible one lay to the west of it (after J. H. Williams and D. C. Mynard).

the north of the region. A fact about the whole area is the scarcity of hill-forts: they simply do not dominate the landscape as is the case to the south and in the Tyne–Forth province to the north. It is difficult to see what, if anything, takes their place, since no one settlement type predominates. While there may be environmental or social reasons for this, possibly the development of nucleation, and a stable settlement pattern in the region, occurred after the period at which the expression of such trends was witnessed structurally by the building of major centres. As has been remarked, no timber-framed rampart north of the Midlands appears to be later than the mid fifth century;[103] whereas all down the eastern side of England from the Tyne to the Wash, despite plentiful scattered evidence of farming earlier, the development of an enclosed and much-used landscape, with a consequential impression of a rapidly rising population, seems to occur in the last two centuries or so BC.

Some 150 hill-top enclosures nevertheless have been recorded between the Trent and the Tyne, mostly along the Pennines and especially their eastern edges. Mam Tor in the southern Pennines appears to have been occupied towards the end of the second millennium, and subsequently enclosed with a palisade and two superimposed ramparts, but otherwise much of the area was probably extensively cleared of forest during the

[103] Challis and Harding, *op. cit.*, p. 110.

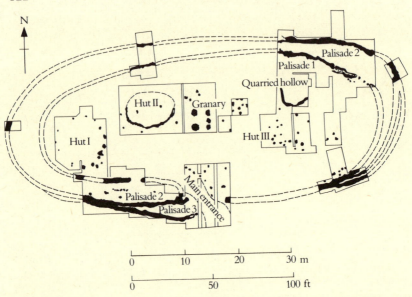

Fig. 23. Plan as excavated of the mid first millennium settlement at Staple Howe, East Riding, Yorks. (after T. C. M. Brewster).

later centuries BC, the major occupation again following during the early centuries AD. Further north, bare pavement limestone and little archaeological field evidence tend to characterize the high Pennine moors of the first millennium BC, while to the east the Wolds do not appear to exhibit the evidence for land pressure again until the late prehistoric period. Hill-forts are virtually absent, the excavated example at Grimthorpe, both stressing the point and raising problems about its functions in the light of its somewhat anomalous evidence, generally dating to the period after *c.* 1000 bc. A somewhat later settlement at Staple Howe is claimed to be typical of small enclosed occupation sites in the area, following a mixed economy of cattle-raising and cereal growing (Figs. 23, 24). A pit in it containing grain is a useful indicator of arable farming on the north-east in the fifth/sixth centuries, particularly as grain itself is only recorded from four other sites in the Trent–Tyne area (below, p. 206). By the end of the millennium, and then on into the Roman period, a 'completely enclosed landscape' is envisaged with linear boundaries dividing up the land, probably for pastoral purposes, with arable, with cemeteries, and with nucleated settlements. The North York Moors, another relatively well-studied area, lack substantive evidence of the earlier first millennium and hill-forts like Eston Nab are peripheral. Again the development of the

Fig. 24. Impression of the Staple Howe settlement in its final phase of occupation (after T. C. M. Brewster).

landscape seems to be a late prehistoric phenomenon represented best by a few field systems, linear earthworks, and beehive querns.

Over the five northern counties generally, the first millennium has proved difficult to recognize archaeologically, though, in some respects, the situation is now changing rapidly (Fig. 12). A scattered population mainly involved in a pastoral economy seems to be implied by the sparse evidence from Lancashire, Westmorland, and Cumberland: "the final prehistoric period... still holds its secrets so far as the Lake Counties are concerned".[104] Such 'secrets' may be beginning to be exposed through an increasing amount of fieldwork, excavation, and air photography (below, p. 189).[105] Meanwhile "hill-fort communities began early here too" and "there is evidence for continued arable farming in the Cumberland Lowlands throughout the 1st millennium B.C.".[106] Over the moors to the east, recent success in identifying first-millennium sites is showing what can be achieved in a 'blank' area by systematic, long-term, and thorough investigation. In County Durham, the excavated enclosed homestead at West Brandon (Fig. 25) is now seen as but

[104] C. Fell, *Early Settlement in the Lake Counties*, Clapham, Yorks., 1972, p. 43. Pp. 36–43 summarize the first millennium BC.
[105] *Curr. Arch.*, 53, 1975, p. 183. Recent work, N. J. Higham and G. D. B. Jones, 'Frontier, forts and farmers...', *Arch. J.*, 132, 1975, pp. 16–53.
[106] Challis and Harding, *op. cit.*, p. 180.

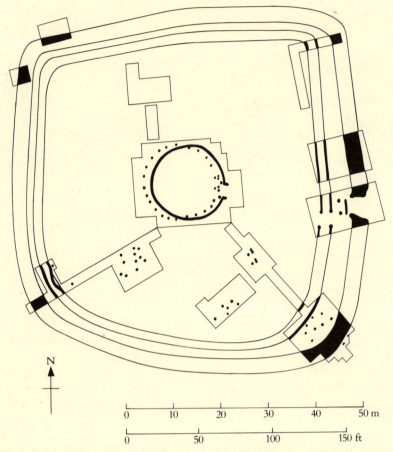

Fig. 25. Excavation plan of enclosed Early Iron Age settlement at West Brandon, County Durham (after G. Jobey).

one of "over a dozen comparable enclosures, mainly on drift-covered central Durham, indicating a pattern of scattered homestead settlement".[107] The possibility of complex ditched settlements, familiar further south, is also envisaged. Across the Tyne in Northumberland and north to Cheviot and southern Scotland, the archaeological picture changes dramatically to one of relatively plentiful evidence in the field though chronology and artifact study continue to be problematical. As in Cumbria, early first-millennium settlements can be suspected under at least some of the many hill-top enclosures which, as now visible, are probably in many cases of the later centuries BC. Certainly, however,

[107] Ibid., p. 182.

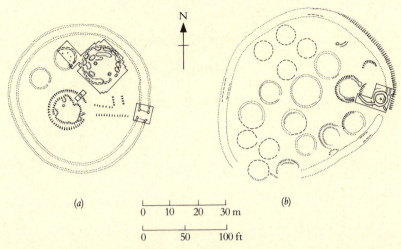

Fig. 26. First-millennium settlements at High Knowes, Alnham, Northumbd: (*a*) showing double palisade, excavated houses and entrance; (*b*) showing palisaded enclosure packed with circular timber buildings, and an excavated, later, stone-walled hut to the east (after G. Jobey and J. Tait).

palisaded enclosures were being constructed in the earlier and middle centuries of the millennium (Fig. 26), followed by stone-walled enclosures often on the same sites as at Huckhoe. Some of the cairn fields may also belong to this period, but of permanent field systems there is so far no record. An economy based on cattle and sheep is therefore envisaged as the basis for a growing population in a generally scattered but locally dense settlement pattern.[108]

Such a generalization also applies to other parts of Scotland, though of course much of the mountainous country was unoccupied and indeed uninhabitable. The variety of settlement type is reasonably well known, ranging from palisaded enclosures and the major hill-fort, Traprain Law, in the south east – an area culturally forming a 'Tyne–Forth province' at least in respect of its field monuments – to local adaptations in stone, notably duns, brochs, and wheel-houses in the west and north (Fig. 27). The remarkable hill-fort concentration between Tyne and Forth stretches down to the south-west along the coasts of Dumfriesshire and Galloway, merging with the southern end of the duns mainly on the west coast and western islands. Brochs also occur to the west though

[108] Most of the relevant literature is synthesized and referenced in P. A. G. Clack and P. F. Gosling and in Challis and Harding, *op. cit.* A first essay on population considerations is G. Jobey, 'Notes on some population problems in the area between the two Roman Walls, 1', *Arch. Ael.*, 5th ser., 2, 1974, pp. 17–26.

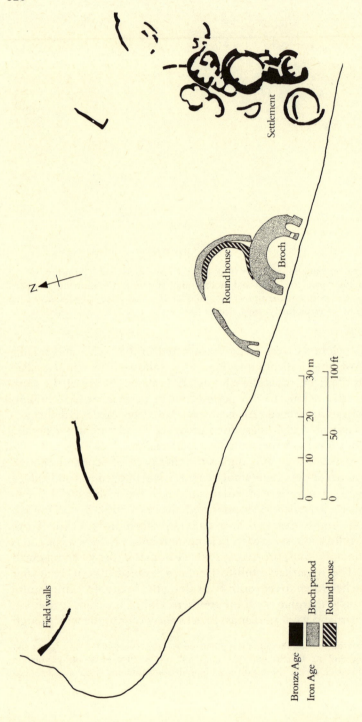

Fig. 27. Jarlshof, Shetland: the three earliest successive structural phases on a complex settlement occupied up to modern times. Occupation over the last 2,000 years has rendered fragmentary the later prehistoric remains (after J. R. C. Hamilton).

their main concentrations are in Sutherland and Caithness in the north east, and on Orkney and Shetland. Scattered through these distributions are vitrified structures of various types, the common denominator being the timber-lacing in their enclosing stonework. Overall, the distribution of these sites surviving as field monuments is markedly coastal and riverine, generally avoiding the mountains and the extensive areas of peat moors and acid grasslands. In the first millennium, as now, they were presumably unusable for farming. The same assumption cannot, however, be made about the other major area apparently 'avoided' by surviving sites, basically the triangle dominated by Aberdeenshire and Angus, east of a line between Perth and Inverness. Here the relative scarcity of settlement archaeology surely reflects land-use in the traditional oats and barley producing area of Scotland. Long-continued arable farming here suggests that much archaeological evidence has been destroyed; also that here too in the first millennium BC, farming is likely to have existed and indeed to have been successful. In other words, eastern Scotland interpretatively faces a problem familiar in eastern and southern England. Some of the settlement evidence which is known, such as the sites with souterrains near Dundee, supports the thesis, and certainly the air photographic surveillance essentially aimed at Roman military history shows the buried existence of former 'native' structures in some numbers.[109] A detailed study of the problem of archaeological distribution in Perthshire makes the point quite clearly.[110]

This briefest of regional summaries serves merely to sketch where the primarily archaeological evidence is for farming in Britain in the first millennium BC, with some slight indication of its nature. There are clear variations between and within regions in the distribution and nature of the evidence, both as originally created, and in its availability for modern study. Clearly too the methods of study have changing emphases from region to region – here a greater dependence on excavation, there on air photography – and, as we shall increasingly see, there have of course been changing interpretations of the evidence through time. As the quantity and, in some respects, the quality of the evidence changes now, and as the objectives of research change too, inevitably different parts of the evidence change in significance in some students' eyes. It would easily be possible to put forward very different interpretations at the moment. Certainly exceptions and even objections could be advanced for every generalization ventured. Nevertheless, as far as the first millennium BC is concerned, in agrarian terms two main

[109] D. R. Wilson, in J. G. Evans et al., CBA Research Report, 11, p. 110.

[110] J. B. Stevenson, in J. G. Evans et al., op. cit., pp. 104–8; and general Scottish references (below, p. 280). Cf. also Vol. I, Part II, pp. 191 n. A modern historical geography, a bit short on later prehistory (pp. 50–2) but with a good bibliography, is R. N. Millman, The Making of the Scottish Landscape, London, 1975.

points seem worth suggesting from the welter of data available. The first is merely quantitative: there *is* not only a huge mass of information, only lightly skimmed here, but it is enormously greater in volume than that available for the second millennium. Yet, curiously at first sight, but leading to the second point, it is not as widespread. The implication seems unavoidable: in the first millennium less land was farmed much more intensively while other land previously exploited was abandoned. In other words, the first millennium saw farming activity concentrated into a relatively restricted number of regions, areas, even localities, where it could be best pursued; and a marked intensification of effort and increase of population occurred in those places. The pattern of settlement which developed as a result persists today – 'the drift to the south-east' – and provided the basic settlement framework in pre-industrial Britain. Of course, parts of the pattern fell into place and became permanent at different times during the last ten prehistoric centuries: continuous farming on the open Sussex Downs cannot seriously be doubted throughout the millennium, for example, while the indications of widespread woodland clearance and settlement nucleation in the east Midlands and further north are cumulatively convincing. Equally, however, certain elements such as some early hill-top enclosures failed to meet the needs of a dynamic situation, and were already ancient monuments by 500 BC.; and elements apparently essential or at least accepted in some areas were not needed in others. The type of permanent field system which developed in Wessex, for example, is not very apparent in the East Riding of Yorkshire; the hill-slope forts of Devon and Cornwall were not appropriate in East Anglia; the rath type of settlement of the farmers in south-west Wales was not the choice of the communities in north-east Scotland. And why were not brochs built in the Cotswolds? – the building stone available was ideal for the purpose. Such archaeological diversity is so well established that to draw attention to it is almost to utter truisms; but as this diversity found expression in these thousand years, some of it prospered and some of it died. Nor was its creation solely a matter of straightforward environmental adaptation, however basic that was; otherwise there *would* be brochs on the Cotswolds. Even if, as will be argued later (below, p. 247), and is already suggested by this summary review, the establishment of a Sub-Atlantic climatic regime was *the* crucial factor in the overall distribution of settlement and pattern of land-use that emerges in the last millennium BC, a compound of cultural factors of both tradition and a willingness to experiment is also apparent. That admitted, then it can be argued that, however anachronistic the phraseology, the farming communities of later pre-history developed an ecological relationship with their environment, and perhaps it is that which, overall, the distribution of settlement represents to us about life 3,000–2,000 years ago.

FARMS AND FARM BUILDINGS

In Part II of this volume (pp. 122–205) three chapters are devoted to, repectively, 'Houses', 'Byres and Stables', and 'Farms and their Uses'. Here no such extended treatment is attempted, though with regret. The reasons are as follows. First, the very concept of a farm, with or without farm buildings, could well be inappropriate in later prehistory, at least in any sense which is meaningful to us. That the author is not alone in this suspicion is rather suggested by the infrequency with which the word 'farm' is used in British prehistoric archaeological writings, the neutral word 'settlement' being much preferred and the frequently used synonym 'homestead' indicating an interpretive bias towards a domestic rather than an agrarian function. The later prehistoric farm has in fact still to be defined, both for us and on its own terms.[111] Secondly, much of the evidence from settlements relevant to a consideration of later prehistoric farms both as an idea and as attested by published and physically surviving data has been made available in convenient, accessible, and reliable forms while this book was in preparation: there seems little point in repeating the same data in a work intended to be synoptic.[112] Thirdly, the very considerable amount of current investigation is not yet ready for synthesis, so that it would be premature to try to supersede these recent statements;[113] any such attempt would be either repetitive or, if consciously innovatory, certainly incomplete and probably wrong. And fourthly, as implied by the first reason, although we can discuss settlements and their contents, including the buildings, the subject of later prehistoric farms has simply not yet been researched. For a farm consists not just of a group of

[111] Harding, *The Iron Age in Lowland Britain*, Section 2, probably now best synthesizes the evidence for one area; R. W. Feachem, *The North Britons*, London, 1965, and *Guide to Prehistoric Scotland*, London, 1963, 2nd ed. London, 1977, and Rivet (ed.), *The Iron Age in Northern Britain*, describe and discuss northern 'farms' with full bibliographies. Conscious attempts to define and discuss specific later prehistoric farms are to be found in the work of G. Bersu, R. Bradley, H. C. Bowen, Aileen Fox and G. Jobey, see the Bibliography (below, pp. 289–98).

[112] Syntheses: Simpson (ed.), *Economy and Settlement*; Cunliffe, *Iron Age Communities in Britain*; Harding, *The Iron Age in Lowland Britain*. The 'Bronze Age' or second millennium lacks a comparable work though R. Bradley and A. Ellison, *Rams Hill: a Bronze Age Defended Enclosure and its Landscape*, British Archaeological Reports, 19, Oxford, 1975, is a major site study for the Wessex chalk country, assembling much evidence of wider significance.

[113] For examples of current work, obviously not yet published definitively, cf. *Curr. Arch. passim* e.g. 53, 1975, pp. 166–71 (Bishopstone, Sussex) and 50, 1975, pp. 81–94.

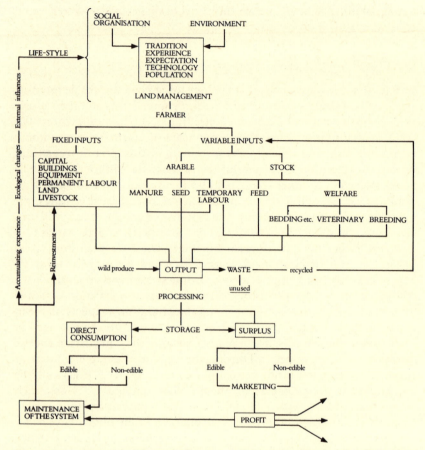

Fig. 28. A simple model of the main factors and their relationships in a farming system (P. J. Fowler).

buildings but also of the resources around it which made possible the act of farming and, further, the maintenance of a group livelihood at however minimal a level (Fig. 28). With very few exceptions, none of which is wholly successful or yet complete, such problem-orientated research has not been carried out.

A very few settlements that could arguably be farms have been completely excavated, many in the same category have been partly excavated, a large number have been surveyed and the great majority of known potential candidates exist on air photographs. On the other hand, recent work in studying landscapes has progressed well but so far without achieving the detail necessary to demonstrate convincingly the workings of an individual farm in its landscape, never mind its social, context.[114] In some respects some of the most useful recent work to this end has been theoretical[115] and experimental, though it has been in the current attempt to try to establish a working experimental farm of *c*. 300 BC (Plate I*b*) 'for education and research' that some of the most acute theoretical and practical problems have been encountered.[116] In many respects, even for the Wessex Middle Iron Age with its quantity of evidence, much of it relatively well recorded and well excavated, the data are not good enough to form an operating base. What validity is there to be sought for earlier times where the evidence is less and often not as good? It would therefore be fanciful to pretend that the subject of 'farms and farm buildings' can be realistically tackled here in the absence of the data-base and the confidence which inspired Chapters VIII–X of 'Roman Britain' in Part II. The following remarks, with all diffidence, relate to only a few selected aspects of the topic, mainly in acknowledgement of the fact that the topic itself is fundamental to an understanding of agrarian history in later prehistoric Britain.

We can only guess at the social, legal, tenurial, and customary constraints which governed the running of later prehistoric farms in human terms; an assessment based on environmental and physical evidence, which is all that can reasonably be attempted, may well be missing the crucial factor (Fig. 28). Nevertheless, a farm can be considered at three levels: in the sense of a 'catchment area' attached to a small community, as a group of buildings (or a single multi-purpose building) central to a localized agrarian economy, and as a series of related buildings with different functions. Our ignorance of the first and last levels in later prehistoric Britain is impressive; at the second level a little can be said, particularly for the last centuries BC. In considering the farm in an extended sense, however, the 'catchment area' model

[114] Recently excavated and illuminating examples of later prehistoric 'farms' include those at Gussage All Saints; Berwick Down, Tollard Royal; Chalton; Shearplace Hill; West Brandon: see Site Index (below, p. 282). 'Landscape' studies include those by Jobey (1968) and Jobey and Tait (1968), Bradley and Ellison (1975) and Lynch (1974), examples being at Chalton, Fyfield, Gwithian and the Somerset Levels: see Bibliography and Site Index (below, pp. 280–98).

[115] From a vast literature see generally M. Chisholm, *Rural Settlement and Land Use*, London, 1966; 2nd ed. London, 1968, P. Haggett, *Locational Analysis in Human Geography*, London, 1965; 2nd ed. 1976, and D. L. Clarke (ed.), *Models in Archaeology*, London, 1972; and specifically, Ellison and Harris, 'Settlement and land use...' and Clarke, 'A provisional model...', in D. L. Clarke (ed.), *op. cit.*, pp. 801–69 and 911–62.

[116] There is so far no substantial or definitive publication about or from the Project for Research and Education on Little Butser Hill, Hants.; but see the *Annual Reports* of the promoting British Assoc./Council for British Archaeology Committee, 1973– (duplicated) and P. J. Reynolds, 'Experimental Iron Age storage pits: an interim report', *Proc. Prehist. Soc.*, 40, 1974, pp. 118–31.

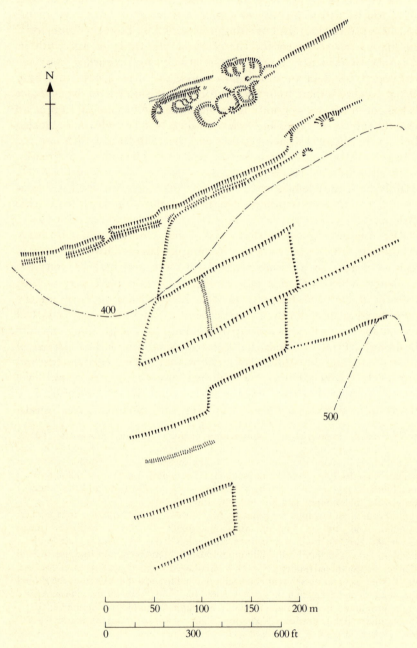

Fig. 29. Itford Hill, Sussex: plan of the settlement of *c.* 1000 bc with adjacent fields and barrow (after G. P. Burstow and G. A. Holleyman, and P. Drewett).

is too static or at least it has to be understood as a series of overlapping and differently shaped areas from within which the farm drew its resources. A farm like that at Gruting, Shetland (Fig. 14), for example, may well have had its arable scattered in patches immediately around it, but it may have been exploiting a much more extensive inland area for feeding its stock, while at the same time gaining its marine food from an extended length of the shore in the other direction. Similarly, while the classic late prehistoric farms (if such they be) at Itford Hill, Sussex (Fig. 29) and Little Woodbury (Figs. 15, 36), Wilts. were, respectively, certainly and presumably surrounded by their much more regular 'Celtic' fields, we do not know that that was their only arable. Furthermore, we can confidently argue that some of their basic needs, like water for stock, hay for winter feed, timber for building, stone for tools, clay for pottery, the materials for daubing walls and sealing pits, and the salt for preserving food, were being met only through a complex series of movements drawing on a widely diversified series of habitats in different directions over an extensive area. Since we cannot really identify confidently the farmlands in the narrow sense of the land directly farmed from, perhaps belonging to the inhabitants of Itford Hill and Little Woodbury, since we cannot assume that even that land formed a single block of land anyway, and since we do not know how the land was owned, it is impossible to consider usefully the idea of a farm in the extended sense implied by the list of necessary materials above. One can guess that some resources might have been derived from 'rights' in the medieval sense, e.g. of bocage, thus drawing the vital distinction between land owned and access to resources outside that land; and presumably entirely non-local material like salt and fine metalwork represents the exchange of goods and services. The only certainties are negative at this level: that all is yet to be learnt, that past reality is unlikely to have been encompassed within the radius of a 2 km circle about the site, and that the idea of the self-sufficient farm, even when we have defined 'farm' in this extended sense, will have to be looked at very carefully indeed.[117]

At the second level of 'farm' as a particular type of settlement – small, detached, and containing a group of buildings and other agricultural features – archaeology has been more successful. Particularly in the recent excavations of Dr G. J. Wainwright, the evidence can be interpreted convincingly in terms of farms. The late pre-Roman settlement on Berwick Down, Tollard Royal, Wilts. (Fig. 30), is a classic example in its structural simplicity: the house, the other timber structures, the pits, the 'working hollows', the open area which is

[117] Discussion of some aspects of this problem occurs in the work of H. C. Bowen and G. Jobey and Bradley and Ellison, *Rams Hill*. See Bibliography (below, p. 289).

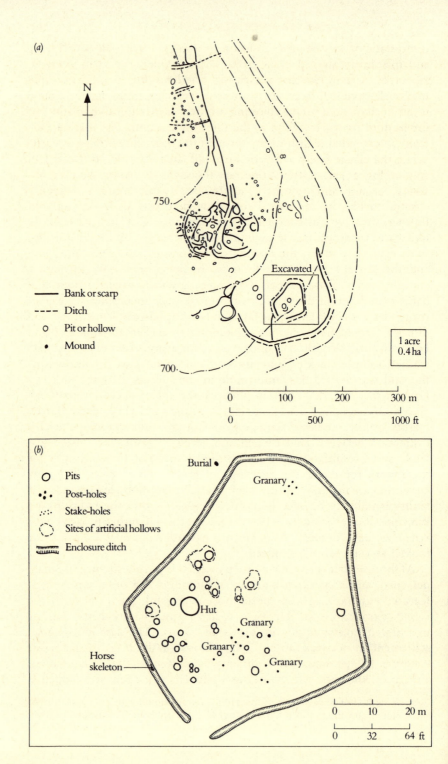

(a)

N

750.

700.

Excavated

— Bank or scarp
--- Ditch
o Pit or hollow
• Mound

1 acre
0.4 ha

0   100   200   300 m

0   500   1000 ft

(b)

Burial •

Granary

o Pits
•.•. Post-holes
.:.: Stake-holes
(○) Sites of artificial hollows
⁗ Enclosure ditch

Hut

Granary

Granary

Granary

Horse
skeleton

0   10   20 m

0   32   64 ft

presumably the farmyard – it looks like what a farm should be upon excavation. While other excavated sites like Gussage All Saints, Dorset (the only other settlement in the south to be totally excavated) (Fig. 31), Walesland Rath, Pembs. (Fig. 32), and Staple Howe, east Yorks. (Figs. 23, 24), are structurally more complex, generally their interpretation as farms is satisfactory up to the point of asking 'What sort of farm?' and 'How did they work?' Similarly in the south-west, notably at Trevisker and Kestor, in Wessex (Plate V), at Shearplace Hill, Dorset, and Chalton, Hants., in the east at West Harling (Fig. 19), Cambs., Draughton and Northampton (Fig. 33) and Colsterworth, Lincolnshire, and in the north in the persistently revealing work of G. Jobey, notably at West Brandon, County Durham (Fig. 25), and Alnham, Northumb. (Fig. 26), we can see sites which can be added to a select list of excavated later prehistoric farms. The list could be further extended with other examples from England, Scotland, and Wales but even so it would not contain more than three or four dozen names. However, arising from this evidence recently synthesized elsewhere,[118] just two aspects are raised here which again suggest limits to current appreciation. In the first place, most of the reliably excavated 'farms' were enclosed sites and therefore usually detected by characteristic earthworks or air photographic evidence. While in certain areas, e.g. the Tyne–Forth province (but cf. Fig. 12) and south-west Wales, it is conceivable that enclosed sites were the characteristic settlement form in the overall pattern, in other areas e.g. East Anglia, the Thames valley, and Wessex, this was not the case. The available evidence may therefore be sufficiently biased as to be misleading at even the elementary level of morphological characterization of farms, especially in the second millennium. A second caveat concerns the characterization of farms as detached or isolated settlements. Present-day Bavarian villages, medieval English villages, and linear Romano-British villages must quickly dispel

[118] See references in n. 112, p. 129.

Fig. 30. Berwick Down. Tollard Royal, Wilts.

(a) Plan of the three adjacent settlements, from north to south, Early Iron Age (two phases), unenclosed with round houses, pits, and ditches; Romano-British, enclosed, with rectilinear structures, a 'through-way' and possibly contemporary (earlier?) structures downhill to the east; early first-century AD enclosed settlement, excavated 1965 (see below). The three major phases of settlement here, each with its own morphological characteristics, are remarkably laid out in the horizontal dimension over c. 600 m and could well represent in ground plan a succession more frequently noted archaeologically superimposed in vertical stratification.

(b) Plan of the southernmost settlement of the early decades AD as excavated, apparently showing a 'classic', single-phase, enclosed farmstead of house, pits and four or six-post buildings with a spacious yard (after Royal Commission on Historical Monuments (Eng.) and G. J. Wainwright).

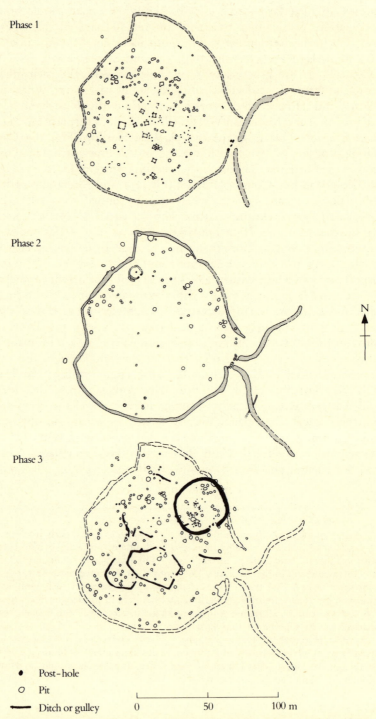

Phase 1

Phase 2

N

Phase 3

●   Post–hole

○   Pit

━━   Ditch or gulley

0   50   100 m

Fig. 31. Gussage All Saints, Dorset: the three main phases of the enclosed settlement as excavated, spanning the 500/600 years up to the mid first century AD (after G. J. Wainwright).

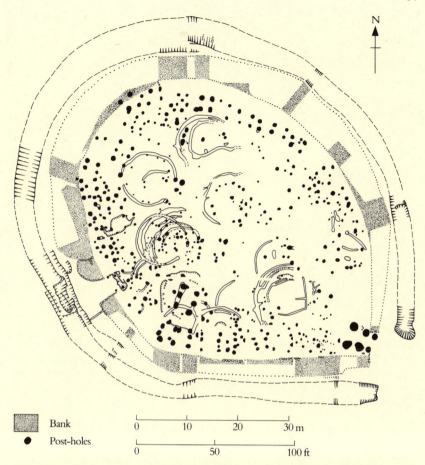

N

Bank

Post-holes

0   10   20   30 m

0   50   100 ft

Fig. 32. Walesland Rath, Pembroke: plan of the late prehistoric enclosed settlement as excavated. The location and succession of round and sub-rectangular buildings is quite distinct from the evidence for ranges of peripheral buildings against the inside of the bank cf. West Marling, Fig. 17 (after G. J. Wainwright).

that concept, for in many cases all three demonstrate nucleated settlements consisting of separate farms.[119] Should we not therefore be looking for our late prehistoric farms as much in *oppida*, hill-forts, and extensive settlements like Boscombe Down West, Wilts., as in the small, discrete enclosure or 'open' hill-side group of hut-circles (Fig. 34)? The

[119] Personal observation; M. Beresford and J. G. Hurst (eds.), *Deserted Medieval Villages*, London, 1971; Thomas (ed.), *Rural Settlement in Roman Britain*; K. Branigan and P. J. Fowler (eds.), *The Roman West Country*, Newton Abbot, 1976.

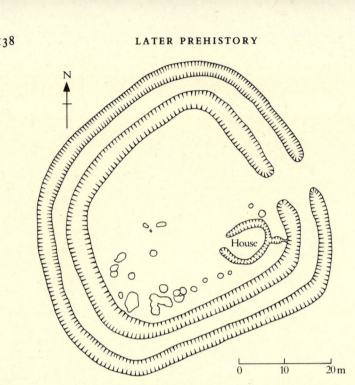

Fig. 33. Plan of a double-ditched settlement enclosure at Blackthorn, Northampton, as exposed and partly excavated during housing development. The site lies on sand, contained a house and twenty-eight pits, and was occupied some time during the last two centuries BC; cf. Fig. 25*b* (after J. H. Williams and M. R. McCarthy).

whole question of farms in later prehistoric Britain is one requiring a great deal more thought and research, even at this second level of its physical existence, form, and situation.

Farm buildings are also a little difficult to discuss for reasons already given or implied. Their existence in round, oval, and rectangular ground plan, large, medium, and small sizes, timber-framed and stone-based, for domestic and other purposes, is not in doubt (Figs. 35, 36, 37); and their reconstruction is currently under detailed investigation (Plates I*b*, VIII).[120] It is in their function or functions that the problem lies. A hearth within one is taken to indicate a domestic purpose – a house or, often wrongly, a hut; but was such a domestic role exclusive of others and does a hearth necessarily point unequivocally to living quarters? Do we have to think of a distinction solely between the human

[120] Background, see n. 112, p. 129; current experiment, P. J. Reynolds, *Farming in the Iron Age*, Cambridge, and 'Experimental archaeology and the Butser Ancient Farm Project', *Rescue News*, 11, 1976, pp. 7–8; and now, *ibid.*, *Iron Age Farm*, London, 1979.

IV. (*a*) Keysley Down, Kingston Deverill, Wilts. ST 872355. Oblique air photograph showing a fragment of an extensive area of prehistoric fields and other features in the south-west corner of the chalk plateau of Salisbury Plain. Although the presence of the fields is revealed by the soil colour (not crop-mark) differences, their outline and relationships are blurred by modern cultivation of early fields, now well on the way to obliteration. The triple-banded lines characteristically mark degraded lynchets; possible ditched features are visible in the centre of the photograph. (Cambridge University Collection *per* J. K. S. St Joseph, AQY 78)

IV. (*b*) Totterdown, Fyfield Down, Wilts. SU 135713. Oblique air photograph looking north across grass downland which has not been ploughed since the Roman period (except top right where twelfth/thirteenth century AD ridge-and-furrow is apparent). As a result, details of Roman and prehistoric landscape features and relationships are determinable in a way not possible in the area of Plate IV*a*. A short length of a linear ditch appearing top left relates to second millennium arrangements; the whole area of the plate was laid out on a north-east to south-west orientation in small, squarish fields in the first millennium, and their lynchets are visible all round the central tree-clump except to the north-west; left of the trees, narrow oblong fields of early Roman date and on a slightly different axis have flattened all but a few fragments of the prehistoric systems. The cottage and tree-clump are eighteenth century. (Cambridge University Collection *per* J. K. S. St Joseph, AAU 85)

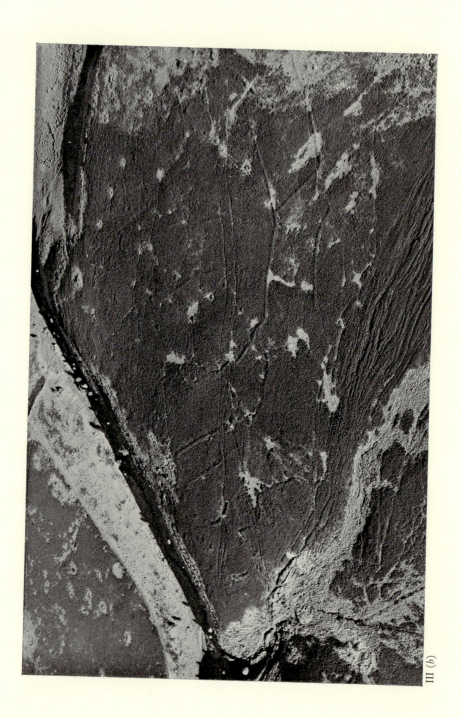

III. (a) Combestone Tor and Holne Moor, Dartmoor, Devon. SX 670717. This oblique air photograph from the north shows rectilinear land allotment defined by terminal and parallel reaves, probably of the second millennium BC. The overall regularity of the major land-blocks is clearly broken up by local subdivisions. The system cuts, or is contemporary with, a circular enclosure bottom right; it is overlain by small, irregular, assarted fields and associated tracks coming up the slope from the north, and by leats of nineteenth-century tin mining. The area encompassed by the photograph is 1 sq. km. (West Air Photography *per* J. White, CA 1893/7)

III. (b) Big Moor, Derbys., from the west, 13 km south-west of Sheffield, near Bar Brook reservoir. An example of a 'derelict', peat-covered Pennine landscape formerly, and probably in the second millennium BC, cultivated in the system of rectilinear fields defined by the low banks showing beneath the heather. (D. N. Riley)

I (a)

I (b)

I. (b) Little Butser Hill, near Petersfield, Hants. A general view from the south of the site of the Butser Ancient Farm Project where numerous experiments relevant to late prehistoric farming are being conducted. Though not primarily intended to represent the appearance of an 'Iron Age Farm', the site with its central linear access, hurdle enclosures, Soay sheep, hay-cocks, seed-beds, round house, pit area, and fields beyond, contains many of the visible elements attested by excavation to have existed on settlements in Wessex c. 300 BC. (Butser Ancient Farm Project per P. J. Reynolds)

II. (a) Knap Hill and Adam's Grave, Alton, Wilts. The derelict, Neolithic earthworks of the causewayed enclosure on the left and of the chambered long barrow on the skyline in the middle distance were already more than a thousand years old by c. 2000 bc when a treeless, downland landscape such as this could well have formed at least part of the Wessex environment in which the agrarian developments of the second millennium occurred. (P. J. Fowler)

II. (b) Bell track terminal, Westhay, Somerset. The remarkable conditions for organic preservation in the Brue valley of the Somerset Levels allow at least a glimpse of where some of the timber and brushwood cleared from the later Neolithic landscape had gone. Here, the track itself is to the left and, in what must have been very wet circumstances, dumped bundles of brushwood have been overlain by heavy timber to provide access to the dry land in the foreground. Date: c. 2300 bc; scale: 6 ft. (Somerset Levels Project per J. M. Coles)

I. (*a*) Long Wittenham, Oxon. SU 557943. Near-vertical air photograph from the north-east of crop-marks *c.* 1 km east of the present village showing features typical of settlement complexes on the gravel terraces of the Middle/Upper Thames valley. The area shown is but a fragment of a multi-period landscape complex known to extend over much of the land enclosed by the loop of the River Thames between Long and Little Wittenham, Oxon., cf. Fig. 39. The photograph shows, over a subsoil network of periglacial cracks, ring-ditches, a block rectilinear mark, and many pits, with numerous enclosures apparently related to a double-ditched road or track. The absence of evidence of enclosed fields in the area around the settlement may be significant though the continuation of the road ditches to the south through the 'blank' area implies land-use on either side. (National Monuments Record, Air Photographs Unit SU 5594/38/273)

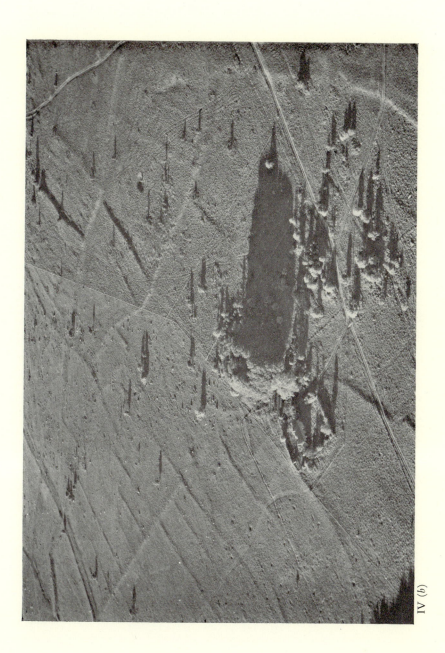

IV (b)

V. Kestor, Chagford, Devon. SX 665868. Oblique air photograph from the north-east showing settlements, discrete hut circles, and small stone-walled enclosures fitting within parallel, oblong land-allotments defined by reaves. Access ways are clearly visible to left and right and the excavated 'Round Pound' is between the ancient and the modern roads on the right. The distance across the bottom of the plate is *c.* 450 m and to its top *c.* 800 m. (West Air Photography *per* J. White, CA 1888/3)

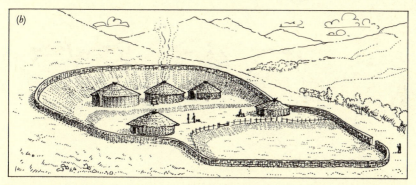

Fig. 34. Reconstructions of: (*a*) an unenclosed platform settlement; (*b*) a scooped settlement (after R. W. Feachem).

house and the other, non-occupied farm buildings? – perhaps the living pattern of the farmers was broken down into different processes like eating, sleeping, and drinking, each of which required a separate building some of which would not require hearths. Perhaps, too, much of the cooking was done out of doors anyway, so that internal hearths might well indicate something else. These are real, not merely theoretical, problems of interpretation, particularly when so many sites excavated have already been ploughed and could have lost their floor levels anyway. What is lacking generally is unambiguous evidence of how known buildings functioned as part of a farm. Granted that many of the known structures are likely to have been lived in, despite these doubts, what is lacking in detail is the evidence for buildings with specific farming functions – barns, byres, stables, sheds, pigsties, and all the other structural impedimenta still cluttering up old-fashioned farmyards today. The rarity of Richmond's specific interpretation of the

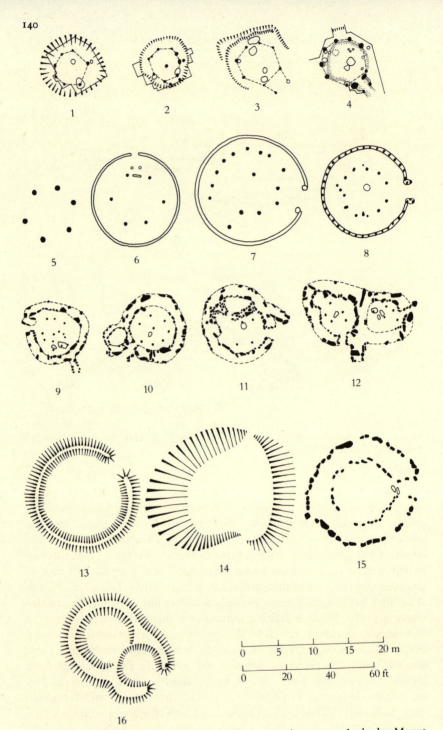

Fig. 35. A selection of buildings from late prehistoric settlements: 1, Amberley Mount, Sussex; 2–4, Itford Hill, Sussex; 5–6, Harehope, Peebles.; 7, High Knowes, Northumb.; 8, West Plean, Stirling; 9–12, Dean Moor, Devon, Huts 1, 7, 8, 5A and B cf. Fig. 10; 13, Davochfin, Sutherland; 14, Green Knowe, Peebles.; 15, Dalruzion, Perths.; 16, Cloughmor, Inverness. (1–4 after C. R. Musson; 5–8 after B. W. Cunliffe; 9–12 after A. Fox; 13–16 after R. W. Feachem).

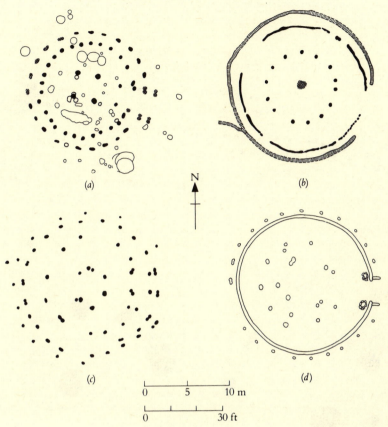

(a)

N

(b)

(c)

(d)

0   5   10 m

0   30 ft

Fig. 36. A comparison of the ground plans of four large Early Iron Age round houses:
(a), Little Woodbury, Wilts., phase I, with conjectural post-holes hatched, possible
repair post-holes in heavy outline, and all other features which could be contemporary
in thin outline; (b), House 2, Llandegai, Caerns., with a central hearth, a wall gully
and external drainage gully (shaded); (c) and (d), the two successive phases of the main
house at West Brandon, County Durham (a, b after C. R. Musson; c, d after G. Jobey).

annex on the side of Hut 56 at Hod Hill as a stable makes the point
(Fig. 37).[121] No doubt later prehistoric farms did have such buildings,
and no doubt the farmyards were cluttered and dirty and smelly and
marvellously interesting, with scarcely a person ever in sight, judging
by farms today; but archaeology leaves that level of reality to the
imagination.

[121] I. A. Richmond, *Hod Hill*, II, 1968, fig. 13. The most cogent discussion of
house-plan interpretation remains C. R. Musson in *Curr. Arch.*, 21, 1970, pp. 267–75,
cf. also D. W. Harding, 'Round and rectangular: Iron Age houses, British and foreign',
in C. F. C. and S. C. Hawkes (eds.), *Archaeology into History*, I, *Greeks, Celts and Romans*,
London, 1973, pp. 43–62.

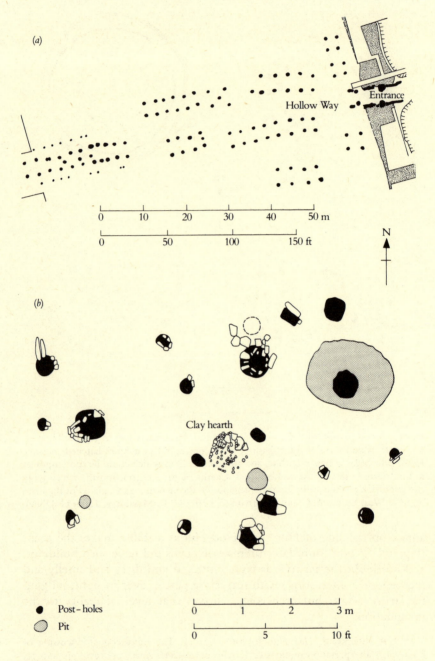

Fig. 37. Rectangular buildings in hill-forts: (*a*), period 2 at Crickley Hill, Glos.; (*b*), Budbury, Wilts. (*a* after P. W. Dixon; *b* after G. J. Wainwright).

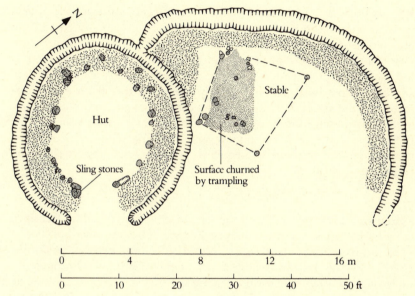

Fig. 38. Hut 56, Hod Hill, Dorset, showing an annexe interpreted as a stable (after I. A. Richmond.

CHAPTER II

AGRARIAN TECHNIQUES AND TECHNOLOGY

ARABLE FARMING

ENVIRONMENTAL circumstances very largely influence the potential and methods of cultivated crop husbandry in any part of the world (Figs. 3, 28). It seems reasonable therefore to assume the converse, i.e. that the products and methods used in any area reflect the local environmental conditions. We have already seen (above, p. 48) how close was the relationship between the British environment and the arable-husbandry of the earlier farmers, and we can now look at the much more prolific evidence for the last two millennia bc. For practical purposes, the review will deal first with arable fields in the Lowland Zone and subsequently (below, pp. 169–203) in the Highland Zone (Fig. 6).

Lowland Zone Field Systems

Systems of cultivated plots of the second and first millennia BC have for long been known in north-west Europe. These are the '*oldtidsagre*' of Scandinavia, the '*eisenzeitliche Fluren*' of Germany, the '*heidensche legerplaatsen*' of Holland and the '*Celtic*' fields of Britain.[1] Undoubtedly most of the known and visible remains of these systems of prehistoric arable fields date to the millennium between *c.* 500 BC and AD 500, but equally clearly the traditional methods of agriculture which they represent, and in some cases the fields themselves, demonstrably go back to the earlier second millennium and probably to at least the second half of the third millennium. It is conceivable that regular field systems were laid out at an earlier date, particularly perhaps in the centuries immediately before *c.* 2000 BC, associated with what appears to be the highly organized 'henge phase' of social development when an agricultural surplus can be postulated; but there is no firm evidence so far of *permanent* field systems with fixed boundaries, though of course there is plenty of evidence of arable farming (above, p. 46). Given the population parameters above (pp. 84–8), there would

[1] G. Hatt, *Oldtidsagre*, Copenhagen, 1949; M. Müller-Wille, *Eisenzeitlicke Fluren in den festlandischen Nordseegebieten*, Keil, 1965; J. A. Brongers, *Air Photography and Celtic Field Research in the Netherlands*, Amersfoort, Holland, 1976; O. G. S. Crawford, *Air Survey and Archaeology*, Southampton, 1st ed. 1924, 2nd ed. 1928; M. C. Bowen, *Ancient Fields*, London, n.d. (1961); C. Taylor, *Fields in the English Landscape*, London, 1975.

seem to have been no need for permanent field systems even if techniques of land-cultivation appropriate to the farming of permanent arable, e.g. cross-ploughing (below, p. 220), had already been developed during the shifting, resource-exploiting agriculture which characterized the Neolithic. The argument will be developed below (pp. 245–9) that the first real husbandry, as distinct from earlier essentially 'exploitation' farming, developed during the early/mid second millennium as one of the several innovations following the 'Beaker' phase of British prehistory.

The 'Celtic' fields[2] of southern Britain are best-known on those areas of lighter soils – on Chalk, limestone, and gravels – which we have already seen to be increasingly populated in later prehistoric times (Plate IV).[3] Such field systems were in use from at least the early second millennium BC to the fifth century AD and, at least arguably, a little later.[4] The systems themselves (Figs. 40, 41) are characterized visually by their extent, often covering many hundreds and sometimes, when fully developed, thousands of hectares; by their organized structural nature in plan, notably in their use of axial lines; by their relationships, often expressed physically by ditches, banks, and trackways, to later prehistoric land boundaries, settlements, and cemeteries; by their shape, edges, and content, especially their component fields or plots; and by their date.

We shall now examine these five characteristics of later prehistoric field systems, considering their extent, plan and components.

Extent

Later prehistoric field systems are known to have been used at some time over much of the Lowland Zone. They have actually been surveyed over a relatively small part of the zone, and they now survive as visible structures on the ground in only a few localities. The best-preserved examples are in Dorset (Valley of Stones, Chaldon Herring, and Penbury Knoll),[5] south-west (Pertwood Down), and

---

[2] By editorial decision, this terminology is not used in this volume. See Appendix 2 (below, pp. 269–74).

[3] For distribution see OS *Map of Roman Britain*, Chessington, 3rd edn. 1956 and, S. Piggott, 'Native economies and the Roman occupation of north Britain', in I. A. Richmond (ed.), *Roman and Native in North Britain*, Edinburgh, 1958, pp. 1–27, Map 1.

[4] P. J. Fowler, 'Early prehistoric agriculture in Western Europe: some archaeological evidence', in Simpson (ed.), *Economy and Settlement*, pp. 153–82; *idem*, 'Continuity in the landscape?...', in P. J. Fowler (ed.), *Recent Work in Rural Archaeology*, pp. 121–36; *idem*. 'Farms and fields...', in K. Branigan and P. J. Fowler, *The Roman West Country*, pp. 162–82.

[5] RCHM, *Dorset*, II and V, 1970, 1075.

north Wiltshire (Fyfield, Overton (Plate IV *b*), and Burderop Downs on the Marlborough Downs);[6] and round Grassington in west Yorkshire (Fig. 52).[7] Otherwise, only fragments visibly remain of what were once very much more extensive systems, for example, on the southern slopes of Mendip, on the Failand Ridge, west of Bristol, on the Isle of Wight, on the Cotswolds, on the Sussex Downs, and in the Peak District.[8] Yet air photography has shown that such systems formerly covered much of the Wessex and Sussex chalklands and parts of the river valleys of southern and midland Britain.[9] In Hampshire, for example, the surviving fields on Woolbury Down are but a fragment of a former arable landscape in a county whose chalk is very widely covered by similar evidence of which virtually none is visible on the ground.[10] In the Fens likewise, the smallest fragments of once extensive field systems now survive (see Part II, Plates I and II), and along the valleys of the Warwickshire Avon and Middle and Upper Thames (Plate I*a*), where nothing is now visible at ground level, air photography shows extensive areas of apparently intensive agrarian land-use (Fig. 39) (see below, pp. 157, 239).[11] Yet this distribution of observable evidence, even if it had all been collated from all sources, certainly would not represent all the land that was cultivated in the last two millennia BC; though of course, in an area lacking such ground or air photographic evidence, it cannot be assumed that other late prehistoric arable land was cultivated in the same or even similar form of field system. This applies in particular to south-east Britain off the Chalk and to East Anglia, areas where scarcely no traces of early field systems are known, yet where thriving late prehistoric populations certainly existed. Did the Cantiaci of Kent and the Iceni of Norfolk farm in 'Wessex-type' field systems? – we do not know.[12]

Looking at the overall distribution of plottable field systems of the later prehistoric period, two of the very few generalizations we can

[6] O. G. S. Crawford and A. Keiller, *Wessex from the Air*, Oxford, 1928; Fyfield and Overton Downs, see Site Index (below, p. 284).

[7] *Yorks. Archaeol. J.*, 33, 1937, pp. 166–74; 34, 1939, pp. 115–50; *Ant.*, XLIII, 1969, pp. 220–1, Pl. XXXV.

[8] Bowen, *Ancient Fields*, references the regional literature to 1960.

[9] The distributional and other aspects of early fields are discussed in H. C. Bowen and P. J. Fowler (eds.), *Early Land Allotment*, British Archaeological Reports, 48, Oxford, 1978; see Appendix 4 (below, p. 278).

[10] O. G. S. Crawford and A. Keiller, *op. cit.*, Pl. XXV; B. Cunliffe, 'Some aspects of hill-forts and their cultural environments', in Jesson and Hill (eds.), *The Iron Age and its Hill-Forts*, pp. 53–69, fig. 16 (also in Cunliffe, *Iron Age Communities in Britain*, fig. 11.16).

[11] See n. 55, p. 93.

[12] For a brief discussion of a topographical-type classification, see below, p. 178, and Appendix 2 (below, p. 269).

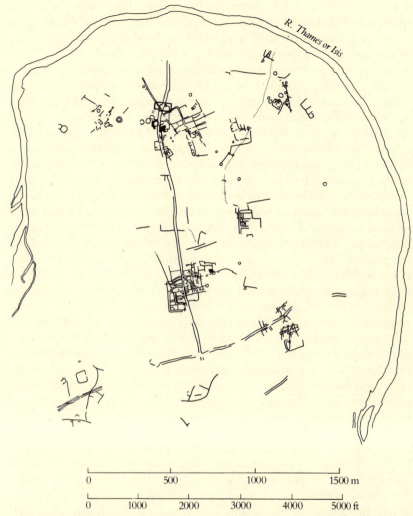

Fig. 39. Multi-period crop-mark palimpsest, as recorded up to 1976, in the loop of the River Thames between Long and Little Wittenham, Berks. (now Oxon). Such is the detail that many features are only shown conventionally. The settlement complex astride the main trackway in the centre is that on Pl. I*a* (after *Royal Commission on Historical Monuments* (Eng.)).

make are, first, that altogether it represents an absolute minimum of land under cultivation sometime during the period, and, secondly, that even the full extent of that minimum is never likely to have been under cultivation at any one time. As usual with contemporaneously undocumented archaeological evidence, we know we are looking at but a fraction of the total evidence; yet we do not know how far, quantitatively or qualitatively, our fraction represents the whole, even in this case with what must have been the most extensive of all types of archaeological evidence from later prehistoric times.

When we consider the extent of individual field systems, as distinct from the overall distribution of late prehistoric field systems in Lowland Britain, difficulties loom large in taking description beyond the stage of the general. The evidence returns assessment to its Wessex bias. In the first place, it is difficult to define a system topographically or physically: either continuous remains cover many hectares in which it is difficult to distinguish distinct field systems or blocks of separate fields, or the fragmentary nature of the surviving evidence obviates attempts to identify the edges of an individual system. Secondly, since we know nothing of the tenurial basis on which the fields were farmed, in a social or legal sense, we do not know what it is that we are trying to define (below, pp. 259–62). Thirdly, even where evidence survives well on the ground and/or shows clearly on air photographs, more often than not it will be on land which, in a medieval context, was marginal, i.e. it lay beyond the edges of permanent medieval cultivation. At least one of the boundaries of the earlier field system will therefore almost certainly lie unrecoverable in the area of the medieval fields, the continual cropping of which will probably have obliterated the traces of earlier land division.[13] This model applies particularly in the Wessex chalklands where characteristically later prehistoric fields can be recorded on the downs at one or both ends of the elongated parishes lying across the valleys (Plate IV *b*), but not in the central area of former 'open' fields spreading outwards and upwards towards the downs from medieval settlements in the valleys.[14]

Nevertheless, even granted these limitations, individual systems of fields can be seen to cover large, even if not closely defined, areas. Minimal areas of what appear to be single field systems can be quoted for a few examples, e.g. Fyfield Down, Wilts., *c.* 280 acres (*c.* 113 ha) where three sides of the system are certain and the fourth probable; 'Ancient Field Group 1', Dorset, "virtually continuous over about 900 acres" (*c.* 364 ha) but "formerly more extensive"; Nutwood Down,

[13] Cf. C. C. Taylor, 'The study of settlement patterns in pre-Saxon Britain', in P. J. Ucko, R. Tringham and G. W. Dimbleby (eds.), *Man, Settlement and Urbanism*, 1972, pp. 109–13. But this statement would not necessarily be true if the 'inner' boundary was ditched and might therefore be recorded by air photography. Furthermore, 'ancient' field boundaries might well survive beneath, and indeed be perpetuated by, existing field and other boundaries (to a much greater extent than is presently realized?).

[14] C. C. Taylor, *op. cit.*, and *idem*, *The Making of the English Landscape...Dorset*. Cf. also P. J. Fowler, 'The distribution of settlement', in C. Thomas, *Rural Settlement in Roman Britain*, pp. 54–67.

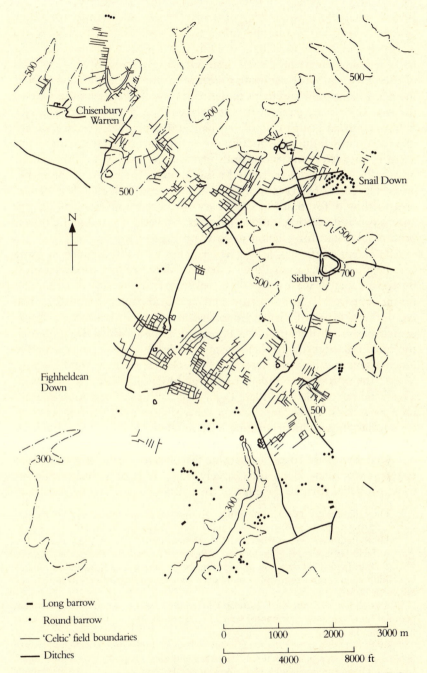

Fig. 40. Prehistoric and Romano-British earthworks in the area of Sidbury hill-fort, Wilts. (after H. C. Bowen and Roman Commission on Historical Monuments (Eng.)).

Berks., where "a massive series of fields...runs continuously for about 4¼ km²" (425 ha).[15] On the other hand, some blocks of fields are relatively small e.g. on Challow Hill, Corfe Castle, Dorset, 34 acres (c. 14 ha), and on Brean Down, Somerset, c. 2.5 acres (c. 1 ha). In each of these two cases, the peninsular position of the fields both constricted their original extent and helps to define it now.[16] Whatever this extent, the caveat must be stressed that we are dealing with extents of *arable* field systems and not of whole agricultural systems. In a sense we are making a misleading distinction in trying to separate arable from pasture, meadow, and woodland, elements of which might well be physically, and would certainly be functionally, included in the arable areas. The extent of a layout of arable fields might well include a 'blank' area within it for pasture, ceremony, or recreation (see below, pp. 162, 239) and, during fallow or after harvest, an arable field was presumably used for grazing (below, pp. 214–15).

The extent of the arable was nevertheless probably defined in some way originally. Occasionally we can see evidence of this, though it must be stressed that, as we now see them, most systems just stop or fade away for no apparently good reason and at no apparent boundary. The commonest types of visible boundary are a ditch, bank, or a track, sometimes in combination. On Pertwood Down, Wilts., for example, the northern edge of the field system is clearly defined as a negative lynchet above which is a trackway; on Overton and Fyfield Downs, Wilts., the northern boundary of a large block of fields is a ditch with a bank on the arable side (Plate IV*b*). The ditch itself was subsequently used as a track.[17] We see field systems deliberately skirting barrow cemeteries, though incorporating individual or small groups of barrows in their layout (Figs. 40, 57), and in the Roman period we see systems bounded by made roads.[18] Natural features too gave shape to field systems: woodland along the Grovely ridge, west of Salisbury, then as now, probably formed the edge of the cultivated land, while elsewhere

[15] These figures are taken from *Wilts. Archaeol. Mag.*, 58, 1962, p. 105; RCHM *Dorset*, II, part 3, 1970, p. 623; Bradley and Ellison, *Rams Hill*, p. 181.

[16] These figures are taken from RCHM, *Dorset*, II, 1970, p. 97 (fig.) and p. 632, Ancient Field Group 27; P. J. Fowler (ed.), *Recent Work in Rural Archaeology*, fig. 85. The block of fields illustrated, though apparently genuinely discrete, should probably be considered in conjunction with a more extensive but unplanned system further east on Brean Down.

[17] A good plan showing this feature on Pertwood Down has not yet been published; personal observation and air photographs. Fyfield ditch, *Wilts. Arch. Mag.*, 58, 1962, p. 107, and F4 on fig. 1.

[18] RCHM, *Dorset*, II–V (1970–75) gives numerous examples of relationships between fields and barrows, a point discussed in Bradley and Ellison, *op. cit.*, P. J. Fowler (ed.), 1971, *op. cit.*, and frequently by H. C. Bowen (see Bibliography). A 'classic' example of a fields/Roman road relationship remains Crawford and Keiller, *op. cit.*, Pl. XXVI.

systems run down to, but not across, streams (but cf. Fig. 41), and to the edge of steep slopes and cliffs, or to an unclearable area dense with surface stones.[19] Where there is no apparent reason for a field system genuinely stopping along an observable line, allowance must presumably be made for an intangible feature, archaeologically speaking, such as an ecological interface, a factor in the tenurial arrangements, a line of sight between two sticks – or just human whim. Unless a boundary is formed by a regularly shaped ditch or similar feature, there appears to be no preferred shape for these late prehistoric lowland field systems other than a somewhat irregular, jagged rectangularity reflecting the shape of the fields themselves.

Plan

Perhaps the subtitle here should be the 'planning of field systems' since the next few paragraphs are based on field systems which have been surveyed and published by modern fieldworkers. On the basis of this evidence it will be argued that at least some field systems were planned in the first place by their originators. The basis for this argument – indeed it is an observation – has arisen independently at a time when 'planning', in the sense of the application of simple geometrical principles to the construction of man-made landscape features amongst later prehistoric communities, has begun to be placed on a sound academic basis (as distinct from the 'old straight track' school of thought to which the idea of prehistoric mensuration remains persistently attractive). Whether or not the more elaborate astronomical arguments behind the planning of major monuments like the Dorset Cursus are followed, an ability to plan both individual structures like stone circles and to relate such structures over tracts of landscape has to be accepted.[20] The same general point has already been made with

---

[19] Grovely: P. J. Fowler, 'Early prehistoric agriculture...', gives earlier references, to which should now be added *Wilts. Arch. Mag.*, 62, 1967, pp. 118–21, and D. J. Bonney, 'Early boundaries in Wessex', in P. J. Fowler (ed.), *Archaeology and the Landscape*, pp. 168–86. The best-displayed examples of field edges are in the many plans in RCHM, *Dorset*, II–V, including ones which are now truncated at cliff edges by post-field erosion and others which cross valleys. A good example of a field system stopping at an area of dense stones is on Overton Down, *Wilts. Arch. Mag.*, 58, 1962, fig. 1. opp. p. 115, where the line of sarsens forming the boundary is on the original OS 6-in. map at 139708.

[20] A. Burl, *The Stone Circles of the British Isles*, London, 1976, is clearly now the standard work but unfortunately it was published too late to influence this text. No examples are indexed, however, of an observed relationship between stone *circles* and prehistoric field boundaries, though Burl suggests (*ibid.*, p. 227) that the 'henge' (?) known as The Lios, part of the Lough Gur complex in Limerick, might lie astride a field wall, and naturally he illustrates (*ibid.*, pp. 244–5) the Beaghmore complex,

regard to the siting of barrow cemeteries and has, of course, for long been established in relation to Stonehenge.[21] Interestingly, such ability, however early it began to develop, seems to have been exercised in particular about 2000 bc with the construction of stone alignments and circles at a time when, on other grounds, there is reason to look for agrarian change. In our field systems we also seem to have evidence of a planning ability better known in a 'ceremonial' context, but here applied in an agrarian context from about the same time.

The evidence in the field consists of two principal observations: first that axial lines run through the superficially irregular layout of the field systems; and, secondly, that these lines often ignore topographical features, in much the same way that the Dorset Cursus continues on its axes across the grain of the rolling chalk landscape, regardless of valleys.

As the commonly used phrase implies, 'Celtic' fields have until recently tended to be studied as fields and not as systems of arable plots. Consequently, the emphasis has been on the morphological characteristics of individual fields rather than on the similar characteristics of a block of fields. It is when we stand back, as it were, from the fields and see them as a complex of single units or parcels making up a greater whole that a landscape pattern emerges. In many cases it appears that the system consists of large blocks of land defined by continuous boundaries, of which the individual fields are subdivisions (Fig. 41). No analogies other than a physical one are intended in comparing this three-tier unit hierarchy with a four-tier 'open field' system subdivided into several large fields each of which is subdivided further into furlongs, which are themselves subdivided into smaller units. Though entirely conjecture, it may indeed be that the land-blocks making up the later prehistoric systems are the units comparable to 'open' fields of medieval times, and should therefore more accurately be called the 'fields', with the subdivisions hitherto called 'fields' being relegated to an inferior status of 'plots' (see below, p. 155).

The existence of long, continuous land or field boundaries in an arable situation presents us with the counterpart of major land divisions for long recognized in a pastoral context (below, p. 233).[22] Their

Tyrone, where three stone *rows* cross two field walls. By implication, the stone circles that the rows are approaching lie inside fields, cf. J. Pilcher, *Ulster J. Arch.*, 32, 1969, pp. 73–91. On the Dorset cursus, cf. H. C. Bowen, 'Air photography: some implications...', in E. Fowler (ed.), *Field Survey in British Archaeology*, pp. 38–49, esp. fig. 12, and RCHM, *Dorset*, v, 1975, pp. 24–5.

[21] For 'landscape planning' inferred from the barrows on the South Dorset Ridgway, see RCHM, *Dorset*, ii, part 3, 1970, map in pocket; for Stonehenge and its environs, see now S. Piggott in VCH, *Wilts*, i, part ii, 1973, fig. 10.

[22] E.g. C. F. C. Hawkes, 'The excavation at Quarley Hill, 1938', *Papers and Proc. Hants. Fld Club*, 14, 1940, pp. 136–94.

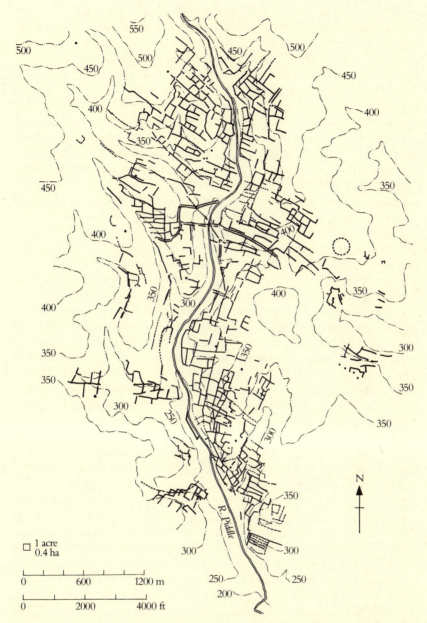

Fig. 41. Early field system and related features in the Dole's Hill area and along the valley of the R. Piddle, Dorset (after Royal Commission on Historical Monuments (Eng.)).

contemporary existence need not therefore occasion surprise, even when it is shown that, in certain cases, these boundaries are themselves following axial lines which continue, or are taken up again, over whole tracts of landscape without there necessarily being a continuous visible boundary feature now. This phenomenon has been recognized over large areas of Hampshire, as well as in Dorset and Wiltshire (Fig. 38), and it can also be seen to be present in the older surveys of 'Celtic field' systems in Sussex. Bowen for example, has demonstrated in central Dorset "an axial arrangement of 'Celtic fields', part of a group of some 2000 acres. . . The deliberate aspect of the arrangement is emphasised by the fact that the axes cross a stream and its narrow uncultivated flood plain" (Fig. 41).[23] It must be stressed that in this case no physically existing line of bank, ditch, or lynchet crosses the flood plain (though a fence might have existed and could indeed still survive in a waterlogged condition) yet the prevailing north-west to south-east axial arrangement of the system (or systems) persists on each side of the valley. Another example, unlike that just quoted, can still be seen: at the south-west corner of the Marlborough Downs, both on Overton Down and on Fyfield Down, excellently preserved blocks of fields survive, separated by the Valley of Stones, an uncleared and uncultivated dry combe littered with sarsen stones. The blocks of fields are physically connected only by a linear ditch forming their common northern boundary, a ditch which cuts its way through the sarsen debris near the head of the combe; yet both blocks of fields, large areas of which are not intervisible, are arranged on the same north-east to south-west axis and there can be little doubt that they form, minimally, a unified cohesive landscape (Plate IV*b*). Arrangements on this scale, ignoring topography, sharing this repetitive characteristic of a common axial orientation, and quite often on what almost seems to be a preferred north-east to south-west axis, cannot be coincidence. They must be attributed to deliberate human action.

Both these examples also raise another question with considerable implications: while we have been discussing the planned element in whole field systems, the natural boundary, a valley in both these cases, provides a physical separation of the blocks of fields on either side. Are we in fact looking at evidence of landscape planning extending from one field system to another? If we look at these two examples in this light, the areas involved do not change, of course, but the concept of a whole field system being deliberately laid out becomes even bigger if the same planning factors are carried over from one field system to another. Who is planning such an agrarian framework and who is

___

[23] H. C. Bowen, *op. cit.*, p. 45 and fig. 47, cf. RCHM, *Dorset*, III, part 2, 1970, plan of Ancient Field Group 45 in pocket.

controlling its execution? What are the sanctions to impose such conformity? Are we dealing with the landscape architecture of a generation, a century or a millennium? – whatever the answers, the implications are considerable (below, pp. 245–61). The recognition of a planned framework within which individual fields were laid out also has implications for the way in which the field systems developed. The traditional, though usually unstated, assumption has been that the superficial irregularity of a 'Celtic' field system reflects its organic, almost cellular growth, a field or groups of fields being added as occasion demanded to the original, nuclear group of irregular fields. It is now necessary to revive a completely different model, first suggested by Curwen in the light of his observations on the Sussex Downs,[24] for in practice a different process seems to have been followed. Its essence was that the *whole* area to be brought under cultivation was chosen and then cleared. Perhaps the clearance itself was carried out in long swathes, thus requiring *ab initio* at least a rudimentary element of surveying, and possibly entailing the working out even at this stage of the main axial divisions of the future field system. Alternatively, these axes could have been laid out after the clearance, when the 'planners' would have been presented with a large open area on which to impose their pattern. On the whole, the former suggestion – that the axial framework of a field system reflects a controlled clearance process – seems the more likely. With an area cleared and already broadly divided up into oblong blocks of land, individual fields and even groups of fields could then be fitted into the existing framework, neatly or otherwise. Even if they followed a systematic pattern of infilling to begin with, a thousand years and more of illiterate farming is bound to have blurred the original arrangements. Fields were doubtless thrown together or subdivided, fell out of use, or were extended further in the normal ebb and flow of agricultural practice, whatever the tenurial and social bases behind the operation of the field system (Fig. 42).

This processual interpretation of the physical evidence is suggested by recent work primarily in Wessex. It need not apply everywhere, though recent and current work on Dartmoor (Figs. 45, 46; below, pp. 170–84) and in the west of Ireland (Fig. 47) is independently producing similar evidence, particularly that of ground clearance and field system planning on the grand scale.[25] As in Wessex but with greater certainty, in both areas the processes postulated were in train in the first half of the second millennium BC, without prejudice to

[24] E. C. Curwen, *Air Photography and the Evolution of the Cornfield*, London, 2nd rev. ed. 1938, 26, followed and expanded by P. J. Fowler, 'Early prehistoric agriculture', pp. 174–7.
[25] See references below, pp. 181–3, H. C. Bowen and P. J. Fowler (eds.), *Early Land Allotment*, and Appendixes 2 and 3 (below, p. 269 and 275).

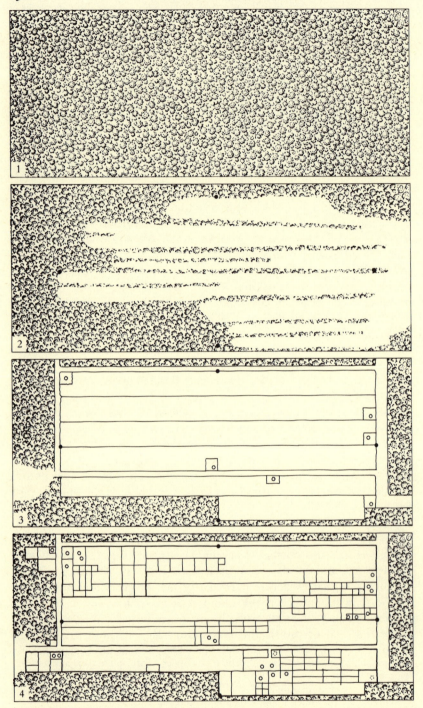

Fig. 42. Diagram to illustrate four hypothetical stages of landscape clearance and infilling as a possible interpretation of field evidence on Dartmoor and in Wessex. 1, Uncleared land; 2, clearance in swathes; 3, structural land allotment with primary man-made boundaries; 4, subdivision and infilling as the landscape is farmed and developed. A fifth stage might well see the breakdown of the structural rigidity with consolidation, expansion and contraction of settlement (P. J. Fowler).

earlier origins and long-continued development (for a discussion of dating, see below, pp. 247–8). On the other hand, it is not everywhere possible to detect the signs of deliberate axes and preferred orientations in field system plans. On the gravels of the Upper Thames (Plate 1*a*), for example, while small blocks of regular enclosures, probably fields, and lengths of double ditches, probably tracks, are detectable, there is little sign of systematic landscape planning, and indeed the overall impression, doubtless in part deriving from the palimpsest in the soil, is of complex irregularity.[26]

Components

A field system in the full sense will clearly consist not only of different physical components, but also of a whole complex of less tangible relationships with other features in both the man-made and natural environments (Fig. 28). When successfully working, it will be integrated with, rather than superimposed on, the landscape. Here we must first, however, examine those artifactual elements which characterized such systems in lowland Britain in the last two millennia BC.

Any field system must consist of at least several smaller units which can be called fields, whatever their function. Here our concern is with arable fields since, although there is plentiful evidence for pastoralism in later prehistoric Britain (below, pp. 232–42), with rare exceptions that side of the rural economy has not been proved to have been associated with extensive systems of permanent confined enclosures, i.e. fields.[27]

Not that fields by definition need to be enclosed, but the essence of a field system, as distinct from 'slash and burn' and 'shifting' cultivation, for example, is that its area should be delineated in some way, and that the units within it should be repeatedly used within that area in a recognized pattern. In other words, a degree of permanence or intended permanence should characterize a field system; its use through sub-divisions called fields should indicate a degree of agrarian stability. This of course can easily become a circular argument but in view of the model of agricultural mobility and exploitation suggested for the early third millennium and before (above, p. 145) and well documented in parts of the contemporary world, clearly major social, economic, and agrarian implications are involved when permanent arable fields were created, delineated, and farmed year after year on the same spot and within the same boundaries.

Fields in later prehistoric southern Britain never occur singly, and

---

[26] Benson and Miles, *The Upper Thames Valley....*
[27] An exception recently claimed is Fengate, see below, p. 239.

were generally rectangular in shape, whatever the geology, with a tendency towards squarishness. Equally, many were markedly oblong, though there is no prehistoric evidence for anything as regular as the groups of very long, narrow fields, characteristic of Denmark.[28] On the Chalk, from which far and away most of the evidence comes, the great majority of fields are of 0.2–0.6 ha, and time and time again the dimensions are of the order of $c.$ 70 × 50 m. As recordable now, they frequently appear larger but, quite apart from the effect of post-Roman ploughing which has tended to blur detail, study of the system of which they are a part will often show how the size and shape of the larger fields probably represents a consolidation of originally smaller units. Many field systems also contain five-sided or polygonal enclosures, perhaps even the D-shaped or circular types. Until proved otherwise, such are best regarded as something other than arable fields, perhaps a relict from an earlier landscape, or a settlement or cattle enclosure in the contemporary one. A 'classic' example is on Overton Down, Wilts., where Crawford's early air photograph showed an apparent, curved lynchet standing out in a series of straight, lynchetted field edges. Excavation subsequently showed that the curved lynchet was indeed genuine and that it was curved because it had accumulated on (and subsequently faithfully reflected) the outer edge of a ditch curving round to enclose a contemporary settlement which had then been ploughed over in the later centuries BC and, apart from that curve, totally obliterated.[29] Bowen shows an excellent example of almost exactly the opposite on Knoll Down, Damerham, Hants., where a curved ditch crosses and destroys, rather than perpetuates, an earlier pattern of rectangular field boundaries.[30]

The boundaries of fields, unlike their shape, to a certain degree reflect the local geology. Field boundaries are known as stone walls, stone or flint banks, earth banks, earth banks revetted with stone or posts, banks and ditches, ditches alone, fences, or simply an unploughed baulk. It can be postulated that hedges, planted or created by simply leaving lines of natural vegetation, might also have formed boundaries. In no case can the type of field boundary by which the fields of later prehistoric Britain are best characterized, the lynchet, have been an original feature. By definition, a lynchet is the product of man-made erosion accumulating against, or downhill of, a defined and permanent field edge (Plate VI). Lynchets therefore developed during the arable use of a field, and

[28] The Danish evidence is displayed comparatively with other European examples, and fully referenced, in M. Müller-Wille, *Eisenzeitlicke Fluren in den festlandischen Nordseegebieten*, 1965.

[29] O. G. S. Crawford and A. Keiller, *Wessex from the Air*, Oxford, 1928, Pl. XIX, supplemented by *Wilts. Archaeol. Mag.*, 62, 1967, pp. 16–26.

[30] H. C. Bowen in P. J. Fowler (ed.), *Recent Work in Rural Archaeology*, Pl. 3a.

were not an original feature of the field. Nevertheless, the fact of their existence is of immense significance for in no better way could it be demonstrated that the individual fields, and not just the field system, were structures intended to be permanent – hence the boundaries around them – and in practice of considerable longevity. The lynchets of the later prehistoric fields of southern Britain are the best witness to the stability and continuity of agrarian practice in the last centuries BC that it would be possible to devise; yet, ironically, they are almost certainly an accidental by-product of the agriculture to which they testify. They might well have been regarded as a nuisance by the farmers whose fields they were gradually reducing in area. Though it is pure speculation to say so, the development of lynchets may have been one of the reasons for the throwing together of adjacent fields since such an act could have released something of the order of 300 m² plus a lot of humus per field, otherwise wasted from the cultivation point of view.[31]

Not a great deal of excavation of field boundaries has been carried out, so that most of the potential information on chalk and other slopes is masked by lynchet formation. On gravels, where of course very little or nothing shows on the ground, most of the information is on air photographs and, again by definition, we can be fairly certain that many of the fields were bounded by a ditch or just an unploughed baulk. They may or may not have had banks, fences, or hedges as well. On the other hand, it may well be that the extensive 'blank' areas were the permanent, unenclosed arable with the defined enclosures serving numerous specialist functions like gardens, paddocks, and stack-yards (Plate I*a*). Air photographs of prehistoric field boundaries on the Chalk are not so revealing since their original nature is obscured by the white bands produced by modern ploughing over lynchets (Plate IV*a*). The ground and excavated evidence from Overton and Fyfield Down, however, provides an indication of the range of original field boundaries.[32] As mentioned above (p. 150) the northern edge of the system, and also of many fields abutting it, was a ditch with a bank on the field side (Plate IV*b*, *top left*). This bank was in part revetted with a drystone sarsen facing back and front. Immediately to the south, without excavation it is possible to see that the adjacent fields were created by clearing the land of the movable sarsen stones, which were then strung out in straight but irregular lines to demarcate the ploughable plots. Lynchets subsequently accumulated against and partly over these stones, which now appear to be sticking out of low terraces.

[31] J. A. Brongers, *Air Photography and Celtic Field Research in the Netherlands*, 1976, contains a useful discussion of field banks.

[32] Summarized up to 1966 in *Ant.*, XLI, 1967, pp. 289–301.

To the south on Overton Down, where similar clearance on a sarsen littered slope has also taken place, the lines of stones running up and down the slope have not been encapsulated in lynchet formation and are quite clear on the ground, almost like parts of Dartmoor (below, p. 192).

A much more deliberate act of field building using sarsens is demonstrated on Fyfield Down where a low drystone wall was put around a field, and indeed presumably many fields. At the points excavated, some of the stones of the wall showed fresh fractures and signs of burning, suggesting that here land-clearance had been much more thorough: probably at least the larger stones were heated by fire and then rapidly cooled by water, causing the sarsens to splinter (as was done in the eighteenth century to the sarsens at nearby Avebury). A proper wall was then built, subsequently acting as revetment to the accumulation of ploughsoil at the field edge during probably discontinuous cultivation over some five hundred years. The wall itself is interesting since it was not originally built high enough to keep animals either in or out: its function was simply to demarcate, so it gives point to thoughts about social capital invested in the construction of field systems and raises thoughts about who built the wall. To answer 'the owner' avoids the real issue of whether the owner was a person, a family, or the community.

By contrast, in an area on Overton Down where sarsens would also have had to be cleared originally, but probably not at the time the particular fields in question were laid out, the division between two fields was marked by a fence with posts at *c.* 1.25 m intervals. The evidence of the post-holes would normally suggest a post and rail fence, but here, in one place only, were small impressions in the chalk suggesting that stakes, perhaps hurdling, had filled the spaces between the posts. The attraction of this interpretation is that while posts alone can divide one field from another for demarcation purposes, and hurdling added to them can keep animals off the growing crops, the removal of the hurdling after harvest could easily throw several fields open to 'common' gleaning and grazing on the stubble, though 'stubble' begs another question (below, p. 223). Other edges of the same two fields divided by this fence were along the line of the filled up ditch of the settlement they replaced, already referred to above (p. 158), providing an example on a minor scale of "the activities of one generation of settlers offering restraints to succeeding generations".[33]

This remarkably preserved, but archaeologically otherwise unremarkable, area of downland offers two other types of field boundary. The fields of a system of the early Roman period were separated only

[33] B. Cunliffe in Benson and Miles, *op. cit.*, p. 7.

by unploughed baulks, subsequently preserved as buried ground surfaces beneath the low lynchets that developed over them (Plate IV*b*).[34] The cut-away in section at each side of the original baulk where the first furrow on each side had been turned away from the thin, unploughed strip of land was therefore preserved and visible in section. In other cases, there was no observed structure at all, so presumably an imaginary line between perhaps two sticks or stones at the field corners was sufficient in practice to keep the ploughmen on either side of their respective fields. Exactly this phenomenon has been observed by the writer in north-west Spain in fields under ard-cultivation: lynchets were developing along the imaginary line between the sticks and therefore giving physical shape and a real edge to the fields.[35] A variant on this observed in Wessex is an accumulation of flint nodules along a field edge, presumably thrown or dumped there year after year as each fresh cultivation brought more flints to the surface (though the process is rather the other way round with the gradual breakdown of the soil revealing more and more flints).

Field boundaries also incorporated existing features. The use of long barrows for field edges (Fig. 38) and of round barrows for field corners is now well-documented for Dorset in particular,[36] though for round barrows at least there is also evidence, crucial for dating, that the relationship was the opposite way round (below, p. 162). Trackways frequently wind their way through field systems, forming the edges of fields, and are sometimes likely to be earlier in date. Often, however, they can equally well be shown to be later. We see this on both chalk and gravel, with tracks and, of course, known roads cutting across existing fields.[37] All the evidence argues for an enormous effort by a few million people during the last two millennia BC to bring large tracks of country under systematic control, not only on the grand scale with their field systems, but also in the detail of many thousands of kilometres of field boundary, every single centimetre of which was constructed in a variety of ways from an imaginary line to major bank and ditch.

[34] Plan of field system: Fowler in Thomas (ed.), *Rural Settlement in Roman Britain*, p. 60, fig. 9; section of baulks, *Ant.*, XLI, fig. 3 opposite p. 290, J and K.
[35] P. J. Fowler and P. J. Reynolds, paper on field evidence in preparation.
[36] RCHM, *Dorset*, II–V, 1970–75, Sectional Prefaces on long barrows.
[37] Overton Down, track cutting through 'Celtic' fields; Pertwood Down, Roman road likewise, *Wilts. Arch. Mag.*, 58, 1962, p. 107 and F4 on Fig. 1; gravel, Benson and Miles, *op. cit.*, e.g. Maps 3, 21 and 22 and fig. 11.

Contents of fields

Though arable fields existed to grow crops, no example has yet been
found containing a crop, part of the crops, or any evidence of the crop
in situ. Our knowledge of the arable product lies literally outside our
field (below, pp. 203–7). On the other hand, surface collection and
excavation have shown that fields contain evidence of how the land they
enclose was used before, during, and after its principle crop-producing
phase, and this evidence itself can indicate, in some degree, the length
and date of that phase. Often, of course, the same piece of land has
enjoyed multiple use through time, with pre- and post-field uses not
necessarily being involved with arable cultivation. One of the most
important pieces of such evidence, certainly for dating purposes, is that
of fields 'containing' round barrows. In a dozen or so instances,
observable or observed on the ground, round barrows appear to be on
the boundary of or inside a field which already existed. Actually
determining such a pre-barrow relationship without excavation presents
some difficulty, e.g. the Grafton Barrows, Wilts.,[38] but on the northern
slopes of Penbury Knoll, for example, there is no doubt that a round
barrow is inside a field, and its post-field date can hardly be doubted
if its position in relation to a well-developed lynchet just downslope
of it is considered. Indeed, the fields must have been old when the
barrow was built.[39]

Barrows, or more precisely ring-ditches once enclosing burial
mounds, also appear on air photographs inside fields on both chalk and
gravel, and they cannot be assumed in all cases merely to have an
accidental relationship to a later, different land-use. In fact, taking into
account also the numerous occasions on which excavation of a barrow
has shown it to lie on cultivated land, the barrow as a feature inside
earlier and disused fields is probably more common than has been
appreciated. On the other hand, the large round-barrow cemetery on
Snail Down, Wilts., is divided off in its own reserved area by ditches
(Fig. 40):[40] and, to quote Overton Down again, there a round barrow
lies in a reserved area formed on at least three sides by field edges of
a system which clearly respects a presumably pre-existing barrow. The
barrow is not, however, strictly speaking, in a field.[41] Just to the south,
to illustrate the multiple use of land cultivated at one stage in its history,

[38] Bowen, *Ancient Fields*, fig. 2, E. Pl. IIa.
[39] P. J. Fowler, *op. cit.*, 'Early prehistoric agriculture...', fig. 35B.
[40] For the ditches in context, see H. C. Bowen in Wilson (ed.), *Aerial Reconnaissance for Archaeology*, fig. 6 at SU 219520; for a revised summary account of Snail Down, see N. Thomas, *Guide to Prehistoric England*, London, 1976, pp. 228–32.
[41] Crawford and Keiller, *op. cit.*, Pl. XIX, K.

a particular small area was used for a Beaker cemetery and a mid first-millennium settlement before its use as an arable field in the later pre-Roman centuries; while in another area to the south again, a late-Roman settlement was fitted into the pattern of lynchetted field boundaries from earlier arable use.[42] All this was revealed by excavating the contents of fields, evidence which is of considerable landscape interest and a topic to which we shall return (below, p. 166); but here we wish to examine a little more closely the archaeological evidence in fields relating specifically to their contemporary arable use.

In the first place the area enclosed within a field boundary may well contain evidence of previous land-use, e.g. arable at Stannon Down on Bodmin Moor, dune formation after cultivation at Gwithian, settlement following cemetery on Overton Down. It may also contain evidence of the land clearance carried out to create that field. Tree, bush, and root holes can indicate not only former vegetation, but the contents and nature of the holes may well suggest the nature of that vegetation and how it was removed. Stones within fields, or the holes from which they have been removed, can provide similar evidence.[43] The two main types of archaeological evidence for the field's use are, however, the marks of cultivation and the residue of manuring.

In numerous cases now throughout Europe – well over one hundred – the marks made by a traction implement used to till the soil in prehistoric times have been identified in excavation (Plate VII). These marks, or 'plough-ruts' as they have been (wrongly) called elsewhere,[44] consist of lines of soil different in colour and/or texture from the surrounding medium. Characteristically as found, this soil lies in a V-shaped groove scratched into the subsoil. The grooves themselves lie in roughly parallel lines almost invariably *c.* 30 cm apart and usually occur in two sets, one at right angles to another. In practice, nearly all the principal British examples appear much more complex because the same area bears the marks of superimposed and successive rectilinear patterns. The main examples of this type of evidence from certain or probable later prehistoric times in Britain have been noted at Carrawburgh and Walker, Northumb.; Rudgeway, Glos.; South Street, Avebury (Figs. 1, 53), West Overton and Amesbury, Wilts.; Fritham, Hants., and, in two separate phases, at Gwithian, Cornwall[45] (Fig. 51 Plate VIIb). To that 1971 list can be added further examples at Chester,

[42] See Site Index for full references; the main one for this point is *Wilts. Arch. Mag.*, 62, 1967, pp. 16–33.

[43] Holes of various origins, soils and environmental evidence are discussed in Evans, *Land Snails in Archaeology*.

[44] Cunliffe, *Iron Age Communities in Britain*, fig. 11, p. 12.

[45] *Ant.*, XLI, 1967, pp. 289–301; P. J. Fowler, *op. cit.*, p. 164.

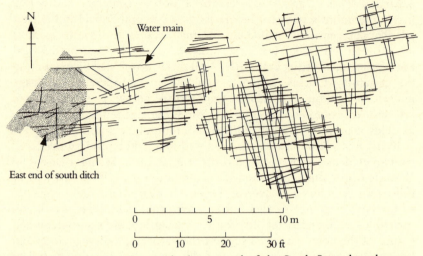

Water main

East end of south ditch

Fig. 43. Plan of ard-marks outside the east end of the South Street long barrow, Avebury, Wilts. The marks cross the filling of the long barrow ditch (*bottom left*) and relate to a Beaker phase of cultivation *c.* 2000 bc (from an original drawing by J. G. Evans).

Rudchester on Hadrian's Wall, and Rosinish in the Hebrides (below, p. 278).[46]

The earliest example, from beneath the South Street long barrow, Wilts., is discussed above (p. 56). Two of the later examples listed here can be looked at in greater detail (a third at Gwithian, Cornwall and a fourth at Rudgeway, Glos., are examined in the Highland Zone section below, pp. 195–8). They are at South Street again and at Overton Down, Wilts., both close together near Avebury but in different geological, topographical, and cultural contexts. The South Street example lay outside and on the east side of the long barrow, the ard-marks being scratched into the surface of the Middle Chalk subsoil (Fig. 43).[47] Their association is with a ploughsoil containing Beaker sherds which developed over the already existing silts in the long barrow ditch. Charcoal from the soil produced a C-14 date of *c.* 2000 bc, and fossil snails indicated a phase of land clearance followed by one of open conditions. The ard-marks themselves, only *c.* 30–40 cm below modern ground level, were very clear and straight, lying parallel and at right

[46] The number of recorded examples is now difficult to list as a result of improved excavation techniques, an increase in relevant excavation and a delay in publication. Probably the total is now well over twenty in Britain.

[47] Evans, *op. cit.*, pp. 328–32; *Ant.*, XLI, 1967, pp. 289–301. No plan of these ard-marks has previously been published. See now *Proc. Prehist. Soc.* 45, 1979, pp. 207–300.

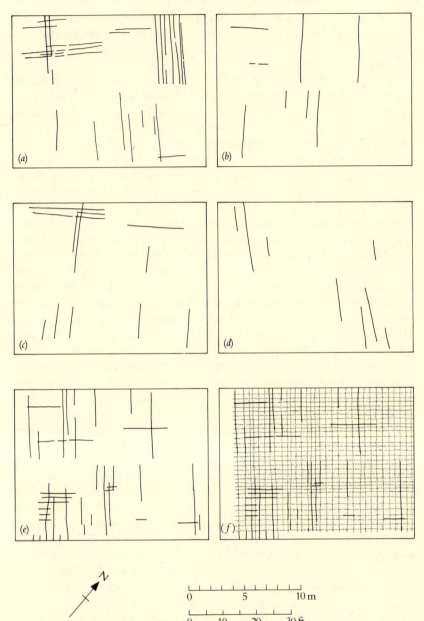

Fig. 44. Ard-marks within a 'Celtic' field at Site XI/A, Overton Down, Wilts., etched into the surface of the chalk bedrock. Five different sets of fragmentary criss-cross marks were tentatively identified in the palimpsest on the basis of their slightly different axes (a–e), with the most complete set (e) here being reconstituted to give an overall impression of what the complete pattern might have been like (f) (P. J. Fowler).

angles to each other almost 1 m apart. Essentially they presented a once-only pattern. No edge to them was located, though presumably they lay in a field of which at least one part of one edge was the millennium-old long barrow.

The recognition of the South Street evidence followed hard on the ard-marks identified on nearby Overton Down (Fig. 44).[48] There they lay only *c*. 20–25 cm below the existing downland turf, existing in the very surface of the crumbling 'split pea' or C horizon of the Upper Chalk bedrock. A few penetrated into the solid chalk but most of the traces could be brushed away. The marks were *c*. 10 cm wide at most, mostly 5–10 cm deep, and V-shaped in section where excavatable. They lay roughly parallel and at right angles to the adjacent lynchet, beneath which was found the evidence for a fence (above p. 160); but the overall pattern they formed was complex, and at least five separate 'ploughings' could be identified. In each, the ard-marks were *c*. 30 cm apart in both directions. Some cut through features of the Beaker cemetery and mid first millennium BC settlement existing in the same plane of the bedrock surface. The ard-marks exist widely over the area, as shown by cuttings away from the main excavations, but an edge to them was found beneath the tail of the lynchet piled up behind the fence. That this edge marked the edge of the cultivated area could not be further demonstrated here because the soil beneath the lynchet and on the bedrock had been disturbed, presumably by the (immediately?) preceding occupation. Molluscan evidence from and beneath the lynchet indicated open conditions throughout the time before and during the formation of the lynchet.

These and the other examples raise several points, some of them basic to our understanding of at least the methods of later prehistoric cultivation. What was making the grooves? Was their creation deliberate or accidental? Do the marks at right angles really represent the two parts of but a single process? Why do we find once-only and palimpsest patterns? Are we looking at the evidence left by the normal, annual cultivation of the soil (Plate VII*a*) or at that from special ploughings when the implement went deeper? Are we indeed looking at the evidence of ploughing at all? Some answers, uncertain and at best a balance of probabilities, can be considered when the Highland Zone evidence is also brought into the account (below, pp. 195–201).

One, at the moment unique and very dubious, variant on the ard-mark type of evidence comes apparently from a mid first millennium context at Weston Wood, Surrey. There the marks, in two groups but all running in the same direction, were broader and much shorter than

[48] Evans, *op. cit.*, pp. 320–1; *Ant.*, XLI, 1967, pp. 289–301; *Wilts. Arch. Mag.*, 62, 1967, pp. 24–6.

ard-marks proper. Whether ancient or modern, they seem best interpreted as having been formed by hand-digging in spits, probably in two small (8.5 × 7 m) plots, rather than as representing part of a field system. Although in this particular case the evidence so far published is unconvincing, the use of a spade for digging in a field is demonstrated at Gwithian, Cornwall (Fig. 53), and the now abundant evidence of second-millennium 'ridge and furrow' in Ireland seems most likely to result from hand-dug ridging of the 'lazy-bed' type (see below, p. 201 and for comparable evidence in north Britain, pp. 198–201).

The other main type of archaeological evidence from within fields consists simply of potsherds and other cultural material. This was first systematically shown by Rhodes using mainly surface material collected during his study of the later prehistoric field systems of the Berkshire Downs,[49] and has since been confirmed by excavation and much further field-walking. Pottery ranging over the whole of the last two millennia BC has thus been recovered, though the most frequently found material is of Roman date. The potsherds themselves are characteristically small, e.g. 3 × 2 cm, weathered and rounded along the fractured edges. The implication is not only that they have been out in the fields for a long time but that they were present during their cultivation. As a result they have been pulversized and rolled during the repeated preparations of the seed bed. The only rational explanation of their presence on arable fields is that, presumably but not necessarily accidentally, they were spread on the fields with manure brought, in part anyway, from domestic middens. By a circular argument, the presence of occupation material on the fields is interpreted as evidence of manuring.

In addition to pottery, other material also occurs in fields, though less commonly. The rest of the domestic rubbish – nails, tile fragments, 'pot-boilers', burnt flints, and bits of stone tools, for example – can reasonably be accounted for by the 'manuring model'. So, too, can most of the struck flints which frequently occur in the chalk country; but occasionally a flint implement, particularly a sickle blade with silica gloss (below, p. 222), may represent a loss in situ and so too could a whetstone. Some of the flint waste might also represent the working of tools out in the fields rather than swept-up debris brought out from settlement or working floor.

Apart from such speculation about material actually lost or used in the fields, there is also a small group of material which was deliberately buried in the fields – quite different from the bulk of the domestic refuse which happened to end up in a field. This principally consists of late second to early first millennium BC bronzes buried in fields and their

[49] P. Rhodes, *Oxoniensia*, 15, 1950, pp. 1–28.

boundaries. Hoards of this type have been recorded, for example, in a field at Ebbesbourne Wake, Wilts., and possibly in a lynchet near Lulworth, Dorset.[50] In both cases incidentally, the evidence presumes the pre-existence of the fields. Whether such hoards should be taken at face value as unrecovered traders' or metal-workers' deposits, or as representing some ritual facet connected with arable fields, is unknown. The more mundane explanation is probably to be preferred. A similar judgment should probably be applied to the occasional burials, invariably inhumation, amongst those so far recorded, found not so much in fields as in their lynchetted edges. None are certainly pre-Roman, though one at West Overton, Wilts., could just conceivably be contemporary with the fields' origins, since it was apparently beneath, rather than in, the lynchet.[51]

Finally, in considering the contents of fields it is all too easy to overlook the principal containing material – the soil. Although once it is enclosed and treated to become a seed-bed it becomes in effect a cultural layer containing the type of evidence just discussed, for present purposes the main importance of soil lies in its 'natural' evidence and the implied relationships between man and his environment.[52] The structure of the soil itself is a source of information hardly yet exploited, while its chemical properties as a result of acculturalization remain of largely unknown potential. In the soil too are the many fossil and living biological data bearing on its past use: the pollen grains and molluscan shells, the scattered fragments of cereals themselves, the skeletons of former insect life, pieces of charcoal and animal bone are the better known types. Such evidence, all constituting 'the soil', represent an enormous reservoir of information as yet barely exploited systematically from the agrarian point of view, although in a sense taken for granted. It is perhaps only when local conditions do not preserve such evidence that it is realized how sterile is the study of agriculture by its artifacts without an environmental context.

In the Lowland Zone, then, we see quite clearly on many of the lighter soils, particularly over chalk and gravels, and also on some of the heavier soils, like Keuper Marl, a tremendous range of evidence for cultivated crop husbandry in the field. The evidence is varied, but underlying it seems to be a remarkable consistency over a relatively large area and through so long a period of time. An attempt will be made

---

[50] Ebbesbourne Wake: the original publication, *Wilts. Arch. Mag.*, 53, 1949, pp. 104–12, makes it quite clear that the hoard was found in a field, *not* in a lynchet, *contra* Rowlands, *The Organisation of Middle Bronze Age Metalworking*, no. 155, perpetuating the error in C. N. Moore and M. J. Rowlands, *Bronze Age Metalwork in Salisbury Museum*, Salisbury, 1972, p. 63. Lulworth, see RCHM, *Dorset*, II, 1970, p. 629.

[51] VCH, *Wilts.*, I, part i, 1957, p. 120.

[52] On soils, see S. Limbrey, *Soil Science and Archaeology*, London, 1975.

to fit the gist of the foregoing descriptive matter into a chronological and cultural context in Chapter III (below, pp. 245–62).

Highland Zone Field Systems

The traditional view of a Highland Zone dominated by, if not exclusively devoted to, pastoralism is not borne out by the archaeological or indeed palaeobotanical evidence in our period. The part played by pastoralism is discussed below (p. 232) and its importance is not to be denied; but, just as we have already seen for the third and fourth millennia, there is also much evidence for arable farming in the Highland Zone from the Beaker horizon onwards. For certain areas west of the Teesmouth–Seaton line, much of what has already been said also applies: in the Cotswolds and on the lower parts of the Derbyshire Peak, for example, traces remain of field systems with small rectangular fields and other associated characteristics. In the Yorkshire Dales too, particularly round Grassington (Fig. 52), similar systems were in use in the Roman period. For much of the Zone, however, the archaeological remains look different, not least in their use of stone, and in some cases such physical differences suggest a different chronology and different agrarian practices from those in the Lowland Zone. Certainly different methods of crop cultivation seem to have been going on simultaneously in the two zones though, equally clearly, much of the evidence from the south-western peninsula in the second millennium shows close similarities with contemporary evidence in the rather different environment of chalkland Wessex. There is some evidence for arable farming from somewhere in the Highland Zone throughout the last two millennia BC but it is by no means so densely distributed as in the Lowland Zone, and whole tracts of landscape bear no structural evidence at all.

Many of the mountainous areas, for example, perhaps already agriculturally 'dead' through previous exploitation, hardly seem to have been used at all, let alone for crop cultivation. Other areas, like Dartmoor, we see becoming agriculturally derelict in the late second millennium while, at the other extreme of Britain, land cultivated in our period by apparently Late Neolithic communities in Shetland does not show an agricultural succession either. In fact, by and large, though ground evidence for later prehistoric cultivation in the west and north is extensive, if sporadic, very few areas preserve or present the landscape palimpsest effect so characteristic of Midland gravel or Wessex chalk. Overall, the impression is much more one of 'exploit and move on', with the result that the transitory farmer often broke the forest regeneration cycle so that the landscape took on the aspect of a wilderness so highly regarded as a 'natural' phenomenon today by a predominantly non-agrarian population. As a result of this exploitive relationship of man with the natural resources, particularly in the second millennium, in sharp contrast to the more balanced, conservationist relationship in the Lowland Zone (below, p. 248), areas once farmed have tended not to be cultivated again, and consequently the monumental remains of the exploited, relict landscape, fossilized in stone, have been well-preserved to the present day. Clearly an account of Highland Zone agriculture in later prehistoric times must lean heavily on such evidence, accepting the unavoidable bias. In mitigation, however, it can be said that, unlike the many examples of field systems recorded on the Wessex downs, comparable evidence in the Highland Zone is not necessarily on marginal land in a contemporary prehistoric context, however marginal it may appear to present-day farmers. In the following, we draw heavily on the south-west, parts of Wales, the Pennines, Northumbria, and the Shetlands, all areas where field systems have been recorded. We can only note that much larger areas have either not been investigated or, after examination, are not known to contain relevant field evidence.

Extent

The areas where extensive field systems with constructed fields are known are few: Penwith in West Cornwall, Bodmin Moor and Dartmoor, Pembrokeshire and Carnaervonshire, and Cumbria. Other large areas have been cultivated, and to them we shall return (below, p. 172). In some of the areas mentioned, the extent and nature of the field systems lead to interpretation similar to those for Wessex. Dartmoor is the most striking case, partly because of the well-preserved evidence but also because of a long tradition of fieldwork and excavation, continuing still and recently linked to parallel palaeo-botanical studies. Current work, as in Wessex, is concentrating on the systems rather than the fields and, as a consequence, major landscape architecture broadly of the mid to late second millennium BC is being recognized (Plates IIIa, V, Figs. 45, 46).[53] Parts of the Moor were divided up into large oblong blocks of territory by long, parallel, and approximately straight 'reaves' or stone and earth banks, in part probably derived from land clearance. It is the scale of the operations, however, which is impressive: typical blocks are many hectares in extent and, to cite one example on Spitchwick Common, the area covered by a whole system of related reaves is minimally c. 13 ha. The recent and

[53] E. Gawne and J. V. Somers Cocks, 'Parallel reaves on Dartmoor', Trans. Devons. Assoc., 100, 1968, pp. 277–91, fig. 2. See now Proc. Prehist. Soc. 45, 1979, pp. 1–33.

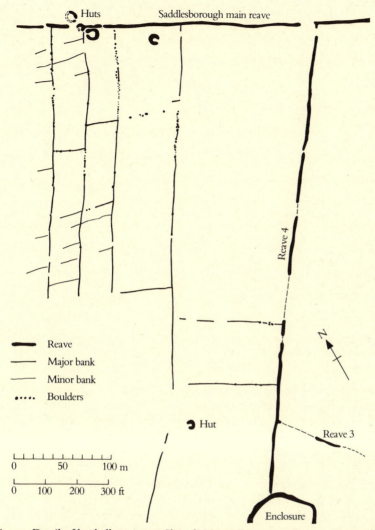

Fig. 45. Detail of land allotment on Shaugh Moor, Dartmoor, Devon. Reave 4 is one of several parallel reaves terminating on Saddlesborough Main Reave. The land on its west is divided up by four slighter, parallel boundaries, the strips they define being further subdivided by cross-banks of similar slight construction. The huts are presumably contemporary (after J. Collis).

current demonstration of the extent of cohesive land arrangements on Dartmoor (and in western Ireland, see p. 201 below; Fig. 47) contrasts with the traditional Highland Zone picture of a single isolated farm with a few hectares of arable land surrounded by rough grazing; but it is not the only such example. Extensive areas of arable also occur over

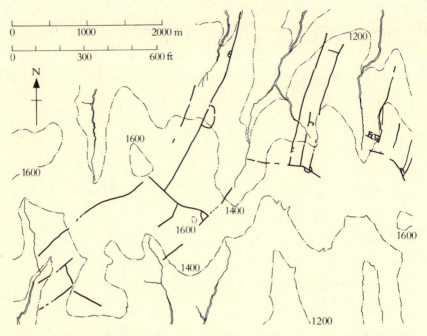

Fig. 46. Reaves and related enclosures between White Ridge and Shapley Tor, Dartmoor, Devon (after A. Fleming).

many other parts of the Highland Zone, though the evidence for it is in many instances so slight that its existence has only recently been recognized (Plate IIIb). The field arrangements in these cases – most of those so far published are in the north of Britain – differ from the regularity seen on Dartmoor, but their *extent* is, in some cases, comparable.[54]

In Wales, for example, around Penmaenmawr in north-west Caernarvonshire, an area of former cultivation marked by lynchets, banks, hut-circles, and clearance cairns originally occupied *c.* 14 ha (Fig. 48*c*). In Northumberland, a cairn field at Chatton Sandyford, which could possibly be of agricultural significance, extends over about 40 ha (Fig. 48*b*); while just over the Border in Peeblesshire, another 'plot-system' of nearly 14 ha has been surveyed on White Meldon Hill. Stanshiel Rig (Fig. 49*a*) to the south-west in Dumfriesshire is one of the best known areas of prehistoric cultivation in Scotland: the area so far recorded, 26.3 ha, contains hundreds of clearance cairns, banks, low lynchets, and various settlement structures. Extensive plot-systems have

[54] R. W. Feachem, 'Ancient agriculture in the highland of Britain', *Proc. Prehist. Soc.*, 39, 1973, pp. 332–53.

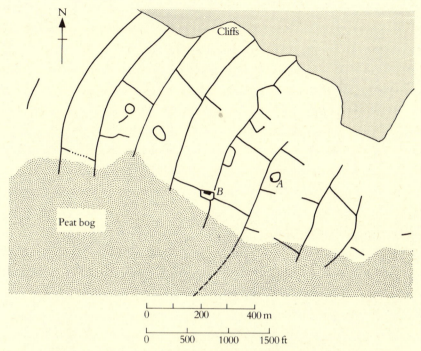

Fig. 47. Land allotment of the late third millennium bc at Behy/Glenulra, County Mayo, Ireland. *A*, excavated enclosure; *B*, court cairn (after S. Caulfield).

also been recorded in Perthshire and Angus, e.g. one of *c.* 9 ha on Middleton Muir (Fig. 49*b*), Perths. Further north still, and only recently recognized, "the countryside bordering the Moray Firth and extending northwards to the Kyle of Sutherland contains hundreds of hectares of plot-systems". One example covers *c.* 43 ha on The Ord near Lairg, Sutherland (Fig. 49*c*).

The new, or newly displayed, evidence stems largely from recent fieldwork by the Ordnance Survey. Important in itself, it also helps to provide a context for longer-known examples of putative Highland Zone agriculture which may have appeared to be isolated, or at least infrequent, occurrences. This is perhaps particularly so in northern England where cairn fields have for long been known. In a recent study[55] these are termed 'extensive settlements' and are identified as having existed (or existing now) in three main concentrations, namely on the gritstone moors of the southern Pennines, in central Blackmore on the North York Moors, and on the peripheral fells of the Cumbrian

[55] A. J. Challis and D. W. Harding, *Later Prehistory from the Trent to the Tyne*, British Archaeological Reports, 20, Oxford, 1975, p. 125, fig. 84.

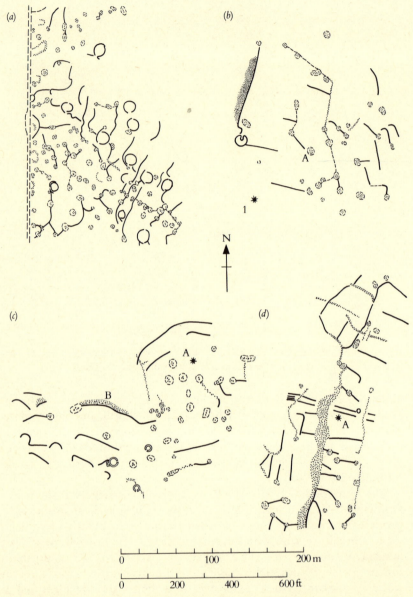

Fig. 48. Examples of former arable areas in the Highland Zone: (*a*), Loch Laide, Inverness.; (*b*), Sandyford Moor, Northumb.; (*c*), Penmaenmawr, Caerns.; (*d*), Gardom's Edge, Derbys. (after R. W. Feachem).

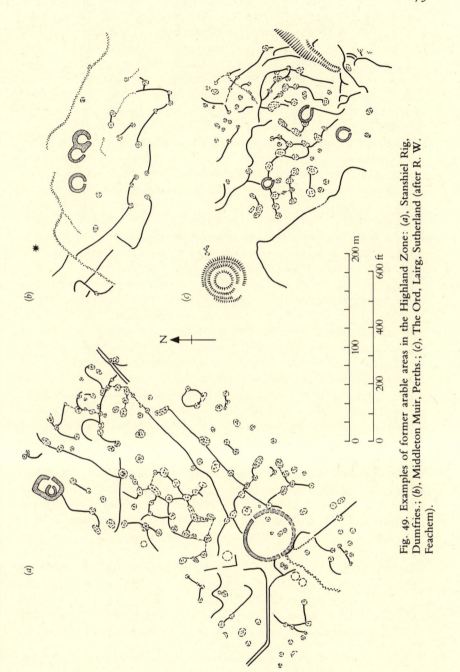

Fig. 49. Examples of former arable areas in the Highland Zone: (a), Stanshiel Rig, Dumfries.; (b), Middleton Muir, Perths.; (c), The Ord, Lairg, Sutherland (after R. W. Feachem).

Lake District. Topographically, they occur within a zone 1000 ± 400 ft. (*c.* 300 m) above OD and, although "the cairns appear as shapeless heaps of stone", *c.* 2–3 m in diameter, here as in the Welsh and Scottish examples quoted above, "lengths of rough walling run between the cairns on irregular alignments, sometimes forming small enclosed areas". The positive evidence from pollen analysis, indicating extensive clearance of alder and hazel scrub "on an unprecedented scale", rather than the negative evidence of very infrequent burial evidence beneath the cairns, suggests that these remains represent crop production rather than a pastoral economy, and that the cairns themselves are primarily clearance-heaps rather than burial mounds. This can certainly be argued for one of the most extensive examples, on Danby Rigg with more than 800 cairns, and the same can be argued for one of the most extensive of all such areas, *c.* 88 ha on Green Crag Slack in the eastern Pennines. Further west, one of the half-dozen examples in Cumbria is at Barnscar where "about 400 cairns, some arranged in lines, and banks and walls suggesting a cultivation system" have been reported. Overall, and in several specific cases, related pollen analytical and C-14 estimates strongly suggest a general clearance of upland wood and scrub for arable farming in the second half of the second millennium BC. That the individual, cleared areas are often so extensive and, never having regenerated, are now wilderness landscapes could indicate intensive but shifting exploitation, terminated during or possibly before the onset of the Sub-Atlantic climatic deterioration.[56]

The extent of former arable, and of field systems now shown to exist in some areas of the Highland Zone, must not be allowed, however, to dominate the picture completely. In many other parts of Britain the small cluster of fields, apparently forming a 'family' or 'farmstead' system related to one settlement, can still be seen as the norm. In the south-west, for example, compact units of unenclosed 'huts with fields' have been remarked on, especially on the east side of Dartmoor, while the later second-millennium site at Gwithian in west Cornwall (Fig. 49) demonstrates two successive phases of a small farm, surrounded by a group of small fields covering, in the earlier layer-5 phase, *c.* 0.5 ha between sand-dunes and a tidal estuary.[57] This area is, however, that established by excavation – none of the relevant evidence is visible on the surface, unlike the Dartmoor situation – and the real extent of the arable may have been considerably more. In Wales, too, there are also extensive field systems, located mainly in the north (Fig. 20) and

[56] Cf. A. Fleming, 'Bronze Age agriculture on the marginal lands of north-east Yorkshire', *Agric. Hist. Rev.*, 19, 1971, pp. 1–24.

[57] A. Fox, 'Celtic fields and farms on Dartmoor', *Proc. Prehist. Soc.*, 20, 1954, pp. 87–102; *idem, South West England.*

south-west of the country.[58] Dating evidence is sparse, though many were probably in use in the early centuries AD, perhaps a little earlier, rather than in the second millennium BC (excepting systems with unenclosed huts and/or cairns, see above, p. 109). They appear, generally to represent conglomerations of small fields, each related to a single farm rather than the larger scale ordering of a unitary landscape. In Caernarvonshire,[59] for example, eight enclosed homesteads have a minimum associated exploitable arable area, estimating from the surviving ground evidence of field remains, ranging only from 16 to $\frac{1}{4}$ acres (c. 6 to 0.1 ha). Another morphologically distinguishable settlement form, the terraced fields associated with enclosed hut groups, do not vary quite so much in their estimable extent, the range in a sample of 10 being from 2–19 acres (c. 0.8–7.6 ha) with, perhaps more significantly, five of the examples being between 10 and 19 acres (4 and 7.9 ha). Perhaps as significant as their extent is their location, tending to be below 1000 ft (c. 300 m) above OD on gentler slopes and within the zone of modern crop-growing arable land. A recent detailed study in this area notes a close relationship between lynchetted fields and dry light soils.[60] It concludes that "the relationship between farm location and soil type is close enough to confirm the commonsense belief that farms are located where their economic base is most likely to succeed". Though such a generalization may seem 'obvious', it is limited to the 'enclosed homesteads', mainly in Caernarvonshire, and provides a contrast with, for example, the earlier, unenclosed settlements on eastern Dartmoor. In considering the distribution and extent of Highland Zone field systems, a significant contribution from this study is its identification, within the mass of field data, of differences of function: upland settlements for animal husbandry, lowland unenclosed and concentric circle-type settlements for arable except where their fields lie on wet soil in which cases "they are often walled and do not show any signs of cultivation".

The shape of these various field systems varies a great deal. We are after all dealing with very different phenomena. All are irregular, if generally rectilinear, in outline, though to varying degrees. Some Dartmoor systems tend to be elongated with long stretches of their boundaries straight (Fig. 46; Plate IIIa) while, at the other extreme, the arable areas around the Shetland farms tend to be amorphous in shape,

[58] RCAM, *Caernarvonshire Inventory*, I–III, London, 1956–64; *idem, Anglesey Inventory*, London, 1937, reprint 1960; *idem, Pembrokeshire Inventory*, London, 1925.
[59] RCAM, *Caernarvonshire*, III, 1964, pp. xciv and ciii.
[60] N. D. Johnson, 'An environmental study of the location of pre-medieval settlement in Caernarvonshire', M.A. thesis, Univ. of Sheffield, 1976. The author is extremely grateful to Mr Johnson for the prolonged loan and consequential use of his helpful thesis.

apparently fading out into the surrounding countryside (Fig. 14). By and large then, the individual fields or plots do not derive their shapes from an imposed overall plan of the systems of which they are a part though, notably in some south-western instances, there are major exceptions.

Typology

The shape of the fields has naturally suggested morphological distinction, recently summarized as:[61]

1. Amorphous walled enclosures, usually associated with some clearance cairns and hut-circles; third/second millennia BC.

2. Systems of small irregular plots formed by lynchets and banks, with clearance cairns, often associated with timber buildings or hut-circles; possibly from latter part of the second millennium BC to about the middle of the first.

3. More regular fields, perhaps starting in the last centuries BC and continuing into the first centuries AD.

Though primarily emphasizing various settlement features rather than the characteristics of fields specifically, Johnson follows a similar three-fold morphological/chronological succession in summarizing his results from the detailed study of his Class II type of settlement – unenclosed huts and associated walls and enclosures – among the evidence for pre-medieval settlement in Caernarvonshire:[62]

(i). Class IIa – unenclosed, upland, dispersed enclosures associated with small, roughly built round huts; pollen Zone VIIb, third/second millennia BC.

(ii). Class IIb – large, well-built round huts associated with enclosures less dispersed than with IIa, often overlain by Romano-British enclosed homesteads; last centuries BC – early centuries AD.

(iii). Class IIc – sub-rectangular huts associated with small paddocks, forming pastoral units contemporary with the enclosed homestead; Romano-British period.

Looking at the Highland Zone as a whole, a slightly more extended categorization could now be reasonably suggested for the surviving field types up to the Roman period. Since types 1, 2, etc. are rather dull labels, possible geographical names are very tentatively suggested in brackets after the Feachem class number.

(a) Irregular, amorphous cleared area, characterized by cairns, but really without obvious lynchets or field boundaries. Typologically the earliest, but can be of any date. (Feachem 1; the Shetland type?)

(b) Irregular but generally rectangular fields characterized by cairns

[61] Feachem, *op. cit.*, pp. 347–8.   [62] Johnson, *op. cit.*, pp. 157–8.

or clearance mounds, lynchets, walls, or stone lines, and sometimes burial mounds, located in mountainous country. Probably all pre-Sub-Atlantic (Feachem 1; the montane type?)

(c) Elongated or geometric fields related to axial lines, so far characteristic of the south-west and probably all pre-sub-Atlantic. (No Feachem number; the south-western type?)

(d) Roughly square or rectangular fields, akin to many Celtic fields on the chalk downs and common in the Highland Zone. Second millennium BC onwards. (Feachem 3; ?)

(e) Somewhat irregular but markedly oblong fields, characteristic of the Pennines and north-west England, but with regional variants, probably mainly of the Roman period. (Feachem 3?; the northern type?)

Type (a) can be of any date, since essentially it represents a first clearance, but in the British Highland Zone examples are likely to be second millennium or earlier. Type (b) seems specifically of the mid/later second millennium, perhaps just coming into the 1st millennium but no later. This is probably true also of type (c). Type (d) is also present by the mid/late second millennium though many surviving examples were almost certainly being cultivated at the end of the prehistoric period and in Roman times. Type (e) has most of its associations in the Roman period. These generalizations must now be looked at in more detail.

Type (a) fields are best exemplified at, and still most fully published from, Shetland.[63] Despite their typologically early nature and 'Neolithic' association, a single, recently obtained C-14 date suggests a mid second-millennium date for their use.[64] A dozen scattered house-sites (Fig. 53) and a 'temple', three of them excavated, were recorded over an area of *c.* 2 square miles (*c.* 518 ha) around Gruting and Stanydale. Near Gruting School *c.* 2 acres (0.8 ha) east and north of two of the houses was marked by 35 'heaps of field-gathered stones', from which it was argued that the area, cleared of stones, had been used as a patch of arable land by the houses' inhabitants. The patch has no definite boundaries and, indeed, is defined by the distribution of the heaps of stones; nor are individual fields delineated. About 1.6 km to the south, however, an area of former cultivation with more developed characteristics was recorded, extending down the southerly slope of the Ness of Gruting almost to the shore of Seli Voe (Fig. 14). The total area involved is *c.* 8.25 acres (*c.* 3.3 ha), again without apparent boundaries but indicated by a scatter of some 50 'heaps of field-gathered stones'. Within this area, however, are slight lynchets, a few low banks and

[63] C. S. T. Calder, 'Stone Age house-sites in Shetland', *Proc. Soc. Ant. Scot.*, 89, 1955–6, pp. 340–97.   [64] BM 441: 1564 ± 120 bc.

'traces of field dykes'; i.e. close-set earth-bound stones, together apparently indicating small, cultivated plots. In other words, individual 'fields' are marked out but the whole 'system' is not. Indeed, not all the 'fields' – 'plots' probably is a better word – are contiguous, so perhaps the remains are best not described as a 'field system'. Nevertheless, there is a high correlation between the observable plots and the clearance cairns, so an interpretation of the evidence as perhaps eight or nine individual, irregular, cultivated plots scattered across a south-facing slope in an area generally used by the occupants of the adjacent house is permissible. Even with three other house sites within 400 m to the west, the impression is that there was little pressure on space and apparently no need to delimit a territory.

That this became necessary with time, or contemporaneously elsewhere, perhaps in preferred locations, is demonstrated a little further to the west at Brouster where five or six fields around a house and containing two other oval structures cover some 2.75 acres (c. 1 ha). The area is again characterized by stone clearance mounds – the fields containing respectively 4, 2, 12, 10, 7, and 9 – but each field is enclosed by a dyke of earth-fast stones, their outer boundaries in effect delineating a ring-fence some 500 m around. Some of the complexes on Shetland, notably in the area around the Stanydale 'temple' itself, to the east at Stromness and on the eastern side of the island at Vassa Voe, develop the ring-fence idea in the form of a field dyke almost completely delineating an irregular or sub-rectangular which apparently contains no subdivisions. At Stanydale such a 'field' encloses some 8 acres (c. 3.3 ha) containing the 'temple', two houses, and about thirty stone mounds but no plots, though two small fields, each about 0.5 acre (0.32 ha), form part of the south-west boundary of the field beside another house. At each of Vassa and Stromness Voes, a single house is apparently related to an enclosed or at least delineated sub-rectangular area of c. 0.75–1 acre (0.3–0.4 ha), with no subdivisions, no cairns, and no other stone structures. Clearly here we have gone beyond a strict definition of type (a) fields, even within the type-area, so clearly a morphological classification has to be used carefully and at best can only be of moderate help at an early stage of enquiry. Nevertheless, we can apparently see on Shetland the archetypal (a) fields in the form of scattered cultivated plots without any built, enclosing boundary, even though much more important, not least for the rarity of its occurrence in prehistoric Britain, is the topographical association of settlements, houses, plots, fields, temples and burial places, closely related to a distinctive environmental context and, so it can be argued, a presumptive way of life which continued until the recent past.

Type (b) fields have already been considered when dealing with the extent of field systems (above, p. 170). They are discussed and clearly illustrated in a recent paper already much quoted here[65] from which Figs. 48 and 49 are taken. Most of the examples published are from Scotland, but for geographical variety I stress two shown here are from Northumberland and Caernarvonshire (Fig. 48b, c: sample surveys of more extensive evidence only). Both show the main characteristics of the type, individually similar to the Shetland examples, i.e. cairns, lynchets, and, occasionally, dykes or lines of earth-set stones. The essential differences, however, appear to be that these fields are contiguous, forming extensive systems. Furthermore, the fields themselves, although showing a wide range of shape and size, give an overall impression of rough rectangularity. Lynchets, for example, tend to be approximately parallel or at right angles to each other. In the Sandyford Moor example (Fig. 48b), cairn 1 contained Beaker inhumations and an enlarged Food Vessel cremation, and cairn E (not on plan) a pit from near the edge of which some charcoal produced a C-14 date of 2890±90 bc; but four other excavated cairns gave no evidence that they were other than stone clearance heaps. Straight ard-marks were recorded on the surface of the subsoil close to cairn A.

The Penmaenmawr example (Fig. 48c) is also in an area already discussed (above, p. 172) and shows the same characteristics as the Northumbrian example; it is, however, quite distinct from the much more common, and probably much later, type of field system ((d) below) well known in the same area. An additional characteristic of this type (b), also present at Sandyford Moor, can be seen at B (Fig. 48c), i.e. the use of natural slopes for dumping stones as well as putting them into heaps within and at the edges of fields. This particular example also contains, as in many other cases, a burial cairn (A) and the round foundations of three stone structures, presumably huts or houses but not necessarily contemporary with the fields. In most of these systems it is difficult to be definite about field sizes but they appear to be generally small, i.e. often less than 0.2 ha. As a result of recent work, type (b) fields are almost certainly the commonest and most extensive among the varieties of late prehistoric fields in the Highland Zone.

Type (c), the south-western type of regular, elongated field, is best known on Dartmoor (Plates, III, V; Figs. 45, 46). Only one detailed account[66] is available, however, and one subsequent published survey[67] has already shown a significant variation on the 'reave' problem. These two publications have, however, prompted intensive work not only on

[65] Feachem, 'Ancient agriculture...'.
[66] Gawne and Somers Cocks, 'Parallel reaves on Dartmoor'.
[67] J. Collis and A. Fleming, 'A late prehistoric reave system near Cholwich Town Dartmoor', *Proc. Devon Arch. Soc.*, 31, 1973, pp. 1–21.

Dartmoor but also on Bodmin Moor and Mendip where similar evidence is now coming to light. This work is current at the time of writing so that the following summary can be no more than an interim statement largely based on two relevant papers and personal observation.

The essence of the systems here categorized as type (c) can fittingly be put in the words of the authors who first realized their significance:

large areas of eastern Dartmoor, sometimes of several square miles are striped with low reaves which are long, parallel and generally straight between one aiming point and the next. They are quite distinct from, and far larger in area than, the field systems surrounding abandoned medieval farmsteads... and over wide areas cannot be accepted as fields at all but rather are land divisions...they ignore physical features such as streams in their lay-out in a way that medieval fields never do. A number of Late Bronze/Early Iron Age[68] settlements lie within them and tend to be aligned with each other in a way which must be outside the limits of chance...the reaves are low banks of stone usually now covered with earth varying in height from under a foot to commonly about 18–24 in. (45–60 cm) or occasionally even more, and several feet in width.... They run virtually parallel to one another continuously for...several hundred yards and often very much more, apparently with a master-line aimed at some marker.... The lateral distances between them vary considerably, but an interval of something around 300 ft (c. 91 m) is a common one though...a group may be found only about half that distance apart and there are many variations in scale. The total lateral distance of any one set can be well over one mile and sometimes even more, while longitudinally they may with interruptions run for several miles. Occasionally...there appears to be a...base line from which at about a right angle the reaves all start.[69]

In case this 1968 statement may seem far-fetched, it can be equally firmly stated now (1975) that subsequent survey has shown its essential correctness, not only on eastern Dartmoor, but also, for example, on the north-eastern edge of Bodmin Moor in the Nine Stones/Fox Tor area.[70]

In the sense that we are here concentrating on fields themselves, these major systems of land allotment, clearly not entirely or even to any considerable extent ever under arable, may seem a diversion; but it is necessary to stress the man-made landscape as a framework to which the individual fields around many settlements can now be seen to relate. One of the larger systems of reaves, for example, covers an area of about

[68] Though Kestor of the excavated settlements seems inescapably 'Early Iron Age', many, perhaps most, of the rest would now be regarded as Middle Bronze Age, generally with a date in the second half of the second millennium, cf. C. Thomas, 'The Bronze Age in the south west', *Arch. Rev.*, 4, 1969, pp. 3–13.

[69] Gawne and Somers Cocks, *op. cit.*, pp. 277–80.

[70] The author is grateful to A. Fleming for introducing him to this area and its current survey.

2,240 acres (c. 900 ha) over a distance of some 2 miles (3.2 km) along a front 1.75 miles (2.8 km) wide, incorporating archaeologically well-known sites such as Horridge Common, Rippon Tor, and Foale's Arrishes. One of the largest reave systems lies just to the west of the last and crosses five river valleys, including that of the Dart, in its compass of more than 12 square miles (31 km²). The settlement sites and their associated fields "occupy only comparatively small areas of each system...no arable farming system would itself ever have required such a layout, but...some prehistoric settlements with their fields are aligned upon the reaves."[71] This is illustrated in Fig. 46, where at least three settlement complexes can be seen orientated within the parallel reave system, two of them with adjacent "elongated or geometric fields related to axial lines". Other similar fields amongst published examples can now be appreciated to be part of larger complexes at, for example, Horridge Common, Yar Tor Down, Foale's Arrishes, Kestor (Plate IV), and Shaugh Moor (Fig. 45).[72] The overall framework, contrasting with the 'discrete small farm with two or three small fields' model of some Dartmoor settlements is clearly hinted at in the well-known plan of the Rippon Tor homestead, which, significantly it can now be seen, shows three boundaries springing off Fields 1 and 3 and the Yard.

Gawne and Somers Cocks concluded in their pioneering study that the systems of parallel reaves were pre-medieval and later than Bronze Age barrows. They looked to the reaves' archaeological associations with settlements and fields in opting for a late prehistoric date. They also suggested that the reaves "represent a form of planned land settlement ...to allow for orderly expansion in a lengthwise and lateral direction as settlements grew in size and number...where groups of huts and fields exist they usually give an impression of having been 'slotted in' to the existing grid".[73] They noted too that the reaves became higher in the vicinity of the subdivisions making up the groups of fields, suggesting clearance of stones for cultivation; and examples of small lynchets at the field edges support this interpretation. But, although the existence of the 'grid system', whatever its significance, and the presence of related, oblong fields cannot be disputed, not all fields were of the type, even on eastern Dartmoor. Furthermore, arable fields need not be associated with reaves at all.

This last point is brought out by the second paper tackling the reave problem.[74] The reave system near Cholwich Town at the south-west corner of Dartmoor covers nearly 1 square mile (c. 260 ha) of

[71] Gawne and Somers Cocks, op. cit., p. 283.
[72] A. Fox, 'Celtic fields and farms on Dartmoor'; C. A. R. Radford, 'Prehistoric settlements on Dartmoor and the Cornish Moors', Proc. Prehist. Soc., 18, 1952, pp. 55–84.
[73] Gawne and Somers Cocks, op. cit., p. 290.
[74] Collis and Fleming, op. cit.

south-west-facing slope, dropping some 600 ft (200 m) from *c.* 1550 ft (472 m) above OD. Essentially it consists of three reaves running roughly along the contours between *c.* 1350 ft and 1050 ft (411 m, 319 m) for *c.* 2.3 km with two similar reaves running roughly at right angles across the contours. There were no fields, arable or otherwise, associated with the reaves, but the important point for present purposes is that they were related to hut-sites, stone-walled enclosures, burial cairns, and peat bog. The detailed field study therefore provides significant dating evidence, generally by association with settlement features of types known elsewhere on Dartmoor, and specifically by dating parts of reaves to a pre-Sub-Atlantic phase of land-use. It is suggested that typologically and perhaps chronologically the Cholwich Town system may be earlier than the eastern Dartmoor systems because it did not develop into a more elaborate system of parallel reaves but, whether or not that is correct, the general dating of these reave systems, and with them the fields where present, to an early first-millennium horizon at latest, and more probably to the second half of the second millennium BC, is very strongly suggested.

Type (d). Some of the best-preserved examples of type (d) fields can be seen along the western side of Britain, particularly in west Cornwall, south-west Wales, north-west Wales, and in modern Cumbria. Unfortunately, few good plans of field systems exist for Cornwall although their location has been exhaustively recorded in the Lands End district.[75] Three excavated settlements have, however, been placed in context with at least some of their fields at Bodrifty, Chysauster, and Goldherring. There the fields are characteristically *c.* 40 m wide and *c.* 60 m long, together forming a somewhat irregular patchwork of roughly rectangular cultivated plots around the settlements, belonging to the late centuries BC and, probably, later.

Presumably earlier fields exist among the recorded evidence on the West Penwith granite plateau but they have not yet been identified. The best examples of earlier fields in the far south-west exist at, and now below, sea-level. In the Isles of Scilly remnants of field walls, still awaiting their authoritative study, exist on some of the islands and continue down the foreshore and across parts of the now submerged land surface between Tresco and Samson (Fig. 50), and off Tean and St Martins (Appendix 3). While such evidence seems to indicate former land allotment, perhaps even of the second millennium, it is difficult to specify the nature of individual fields; and most of the cultivable land on the existing islands has for long been so intensively cropped that not much evidence survives above sea-level except in a few places like

[75] Russell, *West Penwith Survey.*

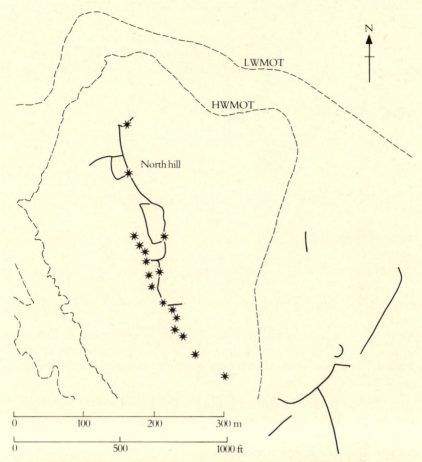

Fig. 50. Samson, Isles of Scilly: walls and enclosures are physically related to the cairns on North Hill, and the walls now on the intertidal Flats to the east appear to be visually related to the structures on the higher ground (from an original field survey by A. C. Thomas and P. J. Fowler).

Halangy Down, St Marys, where the field system of type (d) has associations primarily in the early centuries AD.[76]

On the mainland, the complex at Gwithian where the Red River enters St Ives Bay, provides a rather different sort of evidence (Fig. 51). No prehistoric fields are now visible on the present surface of cropped and coarse grasses on an irregular, wind-deposited, sand-dune system; yet excavation has shown successive cultural layers buried in, and

[76] P. Ashbee, *Ancient Scilly*, Newton Abbot, 1974, pp. 52–69 and 213–15.

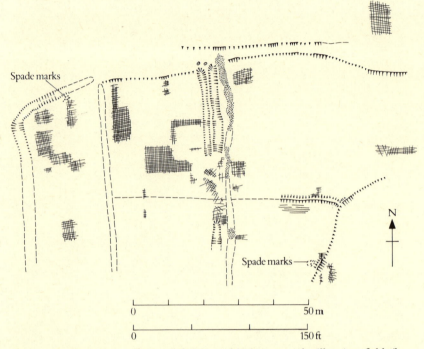

Spade marks

N

Spade marks —

0
50 m

0
150 ft

Fig. 51. Gwithian, Cornwall: simplified plan of the later second millennium fields (layer 5) showing the areas of excavated ard-marks and spade-marks (after J. V. S. Megaw).

covered by, sand-blows from a probably third millennium Mesolithic horizon onwards. Fields have been recorded at two levels, dating respectively to about the fifteenth/fourteenth centuries bc and the thirteenth/eleventh centuries bc. In the earlier level (layer 5), we see part of a field system (Plate VIIb), probably related to an enclosed settlement just uphill of it, with at least eight individual fields measuring, where recordable, about 30 m square. The relevant layer certainly extends c. 200 m to the west so it must be stressed that the field pattern so far revealed by excavation is but a part of a more extensive arable area attractively situated on a gently sloping strip of south-facing land alongside a tidal river mouth. The inevitable impression from limited excavation of a small (? enclosed) farmstead surrounded by a cluster of small fields may be erroneous and initial comparisons made with 'isolated' Dartmoor settlements may also be relevant in future re-assessment of any new evidence (above, p. 171).

The later fields (layer 3) lay in the same situation, though their extent seems to be less. In this phase, however, three or four successive houses, overlying a layer-5 field, were associated with the surrounding, still

(a)

(b)

VI. Butser Ancient Farm Project, Little Butser Hill, Hants. Detail, looking south, in October 1977, of the upper (a) and lower (b) edges of the west-facing Field V on a c. 12° slope on the north-west corner of the Hill. The field, 35 m north to south, 20 m east to west, had been hoe- and ard-cultivated six times in three years for flax, as part of an experiment to study lynchet formation, when the photograph was taken. (a) shows the beginnings of a negative lynchet as a result of the break-up of the turf covering and incipient movement of soil and chalk lumps downhill. (b) shows the bottom edge of the field marked by vegetation, especially thistles, which includes the first hawthorn seedlings. This more concentrated growth is beginning to trap soil and chalk lumps as they tend to move down the slope, and a lynchet several centimetres high has already formed. (P. J. Fowler)

VII. (*a*) Butser Ancient Farm Project, Little Butser Hill, Hants. Ploughing experiment with a reconstructed beam ard. The two Dexter cattle required two years of training to work as a team and are the closest modern counterpart to the *Bos longifrons* of late pre-historic times. Note that, even with a two-animal team and a short, light ard, the physical existence of a field boundary still necessitates a narrow headland at the field edge. (P. J. Fowler)

VII. (*b*) Ard-marks at the base of layer 5 (Middle Bronze Age), Gwithian, Cornwall. SW 590423. Layer 5 was an horizon of cultivated and manured soil contained within a field system, cf. Fig. 51. Here the ploughsoil has been removed, exposing the surface of the underlying windblown sand. Into this surface, soil from layer 5 has been pushed and dragged by the share-point of an ard probably similar to that above in Plate VII*a*. Generally the ard has travelled systematically, and at roughly regular intervals, backward and forward across this view and then, similarly, at right angles away from and towards the camera position. Several successive ploughings are represented but the same axes of cultivation were observed each time. Some of the main furrows seem to have been ploughed more than once, perhaps deliberately. Scales in feet and inches. (Gwithian Excavation Staff *per* A. C. Thomas)

VII (b)

VIII. (a) Butser Ancient Farm Demonstration Area, Hants. A full-scale reconstruction of a large, round, late-prehistoric building, based on a ground-plan excavated at Pimperne, Dorset. The building stands inside a ditched enclosure with an internal bank surmounted by a wattle-and-post fence. Scale: 2 m. (Butser Ancient Farm Project *per* P. J. Reynolds)

VIII. (b) BBC 'Iron Age Village', near Tollard Royal, Wilts., 1978. These buildings, not based on any particular evidence, were used by the various animals: the corner of the byre is extreme left, the pigsties are in the centre, with the henhouse on four posts and the round goat-hut beyond. Together with several other buildings, including a large round house, all were within a ditched, banked and palisaded enclosure, part of which is visible on the right. The site has now been destroyed but this photograph may give some visual impression, possibly approximating to reality, of the preponderance of wood, straw and mud in an 'Iron Age' farm of late prehistoric times. Scales: 2 m foreground, 6 ft background. (Archaeological Advisers Ltd, AA 402)

small, cultivation plots. We shall return to Gwithian in considering other aspects of second millennium agriculture (below, p. 195). Here the important points to stress are the situation, and the burial and consequent preservation of the evidence, since a clear implication must be that similar evidence potentially exists in other dune systems along Britain's western coasts. Whether or not archaeologically recoverable, it is extremely likely that the extensive 'machairs' similar to that at Gwithian have been continually attractive to, perhaps even in part created by, cultivating communities from Neolithic times onwards. It would be quite wrong to regard Gwithian as unique or even exceptional: it merely happens to be an area which has been, by a combination of circumstances, intensively and systematically examined.[77]

Fields of type (d) are also known on Bodmin Moor and Dartmoor, with as yet unstudied examples elsewhere in Devon, for example, near the south coast behind Torbay and along the north coast west of Ilfracombe. On Bodmin Moor, areas of type (d) fields are visible, particularly on its western side, e.g. around Rough and Garrow Tors, and though the field system related to the excavated settlement on Stannon Down c. 2 km to the west is overall of type (c), east of the houses are more squarish enclosures, some of which could be cultivated plots although their interpretation as cattle 'corrals' is attractive.[78] On Dartmoor, though the later prehistoric landscape may have been dominated by the major land allotment systems (above, p. 182 and below, p. 236), groups of fairly regular, squarish fields also existed, sometimes apparently in isolation around a settlement, sometimes fitting into a larger landscape arrangement. At the already-quoted Rippon Tor site, for example, the three fields immediately beside the hut, all c. $\frac{1}{4}$-$\frac{1}{2}$ acre (0.1–0.2 ha) in size, are typical of many Dartmoor settlements.[79] It is, however, a moot point whether they should be called 'fields' – 'plots', 'closes' or collectively, 'the garden' might be more appropriate.

Type (d) fields also visibly survive in the different geological setting of Carboniferous Limestone north across the Somerset Levels. On the south side of Mendip, on Brean Down and, fragmentarily, along the south-facing slopes of Broadfield Down and the Failand Ridge near Bristol, parts of what were once extensive systems, probably of Romano-British date, have been recorded.[80] They are also known on

[77] In addition to the site references in the Index (below, p. 282), see also Evans, *The Environment of Early Man...*, pp. 121, 152, 166; P. J. Spencer in Evans *et al.* (eds.), CBA Research Report, 11, pp. 98–100; Simpson (ed.), *Economy and Settlement...*, pp. 134, 138.   [78] Mercer in *Corn. Arch.*, 9, 1970, pp. 17–46.

[79] A. Fox, 'Celtic fields and farms on Dartmoor', fig. 2.

[80] Summarized in Bowen and P. J. Fowler (eds.), *Early Land Allotment*: see Appendix 3 (below, pp. 275–7).

the Oolitic Limestone around Bath, notably on Charmy and Bathampton Downs and near Marshfield.[81] Again they lack an authoritative
study but, without prejudice to their origins which is likely to be
generally in the (later?) first millennium, most of what is visible seems
to have been in use in the Roman period and perhaps a little later. The
sparse detectable evidence of early fields in the Cotswolds has recently
been investigated, but is not published at the time of writing.[82] One
of the best surviving examples in Barnsley Park near Cirencester, was
laid out around a Roman villa.[83] In Wales, the main concentrations of
type (d) fields are in Pembrokeshire and Caernarvonshire, both counties
which coincidentally have attracted much archaeological fieldwork.
Examples in the former are on St David's Head and off-shore on Skomer
Island (Fig. 21).[84] Another island, Anglesey, contains numerous field
systems:[85] in the western part of Penmon Deer Park, for example,
fragments of type (d) fields cover c. 100 acres (41 ha) also containing
five settlements. Fields are of the order of c. 90 × 70 m. The recorded
distribution of huts and associated field systems, the majority of type
(d), in Caernarvonshire, Anglesey, and Merioneth is shown in Fig. 20,
since it represents, as a result of the concentration of effort in the area,
one of the most complete field records of fields in Britain. Even so, the
fragmentary nature of the total distribution is apparent, and the sparse
evidence on the coastal plateaux and along the river valleys is surely
as significant as the apparent preferred locations around and just below
the 1000 ft (305 m) contour. Good individual examples of field systems
are C. 492 (with an unenclosed settlement), and C. 1063 and C. 1064
(with enclosed homesteads).[86]

Generally similar field systems have for long been known further
north in Westmorland, particularly those at Ewe Close, Crosby Garrett,
and Waitby. Often considered an isolated phenomenon, the last two
have recently been shown to be parts of the same complex covering
8 km², in which "the landscape can be reconsidered in terms of

[81] As note 80 but for Charmy Down: W. F. Grimes, *Excavation on Defence Sites
1939–1945*, I, London, 1960, pp. 196–244: for Bathampton Down: *Trans. Bristol Glos.
Arch. Soc.*, 86, 1967, pp. 42–59; for Marshfield: personal observation, unpublished.

[82] RCHM, *Iron Age and Roman Monuments in the Gloucestershire Cotswolds*, London,
1977.

[83] P. J. Fowler (ed.), *Recent Work in Rural Archaeology*, fig. 8.6, and RCHM, *op. cit.*,
fig. opp. p. 11.

[84] W. F. Grimes, *Arch. Camb.*, 101, 1950–51, fig. opp. p. 1.

[85] RCAM, *Anglesey*, 1960, pp. 125–28.

[86] 'C' identifications from *ibid.*, following N. Johnson, 'An environmental study
of the location of pre-medieval settlement in Caernarvonshire', M.A. thesis, Univ.
of Sheffield, 1976.

agricultural units sub-divided by cross-country dykes ".[87] Within that pattern, type (d) fields roughly 100 yd (c. 90 m) square form part of the settlement complex at Crosby Garrett itself and though the general context appears to be Romano-British, earlier origins are possible. Nevertheless, the 'Celtic' field systems investigated in the 1950s in the Lune valley to the south and in Cumberland to the north produced no evidence that they were other than of the Romano-British period.[88] A similar context, with perhaps similar possibilities for late prehistoric origins, is also suggested for some of the plethora of 'new' settlements recently mapped off the higher ground, with its upstanding evidence on the Solway Plain. There, and particularly on and peripheral to the eskers, the slight sand and gravel ridges rising above the former or existing 'mosses' of the Plain, numerous settlements have been located by air photography. Some have associated field systems, and at the Holme Abbey South complex, for example, type (d) fields are well exemplified, with an apparently unenclosed settlement. Other fields are recorded right on the coast in the Beckfoot area and immediately around Old Carlisle itself.[89]

Though type (d) fields have barely been recorded in Scotland, Feachem illustrates one example of an unenclosed platform settlement at White Meldon, Peebles., associated with oblong fields lying along the contours in a system covering 13.8 ha.[90] This appears to be much more of the (d) than (b) type with which he is primarily concerned. Similarly the system covering 8.9 ha around the settlement on Middleton Muir (Fig. 49b), Perths., consists, to judge from the sample illustrated, of roughly rectangular fields bounded by lynchets and stone banks characteristic of type (d). The possibility of a mid first-millennium BC date should perhaps be treated cautiously for such Scottish examples in general; and in this particular case, there seems as good reason for relating the fields to the burial cairn as to the three, thick-walled huts which lie in their midst and possibly over them.

In many ways, however, the most impressive landscapes of type (d) fields lie on the Pennines of Yorkshire and specifically around Grassington (Fig. 52). Their prolonged and percipient study by Raistrick[91] is well known, showing the fields to lie in extensive systems

[87] B. Jones, 'The north western interface', in P. J. Fowler (ed.), 1975, op. cit., p. 99; generally, RCHM, Westmorland, 1936, and P. J. Fowler, 'Small settlements and their context...', Proc. Roy. Irish Acad., 76C, 1976, pp. 191–206.

[88] R. A. C. Lowndes, in Trans. Cumb. Westmorland Ant. Arch. Soc., 63, 1963, pp. 77–95; B. Blake, in ibid., 59, 1959, pp. 1–14.

[89] N. Higham and G. D. B. Jones, in Arch. J., 132, 1975, pp. 16–53.

[90] Feachem, 'Ancient agriculture...', p. 340, fig. 5; p. 342, fig. 8.

[91] Yorks. Arch. J., 33, 1937, pp. 166–74; 34, 1939, pp. 115–50; Ant., III, 1929, pp. 165–81.

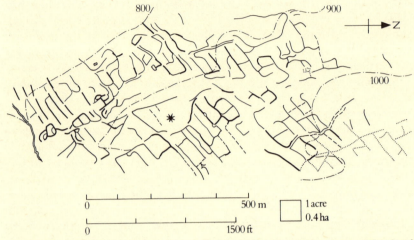

Fig. 52. Grassington, west Yorks.: plan of the surviving field systems and related features. The cairn is probably of the early second millennium and the latest features are of the Roman period. Thick lines show banks, thin lines, scarps, and dotted lines, traces. Although modified, the basic layout shows a marked axial arrangement on a south-west to north-east orientation (after A. King).

related to settlements mainly of the Romano-British period. There are numerous hints, however, that the origins of these lynchetted and stone-banked fields lie in the immediately preceding centuries, though to say so is in no way to gainsay the early centuries AD date of most of what is visible.[92]

Type (e). Among the Yorkshire Pennine fields are examples of type (e) fields, i.e. long, parallel, strip-like fields in blocks. The proposal to distinguish such a field type derives eventually from work in the Lowland Zone which showed such fields to exist and in a Romano-British context (Plate IV*b*; Fig. 40 *top left*).[93] Since then, further examples have been noted, including some in the Highland Zone at, for example, Lye Hole, Somerset, related to a villa,[94] and at Charmy Down, and in several other places on the Cotswolds, generally in Romano-British contexts.[95] Though the field type as such can theoretically appear at any time – those south-east of the later second millennium settlement at Stannon Down on Bodmin Moor,[96] for example, could be considered – at present type (e) seems generally to

[92] See also A. King, *Early Pennine Settlement*, Clapham, 1970; and Appendix 4 (below, p. 278).
[93] H. C. Bowen and P. J. Fowler, in Thomas (ed.), *Rural Settlement in Roman Britain*, pp. 43–67.
[94] *Proc. Univ. Bristol Spelaeol. Soc.*, 12, 1970, p. 176, fig. 27.
[95] RCHM, *Gloucestershire Cotswolds*.   [96] *Corn. Arch.*, 9, 1970, p. 19, fig. 6.

be a Romano-British development and therefore not primarily our concern here. With so much else from the Romano-British landscape still to be examined critically, it would in any case be illogical to isolate and discuss in detail one particular field type in it which simply happens to be morphologically distinctive and relatively well dated.

The five-fold typology based on general field morphology used in the preceding paragraphs is nothing more than a convenient way of breaking down for descriptive purposes a considerable amount of primary data. It is not meant to imply a rigid chronological succession, though dating evidence has been indicated where available and, in Britain at least, types (a), (b) and (c) are not only earlier than (d) and (e) in general but can be argued to be predominantly and characteristically of the second millennium BC. Type (d), however, was also present in the second millennium, as in the Lowland Zone, but probably most frequently belongs to the end of the prehistoric and the Romano-British periods when seen in the Highland Zone. Type (e), as we have briefly indicated, seems to be specifically of the first centuries AD. Nor is this typology meant to imply the prior importance of field shape and size over other factors relevant to understanding the environmental, agrarian, economic, and social significance of late prehistoric fields in Britain's Highland Zone. A host of other factors, ranging from climatic change through technology to tenure, must be taken into account, and basically much of that work has still to be designed and executed, a great deal of it initially within a locally intense research programme. The fact that this section has been reduced to a conceptually old-fashioned and somewhat suspect framework largely reflects the available sources, and makes, by implication, its own comment on our knowledge of the subject.

Field boundaries

It is clear from the foregoing brief survey of physically surviving field remains in the Highland Zone that the *boundaries* of the fields themselves vary enormously. This can be seen on the surface, with stone structures predominating as could be expected, but the amount of excavated evidence on this point is very small. This is a significant limitation, because where excavation has occurred, and notably at Gwithian, considerable additional information has been obtained (below, p. 195). From field survey, however, we can note the different uses of stone in field boundaries: the surface stones collected from the intended arable area and placed in piles within it or at its edges – sometimes in heaps, sometimes in lines, sometimes on natural stony slopes. Mention has already been made numerous times of the cairns demarcating arable areas (above, p. 172). The dumping of stones in rough lines to form the edges of fields and the placing of stones in deliberate lines, sometimes by digging holes in which they sit or stand upright, to define the shape and size of 'enclosed fields' are exemplified in many examples on Dartmoor; the building of revetments on slopes, e.g. in Caernarvonshire, and the construction of actual walls, e.g. at Kestor (Plate V), represent more careful boundary-making, but it is rare to find such walls of more than two or three courses high. Stones were also used, pulled randomly together or set upright, in basically earthy banks, sometimes with a ditch: the 'reaves' on Dartmoor again are a case in point for, whatever else they represent, in parts they functioned as field walls.

That the wooden and ditched boundaries of the Lowland Zone were also present in the Highland Zone was clearly shown in the excavation at Gwithian (Fig. 51). The layer-5 fields there showed considerable variety of boundary structure: a ditch, probably periodically re-dug and perhaps filled with gorse; a ragged line of stones surviving as part of what was, probably, once a clearance bank, even though it ran over earlier ard-marks, and, elsewhere, both composite and negative lynchets. Excavation of a lynchet showed there to have been no original tangible structure, yet its clearly defined 'positive' and 'negative' parts showed that a recognized line of demarcation between adjacent plots had once existed, and for long enough for the lynchet to develop to its height of 0.40 m. In so developing, it buried ard-marks cut into the top of layer 7. The other excavated field boundaries elsewhere in the Highland Zone, notably Goldherring, Kestor, and Caerau, showed different versions of stone field-edge structures. At Kestor, three courses of granite boulders remained *in situ*, cut into or sitting on the peat over which the associated plough-soil lay.[97]

Contents of fields

When we look at the contents of late prehistoric Highland Zone fields, we see a range similar to those in the Lowland Zone though the form of some of the contents is somewhat different in certain cases. The evidence, particularly that from excavation, is, however, much more limited and, as previously noted, neither is there quite the same widespread evidence for land-use succession. This fact may be related to long-term climatic change rather than merely uneven distribution of archaeological investigation (below, pp. 245–9).

In a general sense, some at least of the cairns which characterized some Highland Zone fields, notably types (*a*) and (*b*), are the equivalent of the round barrows related to the prehistoric fields of Wessex, i.e. they

[97] *Ant.*, XLI, 1967, fig. 3 opp. p. 290 illustrates a range of field boundary types.

were used for burial. Examples come from most of the areas already discussed, but specific instances can be quoted from Gardom's Edge (Fig. 48*d*), Derbys., Penmaenmawr (Fig. 48*c*), Caerns., and the North York Moors.[98] Two recent excavations in cairn fields in Northumberland,[99] respectively at Alnham and Chatton Sandyford (Fig. 48*b*), illustrate the difficulty of generalizing on the topic, while pointing to the structural and chronological variety to be expected once a reasonable excavated sample of the many thousands of cairns known only from field observation becomes available. In neither of these cases was there any question from surface evidence of the cairns being part of, or related to, a field system. At Alnham, the interest was a possible link with two, undated but probably late prehistoric, enclosed settlements nearby (Fig. 26), and four cairns were excavated in two cairn-fields. In one, of 22 cairns varying from 10 to 18 ft (3 to 5.5 m) in diameter and 1 to 3 ft (0.3 to 0.9 m) in height, there were also 6 circular ditched enclosures averaging 20 ft (6.5 m) in diameter. One of these proved to consist of a shallow ditch and slight outer bank, broken by opposed entrances in one of which was a stone-hole. Of the two small cairns excavated nearby, one was surrounded by a rock-cut trench, some 18 ft (6 m) in diameter, inside which was a low bank. Its inner edge was marked by a discontinuous kerb of small stones incorporating four small orthostats. This kerb enclosed a layer of charcoal interpreted as the remnants of a cremation pyre. The whole was covered by stones forming the visible cairn. The other cairn covered a grave, probably for an inhumation. A third cairn in another cairn-field lower down the hill was larger (33 ft, 10 m, in diameter) and covered two cremation pits. Of the four, three were probably of Bronze Age and one of Iron Age date; three were certainly burial mounds and all exhibited structural differences.

At Chatton Sandyford, the results were somewhat different. The cairn-field was much bigger: two large round cairns and about 150 smaller stone mounds. Excavation of one of the large cairns showed it to consist of a complex structure, but, with three Beaker inhumations and two cremations, to be very definitely a sepulchral mound. No such clarity emerged from four of the small cairns which "may have been no more than the results of field clearance". The fifth covered a grave from which carbonized material produced a Middle Neolithic C-14 date.

The reason for this apparent diversion into the detail of modern excavations of a few cairns should be all too clear: 'cairn' is clearly an umbrella term for what is superficially the slightest and least impressive of Highland Zone field monuments, which nevertheless occurs in

[98] Feachem, 'Ancient agriculture...', figs. 2 and 1; Fleming, *op. cit.*, note 56.
[99] *Arch. Ael.*, 44, 1966, pp. 5–48; 46, 1968, pp. 5–50.

its thousands and is central to a consideration of settlement studies generally and early agriculture specifically. After the above excavations, Jobey stated "a reluctance to discuss such assemblages of small cairns as arising solely from field clearance".[100] In an important appendix to that paper he clearly defined (*ibid.*, p. 49) the crux of the matter: "the chief difficulty with respect to the majority of the assemblages, and these may include groups of upwards of two hundred small cairns or mounds, lies in the impossibility on present evidence of making a certain attribution to either of the categories, sepulchral or agricultural, or to distinguish those situations where both may be present." Though written in the light of the Northumbrian evidence, the summary is of wide application. The subsequent recognition (above, p. 173) of the extensive former arable over much of the Highland Zone has at least placed many cairn fields in an agricultural context and many individual cairns in or on the edge of fields. Furthermore, Fleming has proposed a model in which, for the North York Moors, the cairns are, indeed, the result of field clearance but in a secondary, not a primary, phase of land use.[101] Possibly there is a line of enquiry to be followed here between this thesis and Jobey's independent observation that in Northumberland "the major concentration and certainly the largest groups (of small cairns) are to be found on the poorer soils of the Fell Sandstone series...".[102] Though cairn fields obviously are a major consideration in discussing 'the contents of fields' in the Highland Zone, nevertheless they are mainly a northern phenomenon: the 'cairn field problem' does not exist on present evidence in the south-west, an apparent fact suggesting an unexplained regional distinction at an early stage in the development of British agrarian history. The 'apparent fact' must, however, be treated with caution, partly in view of the buried Neolithic field clearance cairns found on the slopes of Carn Brea, Cornwall,[103] and partly because the revelatory results from field archaeology in the last two decades especially demand, rather than invite, caution in arguing dogmatically from current distributions.[104]

Small stone heaps are nevertheless a common feature of Highland Zone fields (Plate III*b*). A few have been proved to be funerary, many have been shown to be associated with charcoal, but the great majority have either produced no conclusive evidence of function or have not been excavated. In general, and particularly where associated with types (*a*) and (*b*), it seems reasonable to regard them as likely to be primarily

---

[100] *Ibid.*, 46, 1968, p. 42.   [101] Fleming, 'Bronze age agriculture...'.
[102] *Arch. Ael.*, 46, 1968, p. 49.
[103] R. Mercer, in *Corn. Arch.*, 9, 1970, pp. 53–62; 10, 1971, p. 93; 11, 1972, pp. 5–8; and *idem*, in P. J. Fowler (ed.), *Recent Work in Rural Archaeology*, fig. 2.1, Pl. 2*a*.
[104] Small stone mounds, clearance cairns or otherwise, are in fact already known on both Exmoor and the Quantocks but have not yet been fully examined or assessed.

clearance mounds. It is also likely, however, that communities of the second millennium BC did not make as clear-cut a distinction between the practical and the sacred as is common in modern Western society, and it may well be that, ultimately, there is an element of the agrarian clearance mound tradition in the developed funerary architecture of the Bronze Age. Nevertheless, well-documented examples of barrows proper actually on top of fields are very rare in the Highland Zone, and no proven examples exist of other characteristic field monuments such as stone circles or rows being parts of field systems either.[105] On the other hand, such certainly existed as parts of the contemporary landscape, sometimes, as on Dartmoor, in close juxtaposition. Even if we do not fully understand their significance, and even if such structures are not strictly to be numbered amongst the contents of fields, in places they were part of the physical framework within which agrarian life was pursued, and we can, at the moment anyway, make our choice of their role in the conceptual framework.[106] More prosaically, but significantly again from one of the few settlement complexes extensively excavated, we can point to a small cremation cemetery and ring–ditch stratified at the base of layer 5, immediately below the earlier ard-marks at Gwithian, west Cornwall.

It is at Gwithian too that the best examples of Highland Zone ard-marks have so far been discovered (Fig. 51, Plate VII*b*).[107] They occurred in association with both layers 5 and 3, i.e. in two different and successive contexts in the second half of the second millennium. In both cases they lay in adjacent fields, i.e. they did not occur singly or in isolation but were extensive in the fields of two different systems. Furthermore, although the area uncovered was quite large by the excavation standards of its day, much more extensive areas of ard-marks are known to exist unexamined in the surrounding area, so the source of our information can be tapped again when improved techniques and further research make this desirable. The minimum area of layer 5 over which ard-marks are likely to exist is, to judge from the area actually excavated, *c.* 6,600 m². Only 832 m² of layer 3 was exposed since it was discontinuous. The recovery of the plan of the fields and field system containing the ard-marks was therefore much more difficult than for layer 5. The latter was generally buried more deeply than layer 3 and is consequently better preserved, though in most of the area excavated

[105] See n. 72, p. 183.

[106] Cf. Burl, *The Stone Circles of the British Isles*.

[107] Gwithian references, see Site Index (below, p. 284) and n. 77, p. 187. The author gratefully acknowledges the help of Professor Charles Thomas with the Gwithian evidence. It is set in its regional context in Thomas, 'The Bronze Age in the south and west'; Mercer, 1975, *op. cit.*, pp. 27–43; and in the Trevisker report, *Proc. Prehist. Soc.*, 38, 1972, p. 302–81.

it occurs immediately below the modern turf and a thin layer of wind-blown sand. Clearly, as the history of settlement and farming evidenced by the excavation shows, the environment here has been unstable since Mesolithic times. Indeed, it is largely because of this that the ard-marks have been preserved at all, buried under incipient sand-dunes.

Ard-marks were detected immediately beneath, in, and on top of layer 5. As exposed in plan, except at the very top, they always produced a complex pattern, in fact a palimpsest from the top of the layer down through the layer to the surface of the underlying sand. There the lowest and presumably earliest marks occurred, visible only after total removal of the cultural layer. Nevertheless, the marks generally lay east–west and north–south respectively, along and across the contours of the gently south-sloping contemporary land surface. The marks, though apparently packed close together and, indeed, with fragments cutting across each other at very acute angles, were when assignable to particular sets, c. 30 cm apart, a characteristic width already noted elsewhere (above, p. 166). In plan, they showed up as marks beneath layer 5 because the darker, more humic plough soil had been pushed down into the yellow sand of layer 6; in layer 5 itself they could be recorded fragmentarily because the action that produced them allowed lenses of yellow sand to accumulate along the edges of the 'mark', a process which became accentuated during the later stages of the fields' use. This was presumably due to the increasing amount of wind-blown sand which eventually caused the fields' abandonment. Consequently the latest 'marks' appeared to be of a distinctly lighter colour compared to the brown of the plough-soil, i.e. the reverse effect of the earliest 'marks'.

It is, strictly speaking, inaccurate to refer to these phenomena as 'marks', since the word really reflects their nature as they appear when revealed as a two-dimensional feature recordable in plan; in fact, they are three dimensional, with a depth typically of c. 5 cm (none of those measured was as much as 10 cm deep). Their real nature is that of a groove. They may indeed have existed for a time as open grooves during the preparation of the seed-bed of which their creation was presumbably but one stage. In section, the grooves were V-shaped and quite often asymmetrical with one side nearer the vertical than the other; asymmetry in alternate directions was noted in places. Their filling was mainly of the plough-soil itself, but with the thin lenses of sand, already noted as showing in plan, also showing in section, again suggesting that, however briefly, the grooves lay open for a time. The grooves associated with layer 3 were to all intents and purposes similar to their predecessors. Their pattern was, however, different in two respects. In the first place, the overall pattern was not complex and nothing like the palimpsest of layer 5. Secondly, the grooves really only existed at all convincingly at the base of layer 3.

Part of the top of layer 5 exhibited a remarkable phenomenon: its dark surface was marked by a single grid of yellow lines once all the superincumbent wind-blown sand had been removed. These sand-filled ard-grooves imply that at least part of the field had been abandoned immediately after the creation of the grooves, because the wind had deposited enough sand sufficiently quickly to make it not worthwhile, or physically impossible, to continue preparing the seed-bed.

These two, later second millennium examples on the same site carry certain implications which in some ways conflict with other interpretations of ard-grooves or marks. There can be little doubt that they were produced by dragging a pointed implement through the sandy soil, not least because the broken end of a Cwm Mawr picrite axe-hammer was found actually lying in one of the grooves in layer 5. The palimpsest effect, particularly of layer 5, suggests that we are looking at the evidence of normal cultivation, and not at a rare or special event; the abandoned 'ploughed' top surface of layer 5 suggests likewise, and its criss-cross pattern is proof that the 'ploughing' in opposite directions was the product of a single act. Equally, that same evidence proves that this 'ploughing' was only one stage of several in the whole process of preparing the seed-bed. It is possible that the grooves were actually the seed-drills, but the distance between them (usually 30 cm) makes such an interpretation very unlikely. In any case, animals would not have been necessary to pull a shallow-grooving implement merely making drills.

That animals were almost certainly used at Gwithian is suggested by another piece of evidence there, namely spade-marks (Fig. 51). They occur only in layer 5 and only at the edges of fields in areas not criss-crossed by ard-grooves – presumably the headlands. They appeared in plan in the surface of the field as D-shaped, light-coloured areas in the darker plough-soil. The most complete examples were 22–27 cm along the stroke of the 'D' with a slight, off-centre bulge 'backwards' of this line and an eccentric arc 'in front'. On excavation they proved to be about 10–13 cm deep with a rounded bottom. The excavator has convincingly argued that these sand-filled holes were produced by a long-handled hafted spade with a heart-shaped blade essentially similar to the 'Cornish shovel' still in use today; and further that they represent the hand-digging of the headland at the edge of the field where the ard was lifted up and carried round through 180° behind the draught animal or animals, which, as closely as possible, mark time as they too shuffle around. This is certainly still done today in, for

example, north-west Spain, with an ard essentially of the type envisaged
for Bronze Age Gwithian. Though there were no ard-marks, it is worth
remembering too that the ard-grooves on Overton Down also ended
some 2 m from the field boundary fence (above, p. 166).

In combination the Gwithian evidence is unique. Ard-marks and
other evidence of cultivation have, however, been found elsewhere in
fields in the Highland Zone. Low-lying in position but west of the
Cotswolds, in the traditionally pastoral Vale of Berkeley, for example,
a complex of ard-marks has been excavated on a Rhaetic Clay subsoil
at Ridgeway, Falfield, a few kilometres north of Bristol.[108] The
ard-marks, here showing only as darker, humic lines in the surface of
the yellow/reddish sandy clay, lay beneath the earliest occupation level
of a Romano-British settlement but, apart from having a *terminus ante
quem* of *c.* AD 80, are undated. They are more likely, however, to belong
to the later third to earlier second millennium BC than later. Overall
they presented the most complex pattern of plough-marks yet discovered in Britain, not only in being a palimpsest but also in the
discontinuous nature of so many of the marks. Certain preferred
orientations and groups of lines at right angles to others could
nevertheless be discerned. The marks varied from 2 to 9.5 cm in width
and from 3 to 6.5 cm in depth; they were often clearly asymmetrical
in a V-shaped section. A possible boundary between two separate areas
of ard-marks could be defined along one edge by an area of disturbance
which might have represented earlier vegetation but could just possibly
indicate a hedge-line; certainly the ard-marks respected it. Otherwise
nothing of the field or field system, in which these marks presumably
existed at the time they were made, was recorded, largely because of
the circumstances of discovery during motorway construction.

Several other similar examples have also been recorded from the
north of England since the first in the region was noted beneath the
Military Way, like the Falfield one, scratched into clay.[109] Indeed, all
the known examples here have occurred almost incidentally in the
continuing research on the Hadrianic frontier zone as such (thereby at
least sharing the common denominator of a *terminus ante quem* in the
earlier second century AD). Indeed, it is as yet uncertain whether they
represent cultivation interrupted by recent military occupation or by
some unknown circumstance at a much earlier date. The excavator of
an example at Carrawburgh tends to favour a Neolithic or Early Bronze
Age date.[110] Stratigraphically, the marks lay, and were found only,

[108] A. Everton, in *Trans. Bristol Glos. Arch. Soc.*, 94, 1976, pp. 47–91, fig. 8; and
in Bowen and P. J. Fowler (eds.), *Early Land Allotment*, see Appendix 4 (below, p. 278).
[109] *Arch. Ael.*, 43, 1965, pp. 77–86; *Ant.*, XLI, 1967, pp. 294–5.
[110] D. J. Breeze, in *Tools and Tillage*, 2, 1974, pp. 188–90.

beneath and immediately north of four of the five rooms behind the forts' headquarters building. Two structural phases, namely a ditch and subsequently the Vallum, lay between the marks and the fort, but otherwise there was no evidence of date. The marks themselves, usually 20 or 40 cm apart and only a few millimetres deep, mostly ran north–south with only a few east–west marks in one patch. The topsoil above them was 20 cm thick with no recorded evidence of further ard-marks or any surface features. This could be taken to signify that the soil itself had, in part at least, formed after the cultivation evidenced by the ard-marks, thus tending to favour a date for them perhaps in the second millennium rather than in the immediately pre-Hadrianic years.

In contrast, ard-marks beneath Rudchester fort were both associated with rigg-and-furrow and interpreted with other evidence as indicating "that the land...was under cultivation up to the time of the building of Hadrian's Wall".[111] The excavation was very small – essentially two 4 × 4 m boxes – and only seven east–west ard-marks occurred in the area covered by two complete and two incomplete ridges recorded in section. Other marks, including some on a different alignment, were glimpsed immediately to the north but, as published, were not related to ridges because the relevant level had not been reached. All the marks were scored into the clay subsoil and varied from 1 to 3 cm in thickness; the distance between them averaged c. 50 cm but, like the Falfield examples, they were discontinuous, and a more realistic estimate of the original distance between furrows seems to be c. 15 cm. Overlying the ard-grooves was a plough-soil, the upper surface of which was undulating in flat-topped ridges c. 1.5 m apart crest to crest. As a result, the thickness of the plough-soil varied between 12.5 cm and 5 cm in the furrows. Curiously but significantly, the ard-marks occur under the ridges and not below the furrows suggesting, with other hints, that the rigg-and-furrow need not be associated with the ard-marks. Indeed, since there is clear if fragmentary evidence of two separate phases of cross-ploughing on slightly different orientations, it is very likely that this excavation coincidentally produced evidence of two phases of cultivation, one with an ard of possibly very much earlier date than the later phase which, through the use of a tilted ard, an asymmetrical ard, a plough with mouldboard and coulter, or a spade, produced the narrow ridges. It seems likely too that this later phase, while it may have been continuing up to the time the fort was built, had already lasted long enough for the ridges to become consolidated: it is remarkable that the highly inconvenient corrugations of the land surface were not flattened before the constructions of the fort though, according to the published

[111] *Arch. Ael.*, 5th series, 1, 1973, pp. 81–5; quote from p. 84.

section, a levelled surface was achieved by filling in the furrows with masons' chippings. Whatever the details of the Rudchester evidence and its interpretation, two important points emerge: first, that following the examples at Walker and Carrawburgh and an unpublished one at Halton Chesters, it provided the fourth case of ard-marks being recorded on a clay subsoil in a pre-Roman context in the Hadrianic frontier zone, an area where evidence of early agriculture was, and is, notoriously difficult to identify; and, secondly, the appearance in a pre-Hadrianic context of rigg-and-furrow opened up a new perspective on whole tracts of the northern landscape which are covered with rigg, generally regarded as of medieval or later date.

This particular problem, though of general interest in the north, has focused on Housesteads where the extensive remains of fields have been discussed for some time.[112] It is clear from published plans, air photographs, and fieldwork that at least five successive phases of arable cultivation can be identified on the ground, with the earlier ones likely to be pre-Roman or at latest contemporary with the Roman activity. Two of the terraces for example, are cut respectively by the Vallum road and by buildings of the *vicus*, and they themselves bear rigg-and-furrow and appear to overlie earlier fields. The possibility that rigg-and-furrow could be of Roman date or earlier, long-known at Housesteads, was also hinted at in the Royal Commission's *Westmorland* survey when it described the site at Askham, a Romano-British settlement, as being apparently associated with such ridges.[113] More recent work in Cumbria, independently of the excavated Rudchester evidence, has developed an increasingly strong argument, based upon fieldwork and air photography, for regarding at least some of the rigg as occurring in fields and other enclosures forming parts of Romano-British, possibly very late prehistoric, land arrangements.[114] This is not to suggest, however, that all or even most of the rigg-and-furrow in the northern counties is premedieval: clearly most of it *is* of medieval or later date and, when examined in detail, can or will be found to fit comfortably into a documented context of local land-use.[115] Nevertheless, it cannot now be *assumed* to be medieval or later without further enquiry; this applies particularly to examples of narrow widths on land which is marginal in terms of medieval and modern cultivation, and therefore likely to contain relict features of Romano-British and earlier landscapes. Such examples, however, unless there is good evidence in

[112] *Ant.*, v, 1931, pp. 351–4; *Liverpool Annals*, 24, 1931, 156 ff. Also discussed by B. Jones in P. J. Fowler (ed.), *Recent Work in Rural Archaeology*, p. 100, with excellent air photograph, Pl. 6g.

[113] RCHM, *Westmorland*, 1936, pp. 24–6.   [114] B. Jones, *op. cit.*

[115] For an excellent, modern local land-use study, see D. Austin, 'Fieldwork and excavation at Hart, Co. Durham, 1965–1975', *Arch. Ael.*, 5th series, 4, 1976, pp. 69–132.

support, should not perhaps be automatically assumed to represent ard or plough cultivation, for there is plentiful evidence until recent times of the ubiquity and efficacy of spade cultivation in ridges, a phenomenon to which much of the present Irish landscapes bears witness.[116]

Though strictly speaking not part of the agrarian history of England and Wales, recent and current work on *buried* Irish landscapes is directly relevant to this matter of ard-marks, early rigg, and spade cultivation.[117] Prehistoric 'walls' have for long been known in Irish archaeology, occasionally related to other structures, such as megalithic tombs. Over the last decade, a deliberate search has been made for them along the western side of the country where they can be related to the blanket peat bogs of Sub-Atlantic times which have covered them. The search has produced several dozen examples but, more importantly, a greater appreciation of the considerable extent of land allotment in the second millennium bc, particularly in counties Kerry and Mayo. Generally, stone-walled enclosures of some 3–4 acres (*c.* 1.5 ha) occur in systems covering blocks of land incorporating tombs, settlements, and arable fields. At Behy (Fig. 49), County Mayo, associated with a transepted court grave, was an oval stone enclosure with a mid third millennium bc C-14 date related to rectangular walled enclosures some 6 acres (2.4 ha) in area, arranged in slightly curved parallel strips, recalling in their layout both theoretical and actual land allotments discussed in southern England (above, pp. 151–7). Selective excavation within such complexes has been particularly fruitful: at Carrownaglogh, County Mayo, the definition and clearance of one such enclosure showed it to be 1.6 ha in extent and containing a 'fish-bone' pattern of bundles of ridges *c.* 1.5 m wide. The overall pattern looked very similar in miniature to that of a medieval 'open' field with its bundles of strips within asymmetrical furlongs, but at Carrownaglogh there is little doubt that the ridges represent spade cultivation of 'lazy-beds', thus taking a traditional method of cultivation back to *c.* 2000 bc. At Belderg, *c.* 8 km west of Behy, and also under the peat, was evidence very similar to that at Rudchester: namely, ard-marks, here convincingly in a criss-cross pattern, overlaid by spade-dug cultivation ridges belonging to a separate phase of tillage. One of the implications is clearly that the ard was not necessarily regarded as an improvement on the spade.

[116] A. Gailey and A. Fenton (eds.), *The Spade in Northern and Atlantic Europe*, 1970. On the Irish landscape, see F. Mitchell, *The Irish Landscape*, London, 1976.

[117] Briefly summarized by E. Evans in J. G. Evans *et al.* (eds.), CBA Research Report, 11, pp. 4–5, cf. M. Herity, 'Prehistoric fields in Ireland', *Irish Univ. Rev.*, Spring 1971, pp. 258–65. For an updated account see S. Caulfield in Bowen and P. J. Fowler (eds.), *Early Land Allotment*, Appendix 4 (below, pp. 278–9). The author is grateful to Dr Herity and Mr Caulfield for the opportunity to see and discuss this evidence in County Mayo during its investigation.

Apart from the various structures and features found within Highland Zone fields, portable material is also found, though in nothing like the quantity in fields of the Lowland Zone. Potsherds, for example, simply do not occur on and in fields like the prolific Iron Age and Romano-British pottery on the later prehistoric fields of the chalk downs. In most cases, however, this is perhaps due to the acidity of the soil and/or the non-disturbed state of its surface when investigated. Gwithian is again a striking example because there both of the main, later second millennium cultural layers contained a great deal of artifactual and 'natural', but man-deposited, material. The stone tip of an ard has already been noted as a unique occurrence (above, p. 197). Other utilized stones, potsherds, and fragments of domestic rubbish occur commonly throughout layers 5 and 3 and, equally important, so too do countless comminuted seashells. A differential distribution of such material was noted between the fields west and east of the 'central', north–south stone banks, suggesting that the eastern fields were more intensively manured. Developing the argument that the domestic rubbish represents the tangible debris of midden-derived manure, it seems possible that the sea-shells represent manuring with sea-weed, a common enough practice along the western littoral until fairly recently. The thickness of the two plough-soils of layers 5 and 3 certainly suggests in any case that organic matter was added to the original cultivated surface and topsoil to create the depth of tilth in the fields' developed stage. On the whole, however, such artifacts and man-transported material do not survive on Highland Zone fields, which is one of the main reasons why they are difficult to date.

Exceptions to this generalization, such as the few examples of Romano-British sherds from Caernarvonshire field systems,[118] stress the point, but the absence of evidence cannot allow the firm inference that manuring was not practised. Indeed, the probably greater run-off and erosion in the west could seem to have made it even more necessary than in the Lowland Zone (but cf. below, p. 213). Despite the erosion, soils still exist in Highland Zone fields and remain a great potential source of information.[119] Furthermore, there are large areas of buried cultivated soil even though we may not now be able to see the fields that contained them, e.g. under tombs, hill-forts, and bogs. Indeed, in some cases there may never have been fields in a formal, enclosed sense. This might apply, for example, along the machairs of the western coast,

[118] E.g. Caerau, *Ant. J.*, 16, 1936, pp. 295–320; cf. C. A. Gresham, *Arch. Camb.*, 121, 1972, pp. 51–60.

[119] As demonstrated generally in north-west Wales, even without laboratory analysis, in N. Johnson, 'An environmental study of the location of the location of pre-medieval settlement in Caernarvonshire', M.A. thesis, Univ. of Sheffield, 1976. See also Limbrey, *Soil Science and Archaeology*.

which surely represent preferred and exploited habitats over long periods, and it might apply too to land surfaces now below high water mark or sand-dunes, as at Eskmeals, Cumberland.[120] Nor need the soils necessarily even be buried, for it may be that the existing landscape and its flora provide the best evidence required for postulating prehistoric land use, perhaps arable, perhaps pastoral. Buried soils contain fossil fauna such as molluscs and bear witness to structural and chemical changes induced by anthropogenic activities, just as the present vegetation may be what it is as a result of environmental developments begun in the fourth, third, and second millennia. The changes through which the surface of the land was put in the production of cultivated crops was undoubtedly one of the main factors in promoting such environmental developments during later prehistory.

Cultivated crops[121]

The range of Neolithic crops has been discussed above (p. 52). For later prehistoric times, our knowledge is still based on the survey by Helbaek, published in 1952. As he emphasized, his material was not, on the whole, statistically acceptable.[122] We lack therefore a sound quantifiable base to talk authoritatively about the proportions of individual crops through time, though our evidence probably represents the range of cultivated crops during later prehistoric times. The bias of the evidence towards southern Britain and, furthermore, the chalklands should again be noted. Cereals, and specifically wheat and barley, were far and away the most common crops. In the later third, and for most of the second, millennium, Helbaek argued that barley predominated over wheat, a reversal of the situation amongst the earlier British farmers, but, though his figures justify the suggestion, they are based on too small and select a sample to carry conviction. The proportions appear to alternate again in the first millennium, with wheat, supplemented by the variety called spelt, becoming the favoured crop, a position it maintained through the Roman period (see PART II, p. 108). It is tempting to see these changes, if indeed they occurred, reflecting in part at least the climatic deterioration from the late second millennium, and particularly from the eighth to seventh centuries, onwards, but it seems more likely on general grounds that Helbaek's hypothesis,

[120] J. Cherry in *Trans. Cumb. Westmorland Ant. Arch. Soc.*, 63, 1963, pp. 31–52. On machairs, see for example Evans, *The Environment of Early Man...*, pp. 120–1, 138, 148.

[121] Since this section was written, an article by R. W. Dennell, 'Prehistoric crop cultivation in southern England: a reconsideration', *Ant. J.*, 56, 1976, pp. 11–23, has appeared, arguing along similar lines.

[122] H. Helbaek, 'Early crops in southern England', *Proc. Prehist. Soc.*, 18, 1952, pp. 194–233.

propounded for the whole of southern Britain, could well be masking regional or even more local variations in agricultural regimes, which themselves reflect different environmental circumstances, i.e. in Devon, through Somerset to Wiltshire, the area from which most of the samples come.

More wide-ranging geographically, though still statistically limited, was an earlier survey covering the whole of the British Isles, other than southern England and Ireland.[123] Some 426 impressions of grains and seeds in pottery from Neolithic to early medieval times and 3,442 carbonized plant remains from the Bronze Age to early medieval times were identified. In addition to wheats and barley, among both types of evidence were oats, wild oats, and rye, with flax and woad also appearing in the former. It is difficult, however, to establish relative proportions of species at any one time or in any one area, though the range of crops has not been significantly added to by subsequent work. From the small number of samples available to him, in his southern English survey, Helbaek identified from the early centuries of our period emmer (Fig. 60) and bread wheat, naked and hulled barley, and flax; from his mid to late second millennium samples came eincorn and emmer, naked and hulled barley and, again, flax; while from the centuries either side of *c.* 1000 BC, his samples produced the same range of wheat and barley but minus bread wheat and flax. Overall, in the 'Late Neolithic/Early Bronze Age' phase, barley occupied 70–80 per cent of the samples available, this British result being in accord with the general north-west European picture. At Gruting, for example (above, p. 179), a heap of 28 lb (12.7 kg) of carbonized grain consisted entirely of barley (Fig. 53). Its continued predominance is emphasized by the large quantity of grain from a pit at the Itford Hill settlement (Figs. 29, 60), Sussex, which was "almost exclusively of barley", none of it of the naked variety. These two major grain finds have incidentally, subsequently been used to obtain C-14 estimates, respectively of 1,564 ± 120 bc and 1,000 ± 35 bc (BM441; GrN6167).

In contrast, the other major pit deposit available to Helbaek from the mid first-millennium BC settlement at Fifield Bavant (Fig. 16), Wilts., consisted of about two-thirds barley but "practically entirely of the hulled form", i.e. "the six-row, lax-spiked variety, bere". The remaining third "was spelt with only a few kernels of club wheat, but no emmer, the national wheat of Britain up to that time". One grain of rye was identified, and it also appeared at the nearby hill-fort of Winkelbury. In addition, the Fifield pit contained "a fair proportion of oat of various species, wild oat being the most frequent". Helbaek

[123] K. Jessen and H. Helbaek, *Cereals in Great Britain and Ireland in Prehistoric and Early Historic Times*, Copenhagen, 1944.

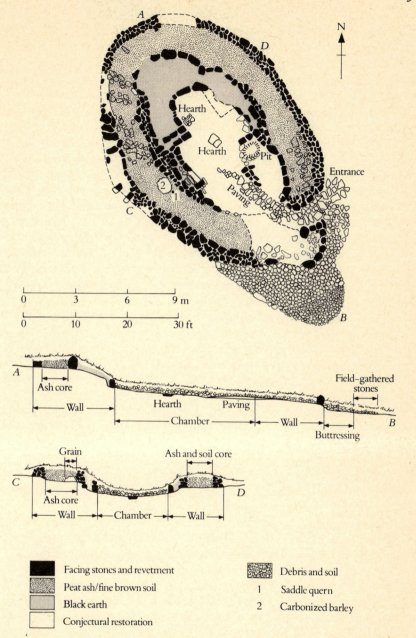

Fig. 53. House I, Ness of Gruting, Shetland, showing cache of barley and adjacent saddle quern (after C. S. T. Calder).

opined, however, that "it is doubtful whether intentional cultivation of this cereal took place in pre-Roman England". He remarked on another characteristic of the late prehistoric crop range, the presence of chess which commonly occurs with spelt.

By and large, our general knowledge of later prehistoric crops, based upon Helbaek's detailed analyses, has been confirmed by more recent information, though little new has come to light for the second millennium, so that a major uncertainty remains about the dominance of barley for that period. No synthesis of the last twenty years' work has, however, yet been made, and no new national research programme following up Helbaek's work has been carried out. We can therefore but look at some examples of the new evidence from those few individual sites where examination of crop evidence has been both executed and published. The mid first millennium BC settlement at Staple Howe (Figs. 23, 24) in the East Riding of Yorkshire, produced a large deposit of carbonized grain (c. 8,000 grains) which consisted solely of club wheat; the same variety only was also represented in another sample from the Phase 2 palisade trench. The samples examined contained "no trace of barley, or of weeds", an unusual fact in the light of Helbaek's point about the 'wild' or unintended varieties of plant in a 'host' crop of the first millennium. [124]

At Croft Ambrey hill-fort, Herefords., a sample of 11 carbonized grains were all identified as 'wheat' or 'probably wheat'. There was no barley in the samples identified, but no systematic search for grains was carried out during the excavation. This was, however, done in the entirely different context of the late prehistoric Berwick Down farmstead, Tollard Royal, Wilts. (Fig. 30), dating to the first decades of the first century AD, where 383 grains of carbonized wheat, probably spelt and emmer, and 163 grains of barley, certainly hulled and probably of the 6-rowed variety, were recorded. An interesting point is that the wheat was mainly related to the pits, and the barley to arrangements of post-holes interpreted as granaries.

In recent years a great deal more attention has been given to the recovery of botanical specimens and to the study of grain impressions on pottery. In particular, the development of flotation methods for obtaining grain and other botanical debris from excavated soils is increasing the amount of evidence out of all proportion to the statistically small quantities on which most of the above paragraphs are based; e.g. at Owslebury, Hants., in one season "all deposits with traces of burning" were filtrated, and some 4,000 carbonized grains and seeds were collected. Unfortunately, none of the new generation of reports

[124] Cf. also R. W. Dennell, 'The purity of prehistoric crops', Proc. Prehist. Soc., 40, 1974, pp. 132–5.

based on these new methods and on norms of thousands of samples recovered comprehensively is yet available; but their appearance shortly should begin to make a profound impact, on the study of what was, after all, the *raison d'être* of later prehistoric farming in Britain. Not merely will they confirm or refute Helbaek's conclusions, they will open up new lines of enquiry. What, for example, was the relationship between the 'host' crop and its weeds? Were the latter controlled or encouraged? Can we see crop-management developing, e.g. keeping the crop 'clean', on a par with the technological developments of our period? These and many other questions are prompted by the analysis of the contents of a single 'corn-drier', just outside our period, but not available when Part II of this volume was written. It contained the expected wheats, including spelt, but also twenty different identified species of weeds and fruit.[125] Numerically, if coincidentally, this compares closely with the twenty-two 'field weeds' listed by Helbaek from nine different contexts spread over some two millennia, with some overlap, as could be expected, in the individual species identified, e.g. fat hen (*Chenopodium album*), common orache (*Atriplex patula*), black bindweed (*Polygonum convolvulus*).

In addition to cereals, the only other cultivated plants in evidence were beans (*Vicia faba*), noted only in a very restricted area in Somerset at three sites, Glastonbury, Meare, and Worlebury. Otherwise, the range of domesticated legumes, brassicas, and fruits known from Roman Britain (PART II, p. 115) is absent, though certainly vetch (*V. sativa*) and chess (*Bromas* sp.) were quite widely grown.

The processes and artifacts of food production

We shall now look at the processes of food production by cultivation over the whole of our later prehistoric period, dividing the topic for convenience into its five main practical stages:

    (i) preparation of the seed-bed,
    (ii) sowing and care of the field crop,
    (iii) harvesting,
    (iv) storage,
    (v) food preparation.

The artifacts of each stage will also be discussed.[126]

[125] H. H. Clark in *Trans. Bristol Glos. Arch. Soc.*, 90, 1971, pp. 48–9.
[126] Acknowledgment is made to the writings of G. E. Evans whose influence will be apparent in the arrangement and content of this section. *The Horse in the Furrow*, London, 1960, and *The Farm and the Village*, London, 1969, have been particularly suggestive.

Preparation of the seed-bed

This stage can be subdivided into various actions, though not all would
necessarily have been carried out every year. The basic aim, as now,
would be to prepare the soil to receive the seed. Initially in any area,
and repeatedly in many places if the pollen evidence is followed, land
clearance would first be necessary, though even before that, in an ideal
model anyway, care and thought would have been expended on the
choice of land to be cultivated. The amount of clearance required – of
forest, scrub, or stones – was presumably one of the factors influencing
the choice. Others would have been slope, aspect, altitude, weather,
drainage, soil structure and type, and, in practice, existing land-use; and,
with the passage of time, other social claims on the land. Although most
of these factors may seem theoretical, it can be argued, certainly in the
first half of our period when population was small (above, pp. 84–8),
that in many cases communities and individuals would have had a free
choice of where to farm, 'free' that is of pressure from other people.
They could therefore have considered and weighed up the 'natural'
factors before making a decision. Of course, we can never know for
certain how deliberate and conscious was the making of a choice, but
it would be inappropriate to deny that considered choices were made
by communities which, in other fields between *c.* 2500 and 1500 bc,
developed considerable abilities in social organization, man-manage-
ment, mineral exploitation, distributive services, architecture, and
astronomy. The point must be emphasized on two grounds: first
because of what we can now begin to appreciate about the nature of
contemporary society in the later third to earlier second millennia bc;
and, secondly, because of the critical importance in terms of consequences of cultivating area x rather than area y. So important a matter,
particularly as agrarian experience accumulated, is hardly likely to have
been simply left to chance, especially bearing in mind the evidence of
detailed geological knowledge, indicated directly by the variety of stone
axe-heads, and indirectly by the consistent sensitivity shown in placing
settlements in relation to their environment.

With virgin land and land to be reclaimed, clearance broadly
involved two activities, separately or together: the removal of vegetation
and/or stones. A model for clearing forest applicable in northern
Europe, but not firmly evidenced in Britain, was 'slash and burn' or
'*Brandwirtschaft*' (above, p. 39). It is doubtful if this was used at all
commonly in later prehistoric Britain, though the widespread occurrence of charcoal fragments in pollen profiles, sediments, and under
stone clearance heaps cumulatively suggests the frequent use of fire for
initial clearance of vegetation. On the other hand, evidence also suggests

that swathes of countryside were cleared, with the debris being moved to the edges (Fig. 42). Possibly lines of existing vegetation were left to form 'natural hedges' around or between the new fields, but otherwise presumably trees and vegetation were burnt as far as possible, perhaps in great bonfires rather than by 'forest fires', i.e. by area conflagration. The felling of trees is indicated well into our period by the incidence and distribution of stone and flint axe-heads (Fig. 13), replaced in the bronze-smith's products by a range of flat-axes. It is not, however, until the Roman period that we again see clear examples of the specifically woodman's axe, then of course in iron (see Vol. I, Part II, pp. 73–82). Perhaps much of the effort in the second millennium was devoted to the clearance of scrub and light woodland rather than primary or 'climax' forest. Alternatively, the lighter axe-heads of the Early and Middle Bronze Age might have been quite adequate either for ringing, instead of felling, large trees or for chopping down mainly trees of lesser girth like ash, alder, hazel, birch or, for example, relatively young beech that was recolonizing an area previously exploited after initial clearance of primary elm and oak. The prevalence of the various forms of palstave throughout the second and on into the earlier first millennium can perhaps be seen as fitting into this sort of context: it is a multi-purpose, general chopping/cutting implement, rather like the small bill-hook or machet, more suited to farmers than to pioneers, for whom a heavy, strongly-hafted tool specifically for timber-felling would have been essential.

The clearance of stones demanded no such specialist tools. As already discussed above (p. 172), stones were piled into heaps in or at the sides of areas to be cultivated or used in lines for various forms of field boundary including built walls. Simple though this sounds, the immensity of this task over much of Britain must not be underrated. Nor was stone clearance necessary only in the Highland Zone, though it is certainly there that the evidence for this having taken place is now visually most apparent in the form of surviving surface structures, e.g. on Darmoor and the North York Moors. Particularly if the recently accumulated evidence for the former distribution of sarsen is accepted,[127] however, stone clearance was widespread in parts of the Lowland Zone too, even if the evidence for it now is, in contradistinction to Dartmoor for example, the actual stone-free appearance of the landscape itself. Certainly in Wessex it now seems that widespread clearance of sarsen must be allowed for, though it is problematic where the stones were put or now are. Without much doubt, many are now

[127] Summarized in J. G. Evans, *The Environment of Early Man...*, fig. 26; new survey results summarized in *Evolution of the Landscape Project: Sarsen Symposium*, News Sheet no. 2, Soc. Ant. Lond., 1975, cf. *Ant. J.*, 53, 1973, pp. 9–13.

buried in erosion products in valley bottoms. River clearance and widening, a pipeline, and the breaking up of water-meadows in the now largely stone-free upper Kennet valley, for example, have recently indicated the density of buried sarsens there. Otherwise, man-made locations must be looked for, and obvious candidates are the mounds of barrows and the thousands of kilometres of early field boundaries now marked by lynchets. Over most of the Lowland Zone, the excavation of many hundreds of round barrows has shown, without denying the existence of stone structures, that they are emphatically not the major repository of debris from massive land clearance.[128] Very few long barrows, on the other hand, have been extensively excavated,[129] and their extended 'tails' represent the location of very many tons of stone debris some at least of which could have come from land clearance rather than ad-hoc quarrying. Indeed, it has been suggested that the 'megalithic' long barrows of Lowland Zone Britain may in part have originated in their local context as field clearance mounds. Both these hypotheses remain to be tested systematically. Meanwhile, all over Britain, wherever stone occurs locally, it can be seen in use in the vernacular buildings of the area and, just as Roman buildings have proved irresistible quarries for later builders, so probably much of the product of prehistoric land clearance has found its way into the structures not only of contemporary but also of medieval and later communities.

The actual cultivation of cleared land was carried out in various ways. It seems reasonable to assume that pasture and ground newly cleared, and probably also cropped land on occasion, would be broken up by hand hoes and other mattock-type implements. Stone axes, palstaves, antlers, and all-wooden tools could have been used, though there is no direct evidence. The importance of spades at this, and indeed later, stages of seed-bed preparation must not be overlooked. Hand-digging of new land, though slow, is as effective as any method of breaking up the soil, particularly any containing pan, and of burying the 'trash' of grasses and weeds. Second millennium evidence from Gwithian and County Mayo, Ireland (above, p. 201), and recent analogy especially from Highland Britain, provide plentiful evidence for the use of the spade for inverting the soil profile, and indeed doing the major work in preparing the soil to receive the seed.[130]

There is, nevertheless, abundant evidence for the use of traction ploughs or, more correctly, ards, if the word 'plough' is reserved for an implement with coulter and mould board. The ard had neither,

---

[128] See generally, P. Ashbee, *The Bronze Age Round Barrow in Britain*, London, 1960.
[129] See generally, P. Ashbee, *The Earthen Long Barrow in Britain*, London, 1970.
[130] Gailey and Fenton (eds.), *The Spade in Northern and Atlantic Europe*.

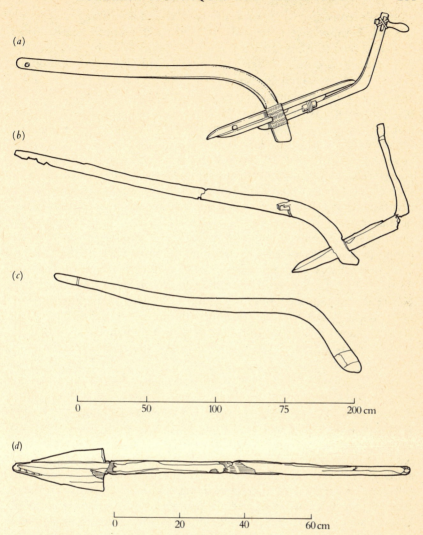

Fig. 54. Ards: (a), reconstruction of the Donnerupland ard, Denmark, showing from left to right, beam with yoke attachment, foreshare, main share and ard-head (all passing through the beam), and stilt with handle; (b), the Hendriksmose ard, Denmark, showing the slightly different arrangement of the foreshare directly on the ard-head at the end of the stilt; (c), beam with dowel-holes from Lochmaben, Dumfries.; (d), ard-head and stilt from Milton Loch crannog, Kirkcudbrights. (a, after H. C. Bowen; b, after H. O. Hansen; c, d, after A. Fenton).

essentially consisting of a point or share which was dragged through the soil, compressing it laterally and lifting it vertically rather than turning it over (the current arguments for 'direct drilling', incidentally, question the wisdom of inverting the soil profile annually). Traditionally, the ard envisaged for later prehistoric Britain has been a light, wooden-framed implement essentially similar to the Donnerupland ard from Denmark (Fig. 54), and there is little doubt that such was in common use, was perhaps the common type, particularly in the first millennium BC in the Lowland Zone.[131] In terms of processes, however, it is difficult to envisage such an implement breaking up recently cleared ground or turf, and it is indeed known from experiment that it is not very effective (Plate VIIa).[132] Hence the suggestion above that the initial breaking up was done by hand, using hoes, mattocks, or spades.

One of the consequences of recognizing ard-marks in Britain, however, has been to raise the question of what it was that produced them and why (above, pp. 163–6). It is possible, particularly with the deep and broad examples like both sets at South Street, Avebury, that they represent a special ploughing, abnormally deep, and occurring only infrequently, rather than the normal, annual ploughing.[133] The difficulty here has been to postulate the sort of implement necessary for such a post-clearance but essentially 'soil-busting' operation. A possibility, still in use in Galicia and noted long ago by Leser, is a type consisting only of a heavy, straight (oak) beam bound to a sharply curving piece of wood on to which is (now) fitted a heavy, socketed, iron bar-share.[134] Locally it is called 'el carbelo' and though impressive in its form and achievements – it is reserved for breaking up new ground – it is essentially simple. Admittedly no certain part of such a plough has been identified in later prehistoric Britain, and indeed the only evidence, and that indirect, is provided by the deep ard-marks apparently beyond the capacity of the normal, light ard. The Galician model, although an 'ancient' type, merely provides a pointer to what could have existed in third/second millennium Britain. Such an implement

[131] P. V. Glob, *Ard og Plov i Nortens Oldtid*, Aarhus, 1951: Bowen, *Ancient Fields*; P. J. Fowler, 'The Abingdon ard-share', in M. Parrington, *The Excavation at Ashville Trading Estate, Abingdon (Oxfordshire), 1974–76*, Oxfordshire Archaeological Unit, Report 1, and CBA Research Report, 28, London, 1978, pp. 83–8.

[132] Hansen, *Reports from Experiments in Lejre 1968*, 1, 1969, and 'Experimental ploughing with a Døstrop ard replica', *Tools and Tillage*, 1, 1969, pp. 67–92; F. A. Aberg and H. C. Bowen, 'Ploughing experiments with a reconstructed Donnerupland ard', *Ant.*, XXXIV, 1960, pp. 144–7.

[133] *Ant.*, XLI, 1967, pp. 289–301.

[134] P. Leser, *Entstehung und Verbreitung des Pfluges*, 1931, p. 332, fig. 182, though without the iron bar-share observed by the author in 1974, see P. J. Fowler and P. J. Reynolds, paper in preparation.

could have been entirely of wood, its share purely a sharpened point, or it could have been fitted with a bar-share of wood, stone or flint. Obviously none would have fitted as well, or been as heavy, as a *socketed* iron share; but the essential characteristics of this type of ard are the weight in the beam, the acute curve from beam to share, and the bar-nature of the share itself. All these conditions could have been met in a pre-iron agricultural context so it is tentatively suggested that such a type of soil-breaking traction implement could have been in existence, at least in the earlier part of our period, for use in the pre-ploughing and periodic 'subsoil-breaking' phases of preparing the seed-bed.

With the land cleared and the soil loosened, by hand and by various implements, the ground might well now be considered ready for 'ploughing'. Land which was newly taken in would presumably be reasonably fertile, and no further preparation would be necessary before such ploughing. Nevertheless the latent fertility could well be supplemented even for the first cultivation by the deliberate creation of a layer of ash from foliage or turf-paring over the area to be cropped.[135] In an operative field system, however, manuring or marling would almost certainly have been an additional and regular operation to be completed before the ard itself was used. This generalization seems to be applicable from the later second millennium onwards, as witnessed at Gwithian in the west and Itford Hill in the south; but, to judge from the number of occasions that Beaker sherds occur in plough-soils, e.g. at South Street, Avebury, and assuming such sherds are manure-derived, then the practice of manuring may well have begun several centuries earlier.[136] Whether it developed as a result of observing decreasing yields in the continual cropping of the same areas, or whether the construction of permanent field systems became possible because the potential of regular manuring came to be realized is impossible to say: the questions may not even be the right ones. But in terms of processes involved in cultivated food production, a manuring stage by one or more of several different methods can certainly be envisaged as a regular practice on the arable, and perhaps the pastoral, fields of Britain in the first millennium BC.

The methods used can only be inferred. The carting of domestic refuse on to fields is implied by the presence of domestic debris in the fields as already discussed (above, p. 167), though the dangers of using a circular argument are apparent. What is surprising, if the thesis is

---

[135] G. Clark, *Prehistoric Europe: the Economic Basis*, London, 1952, pp. 92–4; A. Steensberg, 'Some recent Danish experiments in Neolithic agriculture', *Agric. Hist. Rev.*, 5, 1957, pp. 66–73; above, p. 41.

[136] Discussed further in P. J. Fowler, 'Lowland landscapes', in Limbrey and Evans (eds.), CBA Research Report, 21, pp. 1–12.

correct for the later first millennium especially, is the sheer quantity of
such refuse thrown away, unused as manure, into the thousands of pits
studding Iron Age settlements. The implication seems to be that fields
were not primarily used for disposing of domestic refuse, but that the
artifactual residue now found in them was, perhaps accidentally or just
sporadically, incorporated in dung-heaps or possibly all-purpose
farmyard middens specifically intended for muck-spreading. Another
related problem is the whereabouts of all the material that was dug out
of the ground in making the pits: by and large it is not in the pits as
excavated now, and it is at least arguable that by no means all of the
material would have been used up for construction purposes, e.g. in
walling or in making cob. An inference could be that, where suitable,
as in the case of chalk, it was spread over fields, perhaps on arable, but
equally possibly on pasture as the equivalent of 'liming' grassland today.
'Marling' is also likely on heavier soils. The possibility should also be
borne in mind, while considering the physical transport of material to
fields, that soil itself was taken to the arable as a means of rejuvenating
or perhaps just maintaining fertility. Though speculation in Britain's
case, this has long been known to have been done in medieval and later
Holland with river silts, and the practice has now been demonstrated
on 'Celtic' fields of the late prehistoric period.[137] Though no evidence
yet exists, the possibility that soil was moved on to late prehistoric fields
in Lowland Britain is not entirely remote, particularly perhaps when
one considers the massive erosion which had taken place on the chalk
downs by the end of our period, and the vast, consequential linear
reservoirs of fine tilth lying idle along field edges and at the base of
valley scarps. Specially collected organic materials, like seaweed (above,
p. 202), leaf-mould or peat might also have been used.

   In addition, or alternatively, fertility would probably have been
maintained directly by animals themselves. It is so easy to divide animal
from crop husbandry, as the structure of this chapter shows, but in
practice, and especially in the mixed farming probably characteristic of
all Britain until the Sub-Atlantic deterioration, and in Lowland Britain
thereafter, both were interdependent. Direct animal manuring, the
existence of which is entirely theoretical but nevertheless virtually
certain, could have been achieved in two ways, and its seems likely that
both were used. Sheep and cattle could be allowed to graze *extensively*
over harvested fields and on fallow fields, at one and the same time
manuring the arable and resting the regular pasture. Both, but particularly sheep, could be folded on arable, i.e. penned into a small area
for *intensive* dunging and then moved in succession through a series of
similar areas. The half-acre (0.2 ha) plots of so many late prehistoric field
systems seem particularly well-suited to this practice. Perhaps some of

[137] Brongers, *Air Photography and Celtic Field Research.* . . .

the late prehistoric pottery found on contemporary arable fields arrived there in the hooves of manuring cattle, as in the case of some modern artifacts of fields, rather than in the manure itself. Behind all the speculation, the important point is that from some time in the second millennium BC, we can safely assume that, in many areas and increasingly, a manuring stage occurred in the preparation of the seed-bed, after clearance or harvest and before ploughing. Although muck-spreading is the subject of not inconsiderable bucolic humour even, or perhaps especially, in modern, urban-based societies, it is critical to agrarian stability and, as this brief discussion should imply, involves the fairly skilful, long-term management of numerous human, livestock, and environmental resources.

'Ploughing' is another apparently simple operation involving rather more than just walking behind a team and implement. Not the least of the skills involved is knowing *when* to plough. We can place the event in the sequence of operations making up the whole process of cultivated food production, but knowing when to plough in any given year in any given place is a matter of judgment, based on knowledge and experience, and doubtless custom and even ritual too in the last two millennia BC.[138] The main point of ploughing is to remove surface vegetation, particularly weeds, to induce fertilization by creating a tilth to receive the seeds, and to encourage maximum germination by obviating bad drainage. Later prehistoric ploughing was normally carried out by light, wooden-framed ards of various types, for which the European evidence is consistent and matched by a wealth of ethnographic material. But it must be stressed that no actual wooden ards survive in Britain until the later centuries BC. It is only an assumption, though it seems a reasonable one, that similar ards existed earlier in Britain. The earliest European ard, from Horslev, Denmark, is dated *c.* 1500 bc, though there are many pictographs from the second millennium onwards showing ards and their plough teams, nearly always of two oxen, from the Italian Alps north to Scandinavia.[139] On the other hand, parts of ards and the marks they made in, and below, the plough-soil are well-recorded from the third millennium bc onwards (above, p. 163).

The best-known parts of ards from late prehistoric Britain are stone shares.[140] Coming principally from Shetland but also from Orkney, dating around the middle of the second millennium bc and probably

[138] Cf. G. E. Evans, *The Farm and the Village*, London, 1969, 1974 paperback ed., p. 43.

[139] Glob, *op. cit.*; P. J. Fowler, 'Early prehistoric agriculture...', in Simpson (ed.), *Economy and Settlement...*, pp. 153–82.

[140] A. Fenton, 'Early and traditional cultivating implements in Scotland', *Proc. Soc. Ant. Soc.*, 96, 1962–3, pp. 264–317; S. Rees, 'Tools available for cultivation in prehistoric Britain', in Limbrey and Evans (eds.), CBA Research Report, 21, pp. 103–14.

on into the first millennium BC, are *c.* 400 stone implements best interpreted as bar-shares (Fig. 55*a*). They are of sandstone and characteristically of flattened oval cross-section, but some are round in section. Most survive as broken points, but original lengths probably varied between *c.* 15–45 cm with at least one being nearly a metre long. Widths, in contrast, are fairly constant around 7–8 cm. A distinctive feature is that usually only one side has been smoothed by wear, but some are worn at both ends. Unfortunately, this evidence is at the moment confined to Orkney and Shetland, perhaps in the absence of suitable wood, and it is not known whether it represents a highly developed example of local adaptation to environment, or whether the phenomenon is more widespread. It can, however, be suggested that conventional stone axe-heads could have acted as shares, most appropriately, as in the case of the Orkney/Shetland shares, attached to a bow-ard; but the point is unattested except for the broken tip of an axe-head found in an ard-furrow at Gwithian (above, p. 197). While stone shares, or stone tips to wooden shares, are likely on our third to second millennia ards, the implements would have been basically of wood, a material which, as many late prehistoric examples from Denmark show, was quite adequate for the share itself. Some Danish examples, with pebbles let into wooden shares to make them last longer, led to the suggestion that some pebbles from British sites might have had an aratral function; but this always seemed somewhat tenuous and the originals are probably medieval anyway.[141] There is no evidence that bronze shares were fitted to an ard, though conceivably bone or antler points could have been used; and indeed it is not until late pre-Roman times and the Roman period itself that we have much evidence for iron parts on a plough (Fig. 55*b*, *c*). Excavation of the settlement at Gussage All Saints, Dorset, has, however, recently produced some iron share-tips in a mid first-millennium bc context.[142] Some iron bars, previously thought to be currency bars, have been claimed to be bar-shares from the very end of our period and such were certainly used in the Roman period.[143] For the first millennium BC as a whole, however, largely in the absence of evidence, we have to assume light, nearly all-wooden ards, in principle perhaps almost always the same but in structure varying from the simple to the complex.

[141] C. W. Phillips, *Proc. Prehist. Soc.*, 4, 1938, pp. 338–9; G. Lerche, 'The ploughs of medieval Denmark', and 'Pebbles from wheelploughs', *Tools and Tillage*, 1, 1970, pp. 131–49 and 150. Cf. also D. V. Clarke, *Tools and Tillage*, 2, 1972, pp. 50–1.

[142] *Ant.*, 47, 1973, pp. 109–30; 50, 1976, pp. 32–9. Information about the share-tips from Dr G. Wainwright in advance of publication is gratefully acknowledged.

[143] D. Allen, 'Iron currency bars in Britain', *Proc. Prehist. Soc.*, 33, 1967, pp. 307–35; W. Manning, 'The plough in Roman Britain', *J. Rom. Stud.*, 54, 1964, pp. 54–65.

The Danish Donnerupland ard has often been quoted as the common type in late prehistoric Britain, though it is in fact a relatively sophisticated piece of carpentry.[144] Particularly for the third and second millennia, it is worth considering the possibility that the spade, which certainly existed (above, p. 201), was also used as a traction implement. This suggestion has already been made as a possible explanation of the origins of the ard in Europe, and its use for ploughing as distinct from digging has now been demonstrated by experiment.[145] Perhaps the broad furrows at Weston Wood, Surrey, illustrate the practice.[146] The two best-attested wooden parts of late prehistoric British *ards*, respectively from Lochmaben and Milton Loch in south-west Scotland, nevertheless appear to be of the Donnerupland or bow-ard type.[147] The Lochmaben example (Fig. 54c), ^{14}C dated to 80 ± 100 bc, consists of an alder beam, 2.48 m long, near the base of the curved end of which is a mortice-hole through which would have been pushed, from the front, not only the horizontal cutting share (or ard-head) but also a fore-share, perhaps a bar-share, and the stilt (or handle). At the other end of the beam was another hole for a wooden fitting to take the yoke attachment. The Milton Loch 'ard' (Figs. 54d, 56) in fact consists only of the ard-head and stilt of a type which could well have passed through the beam from Lochmaben. It has a ^{14}C date of 400 ± 100 bc. The whole is 1.28 m long with an arrow-shaped head 29.5 cm long by 13.33 cm wide. This part shows no evidence of, and indeed would not have required, any iron share or 'shoe' fitting over it: it could well have come from an ard with a fore-share fitted with an iron shoe and, despite the generalization about the infrequency of iron ard-parts above, the existence of iron shares, and possibly even of coulters, must be noted. While no definite pre-Roman coulters have been identified, however, some three dozen iron share-tips (Fig. 55b, c) have been claimed, though doubts exist about the exact date and function of some of the individual pieces.[148] The dating of some of the examples from Ireland, for

[144] Bowen, *Ancient Fields*, pp. 7–9. See also Bibliography (below, p. 282), papers by F. G. Payne; W. Manning; A. Aberg; and P. J. Fowler, 'The Abingdon ard- share'.
[145] P. J. Fowler, 'Early prehistoric agriculture...', p. 159; A. Steensberg, 'A 6000 year old ploughing implement from Satrup Moor', *Tools and Tillage*, 2, 1975, pp. 105–18.
[146] Though the evidence is far from convincing and should perhaps be discounted altogether (above, p. 166). Acceptable evidence of spade-marks, or at least of hand-digging, has now been published from Ascot, Berks., *J. Arch. Sci.*, 2, 1975, pp. 95–108, supplementing that from Gwithian, Cornwall.
[147] *Agric. Hist. Rev.*, 5, 1957, p. 74; *Trans. Dumfries. Galloway Nat. Hist. Ant. Soc.*, 45, 1968, 147–52; *Proc. Soc. Ant. Scot.*, 67, 1952–3, pp. 143–4; Fenton, *op. cit.*: Rees, *op. cit.*: *Tools and Tillage*, 1, 1969, p. 128.
[148] Fenton, *op. cit.*; F. G. Payne in *Arch. J.*, 104, 1948, pp. 82–111 and *Agric. Hist. Rev.*, 5, 1957, pp. 74–84; P. J. Fowler, 'The Abingdon ard-share'.

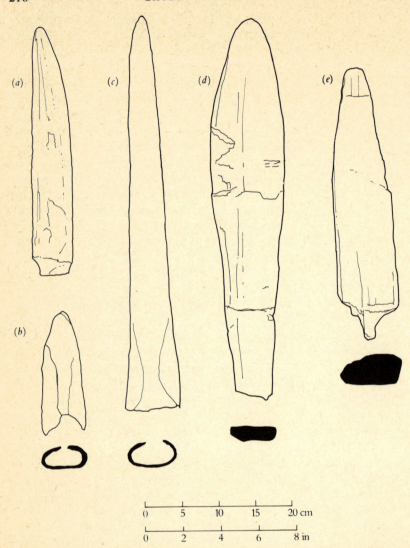

Fig. 55. Ard-shares: (a), bar-share of stone from Orkney, with oval cross-section and collar at back; (b), iron share or share-tip from Hunsbury, Northants.; (c), iron share from Bigbury, Kent; (d), wooden share from Walesland Rath, Pembs.; (e), wooden share from Abingdon, Berks. (now Oxon) (a, after C. S. T. Calder; b, c, after S. Rees; d, after G. J. Wainwright; e, after P. J. Fowler).

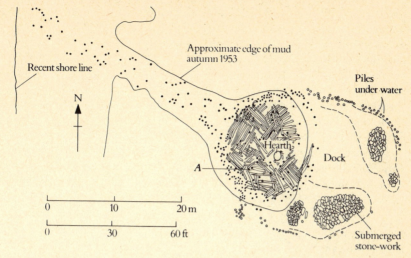

Fig. 56. Plan of Milton Loch crannog I, Kirkcudbrights., before excavation, showing shoreline, causeway and harbour; with selected excavation detail including the position (A) of the ard-head and stilt beneath the house floor (after C. M. Piggott).

example, is uncertain[149] and others may be to sheath digging implements rather than shares.[150]

Two other ard-heads and stilts, both from Virdifield, Shetland, are also not dated closely but are probably late prehistoric,[151] and an oak share, probably of the first century BC, has also now been recognized from Walesland Rath, Pembs. (Fig. 55d).[152] England too can now contribute to the growing list of parts of wooden ards, one example and possibly two, having been found since Part II was published.[153] The possible example came from a gravel pit which was part of an Iron Age/Romano-British settlement complex at Odell, Beds. Dating to the

[149] See generally A. T. Lucas, 'Irish ploughing practices', *Tools and Tillage*, 2, 1972, pp. 52–62; 1973, pp. 67–83; and 1974, pp. 149–60; M. V. Duignan, 'Early historic agriculture', *J. Roy. Soc. Ant. Ireland*, 74, 1944, pp. 124–45.

[150] The author is grateful to the Director, National Museum, Dublin, for access to the shares and other material in the collection. Several papers in Gailey and Fenton (eds.), *The Spade...*, examine Irish spades and detail the considerable literature on the subject.

[151] Rees, *op. cit.*

[152] G. J. Wainwright, *Britannia*, 2, 1971, pp. 94–99; W. Manning, in Evans *et al.* (eds.), CBA Research Report, 11, p. 114.

[153] I am indebted to D. Baker and B. Dix, Bedfordshire County Council, and to D. Miles and M. Parrington, Oxfordshire Archaeological Unit, for the opportunities to examine these two pieces, for the invitations to prepare accounts of them for publication, and for permission to quote them here in advance of the excavation reports. The Abingdon ard-share is now published as Parrington, *The Excavation at Ashville Trading Estate*, see fn. 131, p. 212.

mid first century AD – whether just pre- or post-Conquest is in doubt – the 'ard', if such it is, can be interpreted as the share, sole, and stump of the beam of a crook-ard. If correctly identified, it is the first such example from Britain and, particularly in view of its date, advises caution in generalizing about the ubiquity of the bow-ard in late prehistoric Britain. Though typologically the crook-ard is early, the re-dating of one of the type-specimens, the Dabergotz ard from eastern Germany, to the early medieval period[154] suggests a date of c. 50 AD for the Odell piece need not in itself occasion surprise.

The second English example, a wooden arrow-shaped share (Fig. 55e) also from a gravel-situated Romano-British settlement, might likewise be regarded as a little 'late'. It was found in 1974 at the bottom of a well in a firm third-century AD context at Ashville, Abingdon, Berks. (now Oxon.). It is a piece of oak 36.9 cm long from the broken end of a tang to the tip of a rounded point; 8.3 cm broad at its shoulder below the tang; and varies in thickness from 4 cm at the base of the tang to 2.5 cm just behind the point. All the surfaces were either cut, worn, or broken, and heavy wear was apparent asymmetrically on one edge and across one surface. The point was hardly worn and almost certainly had been sheathed in an iron tip. The object was certainly from a bow-ard but it is difficult to decide whether it formed the fore-share above the ard-head on a 'Hendriksmose-type' ard or the main-share between the fore-share and the ard-head on a 'Donnerupland-type' ard. Clearly the ard it was used on, whatever its construction, was not a Roman introduction, and it is reasonable to see in the Abingdon share the persistence in a heavily Romanized area of a long-lived native tradition with roots certainly in the second millennium, and perhaps in the fourth millennium BC. We can be reasonably confident that, when the ploughing of the arable in later prehistoric Britain occurred each spring and autumn, it was carried out with a light, wooden-framed implement constructed within a limited and very conservative range of types.

Whatever the technical details of the later prehistoric ard in Britain, it was long ago postulated that the ard itself was used to cultivate by cross-ploughing, i.e. by moving backwards and forwards across a field on one axis and then repeating the action at right angles to the first line *as part of the same process*. The evidence of ard-marks, particularly that from Gwithian and Overton Down (Figs. 51, 44), on the whole can be interpreted satisfactorily in terms of this hypothesis. Further, by making various assumptions, it has been tentatively estimated that the cross-ploughing of a typical c. 1 acre (0.4 ha) 'Celtic' field would take about eight hours, thus suggesting that, on Overton Down anyway,

[154] 733 ± 80 AD (Berlin 462), *Tools and Tillage*, I, 1968, pp. 50–5.

there could be some correlation between field shape and size, and the method of cultivation employed on it.[155] Such a process with an ard would tend to churn up the surface soil rather than invert it, though since ard-marks have been noted as asymmetrical in section (above, pp. 196, 198), and shares observed to be asymmetrically worn (above, pp. 216, 220), it can be argued that the stilt was leant to one side, usually the right, to create a semi-furrow with more soil pushed to one side than the other. Leant or not, experiment and observation of such ards still in use shows that the share has frequently to be cleaned of the vegetational 'trash' collected around it.

While cross-ploughing was almost certainly the norm, recent evidence particularly from north Britain and western Ireland suggests that alternatives existed both early and late in our period. Ard-marks at Rudchester (above, p. 199), though crossing each other, have been divided into three sets and seen as representing three separate ploughings, each in one direction only. Furthermore, one set, presumably the latest, is claimed as being associated with narrow rigg-and-furrow, envisaged as being under cultivation in the early second century AD. This, linked as we have seen to the tentative evidence for other rigg-and-furrow of Roman date in the north-west, could suggest either a reversion to spade-cultivation or the emergence of a one-way plough, presumably at least with a coulter and possibly with a mouldboard. The point here is that in considering 'ploughing', while we can envisage criss-cross cultivation with an ard over much of the first-millennium Lowland Zone, in other places and at other times the later prehistoric farmer might have used other techniques, perhaps for specific purposes. Just possibly, right at the end of our period, an improved cultivating implement might also have been developed.

Whether cultivation was carried out by hand or by a traction implement, further work could often have followed in the final stages of preparing the seed-bed. Areas might have been raked to spread unevenness, the field might have been walked with a mattock or hoe to break up remaining clods, the whole might have been harrowed to try to produce a regular tilth. Direct evidence from the past for such actions is nugatory: commonsense and present practice alone suggest the likelihood that they took place.

Sowing and care of the field crop

There is no direct evidence for this stage of the food production process. Presumably sowing was by hand, and, though it is easy to assume that it was done broadcast, it is more than likely that dibbling was frequently

[155] *Wilts. Arch. Nat. Hist. Mag.*, 62, 1967, pp. 24–6, fig. 3.

used. It is simply so much more efficient to put two to four grains into holes arranged in lines: covering of the seeds can be ensured, loss is reduced, weeding is more manageable, the crop is more evenly spread, and harvesting is easier. A case for regarding ard-grooves as seed-drills has been considered – and rejected. Presumably too, while the crop was growing, weeding and bird-scaring were undertaken. The main threat to the growing crops was, however, probably wild, and perhaps domesticated, animals. The development of regular field systems with walls, ditches, and fences as boundaries may have been as much a response to this situation as to any other factor. The danger of human pillage, particularly in the late prehistoric period, was also probably considerable, especially during bad seasons, and it is not difficult to envisage co-operative action to protect their crops by communities whose very livelihood in the coming year depended on the successful harvesting of their cereal food supply.

Harvesting

Harvesting too is largely a matter of conjecture, deriving from some tools – the only archaeological evidence on the topic – traditional practice and commonsense. The tools in question are sickles. In the earlier part of our period flint was used both to make single blades hafted into wooden handles, rather like a penknife in size, and to provide small, sharp edges mounted into a wooden back, so making a serrated cutting tool. Flints of both sorts have been recognized by the characteristic silica gloss on their surfaces caused by friction against the cereal stems. Both types of tool were probably used for cutting the crop just below the ear. There is no evidence until later for either scythes or bill-hooks suitable for cutting the stem at ground level.

With the development of a metal technology, sickles appear first in bronze and then, from the mid first millennium onwards, in iron.[156] Perhaps curiously, Early and Middle Bronze Age sickles are not common, possibly suggesting that the flint varieties continued to be

---

[156] C. Fox, 'The socketed bronze sickles of the British Isles', *Proc. Prehist. Soc.*, 4, 1939, pp. 222–48, and 'The non-socketed sickles of Britain', *Arch. Camb.*, 96, 1941, pp. 136–62; A. Steensberg, *Ancient Harvesting Implements*, Copenhagen, 1943, esp. Parts 1 and 3; V. G. Childe, 'The balanced sickle', in Grimes (ed.), *Aspects of Archaeology*, pp. 39–48. For examples of bronze sickles, see M. J. Rowlands, *The Organisation of Middle Bronze Age Metalworking*, British Archaeological Report, 31, Oxford, 1976, pp. 46–7, and of iron sickles, e.g. Glastonbury and Barbury. A modern study of later prehistoric sickles is badly needed and is now partly provided, *inter alia*, by A. Harding, 'Bronze agricultural implements...', in G. de G. Sieveking, I. H. Longworth and K. E. Wilson (eds.), *Problems in Economic and Social Archaeology*, London, 1976, pp. 513–22.

preferred, but the products of Late Bronze Age technology demonstrate a number of varieties including larger and heavier ones that could have been used for ground level reaping. A common type was socketed on to a handle, and had a characteristic beak-like blade. Iron sickles were socketed, tanged, or riveted, and ranged in size from the small 'ear-sickle' (Fig. 60b) to larger tools which could have been used for ground reaping. There need be no conflict of evidence here: recently, in a field in Galicia, I saw a man removing the ears of wheat with a small bill-hook while his wife followed cutting the stalks with a larger curved sickle. The straw was carefully gathered in bundles to be used for thatching and cattle bedding. The all-important factor in the design of a sickle is that it should be 'balanced', enabling the user to work with minimum effort for long periods.[157]

Clearly the nature of the field operation in gathering the crop affected the other main harvesting operations, threshing and, beyond that, the storage of the harvest. Threshing was almost certainly done using flails but the evidence for this is archaeologically non-existent; it could also have been achieved by animals trampling over the harvested crop. We do not know where the threshing took place – on small, individual threshing floors out in the fields as, for example, in the Peloponnese today; at large communal stone-flagged threshing centres near or in the settlements, as in north-west Spain today; or in private barn or house. Wherever it took place, it would have been a different operation depending on whether the crop to be threshed consisted of ears alone, or ears on the stalk. Considering the cumulatively large amount of evidence for later prehistoric agriculture in Britain, and the critical importance of threshing – the process which turned potential food into a usable form – the absence of hard evidence for threshing and for barns in particular is extraordinary. Possibly it implies that threshing was carried out in the fields as the crop was harvested, but traditional practice, and, one would guess, instinct is to rush the harvest under cover in rick or barn while it is dry, leaving the threshing until later.

For spelt at least it seems highly likely that the ears were cut separately, because this particular wheat variety had to be parched before threshing, not so much to dry the grain as to make the husks brittle so that they would break off during threshing (Fig. 60a). Grain parching areas, and the debris from them, are a characteristic feature of first millennium sites in southern Britain, and the practice they represent certainly has earlier origins. One of the pits at Itford Hill, Sussex, for example, contained a large quantity of parched grain, almost exclusively hulled barley (Fig. 60c). When Helbaek was discussing this

---

[157] Cf. G. E. Evans, *The Farm and the Village*, London, 1969, p. 76: 'The curve of least exertion'.

material and the significance of its carbonization in 1952, he was
naturally thinking of a date in the ninth/seventh centuries BC, but a
C-14 date now takes this grain back to *c*. 1000 bc. A corn-drying oven
was part of the near-contemporary settlement in layer 3 at Gwithian.
Since, however, there is no evidence of grain-drying or parching from
earlier in the second millennium, it is tempting to see in the growth
of the practice a reaction to a worsening climate as early as the later
second millennium (above, p. 73). Though a circular argument, the
phenomenon could itself be evidence of a worsening climate since there
is no botanical reason why barley should be parched: unlike the later
spelt, it was parched primarily to dry it. All this of course has
implications for the methods of storage (below).

We presumably can also envisage winnowing taking place to separate
grain and chaff. The only evidence for this, and indirect evidence at that,
is the grain and particularly husk impressions frequently observed on
prehistoric pottery. When Helbaek carried out his survey, he noted that
the evidence of impressions came almost entirely from before the mid
first millennium BC, an observation which could have several
implications if further work confirmed its correctness. Whether
absolutely correct or not, it does suggest a general practice of
winnowing, perhaps threshing too, in the vicinity of the pot-making
area of a settlement. A picture of chaff blowing about between the
houses and some of it sticking to pots standing out to dry at the
'green-hard' stage is difficult to resist. The straw that was left after the
harvest, the threshing, and the winnowing, would undoubtedly have
been put to many uses as thatch, as bedding for humans and animals,
as winter fuel, and, who knows, as decorative material for corn-dollies
and the like. Here again, however, any straw is not necessarily suitable
for all or any of these purposes, and selection both in cultivation and
in harvesting treatment would have been necessary to obtain, for
example, the right material for autumnal roof repairs.

Storage

Pits are the characteristic archaeological phenomena always associated
with late prehistoric storage, particularly of cereal, and they make their
appearance in the preceding Neolithic period (above, p. 72). For most
of the second millennium BC, however, they are conspicuous by their
absence from the archaeological record, though this may well reflect
the general lack of settlement excavation of this period. On the other
hand, many of the large jars of the period, particularly collared, barrel,
and bucket urns, some with their skeuomorphic applied and impressed
ornament, suggestive of rope containers and lashed on covers, could

well have been and probably were used for storing grain. One can only guess at the wooden and perhaps leather containers used for the same purpose and perhaps slung from the rafters in the roomy, dry, and smoke-filled roof-spaces of houses.

No storage pits were present at Gwithian and Trevisker, Cornwall, or Shearplace Hill, Dorset, broadly contemporary settlements in the south-west in the later second millennium; but, as already noted, they were present at Itford Hill, where one certainly held parched barley grains (Fig. 60c), and at Chalton, Hants., where they could also have been used for corn storage in the later second millennium. It is not, however, until the development of iron-using communities later in the first millennium that pits proliferate: many a site on air photograph or on excavation shows a veritable complex of hundreds of pits, reflecting an apparent pit complex in the minds of our later prehistoric farmers (Fig. 19).[158] Whether or not that is true, the pits can be seen as representing a wetter climate, a considerable increase in crop yield and population, and a greater concern with the winter security of the autumnal harvest.

Storage pits occur over most of the Lowland Zone, to the west on the Cotswolds and in the Welsh Marshes, and to the north on the Yorkshire Wolds and Moors. They do not appear in the settlements of Cornwall and Devon, Wales, Cumbria and Scotland and, with three exceptions, they are absent from the Pennines.[159] In their area of distribution, they were in use throughout the whole range of settlement types – though not necessarily in every settlement – from the largest hill-forts to the smallest farm. Their numbers and arrangement in the former type of site have suggested that they were perhaps used in a few selected foci to store the cereal food supply of a whole area – a sort of regional granary – while at the latter types of settlement they seem to be the silos for holding the bulk of the modest produce of a single family during the winter and spring months. Various pit-types were identified at Little Woodbury, Wilts., and basically the typology holds good. Pits are either cylindrical or bell-shaped in section, characteristically *c.* 1 m in diameter at ground level and 1–2 m deep with a capacity of about a tonne. Much bigger ones occur – the largest at Maiden Castle, Dorset, would hold 4–5 tonnes of cereal – and a few double pits, one on top of the other, are also known. Practice has shown that it takes about 25 man hours to dig a typical pit in chalk; and experiment has shown that

[158] Cf. H. C. Bowen in Rivet (ed.), *The Roman Villa...*, p. 16. For comparison: Little Woodbury, 190 pits from *c.* ⅓ of the settlement; Gussage All Saints, *c.* 400 pits; Hod Hill, *c.* 700 (Bowen and Wood, 'Experimental storage...', p. 14); Danebury, *c.* 970 pits from *c.* 3 acres (in formation B. W. Cunliffe, 1976); but cf. Croft Ambrey, 14 pits, only 4 probably for grain storage.

[159] S. Piggott in Richmond (ed.), *Roman and Native...*, p. 10, Map 2; Challis and Harding, *Later Prehistory...*, fig. 97.

the size of pit does not affect its chemical effectiveness, though clearly larger pits are more efficient from other points of view. The bell-shape also has advantages over the straight-sided cylindrical shape, and firing of an empty pit, plus the cleaning of algae from its sides, has been shown experimentally to prolong the life of a pit very considerably. Lining the sides of pits tends to be counter-productive, and there appears to be no advantage in revetting the side with drystone walling.[160] Nevertheless the anomalous drystone walled beehive-shaped pits on the Isle of Portland seem to be best explained as storage containers.[161]

Such an interpretation, however, begs the questions, not of whether grain was stored in pits – that is certain – but of what sort of grain was stored in the pits and why. Before considering these points, two other factors must be taken into account: the chemistry of successful underground grain storage, and other storage mechanisms available to late prehistoric communities. The concept of tipping precious grain into a potentially, if not actually, damp pit for safekeeping at first sight seems unlikely, so much so that, despite the unequivocal evidence of Tacitus on the point for north German tribes in the first century AD, the British storage pit was for long accepted as the actual dwelling place of the Celtic farmer.[162] The partial excavation and interpretation of the Middle Iron Age settlement called Little Woodbury (Figs. 15, 4), Wilts., in the late 1930s, finally and scientifically disposed of that particular myth. Since then experiment in particular has shown the feasibility of the practice. The essence of the technique is not the provision of a false floor in the pit bottom or the lining of the pit sides with clay or wickerwork, but in making the seal over the top of the pit absolutely airtight. The complete clay domes over pits at All Cannings Cross show how it was done in the chalk country; doubtless other local materials such as cob and dung were used elsewhere, though perhaps broken chunks of lid have not always been recognized in excavation. The function of the seal at ground level was not so much to keep air out as to keep carbon dioxide in. The carbon dioxide produced by the chemistry of the stored grain itself builds up to such a level that it inhibits germination and the development of bacteria, which might otherwise begin to decompose the grain. It also kills any animals which might gain entry, provided always the seal is maintained. Given that condition, grain can be and has been stored successfully in pits through

[160] P. J. Reynolds, 'Experimental Iron Age storage pits...', *Proc. Prehist. Soc.*, 40, 1974, pp. 118–31.

[161] RCHM, *Dorset*, II, 1970, pp. 605–6. One contained carbonized grain, including spelt, hulled barley, oats and chess.

[162] Bowen, in Rivet, *op. cit.*, for classical references and interpretative history; and Bowen and Wood, 'Experimental storage...'.

modern winters, as presumably it was 2,000 years and more ago. The contentious point is that experiment has shown that corn for both consumption and seed can be so stored and subsequently fulfil its very different functions.

Above-ground storage of grain has always been a theoretical alternative to pit storage. Again, this idea was explored by Bersu in considering his Little Woodbury results: he suggested that rectangular groupings of six post-holes represented granaries consisting of six timber uprights supporting some form of enclosed container. A modern but traditional counterpart is the four post granary of Galicia, now mainly used for the winter storage of 'corn on the cob' (English), corn (American), or maize. The interpretation has been widely accepted, and 4, 6, and 8 post granaries have since become a characteristic feature of Lowland (and some Highland) Zone first-millennium settlements.[163] At Danebury hill-fort, Hants., for example, their frequency and regular arrangement have suggested to the excavator that they too represent a regional granary, but not totally dissimilar evidence at Croft Ambrey hill-fort has been interpreted as representing rectangular houses. The evidence at Little Woodbury itself has been taken as typical of the arrangements on non-hill-fort settlements, but that is now supplemented by the more complete evidence from the contemporary settlement at Gussage All Saints (Fig. 33), and at the immediately pre-Roman small farmstead on Berwick Down, Tollard Royal (Fig. 30), Wilts. Until the evidence from the last-named site became available, the acceptance of above-ground granaries was based on the assumption that, since seed-corn could not be stored in pits, it had to be kept dry and vermin-free on top of posts. Now experiment has shown that pit-stored grain can germinate, and the Berwick Down excavation produced slight but suggestive evidence that, there anyway, the two methods of storage were used for two different varieties of cereal (wheat in pits, barley on posts).

It is, in fact, difficult to see a pattern of general practice at this stage, largely because of the lack of sufficiently detailed work necessary to establish patterns at this level of interpretation. The parched barley in the Itford pit (Fig. 60c), and the parched barley and spelt in the Fifield Bavant pit (Fig. 16), clearly would not germinate and so were presumably cereals to be eaten. On the other hand, precisely because of the preserving process in a pit, once opened it could not be easily sealed again without serious risk to its remaining contents, so the fairly rapid removal of pit-stored grain after a pit-opening seems to be required. From that point of view, pits would not have been very

[163] Summarized in Cunliffe, *Iron Age Communities in Britain*..., chaps. 11 and 12; cf. Harding, *The Iron Age in the Upper Thames Basin*..., 78, pp. 110–11.

suitable as the larder for a small family, though, conversely, this limitation would not have affected their use in larger social groups provided the contents were available communally. A pit would, however, have been ideal for seed-corn since it could have been sealed, obscured, and left undisturbed quite safely for some six months from harvest to spring sowing when, following its opening, all its contents could have been used immediately. Meanwhile, the community's corn for consumption, perhaps in large jars or wooden bins, could be stored in an easily accessible shed-on-stilts, aired by slatted sides, and safe from vermin with its edges over-hanging the timber posts, staddle-stone fashion. Grain for meals or grinding (see below) could simply be removed in small quantities as required. It is therefore possible to propose an interpretation in direct contrast to Bersu, i.e. that pits were for seed-corn and above-ground granaries for consumption-corn. Yet the only certain observation is that some consumption-corn was stored in pits. Perhaps pits and granary sheds were used for both purposes, according to local practice and need; but it is worth commenting that, since pits could have been used for storing both types of grain, the six-post structures on sites with pits need not have been used for grain storage at all. Alternatively, pits could have replaced granaries (or vice versa) as storage containers or, following the Tollard Royal evidence, pits and granaries could have been used simultaneously not for differently functioning grain but for different varieties of cereal.

Another imponderable is the extent to which grain stored by either method was already threshed. The major grain finds already often quoted show that some was threshed as well as parched when put into pits, and so far no pits have been found with grain still in the ear, let alone on the stalk. Nevertheless storage in the ear in either, or both, pit and granary is a possibility. One attraction of storing in the ear is of course that threshing can then take place during the winter, thus saving valuable time at the rushed harvest period. Indeed, until the advent of the combine harvester, cereal crops were commonly stored on the stalk until winter-threshing, a line of thought which opens up a whole range of storage variables. Cereals can be stored on the stalk quite safely either in rick or barn provided they are dry when collected. While, however, the identification of a rick site is unlikely archaeologically, the possibility of barns for temporary cereal storage should be borne in mind when looking at any hearthless round and rectangular buildings of first millennium settlements. Bearing in mind too the possibility of rick storage, in the fields or by the settlement, one is struck again by the frequency and sheer number of pits in Lowland Britain. This quantitative aspect has not yet been adequately explained, and the observer of the phenomenon is reduced to wondering again about the psychology of what appears to be a compulsion to dig pits. Agriculturally they are not really necessary, which suggests that perhaps security at a time of growing population pressure was the main stimulant of the apparent compulsion.

Security has in fact often been suggested as the motive for building another possible storage facility, the fougou.[164] These underground stone structures, distributed in places from which pits are absent and belonging to the late pre-Roman period and later in the west, seem best interpreted as places for storage and, probably, other functions too. Presumably grain could have been stored in jars, as it probably was also in south-eastern Britain at the same time. This is an area which almost certainly produced a grain surplus, and yet is almost devoid of pits in the generations immediately before the Roman Conquest. The technical competence of potters influenced by Gallo-Roman prototypes, imported and copied, seems to be the explanation.[165]

The storage of cultivated crops in later prehistory is then a difficult topic. Clearly it was vital to the farming communities to secure their food supply, to the production of which so much of their efforts were devoted, during the winter and spring months; yet, while there is almost overwhelming evidence of the use of pits in the latter part of our period for storage of cereals, there are still too many imponderables in considering the subject from a practical point of view. And even the grain storage function of pits is not often directly evidenced by archaeology for, as found and excavated, they are usually full of rubbish for which they were characteristically and finally used. Such evidence can reveal much about the community originating the rubbish but little about why the pit was originally dug, how it was then used, or why, perhaps most puzzling of all, it was abandoned.

Food preparation

Very little precise information is available about the last stages of the food production process: the actual preparation of the raw material from the fields to make palatable food. The broader issues of nutrition and diet, health and disease, behind the practical considerations are also in the early stages of scientific investigation.[166] Perhaps somewhat curiously, however, there is, at least quantitatively, not a little evidence

[164] C. Thomas, 'Souterrains in the Irish Sea Province...', in C. Thomas (ed.), *The Iron Age in the Irish Sea Province*, London, 1972, pp. 75–8.

[165] For the ceramic range, see A. Birchall, 'The Aylesford–Swarling Culture...', *Proc. Prehist. Soc.*, 31, 1965, pp. 241–367.

[166] As illustrated, for example, by C. Wells, *Bones, Bodies and Disease*, London, 1964; D. R. Brothwell and A. T. Sandison (eds.), *Diseases in Antiquity*, Springfield, Ill., 1967; D. and P. Brothwell, *Food in Antiquity*, London, 1969; and D. Brothwell, 'Diet, economy and biosocial change in late prehistoric Europe', in Simpson (ed.), *Economy and Settlement...*, pp. 75–87.

from the field in the shape of small mounds of burnt stones, largely noted in Shetland and Ireland. They have been interpreted, and shown by experiment to be interpretable as such, as cooking places, presumably of a communal nature.[167] Otherwise, the most obvious 'hard' evidence for food preparation is that provided by stone artifacts used for grinding grain. For much of the later prehistoric period this was done by moving a stone rubber, usually hand-sized and certainly hand-held, backwards and forwards on a larger, flattened stone resting on the ground. This action caused the centre of the lower stone to become dished, and take on its characteristic shape which has given rise to its common name of 'saddle quern'. The method and equipment were ubiquitous in the Old World from the beginning of a crop-gathering economy, and the frequent occurrence on later prehistoric sites in Britain of whole or fragmentary rubbers and 'saddle quern stones' leaves no doubt that this was the normal method of grain treatment. Oddly, however, the two parts of the equipment are rarely found together and *in situ*, one recently discovered exception being in a late prehistoric context at Cadbury Congresbury, Somerset. A broken lower stone or 'trough quern' was found inverted beside the heap of barley under the wall of 'Neolithic' House no. 1 at Ness of Gruting, Shetland (Fig. 53).[168] This method of grinding can produce a reasonably fine flour.

During the first millennium, hand rubbing or crushing was replaced by a rotary machine, the rotary quern or hand-mill, consisting of a stationary, lower round stone, which provided the grinding surface, and an upper round stone which was rotated around a central spindle fixed into the centre of the lower stone. Grinding grain could have been achieved by moving the upper stone backwards and forwards rather than by a continuous circular motion. Grain was fed in through the top of the upper stone and flour was produced around the circumference of the device from the interface of the two stones when the upper was rotated. There were several variants in shape and design, both with time and regionally, in later prehistoric Britain, but the principle remained the same. Hand-powered rotary querns had become the common method of grain treatment by the last centuries BC, and there is no evidence of the principle being extended to larger equipment with other power-sources until the Roman period.[169] There is also some evidence

---

[167] E.g. C. S. T. Calder, 'Cairns, Neolithic houses and burnt mounds in Shetland', *Proc. Soc. Ant. Scot.*, 96, 1962–3, pp. 78–86.

[168] Cadbury: P. J. Fowler, unpublished; Calder, *Proc. Soc. Ant. Scot.*, 89, 1955–6, p. 348., fig. 5.

[169] The basic survey of rotary querns is still J. T. Philips, *Trans. Leics. Arch. Hist. Soc.*, 26, 1950, pp. 75–82. On their earlier presence at Gussage All Saints in mid-first millennium, see now *Ant.*, L, 1976, pp. 35–6.

for the use of pestle and mortar, but it is unknown whether its use was widespread or applied to the products of arable farming.[170]

There is no British evidence comparable to that from the Danish 'bog burials' to provide an insight into what later prehistoric Britons were eating and how the food was prepared.[171] The most concrete evidence, almost literally, comes late in our period from Glastonbury in the shape of fragments of carbonized buns or small cakes – "largely insoluble even in powerful chemicals".[172] Analysis eventually identified "fragments of wheat, hulled barley, wild oat, chess, and a seed of Common Orache" suggesting that the 'bread' was "made up as a stiff porridge, rolled into balls, flattened, and baked, or perhaps only dried". There was no evidence of leavening, but the inclusion of 'weeds' – the wild oat and orache seeds – indicates the growth of crops in a relatively impure state by modern standards, rather than their deliberate collection as food. "They grew and were consumed together with the cereals." We can but assume the making of similar 'coarse bread' in earlier times.

Another assumption has to be that cultivated cereals, particularly barley, were used to make alcoholic drinks, a form of beer and perhaps also a form of wine.[173] Sediments have occasionally been noted and examined on the bases of pottery vessels, and have been interpreted as the residues of such liquids.[174] It has indeed for long been traditionally thought that the 'beakers' of the Beaker People could well have been (communal?) beer-drinking containers, but, although the possible contemporary rise in the production of barley could allow precisely this interpretation, the argument is insecure and circumstantial.

With the abundant evidence for cereal production from so many parts of Britain in later prehistoric times, into the production of which such a large proportion of communal endeavour was invested, it is a fairly severe indictment of the predominantly artifact-orientated nature of British archaeology that really little more can usefully be said about the preparation and nature of man-cultivated foods than what could have been guessed anyway, i.e. that cereal was used to make varieties of coarse

---

[170] E.g. at Chysauster; and in current excavations at Odell, Beds. Further north, the distribution of 'beehive' querns is now conveniently displayed in Challis and Harding, *Later Prehistory...*, fig. 98. A brief discussion on 'boulder basins' used as mortars is in *Corn. Arch.*, 1, 1962, pp. 55–6.

[171] Now readily accessible in P. V. Glob, *The Bog People*, London, 1969.

[172] *Glastonbury II*, 1917, pp. 625–30; Helbaek, *Proc. Prehist. Soc.*, 28, 1952, p. 212; cf. Brothwell, in Simpson (ed.), *Economy and Settlement...*, pp. 75–87.

[173] For the alcoholic potential of grain-storage pits, see P. J. Reynolds, *Proc. Prehist. Soc.*, 40, 1974, p. 126.

[174] Brothwell in Simpson (ed.), *op. cit.*, discusses the types of evidence for diet and some of the implications of preparing and serving food in and from unglazed pottery.

porridge/gruel-type preparations, 'breads', probably usually unleavened, and beer. As we shall discuss later, however, this by no means represents the available food-range, and, despite its gastronomic limitations, it probably provided a sound nutritional base.[175]

PASTORAL FARMING

The landscape evidence

The breeding, herding, and cropping of domesticated animals, principally cattle, sheep, goats, pigs, and horses, played a significant part in the agrarian life of later prehistoric Britain, and has had a lasting impact on the landscape up to the present day. The subject is discussed later in detail from the point of view of animal husbandry (below, p. 320ff). Here our concern is with the archaeological manifestations of the pastoral element in the landscape and economy, with a brief look at its social significance.

A severe limitation on description, let alone narrative and discussion, is that by its very nature pastoralism makes a much less obvious impact on the archaeological record than does the production of cultivated crops by arable farming. This is so despite the fact that the appearance of much of our existing landscape, particularly in the Highland Zone, may owe more to animal than to arable crop husbandry. The critical distinction here is between landscape on the one hand and archaeological sites or single entities on the other. It may well be that, whatever the 'natural' Post-glacial vegetation in any given area, and whatever its early use by man, its subsequent history and consequent appearance has been dominated by the impact of grazing animals. Nor need this hypothesis be restricted to the treeless, moorland tracts of the National Parks (Plates IIIa, V), some Areas of Outstanding Natural Beauty, and the subsidized hill-farms of the west and north today: the traditional treeless skylines of the Lowland Zone's Cretaceous downs (Plate IIa), regardless of whether originally created by arable farming or today framing an arable landscape, have certainly been maintained over the first two millennia AD by thousands upon thousands of sheep.[176] Significantly for our later prehistoric period, it is documentary, not

---

[175] Ibid., again, on nutrition, supplemented now by P. J. Reynolds, op. cit., on nutritional values of primitive cereals suggested by early results from the Butser experiments. The absence of root crops and citrus fruits and, following Brothwell, the non-use of plant sugars, are all important factors in assessing later prehistoric nutrition. Ross, Everyday Life of the Pagan Celts, pp. 105–9, makes good use of documentary evidence for meat-eating and alcohol-drinking, presumptively at the end of our period.

[176] Much of the discussion on the Highland Zone in Evans et al., CBA Research Report, 11, and the companion volume on The Lowland Zone, CBA Research Report, 21, 1978, is relevant to this point.

archaeological, evidence which tells us that. Conversely, over much of the Midlands, where archaeologically we can see the extent of former medieval cultivation while admiring the contribution of trees and shrubs to the present landscape, the hedges containing much of that standing vegetation are essentially the product of pastoral, not arable, farming. They mark the creation in later medieval/early modern times of a landscape fit for sheep rather than the plough team.[177] Pastoralism, it seems, tends to create landscapes rather than produce discrete archaeological sites.

Yet elements of a pastoral landscape, like the Midland hedges, have to be constructed and they can survive. Archaeologically, from later prehistoric Britain direct evidence of pastoralism is probably represented by linear land boundaries, apparently to do with land allotment on a major scale. Their purpose may have been proprietorial or functional or both, but it seems reasonable to see at least some of them as serving to control flocks and herds. Such landscape features take various forms and their ascription to a function in a pastoral context is by no means certain. The sometimes indirect evidence for animal husbandry is much more plentiful and, on the whole, less ambiguous: the bones of domesticated animals themselves often comprise the commonest material collected from excavation of a Lowland Zone settlement, even if their identification and interpretation are not always straightforward. The artifacts produced from animal products (like woollen and leather garments) may have to be inferred, or may actually survive as, for example, 'scapula shovels' and bone handles; artifacts which can reasonably be regarded as having been used for processing animal products, such as flint scrapers, loom weights, and spindle-whorls, for example, abound. More indirect evidence can be identified in the settlements themselves, not only with regard to individual buildings identified as byres, for example, but also in respect of the less tangible considerations of settlement morphology and settlement pattern.

Linear land boundaries are best known in Wessex.[178] Referred to as 'linear ditches', 'linear dykes' or 'ranch boundaries', they occur on the downs of east Dorset, Wiltshire, west Hampshire, and Berkshire north to the White Horse scarp overlooking the Thames valley. Individual ditches can be several kilometres long. They are characteristically 4–5 m wide and 2–3 m in depth, with a bank on one or both sides. There is a little evidence that they were sometimes associated with timberwork, and indeed that their line was continued by a fence on to lower ground; similarly a few examples of associated stone structures, e.g. a revetment,

[177] See generally, *Agric. Hist. England and Wales*, IV.
[178] See Bibliography (below, p. 289) for papers by H. C. Bowen, and especially his paper in Limbrey and Evans (eds.), CBA Research Report, 21, pp. 115–23.

are also known. Much more significant than these physical details, however, is the ditches' evidence, akin to that for the allotment of arable land (above, p. 152), of landscape organization on an extensive scale. Like arable fields, though not quite exclusively, linear ditches seldom occur singly but always as part of a system. The best examples of these complexes tend to be grouped on and around the southern parts of Salisbury Plain (Fig. 40), extending into east and central Hampshire and along the Wiltshire/Hampshire/Dorset border of Cranborne Chase. Other examples in the Rams Hill area of the Berkshire Downs (Figs. 57, 58) have also recently been surveyed and discussed in detail.[179]

Such ditches by their very nature are not easily dated, and have not attracted excavators (with the honourable exception of Pitt-Rivers). On the other hand, the length of individual ditches, and the extent of the system of which they form a part, provide horizontal data across the landscape which relate the phenomena to other landscape features both generally and specifically. Taking the outside chronological limits, these systems and their ditches respect long barrows always, and round barrows usually; they are followed and cut by Roman roads and Anglo-Saxon charter boundaries. Their generally later prehistoric date is not therefore in question. Within that period, they characteristically cross 'Celtic' fields – a point to which we shall return – and underlie hill-forts. On Overton Down, one cuts through Beaker settlement debris and underlies 'Celtic' fields and a Roman track (above, p. 150); other associated excavated evidence, in particular from Pitt-Rivers's work, indicates use after a settlement and fields of the later second millennium BC.[180] While there can be no doubt that, in general, the use of these particular ditch systems dates to the second millennium, their development should be sought at latest in the middle centuries of that millennium and their origins perhaps even earlier.

It is a vexed question whether these ditches define property or land-use and specifically grazing areas. The subject is currently receiving detailed attention by the Royal Commission on Historical Monuments (England) and it would be improper, as well as unwise, to anticipate the results. Where such systems have already been recorded in some detail, and specifically on the Hampshire/Wiltshire border by Crawford and Hawkes,[181] the impression is given that they represent an attempt to divide the land up for practical purposes rather than to designate

[179] Bradley and Ellison, *Rams Hill*.

[180] Overton: author, unpublished in detail; Martin Down: as interpreted by Bowen, *Ancient Fields*, fig. 3A. See now Bowen in CBA Research Report, 21, 1978, pp. 115–21.

[181] OS (O. G. S. Crawford), *Celtic Earthworks of Salisbury Plain*, Sheet 1, 1934; C. F. C. Hawkes, in Quarley Hill report, *Papers and Proc. Hants. Fld Club*, 14, 1939, pp. 136–94; cf. H. C. Bowen, in Wilson (ed.), *Aerial Reconnaissance...*, p. 107, fig. 6.

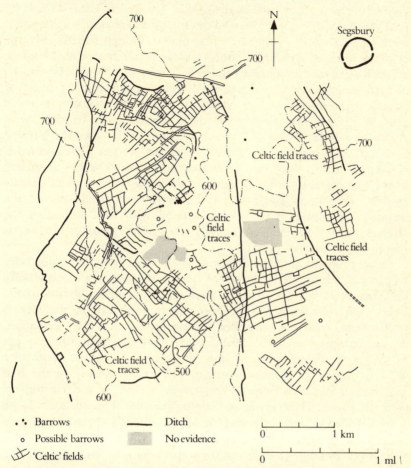

Fig. 57. Plan of later prehistoric landscape south-west of Segsbury hill-fort, Berks., showing barrows, ditches, field systems, tracks and small enclosures. The cohesive nature of the field systems is particularly apparent; the ditches either respect field boundaries or cut across earlier arable; the barrows either lie at the outer edges of the field systems or have been incorporated in field boundaries, sometimes on axial lines (after R. Bradley).

properties. The impression that this zoning was for controlled grazing is increased by the fact that in numerous cases ditches cut through pre-existing arable field systems, apparently putting them out of action, at least for a time, and superficially representing a deliberate change of land-use from arable to pasture (Figs. 40, 57). On Salisbury Plain especially, that change has been perpetuated until the present or very recent past, so that it was fairly decisive in landscape terms. Despite the pattern of change suggested by the similar examples of linear ditch/field relationship, we do not know, and cannot assume, that they came about contemporaneously or as part of a trend, although superficially the evidence seems to suggest this; nor is it easy to point to a cultural context for such a general change from arable to pasture in Wessex. The similar, general change in parts of late medieval England was the result of complex pressures amongst which was that it was simply more profitable, for a time, to invest in sheep for wool than to grow corn. A change in the emphasis of land use, assuming for the sake of argument that such happened in Wessex of the earlier second millennium bc, could reflect, in a way not yet understood, other changes in society as the first metal technology developed, and a warmer, drier climate evolved (below, p. 250); or, if the change occurred later in the second millennium, it may be associated with the 'decline of the Wessex culture' or, environmentally, the early beginnings of climatic deterioration (above, p. 72).

Other elements in the landscape in Wessex and elsewhere could refer to pastoral activity. The pattern of large-scale clearance and enclosure on Dartmoor (above, p. 181) contains large areas without obvious arable fields, and may indeed have been, again probably in the second millennium, more for controlled stock-raising than cereal cultivation. Again, current work will doubtless clarify the picture. Other types of dykes, both in Wessex and, for example, in the Yorkshire Wolds, suggest an agrarian context, this time probably in the first millennium.[182] Cross-ridge dykes, traversing ridges and cutting off spurs in Sussex, Hampshire, and south Wiltshire (Fig. 16) seem to be best explained in terms of both territorial divisions and control of stock movement, in particular to keep livestock off arable fields. Though the type is not closely dated except for some very rare examples of early third millennium date on Hambledon Hill, Dorset,[183] most seem to be related to the filling up of the landscape which we see in other respects from the mid first millennium onwards. Another type of earthwork, seemingly related to stock farming, is the multiple dyke, also probably of the last centuries BC, common in the Yorkshire Wolds and sporadic on the Wessex Downs. Sometimes, as in the case of the three ditches and four banks running west from the west end of the Dorset Cursus down towards the Crichel Brook, they appear to block off one area from

[182] P. J. Fowler, 'Cross-ridge dykes...', *Wilts. Arch. Nat. Hist. Mag.*, 54, 1964, pp. 46–57; R. J. Bradley, 'Stock-raising...', *Ant. J.*, 51, 1971, pp. 8–29; Challis and Harding, *Later Prehistory...*, 1975, pp. 160–2; and, for the Yorkshire Wolds, RCHM *forthcoming*.
[183] 2790±90 bc (NPL 76). I. F. Smith in Simpson (ed.), *Economy and Settlement...*, p. 107.

another;[184] in many other cases they wind for considerable distances across country, and could have served as either or both barriers or trackways. In Wessex, right at the end of our period, such are sometimes associated with small circular or oval enclosures in complexes suggesting the corralling and possibly sorting of stock. Particularly good examples occur at Hamshill Ditches, Wilts., and on Gussage Cow Down, Dorset, though the latter is now virtually destroyed by ploughing.[185]

The place of cattle enclosures in the archaeological record is a vexed one; equally the role of pastoralism in the process of settlement and nucleation during the first millennium is arguable.[186] An enclosure, really or apparently with nothing in it, is easy enough to interpret as having been built for stock but that is actually only one of several plausible interpretations. Evidence to clinch a stock function is, by its nature, difficult to obtain and to date; but several groups of enclosure have been assigned such a function in later prehistoric times. In Devon particularly, a county traditionally associated with cattle, enclosures from the second millennium to Roman times on Dartmoor and in the south of the county, with little or no associated occupation debris, have been seen in this context; similarly over the south-west generally, the hill-slope forts enclosing a considerable area between the outer and inner defences have also been interpreted as a regional adaptation to a dominant element in the economy in the later centuries BC, but the thesis has not been systematically tested by excavation.[187] The same argument has been applied to the extensive areas of, now, good pasture, enclosed by the complex of earthworks regarded as the Brigantian centre at Stanwick, Yorks.[188] Smaller, self-contained rectangular enclosures on Cranborne Chase and the Marlborough Downs have also been seen, largely through lack of finds, as cattle enclosures; their

[184] D. W. Harding, *Proc. Dorset Nat. Hist. Arch. Soc.*, 81, 1959, pp. 110–13.

[185] B. T. Perry, 'Iron Age enclosures...', *Arch. J.*, 126, 1969, pp. 29–43; Hams Hill: *Wilts. Arch. Nat. Hist. Mag.*, 69, 1967, pp. 118–21, Gussage Cow Down: Crawford and Keiller, *Wessex from the Air*, Pls. XV, XVI; RCHM, *Dorset*, V, 1972, fig. opposite p. 24. It is perhaps worth considering that such an idiosyncratic type of enclosure may have had a very specific function: the possibility of horse-breeding rather than general cattle-ranching/shepherding is one suggestion, already made for the Roman period in Volume I, Part II, p. 219.

[186] General discussion: Cunliffe, *Iron Age Communities in Britain*, chaps. 11, 12, 13; Challis and Harding, *Later Prehistory...*, chap. 10; specific examples: *Wilts. Arch. Nat. Hist. Soc.*, 60, 1965, pp. 52–74; *Ant.*, XLI, 1967, pp. 304–6.

[187] A. Fox, 'Hill-slope forts and related earthworks in southwest England and south Wales', *Arch. J.*, 109, 1952, pp. 1–22; 'South western hill-forts', in Frere (ed.), *Problems of the Iron Age...*, pp. 35–60; and, generally, A. Fox, *South West England*, 2nd ed. 1973.

[188] *Rep. Res. Comm. Lond. Soc. Ant.*, 17, 1954, pp. 28–30, and S. Piggott, 'Native economies...' in I. A. Richmond (ed.), *Roman and Native in North Britain*, Edinburgh, 1958, pp., 11–15.

distribution generally relates to that of the linear ditches, and in at least two cases, at Ogbourne Maizey and South Lodge Camp, Wilts., an enclosure, like several of the ditches, is lying on 'Celtic' fields and is probably a settlement.[189] Again, except at Pitt-Rivers's sites on Martin Down and at South Lodge, the thesis has not been put to the test, an extraordinary fact considering the basic importance of their identification and that every such enclosure in Wessex has now been levelled, unexamined, by modern cultivation.[190]

Some of the particularly large univallate enclosures in southern England, loosely bracketed as hill-forts, have been segregated as a special category originating as stock enclosures, perhaps before the middle of the first millennium. Examples are Nottingham Hill in the north Cotswolds, in which a Late Bronze Age hoard was recently found, and Bathampton Down Camp above Bath which, like the linear ditches, cut across an already well-developed field system.[191] Other small, though not necessarily rectangular, enclosures in Sussex and Hampshire have also been interpreted as stock enclosures, with some of them gaining a local importance and providing one of several possible origins for hill-forts proper.[192] There seem in fact to be at least four different situations in this context, all possibly related to stock-management, and all potentially leading to the local pre-eminence of a particular hill top, usually though not necessarily later expressed by a hill-fort. One situation is that of a small, original enclosure, as at Thundersbarrow, beginning as a stock gathering place and successively becoming larger. A second is that, like Little Butser Hill, Hants., of an area of high ground being separated off and internally divided as if for special grazing, or breeding or rearing stock. The third situation involves a particular hill-top like Quarley, Danebury, and Whitsbury, Hants., and Sidbury (Fig. 40), Wilts., each being a focal point in a linear ditch system and subsequently developing into a multi-ramparted hill-fort. And the fourth situation, as at Cold Kitchen Hill, Wilts., is of a hill-top being separated from its spurs and the whole being segregated, as it were, from

---

[189] C. M. Piggott, 'Five Late Bronze Age enclosures in north Wiltshire', *Proc. Prehist. Soc.*, 8, 1942, pp. 48–61; *idem*, 'Late Bronze Age enclosures in Sussex and Wessex', *Proc. Prehist. Soc.*, 16, 1950, pp. 193–5. The relationship of the Ogbourne Maizey enclosure to 'Celtic' fields is stated in *ibid.*, 8, 1942, p. 52, illustrated in *ibid.*, fig. 3, and demonstrated by the air photograph in P. J. Fowler in Simpson (ed.), *Economy and Settlement...*, pl. 8. South Lodge Camp, *Ant.* LII, 1978, pp. 223–7.

[190] Excavation of one of them began in 1977, *Proc. Prehist. Soc.* 45, 1979, p. 333.

[191] Nottingham Hill: *Ant.*, XLVIII, 1974, pp. 306–9. Bathampton: Crawford and Keiller, *Wessex from the Air*, pp. 144–7, questioned by G. J. Wainwright in *Trans. Bristol Glos. Arch. Soc.*, 86, 1967, pp. 42–59; cf. now P. J. Fowler, in Bowen and P. J. Fowler (eds.), *Early Land Allotment*, Appendix 4 (below, p. 278).

[192] R. Bradley, 'Stock-raising...', *Ant. J.*, 51, 1971, pp. 8–29.

the surrounding lower ground by a series of cross-dykes facing up hill towards a temple site. Again, crucial excavated evidence is lacking and the temple manifestation is, of course, of the Roman period; but once more, with circumstantial evidence from late prehistoric times, we seem to see, perhaps deriving from a pastoral background, the recognition and development of a focal point in the landscape.

The dating problem occurs too in the other main setting where archaeological evidence suggests pastoralism, namely on the gravel terraces of the river valleys. Air photography frequently shows patterns of droveways and small closes or paddocks, various types of linear landscape boundaries, and genuine 'blank' areas perhaps indicating former pasture, all suggesting provision for cattle and/or sheep; but while such elements can sometimes be placed in a local, relative chronology, with long-lived occupation so widespread and intense on these gravels it is difficult to date them absolutely. Much undoubtedly belongs to the Roman period but, equally, individual elements have already been shown by excavation to originate in the preceding 2,000 years. At the moment, however, the evidence for pastoral farming on the gravels is potential rather than demonstrable.[193]

One area, however, where some of the potential has been in part realized is at Fengate (Fig. 11), Peterborough. There, situated immediately above the alluvium on the First Terrace river gravels, is a complex of settlement evidence dating from the Neolithic period onwards. The elements relevant here are parts of field systems belonging to two different phases, the earlier related to a 'Grooved Ware' settlement and C-14 dates clustered around c. 2000 bc, the later of Middle/Late Bronze Age date with C-14 dates of c. 1280 and c. 935 bc. Only a fragment of the former was examined but at least two rectilinear fields were defined by ditches pierced at the field corners by entrance-ways. These ditched enclosures were interpreted as being for stock, and existing in an open grassland environment. The later system has been recorded much more extensively: it lay at right angles to the Fens along c. 535 m, stretching inland for c. 400 m, and was also defined by ditches, here paired ones with staggered entrance-ways forming the skeleton of a grid layout. This work too is current and continuing, so no conclusion is possible at this stage; but on present evidence there is no reason to doubt

[193] A situation that will shortly change as the environmental evidence from recent and current excavation by the Oxfordshire Archaeological Unit comes to be published (see n. 153, p. 219). A foretaste is M. A. Robinson, 'A comparison between the effects of Man on the environment of the first gravel terrace and floodplain of the Upper Thames Valley during the Iron Age and Roman periods', in Limbrey and Evans (eds.), CBA Research Report, 21, pp. 35–43; now complemented by M. Jones, 'The plant remains', in Parrington, The Excavation at Ashville Trading Estate, Abingdon..., pp. 93–110.

the pastoral function of these remarkably "elaborate, accurately surveyed series of rectilinear...ditches...used by groups whose primary economic base was livestock.[194] The fields are envisaged provisionally as having been used during the winter by animals which spent the summer grazing around the Fen 'islands' nearby, an interpretation parallelled in the Somerset Levels. Pastoral or not, perhaps the most significant aspect of the land allotment at Fengate is that here, on gravel at the Fen edge, the evidence for extensive landscape planning is strikingly similar to that already discussed from the very different environmental conditions on Wessex Chalk and Dartmoor granite (above, pp. 151, 181).

For the greater part of Britain, however, ironically the stronghold of pastoralism, no such evidence is known. The open spaces of the Highland Zone are both the evidence itself and the main reason why the landscape is not littered with the artifactual fossils of a way of farming which continues today over much of the area. There simply was not the pressure on space that the Lowland Zone continuously and increasingly exhibits, and therefore the need to 'control and confine' did not exist except for purely practical and seasonal activities like lambing and culling. It must be emphasized that the pastoral/arable dichotomy is essentially a generalization about the two zones, perhaps hardly applicable at all in the third and second millennia when, as we have noted, many areas of the Highland Zone were under cultivation (above, p. 169). Even subsequently, it is a matter of emphasis rather than contrasts for, as we have also seen, pastoralism probably played a major part in the Lowland economy and, equally, many a sheltered valley in the mountain region probably supported arable crops. By and large, however, a broad distinction can usefully be made between south and east, and north and west, in terms of agrarian produce in the first millennium: the former has been discussed (above, p. 203), in the latter the economy and life-style reflected a different range of priorities. With increasing emphasis during the first millennium, the security of a food supply and the wealth from its accumulation was in the pastures and on the hoof, rather than in cultivated fields and insulated pits.

Processes and artifacts of pastoral food production[195]

Although direct evidence of the uses to which domesticated animals were put is not plentiful in the archaeological record for our period, it seems fairly safe to assume that cattle were used for meat, hides, and farmwork; sheep for meat, milk, and wool; goats for milk and meat;

[194] *Curr. Arch.*, 46, 1975, p. 336.
[195] See generally M. L. Ryder (below, pp. 310–17); Ross, *Everyday Life of the Pagan Celts*, chap. 4.

horses for transport, traction, riding, and their hair; and pigs for meat. Various parts of these animals could also have been used, as food or raw material, in a variety of ways, e.g. to make bone objects, leather, glue, and candles and, just possibly, parchment.

Archaeologically, we glimpse the uses of animals for food in the animal bones themselves, not least when collections of them from settlements show selective components or individual bones bear the marks of butchery and are split longitudinally to extract the marrow.[196] The meat itself, and its preparation, have to be envisaged, but it is likely that, perhaps with food other than cereals, it was stored in pits or underground larders. Whatever the storage method, salt would have been of crucial importance in preserving meat especially, and the maintenance of a salt supply must have been a constant concern.[197] Pottery fragments of large thick jars, particularly from a first millennium context, often contain a carbonized residue on the interior surface suggesting that stews or soups, perhaps with a meat base and continually simmering and added to on the hearth, were a common feature of the late prehistoric household. A common archaeological object on settlements is the 'pot-boiler', frequently a flint in southern Britain though often a pebble, which has been heated intensely and then presumably placed in a container to heat it internally. Though such stones could have been used in pots, experiment has also shown the feasibility of their use in heating water in large leather containers.[198] Otherwise – and it is easy to overlook the obvious – a very high proportion of the large quantity of later prehistoric pottery, so assiduously studied by archaeologists for other purposes, must actually have been used for the containing, preparation, and consumption of animal food products ranging from neat milk to jellied pigs' trotters. It is unlikely that much of the edible product of animal husbandry was wasted.

Though not edible, the many other uses for animal products must

[196] For a discussion of some of the problems attending the interpretation of 'bone reports', see L. Alcock, 'Dry bones and living documents' and the comments on this paper by R. E. Chaplin in Evans *et al.*, CBA Research Report, 11, pp. 117–23; cf. also R. E. Chaplin, *The Study of Animal Bones from Archaeological Sites*, London, 1971 and R. W. Casteel, 'Some biases in the recovery of archaeological faunal remains', *Proc. Prehist. Soc.*, 38, 1972, pp. 382–8. As an example of a modern bone report from our period, see R. A. Harcourt, in Wainwright and Longworth, *Durrington Walls...*, pp. 338–50.

[197] See generally, K. Riehm, 'Prehistoric salt-boiling', *Ant.*, xxxv, 1961, pp. 181–91, and J. Nenquin, *Salt, a Study in Economic Prehistory*, Brugge, 1961; and, now, for insular evidence, Colchester Archaeological Group, *Salt: the Study of an Ancient Industry*, Colchester, 1975.

[198] M. J. O'Kelly, 'Excavation and experiments in ancient Irish cooking-places', *J. Roy. Soc. Ant. Ireland*, 84, 1954, p. 105; M. L. Ryder, 'Can one cook in a skin?', *Ant.*, xl, 1966, pp. 225–7.

briefly be noted. The provision of clothing was perhaps the most
important. Though Britain has not yet produced any near-complete
examples of woollen garments like those from second-millennium
Denmark, there is plentiful evidence, in the form of scraps of fabric and
impressions of them, to show that weaving was probably a normal task
about the house.[199] Arrangement of post-holes in late prehistoric houses
have been claimed as loom-bases, and loom-weights, spindle-whorls,
and bone needles are common, particularly in later first millennium
contexts. The various types of brooch indirectly suggest the type of
clothing available, and in particular the penannular brooch indicates a
woollen garment held together in folds.[200] For the second millennium,
evidence of weaving is not so common, and there is a suggestion of
greater dependence on leather, not least in the absence of brooches.
Toggles and buttons and other circumstantial evidence imply that it was
the cow rather than the sheep which was providing the raw material
for a lot of the clothing. We see the mastery achieved in the working
of animal skin in a few surviving wooden, hide-covered shields from
the centuries around 1000 BC, and can assume the use of hide for many
other purposes, e.g. for liquid containers, for coracles and perhaps other
craft, and for thongs.[201]

Animals would also have produced much of the other raw material
necessary in an agrarian society: as with their food potential, little is
likely to have been left unexploited. Horn and bone for example, were
used to make tools, to fashion handles for metal tools, as a medium for
decoration, and doubtless to make glue. Food and by-products apart,
however, they provided three essential functions in the society that they
served: they produced the manure basic to the settled agriculture of our
period; they provided the primary source of non-human power in
carrying out the tasks of agriculture; and they peopled, if that is the
word, the religious and ceremonial life of their communities, eventually
so strongly that elements of the native animal pantheism survived the
conformist officialdom of Roman religious adminstration, and can still
be faintly heard as echoes today.

[199] A. S. Henshall, 'Textiles and weaving appliances in prehistoric Britain', *Proc.
Prehist. Soc.*, 16, 1950, pp. 130–62. An updating of this topic, bringing in more recently
discovered evidence, is needed.

[200] E. Fowler, 'The origins and development of the penannular brooch in Europe',
Proc. Prehist. Soc., 26, 1960, pp. 149–77, cf. M. J. Fowler, 'The typology of the brooches
of the Iron Age in Wessex', *Arch. J.*, 110, 1954, pp. 88–105.

[201] J. Coles, 'European Bronze Age shields', *Proc. Prehist. Soc.*, 28, 1962, pp. 156–90,
and, for boats, with references, *idem, Archaeology by Experiment*, pp. 97–110. P.
Johnstone, 'Bronze Age sea trial', *Ant.*, XLI, 1972, pp. 269–74, demonstrates what might
have been a widespread use of hide for boats, cf. H. Case, 'Neolithic explanations',
Ant., XLIII, 1969, p. 176. On leather containers in use, see, for example, G. E. Evans,
The Farm and the Village, London, 1969, *passim*.

OTHER FOOD SOURCES

While cereal and animal husbandry undoubtedly provided the bulk of the later prehistoric food base, scattered archaeological evidence or rural commonsense suggests the exploitation of other resources too. There is some evidence for a domestic fowl in later prehistoric contexts and, of course, though presumably not as a food animal itself, the domestic dog.[202]

On the non-domestic side, the animal and floral kingdoms were there for the hunting, collecting, and fishing. Deer in particular were very important, certainly as suppliers of antler picks earlier in our period (and they could have been used for cultivation as well as the attested digging of ditches), and almost certainly as suppliers of hides and meat.[203] Presumably wolves were also hunted, at least in self-protection, and other quarry amongst the larger mammals probably included fox, badger, wild pig, and wild cat. Fish and eels must surely have provided a significant element of variety in the diet, shellfish were certainly collected, and, particularly early in our period and in coastal situations, were a staple food.[204] Non-marine mollusca could also have been eaten selectively though this is not certain.[205] Wildfowl was, again presumably, an important supplementary food source, especially in favoured locations like the edges of the Fens and in the Somerset Levels.[206] Evans has suggested that the reversion in arrow-head types back to the tranchet form early in our period reflects an increased exploitation of small game and bird in regenerated forest.[207] Birds apart, the eggs of the larger species like swan, duck, seagull, and pigeon would surely have been sought out and wild honey was doubtless prized too.

[202] For references in nn. 202 and 203 see the Site Index (below, pp. 282–8). Domestic fowl: cf. J. W. Jackson in E. M. Clifford, *Bagendon*, Cambridge, 1961, p. 270, with Volume I, Part II, pp. 219–39. Caesar (*de Bello Gallico* v, 12, 6) states that the Britons would not eat fowl or geese, keeping them as pets; but perhaps their eggs were eaten nevertheless. *Meare* (III, pp. 409–10) produced an interesting list of avian remains, obviously reflecting its particular wetland environment; in marked contrast is the *Tollard Royal* (p. 147) evidence where 'the complete absence of farm birds and of sizeable wild ones is noteworthy' – and presumably also reflects its downland environment. Dog frequently occurs on later prehistoric sites e.g. *Jarlshof*, pp. 25, 212–13; *Staple Howe*, pp. 136–7; *Croft Ambrey*, p. 242; *Little Woodbury*, III, p. 23; *Meare*, III, p. 408; *Bagendon*, p. 269; *Tollard Royal*, pp. 146–7.

[203] Antler picks: e.g. *Durrington Walls*, pp. 185–8. Red and or roe deer were present at numerous late prehistoric sites e.g. *Croft Ambrey*, p. 215; *Staple Howe*, pp. 136–7.

[204] Cf. for some general points on a shellfish diet, Evans *et al.*, CBA Research Report, 11, pp. 105–6. *Jarlshof* provides some good evidence of a marine-based food-supply.

[205] Evans, *Land Snails in Archaeology*, pp. 175–6 sees *Helix aspersa* as a first-century AD introduction.

[206] See n. 202 above.   [207] Evans, *op. cit.*, p. 122.

Not very much is known for certain about the range of edible wild plants and fruits, and less about their exploitation.[208] The range could well have been less than in later times, since some of the present 'wild' flora have been imported, e.g. the walnut; but amongst the varieties available were crab apple, bullace, and sloe of the fruits, and extensive list of berries – barberries, blackberries, elderberries, raspberries, and strawberries to name the obvious ones. Then too there were certainly the nut-bearing trees, especially the hazel, and a whole range of other edible fruits, weeds, roots, fungi, spices, herbs, greens, flowers, and seaweeds. Knowledge and exploitation of such sources has really only been generally lost in Britain in the last two centuries, and it is but necessary to look at rural books, particularly herbals of the sixteenth and seventeenth centuries, or indeed of medieval times, to realize the range available.[209] The knowledge persists in some remoter parts of the country, and is of course still cultivated and practised by specialist groups. Proof that such sources were used by later prehistoric communities, collecting herbs for medicinal purposes for example, is almost everywhere lacking, but it is simply inconceivable that people so deeply rooted in the landscape, so 'close to Nature', and so adept in exploiting their environment in other respects should be ignorant of, or choose to ignore, such a range of natural resources available for the taking to supplement and indeed improve their livelihood from field and pasture.[210]

[208] R. Mabey, *Food for Free*, Glasgow, 1972, is one of the most recent in a long line of advocates of the practicality of, at least in part, living off edible wild plants. It, and similar books, probably provide a good indication of what was generally available in the first millennium BC. That this footnote is being written proves that not all wild plants are poisonous; and some are certainly recommended.

[209] E.g. N. Culpeper, *The Complete Herbal*, 1653; Mabey, *op. cit.*, pp. 185–7, provides a useful short bibliography.

[210] One of this author's favourite references is to the apparently authentic modern germination of (wild?) raspberries from seeds found in the stomach of an inhumation 20 ft down in a Bronze Age barrow, quoted by C. Warne, *Celtic Tumuli of Dorset, Tumuli opened at various periods*, no. 62, London, 1866, cf. RCHM, *Dorset*, II, 1970, p. 465.

CHAPTER III

THE ACHIEVEMENT OF LATER PREHISTORIC
FARMING IN BRITAIN[1]

IN assessing the achievement of later prehistoric farming, it is probably
inevitable that some of the applied criteria are anachronistic. What
may appear now, for example, 3,000 years later, to have been a debit
item would not necessarily appear as such to the farmer or his
community living on the Sussex Downs in 1000 BC. A late twentieth-
century standpoint is, however, perfectly valid, for we are entitled to
judge the actions of our predecessors provided we do not represent such
judgment as deriving from a state of mind in the period being studied.
The distinction between contemporary prehistoric and contemporary
present is the critical one to be maintained. In trying to achieve this,
while reviewing later prehistoric agrarian achievement, we could stand
back from the topic and treat it chronologically. Although this is done
in extreme summary form (in Fig. 3), I prefer to continue the topical
treatment and so will review the achievement under four main
subheadings: environment, culture, economics, and social system.
Overlaps are inevitable and, in the reality of the last two millennia bc,
all four aspects were interacting and interdependent.

THE ENVIRONMENTAL ACHIEVEMENT

It may well be that agrarian man's major achievement in later
prehistoric Britain was to make a considerable impact on his environment. Perhaps more subtly and significantly his real achievement was
to develop over these two millennia a productive relationship, a
partnership, a symbiosis, with Nature, which subsequently affected his
actions and his thoughts until the basis of Britain's economy fundamentally changed in the later eighteenth and nineteenth centuries AD.
Arguably, the residual memories of that symbiotic relationship unconsciously lie behind the conscious seeking after an appropriately
satisfactory relationship between a predominantly industrial and urban

---

[1] This chapter has no references except for a terminal quote. It is clearly a subjective
interpretation arising from the data and ideas already itemized in footnotes or referenced
in the Site Index and Select Bibliography. It seems pointless to parade more and
repetitious detail from the same material.

society and its rural hinterland which is one of the characteristics of twentieth-century Britain. Before pursuing the first two points in this proposition, however, it must be recognized that, although the relationship changed through time, elements in the environment were constant and could not be changed by man. Likewise, other elements changed outside the control of man yet critically affected the environment and presumably the relationships within it.

By the period under discussion, the major structural changes in the landscape had already taken place, and were no longer significantly or perceptibly changing. These were constants in the environmental framework of later prehistoric man which are still there today. Given a view of the landscape in 2000 BC, a modern man would have been able to recognize where he was in modern terms. The mountains and hills, the rivers and valleys, the mineral deposits, were where they are now – unlike the situation, for example, in 50,000 BC. Of course, erosion and deposition and all the continuous processes of geomorphology have made alterations in the last 4,000 years but the physical relief is basically the same now as it was then. Man could not therefore change the physical constraints of his environment except by moving and accepting a different set. Nor could he control changes in some of the elements in that environment. The climate changed, for example, and man had to adapt to the consequences. He could not alter the basic range of floral and faunal variety in his environment, yet that too changed through time, perhaps anthropogenically influenced but certainly not controlled by man. Yet clearly with flora and fauna, we can be less sure of our argument, and another critical distinction must be recognized between the validity of a generalization and its applicability in a localized situation at a given time. Man did not radically affect the range of wild-life species in later prehistoric Britain but a community could certainly rid its vicinity of, say, a particular predator or indeed, by over-exploitation, a particular, preferred food source.

Given these constants and the uncontrollable elements in the natural background, man has nevertheless had more impact than any other mammal on the natural environment. In our period he cleared with his own hands many hectares of woodland, scrub, and stone; simply by pasturing his sheep, goats, pigs, and cattle, he grazed open forest clearings, broke up forest edges, and created a grass cover. At one time or another during those two millennia he cultivated, however briefly, much of the land in Britain and over large areas in the south and east he brought under cultivation land which has remained the country's paramount arable ever since. Furthermore, supported by this agrarian base, he prospected and exploited, however minimally in terms of later exploitation, many of the mineral deposits occurring naturally in his environment. The scars of this industry are still visible today as spoil heaps in the flatlands of East Anglia at Grime's Graves, as quarries and debris on the Lleyn peninsula, and as the screes of Upper Langdale.

It is difficult to avoid using the word 'exploit' in describing these activities yet exploitation can hardly be the basis for the symbiotic relationship hinted at above (p. 245). The point is fundamental in assessing the environmental achievement of later prehistoric agrarian communities and involves both a temporal and a topographical dimension. Broadly speaking, in the first part of our period we see man apparently pursuing an exploitive strategy in relation to his environment. He is taking what he needs and not replacing it; arguably, he is a farmer but not yet a husbandman. His principles and concepts in relation to this environment remain essentially 'Mesolithic' despite the 'Neolithic revolution' of the older terminology. Pre-farming communities lived off their environment; but so did the early farmers for, although they planted their own seed and herded their own stock, and were not therefore entirely dependent on the fruits of Nature for their food, they were still absorbing natural resources in producing their own food. Critically, they were exploiting natural fertility and not replacing it. They had no need to: with low population and plenty of space, decreasing fertility was obviated simply by moving to another exploitable niche in the ecosystem and there repeating the process. But in this shifting, and, from our point of view, shiftless agriculture, anthropogenic interferences seem in places to have critically affected the natural cycle of regeneration. Exploitation was of the vegetational cover and of the soil structures and chemistry, and it can be argued that the subsequent history and present appearance of much of what is now the Highland Zone can be traced back to what was happening in the later third and second millennia.

In that thousand years or so the first critical steps were taken towards what in today's terms is considered a scenic amenity and, wrongly, a natural phenomenon of unspoilt beauty; but in pedological and vegetational terms much of northern and western Britain is a landscape of dereliction. Perhaps, however, the process of incipient degeneration from the broken 'natural' cycle of regeneration would not have continued had there not been a climatic deterioration beginning in the later second millennium and only stabilizing into the existing Sub-Atlantic phase in the earlier first millennium. In other words, climate, one of the environmental elements outside man's control, accentuated the trend he had started. It was in particular its increased wetness and the prevailing Atlantic direction from which the weather came that probably created, perhaps for the first time, a real distinction between Highland and Lowland Zones. The impact of the slow climatic deterioration was felt more severely in the west and north where, in part because of the situation already created by early farmers, and in part because of the physical geography, conditions were more suitable for more rapid run-off of the increased rainfall. As a result, erosion, leaching, podsolization, and the ponding which produces active bog growth, all proceeded, in many cases remorselessly, perhaps inevitably, because man had disturbed the soil structure, removed the tree-cover, and could not control the consequences of his action in a changed environmental situation. As the derelict field systems of the second millennium show over much of highland Britain from Dartmoor to Shetland (Plates III, V; Figs. 14, 45, 46, 48, 49), man the farmer was even forced gradually to abandon some of his developed and highly organized attempts at settled agriculture, in addition to abandoning the areas where he had first pushed out his shifting or semi-permanent agriculture in earlier times. When he moved away, however, instead of weeds and scrub and then woodland taking over, his empty fields and extensive pastures, their structure altered, their flora reduced, their fertility drained, supported only heather, bog growth, and the occasional silver birch. This whole thesis is of course an oversimplification but not, it is hoped, grossly so. There will be many exceptions to it, and the chronology and extent of its stages will vary from place to place: but, given the time-scale and the area involved in this survey, the process and its consequences are generally supported by the existing evidence.

In what we can begin to recognize after _c._ 1000 BC as a distinctively Lowland Zone, the man/environment relationship worked out differently though not necessarily entirely deliberately. In the fourth and third millennia woodland areas were cleared, pastures were created, and cultivation was practised here too. In the earlier second millennium we see also the landscape architecture of organized and permanent field systems, and of extensive land allotment, and of individual monuments on the grand scale. Yet around 1000 BC we see a quickening of developments, and throughout the first millennium an increasing technological, material, and social progress. The land itself not only remained in good heart but apparently increased its productivity. Here was no pedological degradation, and, while there was certainly vegetational change, its consequences were not irreversible as was the case further west and north. Yet climatic change occurred here too; why the agrarian differences between Highland and Lowland Zones? Fundamentally it was probably the result of a change in the nature of the relationship between man and his environment, a change in attitude reflected in practice from exploitation to conservation of the environment. There is of course a danger here of projecting backwards present ideas, but by 'conservation' in this context is meant a working with, rather than a taking from, a harmonization of objectives rather than a conflict, the development of the long-term concern of the husbandman rather than the cash-crop philosophy of the 'Mesolithic' farmer and the modern land-investment combine.

The evidence that can be interpreted in this light is archaeological rather than environmental: the extent, longevity, and lynchetting of the field systems themselves, the crucial evidence of manuring on them, the implied control of stock-grazing – undramatic, essentially practical matters but the very stuff of agrarian history. The later prehistoric communities of southern Britain simply had to learn to strike a balance with their environment to survive in a worsening climate; that they learnt to manage a good balance is evident from the rapid increase in their numbers, the slower increase in their material well-being, and the compliment of two Roman invasions. Seashells in the sandy plough-soil at Gwithian and broken potsherds on 'Celtic' fields on the Berkshire Downs are not among the most dramatic of archaeological finds; but, in that they represent the practice of manuring, they are amongst the most significant. Later prehistoric man's environmental achievements were inadvertently to create the now much-prized wildernesses of west and north, to create the farming landscape of the east and south and, above all, to discover and recognize the principle of reciprocity not just in dealing with Nature but rather in being a part of the whole of the 'natural' environment, i.e. of an ecosystem. It is a principle forgotten by industrial man in his reversion to an exploitive strategy; but, as the later twentieth century is learning all over again to its cost, it is one which even urban man, in completely different circumstances from the husbandmen at Little Woodbury, cannot ignore for long.

THE CULTURAL ACHIEVEMENT

It follows from the foregoing thesis that, in many respects, a distinction between 'natural' and 'man-made' is itself artificial. Yet it is not entirely invalid, for man-in-nature nevertheless produced his own distinctive artifacts, just an other mammals produce theirs, and in that context we can ourselves recognize a cultural, i.e. man-made, achievement. Its relevance here is based on the premise that the great bulk of human endeavour in later prehistoric Britain was made physically possible by a reasonably reliable and adequate food supply largely deriving from farming. Put the other way around, had the agrarian base of the last 2,000 years BC not been present the particular cultural achievements of that period would have been impossible. There would have been cultural developments, of course, but they would have been different. In that sense, later prehistoric culture, archaeologically speaking, is the specific and characteristic product of contemporary agrarian achievement.

Thus defined, culture can still usefully be discussed in terms of the old-established, if now old-fashioned, 'Three Age' or technological model. At the start of our period, we see stone-using communities, soon to be infiltrated by the first metal-users. Copper was rapidly replaced by bronze which, for 1,500 years, was the prime material for cutting-edge tools and weapons and, increasingly, a host of other implements. Its successor, iron, had an even longer life in similar terms almost up to the present day. While many of the artifacts in these metals possessed characteristics distinctive of Britain, of their region, of certain workshops, or even of individual craftsmen, in a European context their production and characteristics represent no great cultural achievement; or rather should one perhaps say they represent a common achievement? Yet, in a world context, the success is considerable, as a glance at the prehistories of Africa and America emphasize. Can the British development of metal-working, attaining a high degree of technical competence and aesthetic achievement in its latest stages, be explained adequately by the readily available metalliferous deposits? – presumably not, by American analogy, but equally farming itself is not the full answer either for it also existed across the Atlantic. An answer is in fact not readily available, yet there is something to be said in favour of the stimulus-and-reaction model. Britain was essentially a wooded landscape at the beginning of our period and trees had to be chopped down for agricultural purposes and for building (Plate IIb). Perhaps significantly, along with daggers for self-defence, the earliest copper and bronze products concentrated on axes. Perhaps similarly a thousand years and more later, a wetter climate produced denser, uncleared vegetation and quicker regrowth while society developed an insatiable appetite for timber to enclose hill-tops and build houses (cf. Plate VIII; Figs. 36, 38). About the same time, lead additions to the bronze alloy made the finished products sturdier, products which increased considerably in their variety, and soon afterwards an iron technology developed. The case cannot be pressed, but conceivably there was a direct causal demand-and-supply connection between agrarian need and technological development. The same may also be true of earlier types of pottery, e.g. grain storage jars in the mid to late second millennium and again in the last century before the Roman Conquest, but otherwise pottery does not represent a very great cultural achievement.

Yet cultural expression cannot be confined to portable artifacts, however convincingly they group and distribute themselves; structures and the distribution of settlement are also, on a larger and broader canvas, expressions of what societies manage to achieve. Buildings represent a conscious striving after achievement, particularly large communal structures designed to last. We have already seen that precisely such were produced, in the form of tombs, from early in the history of British farming (above, p. 46) almost as if a considerable proportion of the extra time and energy released by agriculture was invested in a completely new form of communal activity. Further developments of such major cultural manifestations continue in our period: at its start we see the *floruit* of henges, incidentally with their clear evidence for the massive use of timber for building purposes, culminating in the long drawn-out achievement, pre-eminent in its sophistication, at Stonehenge. In the same period of almost inexplicable release of social energy we see too many other examples of circular structures, principally stone circles incidentally showing land clearance, and the development of an interest in linear features exemplified by the cursus and stone rows. Slightly later, the development of the great barrow cemeteries in the south, and of cairn fields in the north and west, continue the theme of cultural expression in the form of major landscape works, and it is surely somewhere in this complex of communal endeavour, however organized (below, p. 259), that fits most appositely the signal agrarian developments of landscape organization already discussed (above, p. 151). Of course a great deal more field data and dating evidence are required, but the thesis can certainly be considered that, within the centuries between *c.* 2000 and 1400 bc a release of unprecented social energy through communal effort created a cultural landscape in which we can now see not only the peaks of achievement, as represented by the major monuments, but also the agrarian base from which these achievements derived. Furthermore, it was that base on which pre-industrial society and economy developed over the next 3,000 years, granted the different modes of social organization over those millennia, and of course the emergence of a market economy in the early centuries AD.

It is not perhaps surprising in terms of cultural history that, broadly in the second half of the second millennium, we can dimly perceive a lull. Major new enterprises are not apparent; indeed the major old ones wane. Agriculturally it appears to be a phase of consolidation or, perhaps more significantly, of adjustment to a changing situation. Perhaps it is now rather than earlier that a part of this adjustment is a switch in places from arable to stock farming (above, p. 236), and now rather than later that upland areas of settlement are abandoned. We see too the growth of the practice of manuring, of grain storage in large pits, of grain drying, and then, towards 1000 BC, the reappearance fairly widely of major communal works – the proto-hill-forts.

The building and functions of hill-forts and their regional variants

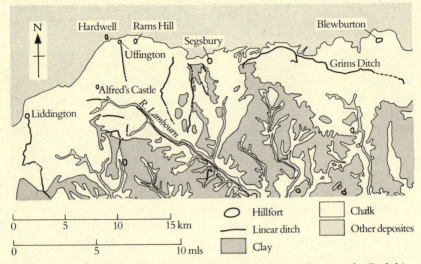

Fig. 58. Hill-forts and linear ditches in relation to surface geology on the Berkshire Downs. The hill-forts are generally on or close to boundaries (after R. Bradley).

come to dominate the first millennium, at least in the archaeological record of cultural achievement, because, unlike earlier major monuments, and whatever other function hill-forts served, many were settlements. As such they represent a new phenomenon in the cultural landscape, the permanent, enclosed communal settlement, significantly a type of settlement which, usually in the guise of a town, has subsequently always been present in at least Lowland Britain. This is not to say that all hill-forts were towns, were permanently occupied, or indeed continually defended – we need only look at the vicissitudes in the lives of individual towns to appreciate the variety of historical experience likely within such a broad category of settlement type. Nevertheless, whether a 'hill-fort' be of the order of Maiden Castle, a humble 'round' in Cornwall, or a small dun in Scotland – in absolute terms representing a tremendous range of social investment – relative to its locality each represents a significant and characteristic cultural expression deriving, amongst other factors, from an agrarian society (Figs. 7, 22, 40, 56, 58). As such, they represent a considerable achievement, physically and conceptually; and the concept has proved enduring even if the physical achievement, unlike what happened to some hill-top sites in Gaul and Greece, but as subsequently happened to Romano-British villas, did not endure in the long term.

Though it was from hill-forts that the Britons confronted the Roman army in the south-west, west, and north, this was not the case in the south-east. Even though the type of settlement may have been conceptually imported, the existence of the Belgic *oppida* in the first centuries BC/AD must be noted because they represent the development of the idea of the 'permanent, enclosed communal settlement'. The significant part of this development for present purposes was the location of the site. Although some *oppida* were on high ground (Minchinhampton) and several included high ground (Bagendon, Prae Wood), unlike the native hill-forts as a class, they were not *dependent* on hill-slopes for their effectiveness. Thus as major settlement foci, the conceptual significance of *oppida* is that in locational terms, as we see at Verulamium and Colchester, for example, they opened up the way for the development in Roman and medieval times of the urban settlement in its preferred situation on low-lying ground, characteristically by a river; while, apart from a brief, interesting, but anachronistic re-use of some in late- and sub-Roman times, the hill-forts fossilized on their hill-tops. The development of *oppida* obviously involves many factors not all of which are our direct concern here; but, in that they emerge as an expression of a still basically agrarian society, and in the light of subsequent urban history, they certainly represent one of the achievements of late prehistoric Britain.

While all these major cultural achievements still attract the eye, individually they are but part of a pattern, the successive patterns of settlement; and cultural expression, sometimes amounting to achievement, can be communicated, perhaps unconsciously, as much through such media as through monumental structures or art. The study of settlement patterns in later prehistoric Britain is topographically sporadic, and, in spatial terms, much is conceptually naive. The topic still leans heavily on artifact distribution rather than on settlement geography incorporating the total available relevant evidence. It is, therefore, difficult to generalize not least because, unsurprisingly, different patterns have tended to emerge where adequate, detailed regional or local studies have been made (Figs. 58, 59). Even then, while a pattern may emerge, few attempts to express it numerically, by area, or as a predictive model, have been made.

Influenced on the one hand by developments in the philosophy and practice of local history and on the other by theory from modern geography, some recent studies have, however, shifted conceptually and methodologically away from a 'portable antiquity' or site-specific orientation in an attempt to study the landscape evolution of a particular area as a step towards understanding the changing cultural environment of the communities which lived there. The 'prehistoric geography' preached by Crawford and Fox from the 1920s onwards, now immensely improved in execution through the techniques of the field

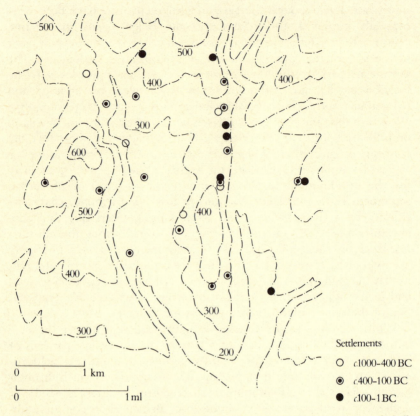

Settlements

O   c1000–400 BC

◉   c400–100 BC

●   c100–1 BC

Fig. 59. Settlement distribution in the first millennium BC over an area of chalk downland at Chalton, Hants. (after B. Cunliffe).

sciences, can be seen in action in the Somerset Levels, in the Brenig Valley, Denbighs., and on the Berkshire, Wiltshire, and Hampshire Downs. In the Somerset Levels the changing patterns of local livelihood from the fourth millennium bc, elegantly linked to subtle but significant topographical variation, palaeobotanical succession, and remarkable organic survival, are informing a detailed appreciation of ecological adaptation and exploitation up to the present day. There the immediate archaeological targets, the wooden trackways (Plate II*b*), along which later prehistoric farmers crossed with their cattle from island to island to Polden shore, are explained in a settlement pattern embracing not just the peat in which they occur but also the sides of the Brue valley and the hill-tops beyond. Similarly, in the totally different environment of the chalk downs, the earthworks, surface debris, and air photographic evidence from above Lambourn and Chalton are interpreted in terms of a settlement pattern including the Vale of the White Horse and the valleys of the Hampshire/Sussex border respectively. Though much of such interpretation is at best limited and necessarily speculative – and in the cases of Rams Hill and Chalton very different in outcome – the overall and unavoidable impression is of local complexity yet basic continuity, of powerful yet subtle environmental influences, and of the creation through time of increasing constraints in the landscape of the present. It was the misfortune of later prehistoric communities that their efforts in managing their land, in converting the wild landscape of their forbears to the cultural landscape inherited by the Romans, were not recorded in writing; it would be our misjudgment if, through lack of written record, we underestimated their achievement then, or its significance now.

THE ECONOMIC ACHIEVEMENT

It could be argued that a measure of the achievement of Britain's later prehistoric agrarian economy was the fact that Rome thought it worthwhile to invade the island. Admittedly, the other parts of Europe were similarly treated but there were good military reasons for so doing, apart from the straightforward desires of imperial aggrandisement. Despite contemporary propaganda to justify the invasion of Britain, the island presented no real military threat to imperial integrity, and was incapable of doing so. At worst, it was of nuisance value. It has been argued, however, and was said at the time, that the real attraction in Britain was not so much its agricultural productivity as its mineral wealth; and the course of the Claudian conquest to some extent gives credence to this view. In that sense, then, perhaps the attempts at conquest were not primarily motivated by agrarian considerations. In the background too were the politics of Rome, and problems of personal status, making a new conquest desirable. So it is not surprising, as with most invasions, to find a complex of reasons but, without giving it pride of place, in reality agrarian productivity was probably a strong motivation. Both before 55 BC and especially in the decades leading up to AD 43, the growth of an export trade from southern Britain to Roman Gaul showed not only the range of produce but the fact that, probably for the first time, British agriculture was producing a surplus. Indeed, the major economic achievement of late prehistoric agriculture was to make Britain, for the first time in its history, a grain-exporting country. Since the efficient Roman official mind would automatically assume that this was being achieved inefficiently, what potential wealth must have seemed likely given organization, technical improvement, and a military presence?

It is therefore a question of some importance to ask how and why British agriculture had managed to develop from its small and limited competence in the third millennium to a surplus-producing economy some seventy-five generations later. The pace of change is of course ridiculously slow compared to modern change from a 'Neolithic' economy to urban-based capitalism in one generation in parts of the Third World today; but the change in Britain was effected largely if not entirely by insular effort. Furthermore, in the early stages of a developing agrarian economy, an extra capacity, a surplus of time and energy for internal consumption, was made available, sufficient to promote the creation of a distinct and idiosyncratic cultural expression. This cultural product of economic progress continued to develop characteristic insular features with regional variants for 2,000 years. Yet, while we can see some of the results of what happened, the rationale and mechanics of economic development during these two illiterate millennia are difficult to postulate and impossible to prove. In any case, the overall achievement leading to the Roman Conquest can easily be exaggerated. Throughout that time except at the very end and only in parts of the country, the British economy was a subsistence economy in which, by and large, communities consumed their produce annually, and were dependent for their livelihood on a repeating cycle of hard work and favourable weather. The margin of error, the difference between subsistence and starvation, must have been small for most people most of the time – a supposition which is borne out by the very significant fact that few grain storage pits out of thousands excavated have been found with their contents intact or indeed with any grain at all *in situ* (Fig. 60c; if, however, most pits were used for seed-corn (see above, p. 228) the point is invalid). There was no room for waste, or forgetfulness, in the late prehistoric economy.

While, however, that economy maintained life at subsistence level, it possessed a stability of expectation probably providing a degree of security which encouraged economic and material development. Of course there would have been bad years and lean spells, but it was unlikely that everything would fail simultaneously, for one of the major strengths of the economy throughout later prehistory was that in agricultural terms it was a mixed economy. Never at any time does there seem to have developed a significant proportion of economically specialist communities. Exceptions could have been mining communities or metal-workers, but the evidence is not conclusive; and, indeed, examination of the life-style of the rural specialists in medieval times often shows them to have been farmers second whatever they were first. So while there were undoubtedly differences of emphasis in the economic base through time and from region to region and community to community, as a whole the British economy proved viable and capable of development because of its lack of specialization. The cereal and arable farmers of Dartmoor in the second millennium perhaps primarily herded cattle and pastured sheep: the pastoral farmers of the first millennium in Northumbria also grew cereals; and the farming communities on the Wessex Downs and in the Midland valleys seem to have kept a balance throughout between the poles of arable and pasture. As an example of the economic sensitivity, or just commonsense, of farming communities in a particular locality reacting to changing environmental conditions through time, we see at Fengate how the emphases in the micro-economy and the *loci* of its principal activities changed with the conditions along the river gravel/fenland edge interface. Furthermore, despite our previous emphasis on clearance, there was probably always woodland and scrub somewhere in any vicinity, and this represented another economic resource, even if not strictly speaking 'farmed', in providing pannage for pigs and a larder of catchable wild-life.

Of increasing importance during later prehistory was another aspect of the economy: industry. Perhaps one of the most far-reaching economic achievements of the last two millennia BC was the discovery of a range of mineral wealth in Britain. Of course these communities did not discover every location by any means, and their exploitation of the resources was minimal, but by Caesar's time the variety of Britain's mineral, and particularly metalliferous, wealth was well known. Metamorphic rocks and flint, suitable for cutting tools, had long been discovered, quarried, and exchanged. Subsequently copper, tin, gold, silver, lead, and iron ores; a whole range of clays and/or minerals for pottery fillers; numerous quartzitic and sandstone rocks for querns, rubbers, and whetstones; a wide variety of rock for building materials including, among those which were used more widely than just in the place of origin, sarsens, oolitic limestone, tufa, and pennant sandstone; and of course, from collection rather than quarrying, a very large number of pebbles, from beaches and inland eocene deposits, for slingstones.

Most of these 'industrial' products were consumed internally and, probably, locally, but there must have been some mechanism of exchange. The model of 'embassies' or 'gifts' has been suggested for groups of the more exotic artifacts early in our period, and that may well cover some of what otherwise appears to be internal trading, e.g. unused mace-heads and the occasional import like Continental jade and non-functional axeheads. But does it explain other rare exotic imports like the south German-type pins from Gwithian or the 'Bavarian' palstave from inside a field at Horridge, Devon? There are hints of minor imports in the second millennium, but it is doubtful whether any 'trade' then was economically significant, and, even if it existed, we can only guess at the exports. Increasingly in the first millennium, however, the manufacture of lead-bronze and then iron objects suggests the existence of an exchange system since clearly individual agricultural communities were acquiring to a greater degree objects which they themselves had not manufactured. The picture of the travelling bronze-smith has long been suggested by the discovery of buried hoards of bronze objects, especially those containing scrap; and a system of barter has been envisaged. Recently the discovery of the debris of bronze-working in a settlement at Gussage All Saints, Dorset (Fig. 31), has tended to confirm the itinerant bronze-smith model but raises the question of what he received in return for his work from the wholly agricultural settlement in which he briefly stopped. Did he leave leading a couple of oxen, loaded with sheepskin and butter, weighed down with currency bars – or checking the coin in his purse?

The development of an insular gold, silver, and bronze coinage from the later second century onwards must rank as another of the major economic achievements of late prehistory. Its immediate effect was to facilitate the expansion of the cross-Channel trade in the first centuries BC/AD which saw consumables like wine and pottery, glassware and personal ornaments flood into south-eastern Britain and spread outwards. The spread, however, was rapidly diluted so that one effect of coinage and Gallic trade was a further accentuation in economic terms of the Lowland/Highland difference. South-eastern Britain moved into a market economy based on imports, exports, and coinage while much of the rest of the country, even if it had coins, remained economically insular and largely self-sufficient with bartering rather than cash probably still the basis of exchange. But despite the material affluence of the south-east, Strabo's (IV, V, 2) list of British exports, interesting in itself as our first written evidence of Britain's surplus produce, also reminds us of the insular agrarian base behind the international trade: grain and cattle first, then gold, silver, iron, hides, slaves, and hunting dogs. Though export was through the south-east and the imports largely benefited that area only, it is clear from the list that the produce being sent across the Channel was truly a British and not just a 'Belgic' surplus. The gold and silver, for example, must have come originally from the west, cattle and the hides perhaps came from the Brigantes or the Welsh tribes, and slaves and hunting dogs also have a western ring about them.

The surprising fact in all this is not so much that there was a surplus but that the agrarian-based British economy had become sufficiently productive to produce a surplus for export at the end of a period of supporting a rapidly growing population. Undoubtedly, its major economic achievement was to feed, and make possible the great increase in, a still predominantly agrarian society without any non-agrarian innovation of major economic importance, e.g. in communication or industry. The advent of iron made a great difference, but archaeology does not indicate that it was commonly in use for farming until the last centuries of our period, and this technological improvement seems agriculturally to have been one of adaptation rather than revolution, e.g. no new types of tool appear until the Roman period. A fair assessment of later prehistoric agriculture then, pin-pointing its achievement on the eve of conquest, would be that far from consisting of the inefficient scratchings of a few barbarous peasants, it represented a combination of factors resulting in a maximum productivity within the contemporary environmental, technological, and social framework.

THE SOCIAL ACHIEVEMENT

The social achievement is perhaps the most difficult of all to assess. The evidence for it is difficult to recognize and easy to misread. There are many suggestions from the archaeological record that later prehistory saw the progressive development of a more cohesive agrarian society; yet when, at the end, our first literary records appear, we read in the pages of Caesar and Tacitus of a society divided among itself, split by economic differences, political ambitions, and even the tactics of repelling the invasions. It took another thousand years of intermittent central government before a nation could begin to be recognized or wished to recognize itself. So the political result of later prehistory was Roman conquest, directly attributable in the field not only to inferior weapons and tactics but basically to a divided organization. In its *mélange* of pre-Roman tribes, Britain was still essentially a land of local communities.

It is, however, difficult to overlook the evidence of social order from earlier times. Furthermore, it is just possible that the fragmentation so clear in the first centuries BC/AD was a relatively recent development, largely created by a rapid growth of population which had broken a social structure evolved for smaller numbers. Nineteenth-century Britain, for example, saw a society with a structure related to a rural, agricultural way of life trying to adjust to a much larger industrial populace in towns. Not that later prehistoric society can ever have been other than hierarchical, but that in itself does not obviate its being cohesive, well-ordered, and productive. We do not know what social mechanics produced the major works of civil engineering from henges to multi-vallate hill-forts but they are unlikely to have been democratic.

The concept of the chief man was fairly well embedded in later prehistory, and the archaeology of the period can produce him if required at the henges, in Beaker graves, under 'Wessex culture' barrows, or in the major hill-forts, the *oppida* and richly-furnished Belgic graves. On the coins at the end we have their symbols, the allegiances, and their names, and one feels that had there been a Beaker coinage the evidence would have been similar. For a brief period in the second half of the second millennium the chief seems to disappear and, perhaps due to a quirk of the data, we see a society of small farmers at Gwithian, Trevisker, Shearplace Hill, and Itford burying their dead in communal, egalitarian cremation cemeteries.

Apart from the absence of chiefs, however, the social picture portrays the bulk of the population as it appears in later prehistory. From all over Britain throughout our period we see the small farms dispersed across the landscape suggesting the prevalence of the 'family unit' at the base of the social hierarchy. There is no evidence for any larger units in the second millennium, though obviously 'families' combined for work if not for living; yet in the first millennium larger social groups appear in hill-forts, in large 'open' settlements and in *oppida* as a trend towards social nucleation developed. It seems reasonable to see these as village, even proto-urban, communities, distinct from the scattered communities of the dispersed farms.

Later prehistoric society in Britain was and is regarded as barbaric. Certainly it did not create a civilization but, arguably, perhaps it would have done so if its culture had not been truncated by Rome. It was nevertheless a dynamic society, adaptable, and inventive, which both encouraged and depended on a wide range of skills and crafts exercised by individuals. It produced no great art, except briefly in the late centuries BC, no literature at all, and no religion which has influenced later times; yet clearly it celebrated an intense religious observance based variously on a belief in the after-life, the animal kingdom, arguably the heavens, and certainly the human head. Equally it surely developed at the very least an empirical learning to have been so agriculturally successful and, presumably, an oral tradition of customary practice or lore, narrative, and poetry. Of law and order we know nothing until the slight documentary evidence at the end, though an assumption about a rough and ready justice emanating from the chiefs could well be near the mark.

Two of the most important aspects of social development have contrasting types of evidence. Archaeology shows that amongst the earliest metal tools were daggers, though it would be yet another assumption to regard them as offensive weapons, for their use may have been as hunting knives, for show or status, or in self-defence against animals. Weapons are singularly absent from the earlier part of our period, yet appear in the later second millennium and proliferate thereafter. On the ground, likewise, there are no convincing sites with military implications until the early hill-forts. Is it just possible that, coincidental with the early climatic decline, warfare began in Britain? Whatever the causes of fighting, pressure on land is a common factor, and that was increasingly present in the first millennium with a worsening climate and a rising population, whereas earlier in our period space was no problem. It can be suggested then that during our period society changed from one essentially at peace with itself to one in a constant state of tension and probably friction. We have noted the clear evidence for the growth of the concept and practice of land allotment, and with them probably goes the idea of 'territory' as observed in the animal kingdom. 'Territory' implies 'mine and not yours', the idea of property, and the need for defence.

Whether this development is an achievement is debatable, but it is connected with an equally basic aspect of social behaviour about which, in contrast, we have virtually no later prehistoric evidence. This concerns tenure, and involves the concept of property which was absolutely fundamental to Britain's agrarian communities. In practice it involved for whom individuals were working (themselves or a master?), whether they were owners or tenants of land, how the land was allotted, grazing, and other 'rights', and the principles of inheritance. Any views on the subject would be guesswork since we simply do not know how, in tenurial terms, the farming of later prehistoric Britain was carried out. Worse, "it is difficult to see how the problem of tenure can be satisfactorily resolved".[2] It is no mean achievement of our later prehistoric agrarian society to have hidden so successfully the basis of its success.

POSTSCRIPT

It is of course virtually impossible for a synthesis to be fully up-to-date, even at the time of completing the typescript, let alone at the time of publication. An attempt has been made in Appendixes 2, 3, and 4 below to go some way towards bridging the gap, specifically in 1976–7 and at least bibliographically, between what was available for assessment when writing the foregoing chapters and what is available now; but of course new data and interpretations cannot always be easily integrated into an existing structure or the basic hypotheses advanced within it. It has seemed best therefore to refer to post-1975 publications, mainly

[2] A. L. F. Rivet, 'The rural economy of Roman Britain', in H. Temporini and W. Maase (eds.), *Aufstieg und Niedergang der römischen Welt*, II, Berlin, 1972, p. 339.

in the Appendixes, but not to attempt to graft their results on to the existing text. The problem is not peculiar to agrarian prehistory but it happens to be a particularly acute one now as the pace and directions of new research are rapidly rendering redundant much of the old evidence and the thinking based upon it (see below Appendix 4).

One particularly interesting, indeed controversial, development during and after the writing of this account has been the reconstruction of 'Iron Age farms'. Experimental archaeology, and some aspects of the early work at Butser Ancient Farm, are referred to above (p. 67; Plates I*b*, VI). In 1976, however, a complete full-scale reconstruction of a farm of *c.* 300 BC was built, specifically for public and educational purposes, on land newly acquired by the Butser Project within the Queen Elizabeth Country Park (Plate VIII*a*), Hants.; and in 1977 a similar full-scale reconstruction (Plate VIII*b*) was built, appropriately, on the Pitt-Rivers Estate on the Wiltshire/Dorset border, by the BBC for a series of television programmes called 'Living in the Past', first screened in the spring of 1978. The Butser reconstruction, carefully designated the Demonstration Farm Area to distinguish it from the research site on Little Butser Hill (Plate I*b*), is essentially a static model in that no-one lives there, although it is surrounded by fields in which crops are grown and animals are grazed; the BBC reconstruction, innocently built on top of genuine 'Celtic' fields, was deliberately burnt down at the end of filming after having been lived in by twelve adults and two children for nearly a year.

Such publicity-seeking exercises, overtly playing to the current popular interest in archaeology, may not seem to provide appropriate material with which to end an 'academic' book; but both reconstructions are important, despite all the caveats one can make about them and their presentation, because, in a very real sense, they provide a three-dimensional physical reality, based very much on the data drawn on here, impossible to achieve by any other means. This is especially relevant in view of the diffident paragraphs accorded to the late prehistoric farm above (p. 129). The reconstructions are of course interpretations, but in wood, straw, and mud (Plate VIII*b*) rather than in prose or through an artist's drawing (cf. Figs. 20, 29); as such, while in a sense representing a culmination, even a fossilization, of interpretative ideas deriving from archaeological research, they also present a challenge, intellectual as well as visual. In this respect, they can properly be seen as a significant and complementary addition to the range of research methods applicable to the many outstanding problems in later prehistoric agrarian history.

May Day, 1978

Fig. 60. Three basic elements of later prehistoric agriculture: (a), wheat, spelt (*Triticum spelte*) on the left and emmer (*T. dicoccum*) on the right; (b), the sickle, in this reconstruction an iron one with split socket and wooden handle shown one-eighth actual size as it might have been used to harvest cereals in the ear only; (c), the pit, here shown in the section as excavated in Pit 26, Hut E, Itford Hill, Sussex, with a heap of carbonized barley on its base (a, b, after P. J. Reynolds; c, after G. P. Burstow and G. A. Holleyman).

APPENDIX 1

A SELECT LIST OF C-14 DATES

Site	Age bc	Uncertainty (1 standard deviation)	Laboratory number	Context
Skara Brae, Orkney	2190 to 1830	120 } 110	Birm. 433–438	Final occupation of settlement
		Second millennium bc		
Somerset Levels				
Abbot's Way	2090	90	GaK 1940	*Alnus* transverse of trackway
Abbot's Way	2068	80	Q926	Peg
Abbot's Way	2014	60	Q908	Peat
Abbot's Way	1990	65	Lu 299	Peg
Abbot's Way	1984	111	BM 386	*Alnus*
Bell A	2071	103	BM 383	*Fraxinus* peg of trackway
Bell B	2025	92	BM 384	*Fraxinus* transverse of trackway
Fengate, Peterborough, Northants.	2030	100	HAR 397 }	Settlement
	2020	70	HAR 399 }	'Kitchen' assemblage
	2010	90	HAR 401	Barrow G71, filling of primary
Earl's Farm Down, Amesbury, Wilts.	2010	110	NPL 77	grave which cut ard-marks
Durrington Walls, Wilts.	2050	90	BM 400	Ditch bottom of henge monument (cf. also BM 398, 399)
	2000	90	BM 396	S. Circle, phase 2, of henge monument (cf. also BM 395, 397)
Marden, Wilts.	1988	48	BM 557	Ditch bottom of henge monument
Collier Gill, Westerdale, N. Yorks.	1965	53	BM 428	Clearance phase
Mount Pleasant, Dorset	1961	89	BM 663	Timber structure inside ditched enclosure (cf. also BM 666, 667)

Site	Lab code	±	bc	Description
Embo, Sutherland	BM 442	100	1920	Passage grave, bones contemporary with construction
Woodhenge, Wilts.	BM 677	74	1867	Ditch of henge monument (cf. also BM 678)
Grime's Graves, Norfolk	BM 775	60	1865	Flint mine, backfilling of gallery 3
	BM 776	60	1839	Flint mine, hearth
	BM 777	61	1831	Flint mine, early filling of shaft
Silbury Hill, Wilts.	BM 842 }	43	1899	Red deer antler from ditch bottom
	BM 841 }	50	1802	
Fifty Farm, Mildenhall, Suffolk	BM 133	150	1850	Beaker occupation site
Stonehenge, Wilts.	C 602	275	1848	Aubrey Hole 32
Knap Hill, Wilts.	BM 208	130	1840	Causewayed enclosure, upper fill of ditch
Mount Pleasant, Dorset	BM645 }	41	1784	Hill-top enclosure, primary silt of ditch
	BM 646 }	59	1778	
Stanydale, Shetland	GrN 6168	55	1760	Burnt grain
Hunstanton, Norfolk	BM 704	63	1736	Settlement, pit
Cambridge Fens	Q684	110	1730	Yew bow
Chatton Sandyford, Northumb.	GaK 800	50	1670	Stake structure under round cairn
Stonehenge, Wilts.	I 2384	110	1620	Phase II
	BM 46	150	1720	Phase IIIa
Northton, Isle of Harris				
Beaker I	BM 706	70	1654	Forest clearance
Beaker II	BM 707	54	1531	Forest regeneration
Durrington Walls, Wilts.	BM 702 }	76	1647	Henge monument, Pit 27
	BM 703 }	72	1523	
Wattisfield, Suffolk	BM 77	150	1570	Deep shaft
Ness of Gruting, Shetland	BM 441	120	1564	Carbonized barley, hulled and naked, cached in base of house wall
Eclipse track, Somerset Levels	HAR 680	60	1510	Longitudinals
Mount Pleasant, Dorset	BM 664	131	1460	Hill-top enclosure, occupation in partially silted ditch
Beckford, Worcs.	Birm. 431	200	1410	Linear ditch beneath EIA settlement
Wilsford, Wilts.	NPL 74	90	1380	Organic material near bottom of shaft

APPENDIX I (*cont.*)

Site	Age bc	Uncertainty (1 standard deviation)	Laboratory number	Context
Fengate, Peterborough	1340	80	HAR 406	Final stage of settlement: wood from pit
Meare Lake track, Somerset Levels	1340	70	HAR 683	Longitudinal
Catcott Burtle, Somerset Levels	1320	110	Q 669	*Taxus* bow
Denny, Falkirk	1300	85	Q1196	Oak bow
Fengate, Peterborough	1280	70	UB 676	Ditch of field system
Chalton, Hants.	1243	69	BM 583	Settlement
Stonehenge, Wilts.	1240	105	I 2445	Phase IIIb/IIIc transition
Earl's Barton, Northants.	1219	51	BM 680	Land surface beneath barrow
	1269	64	BM 681	Land surface beneath barrow
Kaimes, Midlothian	1191	90	GaK 1970	Hill-fort, Hut 3 (contemporaneity uncertain)
Shearplace Hill, Dorset	1180	180	NPL 19	Settlement
Fisherwick, Staffs.	1170	140	Birm. 503	Settlement
Mam Tor, Derbys.	1180	132	Birm. 202 }	Charcoal preceding huts in hill-fort
	1130	115	Birm. 192	
Gwithian, Cornwall	1120	103	NPL 21	Settlement, layer 5
Trevisker, St Eval, Cornwall	1110	95	NPL 134	Settlement, floor of Hut A
Tinney's tracks, Somerset Levels	1090	70	HAR 681	Brushwood in tracks
Croft Ambrey, Hereford	1050	200	Birm. 144	Grain from main quarry ditch
Fengate, Peterborough	1050	70	HAR 398	Wood lining well
Itford Hill, Sussex	1000	35	GrN 6167	Grain
First millennium bc				
Rams Hill, Berks.	1070 to 740	90 to 70	HAR 197,228 to 231,461	Ditched enclosures
Tormarton, Glos.	977	90	BM 542	Skeletons with 'LBA' spearhead
Grimthorpe, E.R. Yorks.	970	130	NPL 137	Stockaded enclosure, primary ditch silt

Site	Date	±	Lab no.	Description
Fengate, Peterborough	895	95	V 122	First rampart
Meare Heath, Somerset Levels	935	135	UB 677	Ditch of field system
Breiddin, Powys	900	110	Q52	Stake from trackway
Westhay, Somerset	868	64	BM 880	Early hill-fort
Fisherwick, Staffs.	850	110	BM 880	Trackway
Fiskerton	850	140	Birm. 502	Settlement
Brigg	846	100	Birm. 502	Dug-out canoe
Balksbury, Hants.	834	100	Birm. 502	Boat
Combe Hay, Somerset	790	170	HAR 442	Hill-fort
Grimthorpe, Yorks.	700	120	Birm. 445	LBA pot and saddle quern
Skinner's Wood, Somerset Levels	690	130	NPL 136	Bones from ditch
Nidon's track, Somerset Levels	680	70	HAR 650	*Fraxinus* peg
Longbridge Deverill, Wilts.	635	100	Q313	Morticed timber
Finavon, Angus	630	155	NPL 105	Post-hole, House 1, Enclosure 2
Shapwick Heath, Somerset Levels	590	70	GaK 1224	Vitrified fort, inner wall face beams
Burnswalk, Dumfries.	520	110	Q39	*Corylus* longitudinal from track
	525	90	I 5314	} Hill-fort, first defences
	500	100	GaK 2203	}
South Barrule, Isle of Man	520	84	GaK 2203	Hill-fort
Wrekin, Shrops.	520	180	Birm. 531	Grain
Huckhoe, Northumb.	510	40	GaK 1388	Palisaded enclosure
Weston Wood, Surrey	510	110	Q760	Grain from pit
Gussage All Saints, Dorset	510	80	Q1204	Settlement, Pit 297, charcoal
	450	75	Q1209	Settlement, Ditch 1, bone
	420	90	Q1203	Settlement, Pit 379, charcoal
Milton Loch, Kirkcudbrights.	490	100	K2027	Oak pile of crannog
Breidden, Powys	479	55	BM 881	Later hill-fort
Platform track, Somerset Levels	460	100	Q311	
Hod Hill, Dorset	460	150	BM 47	Hill-fort, Phase 2 of rampart, charcoal
Dun Lagaidh, Wester Ross	460	110	GaK 2492	Grain burnt with timber fort
Staple Howe, E.R. Yorks.	450	150	BM 63	Grain from palisaded farmstead
Dun Mor Vaul, Tiree, Argyll.	445	90	GaK 1098	Charred grain from pre-broch level

APPENDIX 1 (*cont.*)

Site	Age bc	Uncertainty (1 standard deviation)	Laboratory number	Context
Longbridge Deverill, Wilts.	440	70	HAR 253	Carbonized grain, mainly barley, from base of pit
	420	95	NPL 107	Post-hole, House 2, Enclosure 2
Midsummer Hill, Hereford.	420	190	Birm. 142	Hill-fort, wood in quarry ditch associated with first gate
Milton Loch	400	100	K1394	Ard-head and stilt
Shapwick Station, Somerset Levels	345	120	Q357	Wood from boat
Finavon, Angus	320	90	GaK 12231	Occupation in fort
Holme Pierrepoint, Notts.	230	100	Birm. 132	Canoe
Gussage All Saints, Dorset	230	75	Q1201	Settlement, Ditch 1, charcoal
	210	75	Q1205	Settlement, Pit 437, charcoal
	150	65	Q1207	Settlement, Pit 209, charcoal
Ingram Hill, Northumb.	220	90	I 5316	Charcoal beneath bank of palisaded settlement
Balksbury, Hants.	230	150	HAR 446 } HAR 444 }	Hill-fort, charcoal from pit
	190	80		
Fisherwick, Staffs.	180	100	Birm. 614	Wood from ditch around settlement
Lochmaben	80	100	K1867	Ard-beam
Gussage All Saints, Dorset	70	70	Q1206	Settlement, Pit 209, charcoal
Midsummer Camp, Hereford.	50	100	Birm. 143	Hill-fort, grain associated with eighth gate
Balksbury, Hants.	50	80	HAR 445	Hill-fort, charcoal from pit
Wrekin	10	90	Birm. 532	Grain
	AD			
Gussage All Saints, Dorset	20	75	Q1202	Settlement, Ditch 310, charcoal
	50	65	Q1208	Settlement, Pit 139, charcoal

APPENDIX 2

'CELTIC' FIELDS: A NOTE ON TERMINOLOGY

The term 'Celtic' fields was apparently invented, independently and more or less simultaneously, by O. G. S Crawford and the Curwens in 1923. In the published version of a lecture given on 12 March of that year, Crawford wrote: "There are two kinds [of lynchets] which are not contemporary and which belong to two radically distinct systems of agriculture. The first kind is... arranged in chess-board fashion. This kind I shall, in anticipation, call 'the Celtic type'."[1] In fact, Crawford scarcely uses the phrase 'Celtic field' in this paper, throughout usually referring to "Celtic lynchets", "the Celtic system", "Celtic lynchet system", "the network [of lynchets] which I call Celtic", "an area of Celtic cultivation", "the Celtic type of cultivation", "the Celtic lynchet-system", etc. He first uses 'Celtic field' (without inverted commas) on p. 5,[2] but had, after considerable circumlocution, come round to the concept of an actual prehistoric field which he called 'Celtic' by p. 6, column 2: "on the edges and in the corners of the Celtic fields".

His use of the term is clearly defined and his reason for using it is implied:

"There are many possible systems of agriculture, and I am merely maintaining that the one I have called 'Celtic' was new, not that it was necessarily the first to be used here. I am anxious rather to prove that the system is prehistoric, and not later... Those who believe the neolithic inhabitants of England to have practised agriculture are welcome to believe that the system I have called 'Celtic' originated in neolithic days... The Celtic system began here, I believe, within a century or two of 500 BC. It lasted in England for about a thousand years, and it was brought to an end by the Saxon invasions."[3]

Although Crawford believed the fields to be an introduction by invading immigrants who first brought iron into England – "the first wave of Celtic-speaking peoples" – he is clearly using the apparently appropriate word 'Celtic' as a synonym for 'prehistoric'. He chose 'Celtic', because it was the antithesis of 'Saxon' and people with a

---

[1] Crawford, *Air Survey and Archaeology*, OS Professional Papers, NS, no. 7, 1924, p. 3. The lecture was originally printed in *Geog. J.*, 61, 1923, pp. 342–66. Cf. E. and E. C. Curwen, 'Sussex Lynchets and their associated field-ways', *Sussex Arch. Coll.*, 64, 1923, pp. 1–65.

[2] Crawford, *op. cit.*, p. 5, col. 1.   [3] *Ibid.*, p. 6, col. 1; p. 7, col. 1.

radically different system of agriculture (which he discusses later in the same paper).

'Celtic field(s)' soon became a well-understood and frequently used term for prehistoric and Romano-British (pre-Saxon) fields and field systems in England, particularly on the chalk downs of Wessex and Sussex. It dominates the literature of early British agriculture until *c.* 1960, reaching its apotheosis perhaps in its never-to-be-repeated appearance on the OS *Map of Roman Britain* (3rd ed. 1956) and in Piggott's attempts,[4] unrepeated until 1976 (see below), to show the total distribution of 'Celtic' field systems in Britain. The ubiquity of 'Celtic' fields persists in Bowen's *Ancient Fields* (1961) where, for example, the fields on Skomer Island (Fig. 21) and on Dartmoor (Plate IIIa) are included under that title (*ibid.* p. 14) as well as the more familiar chalkland remains. Although the booklet's title might be taken to imply a slight hesitancy in the use of 'Celtic' as the appropriate adjective for early fields, the subject matter includes much else besides 'Celtic fields' *sensu* Crawford, notably strip lynchets and indeed a new type of 'Celtic' field, the 'Celtic long field' with square enclosed ends (*ibid.*, pp. 24–5).

The term continued to be used throughout the 1960s and indeed persists today but increasing unease has been felt as the racial connotations of 'Celtic' have been seen to be inappropriate with the back-dating of many surviving field systems to the second millennium BC and with the recognition of a wide variety of ancient field types and land allotment systems, both later and probably earlier than conventional 'Celtic' fields and occurring in an enormous range of environments all over Britain. The main reason for the term persisting is, nevertheless, that it is both still useful and because no such convenient term has been coined to supplant it. The fact is, however, that the field data are now too varied and extensive in time and place to be covered by a single all-embracing term and hence the editorial prohibition on the use of the phrase 'Celtic field' here.

The need for a widely understood nomenclature is nevertheless crucial if disciplined study is to develop. Accepting that any new terminology is bound to be more complex than the umbrella simplicity of 'Celtic fields', various alternatives suggest themselves:

1. Based on absolute or relative chronology, e.g. Late Neolithic fields, fourteenth-century BC fields, post-Beaker fields, pre-bog fields.

2. Based on morphological characteristics, e.g. small, square fields, geometric fields, planned fields.

3. Based on structural characteristics, e.g. lynchetted fields, stone-walled fields.

[4] S. Piggott, 'Native economies...', in I. A. Richmond (ed.), *Roman and Native in North Britain*, Edinburgh, p. 8, Map 1.

4. Based on regional characteristics, e.g. Wessex fields, Thames valley fields.

5. Based on functional characteristics, e.g. arable fields, pastoral fields.

6. Based on associations, e.g. villa fields.

The tentative typology for Highland Zone fields suggested above (p. 178) is an amalgam of methods 2, 3 and 4 with method 1 implications. A similar, unsuccessful attempt for the Lowland Zone, e.g. Wessex-type, Sussex-type ancient fields (= 'Celtic' fields) was made in draft but the evidence was found to be at one and the same time too varied and too imprecise for helpful definition at the moment. It might be more useful to try to define types of field or even land-use systems on a regional basis rather than individual field types, e.g. geometric or planned land allotment. Nevertheless, it will remain important in such broader analyses to identify the arable areas, without prejudice as to whether or not they were divided into units of what we can recognize as fields.

It is interesting and possibly unfortunate that, just at the moment when the term and the concept of 'Celtic' fields are under stringent review, there should appear a major study of pre-medieval fields in Holland which gives the term, used without inverted commas, a new lease of life.[5] Brongers's work is of great significance for the recognition of early fields as such and for their interpretation as the arable element in a working economic system. Its presentation now in magnificently published form is without peer not only in Britain but also in Europe, and advances significantly the study of early fields in their continental context beyond the stage synthesized ten years ago by Müller-Wille.[6] "The term Celtic field...does not indicate a typologically or chronologically homogeneous archaeological phenomenon, but is used as a *terminus technicus* indicating land divisions forming a more or less checkboard-like pattern in which the elements are surrounded by low banks" (*ibid.*, p. 7) – the definition is very similar to Crawford's (above p. 269) though the 'low banks' element is not sufficiently comprehensive, either for reference to the original structure or to present archaeological appearance, to embrace all instances of what have been called 'Celtic' fields in Britain (which include, for example, varieties of ditched and walled boundaries). In his Appendix IV (*ibid.*, pp. 102–3), Brongers proposes a typological classification of the 'Celtic' fields in north-west Europe, elaborating his definition thus: "A Celtic field is a prehistoric parcelling system of which the parcels are (almost) completely sur-

[5] J. A. Brongers, *Air Photography and Celtic Field Research in The Netherlands*, Nederlandse Oudheden 6, ROB, Amersfoort, 1976.

[6] M. Müller-Wille, *Eisenzeitliche Fluren in den festländischen Nordseegebieten*, Siedlung und Landschaft in Westfalen, 5, Munster, 1965.

rounded by low banks consisting of stones, sand, or a mixture of the two, and laid out for agricultural purposes."

Although, despite the title of his appendix, Brongers is clearly writing primarily about the 'Celtic' fields in Holland, his characterization of the features by which he proposes to classify 'Celtic' fields typologically is the most detailed published so far and is worth repeating in full.

" (a) Regular or Irregular
Because many Celtic field plans are still incomplete no large-scale attempt has been made to analyse other plans...Even so, the occurrence of strip-like elements is obvious in some Celtic fields, as had already been indicated by Curwen, whereas it is equally clear that they are not found in other Celtic fields. The occurrence of strips seems to me a distinctly cultural phenomenon, so that the symbols 'R' (Regular = strips) and 'I' (Irregular = no strips) could be introduced to distinguish between Regular and Irregular Celtic fields.

(b) Staggered angles
In some cases the four banks around a parcel meet in three instead of four corners thus leaving, as it were, an 'entrance' to the parcel. This seems to be another distinctly cultural phenomenon and could be indicated by an 's'.

(c) Tracks closely connected with the banks
Sometimes tracks have been made through a Celtic field so that their sides are formed by a series of connected banks belonging to the Celtic field. This, again, seems to be the result of human activities and could be indicated by a 't'. Roads running along the outside of the Celtic field, although determining the shape of the system, like the one at Vaassen, do not belong to this category.

(d) Lynchets
Sudden differences in height in arable land on sloping terrain causing the formation of terraces are called lynchets. The terrace boundaries run parallel to the contour lines. Although the environment (the slope) seems to be the decisive factor, yet no lynchets were found on fairly steeply sloping grounds in the Netherlands, a sufficient reason to introduce the symbol 'L' for lynchets.

(e) Stones at the corners of the parcels or at the edge of a Celtic field
Sometimes larger stones are found at the corner of a parcel or at the boundary of the Celtic field itself, obviously meant to mark these spots. Although the application of these stones may have been suggested by the abundance of stones in the subsoil, it may also be considered a typological factor: the stones served as markers during the lay-out of the Celtic field. Their occurrence is indicated by the symbol 'c' (corners).

(f) Composition of the banks
Sometimes the banks of a Celtic field consist almost completely of stones (1), sometimes almost completely of sand (3), whereas an intermediate form – a sandy bank containing many stones – is also possible (2). Although in this case the subsoil is obviously the decisive factor, yet the numbers '1', '2', and '3' might prove useful, as a bank mainly consisting of stones could hardly indicate humus transport.

Theoretically, a combination of these characteristic features could result in ninety-six different categories of Celtic fields in Europe, but it may be assumed that a complete inventory of all Celtic fields will reveal that not all possibilities have materalized. Most Celtic fields in the Netherlands belong to the R 3 type: they have clear, strip-like structures with banks consisting predominantly of sand. In a few cases they belong to the R 2 type; the Celtic field that was formerly supposed to be the legendary town of Hunsow belongs to this category. R 3 c is found once; R 2 c occurs slightly more frequently. Lynchets (L), staggered angles (s), tracks(t), and banks consisting almost completely of stones (I) have not (yet) been found in the Netherlands.

The classification given above is based exclusively on those qualities of the Celtic fields that are directly perceptible to the human eye. Dating elements and invisible structures below the surface, like ditches or palisades along or underneath the banks, are left out of consideration. If, in future, these last-mentioned aspects can also be taken into account, the regional differences in this apparently homogeneous group of archaeological monuments will become even more obvious."

This typological approach does not, however, prevent some important conclusions being reached as a result of the whole study. Brongers summarizes his work (*ibid.*, p. 74) as demonstrating that

"a particular agricultural method was in use on the sandy soils of the northeast part of the Netherlands between *c.* 600 BC and *c.* AD 200. This method is called the Celtic field system; it represents a fundamental change in agricultural technology to meet the growing demands of an expanding economy attended by population increase and perhaps regional specialization.

The important new features introduced in the Celtic field system were: multiple-course rotation and regeneration of soil fertility by means of humus addition to the fields. The characteristic banks were caused by the removal of clearance debris and exhaused infertile arable soil to the boundaries of the parcels. With regard to the shape of the elements, one has to distinguish between a clearance phase and a cultivation phase. The clearance phase is responsible for the shape of the larger striplike elements in the parcelling system, while the subdivision into smaller square units took place during the cultivation phase. It is incorrect to classify the Dutch Celtic fields in the group of *Blockfluren*; the complexes are not haphazard arrangements of small individual square parcels, but systems with a clear macro-structure."

Brongers also provides (*ibid.*, Fig. 1) a map showing the "Distribution of Celtic fields in northwest Europe" – a useful and brave attempt based on Müller-Wille's 1965 *corpus*, with additions from more recent published work and current workers. For Britain, the distribution is essentially as in Piggott's 1958 Map, with major additions in the Fens and East Anglia. It emphasizes by implication the main point of this note, i.e. that one of the prerequisites for further useful developments in the understanding of the land use, particularly of the arable fields, in prehistoric Europe is for an agreed, international terminology. For

'Celtic' fields especially, we must either drop the term altogether, even as a technical one; or define it very specifically and restrict its use to that definition for, despite Brongers's Fig. 1, the prehistoric fields in Drenthe, Store Vildemose, Sussex, and Dartmoor *are* different phenomena; or we can accept its use merely as a general term for any early (pre-medieval) type of land-parcelling. The first alternative is used in this Volume; the last seems pointless when 'prehistoric', 'Bronze Age', 'first millennium', third century BC', 'Roman' or just 'early' or even 'ancient' provide more accurate adjectives than 'Celtic'; and if, as seems likely, the second is used, then inevitably 'Celtic' fields' must be accompanied in any discussion of early agrarian history in Europe by a multitude of other field-types too.

APPENDIX 3

A NOTE ON EARLY FIELD SYSTEMS IN THE ISLES OF SCILLY

The significance of the Isles of Scilly for the study of early agriculture is understated in the main body of the text (p. 184). Reference to them is not full enough, the evidence at the time of writing being summarized in the revision of Lady Fox' synthesis, *South-West England, 3500 BC–AD 600* (1973) and, subsequently, by Ashbee's authoritative *Ancient Scilly: from the First Farmers to the Early Christians* (1974).

It was only when the author visited the Scillies early in 1977 and in 1978 that the extent and nature of the field evidence there began to be apparent to him, a realization enhanced by detailed discussions and fieldwork with, and some interim publications by, Professor Charles Thomas (Institute of Cornish Studies). Though this note clearly breaks the 1975 horizon of the main text, its justification is that the relevant evidence in the Isles of Scilly has simply not been appreciated, and certainly not in print, as is its due. The purpose here is merely to emphasize the existence of a very important body of evidence, extensive, sometimes stratified, often associated with other features, and marvellously preserved, which was, through ignorance, omitted from the text.

Crawford of course drew attention to the boulder walls on Samson Flats fifty years ago,[1] but, as Ashbee's synthesis makes clear,[2] his perception has been shared by virtually no-one since. Exceptions are Ashbee's own long-continuing work on Halangy Down, St Mary's – though even there the field system and its associations "have not as yet been surveyed in detail"[3] – and Charles Thomas's work, both on present islands and submerged land surfaces, now reaching the stage of publication.[4] As Ashbee makes clear, however, Crawford followed

[1] O. G. S. Crawford, 'Lyonesse', *Ant.*, I, 1927, pp. 5–14.
[2] P. Ashbee, *Ancient Scilly*, pp. 52–66, 213–15.
[3] *Ibid.*, p. 213. Professor Thomas and the author completed a detailed survey in 1978.
[4] C. Thomas, 'Recent fieldwork in the Isles of Scilly', *Corn. Arch.*, 14, 1975, pp. 87–94; 'Samson: an Outline History of Settlement', dup. typescript, Institute of Cornish Studies, 1977; 'Pre-Norman Fields in Cornwall and Scilly', in Bowen and P. J. Fowler, *Early Land Allotment*. Professor Thomas and this author are now working towards the publication of a more detailed consideration of the subject matter of this

Borlase in remarking on the signal fact about the field evidence on the Isles of Scilly, i.e. that prehistoric stone walls are to be seen on all the larger islands and some of the smaller uninhabited ones".[5] Nor are they just stone walls: they are of various construction and they form systems of fields.

From Ashbee's diligent collation of previous observations and his own and Thomas's fieldwork, we can summarize the recorded evidence as occurring above and below high water-mark on these islands: Arthur, Bryher, Gugh, Samson, St Agnes, St Martin's, St Mary's, Tean and Tresco. To the detail amassed by Ashbee, we can now add further information about Heathy Hill, Bryher;[6] White Island and other areas; St Martin's; and, above all, Samson (Fig. 50).

White Island, St Martin's,[7] possesses the remains of a field system or systems with several points of particular interest. The fields themselves apparently form a system of parallel plots some 23 m wide across the neck of the island where one upstanding division, of small, upright stones, is partly buried in peat and eroded by the sea at its eastern end. It, and other walls, disappear under the shingle and sand just above present high water-mark along Porth Morran and two continuations of them extend to, and in one case beyond, low water-mark. Another wall at right angles is also below low water-mark, while the fourth side of a boulder-walled enclosure just to the north-west is also eroded at the present, low cliff edge. At least one of at least six small mounds nearby, probably clearance cairns, is partly covered by peat. Just uphill of them is an entrance tomb. Further lines of small standing stones demarcating fields protrude from peat on St Martin's Island proper, notably immediately outside the promontory fort on Burnt Hill between Bull's Porth and Stony Porth on the north coast, and over much of Chapel Down on the east coast. At least two phases are apparent in the latter case, one probably relating to cairns.

Samson is a gem of field archaeology. The walls on the Flats on the east side (Fig. 50) are structurally more complex than is apparent from Crawford's air photograph,[8] being of at least two phases of construction and containing non-local stones in their core. While individual walls have been smashed up in the high-tide zone, the system continued westwards on what is now a buried land surface beneath the sand-dune

Note than is possible here. Cf. also C. Thomas in P. H. Sawyer (ed.), *Medieval Settlement*, 1976, pp. 145–51.

[5] Ashbee, *op. cit.*, 53. On pp. 53 and 54 Ashbee discusses not entirely unfavourably Crawford's later idea that the walls on Samson Flats could have been fish-weirs, a suggestion subsequently added to by Piggott who opted for a medieval date. As far as the walls discussed in this footnote are concerned, the idea can be discarded altogether.

[6] Thomas, 'Recent fieldwork', pp. 92–4.

[7] *Ibid.*, pp. 87–90; plus author's observations.   [8] Crawford, *op. cit.*, Pl. III.

'cliffs'. On the island itself, all the slopes of South Hill especially are an excellently preserved palimpsest of field systems of at least four phases, tied, literally as well as chronologically, at one end to the northernmost of the entrance graves on the hill-top and at the other to mid-nineteenth-century, post-desertion walls to control grazing.[9] The relationships between the different systems, so far merely observed to exist and not yet elucidated, and the range of both field type and field divisions (walls of various structure, lines of stones, lynchets) in so small an area make this, and indeed the whole island and its foreshore, an area of outstanding scientific interest.

For present purposes, one other aspect of the agrarian history of Scilly needs to be emphasized. In several cases there is a direct physical link between fields and chamber tombs; and in others, even if such man-made evidence is not superficially visible, there is at least an implied relationship between the various stone structures built for food production and burial respectively (Fig. 50). Examples are on Bryher, Gugh, Samson (North and South Hills), St Martin's, St Mary's (Halangy Down, north and south of the 'Guardianship' settlement), and Tean. The dating of the funerary monuments of Scilly is a vexed question but a date from c. 2000 BC is currently accepted for the entrance graves.[10] It is very likely, therefore, that the Isles of Scilly possess tracts of preserved landscape as laid out in the first half of the second millennium BC. The insular context of this remarkable occurrence, certainly among the earliest, physically surviving land allotment in Britain, makes its potential all the higher.

[9] Thomas, op. cit. Detailed field survey, but only of the area illustrated in fig. 50, was made by Thomas and the author in 1978. See now Ant., 43, 1979, pp. 175–89.
[10] Ashbee, op. cit., p. 64.

APPENDIX 4

SETTLEMENT, ECONOMY, ANCIENT FIELDS
AND LAND ALLOTMENT

As stated below (p. 281), bibliographically this volume comes up to December 1975; indeed, the end of that year appears to be as real an 'horizon' in studies of British agrarian prehistory as is ever possible in academic matters. Two conferences, both producing published volumes of papers, were held early in 1976, and both take the study of agrarian prehistory to a stage beyond that represented in this volume.

A conference at the University of Newcastle-upon-Tyne in January 1976 was entitled 'Settlement in the later Neolithic and earlier Bronze Age'. It has resulted in a volume of papers published under the title *Settlement and Economy in the Third and Second Millennia BC*.[1] Much of the matter is of general relevance to this volume and of particular significance are papers on "Fenedge land management in the Bronze Age: an interim report on the excavations at Fengate, Peterborough, 1971–75" (*ibid.*, pp. 29–49) and "Gwithian, Cornwall: some notes on the evidence for Neolithic and Bronze Age settlement" (*ibid.*, pp. 51–79). Both papers represent the fullest statements so far on these two key areas and advance their study beyond the discussion here (above, pp. 239 and 185). Other specific material not available at the time of writing includes new evidence on flint-mining at Grimes' Graves (pp. 101–11, cf. p. 138 above), Neolithic activity in north Northumberland (*ibid.*, 113–42, cf. p. 106 above), settlement data from Meldon Bridge, Peeblesshire (pp. 151–79), Islay, Argyll (pp. 181–207), Northton, Isle of Harris (*ibid.*, pp. 221–9), and Skara Brae (*ibid.*, pp. 233–50), and, of particular relevance, ard-marks and sub-peat field walls from respectively, a Beaker horizon at Rosinish, Benbecula, Outer Hebrides (*ibid.*, pp. 209–19), and Black Moss, Achnacree, Argyll. (*ibid.*, pp. 283–7).

A second conference held at the University of Bristol in May, 1976, was more specifically concerned with early fields and land allotment, as indicated by the title of the resulting volume.[2] It contains twenty-eight

[1] Edited by Colin Burgess and Roget Miket, British Archaeological Reports 33, Oxford, 1976.
[2] Edited by H. C. Bowen and P. J. Fowler, *Early Land Allotment*, British Archaeological Reports, 48, Oxford, 1978.

papers and some ninety line drawings, many of the latter contributing to the best available *corpus* of field plans of early field systems in Britain – and indeed Europe. Bibliographically, a conscious effort was made to continue from the references here, terminating at the end of 1975, on to the autumn of 1977 soon after which *Early Land Allotment* finally went to press. It is a sequel to this volume too in the sense that its topographical survey is much more thorough than was possible here (above, pp. 95–129): counties and areas covered by surveys of the available evidence up to the end of 1976 in it include Cornwall and Scilly; Dartmoor; north Somerset, the new county of Avon, and Gloucestershire; Wessex; the Berkshire Downs; Surrey; Sussex; the Upper Thames valley; Essex; Norfolk; south Yorkshire and north Nottinghamshire; Craven, North Yorks.; the North York Moors; north Cumbria; Caernarvonshire; Isle of Arran, Bute; and County Mayo, Ireland. In addition discussions include the Somerset Levels; the Wessex linear ditch system; hedges on early field boundaries; Roman fields and medieval furlongs; Carn Brea and Stannon Down, Cornwall; and ard-marks in Surrey, Hampshire, and south Gloucestershire (now Avon). Curiously, the last three examples all arose in rescue work on motorways. There is also a brief, general review of trends since the publication of H. C. Bowen's *Ancient Fields* in 1961, and an important discussion of pit alignments, an aspect of land division barely touched on in this volume.

Much of the material from these two conferences is new and arises from current work. It was not available, certainly in published and quotable form, when this *Agrarian History* was being written. The study of early, and particularly pre-Roman, agriculture in Britain can now be considered in the light of all three volumes which, together, provide a sort of trilogy centred around the mid 1970s. The two conference volumes fittingly mark the early stages of a renaissance in this field, of which the characteristics happily appear to be a return to the basic evidence on and in the ground, i.e. field survey, and, unlike the conceptual framework for the acquisition of much of the evidence reviewed in this volume, the adoption of problem-orientated approaches related specifically to the answering of questions in agrarian prehistory.

SITE INDEX AND BIBLIOGRAPHY

For individual sites in Scotland, reference should be made to the comprehensive Bibliography by the editor in A. L. F. Rivet (ed.), *The Iron Age in Northern Britain*, Edinburgh, 1966, pp. 131–47; to R. W. Feachem, *A Guide to Prehistoric Scotland*, London, 1963; to E. MacKie, *Scotland: An Archaeological Guide*, London, 1975; and to the County *Inventories* by the Royal Commission on Ancient and Historical Monuments (RCAM) (Scotland). The similar *Inventories* by RCAM (Wales) and C. Houlder, *Wales: An Archaeological Guide*, London, 1974, serve variously as sources of and as leads to the original material. For England, the Royal Commission on Historical Monuments (RCHM) County volumes, especially the recently completed *Dorset*, the recently started *Northamptonshire* and *Gloucestershire*, and the current series of non-county monographs (*A Matter of Time, Peterborough*) provide basic sources, as do some recent volumes of *Victoria County History*, e.g. *Wiltshire* I, parts i and ii, 1957, 1973. J. Hawkes, *A Guide to the Prehistoric and Roman Monuments and Wales*, London, 1951, rev. ed. 1973, has a gazetteer but no bibliography. Site references are included in the selective but authoritative N. Thomas, *A Guide to Prehistoric England*, London, 1960, rev. ed. 1977.

The bibliographical situation has now been conveniently brought under control, while this text was being prepared, for the bulk of the printed material on which it depends is referenced in the following. B. Cunliffe, *Iron Age Communities in Britain*. London 1974: pp. 357–62, appendix C: list of principal sites (with references); and pp. 365–79, bibliography. D. W. Harding, *The Iron Age in Lowland Britain*, London, 1974: pp. 234–49, bibliography. A. J. Challis, and D. W. Harding, *Later Prehistory from the Trent to the Tyne*, British Archaeological Reports, 20, Oxford, 1975: pp. 192–223, bibliography. J. G. Evans, *The Environment of Early Man in the British Isles*. London, 1975: pp. 198–209, bibliography.

Both the following Site Index and the Bibliography are therefore selective. Both are deliberately biased towards sites and publications with an *agrarian* significance and, although there is a large overlap with the bibliographies in the four publications just listed, here it is not so comprehensive.

The Site Index contains at least one significant reference, from which other sources can be found, for all the main sites mentioned in the text (minor sites or single mentions are otherwise referenced in footnotes), and it also includes a few sites not mentioned in the text.

The Bibliography lists the main publications on, or directly relevant to, agrarian history in later prehistoric Britain, i.e. the primary sources and original studies and the main synoptic works. Publications with good bibliographies are starred and no attempt is made to repeat all their sources, e.g. all the palaeobotanical research behind J. G. Evans, *The Environment of Early Man in the British Isles*, London, 1975, is not referenced again here. Sufficient reference, it is hoped, is given to a few general studies dealing with the changing overall interpretation of the chronological framework and the processes of cultural history in later prehistoric Britain, but, again, the detail behind them in, for example, pottery studies, is not this Bibliography's concern. Articles in symposium-type books are not separately referenced unless the article is particularly significant or the book as a whole is not directly relevant.

As stated above (p. 279), the opportunity was taken through the author's joint editorship, with H. C. Bowen, of *Early Land Allotment* to include there bibliographical coverage of 1976–77 as a sequel to that below (pp. 289–98) up to the end of 1975. It has been possible, early in 1980 at page proof stage, selectively to add some significant publications to extend the bibliography to cover 1978–79. Space does not allow this addition (p. 298) to repeat references in *Early Land Allotment*, to which the reader is referred for the period 1976–77, nor of course is the substance of these additional references incorporated in the text.

SITE INDEX

Abbey Farm, Grasswall, Herefords. *Trans. Woolhope Naturalist's Fld Club*, 33, 1950, pp. 112–17.

Allasdale, Isle of Barra. *Proc. Soc. Ant. Scot.* 87, 1953, pp. 80–105.

All Cannings Cross, Wilts. Cunnington, M. E., ... *All Cannings Cross* ... Devizes, 1923.

Alnham (High Knowes), Northumb. *Arch. Ael.*, 44, 1966, pp. 5–48.

Amberley Mount, Sussex. *Sussex Arch. Coll.*, 104, 1966, pp. 6–25.

Amesbury (barrow G.71). *Proc. Prehist. Soc.*, 33, 1967, pp. 336–66.

Ardleigh (Vinces Farm), Essex. *Bulletin Colchester Arch. Gp.*, 13, part 1, 1970, pp. 1–26.

Bagendon, Glos. E. M. Clifford, *Bagendon: a Belgic Oppidum*, Cambridge, 1961.

Balevullin, Tiree. *Proc. Soc. Ant. Scot.*, 96, 1963, pp. 155–83.

Balksbury Camp, Hants. *Papers and Proc. Hants. Fld Club*, 26, 1969, pp. 21–55.

Barbury, Wilts. *Wilts. Arch. Nat. Hist. Mag.*, 58, 1963, pp. 394–402.

Barley, Herts. *Proc. Camb. Ant. Soc.*, 54, 1961, pp. 22–46.

Barmston, E. R., Yorks. *East Riding Archaeologist*, 1, part i, 1968, pp. 11–26.

Barnack, Northants. *Proc. Prehist. Soc.*, 1, 1935, pp. 156; *Ant.* 47, 1973, pp. 145–6.

Barton Hill Farm, Beds. *Bed. Arch. J.*, 1, 1962, pp. 1–24.

Bathampton Down, Somerset. *Trans. Bristol and Glos. Arch. Soc.*, 86, 1967, pp. 42–59.

Belle Tout, Sussex. *Proc. Prehist. Soc.*, 36, 1970, pp. 312–79.

Bigbury, Kent. *Arch. Cant.*, 48, 1936, pp. 151–68.

Big Moor, Baslow, Derbs. *Trans. Hunterian Arch. Soc.*, 10, 1971, pp. 5–13.

Blackbury Castle, Devon. *Proc. Devon Arch. Explor. Soc.*, 5, parts 2–3, 1954–5, pp. 43–67.

Blackpatch, Sussex. *Sussex Arch. Coll.*, 91, 1953, pp. 69–83.

Blagdon Copse, Hants. *Papers and Proc. Hants. Fld Club*, 23, 1968, pp. 81–9.

Blewburton Hill, Berks. *Berks. Arch. J.*, 46, 1942, pp. 97–104; 50, 1947, pp. 4–29; 53, 1955, pp. 21–64; 57, 1959, pp. 52–73.

Bodrifty, Cornwall. *Arch. J.* 113, 1956, pp. 1–32.

Boscombe Down East, Wilts. *Wilts. Arch. Nat. Hist. Mag.*, 47, 1936, pp. 466–89.

Boscombe Down West, Wilts. *Wilts. Arch. Nat. Hist. Mag.*, 54, 1951, pp. 123–68.

Braidwood Fort, E. Lothian. *Proc. Soc. Ant. Scot.*, 91, 1958, pp. 61–77.

Brean Down, Somerset. *Proc. Bristol Univ. Spelaeol. Soc.*, 9, 1960–1, pp. 67–136; P. J. Fowler (ed.), *Recent Work in Rural Archaeology*, Fig. 8.5.

Bredon Hill, Glos. *Arch. J.* 95, 1938, pp. 1–111.

Breiddin, Mont. *Arch. Camb.* 92, 1937, pp. 86–128; C. R. Musson, *forthcoming*.

Broomwood, St Paul's Cray, Kent. *Arch. Cant.*, 76, 1961, pp. 134–42.

Budbury, Wilts. *Wilts. Arch. Nat. Hist. Mag.*, 65, 1970, pp. 108–66.

Burradon, Northumb. *Arch. Ael.*, 48, 1970, pp. 51–95.

Bury Hill, Hants. *Papers and Proc. Hants. Fld Club*, 14, 1940, pp. 291–337.

Butcombe, Somerset. *Proc. Bristol Univ. Spelaeol. Soc.*, 12, 1970, pp. 169–94; P. J. Fowler (ed.), *Recent Work in Rural Archaeology*, pp. 121–36.

Caerau, Caerns. *Ant. J.*, 16, 1937, pp. 295–320.

Cair Mynydd, Caerns. *Ant. J.*, 39, 1959, pp. 33–60.

Camulodunum. *Rep. Research Comm. Soc. Ant. Lond.*, 14, 1947.

Carloggas (St Mawgan-in-Pydar), Cornwall. *Arch. J.*, 113, 1956, pp. 33–81.

Castell Odo, Caerns. *Arch. Camb.*, 109, 1960, pp. 78–135.

Casterley Camp, Wilts. *Wilts. Arch. Nat. Hist. Mag.*, 38, 1913, pp. 53–105.

Castle Dore, Cornwall. *J. Roy. Inst. Cornwall*, 1, 1951, pp. 1–119; *Corn. Arch.*, 10, 1971, pp. 49–54.

Chalbury, Dorset. *Ant. J.*, 23, 1943, pp. 98–121.

Challacombe, Devon. *Proc. Devon Arch. Explor. Soc.*, 4, part 4, 1951, pp. 102–5.

Chalton, Hants. *Ant. J.*, 50, 1970, pp. 1–13; 53, 1973, 173–90.

Charleston Brow, Sussex. *Sussex Arch. Coll.*, 74, 1933, pp. 164–80.

Charmy Down, nr Bath, Somerset. W. F. Grimes, *Excavations on Defence Sites 1939–45*, 1, London, 1960.

Chinnor, Oxon. *Ant. J.*, 31, 1951, pp. 132–48.

Chisenbury, Wilts. *Wilts. Arch. Nat. Hist. Mag.*, 46, 1932, pp. 1–3.

Chysauster, Cornwall. *Archaeologia*, 83, 1933, pp. 237–84.

Cissbury, Sussex. *Ant. J.*, 11, 1931, pp. 14–36.

Clettraval, N. Uist. *Proc. Prehist. Soc.*, 14, 1948, pp. 46–125.

Clickhimin, Shetland. J. R. C. Hamilton, *Excavations at...*, London, 1968.

Clovelly Dykes, Devon. *Arch. J.*, 109, 1952, pp. 1–22.

Cock Hill, Sussex. *Sussex Arch. Coll.*, 99, 1961, pp. 78–101.

Colsterworth, Lincs. Grimes, W. F. in S. S. Frere (ed.), *Problems of the Iron Age in Southern Britain*, 1961, pp. 21–3.

Coygan Camp, Carmarthen. G. J. Wainwright, *Coygan Camp*, Cambrian Arch. Soc., 1967

Credenhill Camp, Heref. *Arch. J.*, 127, 1970, pp. 82–129.

Crickley Hill, Glos. *Ant.*, XLIV, 1972, pp. 49–52; XLVII, 1973, pp. 56–9.

Croft Ambrey, Herefords. S. C. Stanford, *Croft Ambrey*, privately printed, 1974.

Danebury, Hants. *Ant. J.*, 51, 1971, pp. 240–52; 53, 1973, Fig. 2.

Dean Moor, Devon. *Trans. Devon. Ass.*, 89, 1957, pp. 18–77.

Dinorben, Denbigh. W. Gardner and H. N. Savory, *Dinorben*, Cardiff, 1964; *Ant.*, XLV, 1971, pp. 251–61.

Down Barn West, Wilts. *Wilts. Arch. Nat. Hist. Mag.*, 60, 1965, pp. 52–74.

Dragonby, Lincs. *Ant. J.*, 50, 1970, pp. 222–45.

Draughton, Northants. W. F. Grimes in S. S. Frere (ed.), *Problems of the Iron Age in Southern Britain*, 1961, pp. 21–3.

Dray's Ditches, Beds. *Ant. J.*, 41, 1961, pp. 32–43.

Driffield, E. R. Yorks. *Yorks. Arch. J.*, 40, 1960, pp. 183–91.

Dun Ardtreck, Skye. E. Mackie, in P. J. Fowler (ed.), 1975, 72–92.

Dun Mor Vaul, Tiree, Argyll. *Proc. Prehist. Soc.*, 31, 1965, pp. 93–146.

Durrington Walls, Wilts. *Rep. Research Comm. Soc. Ant. Lond.*, 29.

Eaton Heath, Norwich, Norfolk. *Arch. J.*, 130, 1973, pp. 1–43.

Ebsbury, Wilts. C. Thomas (ed.), *Rural Settlement in Roman Britain*, 1966, p. 65.

Eldon's Seat, Dorset. *Proc. Prehist. Soc.*, 34, 1968, 191–237.

Failand Ridge, Somerset. *Proc. Bristol Univ. Spelaeol. Soc.*, 4, 1931, p. 34; 6, 1933, p. 139.

Farley Mount, Hants. H. C. Bowen in C. Thomas (ed.), *Rural Settlement in Roman Britain*, Pl. VI.

Fengate, Peterborough, Northants. *Arch. J.*, 100, 1943, 188–223; RCHM, *Peterborough New Town...*, London, 1969; F. Pryor, *Excavation at Fengate...First Report*, Arch. Monogr. 3 ROM, Toronto, 1974; *op. cit.,...Second Report*, Arch. Monogr. 5 ROM, Toronto, 1978.

Ffridd Faldwyn, Mont. *Arch. Camb.*, 97, 1942, pp. 1–57.

Fifield Bavant, Wilts. *Wilts. Arch. Nat. Hist. Mag.*, 42, 1924, pp. 457–96.

Figsbury, Wilts. *Wilts. Arch. Nat. Hist Mag.*, 43, 1925, pp. 48–58.

Findon Park, Sussex. *Ant. J.*, 8, 1928, pp. 449–60.

Fishbourne, Sussex. *Rep. Research Comm. Soc. Ant. Lond.*, 26, 27, 1971.

Foale's Arrishes, Devon. *Proc. Prehist. Soc.*, 18, 1952, 55–84.

Frilford, Oxon. *Oxoniensia*, 4, 1939, pp. 1–80.

Fyfield (and Overton) Down, Wilts. *Wilts. Arch. Nat. Hist. Mag.*, 62, 1967, pp. 16–33; P. J. Fowler (ed.), *Recent Work in Rural Archaeology*, pp. 121–36.

Garn Boduan, Caerns. *Arch. J.*, 94, 1960, pp. 1–39.

Garston Slack, Yorks. *Curr. Arch.*, 51, 1975, pp. 104–16.

Glastonbury, Som. A. Bulleid, and H. St. G. Gray, *The Glastonbury Lake Village*, 1, 2. Taunton, 1911, 1917; *Proc. Bristol Univ. Spelaeol. Soc.*, 12.2, 1970, pp. 143–67; D. L. Clarke (ed.), *Models in Archaeology*, pp. 801–69.

Glenachan Rig, Peebles. *Proc. Soc. Ant. Scot.*, 92, 1959, pp. 15–24.

Goldherring, Sancreed, Cornwall. *Corn. Arch.*, 8, 1969, pp. 5–39.

Grassington, Yorks. *Yorks. Arch. J.*, 33, 1936–8, pp. 166–74.

Great Woodbury, Wilts. *Proc. Prehist. Soc.*, 6, 1940, pp. 30–111.

Grim's Ditch, Hants./Dorset/Wilts. *Ant.*, XVIII, 1944, pp. 65–71; H. C. Bowen in P. J. Fowler (ed.), *Recent Work in Rural Archaeology*, Fig. 3.4; RCHM, *Dorset*, V, 1975.

Grim's Ditch, Oxon. *Oxoniensia* 33, 1969, pp. 1–13.

Grimthorpe, E. R. Yorks. *Proc. Prehist. Soc.*, 34, 1965, pp. 148–90.

Gussage All Saints, Dorset. *Ant.*, XLVII, 1973, pp. 109–30; L, 1976, pp. 32–9.

Gwithian, Cornwall. *Proc. West Cornwall Fld Club*, 2, 1961, pp. 200–15; *Corn. Arch.*, 1, 1962, pp. 17–60, 61–84; C. Thomas, 'Bronze Age spade marks at...,' in A. Gailey and A. Fenton (eds.), *The Spade in Northern and Atlantic Europe*, pp. 10–17.

Hambledon Hill, Dorset. RCHM, *Dorset*, III, 1970, pp. 82–3.

Ham Hill, Somerset. *Proc. Somerset Arch. Nat. Hist. Soc.*, 70, 1925, pp. 104–16; 71, 1926, pp. 57–76; 72, 1927, pp. 55–68.

Handley Down, Dorset. RCHM, *Dorset*, V, 1975, pp. 70–1.

Harehope, Peebles. *Proc. Soc. Ant. Scot.*, 93, 1960, pp. 174–91.

Harrow Hill, Sussex. *Sussex Arch. Coll.*, 78, 1937, pp. 230–52.

Hawk's Hill, Surrey. *Surrey Arch. Coll.*, 62, 1965, pp. 1–43.

Hayhope Knowe, Roxburghs. *Proc. Soc. Ant. Scot.*, 83, 1942, pp. 45–67.

Heathery Burn Cave, County Durham. *Inv. Arch.*, 9th set, 1968; D. Britton in G. de G. Sieveking (ed.), *Prehistoric and Roman Studies*, London, 1971, pp. 20–38.

Heathrow, Middx. W. F. Grimes, in S. S. Frere (ed.), *Problems of the Iron Age in Southern Britain*, pp. 21–3.

Hembury, Devon. *Proc. Devon Arch. Explor. Soc.*, 1, 1930, pp. 40–63; 1, 1931, pp. 90–120; 1, 1932, pp. 162–90; 2, 1935, pp. 135–70.

Hengistbury Head, Hants. *Rep. Research Comm. Soc. Ant. Lond.*, 3, 1915.

High Rocks, Kent. *Sussex Arch. Coll.*, 98, 1960, pp. 173–221.

Hockwold, Cambs. *Roy. Geogr. Soc. Memoir* 5, 1970; *Proc. Camb. Ant. Soc.*, 60, 1967, pp. 39–80.

Hod Hill, Dorset. J. W. Brailsford, *Hod Hill*, 1, London, 1962; I. A. Richmond, *Hod Hill*, II, London, 1968.

Hog Cliff Hill, Dorset. *Proc. Dorset Nat. Hist. Arch. Soc.*, 81, 1959, p. 94.

Hollingbury Camp, Sussex. *Ant. J.*, 12, 1932, pp. 1–16.

Horridge Common, Devon. *Proc. Prehist. Soc.*, 35, 1969, pp. 223–5.

Howham Rings, Roxburghs. *Proc. Soc. Ant. Scot.*, 82, 1947–8, pp. 193–224.

Huckhoe, Northumb. *Arch. Ael.*, 37, 1959, 217–78; 46, 1968, pp. 293–5.

Hunsbury, Northants. *Arch. J.*, 93, 1937, pp. 57–100.

Ingram Hill, Northumb. *Arch. Ael.*, 20, 1942, pp. 110–33; 34, 1956, pp. 150–60.

Itford Hill, Sussex. *Proc. Prehist. Soc.*, 23, 1957, pp. 167–212; *Sussex Arch. Coll.*, 110, 1972, pp. 70–117.

Ivinghoe Beacon, Bucks. *Records of Bucks.*, 18, 1968, pp. 187–260.

Jarlshof, Shetland. J. R. C. Hamilton, *Excavations at...*, Edinburgh, 1956.

Kestor, Devon. *Trans. Devons. Assoc.*, 26, 1955, pp. 21–62.

Kilphedir, Sutherland. *Scott. Arch. Forum*, 3, 1971, pp. 1–10.

Kimmeridge, Dorset. *Arch. J.* 93, 1936, pp. 200–19; RCHM, *Dorset*, II, part 3, 1970.

Kingsdown Camp, Somerset. *Archaeologia*, 80, 1930, pp. 59–96.

Ladle Hill, Hants. *Ant.* v, 1931, pp. 474–85.

Lakenheath, Suffolk. *Proc. Camb. Ant. Soc.*, 42, 1949, 92–111.

Langford Downs, Oxon. *Oxoniensia*, 11–12, 1946–7, pp. 44–64.

Legis Tor, Devon. *Trans. Devon. Assoc.*, 75, 1943, 273–302.

Lidbury, Wilts. *Wilts. Arch. Nat. Hist. Mag.*, 40, 1917, pp. 12–36.

Liddington, Wilts. *Wilts. Arch. Nat. Hist. Mag.*, 38, 1914, pp. 576–84.

Linton, Cambs. *Proc. Camb. Ant. Soc.*, 46, 1952, pp. 31–42.

Little Solisbury, Somerset. *Proc. Bristol Univ. Spelaeol. Soc.*, 4, 1935, pp. 183–222; 8, 1957, pp. 18–29; 9, 1962, pp. 177–82; 11, 1968, p. 251.

Little Woodbury, Wilts. *Proc. Prehist. Soc.*, 6, 1940, pp. 30–111; 14, 1948, pp. 1–23; 15, 1949, pp. 156–68.

Llyn Cerrig Bach, Anglesey. C. Fox, *A Find of the Early Iron Age from...*, Cardiff, 1946.

Longbridge Deverill, Wilts. *Proc. Prehist. Soc.*, 27, 1961, 346–7.

Lundy Is. *Curr. Arch.* 16, 1969, pp. 138–42; *Ann. Rep. Lundy Fld Club* 20, 1970, pp. 14–17.

Lydney, Glos. *Rep. Research Comm. Soc. Ant. Lond.*, 9, 1932.

'Lyonesse' (Isles of Scilly) *Ant.* I, 1927, pp. 5–14; LIII, 1979, pp. 175–89.

Madmarston, Oxon. *Oxoniensia*, 25, 1960, pp. 3–48.

Maiden Castle, Dorset. *Rep. Research Comm. Soc. Ant. Lond.*, 12, 1943.

Mam Tor, Derby. *Derbys. Arch. J.*, 87, 1967, pp. 158–9; *Curr. Arch.* 27, 1971, pp. 100–2.

Mancombe Down, Wilts. *Wilts. Arch. Nat. Hist. Mag.*, 60, 1965, pp. 52–74.

Marden, Wilts. *Ant. J.*, 51, 1971, pp. 177–239.

Marnhull, Dorset. *Proc. Dorset Nat. Hist. Arch Soc.*, 72, 1951, pp. 20–75.

Martin Down Camp, Hants. A. L. Pitt-Rivers, *Cranborne Chase* 4, 1898; H. C. Bowen in P. J. Fowler (ed.), *Recent Work in Rural Archaeology*, pp. 44–56, esp. Fig. 3.4.

Maumbury Rings, Dorset. *Archaeologia*, 105, 1975, pp. 1–97.

Meare, Somerset. A. Bulleid and H. St. G. Gray, *The Meare Lake Village*, I and 2, Taunton, 1948, 1953; M. A. Cotton *ibid.* 3., Taunton, 1967; *Proc. Somerset Arch. Nat. Hist. Soc.*, 112, 1968, pp. 21–39.

Meon Hill, Hants. *Papers and Proc. Hants Fld Club*, 12, 1933, pp. 127–62; 13, 1935, pp. 7–54.

Milber Down Camp, Devon. *Proc. Devon Arch. Explor. Soc.*, 4, 1952, pp. 27–78.

Mildenhall Fen, Suff. *Ant. J.*, 16, 1936, pp. 29–50.

Millin Bay, County Down. A. E. P. Collins and D. M. Waterman, *Millin Bay*, Belfast, 1955.

Milton Loch, Kirkcudbrights. *Proc. Soc. Ant. Scot.*, 87, 1952–3, pp. 134–52; *Ant.* XLVIII, 1974, pp. 54–6.

Minchinhampton, Glos. E. M. Clifford, *Bagendon – a Belgic Oppidum*, Cambridge, 1961; H. C. Bowen in E. Fowler (ed.), *Field Survey in British Archaeology*, 39–41; RCHM, *Iron Age and Roman Monuments in the Gloucestershire Cotswolds*, London, 1977.

Minnis Bay, Kent. *Proc. Prehist. Soc.*, 9, 1943, pp. 28–47.

Mucking, Essex. M. H. and W. T. Jones, 'The crop mark sites at…' in R. Bruce-Mitford, *Recent Archaeological Excavations in Europe*, London, 1975, pp. 133–87.

Mynydd Bychan, Glam. *Arch. Camb.*, 103, 1954, pp. 85–108; 104, 1955, pp. 14–51.

New Barn Down, Sussex. *Sussex Arch. Coll.*, 75, 1934, pp. 137–70.

North Ferriby, E. R. Yorks. *Proc. Prehist. Soc.*, 13, 1947, 114–38; 31, 1965, pp. 1–24.

Ogbourne Down, Wilts. *Proc. Prehist. Soc.*, 8, 1942, pp. 48–61; P. J. Fowler in D. D. A. Simpson (ed.), *Economy and Settlement…*, Pl. 8.

Overton Down. Wilts. *See* Fyfield Down, Wilts.

Owslebury, Hants. *Ant. J.*, 48, 1968, pp. 18–31; 50, 1970, pp. 246–61.

Park Brow, Sussex. *Archaeologia* 76, 1927, pp. 1–40.

Pimperne, Dorset. *Ant.*, XXXVII, 1963, pp. 63–4.

Plumpton Plain, Sussex. *Proc. Prehist. Soc.*, I, 1935, pp. 16–59.

Porthmeor, Cornwall. *J. Roy. Inst. Cornwall*, 24, 1936, Appendix vol. no. 2.

Portland, Dorset. RCHM, *Dorset*, II, 1970, pp. 605–6.

Portsdown Hill, Hants. *Papers and Proc. Hants. Fld Club*, 24, 1967, pp. 42–58.

Preshute Down, Wilts. *Proc. Prehist. Soc.*, 8, 1942, pp. 48–61.

Quarley Hill, Hants. *Papers and Proc. Hants. Fld Club*, 14, 1939, pp. 136–94.

Rainsborough, Northants. *Proc. Prehist. Soc.*, 33, 1967, pp. 207–306.

Rams Hill, Berks. R. Bradley and A. Ellison, *Rams Hill*, Brit. Arch. Rep. 19, Oxford, 1975.

Ranscombe Camp, Sussex. *Sussex Arch. Coll.*, 102, 1964, pp. 55–67.

Riders Rings, Devon. *Trans. Devons. Assoc.*, 67, 1935, pp. 115–30.

Rippon Tor, Devon. *Proc. Prehist. Soc.*, 20, 1954, pp. 87–102.

Rotherley Down, Wilts. A. L. Pitt-Rivers, *Cranborne Chase*, II, 1888.

Rudchester, Cumb. *Arch. Ael.*, 5th ser. I, 1973, pp. 81–5.

Rumps, The, St Minver, Cornwall. *Corn. Arch.*, 13, 1974, pp. 5–50.

St Catherine's Hill, Winchester, Hants. *Papers and Proc. Hants. Fld Club*, 11, 1930.

St David's Head, Pembs. *Arch. Camb.* 16, 1899, pp. 105–31; *Arch. J.* 119, 1962, pp. 336–8.

St Kew (Trevinnick), Cornwall. *Corn. Arch.*, 8, 1969, pp. 89–97.

St Mawgan-in-Pydar. *See* Carloggas, Cornwall.

Scotstarvit, Fifes. *Proc. Soc. Ant. Scot.*, 82, 1946–48, pp. 241–263.

Shaugh Moor, Devons. *Trans. Devons. Assoc.*, 105, 1973, pp. 87–93.

Shearplace Hill, Dorset. *Proc. Prehist. Soc.*, 28, 1962, pp. 289–328; 35, 1969, pp. 345–51.

Skomer Is., Pembs. *Arch. Camb.*, 101, 1952, pp. 1–20.

Somerset Levels. *Phil. Trans. Roy. Soc. B*, 233, 1948, pp. 233–73; 233, 1948, pp. 275–86; *Proc. Prehist. Soc.*, 26, 1960, pp. 1–36; 29, 1963, pp. 17–49; 34, 1968, pp. 238–58; 36, 1970, pp. 125–51; 39, 1973, pp. 256–93; *Ant. J.*, 52, 1972, pp. 269–75; *Proc. Somerset Arch. Nat. Hist. Soc.*, 113, 1968–69, pp. 17–55; *Somerset Levels Papers*, 1, 1975; 2, 1976; 3, 1977.

South Cadbury, Somerset. L. Alcock, *By South Cadbury is that Camelot...*, London, 1972.

Southcote, Reading, Berks. *Proc. Prehist. Soc.*, 3, 1937, pp. 43–57.

South Lodge Camp, Dorset. A. L. Pitt-Rivers, *Cranborne Chase*, IV, 1898.

Stannon Down, Cornwall. *Corn. Arch.*, 9, 1970, pp. 17–46.

Stanton Harcourt, Oxon. *Oxoniensia*, 28, 1963, pp. 1–19; 31, 1966, pp. 1–27.

Stanwick, N. R. Yorks. *Rep. Research Comm. Soc. Ant. Lond.*, 17, 1954.

Staple Howe, E. R. Yorks. T. C. M. Brewster, *The Excavation of...*, Malton, Yorks., 1963.

Sutton Walls, Herefords. *Arch. J.*, 110, 1953, pp. 1–87.

Swallowcliffe Down, Wilts. *Wilts. Arch. Nat. Hist. Mag.*, 43, 1925, pp. 59–93; 46, 1927, pp. 540–7; 54, 1964, pp. 46–57.

Swarkestone (barrow 4), Derbys. *Derbys. Arch. J.*, 80, 1960, pp. 1–48.

Thickthorn Down, Dorset. *Proc. Dorset Nat. Hist. Arch. Soc.*, 81, 1959, pp. 110–13.

Thorny Down, Wilts. *Proc. Prehist. Soc.*, 7, 1941, pp. 114–33; *Wilts. Arch. Nat. Hist. Mag.*, 47, 1937, pp. 640–59.

Thundersbarrow Hill, Sussex. *Ant. J.*, 13, 1933, pp. 109–33.

Tollard Royal (Berwick Down). *Proc. Prehist. Soc.*, 34, 1968, pp. 102–47.

Torwoodlee, Selkirks. *Proc. Soc. Ant. Scot.*, 85, 1951, pp. 92–117.

Traprain Law, E. Lothian. *Proc. Soc. Ant. Scot.*, 89, 1955–6, pp. 118–226, 284–9.

Tre'r Ceiri, Caerns. *Arch. J.*, 117, 1960, pp. 1–39.

Trevisker, Cornwall. *Proc. Prehist. Soc.*, 38, 1972, pp. 302–81.

Trundle, Sussex. *Sussex Arch. Coll.*, 70, 1929, pp. 33–85; 72, 1931, pp. 100–150.

Twyford Down, Hants. *Papers and Proc. Hants. Fld Club*, 13, 1936, pp. 118–212.

Verulamium. *Rep. Research Comm. Soc. Ant. Lond.*, 11, 1936; 28, 1972.

Walesland Rath, Pembs. *Britannia*, 2, 1971, pp. 48–108.

West Brandon, County Durham. *Arch. Ael.*, 40, 1962, pp. 1–34.

West Harling, Norfolk. *Proc. Prehist. Soc.*, 19, 1953, pp. 1–40.

Weston Wood, Surrey, *Surrey Arch. Coll.*, 61, 1964, pp. 10–17.

West Plean, Stirling. *Proc. Soc. Ant. Scot.*, 89, 1955, pp. 227–51.

Willington, Derbys. *Ant.*, XLVI, 1972, pp. 314–16.

Wilsford Shaft, Wilts. *Ant.*, XXXVII, 1963, pp. 118–19; 40, 1966, pp. 227–8.

Winterbourne Dauntsey, Wilts. *Wilts. Arch. Nat. Hist. Mag.*, 46, 1935, pp. 445–53.

Woodcutts, Dorset. A. L. Pitt-Rivers, *Cranborne Chase*, 1, 1887; C. F. C. Hawkes, and S. Piggott, *Arch. J.*, 104, 1947, pp. 27–81.

Wookey Hole, Somerset. H. E. Balch, *Wookey Hole, its Caves and Cave Dwellers*, Oxford, 1914.

Woolbury, Hants. O. G. S. Crawford and A. Keiller, *Wessex from the Air*, Oxford, 1928, Pl. 25.

Worlebury, Somerset. C. W. Dymond, *Worlebury*, Bristol, 1902.

Worthy Down, Hants. *Papers and Proc. Hants. Fld Club*, 10, 1929, pp. 178–92.

Yarnbury, Wilts. *Wilts. Arch. Nat. Hist. Mag.*, 46, 1933, pp. 198–213.

Yeavering Bell, Northumb. G. Jobey in A. L. F. Rivet (ed.), *The Iron Age in Roman Britain*, p. 97.

Zennor, Cornwall. *Arch. J.*, 98, 1941, pp. 105–30; *Proc. West Cornwall Fld Club*, 1, 4, 1955–6, pp. 164–6; *J. Roy. Inst. Cornwall*, 3, part i, 1957, pp. 66–82.

SELECT BIBLIOGRAPHY

TO THE END OF 1975, WITH SOME ADDITIONS

Aberg, A. 'The Early Plough in Europe', *Gwerin*, I, 1956–7, pp. 171–81.

Aberg, F. A. and Bowen, H. C. 'Ploughing experiments with a reconstructed Donnerupland ard', *Ant.*, XXXIV, 1960, pp. 144–7.

Allen, D. 'Belgic coins as illustrations of life in the late pre-Roman Iron Age', *Proc. Prehist. Soc.*, 24, 1958, pp. 43–63.

'Iron currency bars in Britain', *Proc. Prehist. Soc.*, 33, 1967, pp. 307–35.

Applebaum, S. 'The agriculture of the British Iron Age as exemplified at Figheldean Down, Wiltshire', *Proc. Prehist. Soc.*, 20, 1954, 103–14.

★Ashbee, P. *The Bronze Age Round Barrow in Britain*, London, 1960.

Ancient Scilly, Newton Abbot, 1974.

Ashmolean Museum, Oxford. *Guide to an Exhibition of Air-Photographs of Archaeological Sites*, Oxford, 1948.

Baker, F. T. 'The Iron Age salt industry in Lincolnshire', *Lincs. Architect. Arch. Soc.*, 8, 1959–60, pp. 26–34.

★Benson, D. G. and Miles, D. *The Upper Thames Valley: an Archaeological Survey of the River Gravels*, Oxford, 1974.

Bersu, G. 'Excavations at Little Woodbury, Wilts. part I: the settlement as revealed by excavation', *Proc. Prehist. Soc.*, 6, 1940, pp. 50–111.

'"Fort" at Scotstarvit Covert, Fife', *Proc. Soc. Ant. Scot.*, 82, 1947–8, pp. 241–63.

Blake, B. 'Excavation of native (Iron Age) sites in Cumberland, 1956–58', *Trans. Cumberland and Westmorland Ant. Arch. Soc.* NS, 58, 1959, pp. 1–14.

★Bowen, H. C. *Ancient Fields*, London, n.d. 1961.

'Corn storage in antiquity', *Ant.*, XLI, 1967, pp. 214–15.

'The Celtic background', in A. L. F. Rivet (ed.), *The Roman Villa in Britain*, London, 1969, pp. 1–48.

(ed.) 'Symposium on ancient agriculture in Ireland and N.W. Europe', *Adv. Sci.*, 14, 56, 1958, pp. 365–71.

Bowen, C. and Cunliffe, B. 'The evolution of the landscape', *Ant. J.*, 53, 1973, pp. 9–13.

★Bowen, H. C. and Fowler, P. J. (eds.), *Early Land Allotment*, British Archaeological Reports, 48, Oxford, 1978.

Bowen, H. C. and Wood, P. D. 'Experimental storage of corn underground and its implication for Iron Age settlements', *Univ. Lond. Instit. Arch. Bull.* 7, 1967, pp. 1–14.

Bradley, R. 'Stock raising and the origins of the hill fort on the South Downs', *Ant. J.*, 51, 1971, pp. 8–29.

'Prehistorians and pastoralists in Neolithic and Bronze Age England', *World Arch.*, 4, 1972, pp. 192–204.

★Bradley, R. and Ellison, A. *Rams Hill: a Bronze Age Defended Enclosure and its Landscape*, British Archaeological Reports, 19, Oxford, 1975.

★Branigan, K. and Fowler, P. J. (eds.), *The Roman West Country*, Newton Abbot, 1976.

★Brothwell, D and Higgs, E. S. (eds.) *Science in Archaeology*, London, 2nd ed. 1969.

Bu'Lock, J. D. 'Possible remains of celtic fields at Kelsall in Cheshire', *Trans. Lancs. Cheshire Arch. Soc.*, 64, 1955, p. 24.

Burgess, C. B. 'Goatscrag: a Bronze Age rock shelter cemetery in north Northumberland. With notes on other rock shelters and crag lines in the region', *Arch. Ael.*, 4th ser., 50, 1972, pp. 15–69.

Burgess, C. and Miket, R. (eds.). *Settlement and Economy in the Third and Second Millennia B.C.*, British Archaeological Reports, 33, Oxford, 1976.

Buttler, W. 'Pits and pit-dwellings in south-east Europe', *Ant.*, 10, 1936, pp. 25–36.

Butzer, K. W. *Environment and Archaeology*. Chicago, 1971.

Calder, C. S. T. 'Report on the discovery of numerous Stone Age house sites in Shetland', *Proc. Soc. Ant. Scot.*, 89, 1955–6, pp. 340–97.

Calkin, J. B. 'The Bournemouth area in the Middle and Late Bronze Age, with the 'Deverel-Rimbury' problem reconsidered', *Arch. J.*, 119, 1962, pp. 1–65.

'The Isle of Purbeck in the Iron Age', *Proc. Dorset. Nat. Hist. Arch. Soc.*, 70, 1949, pp. 29–59.

Campbell, J. *et al. The Mendip Hills in Prehistoric and Roman Times*, Bristol, 1970.

★Challis, A. J. and Harding, D. W. *Later Prehistory from the Trent to the Tyne*, Parts i and ii. British Archaeological Reports, 20 (i) and (ii), Oxford, 1975.

Chang, K. C. 'Settlement patterns in archaeology', *Addison-Wesley Module in Anthropology*, 24, 1972, pp. 1–26.

Childe, V. G. 'The balanced sickle' in W. F. Grimes (ed.), *Aspects of Archaeology in Britain and Beyond*, London, 1951, pp. 39–48.

★Clark, G. *Prehistoric Europe: the Economic Basis*, London, 1952.

Clarke, D. L. Review in *Proc. Prehist. Soc.*, 32, 1966, p. 366 (re. Beaker houses and cultivation in E. Anglia).

(ed.) *Models in Archaeology*, London, 1972.

Clarke, R. R. *East Anglia*, London, 1960.

'The Iron Age in Norfolk and Suffolk', *Arch. J.*, 96, 1939, pp. 1–113.

Cleere, H. F. 'The classification of early iron-smelting furnaces', *Ant. J.*, 52, 1972, pp. 8–23.

★Coles, J. M. *Archaeology by Experiment*, London, 1973.

Cotton, M. A. 'British camps with timber-laced ramparts', *Arch. J.*, 111, 1954, pp. 26–105.

'Robin Hood's arbour, and rectilinear enclosures in Berkshire', *Berks. Arch. J.*, 59, 1961, pp. 1–35.

'Berkshire hill-forts', *Berks. Arch. J.*, 60, 1962, pp. 30–52.

Council for British Archaeology. *Archaeological Site Index to Radiocarbon Dates for Great Britain and Ireland*, London, 1971.

Supplements to Site Index, 1973–

Crampton, C. B. and Webley, D. 'The correlation of prehistoric settlement and soils in the Vale of Glamorgan', *Bull. Bd Celtic Studies*, 18, part 4, 1960, pp. 387–96.

Crawford, O. G. S. 'The distribution of Early Bronze Age settlements in Britain', *Geog. J.*, 40, 1912, pp. 184–203.

Air Survey and Archaeology, Ordnance Survey Professional Papers, N.S.7. Southampton, 1924, 2nd ed. 1928.

'Our debt to Rome?' *Ant.*, II, 1928, pp. 173–88.

Air Photography for Archaeologists, Southampton, 1929.

Celtic Earthworks of Salisbury Plain: Old Sarum Sheet, Southampton, 1934.

Archaeology in the Field, London, 1953.

Crawford, O. G. S. and Keiller, A. *Wessex from the Air*, Oxford, 1928.

★Crittall, E. (ed.) Victoria County History of Wiltshire, I, part ii, Oxford, 1973.

★Cunliffe, B. *Iron Age Communities in Britain*, London, 1974.

Curwen, E. C. 'Prehistoric agriculture in Britain', *Ant.*, I, 1927, pp. 261–89.

Prehistoric Sussex, London, 1929.

'Ancient cultivations', *Ant.*, VI, 1932, pp. 389–406.

The Archaeology of Sussex, London, 1937, 2nd ed. 1954.

'Querns', *Ant.*, XI, 1937, pp. 133–51.

'The early development of agriculture in Britain', *Proc. Prehist. Soc.*, 4, 1938, pp. 27–51.

Air Photography and the Evolution of the Cornfield, Econ. Hist. Soc. 2nd rev. ed. 1938.

'More about querns', *Ant.*, XV, 1941, pp. 15–32.

Plough and Pasture, London, 1946.

Dimbleby, G. W. *The Development of British Heathlands and their Soils*, Forestry Memoirs no. 23, Oxford, 1962.

Plants and Archaeology, London, 1967. London, 2nd edn 1978.

'The impact of early man on his environment' in P. R. Cox and J. Peel (eds.) *Population and Pollution*, London, 1972, pp. 7–13.

'The legacy of prehistoric man' in A. Warren and B. Goldsmith (eds.) *Conservation in Practice*, Chichester, 1974, pp. 279–89.

'Archaeological evidence of environmental change', *Nature*, 256, 1975, pp. 265–7.

'Climate, soil and man', *Phil. Trans. Roy. Soc. Lond. B*, 275, 1976, pp. 197–208.

Dimbleby, G. W. and Evans, J. G., 'Pollen and land snail analysis of calcareous soils', *J. Arch. Sci.*, 1, 1974, pp. 117–33.

Dyer, J. F. 'Dray's Ditches, Bedfordshire, and Early Iron Age territorial boundaries in the eastern Chilterns', *Ant. J.*, 61, 1961, pp. 32–43.

Elgee, F. *Early Man in North East Yorkshire*, Gloucester, 1930.

Ellison, A. and Drewett, P. 'Pits and postholes in the British Early Iron Age: some alternative explanations', *Proc. Prehist. Soc.*, 37, 1971, pp. 183–94.

Ellison, A. and Harris, J. 'Settlement and land use in the prehistory and early history of southern England: a study based on locational models' in D. Clarke (ed.), *Models in Archaeology*, London, 1972, pp. 911–62.

*Evans, J. G. *Land Snails in Archaeology*, London, 1972.

* *The Environment of Early Man in the British Isles*, London, 1975.

*Evans, J. G. and Limbrey, S. (eds.) 'The experimental earthwork on Morden Bog, Wareham, Dorset, England: 1963 to 1972', *Proc. Prehist. Soc.*, 40, 1974, pp. 170–202.

*Evans, J., Limbrey, S. and Cleere, H. (eds.) *The Effect of Man on the Landscape: The Highland Zone*, Council for British Archaeology Research Report, 11, London, 1975.

Evans, J. G. and Valentine, K. W. G., 'Ecological changes induced by prehistoric man at Pilstone, Buckinghamshire', *J. Arch. Sci.*, 1, 1974, pp. 343–51.

Farnsworth, G. (ed.) 'Experimental archaeology', *Worcs. Arch. Newsletter*, 9, 1972, special ed.

Feachem, R. W. 'Unenclosed platform settlements', *Proc. Soc. Ant. Scot.*, 94, 1961, pp. 79–85.

'Ancient agriculture in the highland of Britain', *Proc. Prehist. Soc.*, 39, 1973, 332–53.

Fell, C. *Early Settlement in the Lake Counties*, Clapham, Yorks. 1972.

Fenton, A. 'Early and traditional cultivating implements in Scotland', *Proc. Soc. Ant. Scot.*, 96, 1962–3, pp. 264–317.

'Draught oxen in Britain', *Národopisny Věstnik Ceskoslovenky*, III–IV, 1969, pp. 17–51.

*Finberg, H. P. R. (ed.) *The Agrarian History of England and Wales*, I, part ii, A.D. 43–1042, Cambridge, 1972.

Fleming, A. 'Territorial patterns in Bronze Age Wessex', *Proc. Prehist. Soc.*, 37, 1971, pp. 138–66.

'Bronze Age agriculture on the marginal lands of North-east Yorkshire', *Agric. Hist. Rev.*, 19, 1971, pp. 1–24.

'The genesis of pastoralism in European prehistory', *World Arch.*, 4, 1972, pp. 179–91.

Fleming, A. and Collis, J. 'A late prehistoric reave system near Cholwich Town, Dartmoor', *Proc. Devon Arch. Soc.*, 31, 1973, pp. 1–21.

*Forde-Johnston, J. *Hillforts of the Iron Age in England and Wales: a Survey of the Surface Evidence*, Liverpool, 1976.

*Fowler, E. (ed.), *Field Survey in British Archaeology*, Council for British Archaeology, London, 1972.

Fowler, P. J. 'Cross-ridge dykes on the Ebble–Nadder Ridge', *Wilts. Arch. Nat. Hist. Mag.*, 59, 1964, pp. 46–57.

(ed.) *Archaeology and the Landscape*, London, 1972.

(ed.) *Recent Work in Rural Archaeology*, Bradford-on-Avon, 1975.

'The Abingdon ard-share', in M. Parrington (ed.), *The Excavation at Ashville Trading Estate, Abingdon* (Oxfordshire), *1974–76*, CBA Research Report, 28, pp. 83–8.

Fowler, P. J. and Evans, J. G. 'Plough-marks, lynchets and early fields', *Ant.*, XLI, 1967, pp. 289–301.

Fowler, P. J., Musty, J. W. G. and Taylor, C. C. 'Some earthwork enclosures in Wiltshire', *Wilts. Arch. Nat. Hist. Mag.*, 60, 1965, pp. 52–74.

Fox, A. 'Celtic fields and farms on Dartmoor...', *Proc. Prehist. Soc.*, 20, 1954, pp. 87–102.

South West England, London, 1964; rev ed. Newton Abbot, 1973.

Fox, Sir Cyril. *The Archaeology of the Cambridge Region*, Cambridge, 1923.

'The socketed Bronze sickles of the British Isles...', *Proc. Prehist. Soc.*, 5, 1939, pp. 222–48.

'The non-socketed Bronze sickles of Britain', *Arch. Camb.*, 96, 1941, pp. 136–62.

A Find of the Early Iron Age from Llyn Cerrig Bach, Anglesey, Cardiff, 1946.

★*The Personality of Britain*, 1932; 4th ed. Cardiff, 1947.

★*Life and Death in the Bronze Age*, London, 1959.

★Frere, S. S. *Britannia*, London, 1967.

(ed.), *Problems of the Iron Age in Southern Britain*, London, 1961.

★Gailey, A. and Fenton, A. (eds.), *The Spade in Northern and Atlantic Europe*, Belfast, 1970.

Gardner, W. and Savory, H. N. *Dinorben*, Cardiff, 1964.

Gawne, E. and Somers Cox, J. 'Parallel reaves on Dartmoor', *Trans. Devon Assoc.*, 100, 1965, pp. 277–92.

Glob, P. V. *Ard og Plov i nortens oldtid*, Aarhus, 1951.

★Godwin, H. *The History of the British Flora*, Cambridge, 2nd ed. 1975.

Graham, A. 'Cairnfields in Scotland', *Proc. Soc. Ant. Scot.*, 90, 1957, pp. 7–23.

Grimes, W. F. 'Early man and the soils of Anglesey', *Ant.*, XIX, 1945, pp. 169–74.

(ed.) *Aspects of Archaeology in Britain and Beyond*, London, 1951.

Excavations on Defence Sites, 1939–45, I, London, 1960.

Hansen, H. O. 'Experimental ploughing with a Døstrup ard replica', *Tools and Tillage*, I, 1969, pp. 67–92.

Harcourt, R. 'The dog in prehistoric and early Britain', *J. Arch. Sci.*, I, 1974, pp. 151–75.

Harding, D. W. *The Iron Age in the Upper Thames Basin*, Oxford, 1972.

'Round and rectangular: Iron Age houses, British and Foreign', in C. F. C. and S. C. Hawkes (eds.), *Archaeology into History*, I, *Greeks, Celts and Romans*, London, 1973, pp. 43–62.

★*The Iron Age in Lowland Britain*, London, 1974.

(ed.) *Hillforts: a Survey of Research in Britain and Ireland*, London, 1976.

Hatt, G. *Oldtidsagre*, Copenhagen, 1949.

Hawkes, C. F. C. and Piggott, S. 'Britons, Romans and Saxons around Salisbury and in Cranborne Chase', *Arch. J.*, 104, 1947, pp. 27–81.

Hay, T, 'Pit-dwellings or not pit-dwellings', *Trans. Bristol and Glos. Arch. Soc.*, 66, 1947, pp. 233–7.

Helbaek, H. 'Early crops in southern England', *Proc. Prehist. Soc.*, 18, 1952, pp. 194–233.

'Archaeology and agricultural botany', *Univ. London Inst. Arch. Rep.*, 9, 1953, pp. 44–59.

Henshall, A. S. 'Textiles and weaving appliances in prehistoric Britain', *Proc. Prehist. Soc.*, 16, 1950, pp. 130–62.

Hicks, S. P. 'Pollen-analytical evidence for the effect of prehistoric agriculture on the vegetation of north Derbyshire', *New Phytol.*, 70, 1971, pp. 647–67; cf. *Arch. J.*, 129, 1972, pp. 1–21.

Higgs, E. and White, J. 'Autumn killing', *Ant.*, XXXVII, 1963, pp. 282–9.

Higham, N. J. and Jones, G. D. B. 'Frontier, forts and farmers: Cumbrian aerial survey, 1974–5', *Arch. J.*, 132, 1975, pp. 16–53.

Hogg, R. 'Factors which have affected the spread of early settlement in the Lake Counties', *Trans. Cumberland and Westmorland Ant. Arch. Soc.*, NS, 72, 1972, pp. 1–35.

Holleyman, G. A. 'The Celtic field system in South Britain: a survey of the Brighton district', *Ant.*, IX, 1935, pp. 443–54.

Hope-Taylor, B. '"Celtic" agriculture in Surrey', *Surrey Arch. Coll.*, 50, 1952, pp. 47–72.

Huntingford, G. W. B. 'Ancient agriculture', *Ant.*, VI, 1932, pp. 327–37.

Jackson, J. W. 'Derbyshire lynchets', *Derbys. Arch. J.*, 78, 1957, pp. 62–3.

Jessen, K. and Helbaek, H. *Cereals in Great Britain and Ireland in Prehistoric and Early Historic Times*, Copenhagen, 1944.

*Jesson, M. and Hill, D. (eds.) *The Iron Age and its Hill-forts*, Southampton, 1971.

Jewell, P. 'Cattle from British archaeological sites', *Roy. Anthrop. Inst. Occasional Paper*, 18, 1963, pp. 80–101.

(ed.) *The Experimental Earthwork on Overton Down, Wiltshire 1960*, London, 1963.

Jewell, P. A. and Dimbleby, G. W. 'The experimental earthwork on Overton Down, Wiltshire: the first four years', *Proc. Prehist. Soc.* 32, 1966, pp. 313–42.

Jobey, G. 'A note on scooped enclosures in Northumberland', *Arch. Ael.*, 40, 1962, pp. 1–34.

'Hillforts and settlements in Northumberland', *Arch. Ael.*, 43, 1965, pp. 21–64.

'A field survey in Northumberland', in A. L. F. Rivet (ed.), *The Iron Age in Northern Britain*, Edinburgh, 1966, pp. 89–110.

'Early settlement and topography in the Border counties', *Scott. Arch. Forum*, 1970, pp. 73–84.

Jobey, G. and Tait, J., 'Excavations on palisaded settlements and cairnfields at Alnham, Northumberland', *Arch. Ael.*, 4th series, 44, 1966, pp. 5–48.

King, A. *Early Pennine Settlement: a Field Study*, Clapham, Yorks., 1970.

*Limbrey, S. *Soil Science and Archaeology*, London, 1975.

Limbrey, S. and Evans, J. G. (eds.) *The Effect of Man on the Landscape: the Lowland Zone*, CBA Research Report, 21, 1978.

Lowndes, R. A. C. 'Celtic fields, farmsteads and burial mounds in the Lune Valley', *Trans. Cumberland and Westmorland Ant. Arch. Soc.*, NS, 68, 1963, pp. 77–95.

Lynch, F. and Burgess, C. (eds.) *Prehistoric Man in Wales and the West*, Bath, 1972.

Lynch, F. *et al.* 'Brenig Valley excavation, 1973', *Denbigh Hist. Trans.*, 23, 1974, pp. 1–56.

MacKie, E. 'Brochs and the Hebridean Iron Age', *Ant.* XXXIX, 1965, pp. 266–78; 'Radiocarbon dates and the Scottish Iron age', *Ant.* XLIII, 1969, pp. 15–26.

Manley, G. *Climate and the British Scene*, London, 1952.

Manning, W. H. 'The plough in Roman Britain', *J. Rom. Studies*, 54, 1964, pp. 54–65.

Mitchell, G. F. 'Evidence of early agriculture', *J. Roy. Soc. Ant. Ireland*, 76, 1946, pp. 16–18.

Moore, P. D. 'The influence of prehistoric cultures upon the initiation and spread of blanket bog in upland Wales', *Nature*, 241, 1973, pp. 350–3.

Musson, C. 'House plans and prehistory', *Curr. Arch.*, 2, 1970, pp. 267–77.

Nightingale, M. W. 'Ploughing and field shape', *Ant.*, XXVII, 1953, pp. 20–6.

Oldfield, F. 'Pollen analysis and man's role in the ecological history of the south-east Lake District', *Geografiska Annaler*, 45, 1963, pp. 23–40.

OS Ordnance Survey Map of Roman Britain, 4th ed. Chessington, 1959.

Map of Southern Britain in the Iron Age, Chessington, 1962.

Parrington, M. (ed.). *The Excavation...at Ashville Trading Estate, Abingdon (Oxfordshire)*, 1974–6, CBA Research Report, 28, London, 1978.

Payne, F. G. 'The plough in Ancient Britain', *Arch. J.*, 104, 1948, pp. 82–111. 'The British plough: some stages in its development', *Agric. Hist. Rev.*, 5, 1957, pp. 74–84.

★Pennington, W. *The History of British Vegetation*, London, 1969; 2nd ed. 1974.

Perry, B. T. 'Iron Age enclosures and settlements on the Hampshire chalklands', *Arch. J.*, 126, 1969, pp. 29–43.

Philips, J. T. 'A survey of the distribution of querns of Hunsbury or allied types', *Trans. Leics. Arch. Hist. Soc.*, 26, 1950, pp. 75–82.

Phillips, C. W. 'Pebbles from early ploughs in England', *Proc. Prehist. Soc.*, 4, 1938, pp. 338–9.

(ed.), *The Fenland in Roman Times*, Roy. Geog. Soc. Research Ser. 5, London, 1970.

Piggott, C. 'Five Late Bronze Age enclosures in north Wiltshire', *Proc. Prehist. Soc.*, 8, 1942, pp. 48–61. 'Late Bronze Age enclosures in Sussex and Wessex', *Proc. Prehist. Soc.*, 16, 1950, pp. 193–5.

Piggott, S. 'The Early Bronze Age in Wessex', *Proc. Prehist. Soc.*, 1938, pp. 52–106.

★ *The Neolithic Cultures of the British Isles*, Cambridge, 1954.

'Native economies and the Roman occupation of north Britain', in I. A. Richmond (ed.), *Roman and Native in North Britain*, Edinburgh, 1958, pp. 1–20.

★*Ancient Europe from the beginnings of Agriculture to Classical Antiquity*, Edinburgh, 1965.

'A note on climatic deterioration in the first millennium B.C. in Britain', *Scott. Arch. Forum*, 4, 1972, pp. 109–13.

(ed.), *The Prehistoric Peoples of Scotland*, London, 1962.

Pitt-Rivers, A. L. *Excavations in Cranborne Chase*, 5 vols, privately printed, 1887–1905.

Posnansky, M. 'Note on the presence of prehistoric field systems in Derbyshire', *Derby. Arch. J.*, 76, 1956, p. 71.

Powell, T. G. E. *The Celts*, London, 1958.

Radford, C. A. R. 'Prehistoric settlements on Dartmoor and the Cornish Moors', *Proc. Prehist. Soc.*, 18, 1952, pp., 55–84.

Raistrick, A. 'Prehistoric cultivations at Grassington, W. Yorks', *Yorks. Arch. J.*, 33, 1937, pp. 166–74.

'Iron Age settlements in West Yorkshire', *Yorks. Arch. J.*, 34, 1939, pp. 115–50.

Raistrick, A. and Chapman, S. E. 'The lynchet groups of Upper Wharfedale', *Ant.* III, 1929, pp. 165–81.

Renfrew, C. (ed.), *The Explanation of Cultural Change: Models in Prehistory*, London, 1973.

*(ed.), *British Prehistory*, London, 1974.

Reynolds, P. J. 'Experiment in Iron Age archaeology' (pts. 1 and 2), *Trans. Bristol and Glos. Arch. Soc.*, 86, 1967, pp. 60–73; 88, 1969, pp. 29–33.

'Experimental Iron Age storage pits: an interim report', *Proc. Prehist. Soc.*, 40, 1974, pp. 118–31.

Farming in the Iron Age, Cambridge, 1976.

Rhodes, P. 'The Celtic field systems on the Berkshire Downs', *Oxoniensia*, 15, 1950, pp. 1–28.

Riehm, K. 'Prehistoric salt-boiling', *Ant.*, XXXV, 1961, pp. 181–91.

Riley, D. N. 'Archaeology from the air on the Upper Thames Valley', *Oxoniensia*, 8–9, 1943–4, pp. 443–54.

Ritchie, A. 'Palisaded sites in north Britain: their context and affinities', *Scott. Arch. Forum*, 2, 1970, pp. 48–67.

*Rivet, A. L. F. *Town and Country in Roman Britain*, London, 2nd ed. 1964.

*(ed.), *The Iron Age in Northern Britain*, Edinburgh, 1966.

*(ed.), *The Roman Villa in Britain*, London, 1969.

*Ross, A. *Pagan Celtic Britain*, London, 1967.

Everyday Life of the Pagan Celts, London, 1970.

Royal Commission on the Ancient and Historical Monuments of Scotland, *Roxburgh Inventory*, London, 1956.

Peeblesshire Inventory, London, 1967.

Royal Commission on Ancient and Historical Monuments in Wales and Monmouthshire. *Anglesey Inventory*, London, 1937, reprint with additions 1960.

Caernarvonshire Inventory, 3 vols., London, 1956–64.

Royal Commission on Historical Monuments (England). *Westmorland Inventory*, London, 1938.

Dorset Inventory, 5 vols., London, 1952–75.

A Matter of Time: an Archaeological Survey of the River Gravels of England, London, 1960.

Northamptonshire Inventory, 1, London, 1975.

Ryder, M. L. 'Can one cook in a skin?', *Ant.*, XL, 1966, pp. 225–7.

Savory, H. N. 'Valleyward settlement in the Marches during the Middle Bronze Age', *Bull. Bd Celtic Studies*, 15, 1954, pp. 305–7.

Seagrie, F. S. C. 'Pollen diagrams from southern England: Wareham, Dorset, and Nursling, Hants', *New Phytol.*, 58, part 3, 1959, pp. 316–25.

Sheail, J. and Wells, T. C. E. (eds.), *Old Grassland: its Archaeological and Ecological Importance*, Monks Wood Experimental Station Symposium no. 5, 1970.

Simmons, I. G. 'Environment and Early Man on Dartmoor', *Proc. Prehist. Soc.*, 35, 1969, pp. 203–19.

'Pollen diagrams from the North York Moors', *New Phytol.*, 68, 1969, pp. 807–27.

★Simpson, D. D. A. (ed.), *Economy and Settlement in Neolithic and Early Bronze Age Britain and Europe*, Leicester, 1971.

Sims, R. E. 'The anthropogenic factor in East Anglian vegetational history: an approach using A.P.F. techniques', in H. V. B. Berks and R. G. West (eds.), *Quarternary Plant Ecology*, Oxford, 1973, pp. 223–36.

Smith, A. G. 'Post-glacial deposits in South Yorkshire and North Lincolnshire', *New Phytol.*, 57, part 1, 1958, pp. 19–49.

'The context of some Late Bronze Age and Early Iron Age remains from Lincolnshire', *Proc. Prehist. Soc.*, 24, 1958, pp. 78–84.

Stead, I. M. *The La Tène Cultures of Eastern Yorkshire*, York, 1965.

Steensberg, A. *Ancient Harvesting Implements*, Copenhagen, 1943.

Stevenson, R. B. K. 'Notes on early agriculture in Scotland', *Agric. Hist. Rev.*, 8, part 1, 1960, pp. 1–4.

Sutton, J. E. G. 'Iron Age hillforts and some other earthworks in Oxfordshire', *Oxoniensia*, 31, 1966, pp. 28–42.

Taylor, C. C. *The Making of the English Landscape – Dorset*, London, 1970.
Fields in the English Landscape, London, 1975.

Taylor, J. A. (ed.) *Weather and Agriculture*, Oxford, 1967.

Tebbut, C. 'The prehistoric occupation of the Ashdown Forest area of the Weald', *Sussex Arch. Coll.*, 112, 1974, pp. 34–43.

★Thirsk, J. (ed.) *The Agrarian History of England and Wales*, IV, *1500–1640*, Cambridge, 1967.

Thomas, C. (ed.) *Rural Settlement in Roman Britain*, Council for British Archaeology Research Report, 7, London, 1966.

'The Bronze Age in the south west', *Arch. Rev.*, 4, 1969, pp. 3–13.

Thomas, F. '"Celtic Fields" at Blackwell, Taddington', *Derbys. Arch. J.*, 81, 1961, pp. 147–8.

Tierney, J. J. 'The Celtic ethnography of Posidonius', *Proc. Roy. Irish Acad.*, 60, part C, 1960, 189–275.

Trow-Smith, R. *A History of British Livestock Husbandry to 1700*, London, 1957.
Life from the Land, London, 1967.

Turner, J. 'Post Neolithic disturbance of British vegetation', in D. Walker and R. G. West (eds.) *Studies in the Vegetational History of the British Isles*, Cambridge, 1970, pp. 97–116.

Tubbs, C. R. and Dimbleby, G. W. 'Early agriculture in the New Forest', *Adv. Sci*, 22, 1965, pp. 88–97.

Usher, G. *A Dictionary of Plants Used by Man*, London, 1974.

Wainwright, G. J. 'A review of henge monuments in the light of recent research', *Proc. Prehist. Soc.*, 25, 1969, pp. 112–33.

★Walker, D. and West, R. (eds.) *Studies in the Vegetational History of the British Isles*, Cambridge, 1970.

Ward-Perkins, J. B. 'Iron Age metal horses' bits of the British Isles', *Proc. Prehist. Soc.*, 5, 1939, 173–92.

Warren, S. H. 'A probable hunter's trap of the Iron Age', *Ant.*, XXVIII, 1954, pp. 113–14.

Webster, G. and Hobley, B. 'Aerial reconnaissance over the Warwickshire Avon', *Arch. J.*, 121, 1964, pp. 1–22.

White, K. D. *Agricultural Implements of the Roman World*, Cambridge, 1967.

★Wilson, D. R. (ed.) *Aerial Reconnaissance for Archaeology*, Council for British Archaeology Research Report, 12, London, 1975.

Wright, E. V. and Churchill, D. M. 'The boats from North Ferriby, Yorkshire, England', *Proc. Prehist. Soc.*, 31, 1965, pp. 1–24.

ADDITIONAL SELECT BIBLIOGRAPHY, 1978–79
(see above, p. 281)

Bell, M. *Excavations at Bishopstone* (*Sussex Arch. Coll.*, 115, 1977).

★Bradley, R. *The Prehistoric Settlement of Britain*, London, 1978.

Coles, J. M. and Harding, A. F. *The Bronze Age in Europe*, London, 1979.

★Coles, J. M. *et al.* 'The use and character of wood in prehistoric Britain and Ireland', *Proc. Prehist. Soc.*, 44, 1978, 1–45.

Fleming, A. 'The prehistoric landscape of Dartmoor. Part 1. South Dartmoor', *Proc. Prehist. Soc.*, 44, 1978, 97–123.

Fowler, P. and Thomas, C. 'Lyonesse revisited: the early walls of Scilly', *Ant.*, LIII, 1979, 175–89.

Higham, N. J. 'Dyke systems in Northern Cumbria', *Bull. Bd Celtic Studies*, 28, 1978, 142–56.

Lambrick, G. and Robinson, M. *Iron Age and Roman Riverside Settlements at Farmoor, Oxfordshire*, CBA Research Report, 32, 1979.

★Megaw, J. V. S. and Simpson, D. D. A. *Introduction to British Prehistory*, Leicester, 1979.

Rees, S. E. *Agricultural Implements in Prehistoric and Roman Britain*, British Archaeological Reports, 69, 1979.

Reynolds, P. J. *Iron Age Farm. The Butser Experiment*, London, 1979.

Royal Commission on Historical Monuments (England). *Stonehenge and its Environs: Monuments and Land Use*, Edinburgh, 1979.

Smith, C. (ed.). *Fisherwick: The Reconstruction of an Iron Age Landscape*, British Archaeological Reports, 61, 1979.

Thoms, L. M. (ed.). *Early Man in the Scottish Landscape*, Scottish Archaeological Forum, 9, Edinburgh, 1979.

Wainwright, G. J. *et al.* 'The Shaugh Moor project: first report', *Proc. Prehist. Soc.*, 45, 1979, 1–33.

Whimster, R. 'Iron Age burial in southern Britain', *Proc. Prehist. Soc.*, 43, 1977, 317–27.

LIVESTOCK

By M. L. RYDER

Principal Scientific Officer, Agricultural Research Council's
Animal Breeding Research Organisation, Edinburgh
Honorary Lecturer, University of Edinburgh

CHAPTER I

INTRODUCTION[1]

U NTIL relatively recently it was customary in discussions of livestock evolution to quote categorical statements by authors of fifty years previously. In the last fifteen years, however, new techniques have been developed and there has been such increased interest in the subject that many earlier views have been questioned. But such is the state of flux of the subject that few new ideas have become established. The present treatment will therefore be more in the nature of an interim report, discussing the way in which different sources of evidence are being investigated, than a definite statement.

The discussion will also provide the basis for the kind of questions that should be asked by archaeologists and historians, and their progressive refinement. Originally these scholars were solely concerned with the identity of the farm animals present among skeletal remains from excavations, but counts have shown how the relative importance of different species in the economy can be considered. Determination of the age of death of animal remains, and of sex ratios leads to the question of husbandry methods. Finally, analysis of the size of bones and of other characteristics leads to a consideration of the breed or at least the type of animal and its evolution. Size must be determined by accurate measurement: reference to large or small animals begs the question, "What is a large or a small animal?"

After giving an introductory background, the present account will discuss the general level of animal husbandry and the relative importance of each farm animal in all of the main archaeological periods. Following this, each species will be discussed separately in greater detail in order to cover its evolution and any special methods of husbandry.

The classic designations (Neolithic, Bronze Age, etc.) generally used ignore the fact that dividing lines between the different periods are less clear cut than hitherto thought. Thus certain sites that are chronolog-

[1] This chapter was written between the middle of 1969 and the end of 1970, and was accepted by the late General Editor, Professor H. P. R. Finberg in January 1971. His decision, made shortly afterwards, to delay publication until Part I of Vol. I was complete has meant that several relevant books, and numerous papers, have been published in the intervening years. Continuous revision was impossible, and a full revision would have necessitated a complete rewriting, which was out of the question. The author has, therefore, been able to add only brief references to a limited number of new findings.

ically in one period may still have the technology of the previous period
The original ideas of archaeologists that domestic animals could be
considered purely in terms of their economic value or religious
associations have now given way to the understanding that the
relationship of prehistoric man to his livestock was part of the wider
ecological relationship of all living organisms.

The modern agricultural scientist, in his effort to seek maximum
productive efficiency, studies the soil–plant–animal complex, to which
the climate can be added. Thus, before we can consider which animals
were kept at different times, and under what conditions, we must
appreciate the nature of the surrounding vegetation and climate.

VEGETATION AND THE CLIMATIC BACKGROUND

As the climate became warmer after the last Ice Age, open woodlands,
first of birch and then of pine, became established in Britain. In this
woodland roamed deer and wild cattle (*Bos primigenius*) as well as
predatory carnivores such as bears and wolves. This Sub-Arctic climatic
phase corresponded with the end of the archaeological Palaeolithic
period. The gradually improving warm and dry (Boreal) climate
allowed new species of plants and animals to enter Britain, hazel and
pine being the dominant trees in what was then the Mesolithic period.
Then about 5500 BC Britain finally became an island, and the climate
became warm enough to allow alder, oak, elm, and lime to become
established. These produced denser woodland which largely replaced
the pines, so that the plants and animals of open country became
restricted to the hills. But the woodland rose to heights of over 2000
ft (610 m) that are now covered with peat. Deciduous forest dominated
by oak has been the characteristic British woodland ever since.[2] The
weather of this period is known as the Atlantic climate, which as well
as being warmer, was wetter and less extreme. Into this equable climate,
which favours the growth of grass, even in winter, came Neolithic man
with the first farm animals. And, as aptly stated by Trow-Smith these
first pastoralists had to fit the husbandry of their domestic stock and
their slight and unambitious agriculture into the open interstices of the
thick vegetative cover.[3]

The Atlantic climate also favoured the formation of peat bogs, and
it is from the pollen preserved in these that our knowledge of successive
changes in vegetation has come. There has probably been little change
in the range of weather since then. Towards the end of the Neolithic

[2] H. Godwin, *History of British Flora*, Cambridge, 1956. L. D. Stamp, *Man and the land*, London, 1955, p. 3.

[3] R. Trow-Smith, *A History of British Livestock Husbandry to 1700*, London, 1957.

period, about 2000 BC, it became drier and this Sub-Boreal climate persisted for most of the Bronze Age. It helped to clear the Chalk and Upland oolites, which because of their easier drying became less suited for the growth of timber. The grazing and treading of livestock hastened the denudation by preventing regeneration and the growth of young trees (above, p. 25).

About 700 BC the weather became cooler and wetter, and this Sub-Atlantic climate lasted throughout the Early Iron Age and Roman periods, before improvement to warmer and drier weather occurred.

DOMESTICATION

Since the initial domestication of British livestock did not take place in these islands it is not necessary to cover this aspect in detail. This is fortunate because lack of evidence on the process of domestication has led to many theories and much discussion.

The exploitation of animals by man had its origin at the stage in his evolution at which man could be regarded merely as an animal preying on other animals to satisfy his hunger. This crude exploitation of the Palaeolithic age, although it led to progressively better methods of food gathering, culminating in the hunting and fishing cultures of the Mesolithic period, yielded little more than flesh for food, skins for clothing and bones from which weapons and tools could be made (above, pp. 11–22). Although other animal products were available, man on the whole required the leisure of the more settled life following domestication to enable him to exploit these products and develop complicated uses.

Food gathering has the disadvantage that, in general, the wild products of nature are not sufficiently abundant to support more than a small population, and that most of man's time and energy is consumed in searching for food so that little is left for material or mental advancement. The change to the production of food by keeping domestic animals and cultivating plants, although gradual, had such marked results that it was named by Gordon Childe "the Neolithic Revolution". This was regarded by Sir Mortimer Wheeler as a far more important advance than the discovery of fire, or the splitting of the atom, for it enabled mankind to establish large settled communities which provided the basis for civilization. It is now known, however, from plant remains, that settled villages preceded cultivation and domestication in the Near East by several centuries.[4]

We are still a long way from a complete understanding of the way in which domestication came about. Early theorists tended to ignore

[4] Anon, 'Origins of Farming', *Nature*, 228, 1970, pp. 808–9.

the biological background of the problem in their efforts to seek a purposeful economic or religious explanation. It is now known that domestication must be considered in an environmental setting, and from an ecological point of view.[5]

Historical geographers suggest that domestication was stimulated by the desiccation following the last Pluvial period in western Asia, and Zeuner emphasized the biological basis of domestication by pointing out that many of the Mesolithic peoples who initiated domestication would have found it easier to obtain food by hunting than by making experiments in domestication that would not reward their efforts for several generations.[6] Higgs and Jarman have emphasized that domestication need not have occurred only once, nor in only one area.[7] One can regard man in the first stage of domestication as taking merely what natural predators had previously taken from the population. But as man's protection reduced losses and allowed animal numbers to increase, bigger crops could be removed from the population.

Zeuner detailed the various levels of natural association that occur between different animal species, starting with symbiosis. A development of symbiosis is the scavenging in which the wolf for instance probably sought food in the camps of Mesolithic man, who gained from the association by the wolf's removal of waste. It is likely that such a voluntary association led to man's first domestic animal, the dog, and it illustrates another important basis for domestication, viz. that the animals concerned usually form social groups. Since man himself is a social animal, Zeuner considered that the initial phase of domestication can be regarded as an instance of social overlap between man and the animal being domesticated. The idea of incipient domestication first put forward with the reindeer by Zeuner[8] has been developed speculatively by Jarman[9] for other deer and antelopes, and the recent experimental domestication of red deer in Scotland shows that this is possible. But the archaeological evidence indicates the management of a natural resource rather than true livestock husbandry. And one must ask why, if the domestication of red deer was begun, did it not continue.[10]

The next animals to be domesticated, about 10,000 BC, were the goat

[5] K. V. Flannery, 'The ecology of early food production in Mesopotamia', *Science*, 147, 1965, pp. 1247–56.

[6] F. E. Zeuner, *A History of Domesticated Animals*, London, 1963.

[7] E. S. Higgs and M. R. Jarman, 'The origins of agriculture: a reconsideration', *Ant.*, XLIII, 1969, pp. 31–41.

[8] Zeuner, *op. cit.*

[9] M. R. Jarman, 'Early animal husbandry', in J. Hutchinson, G. Clark, E. M. Jope and R. Riley (eds.), 'The Early History of Agriculture', *Phil. Trans. Roy. Soc. Lond.* B, 275, 1976, pp. 99–108.

[10] M. L. Ryder, in discussion of the above paper.

and the sheep, and despite conflicting evidence, the goat is likely to have been domesticated first. There is no biological evidence to support the suggestion of Payne that the sheep and goat formed an interbreeding population as late as the Palaeolithic (below, p. 351).[11] The sheep emerged as the economically superior animal, making an immense contribution to the development of civilization in many parts of the world.

These herding animals were tamed rather than parasitized, and Zeuner considered them to have been domesticated in the pre-agricultural stage of man's development. The wild ancestors of goats and sheep have a relatively narrow distribution centred in the mountains of western Asia, but sheep, at any rate, come down onto lower ground in winter.

Hilzheimer suggested that domestication of the sheep could have taken place during the seasonal migrations of the wild animal.[12] These may have been the origin of transhumance up into the hills in summer, and back to the lowlands in winter, in which Hilzheimer claimed domestic sheep migrate as much by instinct as at the instigation of their owners. Zeuner went so far as to give the credit for domesticating sheep to the dog rather than to man because of the natural ability of the dog to round up ruminants.[13] Man here therefore used one animal to exploit another, and even today the sheepdog forms a vital element of shepherding.

The domesticated goat and sheep provided man with a permanent supply of meat, and allowed him to develop new products, e.g. milk and wool. At this early Neolithic stage man's crops would attract wild herbivores such as the pig and ox. Zeuner termed these not scavengers but crop robbers. Man, however, having already had experience of domestication was probably quick to domesticate such trespassers, and may have had enclosures available to pen them.

As emphasized by Bökönyi it was probably only young animals that were domesticated.[14] Thus a new discipline, animal behaviour, enters the debate on domestication: the young animal is thought to become attached to man (or woman) through the 'imprinting' process which normally helps it to recognize its mother.[15, 16]

---

[11] S. Payne, 'The origins of domestic sheep and goats: a reconsideration in the light of fossil evidence', *Proc. Prehist. Soc.*, 34, 1968, pp. 368–84.

[12] M. Hilzheimer, 'Sheep', *Ant.*, x, 1936, pp. 195–206.   [13] Zeuner, *op. cit.*

[14] S. Bökönyii, 'Archaeological problems and methods of recognising animal domestication', in P. J. Ucko and G. W. Dimbleby (eds.), *The Domestication and Exploitation of Plants and Animals*, London, 1969, pp. 219–30.

[15] H. Spurway, 'The causes of domestication: an attempt to integrate some ideas of Konrad Lorenz with evolution theory', *J. Genet.*, 53, 1955, pp. 325–62.

[16] E. B. Hale, 'Domestication and the evolution of behaviour', in E. S. E. Hafez (ed.), *The Behaviour of Domestic Animals*, London, 1962.

Both the pig and the ox seem to have been first domesticated in the Near East about 6500 BC. Less is known about the domestication of the animals whose main use is transport. The ass seems to have been used in Mesopotamia before the horse was domesticated on the plains of Asia. It is worthy of note at this point that most domestic animals are large herbivores, the ruminants (ox, sheep, and goat), being particularly adapted, because of their specialized digestive system, to the poor nutritional level which domestication might involve.

Zeuner summarized and simplified the stages leading to domestication as follows.

1. Loose contacts of animals with man and no control of breeding.

2. Confinement to the human environment with breeding in captivity; (domestication, unlike the mere taming of a single animal in captivity, involves the control of the reproduction of a group of animals).

3. Selective breeding by man towards certain characteristics, and the occasional crossing with wild forms.

4. The modern planned development of different breeds with desirable economic characters – meat, milk, wool – coupled with the disregard for, and even extermination of, wild and primitive domestic ancestors.

The domestication of animals usually implies the parallel cultivation of plants; stubble provided food for livestock which manure the soil with their dung, and it was the mixed farmer and agriculturalist who established settlements because he had to remain in one place between seed time and harvest. The grazier or pastoralist lived a nomadic life, ever searching for new pastures. Some peoples became very successful at working an economy based almost entirely on animal exploitation, their herds constituting heritable wealth, e.g. the nomads of central Asia who probably gave us the horse, wool felt, and butter.

Finally, before leaving domestication, we must mention the genetical view of Darlington, viz. that domestication can be regarded as part of the evolutionary process of man. [17, 18] He considers that not only were plants and animals selected by man (at first unconsciously) but so close was this relationship that his crops and livestock selected man. This accepted interdependence of all members of an ecosystem might demand an entirely new approach in archaeological interpretation. Thus, briefly, Darlington regards different tribes as having become closely adapted to, and eventually dependent on, the diverse characters

[17] C. D. Darlington, 'The genetics of society', in A. J. Gregor, *A Symposium of Race: an Inter-disciplinary Approach*, Honolulu, 1963, 36 pp.
[18] *Idem*, 'The silent millennia in the origin of agriculture', in Ucko and Dimbleby, *op. cit.*, pp. 67–72.

of the crops and stock which had evolved with them. Men had been selected by the plants and animals to live on only those crops and livestock.

CHANGES FOLLOWING DOMESTICATION

Early workers were perhaps too ready to pin their faith on changes in bone size or shape as necessarily indicating domestication of the animals concerned. But, at the other extreme, the statement by Berry that there are no traits that inevitably accompany domestication is perhaps somewhat misleading.[19] It depends for its truth on the word 'inevitably'; different species have changed in different ways and to differing extents. Such changes, however, take a considerable time to become evident, and so the problem of recognizing domestication is most acute in the early stages when domestic forms can be expected to differ little from their wild ancestors. Bökönyi[20] and Chaplin[21] describe more recent techniques, in which changes from the wild population in the proportions of remains from the two sexes, and of different ages, can indicate domestication. Non-morphological criteria for the study of early livestock will lead us more and more into the biochemical field. Another aspect that is now receiving attention is change in animal behaviour.[22] Blood types have been studied, even in bone remains, and this must surely lead to the investigation and typing of different proteins in bones or other remains. Evidence of a change in bone structure following domestication has also been presented.[23]

The chief way in which changes were brought about was through selective breeding by man, yet we know hardly anything about the breeding methods of early farmers. Archaeologists lacking a detailed knowledge of the variety of breeds may not always have been aware of the immensity of the biological problems, and geneticists have tended to hazard guesses that have not always been supported by the archaeological or historical evidence.

Domestication did not in itself produce any new inheritance, but the changed environment may have allowed the survival of a greater range

[19] R. J. Berry, 'The genetical implications of domestication in animals', in Ucko and Dimbleby, *op. cit.*, pp. 207–18.

[20] Bökönyi, *op. cit.*

[21] R. E. Chaplin, 'The use of non-morphological criteria in the study of animal domestication from bones found on archaeological sites', in Ucko and Dimbleby, *op. cit.*, pp. 231–46.

[22] M. F. Desforges and D. G. M. Wood-Gush, 'Behavioural differences between Aylesbury and wild mallard ducks: a study in domestication', *Vet. Rec.*, 96, 1975, p. 509.

[23] I. M. Drew, D. Perkins Jr and P. Daly, 'Prehistoric domestication of animals on bone structure', *Science*, 171, 1971, pp. 280–2.

of variation (the basis of all selection) through a reduction in natural selection. The differing types surviving could have become fixed by inbreeding, which probably resulted from the breeding unit being smaller than in the wild state. But archaeology has not yet provided information on the size of the first flocks and herds. Evidence from modern nomads suggests a flock of no more than 100 sheep and/or goats, although some settled peasants keep no more than 5–10 sheep for milk and wool.

Evidence from early Neolithic sites in the Near East shows a high proportion of young males being eaten,[24] which would have increased the extent of inbreeding, and could have led to the first artificial selection by man. There is similar evidence from the Bible.[25]

The killing of male animals probably led to the practice of castration. It is essential to be able to neuter particularly male stock in order to select efficiently, and it is likely that castration is very ancient. Trow-Smith[26] regarded as non-proven the claim of Watson[27] that an intermediate ox horn length at Skara Brae indicated bullocks and therefore castration. But Harcourt found the same evidence of castration at the Neolithic site of Durrington Walls, Wilts.[28] Aristotle described in detail the spaying of female pigs in order to promote fatness (below, p. 395). Cranstone describes various mechanical devices used by primitive people today to prevent male livestock from mating.[29] Whatever the cause, evolution became faster after domestication, and the animals changed more, and did so in a shorter period of time than under natural selection.

One of the first changes evident in skeletal remains of livestock is often a reduction in body and horn size. This could have taken place through breeding on a lower plane of nutrition. The reduction in the size of sheep seems to have been a lessening of the height of the animal brought about by a shortening of the limb bones. But the characteristic slenderness of the bones of wild sheep, for instance, remained evident in domestic forms until the Middle Ages. The short, stout bones of modern livestock are probably the result of fairly recent developments for meat. There have also been changes in body proportions which will be detailed when dealing with individual species.

Most of the major changes in sheep, for example in horn shape, tail length, and the change to a white woolly fleece, seems to have taken

[24] Flannery, *op. cit.*
[25] Genesis, xxxi, 38.   [26] Trow-Smith, *op. cit.*
[27] D. M. S. Watson, 'Report on the animal bones', in W. G. Childe, *Skara Brae*, London, 1931, p. 198.
[28] R. A. Harcourt, personal communication, 1970.
[29] B. A. L. Cranstone, 'Animal husbandry: the evidence from ethnography', in Ucko and Dimbleby, *op. cit.*, pp. 247–64.

place by the time that illustrations and records first appeared in Mesopotamia, about 3000 BC. The biologist will probably be less surprised than the archaeologist and historian that the biggest changes occurred during the first half of the domestic sheep's evolution, since this seems to be an example of the principle that evolution along a new line at first proceeds rapidly, and then slows down. In addition, the fact that evolution progresses more rapidly in smaller populations may have been a contributory factor.

It is likely that those characters such as lack of colour, and the absence of horns, which seem to be controlled by relatively few genes, were introduced into the population as a result of mutations. Darwin left such a strong legacy for the view that all mutations must have adaptive value in order to survive, that it has taken some time for it to be realized that many mutations are 'neutral' yet survive during evolution. It is very likely therefore that such neutral mutations have been important in changes following domestication (see p. 374).

Most characters of economic importance, however, such as the structure of the fleece in sheep, and its weight, are controlled by many genes, and show continuous variation. On this basis one can explain the changes wrought by man as being the result of straightforward selective breeding of animals with the desired characters, such as a longer tail, or a woollier fleece. Once some divergence had taken place, human migrations would have allowed wider out-breeding between different types than occurred in the wild state, and cross-breeding in this way has certainly been an important factor in the development of modern breeds.

But the science of genetics dates only from the beginning of this century, and practical breeding appears to have a history extending back little more than two hundred years. How then was primitive man able to breed such wide variety into farm stock?

From the above it will be evident that many of the changes arose from a continuation of natural selection in a modified form, others were the result of unconscious selection by man. It is difficult for us to realize that for centuries man lived far closer to his animals than we care to imagine. In so doing he gained much knowledge of the biology of livestock which was lost before it could be written down.

As a city dweller and laboratory-based biologist I am acutely aware that today we have a very limited experience from which to reconstruct the ways of primitive man. The first farmers lived very close to their livestock, and our civilization is so far removed from this situation that we are groping in the dark unless we start by looking at simple husbandry today, or at that practised in the recent past. The models proposed by Chaplin provide a useful basis, and the present treatment will indicate what can be learnt from an anthropological study of primitive husbandry methods (see below, p. 326).[30] More such studies are vital to the correct interpretation of archaeological data.

The closeness of primitive man to his livestock would have enabled him to observe the variations among his animals, and simple truths, such as 'like begets like', which provided the basis for selective breeding long before Mendel, would be learnt. Man could have been led to selection by the killing of the wildest and least-liked animals, and by the cherishing of particularly attractive or desirable individuals. Just as Palaeolithic hunters appear to have had an anatomical instinct, so Neolithic man may have acquired a breeding sense.[31]

The oldest account of breeding is the so-called Kikulli text of the fourteenth century BC.[32] This is in the Hittite language and deals with the breeding and training of horses, which seems to have attracted more attention than the breeding of other livestock. The work of Aristotle and of later Roman writers on agriculture indicate that selection was practised, but since they contain much that is erroneous, these works are not very helpful in telling us how selection was carried out. Not all apparently fanciful statements, however, lack basis (below, p. 369). On the other hand, except in the Arab world, systematic animal breeding underwent a setback after the Roman period, from which it took a long time to recover. Since breeding was a craft and not a science, the useful facts were probably never written down.

With this sort of approach we are getting away from the idea that animals were necessarily domesticated for a particular purpose. Sheep could not for instance be domesticated for their wool because this only became well developed after domestication. In the same way it is dangerous to infer from the predominant age or sex group among skeletal remains the products, e.g. meat, milk, or wool, for which the different animals were kept. It is doubtful whether any animal was ever kept for a single product. Everything but the proverbial squeal was used; early man used a whole range of animal products some of which we would never suspect today.[33]

ANIMAL PRODUCTS

The less perishable animal products provide sources of evidence on the character of ancient livestock. But when we see hard bone objects in museums it is easy to forget that in addition to his food much of man's

[30] Chaplin, op. cit.
[31] M. L. Ryder, 'The exploitation of animals by man', Adv. Sci., 23, 1966, pp. 9–18.
[32] A. Kammenhuber, Hippologia Hethitica, Wiesbaden, 1961.
[33] Ryder, 'The exploitation of animals...', 1966, op. cit.

equipment, made from what zoologists call the soft parts of animals, is rarely preserved.

The first source of food from animals was meat, but after domestication an animal would tend to be more valuable alive, and so not only would greater efforts be made to preserve meat, particularly for winter use, but new foods (blood and milk) that avoided the need to kill the animal were developed. Not all peoples have thought it necessary to kill their animals to obtain meat from them. Abyssinians in the eighteenth century used to cut flesh from cattle to eat raw, the skin being afterward pinned over the wound, and covered with clay.

Hunters and fishers probably discovered that flesh dried in the sun would resist putrefaction, and it may be that the discovery of the preservative effect of smoke was associated with cooking. When salt was first used, either in food or as a preservative, is not clear. Brothwell and Brothwell give maps to show the distribution of salt-workings, twelve being found on the south and east coasts of England and in north Wales in the Romano-British period,[34] but they were mistaken in believing that salt-panning began in Neolithic times.[35]

Fat varies in amount and consistency between species, that of sheep being particularly hard, enabling it to be used in candles. It has also long been used in making soap.

The use of bone was well developed before domestication in the making of hunting implements such as spears and fish hooks. Antlers are in fact composed of bone, and teeth can be included with bone although of somewhat different material.[36] Some tools, such as antler picks and shoulder-blade shovels, and ribs used as skin scrapers, underwent little preparation, whereas others were intricately carved. Man probably soon learnt that bone can be softened by soaking it in water, making the bone more easily cut with a flint knife.

Bone has been used for such a wide range of tools, from spinning whorls to weaving combs, that it would be tedious to attempt a complete list. The Neolithic dwellers of Skara Brae in treeless Orkney may have used whale bones for roof and door supports, and perforated vertebrae were used later as tethering rings. According to Herodotus, the Scythians, inhabitants of another treeless area, used bones as fuel. In the Middle Ages in Britain ox cannon (ankle) bones were shaped into skate runners.

The organic, collagenous element of bones can be boiled out to give gelatin and glue. If, on the other hand, the mineral part is removed with

[34] D. and P. Brothwell, *Food in Antiquity*, London, 1969, pp. 160–1.

[35] J. Nenquin, 'Salt: a Study in Economic Prehistory', *Diss. Arch. Gandenses*, VI, 1961, pp. 84–5.

[36] M. L. Ryder, *Animal Bones in Archaeology*, Oxford, 1969.

acid, the collagen remains as edible gristle. Bones were in fact prepared to be eaten in this way as *strjugar* in the recent past in Iceland, the (lactic) acid coming from a complicated blood and rye meal preparation in a sheep's stomach.

Skin, too, is composed mainly of collagen, and skins must at first have been used untanned, like the raw-hide of whips and ropes, and later parchment. The first form of tanning to produce leather seems to have been with oil, and this may go back, with smoking, to Palaeolithic times. Tanning with oak-bark extract appears to have begun in Neolithic times.[37] The hair can be removed by allowing putrefaction, but removal is speeded with the use of alkali, an early source of which was stale urine (another animal product).

Skin, like bone, has a wide range of uses, starting with clothing, oiled skins being used until recently by North Sea fishermen, and continuing with footwear, bags and liquid containers. It has been suggested that the first pottery vessels imitated the shape of a skin bag. It is just possible that cooking was carried out in a skin of water into which hot stones were dropped.[38] In more recent times bags made from a whole sheepskin were used to store corn and in the curing of meat, and leather riddles were used in cleaning grain. Bags made from entire animal skins are still in common use as storage containers for liquids as well as solids among nomadic peoples whose economy is based almost entirely on the products of their livestock. The moderately perishable nature of skin makes it likely that these and similar objects have a more ancient origin than one would at first imagine.

The original coracles of Wales and the curraghs of Ireland were made from skins stretched over a wooden frame, and by Roman times leather was used for sails, as well as in tents (which are, however, Palaeolithic in origin). Once the horse became important, elaborate leather harnesses were developed.

The very durable writing material, parchment, is not tanned, but is merely dehaired, stretched and dried.[39] If a similarly stretched skin is oiled, it becomes translucent, and lamb skins prepared in this way were used as windows in the Middle Ages.

Remains of skin provide a source of evidence on the type of ancient livestock from hair or wool persisting within its structure.[40] Leather chiefly gives evidence on cattle (below, p. 382), while different

[37] *Idem*, 'Remains derived from skin', in D. R. Brothwell and E. S. Higgs (eds.), *Science in Archaeology*, London, 2nd ed., 1970, pp. 539–54.

[38] *Idem*, 'Can one cook in a skin?', *Ant.*, XL, 1966, pp. 225–7.

[39] *Idem*, 'Parchment, its history, manufacture and composition', *J. Soc. Archiv.*, 11, 1964, pp. 391–9.   [40] *Idem*, 1970, *op. cit.*

groupings of wool fibres in parchment indicate different kinds of sheep (below, p. 369).

The collection of blood from living animals for food is very widespread, and is probably very ancient. It is still common among nomadic African cattle keepers (below, p. 326). Scottish cattle drovers in the eighteenth century mixed blood with oatmeal, and the same practice was carried out with cows and horses in Ireland in the nineteenth century.[41] Blood was also allowed to solidify for storage, and sheep's blood, in particular, was caught at slaughter (and still is) to make black puddings. These, too, are probably very ancient. The description in Homer's *Odyssey* is comparable with the modern counterpart: "These bellies of she-goats are being cooked on the fire; having filled them with fat and blood, we lay them aside for supper."[42] The mention of bellies provides a link with cooking in a paunch (see below). The Roman word *botellus* for black pudding goes back at least as far as the first century AD.

Milk along with blood, was probably one of the first new products following domestication. It is the most efficient way of converting plant to animal protein, the efficiency being 27 per cent compared with 18 per cent in pig meat, and only 6 per cent in beef and mutton. Man probably soon noticed that animals would let-down their milk more readily in the presence of their young. In seventeenth-century Scotland a calf skin stuffed with straw was put into the byre to assist milking, and similar milking customs are known to go back to prehistoric times over a wide area.[43] Although Proudfoot warns about too precise a projection into the past,[44] the past undoubtedly lives in the present, and it is likely that many similar customs are very ancient.

When primitive customs are abandoned in the interests of progress, it sometimes happens that a similar practice reappears at a later date in a scientific guise. On tackling the question of shelter for sheep, Cresswell, Thompson, and Gill found that appreciable early nineteenth-century knowledge on the subject had been forgotten.[45] Likewise the study of animal behaviour has only recently become respectable: research workers have found that greater success is achieved with

[41] E. Evans, *Irish Folk Ways*, London, 1957.

[42] Homer, *Odyssey*, xviii, p. 45.

[43] E. C. Amoroso and P. A. Jewell, 'The exploitation of the milk-ejection reflex by primitive people', in A. E. Mourant and F. E. Zeuner (eds), *Man and Cattle*, Roy. Anthrop. Inst., Occasional Paper, No. 18, 1963, pp. 126–37.

[44] V. B. Proudfoot, 'Bringing archaeology to life', *Adv. Sci.*, 22, 1965, pp. 125–33.

[45] E. Cresswell, W. Thompson and J. C. Gill, 'The effect of shelter and of tallow dressing of the fleece of fattening Scottish Blackface lambs', *Emp. J. Exp. Agric.*, 32, 1964, pp. 51–4.

artificial insemination of pigs when a record is played of the call of the male!

Souring and curdling is likely to have been discovered as soon as milk began to be used, and the preparation of the curd into cheese that could be stored for winter food may have begun very early. The earliest evidence from Europe, in the form of stone curd strainers, dates from no earlier than the Late Bronze Age, but baskets and cloth can be used for this, and these would not survive.

There is a legend that the way of speeding curdling with the use of the enzyme rennet was discovered by carrying milk in an animal's stomach. If, instead, a skin bag had been used, and the journey had been long, butter would have resulted. The making of butter may have originated with the nomads of central Asia, and came later than cheese. Although cheese was known in the classical world, butter seems to have been unimportant, its place being taken by olive oil. Butter used to be stored in the ground over a wide area of the world, and in some places was preferred rancid. It is now found occasionally as 'bog butter', which incidentally provides a study source of animal hairs, which in turn might provide a source of evidence on livestock. It is said that in the Near East one distinguishes butter made from sheep's milk by the 'fuzz' of wool that is evident along the edge when the butter is held against the light!

The relationship of milk, butter, and cheese is outlined in Fig. 61. The percentage of fat given is that for the modern cow. The figure ranges from 1.5 per cent in the horse and ass through 4.5 per cent for the goat and 7.5 per cent in the sheep to 22.5 per cent in the reindeer.

I have discussed the genetic and environmental hypotheses of lactose tolerance in modern dairying countries.[46] The genetic hypothesis holds that individuals unable to tolerate lactose in milk would have been at a selective disadvantage. The environmental hypothesis states that lactose tolerance arises from the continued drinking of milk into adulthood, and that primitive pastoral peoples would not have been affected by lactose intolerance because the preparation of milk products destroys lactose.

Ghee (clarified butter fat) is an Indian word for the liquid which replaced butter in hot climates. This might be regarded as a combination of butter and cheese because in Africa, at any rate, ghee is butter churned from fresh (whole) milk curdled with cow's urine, which is then boiled and stored in gourds. It may be that cheese manufacture is difficult in a hot climate, except in a cool place. One recalls Polyphemus the Cyclops making cheese in a cave in the *Odyssey*, and the maturation of Roquefort cheese in caves in the south of France.

[46] Animal products with particular reference to sheep have been covered in greater detail in M. L. Ryder, *Sheep and Man*, London (forthcoming).

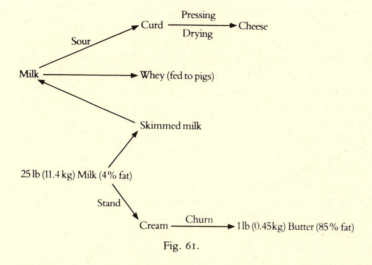

Fig. 61.

Various other milk products originated in Asia. Mare's milk is fermented into *kumiss* to make it keep,[47] just as in the West fruit juice is fermented for storage as wine. These processes depend on the right micro-organisms being present at the right time; cheese is ripened by bacteria, and there must have been many accidents in the past. Yoghurt is formed by *Lactobacillus bulgaricus* and a species of *Streptococcus*, and may have been discovered by the infection of the milk in the udder of a dead cow.

Wool is another important product of domestication, although sheep skins may have been appreciated as clothing before domestication because the outer coat kemps of wild sheep are softer and less coarse than those of deer for instance. Wool may first have been used as a felt, which is frequently formed naturally during the shedding of the fleece, even in wild sheep.[48] There are indications that felt was developed in Asia; it dates back to 400 BC at Pazyryk, and felt is still used by Asiatic nomads for tents, boots and mats. The use of wool in this way enabled cold regions to be occupied. There may be an evolutionary sequence from the tent wall, through the carpet, which is hung on tent and room walls in the east, to the tapestry of Europe, which provided the first house insulation.

Wild and primitive domestic sheep often rub a shedding fleece into long strands of wool, and these strands may have suggested the spinning

[47] B. A. L. Cranstone, 'Animal husbandry: the evidence from ethnography', in P. J. Ucko and G. W. Dimbleby (eds.), *The Domestication and Exploitation of Plants and Animals*, London, 1969, pp. 247–64.
[48] M. L. Ryder, 'The origin of felt making and spinning', *Ant.*, xxxvi, 1962, p. 304.

of wool to Neolithic man.[49] Since weaving, in basketry, was already known before domestication, this could have led to the great Neolithic invention of cloth manufacture. Flax has usually been thought of as the first fibre to be spun, but this could be because only flax has been preserved from the earliest sites. Much preparation is in fact required in order to obtain the fibres from the flax stem.[50]

Remains of wool in textiles provide a source of evidence on coat changes since domestication. There has been a gradual loss of the outer-coat kemp found in wild sheep to give a range of fleece types from hairy ones in which a proportion of kemps is often present, to fine-woolled types with no kemp or hair at all.[51] A fibre diameter distribution can indicate the proportion of different fibre types, and therefore the type of fleece from which a wool has come, which in turn indicates the stage of evolution (below, p. 368). Animal hair (particularly goat hair) although used less extensively has been woven, notably by nomads, into cloth for tents and bags.

The horn of hooves, and the horny covering of the bony core of horns, is composed of keratin, which is the same substance as that of hair and wool, and this has provided another raw material until recent times. Horn casings were probably used first as drinking cups and containers. The chief value of horn is that it can be softened by boiling in water, after which it can be cut, flattened, or moulded into various shapes. Horn was thus the first plastic. One of the earliest examples of this shaping is a horn spoon found in a Bronze Age beaker from Aberdeenshire. By the Middle Ages the horner's craft was well developed, with specialized tools, and a wide range of products. Thin sheets of horn are in fact transparent, and from the use of horn in lantern windows comes the corruption into 'lanthorn'.

Gut takes us back to a material like skin, in that it contains much collagen. The alimentary tract of animals provides a source of containers and tubes, and also of cords for lathes and spinning wheels as well as strings for musical instruments. It was apparently used to make the 'cord' decoration on early Bronze Age pottery. Gut-dressing became a well-developed trade, ox gut being prepared for sausage skins.

The Scottish haggis, made in a sheep's stomach, is probably of great antiquity and, therefore, perhaps to be regarded as a primitive sausage (cf. also black puddings, and the Icelandic stomach preparation, above). Although haggis is now cooked by boiling it in a pan, the original method may have been by suspending it directly over a fire[52] (cf. also

[49] Idem, 'The origin of spinning', Ant., XXXVIII, 1964, pp. 293–4.
[50] Idem, 'The origin of spinning', Textile History, I, 1968, pp. 73–82.
[51] Idem, 'Changes in the fleece of sheep following domestication (with a note on the cost of cattle)', in Ucko and Dimbleby, op. cit., pp. 495–521.
[52] Idem, 'Paunch cooking', Ant., XLIII, 1969, pp. 218–20.

the reference to this in the *Odyssey*, above). This allowed the cooking of liver and other internal organs now discarded.

Last but no less important is dung, being so highly valued as manure in early medieval England that it came third to milk and wool, and before meat in importance. In India, today, shepherds are paid to graze their sheep on stubble in order to have the land manured. The initial effect of fresh, concentrated dung is harmful to grass, and so the observation of its value as a fertilizer must have been made on the periphery of a concentration, or on the run-off from a pen or animal house. Such an effect can be observed on St Kilda today where the Soay sheep shelter in dry-stone *cleits* left by the islanders. At the entrance to each *cleit* is a patch of bright green grass that has been manured by drainage from the accumulated sheep droppings within. Trow-Smith regarded a shippon with a central liquid manure tank at the Bronze Age site of Jarlshof (Shetland) as the first indication of the manuring of crops.[53]

As a source of archaeological evidence human coprolites have provided information on diet from remaining fragments of undigested food[54] and also on internal parasites from surviving worm eggs.[55] Troels-Smith studied the pollen in caprovine dung found within the Swiss early Neolithic site of Egolzwil and showed that either fodder had been brought into the settlement for them, or that they had been allowed to feed outside daily.[56]

This list of animal products aspires to be complete but there were probably others, and certainly many uses in the past that we should never suspect today. A thorough search among primitive communities is essential if we hope to learn about some of these before early customs die out completely.

THE ORIGINS OF BRITISH LIVESTOCK

The original source of British farm animals was the livestock introduced by Neolithic settlers. This largely exotic origin is emphasized by the claim that, had the Incas of South America achieved world domination, we should have had the alpaca and the llama on British hills.

Of the four farm animals, cattle, pigs, sheep, and goats, whose skeletal remains have been found on Neolithic sites, only cattle and pigs were

[53] R. Trow-Smith, *A History of British Livestock Husbandry to 1700*, London, 1957, p. 2.

[54] D. and P. Brothwell, *Food in Antiquity*, 1969, pp. 160–1.

[55] A. W. Pike and M. Biddle, 'Parasite eggs in medieval Winchester', *Ant.*, XL, 1966, pp. 293–6.

[56] J. Troels-Smith, 'Pollenanalytische Untersuchungen zu linigen Schweizerischen Pfahlbauproblemen', in W. Guyan, 'Das Pfahlbauproblemen', *Mon. z. ur-u. Früh. der Schweiz*, XI, Schaffhausen, 1954, pp. 11–57.

at that time still found in the wild state in Britain. These two species were present for instance at the Mesolithic site of Star Carr in east Yorkshire, somewhat before Britain became separated from the Continent.

The wild ox persisted until the Bronze Age, and the wild pig remained until the seventeenth century AD although it had probably interbred with domestic stock for centuries. The so-called wild sheep (the Soay of St Kilda), wild goats, and wild horses in Britain today, are feral domestic animals. Zeuner considered that domestic pigs probably gained from local wild strains,[57] but the view of Trow-Smith that prehistoric domestication of the pig was non-proven since the bones found in domestic contexts could have been from wild animals is clearly too extreme (below, p. 392).[58]

The dog appears to be the only other certain domestic animal of the Neolithic period, having already been domesticated in the Mesolithic period. Other livestock such as the horse and poultry came later. Wild horses lived on the steppes in Britain after the ice had retreated, but no remains were found at Star Carr which was occupied during a period when a tundra fauna was giving way to forest animals. Several sites of the Neolithic Windmill Hill culture have a few bones of wild horses which appear to have been hunted and eaten.[59, 60]

When the domestic horse arrived in Britain is not known, but by the Late Bronze Age there is clear evidence of domestication in the form of bits, cheek-pieces, and other harness remains. Trow-Smith considers that local domestication is possible but the possibly domestic horse bones from the Late Neolithic Rinyo-Clactonian site of Durrington Walls quoted by Murray,[60] are likely to have been wild (below, p. 398). It seems, unlikely, however, that local domestication could have provided the only, or even an important, source of the ancestors of British horses. Since its original use is likely to have been a military one, Trow-Smith suggests that it was first introduced in significant numbers by a militant group of Late Bronze Age invaders. But there is no archaeological evidence for such a group.

[57] F. E. Zeuner, *A History of Domesticated Animals*, London, 1963.

[58] Trow-Smith, *op. cit.*

[59] *Ibid.*

[60] J. Murray, 'The osteological and botanical evidence for Neolithic agriculture in Europe', Ph.D: thesis, Univ. of Edinburgh, 1967; also *idem, The First European Agriculture*, Edinburgh, 1970.

COLONIZATION

How livestock was transferred across the sea has long been a subject of discussion. Johnstone considered that Neolithic man used skin boats to carry his domestic animals,[61] and one has only to observe the islanders of the Aran group off western Ireland ship a calf with its legs tied, and its hooves blunted with sacking, to realize that this was entirely possible. The curragh perpetuates an ancient design, although the covering is now of canvas.

Case has more recently developed this discussion and has attempted to put limits on the time of the year when colonization could have taken place.[62] His allowance for seed planting and harvesting need not, however, be made since the colonizers could have been solely pastoralists. Or, if basically mixed farmers, they could have become pastoralists until settlements had been established, and fields had been cleared and prepared for growing crops. Anthropological evidence, however, suggests that people do not readily change their basic economy and feeding habits.

Only one growing season could have been missed, the original seed brought being stored until it could be sown, or such a stage could have lasted for a few years, any grain required being brought across the sea. Grain would not have been as vulnerable to wetting in an open boat, as implied by Case, if it had been carried in a skin bag.

The need of Neolithic settlers to have winter fodder available, as claimed by Case, is by no means proven. Primitive domestic livestock being much closer to their wild ancestors would almost certainly have been better able to fend for themselves during the winter than the improved breeds with which we are familiar today. What almost certainly was a limiting factor was the area of natural pasture immediately available for grazing, and, indeed, archaeological evidence shows that the chalk downs of southern England were the first areas occupied. As forest clearance proceeded, some low-lying and wetter areas may have retarded animal husbandry through such sheep afflictions as liver-fluke and foot-rot, in the same way as malaria has limited human settlement in some parts of the world. Whether such parasites and diseases were introduced with the livestock, or were found in similar wild species, is an interesting biological problem.

Since this was written the 'Neolithic explanations' of Case have been discussed by Wilkinson, who pointed out that the provision of winter fodder was not essential.[63]

[61] P. Johnstone, 'The Bantry boat', *Ant.*, xxxviii, 1964, pp. 277–84.
[62] H. Case, 'Neolithic explanations', *Ant.*, xliii, 1969, pp. 176–86.
[63] P. F. Wilkinson, 'Neolithic postscript', *Ant.*, xlv, 1971, pp. 193–6.

CHAPTER II

HUSBANDRY IN SUCCESSIVE
ARCHAEOLOGICAL PERIODS

THE NEOLITHIC PERIOD

CLARK in a survey of the evidence from livestock remains concluded that in central, north, and north-west Europe cattle and pigs predominated in Neolithic times, and that by the Late Bronze and Early Iron Ages, the sheep and/or goat had become more important and sometimes predominant.[1] He was one of the first to realize that such differences need not have a cultural basis, and can be explained entirely on ecological grounds. Thus the vegetation encountered by Neolithic man in Europe comprised a dense forest cover, which was more appropriate to the keeping of cattle and pigs than of sheep, which prefer more open country. Pigs, and to a lesser extent cattle, gradually clear forests by killing young trees. The goat, unlike the sheep, is a browser on trees, and has been blamed for forest clearance until recent times. It is happier on more rugged ground than is the sheep.

Clark gave a sequence of radiocarbon dates from Jericho in 8000 bc to Britain about 3000 bc showing the rate at which the Neolithic farming economy spread across Europe.[2] Waterbolk discussed this movement in greater detail with the help of distribution maps.[3] Renfrew's dating of megaliths in western Europe as being earlier than those in eastern Europe may make a modification of these necessary.[4]

Oak forest has predominated in Britain since about 5500 BC.[5] It is, therefore, of interest to consider reports of stock poisoning in the New Forest in recent years through the eating of acorns. These are such a well-known food for pigs that cases of poisoning in other animals seem surprising. They have, when leached, been eaten by man.[6] In fact, acorns are injurious to most species including man, the pig being notably

[1] J. G. D. Clark, 'Sheep and swine in the husbandry of prehistoric Europe', *Ant.*, XXI, 1947, pp. 123–36.

[2] *Idem*, 'Radiocarbon dating and the spread of farming economy', *Ant.*, XXXIX, 1965, pp. 45–8.

[3] H. T. Waterbolk, 'Food production in prehistoric Europe', *Science*, 162, 1968, pp. 1093–1102.

[4] C. Renfrew, 'Carbon-14 and the prehistory of Europe', *Sci. Amer.*, 225, 1971, pp. 63–72. [5] L. D. Stamp, *Man and the Land*, London, 1955, p. 8.

[6] D. and P. Brothwell, *Food in Antiquity*, London, 1969, pp. 160–1.

resistant. Apart from the poison, which is a hydrolysable tannin, acorns tend to give herbivores indigestion, and in particular clog the rumen of ruminants.[7]

Most cases of poisoning today occur in cattle, and in 1968 one hundred animals died in the New Forest, so that in 1969 the ponies and cattle were rounded up early, and pigs were put in to clear up the acorns. Some authorities claim that acorns can be safely fed to ruminants if first allowed to germinate. The amount of poison in the acorns probably varies from year to year, and the fact that by Saxon times only pigs are recorded as being fed acorns suggests an awareness of the problem. Trow-Smith quoted figures showing that acorns have a food value to pigs which is as much as half that of barley meal.[8] But horse-chestnuts have negligible food value, and are repulsive even to pigs. Moore found from pollen analysis of peat in north Cardiganshire that Neolithic people had little influence on the vegetation, and that more intensive forest clearance took place later, possibly in the Bronze Age.[9] In Ireland on the other hand at three Neolithic sites tree pollen was suddenly replaced by cereal pollen, followed by a gradual return to the original situation. This is interpreted as indicating initial clearance of forest for farming activities and eventual abandonment in search of new land.[10]

More recent investigations on the whole confirm the findings of Clark.[11] Even on the Scilly Isles in the Bronze Age sheep predominated over a few goats and cattle.[12]

But Higham found that at the earliest Neolithic level of Egolzwill 3 in Switzerland sheep or goats predominated, pigs came next, although it was not clear whether these were wild or domestic, and that there were only a few remains from domestic cattle.[13, 14] Such anomalies could have an environmental explanation. Wurgler, for instance, showed that at higher altitudes in the Swiss Bronze Age sheep/goats increased at the expense of cattle.[15]

[7] I. L. Mason, personal communication, 1970.

[8] R. Trow-Smith, *A History of British Livestock Husbandry to 1700*, London, 1957.

[9] P. D. Moore, 'Human influence when vegetational history in north Cardiganshire', *Nature*, 217, 1968, p. 1006.

[10] J. Pilcher, A. Smith and A. Crowther, 'Land clearance in the Irish Neolithic', *Science*, 172, 1971, pp. 560–2.   [11] Clark, 1947, *op. cit.*

[12] F. A. Turk, 'Report on the animal remains from Nor-Nour, Isles of Scilly', *J. Roy. Inst. Cornwall*, N.S., v, 1967, pp. 250–66.

[13] C. F. W. Higham, 'A consideration of the earliest Neolithic culture in Switzerland', *Vierteljahrschrift der Naturforschenden Gesellschaft in Zürich*, 112, 1967, pp. 123–36.

[14] *Idem*, 'Stock rearing as a cultural factor in prehistoric Europe', *Proc. Prehist. Soc.*, 33, 1967, pp. 84–106.

[15] von F. E. Wurgler, 'Veränderungen des Haustierbestandes während der Bronze- und Eisenzeit in zwei schweizerischen "Melauner" – Stationen, Montlingerbeg und Moltata Ramosch', *Zeitschrift für Tierzucht. Zuchtsbiol.*, 77, 1962, pp. 35–46.

Higham first used detailed measurements to distinguish between sheep and goats, and then made statistical comparisons of cattle, pig, sheep, and goat numbers at two Swiss Neolithic and two Late Bronze Age sites.[16] At the Neolithic sites there was no significant difference between the numbers of the above species at St Aubin, but at Egolzwill 2 cattle predominated. Of the two Bronze Age sites at Zürich, Alpenquai sheep predominated, but at Zug Sumpf there was no significant difference between the numbers of cattle, pigs and sheep, and goat numbers were negligible.

Higham stressed the ecological basis of cultural changes.[17] He demonstrated a sex difference in cattle remains at Troldebjerg (Denmark), and found that 96 per cent survived their first winter and 80 per cent their second winter. Males were preferentially killed, and these were all killed before the age at which they could be used to draw a plough. There is no basis, however, for Higham's contention that the preferential killing of male sheep in the Swiss and Danish Neolithic necessarily indicates a lack of interest in wool.[16, 17, 18] This practice has been usual from prehistoric times to the present day, and has continued in recent times in Britain even when wool provided 40 per cent of the income from sheep. The use of wether flocks for wool production, e.g. in medieval England or modern Australia, is a specialized practice associated with either high wool prices or poor environments, or both.

It is necessary to have some appreciation of the entry route, and nature of each group of colonizers of Britain, since it is possible that different peoples brought different types of livestock. There is a point of view today which considers that one must not postulate an influx of people to explain every new development in object design. There are, however, certain attributes such as the Celtic language which must have been introduced. Likewise, considerable change in livestock could have taken place within Britain, but we are a long way from being able to distinguish livestock characteristics that could have developed in the British Isles from those that must have been introduced. The occurrence of similar characters on the Continent does not rule out parallel evolution in Britain.

The gene frequencies for human blood groups are known to have remained constant in certain populations for at least 1,000 years and these have been useful in the study of tribal migrations.[19] But the use of blood

[16] C. F. W. Higham, 'Trends in prehistoric European caprovine husbandry', *Man*, 3, 1968, pp. 64–75.

[17] *Idem*, 'Towards an economic prehistory of Europe', *Curr. Anthrop.*, 10, 1969, pp. 139–50.

[18] *Idem*, 'The economic basis of the Danish Funnel-Necked Beaker (TRB) Culture', *Acta Arch.*, XL, 1969, pp. 200–209.

[19] Sir Gavin de Beer, *Genetics and Prehistory*, Cambridge, 1965.

types with livestock is of less value because the gene frequencies are likely to have changed rapidly in recent times owing to the overriding influence of a few males, in what has been termed a genetic bottleneck.

Until the excavation of the Neolithic settlement at Windmill Hill, near Avebury, only fifty years ago, our main information on Neolithic peoples in Britain came from their burials in long barrows. This Windmill Hill culture on the chalk downs of southern England probably represents the initial colonization across the Channel from France, and Piggott recognized several colonizing streams.[20] The Windmill Hill settlers spread along the Icknield Way into East Anglia and thence to the Yorkshire Wolds. The movement continued on two routes: one across the Pennines and across the sea to Northern Ireland, and the other northwards through Scotland to the shores of the Moray Firth.

By this time other groups of colonists – the builders of chambered cairns or megaliths – had settled around the Severn and Clyde estuaries. Of significance to livestock origins is the indication that these peoples came initially from southern Europe, and that this western route of entry was perhaps the most important one during the Neolithic period, whereas during the succeeding Bronze Age, and subsequently, entry from the east was more important.

Piggott distinguished between primary Neolithic cultures, which were entirely exotic in origin, and secondary Neolithic cultures, which arose through the adoption of imported Neolithic ideas by indigenous Mesolithic hunter-fishers but this thesis has now received much destructive criticism. The site of Skara Brae in Orkney regarded as 'secondary', would now be classed rather as simply 'Late' Neolithic. But Piggott attempted to show that even the primary colonists were not averse to the assimilation of Mesolithic techniques – for instance the use of antler combs to dress skins at Windmill Hill – but this is purely hypothetical.

Piggott pointed out that no houses existed within the Neolithic causewayed camps, including Windmill Hill itself, and suggested that they were communal cattle kraals for the primarily pastoral economy, a suggestion that was fully endorsed by Trow-Smith,[21] but has since been severely modified. Such sites were located on chalk, gravel or other soils because of the existing or potential pasture. Piggott claims that the choice of site was not restricted by inability to clear forest. But, as pointed out by Trow-Smith, until grazing changed the flora, the vegetation controlled the type of animal kept, and therefore the pastoral use of the area. Man, and his animals, were dominated by the

[20] S. Piggott, *The Neolithic Cultures of the British Isles*, Cambridge, 1954.
[21] Trow-Smith, *op. cit.*

environment until he became able to control it. Here there may have been seasonal round-ups of stock. Whether or not such round-ups preceded autumnal cropping of stock, followed by feasting and the conversion of skins into clothing, is debatable (see modern evidence below). It has already been indicated that livestock would have been more valuable alive than dead, and there is no compelling reason to believe that with the low stocking density that must have then prevailed, cattle and pigs could not have survived the winter.

Like wild deer, for instance, livestock could graze, over a wide area, the grass remaining from summer growth as well as foliage and bark. There is no evidence that animal feed was preserved for winter use before the Iron Age, but tree branches could have been kept as early as the Neolithic. Clumps of holly were preserved to provide winter feed for sheep in the Middle Ages.[22] In Scandinavia, sheep in winter are still given spruce, pine, and other tree branches from which they eat leaves and finer shoots, as well as gnawing the bark from logs. But except for the clearance of forest such grazing does not leave a mark on the land, as does ploughing (below, p. 345).

A survey of skeletal evidence for Neolithic agriculture in Europe carried out by Murray[23] confirmed the findings of Clark[24] and stressed the overall predominance of cattle in Britain. Cattle were found on all fifteen sites of the Windmill Hill culture of southern England (3200–2600 BC), whereas pigs and ovicaprids (sheep/goats) were found at only half of the sites. Without detailed and laborious measurement it is difficult to distinguish most bones of sheep from those of goats, but both were identified at Windmill Hill.

At Windmill Hill, 90 per cent of the remains were from domestic animals. Table I shows the relative numbers of the different livestock species. Grigson surveyed the three earliest Neolithic sites, Windmill Hill, Wilts., Fussell's Lodge, Wilts., and Maiden Castle, Dorset, and came to the same general conclusions.[25] There is no doubt about the predominance of cattle, but there appears to have been little difference in numbers between pigs and ovicaprids. There is a hint in the table of an increase in the proportion of ovicaprids at a later stage, which, if real, may have been due to increased land clearance.

A similar picture emerges from the later Neolithic period, but at the site of Durrington Walls, Wilts., pig bones predominated (Table 1). This, and nearby Marden, are henge monuments of about 2000 BC,

[22] J. Thirsk, Letter to Editor, *Agric. Hist. Rev.*, 10, 1962, p. 119.

[23] J. Murray, 'The osteological and botanical evidence for Neolithic agriculture in Europe', Ph.D thesis, Univ. of Edinburgh, 1967.

[24] Clark, 1947, *op. cit.*

[25] C. Grigson, 'The domestic animals of the earliest Neolithic in Britain', in H. Schwabedissen (ed.), *Die Anfänge des Neolithikums vom Orient bis Nordeuropa*, Köln, 1971.

Table 1. *Relative percentage numbers of different livestock species on Neolithic sites*

	Cattle	Pigs	Sheep/goat	Horse
Windmill Hill				
pre-enclosure level	70	17	13	—
primary level of enclosure ditch	60	15	25	—
Later Neolithic				
Durrington Walls (percentages calculated from data given by Murray)[26]	35	61	4	0.3
	29	68	1.5 1.5	1
Marden (data from Harcourt;[27] minimum no. of animals)	42	42	10.5	5.5
Abingdon, Berks.[28]				
From bones	57	35	8	—
From minimum no. of animals	49	35	16	—
Puddlehill[29] I	23	43	34 ⎫	not
II	40	60	— ⎬	included
III	33	66	1 ⎭	

which are thought to have been communal, possibly ceremonial, buildings.

A more recent investigation of new material from Durrington Walls by Harcourt yielded one definite goat bone and only five sheep bones (from five individuals) in a total of 8,500 identifiable bones.[30] Percentages from the minimum number of individuals represented in his counts are also shown in Table 1. Harcourt found evidence of castration from the grouping of cattle bones into three sizes which he interpreted as indicating bulls, cows and castrated males. He also recorded wild oxen remains (not included in the count).

Among remains from chambered tombs (2900–2200 BC) according to Murray cattle were most common, ovicaprids next-most frequent and pigs least numerous.[31] Sheep bones predominated however, at Quanterness in Orkney.[32]

Although some of these differences between sites are probably real,

[26] Murray, 1967, *op. cit.*

[27] R. A. Harcourt, personal communication, 1970.

[28] C. L. Cram, personal communication, 1969.

[29] G. W. I. Hodgson, 'A comparative account of the animal remains from Corstopitum and the Iron Age site of Catcote near Hartlepools, Co. Durham', *Arch. Ael.*, 4th series, 16, 1968, pp. 127–62.

[30] R. A. Harcourt, personal communication, 1970.

[31] Murray, 1967, *op. cit.*   [32] J. Clutton-Brock, personal communication, 1977.

it is necessary before placing too much reliance on them to consider the sampling problems discussed by Higham, who gave the statistical basis for the practice that has been current for some time of basing species percentages on the number of individuals represented, and not on the number of bones.[33] Higham found on three Danish Middle Neolithic sites (Troldebjerg, Bundsø and Lindø) that, in percentages, ox comprised 31 on each site, pigs 55, 43, and 39, and sheep/goats 14, 26, and 30.[34] The difficulty of obtaining an overall picture for the Neolithic is illustrated by the ranges in animal numbers over different European sites given by Higham:[35] cattle numbers ranged from 2 to 57 per cent with a mean of 30 per cent, pigs from 8 to 52 per cent with a mean of 23 per cent and sheep from 6 to 51 per cent with a mean of 24 per cent.[36] It will be seen that although cattle numbers predominated each range is similar and the means not very different.

EVIDENCE FROM PASTORAL PEOPLES TODAY

Anthropology, which has contributed to our understanding of Palaeolithic and Mesolithic archaeology, has perhaps not yet been fully exploited as an aid to the understanding of the Neolithic and later periods.

The relatively highly developed mixed farming of the British Iron Age, which forms a recognizable precursor of modern farming, tempts one to project the same detailed organization back to the Bronze Age and Neolithic period, from which few remains survive. Comparisons with the practices of some of the pastoral tribes living in other parts of the world today suggest that the true situation could have been quite different.

Neolithic cattle husbandry has been likened to modern ranching. Thus, R. and N. Dyson-Hudson make the following contrasts between modern American ranching and the subsistence herding of cattle in East Africa, with which British Neolithic husbandry had probably much in common.[37] First, both modern and subsistence herding involve large numbers of livestock, but whereas the first associates the least possible number of people with the livestock, the second associates the maximum population that çan regularly be fed from their produce. Secondly, in subsistence herding, in order to maintain continuity of food supply, the

[33] C. F. W. Higham, 'Faunal sampling and economic prehistory', *Zeitschrift für Säugetierkunde*, 33, 1968, pp. 297–305.

[34] *Idem*, 'The economic basis...', 1969, *op. cit.*

[35] *Idem*, 'Faunal sampling and economic prehistory', 1968, *op. cit.*

[36] I have calculated these from figures given in Table 5 of *ibid*.

[37] R. and N. Dyson-Hudson, 'Subsistence herding in Uganda', *Sci. Amer.*, 220, 1969, pp. 76–89.

main utilization is of blood and milk; meat is eaten only on accidental death, special occasions, and to stave off famine. At once, therefore, we recognize that there is no reason *a priori* why there should have been a seasonal cropping of meat during the British Neolithic.

The Dyson-Hudsons studied the Karimojong tribe of Uganda in which cattle represent property as well as the major source of subsistence. Some collecting and hunting takes place, and the women practice subsistence agriculture. They thus reduce the risks from drought, disease and perpetual war, when depending only on cattle for food. In some tribes cattle are kept for prestige and ritual and the use for food is secondary.

The women live in permanent settlements near rivers, and eat cereal crops supplemented by milk when the herds are nearby, although the goats and sheep remain near the settlements all the time. The herds are moved by the men and boys within the tribal area in search of grass grown by local rainfall. It has been shown that the seasonal migrations of wild animals are synchronized with the availability of specific grasses,[38] and Middle Eastern nomads are known to follow the seasonal maturation of pasture. Land is not owned, and the migration is the most primitive form of transhumance. This is in a Savannah region at 4,000 ft (1,220 m) above sea-level; thus except for a somewhat warmer and probably drier climate, with a seasonal rainfall, the area is perhaps not very different from the downs of southern England in Neolithic or Bronze Age times.

The men live off blood and milk, herd the cattle into thornbush kraals, and sleep in straw huts. This husbandry involves total use of the environment. In a nomadic economy there is no incentive to conserve pasture that may be used by someone else. Thus the aim is the short-sighted one of conserving herds, and not the conservation of pasture. The aim is frequently to own as many cattle as the land will carry rather than to limit numbers to those that will feed the population. According to Allan as many as 40 acres (16 ha) are required per animal in a poor area with little rain, and as few as 7 acres (2.8 ha) on better land with more rain. Where sheep or goats replace cattle the ratio is five of these to one ox. The Masai bleed sheep and goats as well as cattle. All lactating cows are milked each morning and evening. The calf is allowed to feed first to let down the milk, and to suck again after the milking. Four to eight pints (2.3–4.7 l) of blood are taken at three to five month intervals. The dilated jugular vein is pierced by a shot arrow. Blood is drunk mixed with milk.[39]

Also according to Allan, quoting another tribe, two cattle are needed

[38] R. H. V. Bell, 'A grazing ecosystem in the Serengeti', *Sci. Amer.*, 225, 1971, 86–93.
[39] W. Allan, *The African Husbandman*, Edinburgh, 1965, p. 292.

to provide a meal of blood for a family of five or six, and since these could be bled only once in five or six months, 13–16 animals are required per person; taking an average stocking density of 15 acres (6 ha) per cow, the human population density can be only 2 to 3 per square mile (259 ha).[40] An early reference to overstocking appears in Genesis: "Land unable to bear Lot's flocks and herds".[41] It is easy therefore to appreciate the statement of Stamp that from Roman times onwards there has been pressure of population on land in Britain.[42]

Although the Karimojong can dry and store meat, three-quarters of any available has by custom to be shared among friends. This can be interpreted as a social custom rather than as an irregular food supply. Blood is apparently not kept, but milk is stored as ghee (above, p. 314). Despite the large cattle numbers only 12 per cent give milk, and this cannot feed the whole population. Forty per cent of the cattle population are males; cows take $3\frac{1}{2}$ years to mature, the interval between calves is 14 months, and lactation lasts less than eight months. Then only half the cows have excess milk, and this amounts to only 2–4 pints (1.1–2.3 l) per day depending on the pasture. The average amount per person is one pint (0.57 l) a day in the dry season, and two pints in the wet.

The high calf mortality of 17 per cent causes castration to be delayed until the males are a year old. Delayed castration is probably the cause of animal contraception. Different methods – aprons for males or a tied penis, and a pebble in the vagina – are described by Cranstone.[43] Some selection of an illogical nature is carried out; for instance light coloured bulls are thought to give good milkers.

Efforts are made to preserve females. Barren cows and castrated males are killed during religious ceremonies, and since these take place during poor rainfall they constitute a culling. One wonders whether religious sacrifices, to produce rain for example, originated as a necessary culling, which was only later invested with religious significance. Culling is after all a 'sacrifice' made in order to maintain the herd at the expense of individuals. But in some societies it is the best bulls that are sacrificed.

Allan gave a figure as low as 4 per cent for the annual increase in numbers of a herd.[44] This was based on a figure of 45 per cent breeding, and a calf drop of only 40 per cent followed by a one-third neonatal mortality and an overall herd mortality of 8–10 per cent. There are two immediate lessons from these figures for archaeologists: (a) an annual

[40] Ibid., p. 305.   [41] Genesis, xiii, 5–7.

[42] L. D. Stamp, Man and the Land, London, 1955, p. 92.

[43] B. A. L. Cranstone, 'Animal husbandry: the evidence from ethnography', in P. J. Ucko an G. W. Dimbleby (eds.), The Domestication and Exploitation of Plants and Animals, London, 1969, pp. 246–64.   [44] Allan, op. cit., p. 315.

increase as small as 4 per cent means that in order to maintain numbers only this proportion is available for cropping or autumn killing, and (b) skeletal remains from calf losses as high as one-third could give the impression that young animals had been preferentially killed. Drought or disease must in many years have caused much greater overall losses than 10 per cent.

The main manipulation in this system is not of the herd or of the environment, but of the herd within the environment. Some burning of dead grass takes place, and water storage ponds are maintained; cf. the dew ponds of Britain which have been claimed to go back to Neolithic times. But the herd must be taken to food and water. Grazing takes place over 500 square miles (c. 130,000 ha), whereas a settlement of 250 people uses less than one square mile (c. 260 ha).

THE BRONZE AGE

The Bronze Age of nineteenth century nomenclature lasted roughly 1,500 years from about 1900 to 450 BC, but the boundary between the Neolithic period and the Bronze Age is now regarded as not very well defined. The change was rather a gradual process commencing, according to Piggott, when the Beaker folk began to arrive about the middle of the Neolithic.[45] Darlington aptly stated that the patient peasants who made the Neolithic revolution found themselves at the bottom of society in the Bronze Age, and that they have remained there ever since.[46]

Changes in livestock were certainly gradual rather than dramatic. Trow-Smith summarizes the changes as follows.[47]

1. The decline of the ox and pig with receding woodland, accompanied by a rise in sheep.

2. The introduction of a new breed of ox, *Bos longifrons* or the Celtic shorthorn.

3. The establishment of the domestic horse.

4. Husbandry advances involving cattle herding, sheep farming, and the first stock housing.

The Bronze Age coincided with the increasing dryness of the Sub-Boreal period. This either curtailed, or limited the expansion of, arable farming on thin soils, which were then the only ones cultivated. But pastoralism spread over the rest of the Chalk and oolite uplands,

[45] Piggott, 1954, *op. cit.*

[46] C. D. Darlington, 'The genetics of society', in A. J. Gregor (ed.), *A Symposium on Race: an Interdisciplinary Approach*, Hawaii, 1963.

[47] R. Trow-Smith, *A History of British Livestock Husbandry to 1700*, London, 1957, p. 5.

and over less attractive land – the gravel heaths of Cheshire, and the fells of Yorkshire and the Lake District. The Highland zone to the north and west has also been regarded as a haven for refugees from successive waves of invaders from the south and east. The mild climate meant that there was no need artifically to feed or house stock in winter. It also gives one greater confidence in making the comparison with modern African husbandry (above, p. 326). Nomadic pastoralism became highly developed; few habitation sites have been found.

Such nomadism was probably the forerunner of transhumance up bleaker hills in summer, and back to the valleys in winter. Habitations were probably literally camps visited periodically, comprising skin tents. The so-called hut circles of many upland areas may well represent the bases on which such tents were erected. Fleming has studied the density and distribution of Bronze Age barrows and has suggested that these might be used to indicate the grazing areas of different tribes.[48] In fact, as in any pastoral system, the whole range of mostly perishable animal products, discussed in the Introduction (p. 310), was probably highly developed. Bronze Age peoples had little or no pottery, but they did use stone pot boilers. If cooking was not carried out in a paunch[49] it may have been done in water in a skin heated with pot boilers.[50]

The dry climate also contributed towards the clearance of thinner upland forests by discouraging regeneration. This was associated with the decline of the pig and the rise of the sheep. Not only did the sheep provide the basis for the development of wool textile manufacture, but according to Trow-Smith it provided the fertility on which Iron Age arable farming was based.[51]

There is no evidence of textiles or their manufacture in Britain before the Bronze Age. Neolithic finds include bone needles which, it is suggested were used to sew together skins for clothing. Even as late as 55 BC Caesar reported that some of the Britons were clad in skins. The way in which felt-making and spinning could have been suggested from the moulting fleece of a sheep has been discussed in the Introduction. A wooden trackway at Thorne, Yorks., dated 1250 bc by C-14 was found to have dung beetles between the timbers, suggesting that livestock had been driven along it across a marsh between settlements.

Bronze Age cattle ranches are thought to have been built by the Deverel–Rimbury people about 1200 BC. They are bounded by linear earthworks that were first thought to have been tracks along which to drive cattle through arable land, and some may well have been so used.

48 A. Fleming, personal communication, 1970.
49 M. L. Ryder, 'Paunch cooking', *Ant.*, XLIII, 1969, pp. 218–20.
50 *Ibid.*, 'Can one cook in a skin?', *Ant.*, XL, 1966, pp. 225–7.
51 Trow-Smith, *op. cit.*

One such is Grim's ditch on Cranbourne Chase, Dorset. This had a flat bottom along which cattle were thought to have been driven, and was flanked by banks which had the post holes of a fence. Another near Cholderton, Wilts., is 2½ miles (4 km) long by ⅓ mile (0.5 km) wide, i.e. enclosing an area of over 500 acres (200 ha).

Aerial photographs show others to be as large as 1,000 acres (405 ha), with no sign of cultivation. They are also found on Chalk in the East Riding of Yorkshire and were used into the Iron Age since Celtic fields abut them.[52]

Support for the identification of these large enclosures as cattle ranches was thought to come from smaller enclosures less than half a hectare in size, which appeared to lack signs of human habitation, associated with them[53] though this interpretation was based on incomplete excavation. As cattle kraals these would contrast with the much larger Neolithic enclosures of Maiden Castle and Windmill Hill. Trow-Smith considers that these enclosures may have marked the beginning of the interdependence of arable crops and farm animals.

There were similar cattle pounds on Dartmoor, which were later used as summer shielings. Here, as elsewhere, the wetter climate at the end of the Bronze Age may have caused depopulation of the hills and resulted in transhumance back to the hills in summer.

The same period at Jarlshof in Shetland witnessed the first evidence of the housing of animals in a shippon 17 × 13 ft (5.18 × 3.96 m) in size. A central tank to collect liquid manure gives another hint of the move towards mixed farming.[54] Waterbolk described rectangular wooden houses in Holland dating from the Middle Bronze Age, in which cattle were stalled at one end. The heads faced the walls, and there was a central drainage channel. The width of the stalls decreased from 1 m in the Bronze Age to 0.8 m in the Middle Ages, in keeping with the decrease in size of the cattle.[55]

There is virtually no evidence on the methods of sheep husbandry, although one of the smaller enclosures discussed above in connection with cattle was identified as a sheep-fold.[56]

The scarcity of Bronze Age habitation sites means a lack of remains giving an indication of the relative abundance of the different livestock species. Some bones found associated with some Bronze Age pottery in Mill Pot Cave near Wetton, Staffs., are therefore of interest. Percentages, calculated from the number of individuals represented,

[52] *Ibid.*, p. 24.
[53] C. M. Piggott, 'Five Late Bronze Age enclosures in north Wiltshire,' *Proc. Prehist. Soc.*, 8, 1942, pp. 48–61.   [54] Trow-Smith, *op. cit.*, p. 26.
[55] H. T. Waterbolk, 'Evidence of cattle stalling in excavated pre- and protohistoric houses', in A. T. Clason (ed.), *Archaeological Studies*, Amsterdam, 1975, pp. 383–94.
[56] Trow-Smith, *op. cit.*, p. 24.

indicated 76 per cent sheep/goat (one goat skull being definitely identified) 14 per cent cattle, 4 per cent pig and 4 per cent horse.[57] These figures support the increase in sheep numbers in the Bronze Age discussed by Clark and Trow-Smith.[58, 59]

THE IRON AGE

The adoption of iron technology began from the eighth century BC, at a time of cooler, wetter climatic conditions.[60] This Sub-Atlantic phase which became established about 1000 BC has lasted ever since, except for short periods when it has been warmer and drier. It is well known that the characteristic British climate favours the growth of grass, even in winter.

Nevertheless, colder winters do cause a seasonal reduction in the growth of grass, and can make it necessary to house cattle (but not sheep and pigs). Reduced grass growth in winter plus the need for housing may have caused the development of haymaking as a conscious effort to conserve the summer flush of grass for winter use. But the housing of cattle is not inevitable. Hardy beef cattle remain outside all winter in Scotland, although they are fed hay.

Iron Age houses in Denmark had a cow byre, and we have seen that one was already in use in Shetland in the Bronze Age. The cutting of hay would have been facilitated by the development of iron implements, and there is evidence that *Polygonum* (buckwheat) was cultivated in Denmark possibly as a winter feed.[61] This was grown in recent times in eastern England mainly to feed poultry.

Perhaps the major advance between Bronze Age and Iron Age agriculture was the change from nomadic pastoralism to settled mixed farming. Farmoor, Oxon, established about 600 BC appears to have been a specialized pastoral settlement, utilizing ground in summer that was prone to flooding in winter. Villages were established with small square fields cultivated with the light plough or ard. Hansen has shown that these could be drawn by one or two oxen.[62] The heavy, wheeled

---

[57] M. L. Ryder, I. H. Longworth and A. J. H. Gunstone, 'Prehistoric bone and pottery finds from Mill Pot Cave, near Wetton, Staffs.', *North Staffs. J. Fld Studies*, 11, 1971, pp. 40–80.

[58] J. G. D. Clark, 'Sheep and swine in the husbandry of prehistoric Europe', *Ant.*, XXI, 1947, pp. 123–36.

[59] Trow-Smith, *op. cit.*

[60] The Fengate farm near Peterborough, excavated in the 1970s, had an Iron Age post dated 790±80 bc.

[61] E. C. Curwen, *Plough and Pasture*, London, 1946, p. 44.

[62] H-O. Hansen, 'Report on imitative ploughing experiments with copies of a prehistoric ard', *Reports from Experiments in Lejre*, 1968, 1, 1969.

plough was introduced into Britain by the Belgae about 75 BC. This necessitated larger plough teams and longer furrows.

Trow-Smith considered that the Hallstatt and La Tène invaders of the Iron Age A period had little effect on British livestock, although he thought that local varieties would have begun to emerge.[63] The Parisii Iron Age B tribe that settled in east Yorkshire about 250 BC were charioteers and are likely to have introduced horses that were more highly developed than those already here. In 1971 a chariot burial dated about 200 BC was found in this area at Garton slack quarry, Wetwang, a cloven pig's head having been buried with the body. From horse remains at Scarborough, Harcourt gained a hint that horses in the north were taller than those in the south.[64] A possible change in male clothing, associated with the development of horse riding, may have been the adoption of trousers.

In addition to introducing the heavy plough it is likely that the Belgae introduced the domestic fowl and an improved sheep (below, p. 370). They seem to have been such good farmers that they produced a surplus of corn and cattle for export. Strabo mentions the export of salt meat (above, p. 311) and blankets to Gaul. British cloaks became famous, and remained so at least until the ninth century AD. Clark thought that the numerous bone weaving combs, bobbins made from sheep metapodia, loom weights, and loom timbers from Glastonbury suggested more weaving than was required for the villagers themselves.[65]

All Cannings Cross and Little Woodbury, Wilts., have been regarded as typical Iron Age villages yielding remains of cattle, sheep, goats, pigs, horses, and dogs, but Trow-Smith pointed out that regional variation began to be evident about this time, and that one cannot make generalizations for the whole of Britain.[66] The recent excavation at Fisherwick Iron Age Farm near Lichfield indicated that the livestock comprised mainly cattle and horses, with pigs kept in the farmyard.

Little Woodbury is typical of the mixed farming of south-east England. Further west, pastoralism predominated. Little Woodbury on the chalk hills near Salisbury was occupied between the third and first centuries BC and was a single farmstead rather than a village. Cattle remains predominated over those of sheep and horse. Table 2 shows that the order of remains from most Iron Age sites is sheep, then cattle, followed by pigs. The heavier weight of cattle, however, means that the ox provided a greater proportion of the meat than did the sheep. Harcourt made estimates from bone measurements that the weight ratio of cattle:sheep:pig:horse was 10:1:1.5:10 and using these ratios calculated that, at Longbridge Deverill, cattle provided 60–62 per cent

[63] Trow-Smith, *op. cit.*   [64] R. A. Harcourt, personal communication, 1970.
[65] Clark, 1947, *op. cit.*   [66] Trow-Smith, *op. cit.*

Table 2. *Relative percentage numbers of the different livestock species on Iron Age sites*

	Cattle	Sheep	Pigs	Horses	
Woodyates[65]	38	34	2	26	(Bones)
Rotherley[65]	35	43	3	19	(Bones)
Woodcuts[65]	43	32	14	11	(Bones)
Glastonbury[65]	5	91	2	2	(Bones)
Highfield, Fisherton, Wilts.[68]	7	33	33	?	?
The Rumps, Cornwall[69]	14	68	18	—	(Individuals)
Veileby, Denmark[70]	30	35	30	4	(Individuals)
Stanton Harcourt, Oxon.[71]	32	42	21	5	(Individuals)
Twywell, Northants.[72]	22	56	14	8	(Individuals)
Longbridge Deverill, Wilts.[72]					
Phase A	34	26	26	14	(Individuals)
Phase B	29	42	18	11	(Individuals)
Undated	29	48	10	13	(Individuals)
Balksbury Camp, Hants.[73]	29	43	14	14	(Individuals)
Durrington Walls, Wilts.[72]	20	50	20	10	
Grimthorpe Hill Fort, Yorks.[74]	55	25	8	7	(Bones)
Catcote, Durham[75]	42	32	16	10	(Individuals)
Gussage All Saints, Dorset[67,76]	25	54	13	7	

of the meat (although representing only about 30 per cent of the numbers, see Table 2) sheep provided 5–10 per cent of the meat, pigs 3–9 per cent, and horses 23–27 per cent. He assumed that the horses had been eaten because the bones were as fragmentary as those from other species.[67] On medieval sites horse bones (and often skeletons) are usually

[67] R. A. Harcourt, personal communication, 1970.

[68] S. Applebaum, 'Agriculture in Roman Britain', D.Phil. thesis, Univ. of Oxford, 1951.

[69] R. E. Chaplin and J. P. Coy in R. T. Brooks, 'The Rumps, St. Minver: interim report on the 1963 excavations', *Cornish Arch.*, 3, 1964.

[70] C. F. W. Higham, 'The economy of Iron Age Veileby (Denmark)', *Acta Arch.*, 38, 1967, pp. 222–41.

[71] C. L. Cram, personal communication, 1969.

[72] R. A. Harcourt, personal communication, 1970.

[73] *Idem*, in G. J. Wainwright, 'The excavation of Balksbury Camp, Andover, Hants.', *Papers and Proc. Hants. Fld Club*, 26, 1969, pp. 21–53.

[74] M. Jarman, A. Fogg, and E. S. Higgs, 'The animal remains', in I. M. Stead, 'The Iron Age Hill Fort at Grimthorpe, Yorks.', *Proc. Prehistoric. Soc.*, 34, 1968, pp. 148–90.

[75] G. W. I. Hodgson, 'A comparative account of the animal remains from Corstopitum and the Iron Age site of Catcote near Hartlepools, Co. Durham', *Arch. Ael.*, 4th series, 26, 1968, pp. 127–62.

[76] See also G. Wainwright, 'A Celtic farmstead in southern Britain', *Sci. Amer.*, 237, 1977, pp. 156–69.

complete. Trow-Smith considered that the standard of farming at Little Woodbury was little if anything below that of the medieval peasant.

Appelbaum lists the following sites as having goats: Wilbury, All Cannings Cross, Swallowcliffe Down, Glastonbury, and the Belgic period at Hod Hill.[68]

Applebaum gives literary references which suggest that the Bronze Age cattle ranches persisted at any rate well into the Iron Age. Dio referred to the herds of the Caledonians, and Caesar to herds in south-east Britain, which were defended in *oppida* in times of war. Applebaum regarded *oppida* as open grazing areas bounded by woodland and the travelling earthworks already discussed in the Bronze Age (above, pp. 330–1).

The Iron Age cattle were of Celtic shorthorn type and there was no direct evidence of stock housing. Applebaum, however, considered that the scatter of pottery over Iron Age and Romano British fields indicated manuring, and that this in turn indicated overwintering of livestock other than sheep in stalls from which the manure was collected.[77] Ash, identified as coming from cattle dung, is evidence that this was used for fuel in Iron Age Surrey.[78] He suggested that sheep (likened to the Soay) were kept in rectangular enclosures during the growth of crops, and concluded that a 114-acre (46-ha) paddock at Figheldean could have held 40–50 sheep, which would then be turned on to the stubble of a 57-acre (23-ha) grain field to provide manure.

As with all horses in prehistory, the Iron Age ones were small. Harcourt noted at Longbridge Deverill that most horses had been killed between 2½ and 4 years, and, since it seemed illogical to kill a horse when in its prime for draught or riding, he suggested that the bones might have come from wild animals. He thought that this might indicate a periodical round-up to select animals for breaking-in with the subsequent slaughter of unsuitable ones for food. The post-Pleistocene survival of wild horses is, however, not unambiguously established.

Trow-Smith gave the hill fort at Pen Dinas in the hills near Aberystwyth as an example of the more pastoral type of farming which contrasted with the Little Woodbury type discussed above.[79] Here were found the same livestock as at Little Woodbury, plus goats which reflect the hill niche. This no doubt marked the beginning of the dependence on flesh and milk that was to continue for centuries on the Celtic fringe, and Trow-Smith remarks that had archaeologists devoted as much effort to animal remains as they had to field systems, we should know

---

[77] S. Applebaum, 'Agriculture of the British Early Iron Age – Figheldean, Wilts.', *Arch. Prehistoric Soc.*, N.S., 1954, pp. 103–14.

[78] A. Fenton, personal communication, 1976.

[79] R. Trow-Smith, *A History of British Livestock Husbandry to 1700*, London, 1957.

more about prehistoric livestock husbandry and its variations. Cunliffe gave evidence of an increase in sheep numbers during the Iron Age, and stressed the importance of their manure for grain production, yet calculations from body weights indicate that most of the meat eaten came from cattle.[80]

I am indebted to Dr J. P. Wild for a reference from Gildas who wrote in the sixth century, some think in Wales. He mentioned "mountains particularly suitable for the alternating pasturage of animals" which seems to refer to transhumance. This is the earliest reference to transhumance in Britain. Finally, it is worth noting that Turk found an unusual discrepancy of sheep hind limb bones on Nornour, Scilly Isles, from which he suggested that legs of mutton were traded from the island.[81]

THE ROMAN PERIOD

Although it has frequently been suggested that the Romans introduced new breeds of livestock and improved methods of husbandry, a critical examination of the evidence fails to produce overwhelming support for such a view.

Despite the detailed interest shown by Roman agricultural writers on the Continent, it seems that in Britain the largely dominant class, which the Romans constituted, left agricultural pursuits mainly to the lower orders and native elements of the population. Indeed Trow-Smith points out that it is often impossible to distinguish between the agrarian economies of the pre-Roman and Roman Iron Ages, and the post-Roman Dark Age.[82]

The typical Roman farm was the villa, but as late as 1951 Applebaum showed that there were few reliable data on the numbers and kinds of livestock found at villa sites.[83] He indicated that at Hucclecote, Hambledon, West Blatchington, and Appleton, Norfolk, cattle bones predominated, whereas at Langton, Yorks., sheep remains predominated. Although, as pointed out by Applebaum, bones reflect the diet, in a self-sufficient community like that of a villa the different animals are likely to have been eaten in the proportion in which they were kept.

Many villas it is thought became factories, particularly for the manufacture of cloth, but the claim that fulling was carried out at Chedworth, Glos., has not been substantiated. Others are claimed to have had sheep-folds. Collingwood and Myres believed that on the downs of southern England there was a change from corn growing to

---

[80] B. Cunliffe, *Iron Age Communities in Britain*, London, 1973, p. 173.

[81] F. A. Turk, 'A report on the animal remains from Nornour, Isles of Scilly', *Cornish Arch.*, 10, 1971, pp. 79–92.

[82] Trow-Smith, *op. cit.*　　　　　　　[83] Applebaum, 1951, *op. cit.*

sheep farming in later Roman times, the wool produced probably being used at the nearby wool manufacturing centre at Winchester.[84] It is, however, possible that both were combined in a farming system akin to that obtaining on the downs in the Middle Ages and subsequently Trow-Smith thought that sheep numbers continued to rise during the Iron Age and might during the Roman period have reached their highest peak before the wool boom of the later Middle Ages.[85]

Applebaum thought that the salt marshes of Essex were used for sheep rearing.[86] Wild regards the Breckland of East Anglia as the best-attested Roman sheep country[87] and more recently Phillips has argued that animal husbandry was the main occupation of the fenland farmers.[88] Wild questions the view that Cranbourne Chase was converted into a ranch with enclosures for sheep on the ground that the agile Soay cannot be so penned. This is not necessarily a valid argument because I have for several years kept Soay sheep near Edinburgh in relatively small

Table 3. *Percentage animal numbers at Roman sites*

	Cattle	Sheep	Pigs	Horses
Eastwood Villa, Fawkham[89]	56	27	4	13
Hemel Hempstead Villa, Herts.				
first & second centuries	24	44	26	6
fourth century[90]	46	27	19	8
Chew, Somerset (Romano-British)[91]	5	95	—	—
Hadrian's Wall Turrets[92]	31	52	17	—
Corstopitum (Northumb.)[93]	78	12	5	5
Vindolanda (Hadrian's Wall)[94]	58	19	12	3
Shakenoake (Oxon.)	46	27	15	12

[84] R. G. Collingwood and J. N. L. Myres, *Roman Britain and the English Settlement*, Oxford, 1937, p. 223.

[85] Trow-Smith, *op. cit.*   [86] Applebaum, 1951, *op. cit.*

[87] J. P. Wild, *Textile Manufacture in the Northern Roman Provinces*, Cambridge, 1970.

[88] C. W. Phillips, *The Fenland in Roman Times*, Roy. Geog. Soc. Res. Ser., 5, 1970, pp. 14, 64.

[89] J. P. Coy and R. E. Chaplin, 'The Animal Bones', in B. J. Philp, 'The Romano-British Farmstead at Eastwood, Fawkham', *Arch. Cant.*, 78, 1963, pp. 70–2.

[90] R. A. Harcourt, 'Animal remains', in D. S. Nere, 'The excavation of the Roman villa in Gadebridge Park, Hemel Hempstead', *Rep. Res. Comm. Soc. Ant. Lond.*, 31, 1974, pp. 256–61.

[91] *Ibid.* Personal communication, 1970.

[92] R. E. Chaplin, 'Report on the Animal Remains from six Turrets from Hadrian's Wall', *Arch. Ael.*, 4th ser., 43, 1965, pp. 193–200.

[93] Hodgson, *op. cit.*

[94] *Idem*, 'The animal remains, 1970–1975', *Vindolanda* II, Hexham, 1977.

enclosures with normal fences, and, in any case, there is evidence from textile remains that the sheep kept for wool production was an improved, white breed. Wild in fact goes on to acknowledge this, and suggests that the *byrrus Britannicus* capes and *tapete Britannicum* rugs would have been made from the wool of native sheep in the north.

Counts of animal remains from the few more recent Roman excavations give no support for the suggested increase in sheep numbers (Table 3). At Eastwood villa cattle predominated, while at Hemel Hempstead villa sheep predominated in the first and second centuries, but cattle were more numerous in the fourth century, which is the opposite of what has been claimed. This change in the ratio of sheep to cattle has been analysed by the present author with a chi-squared (χ^2) test and found to be not quite significant at the 5 per cent level. The increase in cattle does, however, accord with the suggestion of Applebaum that the enclosures built on Cranbourne Chase and elsewhere in the second and third centuries were for cattle. He contends that a rise in cattle rearing in the later Roman period was associated with increased meat-eating and an increased demand for leather.[95, 96]

The animal numbers from the several Hadrian's Wall turrets described by Chaplin were found not to differ with statistical significance and so have been combined in means (Table 3).[97] Here sheep predominated, but these remains, from their situation, are more likely to indicate the proportions eaten.

On the other hand Applebaum showed that cattle bones predominated at most military sites, one exception being Bar Hill on the Antonine Wall in Scotland where sheep predominated.[98, 99] (See also the contrast between the wall turrets and garrisons in Table 3.) He attributed this to the liking of the Syrian garrison for mutton.

The numerous sheep bones at the Romano-British site of Chew (Table 3) were arranged in ten piles, and Harcourt thought they might represent ritual deposits.[100]

Applebaum stated that goat bones were found at the military sites of Caerleon, Corbridge, and Newstead.[101] The footprint described by Ryder in a tile from Camelon on the Antonine Wall is probably more likely to have been made by a goat than a sheep.[102] Goat skins were

---

[95] S. Applebaum, 'Agriculture in Roman Britain', D.Phil. thesis, Univ. of Oxford, 1951.

[96] *Idem*, 'Agriculture in Roman Britain', *Agric. Hist. Rev.*, 6, 1958, pp. 66–86.

[97] Chaplin, *op. cit.*

[98] Applebaum, 1951, *op. cit.*   [99] *Idem*, 1958, *op. cit.*

[100] R. A. Harcourt, personal communication, 1970.

[101] Applebaum, 1951, *op. cit.*

[102] M. L. Ryder, 'Caprovine foot-prints in a Roman tile', *Proc. Soc. Ant. Scot.*, 99, 1967, pp. 258–9.

found at both Silchester and Manchester, which Applebaum interpreted as indicating use of civilian as well as military personnel. The civil sites with goat bones listed by Applebaum are: Hambledon, Wood Dalling, Folkestone, Otford, East Grinstead, Woolaston Pill, Icklingham, Brislington, Great Witcombe, Grimston, Purwell Mill, Silchester, Caerwent, and London.

Although Trow-Smith states that there are few certain identifications of stock houses dating from the Roman period, he describes a building at Iwerne with living quarters at one end and space for animals at the other which takes back into Roman times the house type known as the Welsh longhouse, which, however, also existed in other parts, notably the Pennines.[103] Applebaum pushes the same basic design back to the Dutch basilican house of the third century BC.[104, 105]

Although the horse was not used for ploughing, Applebaum drew attention to the reference of Varro to geldings being used as pack animals, and the apparent transport by horses of harvested corn, represented on Trajan's column.[106] There are other illustrations of horses carrying burdens, and drawing vehicles. They were also used for threshing, and Applebaum suggests for harrowing as well, since the ox was too slow for such work. Horses were ridden to round up cattle, and Applebaum interprets in this way the occurrence of horse bones in appreciable numbers alongside cattle bones. An inscription from Irchester, Northants., is interpreted by Applebaum as evidence of local, governmental horse-rearing, no doubt for military purposes.[107] The horse was, of course, still used for food at this time (Table 3).

According to the same writer the ass has been identified at Folkstone (a villa) and Newstead, and although there is no record of it before the Roman period, the ass could have been in use since it was recorded in the lake-dwelling of Ballydooloch, Ireland.[108] The mule was common in Roman Gaul but there is no evidence of it in Britain (below, p. 403).

The numbers of pigs at Iron Age and Roman sites are shown in Tables 2 and 3, and Applebaum considers that pig keeping was important at Romanized farms.[108] He lists pig remains as being found at the following villas: Grimston, Norfolk; West Blatchington, Sussex; Nuthills, Wilts.; Hambledon, Bucks.; Park Street, Herts.; Langton, Yorks.; Hucclecote, Glos.; Ely, Glam.; Saunderton, Bucks.; Folkstone and Otford, Kent; Southwick, Sussex; West Meon, Hants.; and Woolaston Pill, Mon., where it composed the greater part of the stock. Pigs appear to have been systematically fattened at Pitney and North Wraxhall.

103 Trow-Smith, *op. cit.*
105 *Idem*, 1958, *op. cit.*
107 *Idem*, 1958, *op. cit.*
104 Applebaum, 1951, *op. cit.*
106 *Idem*, 1951, *op. cit.*
108 *Idem*, 1951, *op. cit.*

Applebaum also lists five villas with no pig remains, but such negative evidence cannot be taken as conclusive. Literary sources show that pork was a popular food with the Romans, and at most military sites except those on Hadrian's Wall pig bones were next in frequency to ox bones. Cram found that the cattle killed at the villa of Shakenoak were old animals, while sheep/goats were killed in their second autumn. From the numbers (Table 3) he concluded that the increase in sheep at the expense of cattle evident in Saxon times began during the Roman period.[109] Hodgson found at Vindolanda on Hadrian's Wall that pigs were killed when young, cattle at three years, and ewes after producing five or six crops of lambs (as in a modern hill flock).[110]

Although the domestic fowl was present at a number of Belgic sites, it was only following Roman introductions that the hen became of economic value (below, p. 403). Applebaum lists the following sites from which fowl bones have been recorded: London; Silchester; Caerleon; Chester; Heronbridge, Cheshire; Pevensey; Hod Hill; Hangling Langford, Wilts.; Woodcuts; Lowbury; Needham and Roden Down; and in villas at Grimston, Gayton Thorpe, Hambledon, Langton, Park Street, Saunderton, and Southwick. It was therefore distributed widely over civil and military sites as well as caves occupied during the period, although some of the remains particularly from military sites may have been from fighting cocks.

No remains of the domestic goose have been recorded before the Roman period, when it was widespread. According to Applebaum, goose bones were found at the following sites: Caerwent, Silchester, Chester, Langton, Lowbury, and Hambledon.[111]

Remains of pheasants have been found on a few sites such as Silchester, and pigeon remains at Caerwent. Applebaum discussed several Roman buildings that have tentatively been identified as dovecots.[111] An excellent review of Roman animal husbandry based on classical writers appeared in 1970, but it concentrates on conditions in Italy.[112]

AUTUMN KILLING, HOUSING AND WINTER FEED

This point seems as suitable as any to discuss the controversial question of whether livestock could be kept over the winter in prehistoric times. It has already been touched upon in the Introduction (p. 319) and in discussing evidence from surviving pastoral tribes (p. 329).

On the one hand, there are wild animals that survive the winter, albeit

---

[109] C. L. Cram, personal communication, 1973.
[110] Hodgson, 1977, *op. cit.*   [111] Applebaum, 1951, *op. cit.*
[112] K. D. White, *Roman Farming*, London, 1970.

with some losses, and on the other there is documentary evidence from Norse sagas and from sixteenth-century writers, e.g. Tusser, of the killing of all but breeding stock in the autumn, and of the weakness of housed cattle at the end of the winter. Best, however, made hay and produced what we call fat lamb before extensive enclosure, and well before the introduction of turnips.[113]

The first domesticated types are unlikely to have differed greatly from their wild ancestors in the ability to withstand winter. Compared with modern breeds, which have been selected for other purposes, primitive livestock was probably more efficient in gaining nutriment from a limited diet. But at some time before the Middle Ages a stage was apparently reached when it became difficult to feed cattle (but not sheep and pigs) through the winter. It has already been mentioned (p. 332) that the worsening climate at the beginning of the Iron Age might have been a contributory factor. Restriction of the grazing area through settlement made it necessary to conserve feed from the summer for use in the winter, and another factor was probably the increased stock numbers resulting from improved husbandry, which made winter an even narrower bottleneck.

The Michaelmas slaughter, to which sixteenth-century writers referred, has led some archaeologists into inaccurate statements that the *majority* of livestock was killed each autumn. This is clearly impossible since by doing so one would soon have no stock at all. Other archaeologists have supported the thesis of autumn killing even when other interpretations were possible.

Before discussing the archaeological evidence it will be useful to look at some simple statistics about animal populations (Table 4). The Soay sheep (an early domestic type that runs feral on St Kilda) has a mortality in the first year of 50 per cent of the females and even more of the males. The differential mortality persists, so that few rams survive longer than four years of age, whereas 20 per cent of the ewes reach ten years.[114] The ecology of Soay sheep has since been discussed in a book.[115]

The Soay on St Kilda has a lambing percentage of over 90 per cent (and over 100 per cent if one excludes the yearling ewes) which is better than the 80 per cent achieved by Scottish Blackface sheep on a poor hill (this figure can be doubled with better nutrition). We have seen (p. 328) that calving in parts of Africa today can be as low as 40 per cent.

[113] H. Best, *Rural Economy in Yorkshire in 1641...*, ed. C. B. Robinson, Surtees Soc., 33, 1857.

[114] Calculated from P. Grubb and P. A. Jewell, 'Social grouping and home range in feral Soay sheep', *Symp. Zool. Soc. Lond.*, No. 18, 1966, pp. 179–210.

[115] P. A. Jewell, C. Milner, and J. Morton Boyd. *Island Survivors: the Ecology of the Soay Sheep in St Kilda*, London, 1974.

Table 4. *Percentage age distribution of Soays on St Kilda*[114]

Age...	Under 1	1	2	3	4	5 and over
Ewes	21	10	16	16	9	28
Rams	44	13	14	19	7	3

The number of females required as replacements depends on their longevity and the annual losses. Sheep breeds in which longevity is fostered may require replacements as low as 15–20 per cent, with consequently more stock available for cropping or 'autumn killing'. Scottish Blackface sheep are kept on the hill for as few as four years, so with this life-span and an annual mortality of 10 per cent, as many as 29 per cent of the flock need to be replaced annually. When losses reach 20 per cent the replacement figure is increased to 34 per cent.

There is evidence (see below) that the majority of Iron Age sheep reached five years of age, so we can consider a hypothetical prehistoric flock in which 20 per cent of the ewes fall into each annual age group from one to five years. If 100 ewes produced 80 lambs and only half survived their first year, all the ewe lambs would be required to supply the 20 per cent needed to replaced natural losses (which could have been eaten). Four rams are likely to have been required and assuming one or two replacements each year this leaves less than 20 ram lambs for 'autumn killing'. But this can be regarded as a cropping process and not a killing to reduce numbers. Even this small proportion of killing is unlikely to have taken place before settlement. Nomadic peoples maintain as large numbers as possible and kill only on special occasions.

The situation with cattle is less easy to follow because of their greater longevity and a possibly longer interval between calving. But with low breeding percentages like those quoted in Africa, there is likely to have been even less surplus stock (cf. African annual increase of only 4 per cent, p. 329).

Whereas the numbers of different species found on different sites have been freely quoted in the present account, the numbers of different ages have been avoided until now. This is because it is not always clear how different authors have arrived at such figures, nor are the age groups quoted always the same for different sites. The methods used are based on observations of present-day livestock.[116] It is likely that tooth eruption and bone growth were retarded in the past so that an animal might in fact have been older than it appears to have been from its bones or teeth. (Limited data from Soay sheep quoted by Boyd *et al.* indicate

[116] Outlined by M. L. Ryder, *Animal Bones in Archaeology*, Oxford, 1969.

several months delay in the eruption of each tooth, compared with modern breeds.[117] Similarly limited observations by the present author have shown some Soays to be as advanced as modern sheep, but others to be a year behind). At the same time the rate of wear of teeth might have been either faster or slower in the past than today. Finally, even with modern livestock, the ages quoted are averages. For example, the milk central incisors in sheep are said to be replaced at 15 months, yet of 850 sheep examined by one author at 18 months, only 84 per cent had got their adult incisors.

With such provisos in mind it is now possible to consider the archaeological evidence. Ryder found with medieval bones that most sheep had been mature, and possibly at least five years of age, at death, and that most cattle had been at least ten years, i.e. had died or been killed probably after a life working as draught oxen.[118] Most pigs on the other hand had died when the last molar was erupting, which today occurs at eighteen months. Even if there had been no retardation of eruption, this would indicate killing in the animal's second autumn, i.e. at an age three times that of today. This in turn indicates a longer time to reach maturity, and therefore slower growth.

Higgs and White re-examined published data on the age of death mainly at Skara Brae and Old Sleaford, Lincs., a site with early Iron Age and Romano-British levels, and came to the conclusion that there was no evidence for autumn killing.[119] One factor in linking age with the month of killing is determination of the month of birth. Thus Higgs and White interpret a peak of death of cattle apparently occurring in November as actually occurring later in the winter, since the month of birth is likely to have been later than today.

Ewbank et al. made a similar study of sheep jaws from the Iron Age site of Barley, Herts., using the sequence of tooth eruption, and again found no peaks indicating autumn killing.[120] If one plots histograms of the percentages of different ages in place of the cumulative graphs used by these authors, peaks can be obtained – 15 per cent dead at 12 months, and 36 per cent which were aged two years at death. Ewbank's lambing date of February–March would then give a killing period of November–March, but evidence from the Soay suggests that lambing would not occur before April, particularly in the north, which would

[117] J. M. Boyd, J. M. Doney, R. G. Gunn, and P. A. Jewell, 'The Soay sheep of the island of Hirta, St Kilda. A study of a feral population', *Proc. Zool. Soc. Lond.*, 142, 1964, pp. 129–63.

[118] M. L. Ryder, 'Livestock remains from four medieval sites in Yorkshire', *Agric. Hist. Rev.*, i, 1961, pp. 105–10.

[119] E. S. Higgs and J. P. White, 'Autumn Killing', *Ant.*, xxxvii, 1963, pp. 282–9.

[120] J. M. Ewbank, D. W. Phillipson, and R. D. Whitehouse, with E. S. Higgs, 'Sheep in the Iron Age: a method of study', *Proc. Prehistoric Soc.*, 30, 1964, pp. 423–6.

lengthen the period of death accordingly. This approach shifts the peak of death towards the end of the winter which is a crucial period in a primitive farming economy. I am indebted to Mr R. A. Harcourt for stressing the possibility of natural death, and pointing out that the above autumn deaths could correspond to the weaning period.

Jarman *et al.* reporting on the animal remains from Grimthorpe, Yorks., found that 70 per cent of the cattle and 26 per cent of the sheep had survived two winters.[121] Higham found at the Danish site of Troldebjerg that 96 per cent of the cattle survived one winter, and 80 per cent survived two winters.[122] Harcourt found that at the Iron Age site of Longbridge Deverill, Wilts., 29 per cent of the cattle remains were from animals under 4 years old, 48 per cent were at least 4, and 23 per cent were over 5 years of age. With sheep he found that 19 per cent had been under six months, 13 per cent under 18 months, 10 per cent from 18 months to 3 years, 40 per cent from 3 to 5 and 18 per cent over 5.[123] Again there is ample evidence of overwintering, most animals being at least mature when killed, suggesting killing at the end of their productive life. But Harcourt points out that animals could have been eaten after natural death. He particularly interprets the remains from young animals in this way, suggesting that they would have had too little flesh to warrant killing before maturity. Pigs of all ages from young to old were represented. Harcourt has more recently approached the difficulty of precise ageing discussed above by placing the finds into groups. At the Neolithic site of Durrington Walls he found that 5 per cent of the cattle were juvenile, 20 per cent young adults, and 75 per cent mature to old. The corresponding figures for pigs were 53, 27, and 20 per cent.[124]

At the Roman villa at Hemel Hempstead, Herts., Harcourt found from the bones that 54 per cent of the cattle were at least mature animals, only 11 per cent being juveniles. From the teeth only 9 per cent were juveniles, 17 per cent were at least mature, 55 per cent had well worn, and 19 per cent heavily worn, molars, which Harcourt thinks could indicate beasts from 10 to 15 years old.[125]

Murray reviewed evidence from pollen analysis and classical authors of the use of tree branches for winter feed, and Simmons and Dimbleby suggested from pollen analysis that ivy leaves might have been collected

[121] M. Jarman, A. Fogg, and E. S. Higgs, 'The animal remains', in I. M Stead, 'The Iron Age Hillfort at Grimthorpe, Yorks.', *Proc. Prehist. Soc.*, 34, 1968, pp. 148–90.

[122] C. F. W. Higham, 'Trends in prehistoric European caprovine husbandry', *Man*, 3, 1968, pp. 64–75.

[123] R. A. Harcourt, personal communication, 1970.

[124] *Idem*, 'Animal bones from Durrington Walls', *Reps. Res. Comm. Soc. Ant. Lond.*, 29, 1971, pp. 338–50.

[125] R. A. Harcourt, personal communication, 1970.

for use in winter as early as the Mesolithic.[126, 127] Tree branches have been given to livestock during the present century in Norway, Switzerland, Italy, Romania, and Greece. I myself saw tree branches being fed to sheep in Yugoslavia in December 1974. Recent analyses of food value suggest that such fodder has limited nutritional value.[128]

Animals dying a natural death were not always eaten. At the Iron Age settlement of Gussage All Saints, Dorset, Harcourt found several articulated skeletons on a rubbish dump, including one of a cow with a calf wedged in the pelvis that had clearly died giving birth.

THE SAXON PERIOD

Only recently has archaeology begun to throw light on this hitherto neglected period. As late as 1957 Trow-Smith listed as the main sources of evidence only such incidental literary records as the Anglo-Saxon Chronicle and Laws, Welsh Laws, a few charters and wills, and stray references in literature, to which can be added place-names.[129]

The Saxon origin of many English place-names stresses the distinctness of the Saxon settlement, but it is almost certain that their agricultural methods at first differed little from those of the Romans. The Domesday survey, however, indicates, according to Trow-Smith, high organization showing centuries of development of techniques.

The Laws of Ethelred II (c. 980) indicate the buying and selling of stock, and safeguards against theft which included the need for two witnesses at slaughter, and the keeping of the head and hide of cattle and sheep for three days in case of enquiry. Urban stockmen could insure against theft from common land at the rate of up to 10 s for a horse, 30 d for an ox, 20 d for a cow, 1 s for a sheep and 10 d for a pig, which gives some indication of their relative value.[130]

There are records of the depredations of Norse raiders, disease and the British winter. A lease of 70 hides of land in Surrey by the Bishop of Winchester to King Edward the Elder (c. 900) lists the stock surviving a severe winter as: 9 (plough) oxen, 114 fully grown pigs, 50 wethers, and 110 fully grown sheep (besides the sheep and pigs the herdsmen could keep).[131]

Trow-Smith considered that pig numbers were at a peak during Saxon times and that they declined with the extension of ploughing and

---

[126] J. Murray, *The First European Agriculture*, Edinburgh, 1970.
[127] I. G. Simmons and G. W. Dimbleby, 'The possible role of Ivy (*Hedera helix* L.) in the Mesolithic economy of Western Europe', *J. Arch. Sci.*, 1, 1974, pp. 291–6.
[128] M. L. Ryder, *Sheep and Man*, London (forthcoming).
[129] R. Trow-Smith, *A History of British Livestock Husbandry to 1700*, London, 1957, p. 43.   [130] London Guild ordinances temp. Athelstan.
[131] *English Historical Documents*, I, p. 501.

Table 5. *Percentage livestock numbers on Saxon sites*

	Cattle	Sheep	Goats	Pigs	Horses
Cadbury Congresbury, Somerset[135]	38	21	4	35	2 (Individuals)
Glastonbury, Somerset[136]	41.5	41.5	—	17	Negligible (Individuals)
Abingdon, Berks.[137]	55	34	—	11	— (Individuals)
Maxey, Northants.[138]	40		39*	12	9 (Bones)
Cassington, Oxon.[139]	47	13	—	32	8 (? Bones)
Hereford pre tenth cent.[140]	28.5 (2)†	14.5 (1)	—	28.5 (2)	28.5 (2)
late tenth cent.	31 (4)	23 (3)	7.5 (1)	31 (4)	7.5 (1)
Crossgates, Scarborough, Yorks.[141]	60	Few	—	10	30 (? Bones)
Hatton Rock (War)[142]	44	21	3	15	16
North Elmham, Norfolk	19	48*		28	5
Ledgeford, Norfolk	27	60*		8	5
Sandtun, Kent	39	52*		8	1
Mawgan Porth, Cornwall[143]	45	50*		3	2

★ Sheep and goats.   † Numbers of individuals in parentheses.

tree-felling.[132] Yet at most of the sites listed in Table 5 cattle bones predominate. This contrasts with the predominance of sheep on most Iron Age and Roman sites. It is probable that by Saxon times one can no longer generalize over all sites. Certainly by the Middle Ages the proportions of different species varied with the type of site.[133] Indeed there is evidence in Saxon times of preference for particular joints.[134]

[132] Trow-Smith, *op. cit.*, p. 550.   [133] Ryder, 1961, *op. cit.*

[134] D. Seddon, D. Calvocoressi, C. Cooper, with E. S. Higgs, 'Fauna', in P. V. Addyman, 'A Dark-Age Settlement at Maxey Northants.', *Med. Arch.*, 8, 1964, pp. 20–73.

[135] B. A. Noddle, 'Animal bones', in P. J. Fowler, K. S. Gardner, and P. A. Rahtz, *Cadbury Congresbury, Somerset, 1968*, Univ. Bristol, Dept. Extra-mural studies, 1970.

[136] R. A. Harcourt, personal communication, 1970.

[137] C. L. Cram, personal communication, 1969.

[138] Seddon *et al.*, *op. cit.*

[139] D. M. Wilson, 'Anglo-Saxon Rural Economy', *Agric. Hist. Rev.*, 10, 1962, pp. 65–79.

[140] R. A. Harcourt, personal communication, 1970.

[141] Wilson, *op. cit.*

[142] B. A. Noddle, in S. Hirst and P. Rahtz, 'Hatton Rock 1979'. *Trans. Birmingham and Warwickshire Arch. Soc.*, 85, 1972, pp. 175–7.

[143] J. Clutton-Brock, 'The animal resources', in D. M. Wilson (ed.), *The Archaeology of Anglo-Saxon England*, London, 1976, pp. 373–92.

Trow-Smith stresses that there is still no evidence of different breeds, although local varieties were probably beginning to evolve. Breeding in isolation would, however, be the cause of this variation, and not the direct effect of the environment as he implies.[144] He had earlier drawn attention to the lack of proof for the theory put forward by Wilson in 1909 (and widely repeated) that red cattle were introduced by the Saxons.[145]

Trow-Smith regarded references in Ine's Laws as indicating the beginnings in the seventh century of the woodland pannage of pigs, that had become so important by Domesday.[146] In pannage, swine were allowed to forage in woods on acorns and herbage, including bracken, and were often penned at night (see pp. 320–1, for discussion on acorns, and pp. 391–2 for pig nutrition). There are wills[147] which indicate herds of pigs several hundred strong, which Trow-Smith thought might have put pressure on food resources. Almost all Saxon references to pigs associate them with woodland, although some seem to have been housed or yarded. "A young pig kept in a sty" was an eleventh-century swineherd's right, which confirms the existence of sties.[148] As Saxon land clearance proceeded, the population of pigs probably decreased and this could have allowed a gradual increase in cattle, sheep, and horses.

There are records of sheep everywhere.[149] Numerous villages embody *sceap* (or Skip, Ship, Shap, or Shep) in their names, indicating the pre-eminence of sheep in the local husbandry. W. G. Hoskins has made a special study of such names, which are widespread from Devon to north Yorkshire, and from Kent to Shropshire. Twenty-one out of forty English counties have such villages – all of them of Saxon foundation. But since their distribution is irregular they cannot indicate the distribution of Saxon sheep farming. Not only do village names indicate sheep husbandry but other names such as Shipbrook, where sheep were washed. Sheppey means sheep island (as, of course, does Soay) and, as it was so named in a charter of 696, W. G. Hoskins thought that it must have already been used to pasture sheep.

Surprisingly, Wiltshire, which was an important sheep area in Roman times, has no such sheep names, and it has been suggested that they were too common to warrant a mention. A charter of 697 gave pasture for 300 sheep on Romney Marsh to the monastery of Lyminge, and it is thought that the reclamation of this salt marsh for sheep dates back to Roman times (see the Charter of 697, quoted by Finberg, Vol. I, Part II). It is tempting to suggest that the Romney sheep itself is of Roman origin (below, p. 374).

Trow-Smith infers from Ine's code (*c.* 690) that one cow gave as much

[144] Trow-Smith *op. cit.*, p. 85.
[145] *Ibid.*, p. 43.
[146] *Ibid.*, p. 50.
[147] *English Historical Documents*, I, p. 495.
[148] *Ibid.*, II, p. 815.
[149] Trow-Smith, *op. cit.*, p. 59.

meat as five sheep.[150] Since the present ratio is 1:20, it seems likely that cattle have increased in size more than sheep. Edgar's Andover code (*c.* 960) fixed the price of a wey of wool (2–3 cwt, 100–150 kg) at 10 s. Trow-Smith thought that this indicated a lower value of wool relative to other products than in the later Middle Ages.

One of the other sheep products was milk, and although the milking of sheep is very ancient, Trow-Smith found no documentation earlier than the ninth century. The rent of Wye marsh, Kent, was forty weys of cheese in addition to twenty lambs and twenty fleeces, which indicates dairying based on sheep. Sheep today yield 1½ to 3 pints (0.9 to 1.7 l) of milk daily, compared with a minimum of 4 (2.3 l) from goats.

The rights of the shepherd are probably as ancient because Trow-Smith quotes the eleventh century *Rectitudines Singularum Personarum* as stating his right to fold the manorial flock on his own land for twelve nights in mid-winter (for manure), to take one lamb and one fleece of the year's crop, and to have the milk of the flock for seven nights after the (spring) equinox, and a bowlful of whey or buttermilk all the summer.

Pre-conquest records[151] quoted by Trow-Smith indicate the existence of sheep farms with sizeable flocks (one had 250 sheep and 47 goats) and there are suggestions of the revival of the Roman woollen trade. Recent excavations at West Stow, Suffolk, have revealed well organized textile manufacture,[152] and more Saxon textiles than Roman ones were fine (below, p. 373).

The rent of a ewe with its lamb at Easter indicates lambing at a date similar to the average date today. Sheep were apparently washed before being shorn, and only became fully grown in their third year. This compares with an average age today of about nine months. At Glastonbury, Harcourt found that 55 per cent of the sheep had been under two at death, 17 per cent between two and three and 28 per cent over three. At Hereford he found that 66 per cent of the mandibles had well-worn molars, and 24 per cent were immature.[153]

In Domesday, sheep were still found almost everywhere, and now in numbers that exceeded all other livestock put together.[154] Since Saxon dairying was based on the sheep and goat, the main use of cattle in Saxon times was to draw the plough. The first literary reference to the oxen team appears in Ine's Laws (*c.* 690). Archaeological evidence, however, suggests plough oxen as early as the Iron Age.

Milk production from cattle occurred only on a cottage scale, and since few were fattened solely for meat, the use of cattle for food implies

[150] *Ibid.*, p. 60.   [151] Anglo-Saxon Charters, 134.
[152] Anon, *Nature*, 219, 1968, pp. 889–90.
[153] R. A. Harcourt, personal communication, 1970.
[154] Trow-Smith, *op. cit.*, p. 74.

prior use for farmwork. Cows were kept to breed replacements for the oxen. There is no evidence of cows being kept solely for milk before the Conquest. Indeed there is unlikely to have been more than a pint or two of milk (0.5–1 l) over after the calf had been fed, and then only for a few weeks (cf. modern African yields, p. 328; see also p. 349). The amount of tribute expected from the Welsh by Athelstan indicates more cattle than were required for the plough, which is in keeping with the belief that hill folk fed more on animal products than did those in the lowlands. Cow's milk was the major source of food in Ireland, too, at that time.[155]

This distinction between the agricultural east, and the pastoral west was already well established by Domesday, which Trow-Smith considered as Saxon evidence since there had been insufficient time for new developments to take place.[156] The eight-ox team was by no means universal, and Trow-Smith thought that it might have comprised a mixture of steers and barren cows.

The oxen began to work at four years, and could continue for six to eight years. This is in keeping with the high proportion of remains from older cattle at Glastonbury and Hereford.[157] At Maxey, however, only 23 per cent were over three years.[158] The average working life was probably four years. As Trow-Smith pointed out, this necessitated two calves a year per team as replacements, and therefore two cows were required to breed animals for each team.

He considered that the *animalia* recorded in Domesday were in fact the cows used for this purpose, and he found that the ratio of *animalia* to each plough team supports this hypothesis. In the east this ratio ranged from 1.5:1 to 3.3:1. The corollary was what has already been noted: the cow played a minor part as a milch animal. In the south-west the ratio of *animalia* to plough teams was greater and Trow-Smith thought that this might indicate the development there of cattle for milk to replace the sheep and goat.

Trow-Smith considered that it is impossible in the Celtic and Saxon world to separate agricultural from other draught use, but that the horse was clearly too highly thought of to be given plebeian tasks.[159] Indeed Trow-Smith quotes a tenth-century Welsh law which restricts ploughing to oxen. Although the horse was valued for the saddle in Saxon times, probably little attention was given to breeding – it was allowed to run wild or half-wild in the forest. Horses, and often whole stud farms, were left in wills, however, and Trow-Smith thought that these

[155] A. T. Lucas, 'Cattle in ancient and medieval Irish Society', *O'Connell School Union Record 1937–1958* (presented at British Association, Dublin, 1957).
[156] Trow-Smith, *op. cit.*
[157] R. A. Harcourt, personal communication, 1970.
[158] Seddon *et al.*, *op. cit.*   [159] Trow-Smith, *op. cit.*

might have continuity with Roman studs. In all these records there is no indication of agricultural use, yet within fifty years of the latest bequest, the horse was being used to draw the plough. Dent and Goodall reproduce a well-known illustration from the Bayeux tapestry showing a Saxon farmer harrowing with a horse.[160] From this, and evidence concerning the faster speed of ploughing with horses, Trow-Smith suggests that the use of the horse for ploughing might have begun in Saxon times (below, p. 400).

There are few references in Domesday to specifically agricultural horses, and there appears to have been about one riding horse per village. Feral and unbroken horses roamed the woods, but their numbers declined considerably between 1066 and 1086 presumably owing to the same forest clearance that caused a decline in goats and pigs. The smaller percentage of horse remains in Table 5 than in previous periods is noteworthy in indicating a decline in the eating of horses.

[160] A. A. Dent and D. M. Goodall, *The Foals of Epona: A History of British Ponies from the Bronze Age to Yesterday*, London, 1962, p. 3.

CHAPTER III

INDIVIDUAL LIVESTOCK SPECIES

THE GOAT (*Capra hircus*)

The main ancestor of the domestic goat was the wild bezoar or pasang (*Capra aegagrus*) which still exists in Asia Minor and Iran. It has been suggested that the markhor (*Capra falconeri*) of north-west India contributed towards the Asiatic breeds, and that the Abyssinian ibex (*Capra nubiana*) influenced the Nubian breeds of north and east Africa.[1] Since these different types of goat will no doubt interbreed, they should probably be regarded as varieties and not species. But the European ibex (*Capra ibex*) was apparently never domesticated, although according to Zeuner it will interbreed with other goats.[2]

It is extremely unlikely, as claimed by Payne,[3] that the goat and sheep formed an interbreeding population as late as the Pleistocene. Curtain[4] outlined chromosome, antigenic, and blood type evidence, and I[5] gave coat evidence, both opposing Payne (below, p. 357). It has more recently been pointed out that Payne's suggestion must be rejected because differences in the cranium, and in behaviour, between sheep and goats must have taken several million years to evolve.[6]

The goat was probably the first farm animal to be domesticated, somewhat before the sheep. Doubt still exists about the first stages, however, owing to the difficulty of distinguishing wild from domestic goats, and also of distinguishing goats from sheep. The evidence quoted by Reed indicates prior domestication of the sheep.[7] Bökönyi and Chaplin described more recent techniques, in which changes from the wild population in the proportions of remains from the two sexes, and

[1] D. R. Harris, 'The distribution and ancestry of the domestic goat', *Proc. Linn. Soc. Lond.*, 173, 1962, pp. 79–91.
[2] F. E. Zeuner, *A History of Domesticated Animals*, London, 1963.
[3] S. Payne, 'The origins of domestic sheep and goats: a reconsideration in the light of fossil evidence', *Proc. Prehist. Soc.*, 34, 1968, pp. 368–84.
[4] C. C. Curtain, 'On the origin of domesticated sheep', *Ant.*, XLV, 1971, pp. 303–4.
[5] M. L. Ryder, 'The status of non-domestic sheep', *Ant.*, XLV, 1971, pp. 220–2.
[6] W. M. Schaffer and C. A. Reed, 'The co-evolution of social behaviour and cranial morphology in sheep and goats', *Fieldiana Zool.*, 62, 1972, pp. 56–8.
[7] C. A. Reed, 'The pattern of animal domestication in the prehistoric Near East', in P. J. Ucko and G. W. Dimbleby (eds.), *The Domestication and Exploitation of Plants and Animals*, London, 1969, pp. 361–80.

of different ages, can indicate domestication.[8, 9] The external distinguishing feature of goats include a beard, erect tail, and straighter more
vertical horns, and the horns form the only simple distinction in the
skeleton.[10] But with more detailed measurement it is now possible to
distinguish most bones of goats from those of sheep.

In the present context the significance of the difference between sheep
and goats lies more in their ecology and the materials they supply. The
goat is more of a browser on trees than is the sheep, and can even climb
trees to reach the foliage. It is happier in rough mountainous country,
but likes and seeks shelter since it withstands cold and wet conditions
less well than the sheep. Indeed, the reputation of goats for sensing the
approach of bad weather has been one reason why they have been run
with other livestock: they provide a warning to the farmer.[11] The goat
has adapted better to hot desert regions with shrubs. Sheep could feed
on grass grown by soil impoverished by primitive agriculture, and so
became dominant in temperate regions.

The goat may have first been valued for forest clearance, a role in
which it later became a menace. The main product of goats is milk and
its derivatives, butter and cheese being made for winter food, and
Zeuner considered that milking was probably fully developed with
goats before cattle were domesticated.[12] It has long been used to provide
milk for livestock and human orphans, and some primitive peoples
allow babies to suck direct.

Being less docile and more unpredictable than sheep (hence the term
capricious) goats cannot be kept in large flocks without a goatherd. Yet
the goats of north Africa are sufficiently intelligent to find their own
way home each night, once within the town walls. But two or three
can readily be tethered, so the goat has been an animal of individual
households like pigs and poultry, being very aptly described as the 'poor
man's cow'. It may never have been widely important in Europe since
the Neolithic period (or since the cow was domesticated), the decline
being accelerated by its single purpose and by forest clearance. Only
its skin is comparable in value with that of the sheep; it was used to
make parchment,[13] and some claim that goat leather is the more

[8] S. Bökönyi, 'Archaeological problems and methods of recognizing animal
domestication', in Ucko and Dimbleby, *op. cit.*, pp. 219–30.

[9] R. E. Chaplin, 'The use of non-morphological criteria in the study of animal
domestication from bones found on archaeological sites', in Ucko and Dimbleby, *op.
cit.*, pp. 231–46.

[10] M. L. Ryder, *Animal Bones in Archaeology*, Oxford, 1969.

[11] J. C. Greig, 'The ecology of feral goats in Scotland', M.Sc. Univ. Edinburgh,
1970.   [12] Zeuner, *op. cit.*

[13] M. L. Ryder, 'Parchment – its history, manufacture and composition', *J. Soc.
Archiv.*, 11, 1964, pp. 391–9.

durable. The hair is on the whole too coarse for textiles, and the flesh, lacking fat, is less desirable in temperate regions, although it provides the only meat in many hot areas.

The distinction between sheep and goats is clearly shown by many Biblical references, e.g. "The lambs are for thy clothing, and the goats are the price of thy field. And thou shalt have goats' milk enough for thy food, and for the food of thy household..."[14] This also illustrates the point, already alluded to in the Introduction, that the herds of primitive tribes provided food in the form of milk rather than flesh.

Domestic goats with scimitar-like horns appear to have entered Europe with the Danubian invaders during the Neolithic period. Later there was another type of goat with horns twisted into the shape of a corkscrew. In the Neolithic Swiss lake-dwellings the goat was at first more common than the sheep. Then during the later Neolithic and Bronze Ages the sheep became more common.[15, 16] This supports the above suggestions regarding the initial importance and later decline of the goat.

The same sequence has been observed elsewhere, and Harcourt[17] found sheep to be more numerous than goats at the Neolithic site of Durrington Walls. During the Neolithic and Bronze Ages goats and sheep may have run together in Britain as they do today in some Mediterranean countries, where, too, a goat is often used as the leader of a sheep flock. A single goat skull was found among identifiable bones with Bronze Age associations from a cave at Wetton Mill, Staffs.[18] Another more recent reason for running sheep with goats was the almost certainly baseless belief that goats reduce the amount of disease amongst sheep.[19]

Trow-Smith considers that by the Iron Age the goat had filled the hill niche, basing this inference on the fact that goat remains were found at Pen Dinas in the hills near Aberystwyth in Wales, but not at Little Woodbury, Wilts.[20] It was, however, found at All Cannings Cross. Megaw drew attention to the importance of the goat in the Scottish Highland economy, but pointed out that it was a peasant animal, those who kept it being looked down upon – a social distinction which he

---

[14] Proverbs, xxviii, 23-7.

[15] Zeuner, *op. cit.*

[16] C. F. W. Higham, 'Trends in prehistoric European caprovine husbandry', *Man*, 3, 1968, pp. 64-75.

[17] R. A. Harcourt, personal communication, 1970.

[18] M. L. Ryder, I. H. Longworth, and A. J. H. Gunstone, 'Prehistoric bone and pottery finds from Mill Pot Cave, near Wetton, Staffs.', *North Staffs. J. Fld Studies*, 11, 1971, pp. 40-8.

[19] Greig, *op. cit.*

[20] R. Trow-Smith, *A History of British Livestock Husbandry to 1700*, London, 1957.

thought might date back to the Early Iron Age, when Celtic invaders imposed themselves on native Bronze Age graziers.[21]

Roman writers such as Columella and Varro gave details of goat husbandry, their diseases, and different breeds. Columella said that a good he-goat should have a large body, thick legs, a full and short neck, and flaccid, very long, shiny hair. He also considered that they should have wattles beneath the lower jaw. These apparently useless appendages today appear to be more common in goats than other livestock, but, according to Greig,[22] were not characteristic of British native goats. Goats were divided by Columella into those with shaggy hair whose horns were allowed to grow, and those with fine hair and sawn-off horns, the sawing being presumably carried out to protect the coat from scratching.

Goats were plucked or shorn like sheep. The Greeks sheared goats with a *Tragokourice machaira*.[23] Goat hair has been used to make ropes that last longer than hemp ropes in water, and nomadic peoples in the Middle East use goat hair to make tent cloth. According to Columella it was used for ropes, tents, and sails, but Pliny said that only the poorest people wore goat hair cloth. I examined one coarse tent yarn (in fact from a hairy sheep) from Daliyeh near Jericho and there was no indication that an attempt had been made to separate coarse from fine fibres[24] and it is possible that similar coarse cloth was made in goat-keeping areas of Britain. Goat hair cloth was made in Sweden in the Middle Ages.[25] In the Middle East, goat hair is mixed with coarse wool in carpet making.

The coat of goats is typically double, consisting of coarse outer hair and fine underwool.[26] In only two breeds has the coat been widely utilized for clothing. In the Cashmere goat of Asia the outer hair is extremely coarse and the underwool very fine, and the wool is still separated from the hair during plucking by special hand combs, one of which is illustrated by Burns, Von Bergen, and Young.[27] The Angora breed which originated in Turkey has evolved a single coat of

[21] B. R. S. Megaw, 'Goat-keeping in the Old Highland Economy', *Scot. Studies*, 7, 1963, 201–9; 8, 1964, pp. 213–17.

[22] Greig, *op. cit.*

[23] Lucian, *Piscator*, 46.

[24] M. L. Ryder, 'Changes in the fleece of sheep following domestication (with a note on the coat of cattle)', in Ucko and Dimbleby, *op. cit.*, pp. 495–521.

[25] A. W. Franzen and A. Geijer, 'Textile finds from excavations in Swedish towns 1960–1966. A preliminary report', *Särtryck ur Res Mediaevales*, 1966, pp. 129–34.

[26] M. L. Ryder, 'Structure and seasonal change of the coat in Scottish wild goats', *J. Zool.*, 161, 1970, pp. 355–62.

[27] R. H. Burns, W. Von Bergen, and S. S. Young, 'Cashmere and the undercoat of domestic and wild animals', *J. Text. Inst.*, 53, 1962, T45–T68.

lustrous, relatively coarse, but not hairy, wool that is still widely used in textiles as mohair.

Such Roman illustrations as there are indicate an animal comparable with those of today, in particular, like that of the Scottish Highlands.[28] These have *dorcas* horns, i.e. rising vertically from the skull, then diverging.

Goats have tended towards single purpose (milk-producing) animals, at any rate in Europe and the Middle East, and little selection for other characters has apparently taken place. There has almost certainly been no development of the carcass, which still retains the conformation of a wild ruminant. The flesh of kids is more desirable. Although many breeds have developed, these are very variable as regards horns, colour, and coat length. The early banishment of goats to the hills and their restriction to peasant husbandry, are probably factors removing them from the attention of improvers.

Most modern British breeds of goat are of exotic origin, e.g. Nubian and Swiss types – brown Toggenburgs and white Saanens; in medieval times white goats were thought to give more milk. According to Peglar the unimproved English goat had a fairly short coat varying from black to brown, but often light or dark fawn, and with white patches.[29] Other sources describe the 'old English goat' as a small animal with a rough coat, both sexes being horned and bearded. According to Greig it weighed no more than 100 lb (45 kg), compared with weights up to 250 lb (113 kg) in improved breeds.[30]

Peglar stated that in Wales the original goats were large and white, but later resembled the Irish goats owing to importation. In Wales, the hind leg of goats used to be cured like ham as *coch yr wden*. In the Scottish Highlands this was known as goat ham. Peglar regarded the Irish goats as representing a more primitive type because there had been less importation. These had large horns, long hair, and were reddish black and white or yellowish grey and white.

The feral goats of Britain must represent the domestic type of earlier times, and most seem to have large horns, and a long black or grey coat, which is frequently blotched with white. Walton stated that the feral goats of north Wales are white with black face, shoulders, and forelegs.[31] Greig gave the colours of Scottish feral goats as grey, brown, or piebald, with relatively few white animals.[32] Harris quoted evidence showing that black and dark breeds are more primitive than variegated and white breeds.[33] Zeuner regarded feral grey goats with a dark stripe

[28] Zeuner, *op. cit.*, pp. 147, 148.
[29] H. S. H. Peglar, *The Book of the Goat*, London, 5th ed., 1918.
[30] Greig, *op. cit.*
[31] K. Walton, 'Feral goats in North Wales', *J. Brit. Goat Soc.*, Apr. 1968, pp. 40–1.
[32] Grieg, *op. cit.*   [33] Harris, *op. cit.*

along the back, and black and white fetlocks, as having reverted to the wild coloration.[34] But it seems more likely that the colour pattern is that of the goats when they became feral, as did the Soay sheep. Reversion to a longer coat would also appear unlikely since, according to Hards, short hair is genetically dominant to long.[35] Greig discusses the arguments against reversion.[36]

The coat samples of Scottish wild goats examined by Ryder[37] (from the study of Greig)[38] indicated a primitive structure having undergone little if any selection of the coat compared with sheep. One herd into which modern goats might have been introduced more recently had a greater proportion of fine fibres, but this could indicate variation rather than selection for more wool. Greig gave evidence that the wild goats of Scotland only became fully feral about the end of the eighteenth century.[38]

Trow-Smith considered that during Saxon times goats were as important as sheep, cattle, pigs, and horses, although they were not documented until the surveys of 1066 and 1086.[39] Relatively large herds were often associated with large flocks of sheep, e.g. a Saxon record of 250 sheep and 40 goats at Hatfield. There appears to have been a concentration around Mendip, which Trow-Smith thought might be associated with the origin of Cheddar cheese. Continued decline of woodland during the Saxon period no doubt contributed to the decline of the goat as it did to that of the pig.

The main breeding season of goats is from October to December, and with the average gestation period of twenty-one weeks, comparable to that of sheep, the kids are born from March to May; some goats can breed from August to February and some female kids will mate as young as three months (while still sucking), but the males not until six months. Mascall,[40] quoted by Greig,[41] noted the early breeding season of goats and recommended withholding the male until late autumn so that the kids should not be born before the spring growth of grass. Twins are usual, and larger litters common.[42] The primitive breeds of Britain used to cease to give milk by the end of July. Low regarded the goat as giving a high milk yield compared with other livestock, producing 4 pints (2.3 l) a day for 5 or 6 months.[43] This compares with the moderate yields of today (100 gallons (455 l) annually). The maximum from average

[34] Zeuner, op. cit.
[35] E. R. Hards, 'The inheritance of coat characteristics in the goat of the British Isles', Brit. Goat Soc. Year Book, 1950, pp. 67–9.   [36] Greig, op. cit.
[37] Ryder, 'Structure and seasonal change...', 1970, op. cit.   [38] Greig, op. cit.
[39] Trow-Smith, op. cit.
[40] L. Mascall, The Government of Catell, London, 1627.   [41] Greig, op. cit.
[42] D. Mackenzie, Goat Husbandry, London, 1967.
[43] D. Low, The Domesticated Animals of the British Isles, London, 1840.

milk sheep today is about 3 pints (1.7 l) per day. Little wonder a goat was used by the ancients to represent the god Pan who symbolized procreative power and rustic plenty. Importation of exotic breeds has increased the daily yield to 6–8 pints (3.4–4.6 l), and extended the period in milk by at least two months, giving a maximum annual yield of 200 gallons (910 l).

Mackenzie aptly puts the place of the goat in the modern dairy industry as on land that is too poor, too hot, or too steep to support dairy cattle.[44]

SHEEP (*Ovis aries*)

Of the three possible wild ancestors of domesic sheep the Urial (*O. orientalis*) of south-west Asia was long thought to have been the first type domesticated, mainly because it was in this region that the initial domestication apparently took place. Recent chromosome evidence suggests that the only ancestor of domestic sheep was the Mouflon.[45] The Argali (*O. ammon*) of central Asia almost certainly contributed to Asiatic breeds, and, as will be indicated later, some British breeds appear to have affinities with certain of those of Asia.[46]

The European wild sheep, the Mouflon (*O. musimon*) died out early in north-west Europe, possibly as a result of the spread of forest in post-glacial times, but survivors in southern Europe, probably contributed to European domestic sheep. In order to accept Payne's[47] suggestion that all modern wild sheep are feral domesticates, one would have to explain why escapes subsequent to the Neolithic period have not caused changes through interbreeding such as a lengthening of the tail, or a change in the colour and structure of the coat. Herre and Kesper gave evidence of the existence of wild sheep in pockets in central Europe as late as the Neolithic period, from which they concluded that local domestication was possible.[48] Whether or not such sheep were domesticated as early as the Mesolithic period was discussed by Murray, and will not be considered in the present account.[49]

The main domestic stock, however, almost certainly reached Europe from the East, and there is no doubt that sheep arrived in Britain with Neolithic settlers. Domestic sheep have a wide range of gestation periods from about 140 days to over 150. Wild sheep appear to have

---

[44] Mackenzie, *op. cit.*

[45] M. L. Ryder, *Sheep and Man*, *op. cit.*

[46] M. L. Ryder, 'The history of sheep breeds in Britain', *Agric. Hist. Rev.*, 12, 1964, (1), pp. 1–12; (2), 65–82.　　　[47] Payne, *op. cit.*

[48] W. Herre and K. D. Kesper, 'History of the distribution of *Ovis ammon* in Europe', *Zool. Anz.*, 151, 1953, pp. 204–09.

[49] J. Murray, 'The osteological and botanical evidence for Neolithic agriculture in Europe', Ph.D. thesis, Univ. of Edinburgh, 1967.

the longest periods, and early maturing breeds the shortest, the mean in the Soay being 147 days.[50]

The main source of evidence in prehistory is from excavated skeletal remains, and only from the skull is it readily possible to distinguish sheep from goats. It is thus the practice in archaeological reports, particularly if goat as well as sheep skulls are found, to record the remaining bones of the skeleton as 'sheep/goat' or ovicaprids.

Early workers likened individual bone remains to those of different modern breeds on a general impression, or at best on a few measurements only. Pitt-Rivers was the first to liken prehistoric bones to those of the Soay. Today it is realized that any such attempt must be made on many detailed measurements and their ratios, together with statistical treatment. Such an approach has already made it possible to distinguish bones of sheep from those of goats.[51, 52] But it has been pointed out that it is going to be an enormous task to distinguish differences in size due to breed, from within-breed variations due to sex, nutritional status, or genetic variation.[53] This is already being attempted with suitable collections, e.g. Higham.[54, 55]

The palustris–studeri controversy

Archaeological remains of domestic sheep were first found in the Neolithic lake dwellings of Switzerland, and were described by Rütimeyer in 1861. These were small sheep with small, only slightly curved horns which suggested that the breed had been derived from the Urial. This urial-horned sheep was named *Ovis aries palustris*, or the 'Turbary' sheep, and since then small sheep bones from prehistoric sites have frequently been described as being of 'Turbary' type.

It is unfortunate if such a label has led to the impression that the 'Turbary' was a distinct breed, because prehistoric sheep were almost certainly far more variable than are modern breeds of livestock. Because of this variability and the apparent lack of change with time during the whole period under review, I prefer to use the term 'prehistoric' sheep. These are probably represented today by the Soay sheep that now lives

[50] M. L. Ryder, 'Post-natal fleece development in some primitive sheep and cross', *Zeitschrift für Tierzüchtung. und Züchtungsbiol.*, 86, 1970, pp. 372–91.

[51] M. Hildebrand, 'Skeletal differences between deer, sheep and goats', *California Fish and Game*, 41, 1955, pp. 327–46.

[52] J. Boessneck, H.-H. Müller, and M. Teichert, 'Osteologische Unterscheidung-merkmale zwischen Schaf und Zeige', *Kühn-Archiv*, Halle 78, 1964, pp. 1–129.

[53] M. L. Ryder, *Animal Bones in Archaeology*, Oxford, 1969.

[54] C. Higham, 'Size trends in prehistoric European domestic fauna, and the problem of local domestication', *Acta Zool. Fenn.*, 120, 1968, pp. 1–21.

[55] *Idem*, 'The metrical attributes of two samples of bovine limb bones', *J. Zool. Lond.*, 157, 1969, pp. 63–74.

feral on St Kilda, and not as has been claimed, for instance, the Dutch Heath sheep, as I have pointed out previously.[56]

In 1882 the Swiss lake-dwellings yielded some larger sheep remains with stouter horns, which led to the belief that this sheep had affinities with the Mouflon (European) type of wild sheep. It was given the name *O. a. studeri* after the discoverer, and was thought to belong to a later period, the Copper Age, at the beginning of the Bronze Age. Even though these sheep might be shown to be distinct types, modern biology would regard them as varieties, or breeds, and not give them Latin sub-specific names. It seems that all types of wild and domestic sheep will interbreed, and therefore, on one view, should be regarded as belonging to a single species.

Although the 'Turbary' (*palustris*) and the Copper Age sheep (*studeri*) are still quoted as being distinct types[57] there is no conclusive evidence that they are. Ewart thought that *palustris* and *studeri* represented a mixed Urial–Mouflon race, and that the finding of hornless skulls among the remains with large horns suggested Mouflon influence, since Mouflon ewes often lack horns.[58] It is now known, however, that Urial as well as Mouflon ewes can be polled, so lack of horns cannot be used to indicate ancestry, nor can the lack of horns be regarded as a result of domestication, because other wild ungulates lack horns. Ewart pointed out that although Mouflon-type horns are found in the Soay, this and other primitive types such as the Shetland sometimes have Urial-like horns suggesting 'simple Turbary blood'.

In my experience, however, the large (Mouflon-type or *studeri*) horns occur only in the rams, and the small (urial-like or *palustris*) horns only in the ewes. I, therefore, subscribe to the view put forward by Hilzheimer,[59] but opposed by Adametz,[60] that both types belong to the same period, and that *studeri* is the ram and *palustris* the ewe of a single type of sheep.

This does not, however, invalidate the contention of Ewart that the Soay contains Mouflon influence, although today we would perhaps regard the expression of such influence in less simple terms. Ewart in fact regarded the light brown type of Soay as coming from the Urial,

---

[56] M. L. Ryder, 'The evolution of Scottish breeds of sheep', *Scot. Studies*, 12, 1968, pp. 127–67.

[57] For example see F. E. Zeuner, *A History of Domesticated Animals*, London, 1963, p. 187.

[58] J. C. Ewart, 'Domestic sheep and their wild ancestors. I. Sheep of the Mouflon and Urial types', *Trans. High. & Agric. Soc. Scot.*, ser. 5, 25, 1913, pp. 160–91.

[59] M. Hilzheimer, 'Sheep', *Ant.*, x, 1936, pp. 195–206.

[60] L. Adametz, 'Uber die Rassenzugehörigkeit des "ziegenhörnungen" Torfschafes der neolithischen schweizer Pfahlbauten und seiner Abkömmlinge', *Zeitschrift für Tierzüchtung. und Züchtungsbiol.*, 38, 1937, pp. 113–29.

and the dark brown type as coming from the Mouflon. Another feature of the wild sheep, found in the Soay, is the short tail.

It does, however, appear that only *studeri* is represented on prehistoric sites in Scotland[61] and Zeuner[62] interpreted this as evidence for an introduction of Mouflon-type sheep by a western route into Britain probably with the megalith builders, whereas the *palustris* type would have reached Britain by the more direct route across the Channel. The full significance of Renfrew's finding that the megaliths of western Europe pre-date similar structures in the East has not yet been worked out for archaeology as a whole, let alone the diffusion of livestock.[63] On this view, the Soay sheep would be entirely of Mouflon type and no variation within it could be related to the Urial. This accords with the recent chromosome evidence (above, p. 357).[64]

The occurrence of *studeri* in Scotland is interpreted by Applebaum as indicating the preferential killing of males, *studeri* being, as already indicated, merely the male of prehistoric sheep comparable with the Soay.[65] This could also reflect nothing more than the greater natural mortality of Soay males (above, p. 341), which could then be eaten.

Polled sheep

The loss of horns in livestock is one of the products of domestication. That some wild Mouflon ewes in Corsica and Sardinia lack horns has been taken as indicating the Mouflon as the source of the hornless character in domestic sheep. It is by no means certain, however, that such a lack of horns is an original feature, since it is possible that Mouflon ewes have become polled through crosses with escaped domestic sheep carrying the hornless character. Bökönyi found hornless sheep on an Early Neolithic site in Hungary from which he suggested that loss of horns was one of the earliest changes following domestication.[66]

When hornless sheep reached Britain is not clear, since, owing to breakage, it is rare to find complete skulls, whereas detached horns can indicate horned sheep. A hornless sheep at Jarlshof has become established in the literature but does not appear from the excavation report to be from a prehistoric level.[67] Harcourt has noted horns in both sexes

---

[61] Newstead: for example see Ewart, *op. cit.*   [62] Zeuner, *op. cit.*
[63] C. Renfrew, 'Carbon-14 and the prehistory of Europe', *Sci. Amer.*, 255, 1971, pp. 63–72.
[64] M. L. Ryder, *Sheep and Man*, London (forthcoming).
[65] S. Applebaum, 'Agriculture in Roman Britain', D.Phil. thesis, Univ. of Oxford, 1951.
[66] S. Bökönyi, 'The vertebrate fauna of the Neolithic settlement at Maroslele-Pana', *Különlenyomat az Archaeologiai Értesító*, 91, 1964, pp. 87–94.
[67] Ryder, 'The evolution of Scottish breeds...', 1968, *op. cit.*

on prehistoric sites and has recorded a polled skull from a second to fourth century Romano-British site in Rutland, and Findon in Sussex.[68] I am not aware of any other evidence for hornless sheep before the Middle Ages.[69]

Changes in size

The wild ancestors of domestic sheep tend to have shoulders that are larger than the hindquarters, which Hammond considered to be due to the retardation of late-developing parts through continual breeding on a poor diet.[70] This is regarded today as too simplified an explanation.

It is difficult to trace changes in size because single sites frequently yield no more than a few bones complete enough to be measured which are likely to be from different parts of the body. One cannot stress too much the importance of keeping every bone found. It is only from large collections that one can hope to obtain sufficiently large samples of the same bone for a statistical analysis to be carried out.

A bone that preserves well, and is often used in implements is the metapodial (cannon bone) of the ankle. The metapodials – metacarpal or fore-cannon, metatarsal or hind-cannon – can also be measured in life, and so I have concentrated on accumulating measurements from these two particular bones. A survey was made of bones from Scottish sites: included were measurements from the wild Mouflon, some bones from English sites for comparison, and measurements of implements in museums made from cannon bones, which do not usually pass through the hands of the bone investigator.[71]

The Mouflon is a longer-legged and therefore taller animal than the present-day Soay.[72] It is therefore of interest, that the few Skara Brae (Neolithic) and Jarlshof (Bronze Age) bones were longer than Soay bones and any of the other prehistoric bones measured. Although there is little evidence to support it, I have suggested that one of the first changes on domestication might have been a reduction in stature brought about by a shortening of the leg bones.[73] Since these chapters were written, I have seen Neolithic sheep bones in Poland that were about twice the length of medieval bones, so supporting this general

[68] R. A. Harcourt, personal communication, 1970.
[69] M. L. Ryder, 'Livestock remains from four medieval sites in Yorkshire', *Agric. Hist. Rev.*, 9, 1961, pp. 105–10.
[70] J. Hammond, 'Some changes in the form of sheep and pigs under domestication', *Zeitschrift für Tierzüchtung. und Züchtungsbiol.*, 77, 1962, pp. 156–8.
[71] Ryder, 'The evolution of Scottish breeds...', 1968, *op. cit.*
[72] *Idem*, 'Post-natal fleece development in some primitive sheep and cross', *Zeitschrift für Tierzüchtung und Züchtungsbiol.*, 86, 1970, pp. 372–91.
[73] Ryder, 'The evolution of Scottish breeds...', 1968, *op. cit.*

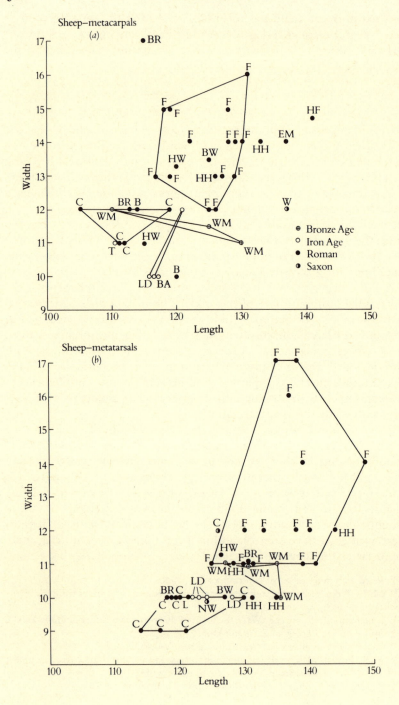

Sheep–metacarpals (a)

Sheep–metatarsals (b)

statement. The supposedly Bronze Age bones from Mill Pot Cave, Wetton, Staffs., were of a size comparable to that of the remaining prehistoric bones measured.[74]

In comparison with modern breeds the limb bones of most prehistoric sheep are on the whole more slender, and, are either of similar or greater length. Hammond interprets this in terms of length-growth taking place before growth in thickness.[75] An index of slenderness is given by plotting the length of bones against the minimum width at the mid-point of the shaft. This was done with the bones which I investigated,[76] and has been done with a further group for the present study (Fig. 62a, b).

This approach revealed no trends among the measurements of prehistoric bones (except that already mentioned with those from Jarlshof) which were seen to have dimensions comparable to those of modern Soay and Shetland sheep. The only obvious difference was the considerable change in width (from roughly 10 mm to 15 mm) between the ancient and the modern bones which has presumably been brought about by the more recent development of the carcass for meat. In the modern bones, where sex was known, it was seen that those of rams were longer than those of ewes, although the width was the same.

English medieval bones included in the graph fell within the range of dimensions of prehistoric bones, so there was no evidence of any change in size until after the Middle Ages.[76] Harcourt has followed the same general approach and come to the same conclusions.[77] His figures have been freely drawn upon in the preparation of the graphs in the present account. Some distal metatarsal widths (24 and 25 mm), which he records from the Neolithic site of Durrington Walls, appear large,

[74] M. L. Ryder, I. H. Longworth, and A. J. H. Gunstone, 'Prehistoric bone and pottery finds from Mill Pot Cave, near Wetton, Staffs.', *North Staffs. J. Fld Studies*, 11, 1971, pp. 40–8.
[75] Hammond, *op. cit.*
[76] Ryder, 'The evolution of Scottish breeds...', 1968, *op. cit.*
[77] R. A. Harcourt, personal communication, 1970.

Fig. 62. Length plotted against minimum width of sheep (a) metacarpals (fore ankle bones); (b) metatarsals (hind ankle bones). Each point (given a symbol for the period) indicates one or more bones. All those from a single site have been enclosed by a line. WM = Wetton Mill (M. L. Ryder *et al.*, *North Staffs. J. Fld Studies*, 11, 1971, pp. 40–8); BA = Balkesbury Camp (R. A. Harcourt in G. Wainwright, *Papers and Proc. Hants. Fld Club*, 26, 1969, pp. 21–53); LD = Longbridge Deverill (R. A. Harcourt, personal communication); T = Twywell (*ibid.*); BR = Brough (*ibid.*); HF = Higham Ferrers (*ibid.*); B = Birchington (*ibid.*); EM = East Malling (*ibid.*); C = Chew Valley (*ibid.*); F = Findon Well (*ibid.*); HH = Hemel Hempstead; G = Glastonbury; BW = Bagwood Coppice (B. A. Noddle, personal communication); L = Llanymyneck (*ibid.*); NW = New Winters (*ibid.*); HW = Hadrian's Wall (R. E. Chaplin, *Arch. Ael.* 43, 1965, pp. 193–200); W = Whitehall (*ibid.*). For discussion see text.

but in fact correspond with the greatest widths recorded from Skara Brae, Jarlshof, and Wetton Mill, Staffs.

Harcourt used Tsalkin's index[78] to calculate height (at the shoulder) from the length of the metapodials, and found all sheep from the Neolithic to the Middle Ages had the same range of height, which was from 21–25 in. (53–64 cm) when calculated from the metatarsal, and 22–26 in. (56–66 cm) when calculated from the metacarpal. His comparison of this size with that of the Soay sheep is supported by my measurements of Soays. Six ewes ranged from 49 to 54 cm with a mean of 52 cm, and six rams ranged from 51 to 61 cm in height with a mean of 56 cm. Pitt-Rivers thought that bones from Roman farms on Cranbourne Chase indicated a long-legged sheep 23 in. (58 cm) high.

Jarman et al. noted that the sheep as well as cattle were larger at the Iron Age hill fort of Grimthorpe (Yorks.) than on the similar site at Barley (Herts.).[79] The proximal width of sheep metapodials, for instance, ranged from 20.4 to 22 mm with a mean of 21.2 mm at Grimthorpe, compared with 17.9 to 22 and a mean of 19.3 mm at Barley, but the difference was statistically significant at only the 5 per cent level. It is not clear what importance one should attach to this difference. Variations of this sort will almost certainly exist between breeds, and very possibly between flocks of the same breed, but I am not aware of any modern studies indicating the extent of variation in sheep. The difference is in any case quite small, and so it would be unwise to postulate two distinct breeds as the cause of a difference that may be due to nutritional variation, although nutritional variation affects the length of bones more than it does width.

There have been reports by previous workers of occasional larger sheep bones on Roman sites (Cranbourne Chase and Bar Hill, Scotland).[80] These have provided a source of evidence for suggestions, such as that of Trow-Smith,[81] that the Romans introduced an improved sheep.

It is therefore of interest to note that Harcourt has recorded larger bones on several Roman sites notably the villa at Hemel Hempstead, Herts., the Romano-British site at Higham Ferrers, Northants., and among the group from Findon Well, Sussex.[82] This does not necessarily prove that larger animals were introduced; they could have increased in size in Britain. Since the latter group date from the second to fourth

[78] Quoted in M. L. Ryder, *Animal Bones in Archaeology*, Oxford, 1969.

[79] M. Jarman, A. Fogg, and E. S. Higgs, 'The animal remains', in I. M. Stead, 'The Iron Age Hill Fort at Grimthorpe, Yorks.', *Proc. Prehist. Soc.*, 34, 1968, pp. 148–90.

[80] M. L. Ryder, 'The history of sheep breeds in Britain', *Agric. Hist., Rev.*, 12, 1964, (1), pp. 1–12; (2), pp. 65–82.

[81] R. Trow-Smith, *A History of British Livestock Husbandry to 1700*, London, 1957.

[82] R. A. Harcourt, personal communication, 1970.

centuries they can indicate only the range over the whole of this period, and not that within a contemporary population. But is is striking that the Findon bones appear both broader and longer than the group from the Romano-British site at Chew, Somerset (Fig. 62a, b). The length:mid-width ratio of the metacarpals, however, does not differ significantly between the two sites although the difference in the metatarsals is significant at the 1 per cent level. Some additional bone measurements made since this chapter was written are given in Table 8, p. 377.

Evidence from the fleece and skin

Since skeletal remains from prehistoric sites suggest a sheep comparable to the Soay that now remains feral only on St Kilda off north-west Scotland, it is of interest to see what information can be gained from the fleece of the Soay and from prehistoric textiles. The Soay's fleece, compared with that of the Mouflon, shows considerable reduction in the diameter of the outer coat hairy fibres, but it still moults completely each spring. Elsewhere man must have selectively bred for sheep that did not shed, whereas on St Kilda such animals would have been at a selective disadvantage, and so shedding persisted there through natural selection.

The common colour pattern in the Soay, of pigmented upper parts and white belly, together with white rump patches at the side of the tail, is comparable to the pattern in wild sheep and indicates a primitive animal not far removed from the wild type. Its overall brown colour suggests an affinity with the Mouflon rather than other wild sheep because the Urial tend to be grey and the Argali white.

There is a division into dark and light animals, the ratio of dark to light on St Kilda being 3:1. Test matings I have carried out have shown that dark is genetically dominant to light. Dark animals have black as well as dark brown wool fibres and appear to be genetically black, whereas light animals have only light brown wool.

There is a further subdivision between wild-pattern sheep (described above) and self-colour animals with a coloured belly. Wild-pattern is dominant to self-colour. Light self-colour Soays are similar in appearance to brown Shetland sheep and are probably of the same colour genotype.[83] Indeed there may be a fairly direct evolutionary link between light self-colour sheep of Soay type and brown Shetland sheep. The inheritance of these colours has since been worked out in detail.[84]

[83] M. L. Ryder, 'Fleece structure in some native and unimproved breeds of sheep', *Zeitschrift für Tierzüchtung und Züchtungsbiol.'*, 85, 1968, pp. 143–70.
[84] M. L. Ryder, R. B. Land, and R. Ditchbourn, 'Colour inheritance in Soay, Orkney, and Shetland sheep', *J. Zool.*, 173, 1974, pp. 477–85.

If the Soay is regarded as a prehistoric sheep, then the Orkney and Shetland group which represents a more advanced stage of evolution than the Soay, might perhaps be regarded as a medieval type. This group has black, white, and grey, in addition to brown individuals. Independent of the different colours, Soay, Orkney, and Shetland sheep have either hairy or woolly fleeces.[85, 86]

After the above brief survey of the fleeces of surviving primitive sheep, we can discuss the types of fleece found in wool textile remains. Unfortunately, there appear to be no certain survivals of sheep skin or wool from the Neolithic period anywhere in the world. I therefore assumed that the fleeces of Neolithic sheep would have been little different from those of wild sheep, and pointed out that primitive 'hair' sheep in the tropics have a similar short coat with an outer coat of hairy fibres known as kemps, and an undercoat of fine wool.[87] The assumption here is that, for clothing, in a hot climate man had no incentive to select for more wool and less kemp. The earliest wool that it has been possible to examine from northern Europe is of Bronze Age date, and the first workers to study such specimens thought that the wool had been mixed with deer hair. It is now realized that the 'deer hairs' are in reality kemps which are found in the fleeces of mostly primitive sheep such as the hairy type of Soay. Fibre diameter measurements I have listed indicate a range comparable with that of Soay fleeces,[87] and since these ancient wools usually have natural pigmentation, textile evidence supports the skeletal evidence, identifying the Soay as the prehistoric type.

The fibre diameter measurements in Bronze Age clothing from Skrydstrup (Denmark) indicate coarser kemps than found in the hairy Soays. This was interpreted as indicating a fleece intermediate between the hairy Soay and that of the wild type, and may well have been typical of Neolithic fleeces.[88]

The contention of Higham that the killing of immature males on Swiss Neolithic sites necessarily indicated a lack of interest in wool has already been refuted in the Neolithic section (above, p. 322).[89]

The fibre diameter distribution found in many prehistoric textiles has been termed a 'generalized medium wool'.[90, 91] The main feature in

[85] M. L. Ryder, 'Coat structure in Soay sheep', *Nature*, 211, 1966, pp. 1092–3.

[86] Ryder, 1968, *op. cit.*

[87] *Idem*, 'Changes in the fleece of sheep following domestication (with a note on the coat of cattle)', in P. J. Ucko and G. W. Dimbleby (eds.), *The Domestication and Exploitation of Plants and Animals*, London, 1969, pp. 495–521.   [88] *Ibid.*, Table I.

[89] C. F. W. Higham, 'Trends in prehistoric European caprovine husbandry', *Man*, 3, 1968, pp. 64–85.

[90] M. L. Ryder, 'Fleece evolution in domestic sheep', *Nature*, 204, 1964, pp. 555–9.

[91] *Idem*, 'Changes in the fleece...', 1969, *op. cit.*

histograms of the diameter distribution is a skewness towards the finer end of the range. The upper limit is of a diameter about 55 μm (1 μm = 0.001 mm) corresponding to the woolly Soay. But in the hairy Soay the 'tail' at the coarser end has hairy (medullated) fibres that can be over 100 μm in diameter in addition to the non-medullated medium fibres that have a mean about 40 μm, and which are the only fibres in the 'tail' of the woolly Soay. I have argued that since these medium fibres are invisible to the naked eye, a white generalized medium wool was the fine wool of the ancient world.[92]

In addition to the kempy wool already mentioned, I listed nine Bronze Age yarns mainly from Germany or Scandinavia, but including three from the oak-coffin burial at Rylstone, Yorks.[93] These included three hairy medium wools, four generalized medium wools, and two possibly true fine wools. I also put forward a possible scheme of evolution from the wild coat through the hairy Soay, in which successive narrowing of the kemp fibres gave rise to the medium fibres of the woolly Soay (the generalized medium wool).[94]

This type appears to be in an intermediate position forming an evolutionary link between the more primitive hairy fleeces and several of the fleece types found in modern sheep. Fig. 63 shows how a further narrowing of the medium fibres could have led to the symmetrical (statistically normal) distribution of the modern, true fine wool. On the other hand, a coarsening of the fine fibres could have led to the fleece composed entirely of fibres of medium diameter found in the modern longwool. If both these changes had taken place simultaneously, resulting in a shortening of the diameter range, then the fleece type of the British shortwool, represented in Fig. 63 by the Down type, would have been produced.

One Bronze Age wool from Denmark, and another from Norway, had an impossibly high proportion of fine fibres, and only a few medium fibres.[95] Since in primitive hand-spinning the wool is taken direct from the staple, one would expect the distribution of fibre diameter in the yarn to be the same as that in the fleece. This unexpected distribution was therefore puzzling until I visited St Kilda to observe the moult in Soay sheep. Here it was found that many of the hairy fibres shed at a different time from the wool. Sheep that moult are plucked to obtain their fleece (the Latin *vellus*, a fleece comes from *vello*, I pluck) and this retention of the hairy fibres suggests that the plucking of primitive breeds might often have yielded wool with a greater proportion of fine fibres than would otherwise be obtained if the fleece were shorn, and the hairy fibres included.

[92] *Idem*, 'Fleece evolution in domestic sheep', 1964, *op. cit.*
[93] *Idem*, 'Changes in the fleece...', 1969, *op. cit.*   [94] *Ibid.*, Fig. 2.   [95] *Ibid.*

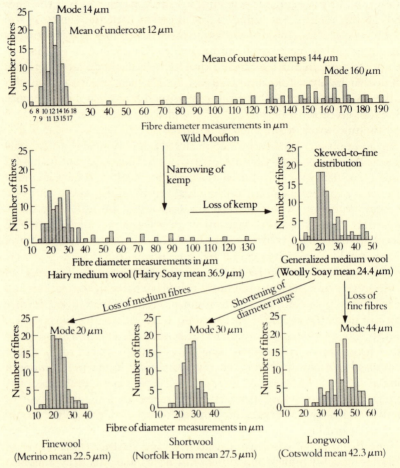

Fig. 63. Probable changes in diameter distribution during fleece evolution based on actual measurements of different fleece types (from M. L. Ryder, in P. J. Ucko and S. W. Dimbleby (eds.), *The Domestication and Exploitation of Plants and Animals*, London, 1969, pp. 495–521). See text for description.

It has already been mentioned in the Introduction (p. 315) that the matting of shed wool in the fleece probably suggested to man the making of felt, and the observation that the shedding fleece was sometimes rubbed into long strands may have given rise to the spinning of wool.

The origin of sheep shearing must have been associated in some way with the change from a moulting fleece to one of continuous growth. Since moulting can result in considerable loss of wool, man would wish to breed selectively against it by culling those animals that shed most. There is appreciable variation in the extent of fleece loss in the Soay, which suggests the existence of the necessary variation that would allow selection for sheep that did not cast their fleece. But this is unlikely to have been worthwhile until an alternative method of removing the fleece was available. Sheep shears seem to have become fully developed only in the Iron Age, but there is evidence that before this a bronze knife or comb was used to obtain wool. It is of interest that in some areas where plucking persisted until recent times, such as Faroe and St Kilda, a knife was used first before shears were adopted.

Whereas many of the technological advances of the Neolithic period were dependent upon the prior biological advance of domestication, the biological change to continuously-growing wool could be considered as having depended on the prior invention of sheepshears. The biological change was in fact so great that it appears to have been the origin of a new type of hairy fibre. The two main types of fibre, kemp and true wool, in the coat of the wild sheep had added to them, apparently in the Iron Age, a third main type, the long continuously growing or heterotype hair. Heterotypes are apparently intermediate between kemp and wool in that they are coarse and kemp-like in summer, but thin and wool-like in winter. When kemps cease to grow during winter, heterotype hairs merely thin down and continue to grow.[96]

The other big change in Iron Age wool in Europe was the lack of natural pigment in many wools. The loss of pigment indicates considerable experience with selective breeding and the change had occurred earlier in the Near East. Virgil and Varro both state that in order to maintain whiteness it is essential to avoid rams with a black tongue.[97, 98] In the present scientific age it is all too easy to jump to the conclusion that such a statement is mere superstition. Ryder and Stephenson, however, drew attention to work on the Karakul sheep and the Swedish Gotland breed, which demonstrated that there is a genetic correlation between a pigmented tongue and pigmented fibres in the fleece.[99]

I have described two Iron Age samples, both pieces of skin with wool intact.[100] One from a Scythian burial at Pazyryk in central Asia, dated 400 BC, had rudimentary heterotype hairs. The other from the Hallstatt salt workings apparently had kemps rather than hairs. The staple form

[96] Ibid.
[97] Virgil, Georgics, At. III, pp. 386–90.   [98] Varro, Res Rusticae, II, 2, 4.
[99] M. L. Ryder and S. K. Stephenson, Wool Growth, London, 1968, esp. pp. 455, 477.
[100] Ryder, 'Changes in the fleece...', 1969, op. cit.

of the Scythian fleece was comparable to that of a short-woolled Scottish Blackface sheep. This is of interest because heterotypes are a feature of the fleece of the black-faced horned stock of Britain, and there are suggestions that this stock originally came from Asia.

Although the main type of sheep in Britain before the Roman occupation appears to have been a small, brown breed comparable to the Soay, Wild suggested from evidence in Strabo that the Belgae might have introduced an improved, fine-woolled sheep, that was presumably white, even before the Roman occupation.[101] It had previously been suggested that the Romans introduced an improved sheep into Britain.[102, 103] There is ample evidence that the Romans had a fine-woolled sheep (which were frequently jacketed to protect the wool), and it is logical to assume that such sheep would have been brought to Britain to be added to any introduced earlier. I am indebted to Dr J. P. Wild for pointing out to me that the much-quoted statement of Dionysius Periegetes that British wool was comparable with a spider's web has no basis. Re-reading of the poem has failed to discover any reference to Britain.

It is tempting to link these sheep with the larger bones found on some Roman sites, and there could well be such an association. Although fine-woolled sheep today tend to be small, the Soay is much smaller, and no remains as large as the big mutton sheep of long-woolled type have been found.

I tabulated thirteen yarns of the Roman period from British sites ranging from London to the Antonine Wall.[104] Of these nine were pigmented and the following fleece types were represented: six hairy medium wools, two generalized medium wools, one true medium wool, and as many as four true fine wools. These show that sheep of Soay type (hairy medium wool and generalized medium wool) were still kept, but that different types had already evolved or been introduced. No shortwools were found, but one was recorded from the Continent. The finding of this range of fleece types among Roman remains lends support for the divergence proposed above (Fig. 63), and shows that these types were in existence at that time, whether or not they arose locally or in exactly the way suggested.

More recently I have examined the wools from the Roman fort and civilian settlement of Vindolanda at Chesterholm on Hadrian's

[101] J. P. Wild, *Textile Manufacture in the Northern Roman Provinces*, Cambridge, 1970.
[102] R. Trow-Smith, *A History of British Livestock Husbandry to 1700*, London, 1957.
[103] M. L. Ryder, 'The history of sheep breeds in Britain', *Agric. Hist. Rev.*, 12, 1964: (1) pp. 1–12; (2) pp. 65–82.
[104] *Idem*, 'Changes in the fleece...', 1969, *op. cit.*

wall.[105, 106] These are closely dated to the end of the first century AD
and Dr J. P. Wild considers that the cloth is of local manufacture.

In all, fifty-six yarns were examined plus a rare unspun staple. This
had a pointed tip not unlike that in the staples of a modern Scottish
Blackface sheep, but the length of 40 mm is unlikely to have been the
total (annual) growth. The wool lacked pigment and represented the
first true hairy fleece type from a Roman context.

Table 6. *Comparison of Vindolanda wools with previous examples*[107]

	Hairy medium (%)	Generalized medium (%)	Fine/gen. medium (%)	Fine (%)	Medium (%)	Short (%)
Other	20	11	31	29	6	3
Vindolanda	34	34	18	9	2	4

There were nineteen hairy medium wools (34 per cent of the total)
and all these were pigmented, the coarser fibres having more dense
pigmentation than the finer fibres. This gives a grey appearance, and
is the earliest date at which this distribution of pigmentation has been
found. It is found today for instance in grey Orkney and Shetland sheep.

There were also nineteen generalized medium wools (34 per cent)
and these had varying amounts of pigmentation. The remaining wools
had little or no pigment. These comprised ten (18 per cent) fine
generalized medium wools, five (9 per cent) of true fine type, one true
medium fleece (2 per cent) and two shortwools (4 per cent). This again
shows the early appearance of the last two types in Britain.

Table 6 shows that on the whole the Vindolanda wools were more
hairy than the wools from all other sites (above) grouped together,

The first two or three types in the table could well represent native
sheep, while the last four types may have been introduced.

The ubiquity of sheep in England during the Saxon period is clearly
shown by the many Saxon place names such as Shipley or Skipton
embodying a reference to sheep (see Saxon section, p. 347) and the
importance of wool (and the excellence of its quality) is indicated by
the well-known letter from Charlemagne to the king of Mercia
regarding the supply of cloaks. Recent excavations at West Stow,
Suffolk have provided evidence of well-organized textile manufacture.

Insufficient evidence, either skeletal or pictorial, is available to enable

---

[105] *Idem*, 'Wools from antiquity', *Textile History*, 5, 1974, pp. 100–10.
[106] *Idem*, in J. P. Wild, 'The textiles', *Vindolanda* III, Hexham, 1977, pp. 31–41.
[107] *Idem*, *Sheep and Man*, London (forthcoming).

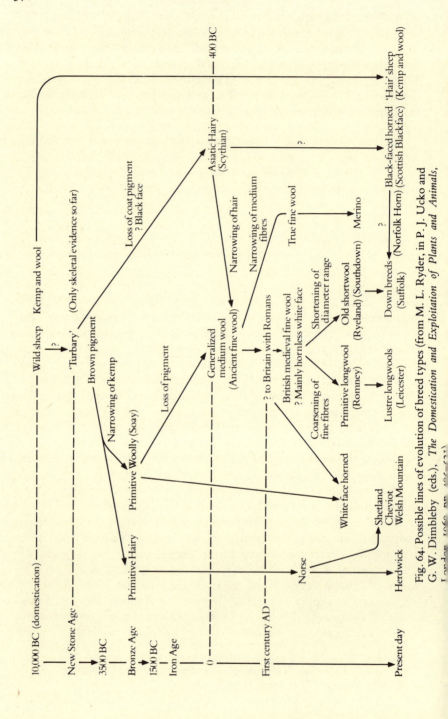

Fig. 64. Possible lines of evolution of breed types (from M. L. Ryder, in P. J. Ucko and G. W. Dimbleby (eds.), *The Domestication and Exploitation of Plants and Animals*, London 1969, pp. 495–521)

one to reconstruct Saxon sheep adequately, as attempted by Chaplin.[108] The slender legs are shown well, but the body is likely to have been shorter and less deep. Of fourteen yarns I listed from the Saxon sites of Coombe, Kent, Broomfield Barrow, Essex, and Sutton Hoo, Suffolk, only five were pigmented.[109] The same range of types as those from Roman sites was found but there were as many as seven fine wools, six generalized medium wools (half of which were finer than usual) and only one hairy medium wool.

From such textile evidence, and the distribution of different breed types, recorded in the first breed descriptions of the eighteenth century, I proposed two or three main introductions of sheep and the possible origin of some of the main types still evident today.[110]

It is possible that the white-faced horned type of sheep was the result of crosses between the brown native Soay, and the white Roman sheep. When horned today, only the rams of this type have horns, and any pigment is usually brown, breeds of this type being frequently tan-faced in the past. When it emerged into history, the white-faced horned type was found in the northern and western parts of Britain that received least Roman influence. The type remains today in such breeds as the Cheviot of the Scottish Border, the Welsh Mountain breed, and possibly the Exmoor Horn, which, however, is horned in both sexes. These breeds in general have no heterotype hairs; any hairy fibres occurring are kemps (Fig. 64).

Some northern sheep, notably those of Orkney and Shetland, have Norse influence. Affinity with the native sheep of Scandinavia is shown by the short tail and colour range found in both groups, each indicating animals more primitive than the Roman white, long-tailed breed (see below, p. 374).[111, 112] The Herdwick of the Lake District too, appears to have some Norse influence, but it differs in having a long tail and heterotype hairs in its fleece.

The true fine wool, which could have been derived from the generalized medium wool by a narrowing of the medium fibres, emerged on the Continent notably as the Merino breed of Spain. This has horned rams, and polled ewes, and so it is tempting to suggest that

---

[108] R. E. Chaplin, 'The use of non-morphological criteria in the study of animal domestication from bones found on archaeological sites', in P. J. Ucko and G. W. Dimbleby (eds.), *The Domestication and Exploitation of Plants and Animals*, London, 1969, pp. 231–46.

[109] Ryder, 'Changes in the fleece...', 1969, *op. cit.*

[110] *Idem*, 'The history of sheep breeds', 1964, *op. cit.*

[111] *Idem*, 'Fleece structure in some native and unimproved breeds of sheep', *Zeitschrift für Tierzüchtung. und Züchtungsbiol.*, 85, 1968, pp. 143–70.

[112] *Idem*, 'The evolution of Scottish breeds of sheep', *Scott. Studies*, 12, 1968, pp. 127–67.

only the rams of Roman sheep were horned. A number of Roman sculptures, such as one from the Antonine Wall, have horned sheep which could be rams. What is probably one of the earliest coloured illustrations, 'The Good Shepherd' on the fifth-century Galla Placidia mausoleum at Ravenna (northern Italy) has six long-tailed, white-faced, polled sheep that appear to be ewes. The tenth-century Caedmon manuscript has what are probably the first illustrations of sheep in Britain: horned rams and polled ewes. Harcourt found that eleventh-century sheep skulls from Hereford had a range of horn sizes suggesting that both sexes were horned.[113] English medieval illustrations show mostly white-faced polled sheep, with a proportion of horned animals that are presumably rams. The fleece invariably appears to be of shortwool type.[114]

English medieval sheep could have evolved fairly directly from the Roman generalized medium wool, the shortwool by a shortening of the diameter range, to give white-faced polled sheep like the Ryeland breed of Hereford remaining today. A coarsening of the fine fibres could have given the diameter range of the primitive longwool, an example of which is the modern white-faced, polled Romney breed whose original home was Kent.

When the lustre longwool, prominent in the eighteenth century, evolved is not clear. It certainly did not develop as a direct result of better nutrition following enclosure.[115]

The biologists of my generation, nurtured on the Darwinian concept that, in order to survive, genetic variations must have adaptive value, have long sought an explanation for the origin of different fleece types (notably the longwool) which did not appear to have any adaptive value. That they were selectively bred by man is far from being a complete answer, because mutant variations probably existed for centuries before they were consciously selected. In recent years a new concept of the origin of species, namely neutral mutation, has come to be accepted, and it seems likely that this was important in the origin of different fleece types. Earlier stages of this argument, with more detail, have been given elsewhere.[116]

It is tempting to suggest that fewer coat types have arisen in cattle and goats because these species have lower mutation rates. But geneticists regard this as unlikely, and attribute the difference entirely to selection by man, since in the absence of selection not all neutral mutations become fixed, and there is a tendency for movement towards a single type.

[113] R. A. Harcourt, personal communication, 1970.
[114] Ryder, 'The history of sheep breeds', 1964, *op. cit.*
[115] *Idem, Agric. Hist. Rev.*, 13, 1965, p. 126.
[116] *Idem*, 'The history of sheep breeds', 1964, *op. cit.*

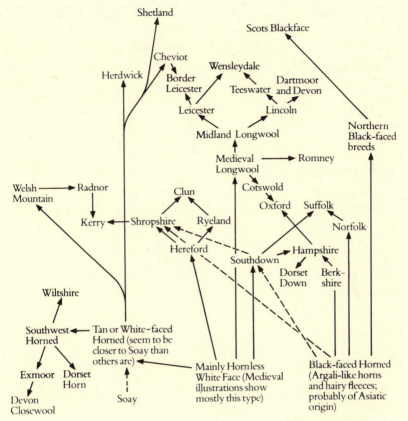

Fig. 65. Probable lines of evolution of British breeds of sheep (from M. L. Ryder, *Agric. Hist. Rev.*, 12, 1964, (1) pp. 1–12; (2) pp. 65–82). This diagram is best interpreted as indicating affinities rather than direct evolutionary links. For instance, the Shetland, although having some affinity with the Cheviot, may owe more to Scandinavian sheep than to native stock.

Two broad modern types of sheep have already been discussed. These are the white-faced, horned, and the white-faced, polled (divided into shortwools and longwools). The third main type is the black-faced, horned and hairy group, but when this arrived is not clear. This type has a number of affinities with Asiatic sheep, notably the black face, the long hairy fleece, and wide-spreading Argali-type horns with a second curve. Ewart laid more stress on horn shape than perhaps we would do today, because for instance Argali-type horns are found in a range of breeds including the Merino.[117] He claimed to have detected Argali

[117] J. C. Ewart, 'Domestic sheep and their wild ancestors. II. Wild sheep of the Argali type', *Trans. High & Agric. Soc. Scot.*, ser. 5, 26, 1914, pp. 74–91.

Table 7. *Classification of main modern British breeds*[121]

Brown short-tail	*Vari-coloured short-tail*
Soay *xx/x*	Shetland *x*
Manx Loaghtan *xx*	Orkney *x*
White-faced, horned mountain	*Black-faced, horned mountain*
Cheviot *x* (now polled)	Scottish Blackface *xx*
Herdwick *x*	Swaledale/Dalesbred *xx*
Welsh Mountain *x*	Lonk *xx*
Radnor *x*	Derbyshire Gritstone
White-faced shortwools	*Black-faced shortwools*
Ryeland	Clun Forest
Kerry Hill	Shropshire
Wiltshire Horn *xx*	Oxford Down
Dorset Horn *xx*	Suffolk Down
Exmoor Horn *xx*	Hampshire Down
Devon Closewool	Dorset Down
	Southdown (now has white face)
Demi-lustre longwools	*Lustre longwools*
Romney Marsh	Teeswater/Wensleydale
Border Leicester	Leicester
	Lincoln
	Dartmoor
	Devon/South Devon

xx ram and ewe horned; *x* ram only horned.

blood in sheep cannon bones of Bronze Age date from the Thames valley.

I[118] developed a suggestion of Trow-Smith[119] that the black-faced, horned type was introduced by the Danes. This was based on the observation that, when records first began, this type was found in an area over the east and north of England that roughly coincided with the pre-conquest Danelaw. There appears to be no archaeological evidence to support this suggestion, but support can be gained from the existence of a similar sheep in the past in Denmark.[120] The same type still persists as the Dutch Heath sheep and the German Heath sheep (*Heidsnucke*). There are other similar breeds further east with which we are less familiar that probably provide continuity with the black-faced hairy sheep of Asia. The Scythian sample already mentioned from Pazyryk in central Asia (above, p. 369), dated 400 BC, appears to have been an early version of this fleece type.

[118] Ryder, 'The history of sheep breeds', 1964, *op. cit.*

[119] R. Trow-Smith, *A History of British Livestock Husbandry to 1700*, London, 1957.

[120] R. Lydekker, *The Sheep and its Cousins*, London, 1912.

[121] Modified from *idem*, 'The history of sheep breeds', 1964, *op. cit.*, and M. L. Ryder and S. K. Stephenson, *Wool Growth*, London, 1968.

Table 8. *Additional sheep bone measurements (mm)*

	Lengths	Shaft width
Metacarpals		
Quanterness, Orkney, Neolithic[124]	129.3–145.8	9.5–12.3
Gussage, Dorset Iron Age[125]	104–122 (33)	Shoulder height 53–59 cm
Tripontium[126]	122–123	12.0–15.0
Balksbury, Hants Iron Age[127]	117	10
Corstopitum (Corbridge) Roman[128]	105–130 (28), mean 117.2	11–13 (28), mean 12.6
Vindolanda, Hadrian's Wall[129]	106–137 (19), mean 119.0	10–15 (19), mean 13.0
Metatarsals		
Quanterness[130]	119.5–120.6	11.5–12.3
Tripontium[131]	125–137	11.0–14.0
Gussage, Dorset[132]	115–137 (29)	Shoulder height 54–64 cm
Corstopitum[133]	121–146 (5), mean 131	10–14 (5), mean 11
Vindolanda[134]	113–132 (16), mean 123.3	10–14 (16), mean 10.6

I included blood types in the discussion of breed affinities, and showed that breeds that are known to have diverged fairly recently have similar blood type value (Fig. 65).[122] But as indicated in the Introduction, this approach is less informative about ancient relationships because of the breeding changes that have taken place in the recent past. Table 7 shows a brief classification of modern breeds.

Nineteen yarns from a tenth-century Danish level of the Lloyd's Bank site, Pavement, York, were described as being of relatively coarse wool.[123] They comprised three true hairy types, seven hairy medium

[122] Ryder, 'The history of sheep breeds', 1964, *op. cit.*

[123] *Idem*, 1974, *op. cit.*

[124] J. Clutton-Brock, 'The animal remains', in A. C. Renfrew, *Investigations in Orkney*, London, 1979.

[125] R. A. Harcourt, personal communication, 1977.

[126] B. A. Noddle, 'Animal bones from two wells at Tripontium', *Trans. Birm. and Warwick. Arch. Soc.*, 85, 1972, pp. 136–42.

[127] R. A. Harcourt in G. J. Wainwright, 'The excavation of Balksbury Camp, Andover, Hants.', *Papers and Proc. Hants. Fld Club*, 26, 1969, pp. 21–53.

[128] G. W. I. Hodgson, personal communication, 1976.

[129] *Idem*, 'The animal remains, 1970–1975', *Vindolanda* II, Hexham, 1977.

[130] Clutton-Brock, 1979, *op. cit.*

[131] Noddle, 1972, *op. cit.*

[132] R. A. Harcourt, personal communication, 1977.

[133] G. W. I. Hodgson, personal communication, 1976.

[134] *Idem*, personal communication, 1977.

wools, five of generalized medium type, and four of true medium type. Several features suggest affinities with modern Scandinavian sheep, and the hairiness compares with Norse wools from Scotland, which were coarser than earlier and later samples. On the other hand the same range of fleece types was found in a medieval level of the Petergate site, York.

It is tempting to use the true hairy fleeces in support of a Danish introduction of the hairy black-faced horned type of sheep which emerged into history in northern and eastern England in such breeds as the Swaledale (as discussed above, p. 376).

I described the two yarns in some cloth from Quernmore, Lancashire, dated by C-14 as being 1300 years BP, as hairy medium and true medium.[135] Wool on the remains of a sheepskin from a Saxon level in Durham, dated about AD 1000 was of true medium type with a similar fibre diameter to the medium wool from Quernmore.

I have summarized the Saxon wools examined elsewhere.[136]

CATTLE (*Bos taurus*)

The wild ancestor of domestic cattle was *Bos primigenius*, the urus or aurochs which became extinct, in Poland, as late as the seventeenth century. Zeuner thought that the almost universal prehistoric distribution of wild cattle in the temperate zones of the Old World made it difficult to determine the original centre of domestication.[137] More recently, however, has come evidence of domestic cattle in Greece and at Catal Hüyük in Anatolia as early as 6500 BC, so it seems likely to have taken place somewhere in the Near East.[138]

Zeuner considered that the domestication of cattle was the most important step in animal exploitation following the initial domestication of the dog. The larger size and food requirements of cattle would have presented problems which he thought rendered it highly likely that their domestication was preceded by settled agriculture. Cattle have a gestation period of 9 months compared with 5 months in goats and sheep, and the first calf is not born until the cow is $2\frac{1}{2}$ years old, compared with as young as one year in some sheep. Although various authors have put forward religious reasons for domesticating cattle (and there is evidence of the later association of cattle with religious practices), Zeuner plumped squarely for the economic explanation of the initial stages. Man already had considerable experience of domesti-

[135] M. L. Ryder, 'Some miscellaneous ancient-fleece remains', *J. Arch. Soc.*, 4, 1977, pp. 177–81.

[136] *Idem, Sheep and Man*, London (forthcoming).

[137] F. E. Zeuner, *A History of Domesticated Animals*, London, 1963.

[138] C. A. Reed, 'The pattern of animal domestication in the prehistoric Near East', in P. J. Ucko and G. W. Dimbleby (eds.), *The Domestication and Exploitation of Plants and Animals*, London, 1969, p. 372.

cation and exploitation and Zeuner thought that the supply of blood, milk, and thicker hides than could be obtained from goats and sheep, provided ample reason for the domestication of cattle. But its most important role, as a draught animal, which Zeuner thought might have been associated with the development of wheeled transport, came later. I am indebted to Mr I. L. Mason for pointing out the unlikelihood of this ferocious animal being domesticated merely for the products that could be more easily obtained from goats and sheep. Possibly its strength and virility were desired for religious reasons, and other authorities[139] are coming back to religious explanations. Zeuner considered that by 2500 BC different breeds of domestic cattle had been developed in the ancient civilizations. In Europe, however, notably from the Swiss Neolithic lake dwellings, a type was found in addition to the domesticated long-horned *primigenius*. This was smaller than the *primigenius*, but comparable in size to modern cattle. It had short horns and a pronounced forehead, hence the names *brachyceros* and *longifrons*. This difference has been recognized for a hundred years, but the way in which the difference should be interpreted is only becoming clarified as more and more detailed measurements are carried out.

Trow-Smith pointed out the confusion that existed regarding British Neolithic cattle through the identification of domestic cattle of *primigenius* type as wild animals, *longifrons* being regarded as the only domestic type.[140] Wild animals were still found at this time, however, showing the possibility of local domestication, and these continued at least into the Bronze Age.[141] Clarification began when Piggott pointed out that *longifrons* had not been recorded from any undoubted Neolithic site, and that of the two sizes of *primigenius* cattle, the smaller were presumably domestic.[142] Trow-Smith wrote that one should compare Neolithic cattle with the half-wild Hereford prairie steer, rather than the doe-eyed Jersey heifer.[143]

He also thought that the decrease in size following domestication could be due to a deterioration in the quality of Neolithic herbage which could have caused a degree of stunting, so that the remains found might be from animals that did not reach their potential genetic stature.[144] It has been said, for instance, that much of the pedigree (milk production) of dairy cattle in recent centuries went in at the mouth. Jewell quoted work relating diet to the density of bone,[145] and the work

[139] For example, Reed, *op. cit.*, p. 373. [140] Trow-Smith, *op. cit.*, p. 5.
[141] F. W. Shawcross and E. S. Higgs, 'The excavation of a *Bos primigenius* at Lowe's Farm, Littleport', *Proc. Camb. Ant. Soc.*, 54, 1961, pp. 3–16.
[142] S. Piggott, *The Neolithic Cultures of the British Isles*, Cambridge, 1954, p. 90.
[143] Trow-Smith, *op. cit.*
[144] *Ibid.*, p. 12.
[145] P. A. Jewell, 'Changes in size and type of cattle from prehistoric to medieval times in Britian', *Zeitschrift für Tierzüchtung und Züchtungsbiol.*, 77, 1962, pp. 159–67.

now being carried out by Miss B. A. Noddle on the mineral composition of bones in an archaeological context is adding to this knowledge. A more likely explanation for small size, however, is that of natural selection on a poor diet. There are breeds today that are genetically small, and whose size would not be increased by better feed.

Jewell pointed out that few of the statements on prehistoric cattle made by earlier authors were based on adequate measurements and no description or measurements of the Windmill Hill ox had ever been published.[146] He thought that on the available evidence there was no reason to believe that the Skara Brae (Orkney) cattle were larger than other Neolithic cattle, as had been claimed. He re-examined and measured the Windmill Hill material and made comparisons with other measurements. From this he was able to state that Neolithic cattle were bigger than Bronze Age, Iron Age, and most medieval cattle. They were in fact as large as the bigger Roman cattle and modern breeds of medium size. More recently Cram had compared Neolithic cattle bones from Abingdon, Berks. with those from Windmill Hill, and found that most measurements from Abingdon were smaller (e.g. distal metatarsal width 54.3 mm compared with 60.3 mm).[147]

A distinguishing feature of Neolithic cattle is the length and robustness of the horns, but Jewell found continuous variation in size, and thus no peaks that would indicate differences of breed or sex. He pointed out that the division of the Skara Brae cattle into groups identified as cows, bulls, and bullocks (castrated males) was not supported by measurements. Trow-Smith had earlier regarded the case for castration at Skara Brae to be not proven.[148]

Jewell showed that the wild cattle of the Mesolithic site at Star Carr, Yorks., were smaller than cattle remains from Maiden Castle, Dorset.[149] Since it is highly likely that these animals were not wild, he put forward the fascinating speculation that they represented hybrids of domestic with wild cattle.

Higham studied a collection of limb bones from modern Aberdeen Angus and Red Danish cattle, and demonstrated the range of sex difference to be expected in a modern breed, and the change due to the castration of males, particularly in metacarpal bones.[150] Grigson made detailed studies of the size range of wild cattle, and demonstrated the

---

[146] *Idem*, 'Cattle from British archaeological sites, in A. E. Mourant and F. E. Zeuner (eds.), *Man and Cattle*, Occasional Paper No. 18 of the Royal Anthropological Inst., 1963, pp. 80–101.

[147] C. L. Cram, personal communication, 1969.

[148] Trow-Smith, *op. cit.*, p. 11.

[149] Jewell, 1963, *op. cit.*

[150] C. Higham, 'The metrical attributes of two samples of bovine limb bones', *J. Zool. Lond.*, 157, 1969, pp. 63–74.

existence of sexual dimorphism.[151, 152] From this she suggested that the Star Carr animals were cows and that large Neolithic examples were bulls. While accepting the possibility of local domestication and also of hybridization, Grigson tends to the view that the large cattle at Maiden Castle were, after all, wild. She does admit, however, that one cannot be certain of this unless one can determine the size range of the *local* wild cattle.

Higham, using measurements of the mean length of the lower third molar in Denmark, demonstrated a progressive decrease in size from wild cattle to medieval cattle, the length in each period differing, with statistical significance, from that in the preceding one. The mean measurements (mm) were as follows: *primigenius*: 48.7; Neolithic: 39.2; Bronze Age: 35.4; Roman Iron Age: 34.7; medieval: 34.0; modern Danish: 39.0 (cf. Neolithic measurement).[153]

Harcourt found several bones of wild cattle amongst the remains at the Neolithic site of Durrington Walls, Wilts. He determined the sex of the metapodials from domestic cattle with the use of Howard's length/breadth indices, and found that they fell into three groups, cows, bulls, and steers (castrated males). Using further factors he calculated the height of cows at the withers to be 47–51 in. (120–129 cm); the one certain bull was 52 in. (131 cm) in height, and the one certain steer was 54 in. (138 cm).[154]

The smaller *longifrons* ox, also known as the 'Celtic' Shorthorn first appeared in Britain on Bronze Age sites.[155, 156] At the Middle Bronze Age site of Snail Down, Everleigh, Wilts., Jewell also found larger animals comparable to those at Star Carr, from which he argued that wild cattle still existed side by side with these much smaller domestic cattle. Although wild cattle undoubtedly remained during the Bronze Age,[157] the latter remains were larger still, and one wonders whether more recent studies would reveal the apparent wild animals at Snail Down as really large examples of the Neolithic ox.[158] Clearly much

[151] C. Grigson, 'The uses and limitations of differences in absolute size in the distinction between the bones of aurochs (*Bos primigenius*) and domestic cattle (*Bos taurus*)', in P. J. Ucko and G. W. Dimbleby (eds.), *The Domestication and Exploitation of Plants and Animals*, London, 1969, pp. 277–94.

[152] *Idem*, 'The domestic animals of the earlier Neolithic in Britain', in G. Nobis (ed.), *Naturwissenschaftliche Beiträge zu den Anfängen des Neolithikums* (forthcoming).

[153] C. Higham, 'Size trends in prehistoric European domestic fauna, and the problem of local domestication', *Acta Zool. Fenn.*, 120, 1968, pp. 1–21.

[154] R. A. Harcourt, personal communication, 1970.

[155] R. Trow-Smith, *A History of British Livestock Husbandry to 1700*, London, 1957, p. 20.

[156] Jewell, 1963, *op. cit.*   [157] Shawcross and Higgs, *op. cit.*

[158] See for example Grigson, *op. cit.*

detailed work is required before definite answers can be given to such questions.

Clutton-Brock and Jewell found an interesting small ox with long horns in a Bronze Age Barrow on Lamb Down, Codford St Mary, Wilts., but the remains were unfortunately very few.[159] Two metatarsals with Bronze Age associations from Wetton Mill, Staffs., were comparable in length with those of smaller Neolithic cattle but were 15 mm broader (Fig. 66).[160]

Another source of evidence on prehistoric cattle is skin and hair.[161] Less is known about variation of the coat of modern cattle than about the fleeces of sheep, but it seems that fewer and less-marked types have evolved. In addition, the relative wealth of material from wool textiles is lacking. The main source of material is leather, and this has fewer hair remains even than parchment.

Roman and medieval leather has shown no differences in hair type and grouping from modern cattle. The first difference from obviously cattle hair was found in a fragment of skin from a Neolithic bow from Meare, Somerset, dated 2600 BC.[162] This contained hairs which were apparently bovine, but they were much finer than the average hairs of modern cattle.

Bronze Age burials have yielded other samples of bovine hair, because bodies were often buried in a skin, and even when this has decayed, archaeologists have sometimes been able to retrieve a specimen of the hairs. Some of these have been similar to the hairs of modern cattle, whereas a group of four from Fife and Angus in Scotland had the same fineness as the hairs in the Meare skin. The identify of this bovine species is uncertain. The hairs had a skewed-to-fine distribution of fibre diameter, and two had an asymmetric distribution of pigment within the hair. Both these are characteristics of bison hair, but the bison is thought to have died out in Britain before separation from the continent. The wild ox, a close relative of the bison, as we have seen, persisted into the Bronze Age, and so it is possible that this unidentified bovine with finer hair was in fact *primigenius*.

---

[159] J. Clutton-Brock and P. A. Jewell, in F. de Mallet Vatcher, 'The excavation of the barrows on Lamb Down, Codford St Mary', *Wilts. Arch. & Nat. Hist. Mag.*, 58 (n.d.), pp. 417–41.

[160] M. L. Ryder, I. H. Longworth, A. J. H. Gunstone, 'Prehistoric bone and pottery finds from Mill Pot Cave, near Wetton, Staffs., *North Staffs. J. Fld Studies*, 11, 1971, pp. 40–8.

[161] M. L. Ryder, 'Remains derived from skin', in D. R. Brothwell and E. S. Higgs (eds.), *Science in Archaeology*, London, 2nd ed., 1970, pp. 539–54.

[162] *Idem*, 'Changes in the fleece of sheep following domestication (with a note on the coat of cattle)', in P. J. Ucko and G. W. Dimbleby (eds.), *The Domestication and Exploitation of Plants and Animals*, London, 1969.

In contrast to sheep, which have clearly been selected for fine wool, the change following domestication in cattle may have been towards a coarser, more hairy coat. Support for this suggestion comes from the relatively fine mean diameter of some prehistoric 'true' cattle (range 35–40 μm compared with 42–44 μm in modern ones). The supposedly primitive Scottish Highland breed has a mean of 41 μm. Exceptions are the modern Galloway breed which has a mean of 30 μm (perhaps indicating a primitive status), and the Chillingham cattle which have coarser hair with a mean of 56 μm.[162]

Until more evidence becomes available, however, the possibility that this unidentified bovine is the wild ox must remain a suggestion. But it does seem certain that two types were present, so an alternative (but less likely) interpretation would be that the finer type was the Neolithic ox and the coarser type the Celtic ox. More recently I have examined hairs found adhering to an ox skull in new excavations at Skara Brae, Orkney, and identified by B. A. Noddle as of early domestic, *primigenius* type, and the hairs were fine like the finer category described above.

The smaller Celtic ox or Celtic Shorthorn (*Bos longifrons*) first appears at the Bronze Age Beaker settlement of Eastern Down, Wilts., and in the Beaker levels of the Skendlebury long barrow, Lincs. It appears to have been introduced from the Continent.[163] Larger cattle were found alongside the Celtic Shorthorn, but these gradually diminished until, by the beginning of the Iron Age, the Celtic ox was dominant. These larger remains were found at All Cannings Cross, and Glastonbury for example, but since they were in fact smaller than Neolithic cattle, Jewell regarded them as hybrids of the Neolithic *primigenius* type with *longifrons*.[163] Trow-Smith, however, pointed out that since there were no intermediate horn types, one horn type must have been genetically dominant.[164] Although there is no reason to suppose that the Continent was not the source of the British examples, Jewell pointed out that the progressive nature of the reduction in size allows one to make a case for the diminution being entirely insular.[165]

Although there is a suggestion of a polled animal at Skara Brae, the first authenticated hornless ox skull is from the Iron Age site of All Cannings Cross. Trow-Smith likened this polled skull to the Aberdeen Angus rather than to the Galloway breed. Harcourt has found polled cattle skulls at Iron Age sites quite close to one another in Wessex.[166] But many centuries were to elapse before polled cattle were common. When a hornless skull breaks up, however, it leaves no evidence as to whether or not it had horns, whereas the horn cores always survive when a horned skull is broken. Hornlessness in cattle is dominant to

[163] Jewell, 1963, *op.* [164] Trow-Smith, *op. cit.*
[165] Jewell, 1963, *op. cit.* [166] R. A. Harcourt, personal communication, 1970.

their presence, whereas mutations are usually recessive to the form from which they are derived.

Not only was the Celtic ox smaller than Neolithic cattle, but it was smaller even than the 41 in. (104 cm) Kerry cow which Pitt-Rivers compared to Romano-British cattle, and which has since been used to exemplify cattle of the period.[167] In fact, the Kerry at 1000 lb (454 kg) is not particularly small; the Dexter, weighing about 650 lb (295 kg) provides a better comparison with the Celtic ox. The 2–4 in. (5–10 cm) horn cores, which means horns no longer than 8 in. (20 cm), made Trow-Smith liken the Celtic ox to a modern, small-horned Shorthorn, but the skull indicates a narrow face like the modern Channel Island or Ayrshire breeds. Trow-Smith speculates that while the *primigenius* type remained a beef animal, *longifrons* might already have been developed as a milch cow, but that necessity could have caused both types to be used as dual purpose animals.

Harcourt found that cows from the Iron Age farm site of Longbridge Deverill, Wilts., ranged from 42 to 44 in (107 to 112 cm) in height, steers from 43 to 46 in. (109 to 117 cm) and two bulls were 44 and 45 in. (112 and 114 cm) in height respectively.[168] Other measurements of 41 in. (104 cm) from Balksbury Camp, Hants.,[169] and two cows 41 and 45 in. (104 and 114 cm) from the Iron Age levels at Durrington Walls were comparable in size, but one metatarsal from Durrington Walls gave a height of 49 in. (125 cm), which is within the Neolithic size range.

Harcourt compared these remains with others from the Celtic ox, and found polled animals at Longbridge Deverill. Although these measurements clearly indicate a smaller animal than that of the Neolithic period, when one considers that the reduction in height was from about 54 in. (137 cm) to no less than 42 in. (107 cm), the descriptions 'large' and 'small' put on a new perspective.

Those familiar with Celtic art will have been impressed by the wealth of cattle representations in metalwork. Trow-Smith has looked at the heads on bronze bucket handles and with many reservations and qualifications claims to have detected four types.[170] The first two of these are the long-horned *primigenius* and the short-horned *longifrons* which have been confirmed by excavated skulls. But there was also a type with vertical horns which Trow-Smith compared with those of the modern Ayrshire breed. This was presumably the 'lyre' horn shape which Applebaum regarded as representing a real and not an imaginary

[167] Trow-Smith, *op. cit.*
[168] R. A. Harcourt, personal communication, 1970.
[169] *Idem*, in G. J. Wainwright, 'The excavation of Balksbury Camp, Andover, Hants.', *Papers and Proc. Hants. Fld Club*, 26, 1969, pp. 21–53.
[170] Trow-Smith, *op. cit.*

animal.[171] Another with horns of Channel Island (Jersey) type, was identified by Trow-Smith, the last two being in fact more common than the first two.[172] One must not use this evidence to jump to the conclusion that it indicates the ancient origin or great antiquity of specific breeds. It is more likely that prehistoric cattle were very variable in appearance, and exhibited a range of horn shapes that are only now associated with particular breeds.

Ryder found four horn types among a collection of one hundred and seven cores from medieval York. But frequency diagrams[173] of both length and diameter indicated a homogeneous population, and it was considered that the variants were no greater than one would expect within a primitive breed.[174] In addition to the typical shorthorn type, a few of the shorter ones curved sharply upwards. A few after curving sharply upwards twisted in the terminal part in a posterior direction (cf. Ayrshire). Finally, there were some that were straighter and flattened dorso-ventrally.

Following the diminution of cattle to the small size of the Celtic ox in the Iron Age, a larger variety began to appear alongside it in Roman times. Applebaum discussed the ideas of authors such as Cossar Ewart and McKenny Hughes concerning the supposed importation of a larger breed by the Romans which they thought had been crossed with *longifrons* to produce a larger type.[175] Ewart thought the feral, white herds of Chartley and Chillingham cattle represented survivors of this imported stock.

The identification of these 'wild', white park cattle as remnants of Roman imports owes much to their superficial resemblance to modern white cattle of similar appearance in northern Italy. But Applebaum rightly found the comparison of skulls illustrated by Hughes as unconvincing (today a strict statistical comparison of many measurements would be required before such a suggestion could be accepted), and concluded that there was no reliable evidence for the importation of new breeds of cattle by the Romans. I am indebted to Mr I. L. Mason for the information that the white cattle of Italy are mostly post-Roman, and have a different colour genotype from British cattle.

In addition to the much quoted polled ox at All Cannings Cross,

[171] S. Applebaum, 'Agriculture in Roman Britain', D.Phil. thesis, Univ. of Oxford, 1951.

[172] Trow-Smith, *op. cit.*

[173] Illustrated in P. A. Jewell, 'Cattle from British archaeological sites', in A. E. Mourant and F. E. Zeuner (eds.), *Man and Cattle*, Occasional Paper No. 18 of the Royal Anthropological Inst., 1963, pp. 80–101.

[174] The horn types are illustrated in M. L. Ryder, 'The animal remains from Petergate, York, 1957–58', *Yorks. Arch. J.*, 42 (168), 1970, pp. 418–28.

[175] Applebaum, 1951, *op. cit.*

which seems to have been derived from *longifrons* and which he likened to the modern Aberdeen Angus, Trow-Smith drew attention to a neglected polled animal reported by Ewart at Newstead which he regarded as having a flat-topped skull suggestive of that of the Galloway.[176]

Jewell re-examined the measurements made by Meek and Gray in 1911 of cattle remains from Corbridge, and came to the conclusion that the bones were all more slender than those of modern cattle, but that the length indicated a size range spanning several modern breeds. Some were smaller than the Kerry and others as large as the Shorthorn breed. Jewell regarded this diversity of types as significant in relation to the later emergence of distinct local breeds.[177]

Hodgson made a more detailed investigation still of the Meek and Gray measurements, together with others made of bones excavated at Corbridge in 1966 and 1967.[178] He first demonstrated that the two series of measurements had means which did not differ with statistical significance. He illustrated histograms of the distal width of 155 metacarpals and of 173 metatarsals. The metacarpals ranged from 45 to 73 mm in width with a mean of 53.8 mm. Hodgson stated that these included bones which were shorter as well as narrower than any (except a single Iron Age bone) reported from the Mesolithic to the medieval period. They also included bones that were longer and wider than most other reported Iron Age and Romano-British specimens. Hodgson considered that the great range in size could be due to the large sample. The metatarsals ranged from 42 to 67 mm in distal width with a mean of 49.9 mm. The distribution of each had a marked skew so that most bones had smaller widths. He discussed four possible causes for this skewing, which was the same as that which I found in medieval cattle horns from York:[179] (1) The few bones with greater widths were from bulls. Support for this suggestion was gained from the use of Howard's index with the smaller number of complete bones. This showed that some bulls were present, but that most were from cows or steers (castrated males). (2) The introduction of larger stocks. This would seem less likely when a sex difference could be demonstrated. (3) The killing of a particular age class in which the preference for age or size is not completely fulfilled, hence the skewing. Support for this can be gained

---

[176] R. Trow-Smith, *A History of British Livestock Husbandry to 1700*, London, 1957, p. 20.

[177] Jewell, 1963, *op. cit.*

[178] G. W. I. Hodgson, 'The difficulties of interpreting the metrical data derived from the remains of cattle at the Roman settlement of Corstopitum, in P. J. Ucko and G. W. Dimbleby (eds.), *The Domestication and Exploitation of Plants and Animals*, London, 1969, pp. 80–101.

[179] Ryder, 'The animal remains from Petergate...', 1970, *op. cit.*

from the lack of very young or very old animals, but I still favour sex difference. (4) The sample is atypical. This would appear to be an unduly cautious interpretation, considering the conclusions that have been drawn on such aspects as animal size from far smaller collections.

Metapodial measurements carried out by Harcourt with bones from the Roman villa at Hemel Hempstead, Herts., indicate animals ranging from 45 to 53 in. (114–135 cm) in height.[180] He detected no difference in size between the first and fourth centuries. The cattle at Brough, Yorks., were 48–50 in. (122–127 cm) in height. These measurements indicate cattle larger than the Celtic ox and comparable in size to Neolithic cattle. Harcourt compared them in size to Chillingham cattle. This raises again the question of whether the Romans did in fact introduce a larger type (although not necessarily like Chillingham cattle in appearance).

We have seen from the husbandry section (pp. 348–9) that Saxon dairying was based solely on goats and sheep, and that the ox was basically a draught animal. It is of interest, therefore, that Jewell found not only larger but more robust bones than those of the Celtic ox at the Saxon site of Sedgeford, Norfolk.[181]

Harcourt found that the cattle from Glastonbury Tor, Somerset, ranged from 42 to 45 in. (107–114 cm) in height.[182] This is smaller than the Roman cattle, but not as small as the Celtic ox. Inclusion of a group of bones from Hereford which extended from the pre-tenth to the fourteenth century reduced the lower limit of the height to 38 in. (97 cm). Because the Hereford bones included other than Saxon material they were not included in Fig. 66, but Harcourt remarked that the remains formed a homogeneous group with little size variation, which suggests persistence of the Saxon type of cattle into the Middle Ages.

Fig. 66 was prepared with data from R. A. Harcourt and B. A. Noddle. It plots length against mid-width of cattle metapodia from the Neolithic to Saxon periods. The figure shows that Neolithic cattle had the longest bones (and were presumably the tallest animals) and the Iron Age cattle had the shortest bones. The Saxon, Roman, and Romano-British bones lay in an intermediate position, but whereas there is little difference in width between the Neolithic, Iron Age, and Saxon, the Roman and Romano-British bones are noticeably stouter. Table 9 was added during revision to include additional measurements.

Although we have seen that the Saxon cow was not a dairy animal,

[180] R. A. Harcourt, personal communication, 1970.
[181] P. A. Jewell, 'Changes in size and type of cattle from prehistoric to medieval times in Britain', *Zeitschrift für Tierzüchtung und Züchtungsbiol.*, 77, 1962, pp. 159–67.
[182] See note 180.

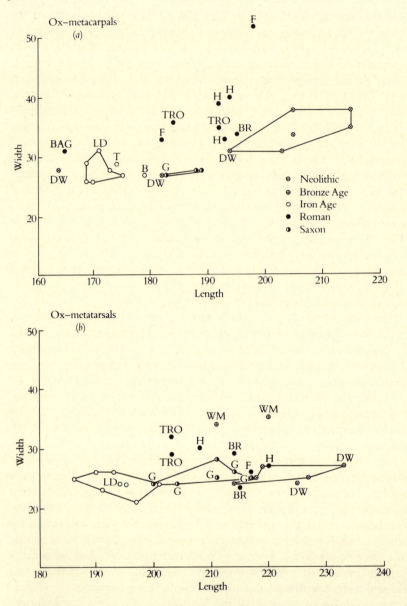

Fig. 66. Length plotted against minimum width at mid-point of cattle (*a*) metacarpals and (*b*) metatarsals. Each point (marked with a period symbol) indicates one bone. Where several bones come from a single site they have been connected by a line. Site key as for Fig. 62 plus the following: DW = Durrington Walls; H = Hemel Hempstead; Tro = Trocester (B. A. Noddle, personal communication). For discussion see text.

Table 9. *Additional cattle bone measurements (mm)*

Metacarpals	Length	Width
Gussage All Saints, Dorset, Iron Age[183]	164–185 (21)	Shoulder height 100–113 cm
Hatton Rock, Warwick., Saxon[184]	195	23

	Distal widths
N. Elmham, Norfolk	50–70
Thetford, Norfolk	44–64
Sedgeford, Norfolk	50–60
Sandtun, Kent	50 only
Mawgan Porth, Cornwall, Saxon[185]	48–62

Metatarsals	Length	
Gussage, Dorset[186]	189–206 (18)	Shoulder height 103–112 cm

Trow-Smith estimated that its lactation period was 150 days, and the annual production 100 gallons (455 l).[187] If a calf consumed ¾–1 gallon (4.5 l) a day, there can never have been more than a pint or two (0.5–1 l) left for milking, and then only for a few weeks (cf. primitive African cattle today in which only half the cows have excess milk, and then only 2–4 pints (see p. 328).

At what stage the almost ten-fold increase in production to today's values took place is not clear. Trow-Smith has shown from eighteenth-century records that then cows in an average extensively grazed herd produced 450–500 gallons (2050–2275 l) a year, and that better feeding increased this amount to 650–800 gallons (2960–3640 l). When milk recording started in the Ayrshire breed in 1913 the qualifying yield was 800 gallons (3640 l), and Trow-Smith suspects that much of the improvement attributed to breeding is in fact due to better nutrition.

We return finally to the coat and consider colour. One of the sources of cattle hair is bog butter, and Trow-Smith quotes the claim of earlier authors that cow hair from Celtic and earlier sources was red or

[183] R. A. Harcourt, personal communication, 1977.
[184] B. A. Noddle, 'Animal bones from two wells at Tripontium', *Trans. Birm. and Warwick, Arch. Soc.*, 85, 1975, pp. 136–42.
[185] J. Clutton-Brock, 'The animal resources', in D. M. Wilson (ed.), *The Archaeology of Anglo-Saxon England*, London, 1976, pp. 373–92.
[186] R. A. Harcourt, personal communication, 1977.
[187] Trow-Smith, *op. cit.*, p. 58.

brown.[188] In my experience, while one can usually determine the intensity of pigmentation under the microsope, it is difficult to be sure about colour or shade. Dense pigmentation is likely to be black, and not only can black fade to brown or grey (even on the animal's back), but it is difficult to distinguish grey from brown under the microscope since both have a similar density of pigment granules.

Trow-Smith points out that heads of the so-called 'red' Devon, Hereford, and Sussex cattle were not represented in Celtic art,[189] but he counselled caution on the old idea that colour can indicate origin.[190] It is noteworthy that the breeds of the Celtic fringe are black: Aberdeen Angus, Galloway (although some are Dun), Kerry, Dexter, Welsh Black, and Gloucester (but the Highland breed is now red). White cattle were supposed to originate from Roman imports, and red cattle (the above three breeds) have been thought to have been introduced by the Saxons. The Lincoln Red seems to have developed from the Shorthorn.

Medieval illustrations of plough oxen show teams containing both black and red animals. White cattle seem to have been rare and undesirable. Mascall,[191] writing in 1627, stated that red or black cattle were best. He lived in Sussex where the local cattle are likely to have been red.

THE PIG (Sus scrofa)

Domestic pigs are derived from a species-group of wild pigs which ranges from Sus vittatus in eastern Asia to S. scrofa in Europe,[192] and this was present in Britain when Neolithic settlers arrived. Western Asiatic varieties were probably domesticated first in the Near East about 6500 BC, later than sheep and goats and at about the same time as cattle.[193] The extent to which each type of wild pig has contributed to modern pigs was discussed by Towne and Wentworth.[194] The main use of the pig must have always been food, and since it is not readily driven, the pig is an animal of settled communities rather than of nomadic tribes.

Antonius considered that pig meat acquired religious taboos since it was not eaten by superior nomadic tribes.[195] In addition to the difficulty of driving pigs, they supply little more than meat. He dismisses as a

---

[188] Ibid., p. 22.

[189] Ibid., p. 34.   [190] Ibid., p. 44.

[191] L. Mascall, The Government of Catell, London, 1627.

[192] F. E. Zeuner, A History of Domesticated Animals, London, 1963.

[193] C. A. Reed, 'The pattern of animal domestication in the prehistoric Near East', in P. J. Ucko and G. W. Dimbleby (eds.), The Domestication and Exploitation of Plants and Animals, London, 1969, pp. 361–80.

[194] C. W. Towne and E. N. Wentworth, Pigs from Cave to Corn Belt, Univ. Oklahoma Press, 1950.   [195] Quoted by Zeuner, op. cit.

reason the proneness of pigs to infestation with the intestinal roundworm (*Trichina spiralis*). This causes trichinosis in man, the alternative host. Hyams points out that the connection is very unlikely to have been understood by primitive man.[196] Coon and Harris both favour the ecological explanation that pigs did not adapt well to the hot areas inhabited by Middle Eastern nomads, and competed with man for food.[197,198] Pig production also threatens the entire subsistence economy.[198]

Zeuner considers that the earliest domestic type was introduced into Europe from the East by Neolithic man.[199] It occurs alongside the European wild pig in the Neolithic lake-dwellings of Switzerland as the smaller *Sus palustris* or 'Turbary' pig (since this is a domestic variety it would not today be given a Latin specific name). But local domestication of pigs has everywhere been important. This was facilitated by their omnivorous diet, and their family grouping in autumn into packs of ten to thirty sows and young. Anthropological evidence shows that young pigs are readily brought into the home, and are even suckled by women. The Welsh Book of Taliesin mentions the introduction of pigs into Wales which Trow-Smith thought might preserve a folk memory of domestication.[200] The wild pig is on heat from November to January, and has a gestation period of 112 days, so that the young are born in April or May.

According to Zeuner, from the first, a small pig for the house or sty has been bred as well as a larger herd type.[201] In the Swiss lake dwellings Zeuner regards the 'Turbary' pig, and especially a small form of it, to be the house type, while the locally domesticated *S. scrofa* was the larger herding type.

The rooting habit of pigs has been important in forest clearance, particularly around settlements, since they eat tree seeds and uproot tree seedlings. They also enrich the soil with humus. Because pigs are resistant to acorn poisoning they are likely to have predominated in oak woods (above, p. 347). Saxon place names indicating a pig sty suggest that the animals were brought in from the woods at night. Medieval illustrations show swineherds knocking acorns down from the trees, and this was the task for November when pigs were fattened for killing in December. In this way woodland was replaced by grass which was used for sheep, as in the Bronze Age of northern Europe, or was ploughed

---

[196] E. Hyams, *Animals in the Service of Man*, London, 1972.

[197] C. S. Coch, *Caravan: the Story of the Middle East*, London, 1952.

[198] M. Harris, 'Riddle of the pig', *Nat. Hist.*, 81, 1972, pp. 32–6; M. Harris, *Cannibals and Kings*, Glasgow, 1978.   [199] Zeuner, *op. cit.*

[200] Quoted in R. Trow-Smith, *A History of British Livestock Husbandry to 1700*, London, 1957.   [201] Zeuner, *op. cit.*

for use in agriculture. As well as nuts, pigs eat fruit and fungi, a fact
that was later exploited in the training of pigs to locate truffles.
Although mainly vegetarian, they also eat worms, slugs, insects, and
even small rodents and so were important pest destroyers.

Trow-Smith discussed the range of natural foods of pigs and their
nutritive value, and pointed out that seeds would only support pigs
during autumn and winter.[202] At other times they would have required
pasture in which their snout can reach fibrous roots and rhizomes,
several inches below the surface, or bracken and couch-grass (*Agropyrum
repens*).

The pig is today one of the most productive farm animals, growing
rapidly, living long, and having large litters twice a year. It converts
food to meat economically, and has a high dressing-out percentage
(dead to liveweight ratio).

Whether improvement dates only from 200 years ago, when Chinese
pigs were introduced into Britain, or from earlier times, is difficult to
determine since it is not easy to distinguish the remains of domestic pigs
from those of wild animals. Because of this Trow-Smith, with the
iconoclastic fervour of a true scientist, regards Saxon literary records
as the first proof of domestication in Britain, although elsewhere he
suggests that the Romans could have introduced Chinese stock into
Britain (see pp. 318 and 394).[203]

The interbreeding of wild and domestic pigs for centuries, suggests,
however, that improvement, despite its apparently great extent, came
later than in other livestock, at any rate in Britain (below, p. 395).

One can of course list the major and obvious differences between
domestic and wild pigs. These are loss of the banded colour pattern of
the wild young (though the Mangalica breed of Hungary is banded),
decrease in the amount of hair, and in many breeds selection for loss
of colour altogether. The overall size first decreased and then remained
small until recent breeding for larger animals. There have also been
changes in the body proportions, with an increase in the size of the
hinder parts at the expense of the shoulders which were important in
fighting. Hammond thought this was because the late-developing
hinder parts have a greater opportunity to reach maturity when
successive generations are bred on a better diet.[204] Current ideas are
likely to attribute this more to selection than to diet. Presumably there
has also been an increase in litter size and in the number of teats, which
were probably kept roughly equal in the wild state through natural

[202] Trow-Smith, *op. cit.*, p. 82.
[203] *Ibid.*
[204] J. Hammond, 'Some changes in the form of sheep and pigs under domestication',
Zeitschrift für Tierzuchtung und Züchtungsbiol., 77, 1962, pp. 156–8.

selection. The large number found in domestic pigs indicates considerable selective breeding, and suggests appreciable variation of this character in the wild state.

It is certain, for instance, that the different skull shape and shortness of the jaw in the domestic pig is a quite recent change, and this makes modern skeletal material from pigs of little value for comparison with ancient remains.[205] Likewise the similarity in size between modern pig bones and those from the Mesolithic site of Star Carr hides first a decrease in skeletal size following domestication, and then a more recent increase.[206] Yet domestic pigs do have specific tooth differences. The tusks are certainly smaller, and workers with the first domestic pigs in southwest Asia recognize a progressive reduction in the size of the third molar.

Tringham states that size is used to distinguish domestic from wild pigs in south-west Russia, but provides evidence of large and small wild pigs from Palaeolithic caves in the Crimea.[207] One wonders whether this difference in size is due to sex and not to different wild strains. Whereas today domestic boars are larger, in the wild state they are smaller than the sows.

Zeuner quotes work indicating that the domestic pigs of Neolithic and Bronze Age Europe, although smaller than wild pigs, were still relatively large.[208] The size decreased until Roman times, when the bones became broader, which is usually associated with improvement.

Curwen noted that the resemblance between domestic and wild pigs in Denmark was closest in the Neolithic period and that their size diverged later.[209] More recently Higham using a statistical approach, confirmed that from the Danish Neolithic onwards the lower third molar of domestic pigs was significantly shorter than the mean figure of 45 mm in wild animals.[210] Clason,[211] quoted by Harcourt,[212] regards any lower third molar of greater than 40 mm as being from a wild animal. There was no difference in its length between Neolithic (36.1 mm) and Bronze Age (35.9 mm) pigs, but the molars of pigs of

[205] This is vividly illustrated in D. and P. Brothwell, *Food in Antiquity*, London, 1969, Pls. 14 and 15.

[206] F. C. Fraser and J. E. King, 'Second Interim Report on the animal remains from Star Carr, Seamer', *Proc. Prehist. Soc.*, n.s., 16, 1950, pp. 124–9.

[207] R. Tringham, 'Animal domestication in the Neolithic cultures of the south-west part of European U.S.S.R.', in P. J. Ucko and G. W. Dimbleby (eds.), *The domestication and exploitation of Plants and Animals*, London, 1969, pp. 381–92.

[208] Zeuner, *op. cit.*

[209] E. C. Curwen, 'Early agriculture in Denmark', *Ant.*, XII, 1938, pp. 135–53.

[210] C. Higham, 'Size trends in prehistoric European domestic fauna and the problem of local domestication', *Acta Zool. Fenn.*, 120, 1968, pp. 1–21.

[211] A. T. Clason, 'Animal and man in Holland's past', Vol. A, Thesis, Groningen, 1967, p. 63.

[212] R. A. Harcourt, personal communication, 1970.

the Roman Iron Age were significantly shorter than those of the preceding two periods (32.6 mm). During the Neolithic and Bronze Age periods the swine of Denmark appear to have been larger than those of Switzerland.

Murray stated that most British Neolithic sites had both large and small pigs, which she considered indicated wild as well as domestic animals, and suggested local domestication.[213] But, without detailed measurements like those discussed above, such conclusions must be tentative.

Cram quotes a few measurements of pig bones at the Neolithic causewayed camp of Abingdon, Berks., and found two sizes, which he thought might indicate a sex difference, if not wild and domestic animals.[214] Again a proper statistical analysis is lacking, mainly owing to the small number of finds. Harcourt found the Saxon pig remains from Hereford to be comparable to the Neolithic ones from Durrington Walls, Wilts.[215] The Saxon ones from Glastonbury indicated a slender animal 24 in. (61 cm) in height.

Trow-Smith considered that until after the Middle Ages the British pig was long-legged, long-haired, razor-backed, slow-maturing, and lean-meated, but suggested that the Romans might have introduced improved breeds based on the short-legged and well-fleshed Chinese pig.[216]

Applebaum listed the following main Roman villas at which pig bones had been found: Grimston, Norfolk; West Blatchington, Sussex; Nuthills, Wilts.; Hambleden, Bucks.; Park Street, Herts.; Langton, Yorks.; Hucclecote, Glos.; Ely, Glam.; Llantwit Major, Glam.; Saunderton, Bucks.; Folkestone, Kent; Otford, Kent; Southwick, Sussex; West Meon, Hants.; Woolaston Pill, Mon.[217]

Pig remains were not found at the following villas: Newport, Isle of Wight; Waggonholt, Sussex; Gayton Thorpe, Norfolk; Appleton, Norfolk. Remains were common on military sites, and it appears that pork came second to beef in popularity.

Roman illustrations given by Zeuner show a long-legged, naked sow with lop ears.[218] Among Celtic illustrations, those of boars were second in frequency only to the horse, and apparently show a mane along the backbone; some medieval pictures show hairy pigs. The Welsh *Mabinogion* perpetuated a legend concerning a different type of pig new

[213] J. Murray, 'The osteological and botanical evidence for Neolithic agriculture in Europe', Ph.D. thesis, Univ. of Edinburgh, 1967.

[214] C. L. Cram, personal communication, 1969.

[215] R. A. Harcourt, personal communication, 1970.

[216] Trow-Smith, *op. cit.*

[217] S. Applebaum, 'Agriculture in Roman Britain', D.Phil. thesis, Univ. of Oxford, 1951.   [218] Zeuner, *op. cit.*

to Britain, with a hint that it was a cross between the wild and domestic varieties. Primitive pigs remaining in Iberia and illustrated by Davidson and Zeuner are thought to be typical of medieval pigs.[219, 220] These appear naked, having large shoulders, small hindquarters, and a relatively long snout. They have only eight teats, and it is therefore of interest to see what indications of teat number can be gained from ancient illustrations.

It is possible that teat number in wild pigs ranged from eight to twelve (I have received one report of ten). A coin of Antoninus Pius (AD 140) bears a side view of a sow with six teats visible, indicating a total of twelve.[221] One cannot be certain, however, that the six suckling pigs shown indicate a litter of twelve. A pig in a Roman sculpture illustrated by the same authors has at least six piglets, but the teats are not visible. Medieval illustrations commonly show five piglets on five teats (indicating a total of ten) but one cannot be sure to what extent such representations are stylized. In modern European breeds teat numbers range from eight to sixteen, a minimum of twelve functional ones being required by British breed societies, whereas in Chinese breeds there are up to twenty.

The litter size of wild pigs could have been as low as five (I received one report of eight), whereas in domestic breeds today it is at least twelve. Chinese breeds seem to be the most prolific, some having a litter size ranging from fifteen to twenty-seven.[222] One wonders whether the main selection for increased teat number and litter size took place in China, such selection being facilitated through pigs being house animals. In Britain, until livestock ceased to roam on common land following the Middle Ages, any form of selective breeding must have been extremely difficult.

One of the requirements of selection is the ability to castrate, and it is likely that this practice goes back to the Neolithic period. It was also carried out to aid fat production, and female as well as male pigs were castrated by quite elaborate methods. In the spaying of female piglets the ovaries were extracted with a hooked tool through two cuts 2 cm long.[223] In the wild state, large litters are usually associated with high infant mortality, and even in modern domestic pigs under good husbandry conditions only eight out of ten will survive to weaning at six to eight weeks. Since early man was not against eating animals that had died from natural causes this may have been the origin of roast 'sucking pig'.

---

[219] H. R. Davidson, 'The evolution of the pig', Span, 6(2), 1963, pp. 59–63.
[220] Zeuner, op. cit., p. 268.
[221] Illustrated in F. C. Sillar and R. M. Meyler, The Symbolic Pig, Edinburgh, 1961.
[222] H. Epstein, Domestic Animals of China, Comm. Agric. Bur., 1969.
[223] F. E. Zeuner, A History of Domesticated Animals, London, 1967.

Piglets, hams, and pork chops have been found in graves, and pigs were sacrificed to various Greek and Roman gods. Pig meat has a special association with preservation. This is because of its fatty nature, and particularly the thick layer of back fat. The rendered product, lard, has a particulalrly soft and delicate constitution.

Hams were salted and smoked from Asia Minor to Gaul. Strabo records salt-pork as one of the products of Gaul. The Greeks are known to have preserved sides of pork and used them as votive offerings, and the making of sausages by filling intestines with chopped meat was a Graeco-Roman practice. Pork dishes became very complicated in Roman times. Whole pigs were roasted after fattening on special foods.

Davidson defined bacon as meat preserved by drying or salting.[224] European peoples have preferred salting, and salt production goes back to the Iron Age in England. But whereas lean meat becomes hard and unpalatable when salted, fatty meat requires less salting to ensure preservation, yet remains succulent when cooked. Hence the pig was favoured for preservation.

The Romans used a 'dry cure' method in which salt was repeatedly rubbed into the meat stored in a cool place. The modern Wiltshire cure involves immersion in brine for four to five days, and Ayrshire bacon is similarly cured but rolled after preparation. In smoking, the bacon is hung over smouldering oak chips. Modern tastes and the development of refrigeration have demanded less fat, and milder cures. Davidson considered that bacon preparation reached its highest development in England,[224] but it clearly goes back earlier than the first reference he found in Piers Plowman (fourteenth century); the term 'flitch' for instance is the Saxon word for a bacon half or 'side'. The legs were cured separately as ham. After division of the trunk into the two sides, the lean meat from inside was removed and eaten fresh or was mildly preserved in sausages. This left a thick layer of back fat covered with skin which was cured as 'bacon'. Thus bacon really means 'back-fat', and it is of interest that the value of pigs was judged by the thickness of back-fat in Saxon times (measured in finger-widths, see Vol. I, Part II, p. 407) because thickness of back-fat is one method of grading pigs for sale today. But the eating of pure fat began to be disliked by the time of the industrial revolution, and although more lean has since been left in, the product is still called bacon. As late as the 1930s, however, the above method was still common in the Midlands as the 'Midland cure'.[225]

[224] Davidson, op. cit.

[225] G. R. Bishop, personal communication, 1970.

THE HORSE (*Equus caballus*)

The period under discussion saw the rise of the horse to its position of importance in transport, and it is difficult for anyone born after say 1920 to realize how vital the horse was to man for over 2,000 years, its value extending far beyond the farmyard into all corners of the earth, although it only finally took the place of the ox on the British farm in the eighteenth century. This relatively recent importance in agriculture means that less detailed treatment need be given than for other livestock.

Evidence for the location and date of the domestication of the horse is particularly scanty. The main centre is thought to have been the steppes of southern Russia, at *c.* 3500 BC and in south Russia the local variety of wild horse, the Tarpan (*E. caballus gmelini*), became extinct little more than a hundred years ago. The Tarpan was smoky grey (blue dun) in colour. Another possible area was Mongolia where a small herd of Przewalski's horse (*E. c. przewalski*) remains truly wild. This horse has tawny (sandy dun) upper parts, black legs, and cream under parts. A third area that has been suggested is Spain, but the evidence is inconclusive. A wild horse did in fact persist in Poland until the eighteenth century; this was the forest horse (*E. c. silvestris*).[226, 227]

All breeds of horse today interbreed freely, and it is most likely that the three (or possibly more) ancestors (above) represent varieties rather than species.

Zeuner considered that the use of the horse for transport came relatively late. It may first have been eaten, and milked. The relatively late domestication means that transport was probably first developed with the slower cattle. Initially horses may have merely carried packs in imitation of the donkey (below). With the horse, riding probably followed its use for draught in most areas. But the evidence from harness may be misleading, since a horse can be ridden with a nose-string only.

Evidence from Late Neolithic sites suggests that the domestic horse was present in Europe beyond the Ukraine by about 2000 BC, but ox-drawn vehicles are known from the earlier third millennium onwards. There is an enormous difference between the 280 lb (127 kg) that can be carried by a pack horse, and the 1–8 tons (1.02–8.13 tonnes) (depending on the nature of the road) in a wagon.[228]

Horse-breeding may have begun on a large scale in the first

[226] Zeuner, *op. cit.*

[227] M. S. Drower, 'The domestication of the horse', in P. J. Ucko and G. W. Dimbleby (eds.), *The Domestication and Exploitation of Plants and Animals*, London, 1969, pp. 471–8.

[228] I. L. Mason, 'Draught animals', *Encyclopedia Britannica*, 1970.

millennium BC and local domestication could have provided additional stock. It may have been at this time that the eating of horseflesh became taboo. To what extent religion was involved in this is not clear, but the horse did appear to be endowed with a sacred character or superior quality that may have been associated with its swiftness and resistance to taming compared with ruminants.

Murray considered that the horse was transmitted to north-western Europe by the peoples of the Single Grave Complex, and the problem of post-Pleistocene survival of wild equids is still unresolved.[229] Domestic horses appear to be present in second millennium BC. The few horse finds of the Neolithic period could have been from wild animals (if such existed), hunted and eaten, but these could have contributed to local domestic stock. The three horses from Durrington Walls measured by Harcourt ranged from 12.3 to 14.2 hands (129 to 148 cm) in height (one hand = 4 in.), i.e. the size of wild horses.[230] Bits and cheek pieces appear during the Bronze Age, and indicate domestication. By the late Bronze Age equine trappings are relatively abundant. Trow-Smith lists three hoards of these from Wales, and the bone remains with them indicate an animal about 13 hands (132 cm) high. He likened similar remains from Jarlshof to the much smaller Shetland pony.[231]

Slender-limbed ponies were found at the Early Iron Age site of All Cannings Cross (about 500 BC), and in the pre-Roman levels at Camulodunum many bones of pony size were found. Trow-Smith quotes J. W. Jackson as considering these horses to have pulled wheeled vehicles. It is likely that the first use in transport was a military one; the chariot was in use by the early Celts and the horse is the most common animal illustrated on Celtic coins. Trow-Smith considered that the horse began to be used in agriculture in addition to hunting and war only during Roman times.[231]

By the beginning of the Christian era there are indications of a horse-breeding economy in Britain and it appears that horses had begun to assume the importance they were going to have for 2000 years. This is illustrated by numerous finds of chariot remains such as iron wheel tyres and bridle-bits of pony size. The horse-shoe may have been invented in Roman Gaul.

At the beginning of the present century Cossar Ewart regarded the wild horses of Europe as comprising three types: the steppe type (*E. przewalski*), the forest type, and the plateau type, which he named *E. agilis* and considered to be the ancestor of the British pre-Roman

[229] Murray, *op. cit.*
[230] R. A. Harcourt, personal communication, 1970.
[231] R. Trow-Smith, *A History of British Livestock Husbandry to 1700*, London, 1957.

domestic, small, and slender-limbed 'Celtic' type. Trow-Smith regarded this as having no agricultural significance, and thought that the Romans might have introduced larger horses.

The native military horses recognized by Cossar Ewart at the Roman fort of Newstead near Melrose on the Scottish border were the Celtic pony of Shetland type and less than 12 hands (121 cm), and a broad-browed forest pony of similar size but more "thick set". In addition to these there were three apparently imported types: a coarse-limbed pony of 12–13 (121–132 cm) hands similar to a small modern Arab horse, a horse of 14 hands (142 cm) comparable to the Arab type, thought to be from Gaul, and a large horse related to the Siwalik type, which was thought to be from Germany. Finally, Cossar Ewart thought he could detect cross-breds between these main types. It is possible that modern osteology might regard this relatively large number of breeds identified by Cossar Ewart as representing no more than variations within only one or two basic types.

Harcourt found horses of 11 hands (112 cm) to 13 hands (132 cm) on Iron Age sites.[232] Those at Hemel Hempstead Roman villa were 13–14 hands (132–142 cm). But Saxon ones from Hereford were only 12–13 hands (121–132 cm).

Horse remains were abundant at some Roman villas, and Trow-Smith thought that these might represent studs that could have been the ancestors of Saxon studs for which there are records (below, p. 400).

The use of the horse to pull ploughs in Roman Britain has not been confirmed (above, p. 339). According to Trow-Smith the horse is said not to have been harnessed until the eleventh-century continental invention of the padded collar. Davis and Dent stated that there are only two methods of harnessing a horse so that it can pull with all its strength in a horizontal direction, and both depend on traces fastened to the front corners of the vehicle.[233] Such traces were unknown in antiquity, and the harness for chariots, for instance, involved a collar that pressed against the windpipe.

Traces can be attached to either a breastplate or a rigid collar that is born on the shoulders. According to Davis and Dent the rigid collar, like the stirrup, was invented somewhere in central Asia and brought to the West by the Mohammedans about AD 700. They state that what appears to be a breast harness is illustrated on a tapestry found in a ninth-century Viking ship grave in Norway. They also considered that the Romans, although unable to overcome the weakness of the ancient harness, were aware of its handicap, but realized that it would not be overcome by heavier horses and so did not breed for them. They did,

[232] R. A. Harcourt, personal communication, 1970.
[233] P. D. C. Davis and A. A. Dent, *Animals that Changed the World*, London, 1966.

however use only stallions for driving because their neck muscles are more fully developed. According to Davis and Dent, this is the reason for the comparative rarity of geldings in classical times.

Trow-Smith considered it impossible in the Celtic and Saxon world to separate agricultural from other draught use, but that the horse was clearly too highly thought of to be given menial tasks.[234] Indeed, there is a tenth-century Welsh law which restricts ploughing to oxen. Although the horse was valued for the saddle in Saxon times, probably little attention was given to breeding – it was allowed to run wild or half-wild in the forest. Horses and often whole stud farms were left in wills, however, and Trow-Smith speculated that these might have continuity with Roman studs. There are rare mentions of colour – black, white, or pied. In all these records there is no indication of agricultural use, yet within fifty years of the latest bequest the horse was being used to draw the plough. From this, and evidence concerning the faster speed of ploughing with horses, Trow-Smith suggests that the use of the horse for ploughing might have begun in Saxon times. This is in keeping with the seventh- or eighth-century introduction of the rigid collar (above, p. 399) rather than the eleventh-century date given by Trow-Smith. There is an ancient practice of slitting the nostrils of horses and donkeys in order to assist breathing, and to prevent whinnying during military patrols.[235] This was apparently practised in Saxon England because two Italian bishops who attended the Synod of Chelsea in AD 786 disapproved of the custom.[236]

There are few references in Domesday to specifically agricultural horses, and there appears to have been about one riding horse per village. Feral and unbroken horses roamed the woods, but their numbers declined considerably between 1066 and 1086 presumably owing to the same forest clearance that caused a decline in goats and pigs.

As to the type of horse found in the Saxon forests, Trow-Smith considered that those in eastern England were blends of Celtic, Roman, Saxon, and Scandinavian types. But in the west they were probably descendants of the Celtic pony. Feral ponies have persisted until recent times in the Lake District, the Pennines, and Wales, but perhaps the best known are those of the New Forest and Exmoor. Such are the wild characteristics of the Exmoor pony, for instance, that it has been deemed a truly wild horse,[237] just as others assert those of the Camargue in France to be wild.

[234] Trow-Smith, *op. cit.*
[235] M. A. Littauer, 'Slit nostrils on equids', *Zeitschrift für Saugetierkunde*, 34, 1969, pp. 183–6.
[236] A. A. Dent and D. M. Goodall, *The Foals of Epona*, London, 1962.
[237] M. G. Speed, 'An indigenous British horse', *Brit. Vet. J.*, 112, 1956, pp. 483–90.

According to Davis and Dent man has done little to change the build and proportions of the horse, the main variation being in height (from 36 in. (9 hands, 91 cm) in the Shetland to 72 in. (18 hands, 183 cm) in the Clydesdale). All wild varieties are about 52 in. (13 hands, 132 cm) in height, (weighing 275 kg or 600 lb) and few remains from antiquity are more than 60 in. (15 hands, 152 cm) high. They considered that considerable food in the form of excess grain and large quantities of hay for winter feed are necessary in order to breed large horses, and the requisite conditions were not present in Britain until about the time of the Norman Conquest.[238] Not least important is the possession of a scythe to cut large amounts of hay, and, although introduced by the Romans, this was not widely used until the Middle Ages.[239]

The first new type to develop in the Middle Ages was a heavier horse that may have had affinities with the heavier primitive type of Scandinavia. This is said to have emerged as the Great English War Horse, which had to be strong to carry the armour of its rider and itself. R. A. Harcourt, however, points out that no medieval remains exceed a height of 15 hands (152 cm) (below). It gave rise to the 17–18 hand (173–183 cm) Shire horse of the English Midlands, and eventually to the cart horse of today or the recent past, a modern version being the Suffolk Punch of 16–17 hands (163–173 cm) which weighs over a ton. The Clydesdale is a taller, but lighter, Scottish version.

The second main type is the tall horse which emerged as the modern racehorse and hunter. This owes much to the importations of Arab horses, which are said to have taken place as early as the twelfth century. The Hackney horse was a cross between the Arab and the Shire.

It is of interest that remains from the Middle Ages indicate horses of a size intermediate between the small ancient ones and modern breeds. Harcourt calculated that the remains I described from the deserted village of Wharram Percy[240, 241] ranged from 11 to 15 hands (112 to 152 cm), and those from Petergate, York from 13 to 14 hands (132 to 142 cm).[242]

THE ASS (*Equus asinus*) AND MULE

The Sumerians had a domestic equine possibly as early as 3000 BC and long before the camel or horse reached Mesopotamia. This was the Asiatic wild ass, the half-ass, hemione, or onager (*E. hemionus*).

[238] Davis and Dent, *op. cit.*

[239] E. C. Curwen, *Plough and Pasture*, London, 1946.

[240] R. A. Harcourt, personal communication, 1970.

[241] M. L. Ryder, 'Report of the animal remains from Wharram Percy', *Yorks. Arch. J.*, 46, 1974, pp. 42–52.

[242] *Idem*, 'The animal remains from Petergate, York, 1957–58', *Yorks. Arch. J.*, 42(168), 1970, pp. 418–28.

The home of the true ass is Africa, and the Nubian race, which is now almost extinct, was the ancestor of the domestic ass or donkey. The ass was first domesticated in the Nile valley, and there is evidence of it in Egypt from protodynastic times.[243]

There is little evidence of the history of the donkey in Europe. It appears to have been introduced via Greece, after the horse, but before 500 BC. Skeletal remains of about the same date were found in Sicily.[244] The ass needs less water and less food than the horse in terms of both quality and quantity, which makes it adaptable to desert conditions. But it does not thrive in a cold, wet climate, and its body size has decreased in northern Europe. It appears to have been distributed throughout Europe and introduced into Britain with the Roman army.

Few archaeological remains have been reported. Applebaum states that the ass was found on one or two Roman sites in Britain, including a villa, and Bökönyi recorded a single ass bone from Zalavar in Hungary dating from the medieval occupation of the Turks.[245, 246] More recently Noddle identified bones from one donkey in a Roman well at Tripontium, near Rugby.[247]

Donkeys have been used for draught, ploughing, and notably to work mills, but perhaps more than anything else as pack and riding animals, their need of little attention having led to the name 'poor man's horse'. The role as beast of burden to the smallholder, originating in ancient Greece and Rome, is still important in Ireland. Dent illustrates a Saxon miniature in the British Museum showing four donkeys pulling a person in a cart.[248]

The taboo on eating horse meat seems to have extended to the flesh of the donkey, but its milk was esteemed. Its skin is hard but elastic and has been used to make parchment, to cover drums, and to make shoes.

The ass is in many ways like the horse. It is broken at two years, which is the earliest the females can breed, the males not being sexually mature until $2\frac{1}{2}$ years. Mating takes place at the end of May and the gestation period is at least a month longer than the 11 months of the horse, so foals are not born until the third or fourth years, at which ages the adults are old enough to work. The late maturity and long gestation period

---

[243] Zeuner, *op. cit.*

[244] M. L. Ryder, 'Some Phoenician animal remains from Sicily', in A. T. Clason (ed.), *Archaeological Studies*, Amsterdam, 1975, pp. 213–18.

[245] S. Applebaum, 'Agriculture in Roman Britain', *Agric. Hist. Rev.*, 6, 1958, pp. 68–86.

[246] S. Bökönyi, 'Rapport préliminaire sur l'examen des ossements d'animaux recueillis au cours des fouilles de Zalavar', *Act. Arch. Acad. Sci. Hung.*, 4, 1954, pp. 281–6.

[247] B. A. Noddle, 'Animal bones from two wells at Tripontium', *Trans. Birm. and Warwick. Arch. Soc.*, 85, 1972, pp. 136–42.

[248] A. Dent, *Donkey: the Story of the Ass from East to West*, London, 1970, p. 55.

makes the donkey a slow breeder, but it has a long life, living 25–30 years, like the horse. Finally, it will interbreed with the horse.

The result of crossing an ass with a mare is the mule, which is often as big as a horse (12–17½ hands, 122–179 cm),[249] but requires less food and water. Only male mules are infertile, the females can mate with donkeys and horses and produce offspring.[250] The mating of a stallion with a she-ass produces a hinny or jenny. This is smaller than the mule, less hardy, and less useful. The breeding of mules seems to have begun with the Hittites in the Near East about 1000 BC to give extra height to leaders in battle. This height, which often exceeds that of the horse, but is not accompanied by its nutritional requirements, seems to have been an important feature, and mules have often been used for riding.

According to Applebaum the mule was common in Roman Gaul, but there is no evidence for it in Roman Britain.[251] Dent illustrates a pictorial stone carving of the Dark Ages, now in the Antiquities Museum, Edinburgh, showing 'the Mule of Inchbrayoch'.[252] Although perhaps unimportant in Britain, Davis and Dent[253] state that mules were bred in the New Forest before 1800. The feet of mules were often shod, or wrapped with cloth, Shakespeare referring in Henry VI, Part II, to "my foot-cloth mule". Their use as military transport in mountainous regions and their stubbornness is almost legendary. They were used on campaigns by the British Army until at least as late as 1945, and its mule corps has only recently been disbanded.

POULTRY

The domestic fowl originated from the red jungle fowl (*Gallus gallus*) of India and was fully domesticated in the Indus Valley civilization by 2000 BC. Zeuner considered that, although apparently recorded at Glastonbury about 250 BC, it was introduced into Britain by the Belgae, because more certain remains, including the representation on coins, come from Belgic sites, e.g. a level at Colchester dated AD 10–43.[254] According to Caesar the Britons did not eat the fowl, but used it for fighting. Fowl bones were found at the Romano-British site of High Ferrers, Northants., and Hemel Hempstead, Herts., Roman villa by Harcourt.[255]

Bone remains are common on Roman sites, and leg bones with large spurs have led to the suggestion that these came from fighting cocks.

[249] T. H. Savory, 'The Mule', *Sci. Amer.*, 223 (6), 1970, pp. 102–9.
[250] Dent, *op. cit.*   [251] Applebaum, 1958, *op. cit.*
[252] Dent, *op. cit.*   [253] Davis and Dent, *op. cit.*
[254] F. E. Zeuner, *A History of Domesticated Animals*, London, 1963.
[255] R. A. Harcourt, personal communication, 1970.

One must beware in drawing this conclusion, however, since the bone supporting the spur in old 'roosters' can reach 30 mm in length.[256] Cock-fighting has been said to have been more responsible than food for the dispersion of the chicken, and its use as a sacrificial animal was widespread.[257] Cocks also acted as an alarm clock.

Roman meals, however, frequently began with an egg course, and a number of methods were used by the Romans to preserve eggs.[258] Hens probably did not begin laying until the end of March, hence the Easter egg, which may date back to early Christian times.

The writings of Columella and Pliny show that Roman poultry husbandry was highly developed.[259] Different breeds suitable for different purposes are recorded, and Columella gave advice on the selection of birds for breeding, prolificacy being one of the characters sought. Housing, feeding, breeding, rearing, culling, and disease control were all discussed in detail, and Columella's writings show that the Romans had a complex and well-organized poultry industry which Wood-Gush considers was not to be matched until the nineteenth century.[260]

The medieval poultry yard was under the care of a dairywoman, and produce rents were often paid in poultry and eggs. The anonymous thirteenth-century author of *Hosebanderie* gave instructions for the produce to be accounted for by the dairywoman.[261] Each hen ought to produce 115 eggs and seven chickens, three of which ought to be made into capons, and, "if there be too many hen chickens, let them be changed for cocks while they are still young, so that each hen may answer for three capons, and four hens in a year".

Eleven fourteenth-century estates listed by Rogers,[262] and quoted by Wood-Gush,[263] had only seven to forty-nine fowls, indicating a minor role in the economy. They were no doubt of greater importance to the peasants. Poultry later became scavengers, but were expected to provide the housekeeping money for the farmer's wife.

Symon doubted the figure of 115 eggs quoted above, because he says

[256] M. L. Ryder, *Animal Bones in Archaeology*, Oxford, 1969.

[257] D. G. M. Wood-Gush, 'A history of the domestic chicken from antiquity to the 19th century', *Poultry Science*, 38, 1959, pp. 321–6.

[258] D. and P. Brothwell, *Food in Antiquity*, London, 1969.

[259] See, however, O. F. Gandert, 'Beitrag zur Geschicht des Haushuhnes in der Hallstattzeit des nordwestalpinen Gebietes', in A. T. Clason (ed.), *Archaeozoological Studies*, Amsterdam, 1975, pp. 362–6.

[260] Wood-Gush, *op. cit.*

[261] Quoted in Lord Ernle, *English Farming past and present*, 5th ed., ed. A. D. Hall, London, 1936.

[262] J. E. T. Rogers, *A History of Agriculture and Prices in England*, London, 1866.

[263] Wood-Gush, *op. cit.*

that if this was achieved there can have been no improvement until after the First World War. He stated that in the Middle Ages only two eggs were demanded as Scottish teinds, from which he argued that if these represented one-tenth of the other-than-hatching requirements, then annual production may have been as low as 30–40 eggs.[264] This would appear to be appreciably greater than the clutch size of 24 eggs of the wild jungle fowl. But it is unlikely to represent the total potential production, which can only be determined by the removal of eggs as they are laid. Hyams gave the clutch size as 30, and the maximum production as 80 eggs.[265]

Geneticists have been interested in past egg production figures in order to ascertain the extent of genetic improvement that had taken place before modern theory began to be applied at the beginning of this century. Wood-Gush quoted Aristotle as saying that the best birds would lay 60 eggs before going broody, and Pliny as claiming that the best birds laid daily.[266] He considered that even if exaggerated this indicates a performance comparable to that of modern birds. This coupled with records of over 200 eggs by 1912, quoted by Clayton,[267] shows that a medieval figure of 115 is by no means impossible, but the average production was probably much smaller. The modern maximum production appears to be about 270 eggs a year, and they are bigger than in antiquity.

The domestic goose was derived from the greylag goose (*Anser anser*) which ranges from northern and western Europe to China, but does not breed south of lat. 45°. Zeuner considered that the goose must have been kept by man since the Neolithic period, and he suspected that domestication, which must have occurred in its breeding area, first took place in south-eastern Europe.[268] Hyams considers a north-Eurasian domestication more likely.[269]

Riddell pointed out that the greylag could have been domesticated independently over a wide area.[270] Since the Aryan root *ghans* (an imitation of the wild call) is the basis for 'goose' in all Indo-European languages, he suggests that the Aryans might have domesticated it.

Domestication may have begun as game preservation by hunters, or while feathers were being collected to fletch arrows. Goose feathers are very good for this purpose, and geese provide a big supply. Removal

[264] J. A. Symon, *Scottish Farming Past and Present*, Edinburgh, 1959.
[265] E. Hyams, *Animals in the Service of Man*, London, 1972.
[266] Wood-Gush, *op. cit.*
[267] G. A. Clayton, 'Some Implications of Selection Results in Poultry', *World's Poultry Science J.*, 24, 1968, pp. 37–57.
[268] Zeuner, *op. cit.*   [269] Hyams, *op. cit.*
[270] W. H. Riddell, 'The domestic goose', *Ant.*, XVII, 1943, pp. 148–55.

of the wing feathers would have had the effect of restricting flight and so helped domestication. Riddell suggests that the provision of feathers could have been the first use of domestic geese.[270] The difficulty of obtaining proof of domestication might be overcome on, say, a Scandinavian site if one could find goose bones in a definite winter context, because then no wild birds would be present.

The greylag is the only goose to breed in Britain, so it could have been separately domesticated here. Indeed, where it bred in the Fens before they were drained, young birds were caught and added to domestic flocks. The domestic goose will readily cross with the wild ancestor, and probably much crossing has taken place; few breeds have developed.

The only changes following domestication have been an increase in size, and possibly in fecundity, a decrease in the intensity of coloration, and an increase in the tendency for whiteness found already in the greylag. The lack of change does not, however, indicate recent domestication since the tame white geese that saved Rome in 390 BC were already ancient. White geese were then sacred, whiteness did not indicate cowardice as it did later in game-cocks. The goose was certainly developed by the Romans. According to Caesar it was regarded as sacred by the Britons, and not eaten. This accords with uses other than food indicated above, but Pliny referred to a small, specifically British variety, the *cheneros*, that was valued for food during the Flavian period. Another possible use was as a decoy in hunting, for which Riddell provided interesting evidence from Egypt of about 2000 BC.[270]

The word goose comes from Anglo-Saxon *gos*, and gander from *gandra*, which has been taken as indicating importance in Saxon times. It may have been at this time that the goose began to be tended by a gozzerd in flocks of up to 1,000. Geese were driven to water and to pasture. They are omnivorous, exterminating grubs and pests in orchards, but tend to foul the land.

Geese were driven long distances to market in autumn, e.g. from the Fens to London. They covered only 10 miles (16 km) a day at a rate of 1 mile (1.6 km) per hour. This slow speed led Riddell to state that nomads could only have kept geese in carts.[270] According to classical authors, the Romans obtained their best geese from northern France, and in 1966 Glyn Daniel quoted on television an experiment designed to determine how far geese could walk in a day. The above speed and distance was confirmed, showing that it would take three months for them to walk to Rome. But according to Riddell not all geese could manage the walk from East Anglia to London, and had to complete the journey in carts, so one wonders whether geese did in fact walk all the way to Rome.

The droving of geese in England continued until the eighteenth century, and in later times at any rate the geese were driven through tar, and then sand, in order to give their feet some protection.

Plucking of the contour feathers to fill pillows took place twice a year in spring and summer, at least from the Middle Ages. Eider feathers were collected (from nests) as early as Norse times, judging from at least one 'Fidra' (feather island), and eider ducks were 'farmed' for this purpose until recent times in Scandinavia. A feather was found among textile remains in the Saxon, Sutton Hoo burial.[271] From the twelfth century on, following the introduction of the pen to Europe by the Arabs, the wing feathers were plucked for quill pens in addition to arrows. Finally one might mention *pâté de foie*, and that goose grease was a valuable emollient owing to its slow drying properties. According to the anonymous thirteenth-century author of *Hosebanderie* there should be one gander to five geese, and each goose should have five goslings annually.[272]

The domestic duck is derived from the mallard (*Anas platyrhyncha*) which ranges throughout Europe and Asia. Zeuner considered that it could have been first domesticated in Mesopotamia, but the Greeks and Romans rarely kept it.[273] Bones of probably domestic duck were found at the Romano-British site of High Ferrers, Northants., and others of mallard size were found at Hemel Hempstead Roman villa by Harcourt.[274] Domestic ducks are little different from the wild form, although wild drakes are monogamous and domestic ones polygamous. It has also been shown that domestic ducks are less aggressive, and have no seasonal territorial behaviour.[275] Since the eggs have a strong flavour, ducks are kept today mainly for meat, maturing quickly and reaching 5 to 7 lb (2.3 to 3.2 kg) in 10–12 weeks. Modern ducks can, however, produce eggs over a longer period than the fowl, reaching a total of about 300 a year compared with 270 in the fowl.

According to Ernle ducks are rarely mentioned in medieval records, although large numbers of geese and fowls were kept.[276] Among skeletal remains the fowl is usually the most common, the goose next, and the duck third.[277]

The white Aylesbury breed of duck was bred in the Vale of Aylesbury, Bucks., by cottagers in their houses, but they dug small

[271] M. L. Ryder, unpublished, 1977.
[272] Quoted by Ernle, *op. cit.*
[273] Zeuner, *op. cit.*
[274] R. A. Harcourt, personal communication, 1970.
[275] M. F. Desforges and D. G. M. Wood-Gush, 'Behavioural differences between Aylesbury and wild mallard ducks: a study in domestication', *Vet. Rec.*, 96, 1975, p. 509.
[276] Ernle, *op. cit.*   [277] Ryder, 1961, *op. cit.*

ponds in their gardens mistakenly believing that it had to be fed in water. Perhaps the duck has been kept, or has kept itself, as long as village ponds have existed.

The Romans bred the pigeon. This was derived from the rock dove (*Columbia livia*) which lives on cliffs of the east coast of Britain, and so it could have been domesticated here. But Fitter found records of domestication only in Scotland,[278] and so native pigeons are unlikely to have been the only source of the British domesticated form (which has now become feral in many big cities). During the Middle Ages the lords of the manor kept pigeons in dove-cotes for meat and manure, providing a profit for him and a loss to the tenant whose grain they ate. Hyams noted that the homing instinct was exploited by the Romans to transmit messages, but when this began in Britain is not clear.[279]

We do not think of the pheasant (*Phasianus colchicus*) as domesticated, but it was taken as such from Italy by the Romans to all parts of the empire. Bones identified as 'pheasant' in Britain are now known to be domestic fowl. The Romans also bred peacocks (*Pavo cristatus*) and so could have introduced them to Britain. As well as peacocks, swans are often mentioned on medieval estates, but Zeuner omitted the swan and so apparently did not regard it as being domesticated.[280] Swans are closely related to ducks and geese. Ornithologists regard the mute swan (*Cygnus olor*) as a feral descendant of medieval semi-domesticated stock that may have originated from the native wild population of eastern England, which opposes the legend that it was imported by Richard I.

HONEY BEES

He that hath sheep, swine, and bees,
sleep he, wake he, may thrive.
Ancient proverb

Zeuner considered that the honey bee (*Apis mellifera*) has been of great economic importance back even to Palaeolithic times. Honey was the only sugar available until a few hundred years ago; the drink mead is of great antiquity; and in the Middle Ages honey as well as beeswax had a medicinal use, the wax being also used in candles.[280]

At first honey would have been collected from the colonies of wild honey bees either without smoke, or after they had been smoked out, either permanently or temporarily. Man may have offered an artificial home to bees as early as the Neolithic period, a possible hive being a hollow tree trunk, which is often used by wild bees.

[278] R. S. R. Fitter, *The Ark in our Midst*, London, 1959.
[279] Hyams, *op. cit.*   [280] Zeuner, *op. cit.*

Later, wooden hives were used, and Fraser considered that wicker skeps were in use in Britain before the Romans arrived.[281] Although Strabo (7 BC) quoted Pytheas, who wrote about 300 BC, as saying that the inhabitants of Thule made a drink from grain and honey, there are no traces of bee-keeping in Britain prior to the Roman occupation. Many Roman (and earlier) writings on bee-keeping exist.[282] The bees of a Roman villa were kept in an enclosure, and tended by a slave, the *mellarius*.

Ancient Irish and Welsh Laws concerning bees are thought to indicate pre-Roman conditions. From the Irish ones, Fraser deduced that the queens were not very prolific, and that the hives sent out three or four swarms a year.[283] The mention of the division of swarms indicates the knowledge that they often contain more than one queen. Absconding swarms were frequent, and the man who followed one and kept it in sight was rewarded. There were severe fines for the stealing of hives, and an owner was responsible for any harm done by his bees.

The Welsh Laws (codified by Howell the Good in AD 918) stated that each free village had to provide the king with a vat of mead. The values of different kinds of colony were carefully recorded, from 24d. for an old stock to 4d. for a swarm after August, called a wing swarm. Fraser considered that the implication of August swarms supports the suggestion that hives were taken to the heather. One wonders whether the taking of hives to the heather could have originated with transhumance?

Fraser considered that the Anglo-Saxons introduced to East Anglia the straw skep, which replaced the native wicker hive in that area.[283] In western counties the wicker hive persisted until 1885. Among the many Saxon references to bees, few give details about bee-keeping. The bee-keeper (*beo-ceorl*) was grouped next to the swineherd, and was often a slave. Laws governed the theft of honey, which was mentioned as a liquid.

The Domesday survey gives some indication of the extent of bee-keeping, but a *custos apium* is mentioned in few places. At Westbury, Wilts., nine *mellitarii* (honeyers) are mentioned; Fraser considered that these might have been collectors of wild honey rather than bee-keepers.[283]

Where hives are mentioned the word *vascula* meaning 'small hives' is used in the west, which appears to indicate wicker hives. In eastern counties the word used is *vasa apium*, possibly indicating the larger straw

---

[281] H. M. Fraser, *History of Beekeeping in Britain*, London, 1958.
[282] *Idem, Beekeeping in Antiquity*, London, 2nd ed., 1951.
[283] Fraser, 1958, *op. cit.*

skeps of the Saxons. Only in East Anglia is the number of hives in each manor given, and in many there were only two or three. Medieval miniatures frequently show three or four beehives supported on a bench in a garden or farmyard, and frequently under cover.

In his thirteenth-century *Husbandry*, Walter of Henley stated that each hive should give on average two swarms a year. If the honey was collected every other year, two gallons should be obtained from each hive. By feeding the bees it was possible to maintain eight hives through the winter on a gallon (4.55 l) of honey, but feeding was not carried out everywhere.

INDEX

References to figures, plates and tables are shown in italic (e.g. *70*).

settlement (*cont.*)

125, *126*; huts, 111, *118, 122, 125*; linear
boundaries, 122, 123; multi-period
settlements, 115, *116*; nucleated, 111,
118, 121, 122, 128; oppida, 112–13, 115;
palisades and ramparts, 121, *122*, 125,
125; rounds, 112; unenclosed, 111, 112;
vitrified structures, 127

topography: clay, *121*; coasts, 113, 117,
119, 121, 127; gravel terraces, *116*;
moors, 111; river valleys, 113, 115, 117,
118–19, 120, 127

settlement distribution of 2nd millennium
areas: Bodmin Moor, 96; colonization of
marginal, 110; consolidation of
Neolithic, 110; Cornwall, 96;
Cotswolds, 98–9; Co. Durham, 107;
Dartmoor, 96, *97*; East Anglia, 103–4;
eastern Midland valleys, 102–3; Exmoor,
96; focal, of intensive exploitation, 110;
implied from burial sites, 95–6, 97;
Mendip Hills, 98; Midland valley
gravels, 102; nature of evidence on, 95;
northern England, 105–9, *106, 107*;
Northumberland, 107, 109; Orkney and
Shetland, 109, *110*; Peak District, 105;
Scotland, 109, *110*; Severn estuary, 98;
Somerset Levels, 98; south of the
Thames, 101–2; south-west peninsula,
96–7; Sussex, 96, 99, 101, *101*; Thames
valley, 102; Trent–Tyne, 104–6; Wales,
97–8; Wessex, 96, 99, 110

remains: axes, *108*; barrows, 109; Beaker
occupation features, 103, *104*, 109; cairn
fields, 109; cairns, 97, 105, *108*, 109;
crop marks, *104*; cup-marks, 97, 109;
ditches, 100, 101, 102; *104*; enclosed, 96,
97; field dykes, *110*; field monuments,
96, 97, 105; fields, 96, 99, *101*, 103; field
systems, 97, 109; flints, 99, 103, 105;
houses, *110*; 'isolated hut' sites, 105;
long barrows, *108*; 109; round barrows,
97, 98, 99, 103, 105; standing stones, 97,
108, 109; stone circles, *108*, 109; stone
cist burials, 107, 109; stone clearance
mounds, 105, 109, *110*; stone structures
of West, 95, 97; trackways, 98, *101*;
upstanding remains, 96, 97, 98, 99, 102;
urnfields, 103

topographical: clay lowlands, 99, 103;
coasts, 96–7, 101, 105, 109; downs, 101,
102, 103, 110; gravel terraces, 102, *104*,
116; heaths, 99, 103; moors, 96, 97, 102,
106, 109; 'natural' woodlands, 99; river
valleys, 96–7, 99, 102–3, 107, 109, 110;
upland land use, 105, 106, 109,
110

settlement(s)
and climatic deterioration, 93
distribution of 1st and 2nd millennia BC,
see settlement distribution
Early Prehistoric: ambiguously agrarian, 7;
bases of stable and continuously
occupied, 5; distinct areas of Mesolithic
and Neolithic, 32; distribution pattern,
44, 45; *Einzelhof* type, 47; of first
colonists, 34–5; problem of recurrent or
permanent occupation, 5; social
inferences from, 44, 48; types of, 44–5
enclosed, 93, 111, *139*
foci, as distinct from ceremonial centres, 93
geography, 253
hill forts and oppida as permanent enclosed
communal, 252–3
in land use sequences, 162–3
patterns, study of, *252*, 253–5, *254*
unenclosed, 93, 111, *137*
use of term in preference to 'farm', 129
sex ratios, 301, 307, 310, 322
Shakenoak, 340
Shamanism, 53, 53n63
Shapley Tor, Dartmoor, 172
Shaugh Moor, Dartmoor, *171*, 183, 287
Shaw, T., 40n34
Shawcross, F. W., and Higgs, E. S., 15n19,
379n141, 381n157
Sheail, J., and Wells, T. C. E., 297
Shearplace Hill, Dorset, 131n114, 135, 225,
260, 266, 287
sheep (*Ovis aries*)
ancestry of: Argali, of central Asia, 357,
365, 375, *375*; chromosome evidence,
357, 360; horns and, 359, 373–4;
megalith chronology and, 360;
Mouflon, of Europe, 357, 359–60, 365;
Urial, of south-west Asia, 357, 358, 359,
360, 365
arrival in Britain, 357
as a food animal, 32, 240, 305, 334, 348
behavioural differences between goats and,
351, 352
Biblical references to, 353
black-faced horned: Argali-type horns,
375, 375; Asiatic affinities of, 370, *372*,
375, 375–6; evolution of, *375*; hairy
fleece, *375*, *375*, 376; introduced by
Danes, 376–8; modern horned
mountain, 376; of Denmark, Holland
and Germany, 377
blood, 313
bones: cranial, 358; distinguishing goat
from, 351–2, 358; from Scilly, 336;
genetic variation and, 358; large, of
Roman sites, 364–5, 370; leg length,